YOUNG
Disraeli

YOUNG *Disraeli*

1804–1846

JANE RIDLEY

CROWN PUBLISHERS, INC.
NEW YORK

FOR
TOBY AND HUMPHREY

Originally published in Great Britain by Sinclair-Stevenson, an imprint of Reed Consumer Books, Ltd., London, in 1995.

Published by Crown Publishers, Inc., 201 East 50th Street, New York, New York 10022. Member of the Crown Publishing Group.

Random House, Inc. New York, Toronto, London, Sydney, Auckland.

CROWN is a trademark of Crown Publishers, Inc.

Manufactured in the United States of America

Library of Congress Cataloging-in-Publication Data

Ridley, Jane.
  Young Disraeli, 1804–1846 / by Jane Ridley.
     p.   cm.
  1. Disraeli, Benjamin, Earl of Beaconsfield, 1804–1881.
  2. Prime ministers—Great Britain—Biography. I. Title.
  DA564.B3R53 1995
  941.081'092—dc20
  94-25543
  CIP

ISBN 0-517-58643-6

10 9 8 7 6 5 4 3 2 1

First American Edition

Contents

List of Illustrations

Acknowledgements

I am especially grateful to Professor M. G. Wiebe, General Editor of the Disraeli Project at Queen's University at Kingston, for permission to quote from *Benjamin Disraeli: Letters*. Christopher Wall of the National Trust, Hughenden Manor kindly loaned transcripts of the Account Books of Mary Anne Disraeli. The Bodleian Library gave permission to quote from the Hughenden Papers in their possession. I should like to thank my aunt, Moyra Campbell, for permission to quote from the journals and memoirs of Lord Campbell. Like all students of Disraeli, I owe a debt to Robert Blake whose *Disraeli* (1966) first kindled my enthusiasm for the subject.

Anthea Palmer of the National Trust generously threw open the doors of Hughenden. David Gordon provided coffee in the room that was once Disraeli's upstairs smoking room. The Grosvenor Estate gave access to the Disraelis' house at Grosvenor Gate. For help and information I am grateful to Fiona Campbell; Mary Lutyens; Valerie Sanders; Mary Skinner; John Clarke; Martin Gilbert; Mark Amory; James Knox; Baron Dombovary von Treuenburg; Duncan Bull of the *Burlington Magazine*; Kay Dawson. The Historical Society of Sheffield University gave a stimulating discussion in response to a paper I read on Disraeli.

A grant from the Nuffield Foundation helped buy time for writing; I should like to record my thanks. This book was begun on maternity leave; I should like to thank my colleagues at Buckingham for coping with the problems this caused. My students have cheerfully tolerated a Disraeli-centred view of nineteenth-century British history, and I have learned much from their responses. The James Roberts Memorial Bequest to Buckingham University Library proved especially useful. The London Library has been invaluable as ever; more than a library, it is a womb, and much of this book was written there.

Peter Ghosh and Lord Beloff read the manuscript, and their comments have been perceptive and constructive. I am especially grateful to Lord Beloff for his sagacious help and enthusiasm, which has sustained this project. My mother Clayre Percy not only read and commented on the manuscript; she also compiled the index.

Caroline Dawnay, my agent, has been warmly supportive and protective of this book ever since its conception. Penelope Hoare of Sinclair-Stevenson has been all an editor should be and more, negotiating difficulties with calm professionalism. Thanks also to Jim Wade and Roger Cazalet. Angela Brown of Buckingham University word-processed my barely legible handwritten drafts with wonderful efficiency and accuracy, meeting impossible deadlines at very short notice.

My husband Stephen Thomas is also my collaborator. Together we researched the book and planned it. He knows as much about the Young Disraeli as I do. He has guided the book and shaped it, told me what won't do and what will. Above all, he has made the book fun to write.

Introduction

BENJAMIN DISRAELI was an extraordinary man; and the more that becomes known about him, the more remarkable he appears. Writer and man of action, dandy and Romantic, self-made politician and man of ideas – Disraeli was all of these. He was also a near-bankrupt speculator, an adventurer and intriguer, a philanderer and depressive. This book explores the many sides of his complex nature, illuminating the many different worlds in which he lived, and the tensions and the links between them. The rich world of imagination, which Disraeli created in his novels, is related to the story of his life.

He has not lacked biographers. Robert Blake's *Disraeli* (1966) was essentially a biography of Disraeli the politician. Writing over thirty years ago, at a time when little was known about Disraeli's father Isaac, Blake tended to see Disraeli's youth as the rackety and somewhat frivolous prelude to the later political career, which was Blake's main interest. Sarah Bradford's biography of 1982 added to the story of Disraeli's personal life; Stanley Weintraub's biography of 1993 enlarged on Disraeli's Jewishness.

This book is not an exclusively political biography; it attempts to draw together these and other strands, giving a detailed and integrated picture of Disraeli's youth. 'Read no history,' wrote Disraeli, 'nothing but biography, for that is life without theory.'

The publication of Disraeli's letters in a definitive edition has transformed the study of Disraeli. Four hefty volumes comprising 1500 letters exist for the years of Disraeli's life covered by this book. Thanks to the Disraeli Project of Queen's University at Kingston, it is possible for the first time to reconstruct with a degree of certainty the sequence of events in Disraeli's early life. Episodes and personalities that were once vague and uncertain have come sharply into focus; and new and sometimes startling evidence has come to light.

Disraeli published his first novel, *Vivian Grey*, in 1826 at the age of twenty-one. By the time he entered Parliament in 1837, aged thirty-three, he had published eight novels, five pamphlets, an epic poem, several satires and a constitutional treatise. He had also published a significant quantity of journalism, much of it promoting the views of his political patron Lord Lyndhurst. The political trilogy, *Coningsby, Sybil* and *Tancred*, followed between 1844 and 1847. 'My works are my life,' declared Disraeli in old age. 'They are all written from my own feelings and experience.' Driven by a compulsion to write about himself, Disraeli poured out his fantasies, his ideas, his ambitions. His novels are a rich mine of biographical material that has been little quarried by previous biographers.

The odds against Disraeli's success were very high indeed. He was an outsider, the grandson of a humble Jewish immigrant. He attended neither public school nor university. From the moment he achieved notoriety with *Vivian Grey* he encountered anti-semitic abuse, the full unpleasant extent of which has only recently emerged. He was prone to ill health and depression. A mysterious illness that crippled him in his twenties turns out to look very like nervous breakdown.

Aged twenty, Disraeli lost a borrowed fortune speculating in South American mines. For the next twenty years debt shaped the pattern of his life. Ruin and disgrace were never far away; his escapes from bankruptcy and debtors' prison were perilously close. He learned to lie to his creditors; he played the part of gigolo. For a youth of ambition, Disraeli displayed an astonishing lack of judgement. With a fecklessness that is truly breathtaking (and that has made his biography a joy to write) he plunged into public quarrels, duels, scrapes and sexual scandals. How, despite all this, Disraeli survived and indeed succeeded is one of the questions this book sets out to answer. His relationship with his father Isaac D'Israeli, himself a remarkable man, has received little attention, but it was crucial to Benjamin Disraeli's self-confidence. Isaac was Disraeli's link with the Romantic movement. The father knew and admired Byron, and wrote an influential study of literary genius. The son, who sometimes wrote under the name of D'Israeli the Younger, worshipped Byron and he often described himself as a genius. Failure and hostility are easier to bear if, like Benjamin Disraeli, you are firmly convinced of your own innate genius.

In an odd way, being Jewish also helped. Disraeli's response to anti-semitism was not to suppress his Jewishness but to assert it. Many Jews in nineteenth-century England chose the path of assimilation. Not so Disraeli. Despite having been baptised a Christian at the age of twelve, he increasingly stressed his separate racial identity as a Jew. His tour of the Middle East in 1830–1 was an important journey of self-discovery. He returned to England

and publicly demonstrated the superiority of the Jews, himself included. Stressing his own ancient descent made him feel the equal, if not the superior, of the aristocrats who ruled Victorian Britain. But his theory of Jewish superiority exposed him to anti-semitic attacks of a more dangerous kind than the pieces of stinking pork that the mob thrust in his face as he stood on the hustings at elections.

Looking back in old age, Disraeli reflected on the debt he owed to women. Nineteenth-century Britain was supposedly a male-dominated society, but in *Endymion* (1880), Disraeli's retrospective novel, it is the women who shape events. Disraeli knew what he was talking about. His first novel *Vivian Grey* would never have made the impact it did without the help he received from a woman. It was through another woman, the forbidding Lady Londonderry, that he gained admission to the dazzling aristocratic saloons that he idealised in his novels. Thanks to the generosity of his mistress, Henrietta Sykes, Disraeli gained a patron, Lord Lyndhurst. Mary Anne Lewis, the woman who later became his wife, provided him with his first seat in Parliament. Her money and her shrewdness were essential to his political survival.

Victorian liberals such as John Stuart Mill complained that the influence of women in society was 'illegitimate' because it depended upon manipulation rather than opinion. Had Mill possessed an ounce of Disraeli's sardonic wit and epigrammatic brilliance he might not have disapproved so vigorously. Disraeli was the least earnest of eminent Victorians, refreshingly free of the Victorian vices of humbug and hypocrisy.

In politics, Disraeli speedily acquired a reputation for opportunism and lack of principle. 'A mighty impartial personage', he stood first at Wycombe as a Radical in 1832, eventually entering Parliament as a Tory in 1837. Mortified by the refusal of Prime Minister Robert Peel to give him office in 1841, he destroyed Peel's government in 1846 in a series of brilliantly vitriolic speeches over the Corn Laws, an issue about which he cared very little. No wonder men asked whether Benjamin Disraeli believed in anything except himself.

He did. But because he worked them out for himself, his ideas are sometimes bizarre and often boldly original. Intellectually, Disraeli was in many ways an outsider. Evangelical Christianity, the all-pervasive creed of early Victorian England, was alien to him. So were the two leading political systems of the 1830s, Benthamite Utilitarianism and Peel's Conservatism. Both had their roots in the rationalism of the eighteenth century, and Disraeli distrusted reason in politics. A true Romantic, he consistently stressed the role of imagination.

Disraeli's early Radicalism was not really thought out. Far more coherent was the Tory Radical position that he developed after 1835. Liberals jeered at

Disraeli's idea of the Tory party riding to power on the shoulders of the mob, and Karl Marx poured scorn on Disraeli's Young England movement, which called for an alliance of aristocracy and proletariat against the bourgeoisie. But Disraeli's Tory Radicalism anticipates in a remarkable way the strategy of playing both sides against the centre which he was later to implement with the Second Reform Bill of 1866–7. Disraeli's position shifted during the 1840s, after Peel's refusal of office. Driven by a new-found fear of democracy, he developed a searing critique of parliamentary government, individualism and all the values of Victorian liberalism. Disraeli foresaw that liberalism by itself could never hold the allegiance of the masses; that way revolution lay.

'I love fame,' he declared in 1844. 'I love public reputation; I love to live in the eyes of the country; and it is a glorious thing for a man to do who has had my difficulties to contend with.' How he got there is the story of this book. Disraeli's public face, his ideas, speeches and books, are only part of the story. Equally important is his marriage (a fascinating book in itself); his intense emotional relationships with younger men; his complex relationship with his patron, Lord George Bentinck.

Disraeli is forty-two when this book ends. He lived to dominate English politics for another thirty-five years. The story of his climb to the top of the greasy pole – to the Tory leadership, to office as Chancellor of the Exchequer and, eventually, to power as Prime Minister, is the subject of another volume.

ONE

Isaac's Library

1804–24

BENJAMIN DISRAELI claimed not to know the year he was born, and he was notoriously vague about where the happy event took place. He often said, rather improbably, that he was born in a library. As a man of imagination – a phrase he loved to use – Disraeli despised mere fact, and could not resist cloaking even the most basic facts in mystery and romance.

Benjamin D'Israeli was born on Friday, 21 December 1804, at 5.30 a.m. at 6 King's Road, Bedford Row (today 22 Theobald's Road) in London, the home of his parents, Isaac and Maria D'Israeli. When Benjamin said he was born and bred in a library, he meant, he once explained, that the rooms in his father's house were full of books.

To the boy Benjamin, his father Isaac seemed to live in his library. Isaac wore thick, metal-framed spectacles over his large bulging brown eyes; his tousled fair hair was pushed back from a broad forehead, curling down over his collar; his nose, which his son later described as Bourbon, was thick and shapeless. The weak point was the chin, which he buried in a high white neckcloth. Most mornings, dressed in a blue or brown coat with brass buttons and with slippered feet, Isaac shuffled into his library and spent the day in an easy-chair among his books. At night, his lamp burned late as he read, short-sighted eyes peering closely in the flickering yellow light. He lived with his books. When he died he left a collection of twenty-five thousand volumes, the fruit of countless hours' browsing in booksellers' shops. He loved to handle and rearrange them. 'The Octavos', he would say, 'are my Infantry, my Cavalry are the Quartos, and the Folios are my artillery.'[1]

Isaac was always busy in his library. The man who passed his time in a library and did not aspire to add to it with his own work was, he said, as 'indolent as that animal called the Sloth, who perishes on the tree he climbs after he has eaten all its leaves'. Bibliomania, or collecting a heap of books without intelligent curiosity, was an infection of weak minds, who imagine they acquire knowledge when they merely keep it on their shelves. 'Their motley libraries have been called the *madhouses of the human mind*, and again, the *tomb of books*, when the possessor will not communicate them, and coffins them up in the cases of his library.' Untouched collections like this, said Isaac – and one can almost hear him giggling at the pun – were without a *Lock on the Human Understanding*.[2]

Day after day, year after year, Isaac scratched away with a goose quill, filling his notebooks in the stillness of his library. Any scrap of paper that came to hand was scribbled over in his small, crabbed writing, leaving a chaos of fragmentary notes. His son Benjamin's first surviving letter ('Dear Mama, I have arrived safe, B. D'Israeli') was preserved only because his father appropriated it to write notes on the back.

Some mornings, he walked to the British Museum, about twenty minutes away from Bedford Row. He had worked at the museum since the 1790s, when there were barely enough men in the reading room to make up a jury. Isaac used to sit between the Abbé de la Ruse and Mr Pinkerton – between Norman antiquity and Scottish history, as he put it. Often whole days went by as he mused in silence and oblivion, waiting for the volumes to appear that he had so eagerly ordered.

At the time Benjamin was born, Isaac was thirty-eight. He was writing a novel, his second, which he called *Flim Flams, or the Life and Errors of my Uncle, and the Amours of my Aunt, with Illustrations and Obscurities, by Messrs Rag, Tag and Bobtail*. It was a satire, modelled on Sterne's *Tristram Shandy*, in which 'My Aunt', a thinly disguised portrait of the astronomer Miss Caroline Herschell, then well over fifty, gives birth to an ape. Isaac, whose mind was evidently full of his wife's pregnancy, had high hopes of the novel, which he thought was a heap of extravaganzas bound to provoke perpetual laughter. The critics did not agree. *Flim Flams* was slated for its poor taste, indiscriminate satire and indecent attack on the unfortunate Miss Herschell. There was talk of a libel action. Isaac lost his nerve, and wrote to his publisher, begging him to stop the second edition and return the manuscript; the book, he said, was bunglingly written and full of errors. After looking through the book again, he ventured to think that it was '*not half so bad*' as some chose to think, but he still worried about it. In the bookshop he dropped hints about book sales in general, meaning *Flim Flams* in particular; the bookseller failed to take the hint, was blind to his blushes, deaf to his sighs and kept an ominous silence about the sales.[3]

Isaac had always wanted to be a poet or a novelist; and his unhappy experience with *Flim Flams* hurt. It was as a poet that he had first edged on to the literary scene. As a young man of twenty-three, he had published some anonymous verses 'On the Abuse of Satire', attacking Peter Pindar's satires on the private life of George III. Wolcot (alias Peter Pindar) mistook Isaac's verses for the work of his rival, Hayley, and published a reply; Isaac was amazed to find his verses reprinted in the newspapers. Since then he had published a couple of volumes of poems which attracted little notice. He thought his leg was being pulled when, years later, he was introduced to Sir Walter Scott, who saluted him by reciting one of his poems, 'To Laura', which Scott published in the *English Minstrelsy*. 'If the writer of these lines had gone on,' said Scott, 'he would have been an English poet.' Maybe; but as his son Benjamin later wrote, the most that Isaac could have achieved was to have become the author of an 'elegant and popular didactic poem' which might have served as a prize volume at ladies' schools.[4]

Isaac's first novel, *Vaurien*, published in 1797, had been a tract against the French Revolution, caricaturing utopians and radicals such as Godwin. He followed it in 1799 with a collection of romances or short love stories. The most successful, 'Mejnoun and Leila', was a Persian love story featuring the son of a sheik and the daughter of an emir; later made into an opera, 'Love in the Deserts', it was an early and rather daring attempt to devise an authentic eastern story, inspired by oriental literature. By the time Benjamin was born, Isaac had failed as a poet and achieved only minor success as a novelist. As a man of letters, however, he had been almost embarrassingly successful.

The man of letters, Isaac once wrote, lives not in the world of men and affairs, but in the solitude of his library. Tranquillity is essential to his existence: 'if the painful realities of life break into this visionary world of literature and art, there is an atmosphere of taste about him which will be dissolved, and harmonious ideas which will be chased away as it happens when something is violently flung among the trees when the birds are singing; all instantly disperse.' Viewing the world from the calm of his study, the man of letters is detached, objective. Learning is an international currency, so the man of letters hates war, and 'only calls for peace and his books, to unite himself with his brothers scattered over Europe'. Nor does he belong to any party: indeed Isaac, who prided himself on his independence, said he had studied to avoid connecting himself with any party – literary, religious or political – 'I have always believed that where there is party there is deception.'[5]

His career as a man of letters dated back to 1791, when, in his mid-twenties, he published a collection of anecdotes, *Curiosities of Literature*. Isaac had found a friend and patron in the shape of Mr Pye, a literary gentleman of good family and a strong Tory, whom Pitt made poet laureate in 1790 for his Toryism rather than his poetry, which was rotten. Pye was a keen collector of anecdotes, made fashionable by Horace Walpole, and he introduced his young protégé Isaac to two friends who had recently published collections of them: James Petit Andrews and William Seward. Isaac thought their books were mere confectionery, and that he could do better. He remarked that a well-read man could compile a more interesting and instructive collection from the library in which he lived; and to prove the point he did just that.

Curiosities of Literature is a collection of short essays and anecdotes on subjects ranging from Libraries to the Talmud, from the History of Fashion to Hell; there are essays entitled, reassuringly, 'Men of Genius Deficient in Conversation', and, intriguingly, 'Virginity', or again, 'On the Custom of Saluting after Sneezing'. It is the commonplace book of a dilettante man of letters, an elegant rag-bag into which Isaac tipped the reading notes he had made from the classics, through France to the orient. There is no unifying theme, unless it is his preoccupation with writers in every recorded culture – their amusements, their poverty, their imitators, the titles of their books. His main source was the collections of French *ana* (anecdotes); the genre of secret history or anecdotes was far better established in France than in England.

Curiosities was an ideal book for dipping into on rainy days or candlelit winter evenings, and it sold well in England. A second edition came out in 1792, and a third a year later: one of the joys of a book like *Curiosities* was that it could be easily revised and added to, and by 1834 six volumes had been published. Isaac claimed in 1794 that *Curiosities* was aimed at the reader with a classical education who was ignorant of the 'characters and revolutions' of modern literature. In the debate between the classics and the new literature of the French Enlightenment, Isaac was firmly on the side of the moderns; he was a man of letters and a populariser, communicating the learning of his library through widely read *belles lettres*.

In the second volume of *Curiosities*, Isaac charged the Whig republican historian, Mrs Catherine Macaulay, with destroying documents in the British Museum which favoured the Stuarts and discredited the Whigs. Mrs Macaulay had died in 1791, and Isaac and Mrs Macaulay's husband wrote acrimonious letters debating whether she had torn out four leaves of the Harleian MS 7379 on 12 November 1764 and was consequently banished from the museum. Nothing could be proved against Mrs Macaulay; but that Isaac made public such heinous charges against a republican and a woman (Mrs Macaulay was Dr Johnson's *bête noire*) says something about his politics. Though attached to no party, his political sympathies were strongly Tory.

He hadn't always been against reform. As an adolescent, Isaac was passionately fond of the rationalist writers of the Enlightenment – Voltaire, Rousseau and Montesquieu – and contemptuous of the classics. He was on the fringes of English 'Jacobin' circles in the 1790s; he may have known

Godwin, and he collected Blake's illuminated books. But he was frightened by the bloody excesses of the French Revolution, which jolted him out of his shallow intellectual optimism, and in *Vaurien* (his novel of 1797) he satirised Godwin's utopian ideas; in 1796 he had also published a collection of essays attacking the revolutionaries' belief in the perfectibility of man. At bottom, he remained an eighteenth-century sceptic. Like Gibbon, whom he much admired and whose Frenchified style he shared, Isaac was an English *philosophe*, a rationalist who could not help sneering at and belittling moral certainties and organised religion.

Prolific and industrious, Isaac flourished as a man of letters. Washington Irving observed him manufacturing his wares in the British Museum in 1817, 'a dapper little gentleman in bright coloured clothes, with a chirping gossipy expression of countenance, who had all the appearance of an author on good terms with his bookseller'. Making a great stir of business, he dipped into various books, 'fluttering over the leaves of manuscripts, taking a morsel out of one, a morsel out of another'.[6] In 1849, the year after he died, *Curiosities of Literature* was published in its fourteenth edition. Various editions of his non-fiction literary works take up two substantial shelves in the London Library (and this excludes the multi-volume historical works he later published). His success was the more remarkable because he was a Jew, the son of an immigrant; it has even been claimed that he was the first European Jew since the Renaissance, excepting Mendelssohn in Germany, to reach the front rank in the Republic of Letters. Isaac, a modest man, would probably not have pitched his claims so high. He once wrote, however, that 'literary Jews must always be rare ... their most malignant and powerful enemies will be found among their domestic associates.'[7] This was certainly his experience.

Benjamin Disraeli gave a characteristically flowery and exotic account of Isaac's ancestry in a memoir he wrote in 1849. 'My grandfather,' he wrote, 'who became an English denizen in 1748, was an Italian descendant from one of those Hebrew families, whom the Inquisition forced to emigrate from the Spanish Peninsula at the end of the fifteenth century, and who found a refuge in the more tolerant territories of the Venetian Republic.'

His ancestors had dropped their Gothic surname on their settlement in the Terra Firma, and grateful to the God of Jacob who had sustained them through unprecedented trials and guarded them through unheard of perils, they assumed the name of DISRAELI [*sic*], a name never borne before, or since, by any other family, in order that their race might be for ever recognised. Undisturbed and unmolested, they flourished as merchants for more than two centuries under the protection of the lion of St Mark.... But towards the middle of the eighteenth century, the altered circumstances of England, favourable, as it was then supposed, to commerce and religious liberty, attracted the attention of my great-grandfather to this island, and he resolved that the youngest [*sic*] of his two sons, Benjamin, the 'son of his right hand', should settle in a country where the dynasty seemed at length established through the recent failure of Prince Charles Edward, and where public opinion appeared definitively adverse to persecution on matters of creed and conscience.[8]

This rococo extravaganza is Disraelian myth-making. Jewish scholars have examined Disraeli's claims about his ancestry, and found almost all false, unproven, confused or seriously misleading.[9] There is no evidence that Isaac's ancestors were expelled from Spain by the Inquisition; Disraeli does not seem to have made up his mind whether they were expelled at the end of the fifteenth century as professing Jews, or whether they were among the Marrano Jews who stayed in Spain for several generations, assuming a gothic surname and professing Christianity to avoid the Inquisition. Perhaps the hint of Marrano ancestry says more about Disraeli than about his forebears: the Marrano *mentalité* – the secret Jew, outwardly observing Christian rites – was an important element in his make-up. He loved to imagine his ancestors as Spanish nobles, privately adhering to the laws of Moses; he gave an exotic Marrano ancestry to Sidonia in *Coningsby*.

Equally revealing is his claim that his ancestors settled in Venice. There is no evidence for this: on the contrary, his grandfather Benjamin came from Cento, near Ferrara in the Papal States. The line can be traced back no further than this Benjamin's father, another Isaac, who probably came from Ferrara and who may or may not have been related to a family named Israel living in Venice in about 1600. Tenuous though the Venetian connection was, the *belief* that his ancestors had lived in Venice was very important to Disraeli. It became a spiritual home for him; as the point where the orient meets the west, Venice was the symbol of Disraeli's self-appointed role as a link between east and west, between Judaism and Christianity, the old testament and the new. The truth was more mundane: his great-aunts, Rachel and Venturini, sisters of his grandfather Benjamin, kept a humble girls' school in the Venetian ghetto well into the nineteenth century.

The name Disraeli was by no means unique, as Benjamin claimed. It was common enough in Moorish Spain and the Levant, where Israeli simply meant 'of the family of Israel' or 'the Jew'. The prefix D' was adopted by Benjamin senior after his arrival in England, presumably because it sounded better; it certainly did not denote nobility. And Disraeli's grandiose claim that his grandfather was drawn to England by its reputation for freedom of commerce and religion is hard to credit. Benjamin D'Israeli came to England in 1748 at the age of eighteen and found work as a poorly paid clerk in the Fenchurch Street counting house of Joseph and Pelligrin Treves, Venetian Jews specialising in trade with Italy. For Benjamin, the attraction of England was less the stability of the dynasty than the vogue for large straw bonnets made of Leghorn chip. In 1756, when still a clerk, he made a good marriage to a Spanish Jew, Rebecca Mendes Furtado, who was related to the Lara family, and in 1757 he set up business on his own account as an importer of Leghorn straw hats, then all the rage thanks to the Gunning sisters, the beauties of the day. In 1764 Rebecca died, leaving a daughter, Rachel, and four months later Benjamin married again. His grandson Benjamin boasted of his descent from the House of Lara, believing that old Benjamin's father was a Lara; but Disraeli was descended from his grandfather's second wife, Sarah Siprut de Gabay, daughter of a wealthy Jewish merchant. In any event, Rebecca D'Israeli had been related not to the noble Spanish House of Lara (the 'haughty Lara' Disraeli claimed as his kinsman) but to unrelated Portuguese Marrano Jews of the same name.

Old Benjamin's second wife Sarah saw Judaism not as a religion but as a misfortune; intelligent, bitter and mortified by her social position, she never forgave her husband his name, and lived until eighty without voicing a tender expression. Benjamin junior remembered his grandmother as a demon, equalled only by Sarah, duchess of Marlborough, his friend Frances Anne, marchioness of Londonderry and Catherine of Russia. As a boy he dreaded Sunday visits to his grandmother: 'no kindness, no tea, no tips – nothing'. When, at the age of eighty-two, she came to stay with her family and was kind to all, her daughter-in-law remarked, 'Depend upon it, she is going to die.' She did.[10] But he recalled his grandmother with pride as well as horror: through her he claimed descent from the Villa Reals, a famous and wealthy Anglo-Jewish family, heroes of the Portuguese Inquisition. In fact, she was related to a different family of Villareals who derived, less glamorously, from Leghorn.

Grandfather Benjamin was cheerful, even-tempered and prosperous. Not content with his successful trade in Italian bonnets and coral, he branched out into speculation on the stock market, where he lost most of his money in 1759. His second wife, Sarah, brought a welcome dowry of £2000 in 1765, and Benjamin's business revived. Having set up as an unlicensed stockbroker in 1776, he was admitted to the inner circle of stockbrokers who met at the Stock Exchange Coffee House, and was a member of the committee which built the Stock Exchange in 1801. Spurred by the ambitious Sarah, he rented a large and distinguished country house (designed by Wren) at Enfield,

Middlesex, and here, according to his grandson's account, he played whist and ate exquisite macaroni dressed by his great friend Sir Horace Mann, the Venetian consul. (His friend was not Horace Mann, but his nephew Horatio Mann.) Old Benjamin retired in 1803, just when the wars and loans of the Revolution were about to create families of Jewish millionaires among whom, his grandson liked to think, 'he might probably have enrolled his own'. This was wishful thinking; Benjamin D'Israeli ended his days in bourgeois comfort in Church Street, Stoke Newington, where he was known as 'Old Mr Israel', no doubt to the fury of his fierce wife. He left an estate, real and personal, valued at £35,000 on his death in 1816.[11]

Isaac (b. 1766) was the only child of old Benjamin and Sarah D'Israeli; his half-sister Rachel* was ten years older, and his father wanted Isaac to succeed him in the family business. Old Benjamin was disappointed. Isaac was a pale, pensive, solitary child; his son described him as 'timid, susceptible, lost in reverie, fond of solitude, or seeking no better company than a book'.[12]

Disraeli wrote an account of his father's childhood which is probably not to be trusted. Suspiciously similar to the romantic childhoods described in his novels, it probably owes a great deal to imagination. It seems likely, though, that Isaac's sharp-tongued mother bullied her son with sarcastic comments and tart remarks. Probably there were scenes, and once the boy is alleged to have run away from home. His father found him lying on a tombstone in Hackney churchyard, embraced him and gave him a pony. Isaac was sent to a private school run by a nonconformist minister near his parents' home at Enfield. More scenes followed, and then Isaac wrote a poem. His father, haunted by nightmares of Hogarthian garrets, was horrified, and Isaac, then fourteen, was packed off to Amsterdam. Four years later he returned, a disciple of Rousseau, gaunt, long haired and strangely dressed. His mother shrank from his embrace, his father found him a post in a counting house in Bordeaux. Whereupon Isaac announced that he had written a poem against commerce.

Desperate to escape his father's business, he sought a literary patron. He tried Johnson, who died, and his cringing yet pushy appeals to the Reverend Vicesimus Knox were rebuffed. At length he was taken up by the poet

---

* Disraeli seems not to have known of the existence of Rachel D'Israeli; he believed his father was old Benjamin's only child. She married her cousin Aaron Lara and, later, Angelo Tedesco; after his death in 1798 she settled in Leghorn, where she died in 1807. Her grandson was the distinguished Italian lawyer and economist, Vittorio de Rossi. In the 1920s Cecil Roth stayed in the same *pensione* in Florence as Rachel's great-grandson Gustavo de'Rossi, a painter and devout Jew. Each morning in winter Roth was woken by 'an awkward body stumbling over the furniture in the adjoining room in the half light. It was the first cousin (at two removes) of an English prime minister, on his way to attend morning service at Synagogue.'

laureate, Pye; more important, in 1791 when he was twenty-five, the year he published *Curiosities of Literature*, he inherited a legacy from his maternal grandmother, making him financially independent of his father.

Benjamin was an easy-going member of the Spanish and Portuguese Synagogue at Bevis Marks in the City. He contributed liberally to the synagogue: his synagogue tax increased as he grew wealthier, from 10s to £22 13s 4d in 1813, and he held minor office briefly.[13] He probably remained a broadly conforming orthodox Jew throughout his life, but, perhaps influenced by the socially ambitious Sarah, he mixed little with the Jewish community. His son Isaac was circumcised; but, thanks to his mother who foresaw only a future of degradation for him as a Jew, Isaac was not taught Hebrew, and received little Jewish education. Though he remained a member of the synagogue as a young man, he was a religious sceptic in the fashion of the Enlightenment – in *Curiosities of Literature* he described the Talmud as 'a compleat system of the barbarous learning of the Jews'.[14]

Isaac greatly admired the Enlightenment Jewish thinker Moses Mendelssohn (1729–86) and wrote an article praising him in 1798. Not only, he wrote, was Mendelssohn that rare being, a Jewish man of genius; he pointed the way forward for Jews of liberal views, like Isaac himself. Mendelssohn argued that Jews could remain Jewish while participating in common European culture. On the one hand, he called for their emancipation and on the other he implored Jews to abandon religious practices which restricted freedom of thought; his ideas were to lead to Reform Judaism. Mendelssohn's view that Jews need only believe in the existence of God, divine providence and the immortality of the soul appealed to the rationalist Isaac, who was repelled and embarrassed by their ceremonial observances and social exclusiveness.

Judaism, it is sometimes suggested, was the subject of furious argument within the D'Israeli household, Isaac's ferocious, strong-minded mother taking the side of her rationalist son against old Benjamin, the orthodox Jew. Sarah D'Israeli reacted so strongly against her Judaism that she died an informal Protestant and was buried in Willesden church. Isaac's biographer believes, however, that the Mendelssohnian reform movement had little impact on the family, and the quarrel remains a matter of speculation.[15] We can only speculate too about how Isaac's Jewishness shaped his character. The transition from the close-knit, inter-related London Jewish world of business to the non-Jewish world of letters was not accomplished without pain, though he was not a Jew who sought assimilation yet resented it, floating between bouts of self-hatred and self-pity, and exaggerated arrogance. His son tells us that he lacked self-esteem and suffered from bouts of depression throughout his life. But he seems to have found security in his library, shutting himself away from the Jewish world he had rejected.

For a young man like Isaac, desperate to escape from the darkness of mercantile Jewry into the pure light of reason, the Enlightenment held out the promise of emancipation, and the French Revolution initially fulfilled it. The Jews were liberated in France in 1791, and French conquest brought liberation to the Jews of the Netherlands in 1796 and Italy in 1796–8. During the bloody 1790s, however, Isaac repudiated the doctrines of the French Revolution, though he grew more interested in the cause of Jewish emancipation. Perhaps he realised that the French *philosophes*, and especially Voltaire, were more anti-Jewish than anti-clerical, attacking the Jews as the most superstitious of all peoples. Enlightenment rationalism was on the side of the Jews only if they stopped being Jews.[16]

That Isaac should incline to Toryism is less surprising than it seems; there were strong affinities between Jews and Tories in England. The Jews, as Disraeli wrote in *Coningsby*, were of their nature Tories – 'a race essentially monarchical, deeply religious, and shrinking themselves from converts as from a calamity, are ever anxious to see the religious systems of all the countries in which they live flourish'.[17]

If anything, the French Revolution intensified the loyalty of English Jews. Revolution raised the spectre of international Jewish conspiracy, and Jews were suspected as spies and crypto-Jacobins. Their response was to proclaim their loyalty more loudly than before; in 1792 the wardens of Isaac's synagogue instructed their dayan to preach a sermon stressing the duty of Jews to uphold king and constitution. In October 1803, when war was again declared with France after the short-lived Peace of Amiens, the Jews were quick to demonstrate their patriotism. In London they enrolled as volunteers, swearing oaths of fidelity to king and country on the Book of Leviticus, and marching past George III in a review in Hyde Park. What a lot of quadrupeds, quipped the king as the Jews marched past, bearing names like Fox, Wolf, Lyon and Bear.[18]

In his late twenties, Isaac D'Israeli had a breakdown. A doctor diagnosed consumption, and prescribed a warmer climate. Benjamin describes his father's illness, which was characterised by lassitude and despondency, as a 'failing of nervous energy' to which literary men are prone, the consequence of study and sedentary habits. The cause, he thought, was his 'inability to direct to a satisfactory end that intellectual power which he was conscious of possessing'. Isaac's breach with his parents and his ambivalence about his Jewishness had imposed a considerable psychological strain.[19]

The war with France prevented him from going abroad in search of warmth, and he went to convalesce in Exeter. Here he socialised with the local literati, and wrote the first version of the most influential of his books,

An Essay on the Literary Character. Two years later, in 1796, he returned to London and set himself up as a writer of taste in a bachelor apartment in the Adelphi, Robert Adam's Thames-side masterpiece. Still depressed, he told his friend the antiquarian bookseller Douce that he hankered after the 'bustle and literary circles in London'. In retrospect, Isaac spent those years as a 'young *littérateur* about town', dining out and lounging in Hatchard's bookshop, the meeting-place for Tory literary gentlemen. Often, though, London meant solitude, and his spirits sank as he gazed out over the Thames from the lonely and seedy splendour of his Adelphi chambers.[20]

In 1802, to the surprise of his friends, Isaac married; he was thirty-six. His wife was Maria Basevi (1775–1847). Maria was the daughter of Naphtali Basevi, a London merchant and prominent member of the synagogue at Bevis Marks. The Basevis were not Spanish or Portuguese Jews, but Italians – Maria's father came to England in 1762 from Verona. The Basevi family were more distinguished and more cultured than the D'Israelis, and claimed descent from the seventeenth-century Baron Basevi von Treuenburg, the court Jew of Prague ennobled by the Emperor Ferdinand. Through her mother, Rebecca Rieti, Maria came from three generations of English-born forebears, settled in London since the seventeenth century; and Rebecca Rieti's ancestry was, in Lucien Wolf's words, 'of the utmost distinction in Jewish history'. She was descended from the Aboab family, whose genealogy reached back without a break to Israel Aboab, 'the last Gaon of Castile, who, at the time of Torquemada's expulsion of the Jews from Spain in 1492, led a contingent of twenty thousand of his brethren into Portugal'. Disraeli's ancestry did go back to the Spanish exodus of 1492, as he claimed; but the line of descent was not, as he supposed, on his father's side but on his mother's.[21]

Isaac had no cousins in England, but through his marriage to Maria he became connected to the leading Anglo-Jewish families: Lindos, Mocattas, Mendez da Costas, Goldsmiths and Montefiores, through whom he was connected to the Rothschilds. Both Maria's brother Joshua Basevi and her sister Sarah were married to Lindos, and the Lindos' ancestry was even more brilliant than the Basevis'. Not only were they fugitives from the Lisbon Inquisition, proud and obstinate Marranos, but they were related to the Abarbanels, the premier family in Jewry. Don Isaac Abarbanel, who claimed direct descent from King David, was minister of finance to Ferdinand and Isabella of Castile when Torquemada ordered the Jewish diaspora in 1492, and he headed an exodus to Sicily at the time that Aboab escaped to Portugal.[22]

Soon after their marriage, Isaac and Maria moved into the house that is now 22 Theobald's Road, an elegant three-storeyed brick house with stone string-courses above the ground and first-floor windows, built about 1750, facing south on to a picture-book view over Gray's Inn Fields. Their first child, Sarah, was born in December 1802, almost exactly two years before Benjamin. Naphtali, born in 1807, died in infancy. Two more sons followed: Ralph (May 1809) and James (January 1813).

Maria D'Israeli is an enigma. In a family of letter writers, she wrote very few. In the memoir he wrote of Isaac, Benjamin did not mention her at all – to the dismay of his sister Sarah, who wrote: 'I do wish that one felicitous stroke, one tender word had brought our Dear Mother into the picture.' Isaac's biographer believes that his marriage to Maria was a happy one; Isaac told his friend Douce a year after his marriage, 'I have never yet found her desires interfere with my wishes, my pleasures are her pleasures, and my friends are her friends.'[23] Benjamin's silence about his mother says more about his relationship with Maria than it does about Isaac's. Benjamin wanted to blot his mother out.

Monypenny, Disraeli's Edwardian biographer, thought Maria had little influence on Benjamin. 'The Basevi family', he wrote, 'were ... not devoid of intellectual distinction, but no portion of it seems to have fallen to the lot of Maria Basevi.'[24] The few letters of Maria's that survive belie this harsh and condescending judgement; certainly she was no bluestocking, but neither was she stupid. A portrait of her made the year after Benjamin was born, when she was thirty, shows a strikingly handsome woman, black ringlets worn in Empire style, proud of her strong chin, straight-nosed profile and large dark eyes. It was from Maria, not Isaac, that Benjamin inherited his looks, the distinctive nose and luxuriant black curls. It is hard to believe that she was the colourless, passive creature, the 'excellent wife and mother', that biographers have described. Her ancestry and family was far more distinguished than Isaac's, yet Disraeli ignored the Basevi side of his pedigree and concocted a phoney ancestry for Isaac. His silence about his mother points perhaps to Benjamin's hurt and rejection rather than her insignificance.

The major source for his childhood relationship with his mother is his novels. Three of his early works – *Vivian Grey*, *Alroy* and *Contarini Fleming* – form a kind of fictionalised autobiography; Disraeli called them a psychological trilogy: a description of the 'secret history of my feelings'. Fathers and father-figures predominate: in *Vivian Grey*, written when Benjamin was twenty-one, Isaac is easily recognisable as Horace Grey, Vivian's father, but Mrs Grey is barely mentioned and there is little about Vivian's childhood. Disraeli writes that Mr Grey 'made an excellent domestic match; and, leaving the whole management of his household to his lady, felt himself as independent in his magnificient library, as if he had never ceased to be that true freeman, A MAN OF CHAMBERS'.[25] As a small boy, Benjamin probably saw very little of Isaac who, like Mr Grey, shut himself in his library all day, emerging only to give the boy a glass of claret.

Contarini Fleming, written five years later, is more revealing, though it is more self-conscious and harder to use as evidence than *Vivian Grey*. Subtitled a psychological romance, *Contarini Fleming* is a study of the formation of the poetic character – it explores the hero's emotional development. Contarini's mother, a noble Venetian, is dead; his father, whom he dearly loves, is a minister in a northern court who is too busy to pay attention to his son. Contarini is brought up by his step-mother, a beautiful northern woman, modelled very loosely on Maria. As a child, he is unhappy; his father and step-mother have two sons whom Contarini views with 'passive antipathy. They were called my brothers, but Nature gave the lie to the reiterated assertion. There was no similitude between us.' They do not even look the same as dark, Venetian Contarini. Had there been a half-sister, all might have been different. 'In that sweet and singular tie I might have discovered solace.' Contarini's step-mother does not love him; though she observes the strict line of maternal impartiality and the etiquette of maternal duty, she far prefers his younger brothers. She thinks Contarini stupid. He is silent and sullen. He hits his younger brother and is locked in his room by his step-mother and the 'domestic police'. He bolts the door on the inside, and refuses to come out or eat or speak all day. Half-fainting, his step-mother has the door forced. He stamps and growls and refuses to move. Distraught, she calls his father. Contarini hears the well-known step upon the stair and rushes sobbing into his father's arms. 'For the first time in my life I felt happy, because, for the first time in my life, I felt loved.'

Contarini withdraws into a private world of day-dreams and imagination. At the age of eight he falls in love with the beautiful Christiana, eight years his senior. A tutor is engaged, and he is formally emancipated from 'the police of the nursery and the government of women'. He visits the theatre, where for the first time he sees people 'conducting themselves as I wished', and it becomes a mania with him. At home, alone and without an audience, he becomes an actor on a stage, but he is still prone to fits of dark humour, moments when all seemed 'vapid, dull, spiritless and flat. Life had no object and no beauty; and I slunk to some solitary corner, where I was content to lie down and and die'. At the age of ten or eleven he has a lengthy fit, and scarcely speaks or eats for days. His step-mother calls in the doctors; Contarini lies upon the sofa with his eyes shut, feigning sleep and listening to their consultations. They are puzzled, for the real cause of his dark humours is 'want of being loved'.[26]

How authentic is all this? When one adds what is already known about Benjamin's relations with his family, reality slides into place. Disraeli adored his sister Sarah, to whom he was very close. His relations with his younger brothers, Ralph and Jem, were more distant. Like Contarini, Benjamin may have resented his younger brothers because his mother preferred them. The death of his baby brother Naphtali may have been transposed into the death of Contarini's mother in childbirth; perhaps it changed Maria's attitude towards Benjamin. Maria probably had more in common with her boisterous younger sons than with her two bookish older children, particularly the difficult Benjamin, who possibly felt his mother did not recognise his genius. Probably Benjamin did have the kind of rows with his mother that he described in *Contarini*, and like Contarini, Disraeli was seriously ill when he was eleven; he also had a passion for theatre. As a child, his relationship with Isaac was far easier than with Maria. He despised his mother because he thought she did not love him. He adored his father; and it was Isaac who gave him his astounding self-confidence.

When Benjamin was eight days old, he was circumcised according to Jewish rites, as were his younger brothers. Isaac D'Israeli rarely attended the synagogue and he defied Jewish dietary laws, but he paid his annual tax of £10 and brought his children up in the Jewish faith.

At the age of six Benjamin was sent to Miss Roper's school in Islington, then on to a school in Blackheath, kept by the Reverend John Potticary, an Independent minister. The school was liberal in politics and religion, and his schoolmates included members of the Quaker Gurney family, as well as Milner Gibson, the future Radical MP and Disraeli's political associate. Benjamin stood at the back of the classroom during prayers, and on Saturdays he and another Jewish boy received instruction from a Hebrew rabbi.[27]

In 1813, when Benjamin was nearly nine, Isaac was elected warden of the synagogue of Bevis Marks, but he declined to hold office. He was fined £40, and refused to pay. In December he wrote to the elders, explaining his reasons.

A person who has lived out of the sphere of your observation, of retired habits of life, who can never unite in your public worship, because as now conducted it disturbs instead of exciting religious emotions, a circumstance of general acknowledgement, who has only tolerated some part of your ritual, willing to concede all he can in those matters which he holds to be indifferent; such a man, with but a moderate portion of honour and understanding, never can accept the solemn functions of an elder of your congregation, and involve his life and distract his business pursuits not in temporary but permanent duties always repulsive to his feelings.[28]

The synagogue of Bevis Marks was in decline at this time. Members were leaving, and services were conducted in an 'indecorous, slovenly and unattractive manner'. As a follower of Mendelssohn, Isaac was repelled by the rigid orthodoxy of the elders. In March 1817, the synagogue again pressed for payment of the fine. Isaac was no longer inhibited by the fear of offending his father Benjamin, who had died the previous year, and he resigned his membership. Maria's brother, George Basevi, resigned at the same time.

Isaac was content to be a non-practising Jew. Breaking with the synagogue was a rational course for a man of enlightened views; Mendelssohn had argued that membership of churches should be voluntary, and that no man should be compelled to belong to the synagogue against his will. Isaac was openly critical of practices which separated Jews from Christians, such as circumcision, forbidden food and sabbath observance. Jewish authorities have criticised Isaac's opinions as 'facile'; but to the end of his life he was interested in the reform of Judaism and the emancipation of the Jews, and he published a book on *The Genius of Judaism* in 1833. There is a tradition that in 1841, as an old man of seventy-five, suffering from gout and nearly blind, Isaac travelled to London to attend the consecration of the Reform Synagogue opened by dissidents from the Spanish and Portuguese communities.[29]

Isaac's break with Bevis Marks prevented the bar mitzvah of his son Benjamin, which might otherwise have taken place in December 1817. He was content for his children to float in the same unattached state as himself, but he certainly had no intention that they should become Christians, a course which Mendelssohn had abhorred. According to Benjamin, it was Isaac's friend Sharon Turner, the Jewish historian of Anglo-Saxon England, who persuaded Isaac to allow his children to be baptised. Benjamin was baptised on 31 July 1817 by the Reverend Mr Thimbleby at St Andrew's, Holborn.*

Old Benjamin D'Israeli's death in 1816 left Isaac, now fifty, a wealthy man, and the following year he moved his family and growing library from 22 Theobald's Road to a larger house nearby: No. 6, Bloomsbury Square.

Bloomsbury Square was the first London square, laid out by Lord Southampton at the end of the seventeenth century. During the eighteenth century it had been a sought-after suburban outpost – Lord Chesterfield lived there, and so did Lord Mansfield, whose house was burned by the

---

* Ralph and James were baptised earlier in the month, and Sarah followed on 28 August. Cecil Roth has speculated that Benjamin's religious education and Hebraic consciousness were by this time so pronounced that he resisted baptism, refusing to go with Ralph and James. Tempting though this theory is, it is pure conjecture.

Gordon rioters in 1780. By the time the D'Israelis moved there, Bloomsbury Square was a respectable neighbourhood much favoured by lawyers, but no longer fashionable. No. 6, which is still standing, is a substantial grey-brick house, probably built about 1740 by Flitcroft, the architect of the Bedford Estate. Facing east on to the gardens in the centre of the square, it is a wide-fronted, handsome London house with a prosperous, no-nonsense eighteenth-century look about it.[30]

About the same time as the family went to Bloomsbury Square, Benjamin left Mr Potticary's school. As a baptised member of the Church of England, he was no longer disqualified from attending a major Anglican public school, and there may have been a family argument about where he should go.

It is possible (as *Vivian Grey* suggests) that Isaac wanted to send him to Eton, but was overruled by Maria who, fearful perhaps for Benjamin's health, insisted on a private school.[31] It was to a private nonconformist school that Benjamin was sent: Higham Hall, near Walthamstow in Epping Forest, kept by a Unitarian minister, the Reverend Eli Cogan, whom Isaac had met in a bookseller's shop.

The decision to send him to a private school was not remarkable. Dr Arnold's rule at Rugby began only ten years later (in 1827), and public school was not yet the automatic choice for the sons of the upper-middle class. In the 1810s and 1820s Eton followed by Christ Church was the norm only for the aristocracy. Here, as Disraeli recalled in *Endymion* (1880), were read 'very little more than some Latin writers, some Greek plays, and some treatises of Aristotle. These with a due course of Bampton Lectures and some dipping into the *Quarterly Review*, then in its prime, qualified a man in those days, not only for being a member of Parliament, but becoming a candidate for the responsibility of statesmanship.'

Disraeli of course was not trained to be a statesman, and when he became one he was sensitive to the charge that he had not received a proper classical education. Some of his political contemporaries were distinguished classical scholars – Lord John Russell translated a book of the *Odyssey* to pass the time at Geneva; Gladstone published prolifically on Homer; and Lord Derby made a successful blank verse translation of the *Iliad*. A sound grasp of the classics, and particularly Greek, was by mid-century seen as essential training for the statesman as well as the gentleman. Greek conveyed social status; it was also thought, rather oddly, to instil Christian morality. When in 1850 Richard Cobden declared that a single issue of *The Times* contained more useful information than the whole of Thucydides, he was greeted with howls of derision. Victorian statesmen could not afford to be ignorant of Greek.

In the autobiographical notes Disraeli wrote in old age for Monty Corry, his secretary and prospective biographer, he claimed that, though he did not reach the top class at Cogan's school (which consisted of only one boy) he read a great deal and received a very thorough grounding in Greek and Latin.[32] The account in *Vivian Grey*, written much closer to his schooldays and well before he had a political reputation to protect, is probably nearer the truth. Here he claims that 'Although more deficient than most of his own age in accurate classical knowledge, [Vivian Grey] found himself in talents, and various acquirements, immeasurably their superior.' Vivian's talents soon attract the admiration of the school, while boys who turned out perfect Latin dissertations and Greek odes are despised as dunderheads. He is the ringleader of the gang of *Romantiques* who rebel against the leadership of the *Classiques*. He stages illicit private theatricals, and he beats the leader of the *Classiques* in an epic fight – 'Oh! how beautifully he fought! how admirably straight he hit! and his stops as quick as lightning! and his followings up confounding his adversary with their painful celerity!'*[33]

Contarini Fleming's schooldays are similar to Vivian Grey's, though more romantic. Like Vivian, he is at first the hero of the school, 'caressed, adored, idolised'. He does badly in school lessons; his teachers, who treat their pupils like 'machines, which were to fulfil a certain operation, and this operation was word-learning' think him lazy, when he is hungry for ideas instead of words. And Contarini far prefers Greek love to Greek verses:

There was a boy and his name was Musaeus. He was somewhat my elder. Of a kind, calm, docile, mellow nature, moderate in everything, universally liked, but without the least influence, he was the serene favourite of the school. It seemed to me that I had never beheld so lovely and so pensive a countenance. His face was quite oval, his eyes deep blue: his rich brown curls clustered in hyacinthine grace upon the delicate rose of his downy cheek, and shaded the light blue veins of his clear white forehead.

I beheld him: I loved him. My friendship was a passion. Of all our society he alone crowded not around me. He was of a cold temperament, shy and timid. He looked upon me as a being whom he could not comprehend, and rather feared. I was unacquainted with his motives, and piqued with his conduct. I gave up my mind to the acquisition of his acquaintance, and of course I succeeded. In vain he endeavoured to escape....

Oh! days of rare and pure felicity, when Musaeus and myself with arms around each other's neck, wandered together amid the meads and shady woods that formed our limits! I lavished upon him all the fanciful love that I

* Sir Henry Layard (b. 1817) remembered being taken as a child to visit Mrs D'Israeli and seeing 'Ben', who appeared in shirt-sleeves and boxing-gloves, having been interrupted in the middle of a boxing lesson.

had long stored up; and the mighty passions that yet lay dormant in my obscure soul now first began to stir in their glimmering abyss.[34]

Contarini soon tires of Musaeus. Musaeus's friend challenges him, and a great fight takes place which Contarini wins. Like Vivian Grey, Contarini then becomes a loner and shuns the other boys.

Both Vivian Grey and Contarini thrash their enemies, become unpopular, and leave soon afterwards (Vivian is expelled). The sub-text to this story is surely anti-semitism. At school, Disraeli was taunted, bullied and persecuted for his Jewishness; anti-semitism was rife among schoolboys, and Disraeli suffered. He may also have been bullied on account of homosexuality. He left Cogan's in 1820, before he was sixteen. Isaac and Maria sent their two younger sons, Ralph and James, not to Cogan's but to Winchester.

Disraeli was too young for university, and seemed behind in his studies. Isaac decided that 'Ben' (as he was then called) should spend a year at home. No tutor was engaged; instead, he gave his son the free run of his library, and kept a rather distant supervision over his reading. Ben sat down to master the classics. In *Vivian Grey* he claimed that 'twelve hours a day, and self-banishment from society, overcame in twelve months, the ill effects of his imperfect education'. A diary of studies that he kept in 1820 shows him ploughing through a solid course of classical reading – Virgil, Lucretius and Lucian, lightened by Gibbon's *Decline and Fall* (which he enjoyed) and interspersed with the dry but necessary study of Greek metres and a heroic assault on Homer: 'Friday. Again at the Greek Metres – bewildered! lost! miserable work, indeed. Writing. Prepared Greek. Read Gibbon, vol. 9. Homer – the *Iliad*, Bk. 1st by myself.'[35]

Monypenny noted errors in Disraeli's Greek spellings, and concluded that, despite his strenuous efforts to teach himself, his Greek remained patchy to the end. Isaac, who was no classical scholar, could not have been much help. Yet, despite Disraeli's inadequate grasp of Greek language, he read it well enough to respond to the oratory of Demosthenes: after reading a famous passage, he wrote that 'our imagination is fired, our enthusiasm awakened, and even I, I who have been obliged to wade through his beauties, with a hateful lexicon at my side, have often wished to have lived in the olden time, when Philip was King of Macedon and Demosthenes demagogue of Athens'. Judged by the mandarin standards of Victorian classical education, Disraeli's Greek was no doubt poor; he never carried a slim, calf-bound volume of Homer or Thucydides in his pocket. Yet though he was no linguist, his mind was soaked and shaped by Greek and Latin literature. Classical characters, plots and allusions came naturally to him; to read his fiiction and journalism today without a classical dictionary is to miss a whole layer of meaning and reference. Like Vivian Grey, Disraeli at sixteen was an ardent classicist, who had discovered that 'all the wit and wisdom of the world were concentrated in some fifty antique volumes, and he treated the unlucky moderns with the most sublime spirit of hauteur imaginable. A chorus in the Medea, that painted the radiant sky of Attica, disgusted him with the foggy atmosphere of Great Britain; and while Mrs Grey was meditating a *séjour* at Brighton, her son was dreaming of the gulf of Salamis'.[36]

One Saturday in 1820 Disraeli also read a book by his father: *The Literary Character*. This was the revised edition of *Essay on the Literary Character* which Isaac had published in 1795 and it had a romantic history. In 1816, when Byron left England in disgrace and went into exile in Italy, he sold his books, among them copies of Isaac's works. These were bought by John Murray, Byron's publisher, who discovered that Byron had made marginal notes when he read them in Athens in 1810–11. Murray showed the *Essay on the Literary Character* to Isaac, who was thunderstruck. Here, scribbled in the margins of Isaac's reflections on the character of literary genius, were the authentic comments of one of the great geniuses of the age. Isaac set to work to produce a new version of the *Literary Character*, which came out in 1818, incorporating Byron's comments. Murray sent the book to Byron, who was flattered, though he pretended to be annoyed with Murray for giving away his juvenile flippancies. 'I have a great respect for Israeli and his talents,' Byron told Murray, 'and have been amused by them greatly, and instructed often ... I don't know a living man's book I take up so often, or lay down more reluctantly, as Israeli's.'[37]

Byron – brilliant, youthful, rebellious – seems an unlikely admirer of bookish, Jewish Isaac. When they first met in about 1812, Byron greeted him with so much respect that Isaac 'being a somewhat modest and retiring man' thought his leg was being pulled, but he soon found that Byron was in earnest. 'The fact is my works being all about literary men were exceedingly interesting to him. They contained knowledge which he could get nowhere else. It was all new to him.'[38] The *Literary Character*, which had started out as an essay on the characteristic disposition of literary men, grew, almost without Isaac's realising it, into a study of the pathology of literary genius. The 1818 edition was sub-titled, revealingly, The History of Men of Genius. The idea of genius – of innate brilliance – fascinated the Romantic generation, with their cult of youth. Genius, Isaac argued, was born, not made; it flowered in youth before education, society and experience had deadened it. Byron, a self-conscious genius, had much to learn from D'Israeli's work. So, perhaps, did Isaac's son Benjamin. The youth of genius, wrote Isaac, spends hours in solitary reverie which is often mistaken for melancholy. 'He [Isaac's geniuses were all men] is a day-dreaming dawdling child, often delicate and sometimes physically clumsy. He takes no part in the sports of his school mates; his parents find him difficult and sullen, and his teachers find him slow and dull.'[39]

The similarity between Isaac's description and Ben's youthful experience was extraordinarily striking. It was almost as if Benjamin's childhood and schooldays had been formed on the template of genius. His genius explained his difficulties with Maria, his failure at school. He had been unpopular not because he was Jewish but because he was different – a genius. He had felt different from the other boys at first because he was Jewish; now he knew that he was different because he was a genius.

In the memoir he wrote of his father, Disraeli described him as a shy, scholarly recluse, living in isolation from society. This was very misleading. Isaac was a fierce controversialist, freely attacking his critics; of one critic he wrote that his work was like 'a filthy platter heaved at us by the hoof of a literary yahoo'. He was also rather a glutton – he held comforting theories about the dependence of the mind's cultivation on the good feeding of the body – and the food at Bloomsbury Square was good. 'The *cuisine* of Mr Grey was *superbe*,' as Disraeli wrote in *Vivian Grey*: guests enthused about Maria's dinners as 'the most capital grub' – new potatoes, asparagus (this was March), wet and dry dessert.[40]

'Neither the fortune nor the family of Mr Grey entitled him to mix in any other society than that of what is, in common parlance, termed the middling classes,' wrote Disraeli in *Vivian Grey* – at twenty-one he had not yet concocted the picture of Isaac as the isolated aristocratic scholar Jew – 'but from his distinguished literary abilities he had always found himself an honoured guest among the powerful and the great.' Isaac's chief connection among the powerful and the great in the 1810s and 1820s was his publisher John Murray. Isaac had known Murray since 1795, when the seventeen-year-old took over the Murray family business and Isaac acted as a literary adviser; later, Isaac was a marriage trustee, and during the 1810s, when Murray held a kind of literary salon in his grand house in Albemarle Street, Isaac naturally had an entrée. Here, in Murray's drawing-room in the afternoons or at dinners, Isaac met the literary talents he wrote about – Byron, Scott, Southey – most of whom were published by Murray. Not that Isaac was immediately accepted; Southey thought he looked like 'a Portugueze who being apprehended for an assassin is convicted of being circumcised. I don't like him.' Southey was later won over by Isaac's broad good nature, and they became friends, though Southey noted what an odd sort of creature he was – 'the strangest mixture of information and ignorance, cleverness and folly'.[41]

The D'Israelis later quarrelled with Murray, and in his memoir Benjamin suppressed the friendship, but Murray was a frequent guest at Bloomsbury Square and a family friend. Benjamin had known Murray since boyhood, and as he grew up he was asked with Isaac to Murray's literary dinners. He took notes of one of these dinners in November 1822. Tom Moore, Byron's friend was there, and Isaac asked him whether Byron was much altered.

M: Yes, his facing has swelled out and he is getting fat; his hair is grey and his countenance has lost the 'spiritual expression' which he so eminently had. His teeth are getting bad, and when I saw him he said that if ever he came to England it would be to consult Wayte about them.

B[enjamin] D[israeli]: Who is since dead, and therefore he certainly won't come.

M: I certainly was very much struck with an alteration for the worse. Besides he dresses very extraordinarily.

D['Israeli]: Slovenly?

M: Oh, no! He's very dandified, and yet not an English dandy. When I saw him he was dressed in a curious foreign cap, a frogged great coat, and had a gold chain round his neck and pushed into his waistcoat pocket. I asked him if he wore a glass and took it out, when I found fixed to it a set of trinkets. He had also another gold chain tight round his neck, something like a collar.[42]

Three years later, Disraeli put these words into the mouth of one of the characters in *Vivian Grey*. But the seventeen-year-old scribbled notes not because he wanted copy for a novel but because Moore's talk seemed to bring him close to the glorious being, Byron, and to the world of great men.

Murray had a soft spot for Benjamin, in whom he saw a likeness of himself when young, and gave him the kind of support that Isaac had given *him* as a fledgling publisher; he acted as father-figure and patron. When Benjamin was only fifteen, Murray asked for his comments on the manuscript of a play. 'Notwithstanding the many erasures the diction is still diffuse, tho not inelegant,' wrote the young critic with great assurance. 'I cannot imagine it a powerful work as far as I have read.'[43] It was impossible to say, however, what a clever actor like Macready might make of it. Two years later, in 1822, on Disraeli's advice Murray published Crofton Croker's *Fairy Legends of Ireland*, a compendium of violent and nightmare-inducing tales which became a nursery bestseller.

In November 1821 Benjamin was articled to William Stevens, a partner in a firm of City solicitors – Swain, Stevens, Maples, Pearse and Hunt of Frederick's Place, Old Jewry. Mr Maples, the head of the firm, was an old friend of Isaac's, and, according to Benjamin, Maples and Isaac planned that he would become a partner in the firm and marry Maples's only daughter.

'My father', Disraeli recalled, 'was very warm about this business: the only time in his life in which he exerted authority, always, however, exerted with affection.'* At Frederick's Place, Benjamin worked in Mr Stevens's office, taking dictation of letters and sitting through interviews with clients. As an old man, his memories of this period were all about the drama of City life: 'extraordinary scenes when firms in the highest credit came to announce and prepare for their impending suspension; questions, too, where great amounts were at stake'.[44]

Ben was still living at home. After work, he went back to Bloomsbury Square, where he remembered spending the evenings 'alone, and always in deep study'. He put aside the dry technical books on law he was supposed to be studying, and plundered the shelves of Isaac's library. His appetite for the classics began to flag. His reading, he wrote as an old man, 'developed at last different feelings and views to those which I had willingly but too quickly adopted when I was little more than seventeen'. He experienced a kind of intellectual conversion. Greek, which he had slaved to teach himself the year before, now seemed futile. Vivian Grey, who had been utterly absorbed in the study of Plato and hungry for the works of the later Platonists, is laughed out of the later Platonists by his father, and soon becomes convinced of 'the futility of that mass of insanity and imposture – the Greek philosophy'. Contarini who, like Benjamin, had taught himself Greek, is absorbed in an esoteric study of the Dorian people, when his father tells him to read Voltaire. He stands before the hundred volumes on the shelf, takes one down and is instantly captivated. He roars, laughs, shouts with wonder and admiration. Voltaire's withering mockery of pedants, priests and tyrants alerts Contarini to the 'long, dull system of imposture and misrule that had sat like a gloating incubus on the fair neck of Nature'; he realises man's folly and imperfection, and abandons his work on the Dorians with disgust.[45]

He now signed himself Disraeli, dropping the foreign-looking apostrophe, though Isaac and Maria still kept it. He dressed in black, in the fashion of the Byron-crazed youth of 1822, shocking the wives of the respectable solicitors of Frederick's Place by appearing at their dinners in a black velvet suit with ruffles and black stockings with red clocks. Theatre was a passion with him. It has been suggested that he was the author of a melodrama called *Cherry and Fair Star or, The Children of Cyprus* which opened on the London stage at Easter 1822.[46] Certainly, he tried his hand at writing plays. In 1823 he wrote a play entitled *Rumpal Stilts Kin* in collaboration with his friend William Meredith. The Merediths were family friends of the Basevis, and William,

* We find Disraeli writing to congratulate Maples on the birth of a daughter in 1823, which suggests that his memory may be inaccurate – or the marriage plans exceedingly long-term.

two years older than Benjamin, was informally engaged to Sarah. He was the heir to his wealthy uncle, another William Meredith, who had been patron to the Platonist Thomas Taylor, an acquaintance of Isaac's whom he had satirised. Young William was bookish, rather pompous and long-winded. He was then an undergraduate at Oxford, where he and Benjamin wrote the play together.

Rumpal Stilts Kin is a verse extravaganza based on the fairy tale by Grimm, whose stories appeared in English translation in 1823. Short, slight and rumbustious, it was no doubt performed amid guffaws of laughter by the Meredith and D'Israeli families, and one copy was transcribed for each family by William. Disraeli seems to have written most of the play, which transposes the fairy tale to somewhere remarkably like Britain in 1823. When King Doronibon announces 'Exhausted treasures, and a bankrupt state', he summons his chancellor of the exchequer, whose solution is to marry the king to the miller's daughter who turns stone to gold (This joyful news [says the chorus] Will make the Blues/With envy fret and stare),[47] and when Rumpal Stilts Kin threatens to grab her baby, the chorus worries lest the child 'prove a second Caroline'.

In May 1824 Disraeli sent Murray the manuscript of a novel, *Aylmer Papillon*, in which he mixed observations on the state of society and the fashion for getting on in the world with the bustle and hurry of a story, so that 'my satire should never be protruded on my reader'. A month later Murray wrote rejecting the novel, and Disraeli told him to burn it – 'and as you have some small experience in burning MSS you will be perhaps so kind as to consign it to the flames'.[48] Disraeli was referring to Byron's *Memoirs*, which had been ceremonially burned in Murray's drawing-room amid much controversy in May; it was an astounding taunt for a nineteen-year-old to make.

The truth was he thought of himself as a youth of genius. William Archer Shee, a contemporary of Ralph and Jem, remembered the eighteen-year-old Disraeli at children's parties at Bloomsbury Square, 'in tight pantaloons, with his hands in his pockets, looking very *pale, bored* and *dissatisfied*, and evidently wishing that we were all in bed. He looked like Gulliver among the Lilliputians, suffering from chronic dyspepsia.'[49]

Disraeli grew restless at Frederick's Place and indifferent towards the law. Nothing would satisfy but foreign travel. In July 1824 he, Isaac and William Meredith embarked on a tour of the Low Countries.

TWO

Vivian Grey

1824–6

A FEW DAYS AFTER Byron's funeral procession came through the streets of London, Benjamin, his wheezing father and William Meredith clambered aboard a passenger boat moored at Ipswich on England's Suffolk coast. From Bruges, Isaac wrote assuring the family that the young travellers had been 'more sleepy than otherwise indisposed' during a 'tedious' journey. Benjamin's account was much more dramatic. His first voyage to the mainland of Europe was momentous, and nature of course was in harmony with his adventurous spirits. He told his family of a 'very stiff breeze and almost every individual was taken down stairs save ourselves, who bore it out in the most manly and magnificent manner, not even inclining to indisposition. We came in with a very fresh sea, the night was most magnificent, indeed I have never witnessed a finer night.'[1]

Bruges, Ghent, Antwerp, Brussels, Aix … Disraeli's jaunty letters home detailed their progress across Flanders, staying in 'crack' hotels, eating at *tables d'hôte*, their carriage surrounded wherever they went by crowds of beggars. ('The old women seem to have the best breath,' he wrote in his diary.) Their travels were made memorable by the food: 'a fricandeau the finest I ever tasted, perfectly admirable, a small delicate capital roast joint, veal chops dressed with a rich sauce piquante, capital roast pigeons, a large dish of peas most wonderfully fine, cheese dessert, a salad pre-eminent even among the salads of Flanders which are unique for their delicate crispness and silver whiteness, beer and bread ad lib, served up in the neatest and purest manner imaginable, silver forks etc.' All for six francs. At Brussels among the English visitors Disraeli found a 'Vulgar but lucky prejudice against frogs. Had the pâté to myself. Eat myself blind.'[2] Benjamin and Meredith lounged about, playing dominoes and billiards; by the time they reached Spa he had become, he wrote, 'a most exquisite billiard player'. Isaac haunted the cafés, reading Flanders papers which were stale copies of

Parisian copies of the English papers, discovering new ices and lecturing the young men on sorbets and liqueurs. He wore a black stock and left off powdering his hair which, together with Ben's habit of calling him 'the Governor', caused him to be mistaken for an English general.

They inspected the battlefields of Waterloo, guided by Koster, the peasant who had shown Napoleon over the battlefield, and who harangued them in a 'belle alliance' lingo of English, Flemish, French and Dutch. But their main concern was with the paintings of the Flemish school. Rubens and Van Dyck they hunted down in cathedrals, in public galleries and private collections, Disraeli making appreciative comments in the diary he kept on the tour.

At Ghent they heard high mass in the cathedral. 'A dozen priests in splendid unity, clouds of incense, and Mozart's sublimest masses by an orchestra before which San Carlo might grow pale,' he wrote in his diary. 'The effect inconceivably grand. The host raised, and I flung myself on the ground.'[3] It was his first encounter with Catholicism, and, starved of religion since his Anglican baptism, his response was intensely emotional. Flanders sowed the seed of the emotional sympathy with Catholicism which recurs in Disraeli's novels, from *The Young Duke* to *Sybil*.

From Aix they travelled to Cologne and up the Rhine as far as Koblenz. The Governor looked on as Ben and William gorged themselves on Rhine wines, downing umpteen bottles of Hochheim, Johannisberg, Rüdesheim and Assmannshausen. Two years later, in the second part of *Vivian Grey*, Disraeli imagined an elaborate drinking scene with the Archduke of Hochheimer, the Grand Duke of Johannisberger, the Margrave of Rüdesheimer given the characters of their wines.[4] His travel diary stops abruptly at Aix, but that he kept some record of the rest of the tour is suggested by the carefully observed descriptions in *Vivian Grey* Part Two, which describes a journey through the Rhineland. William Meredith instantly recognised its authenticity, and the German Prince Pückler-Muskau admired the book for its 'rather baroque, but often witty and faithful delineations of continental manners. The description of a ball at Ems is stinging.'[5]

Ems, the most fashionable watering place on the continent, was a very Castle of Indolence, Disraeli told his family. Here, gratifyingly, they found no English people, and such was the 'utter void of all thought and energy' that even the gambling tables and billiard room were deserted. He was struck by the prince of Nassau's astute commercial exploitation of the baths: the vast hotel was one of his palaces. 'The company at the Archduke's fête was *most select*,' he wrote in *Vivian Grey*; 'that is to say, it consisted of every single person who was then at the Baths: those who had been presented to his Highness, having the privilege of introducing any number of their friends; and those who had no friend to introduce them, purchasing tickets at an enormous price ..."[6] He was fascinated by the comic-opera world of the small south German states, their sleepy, indolent life, the Mozart opera and casinos; the intricate diplomacy of inter-state rivalry and mediatised princes manipulated by the masterly Metternich. 'The greatest enemy of the prosperity of Germany is the natural disposition of her sons; but that disposition, while it does now, and may for ever, hinder [them] from being a great people, will at the same time infallibly prevent [them] from ever becoming a degraded one.'[7] Few predictions have proved more wrong; but Disraeli's youthful exposure to the 'good Germans' of the south left him with a lifelong sympathy for Germany.

From Ems they journeyed to Frankfurt, a bustling, dashing city, where they feasted on opera (Mozart's *Magic Flute*) and 'Gatteau de Pouche' [*sic*], a sweet that Disraeli thought 'superb beyond conception'. Isaac bought prints for his collection at home – Dürer, Marcantonio Raimondi, Giulio Bonasone, and Rembrandt, 'very magnificent impressions and very reasonable'. On to Darmstadt, where they saw Rossini's *Otello*. 'The Duke himself, in grand military uniform, gave the word for the commencement of the Overture, standing up all the time, beating time with one hand and watching the orchestra thro' an immense glass with the other.' In *Vivian Grey* Disraeli satirised Darmstadt and its duke. 'The Grand Duke himself was a military genius, and had invented a new cut for the collars of the Cavalry.'[8]

After Heidelberg and Mannheim, they began their descent of the Rhine. So much had been written about it, Disraeli told Sarah, that he expected her to know the scenery as well as he did.[9] Nine years later Disraeli recalled that it was while descending the magical waters of the Rhine that he determined not to be a lawyer;[10] in Germany he had decided to try his hand as a writer.

On his return to England, Benjamin persuaded Isaac to let him abandon his clerkship at Frederick's Place. He joined Meredith reading for the bar at Lincoln's Inn, where he was admitted in November. His cousin, Nathaniel Basevi, twelve years his senior, was the first Jewish-born barrister to practise in the English courts, and Isaac had arranged for Ben to read law in Nathaniel's chambers; but it seemed unlikely that Ben would follow his cousin's example. The bespectacled, prematurely serious, physically minute and precise Basevi was shocked when Benjamin turned up in his chambers in Old Square with Spenser's *Faerie Queene* under his arm. 'THE BAR,' says the scornful Vivian Grey, 'pooh! law and bad jokes till we are forty; and then, with the most brilliant success, the prospect of gout and a coronet. Besides, to succeed as an advocate, I must be a great lawyer, and, to be a great lawyer, I must give up my chance of being a great man.'[11]

Disraeli was still restless. Far from satisfying him, travel had merely whetted his appetite for change. He craved fame, power, adventure; and he wanted it *now*. Isaac made a feeble suggestion of Oxford but, as Disraeli later recalled, 'the hour of adventure had arrived. I was unmanageable'. In *Vivian Grey*, Isaac/Mr Grey tries to persuade Disraeli/Vivian to go to Oxford, warning him against seeking to become a great man in a hurry. As they talk, there dashes by 'the gorgeous equipage of Mrs Ormolu', the wife of a man who was working all the gold and silver mines in Christendom. '"Ah! my dear Vivian," said Mr Grey, "it is *this* which has turned all your brains. In this age everyone is striving to make an immense fortune, and what is more terrific, at the same time a speedy one. This thirst for sudden wealth it is, which engenders the extravagant conceptions, and fosters that wild spirit of speculation which is now stalking abroad ... Let us step into Clarke's and take an ice.""[12]

Disraeli had returned from the Low Countries to find England in the grip of the first great speculative boom since the peace of 1815. Chancellor of the exchequer 'Prosperity' Robinson presided over soaring revenues as the Tory government cut tariffs, and in the City the bull market surged. The recognition by Canning, the foreign secretary, of the emergent new states of Latin America liberated from the moribund Spanish Empire cracked open a new source of fabulous wealth. Traditional Tories like the duke of Wellington and his confidante Mrs Arbuthnot fumed and fretted at Canning's seemingly irresponsible policy of breaking with the European Great Powers and allying himself with South American revolutionaries like Bolívar; but in the City Canning was a hero. City brokers charged fat commissions for loans to the new republics, and floated doubtful joint-stock companies to exploit the gold and silver mines of South America.

Disraeli, who did not possess fifty guineas in the world, was astonished by the revolution taking place in the financial relations of England and America. 'It immediately struck me', he wrote a few months later, 'that if fortunes were ever to be made this was the moment and I accordingly paid great attention to American affairs.'[13]

At Frederick's Place, Disraeli had made contact with John Powles, a director of J. & A. Powles & Co., a City merchant bank, who was the promoter of three companies – the Anglo-Mexican Mining Association, the Colombian Mining Association and the Chilean Mining Association. Disraeli went to dinner at the Powleses' luxurious house out of town; in *Vivian Grey*, where Powles features as Premium, he recalled how he drank in the glamour and drama of it all, feasting on Powles's ebullient plans to cut a canal through the isthmus of Panama or build a railway over the Andes.

In one part of the room was a naval officer, just hot from the mines of Mexico,

and lecturing eloquently on the passing of the Cordillera. In another was a
man of science, dilating on the miraculous powers of a newly-discovered
amalgamation process, to a knot of merchants, who, with bent brows and eager
eyes, were already forming a company for its adoption. Here floated the latest
anecdote of Bolívar; and there was a murmur of some new movement of
Cochrane's. And then the perpetual babble about 'rising states', and 'new
loans' and 'enlightened views' and 'juncture of the two oceans' and 'liberal
principles', and 'steam boats to Mexico'; and the earnest look which everyone
had in the room. Oh! how different to the vacant gaze that we have been
accustomed to! ... Everyone looked full of some great plan; as if the fate of
empires was on his very breath. I hardly knew whether they were most like
conspirators, or gamblers, or the lions of a public dinner, conscious of an
universal gaze, and consequently looking proportionately interesting.[14]

Though Premium's/Powles's silver plate was magnificent, his crest was a
bubble. Disraeli, however, was taken in. In November 1824 he and Thomas
Evans, a solicitor's clerk from Frederick's Place, began to buy South
American shares. Canning's formal recognition of the South American
republics at Christmas time 1824 pushed up Anglo-Mexican Mining
Association shares from £33 on 10 December to £158 on 11 January, but
Disraeli did not sell out and take a profit. Anticipating further rises, he
bought South American shares for John Murray at the end of January, and by
February Disraeli and Evans together owed over £2000 to their friend
Robert Messer, the son of a wealthy stockbroker, who bought their stocks for
them. Then share prices slumped. Enraged investors attacked the Anglo-
Mexican and Colombian Associations as fraudulent, and Lord Eldon, the
lord chancellor, threatened to intervene under the Bubble Act of 1720.

Enter the young Disraeli – or so he liked to think; at this point reality began
to blur into fiction, and the account he wrote for the moneylender Robert
Messer in April 1825 of his role over the previous few months is highly
romanticised. At the crisis caused by the February panic, Disraeli told
Messer, 'I stepped forward and offered my services to a dismayed and
despairing party.' He proposed measures which Powles took up: lobbying
MPs and organising deputations to ministers to oppose Eldon's intervention.
To no avail; the press and the public were still hostile, and 'a cry of Bubble
was raised which was echoed even in the houses of Parliament'. Our hero
tried another tack. He dashed off a 100-page pamphlet, entitled an 'Inquiry
into the Plans, Progress and Policy of the American Mining Companies'. His
first venture into print, it was published anonymously in March by Murray
(who, thanks to Disraeli's speculation on his behalf, had much to lose from
Eldon's intervention), and, according to its author, it successfully exposed

the fallacy of Eldon's parallel with the South Sea Bubble of 1720. (The pamphlet did indeed go through three editions, though one reviewer commented that 'Whoever wrote it is an ugly customer'.) 'After exertions during which for many nights I did not even sleep', Eldon abandoned his threat to interfere.

> I published the 3rd edit. of my Inquiry and found myself in possession of shares in all the great mining Companies to the amount of many thousand pounds.
>
> All the information which is now received from America passes thro' my hands ... I have perused secret reports which have not even been seen by many of the Directors themselves. I have read every book upon the subject and conversed with secret agents of the Companies in which I am interested and I have come to the conviction that the 100£ shares in the Mexican mining Companies will in a very few years be worth upwards of 1000£ apiece.[15]

Mrs Arbuthnot, confidante to the duke of Wellington, noted in March that the House and the country were obsessed with City speculation to the exclusion of all else. 'I am', she wrote, 'very fond of these speculations and should *gamble* greatly in them if I could; but Mr Arbuthnot does not like them and will not allow me to have any of the American ones as their value depends upon political events.'[16] The caution of Mr Arbuthnot was not shared by the twenty-year-old Disraeli. South American share prices remained stubbornly low, but he was optimistic, predicting terrific increases when the mining companies declared their dividends. He went on buying Anglo-Mexican, and formed a partnership with John Murray, who owned two-thirds of the South American mining shares held in an iron box in Disraeli's room, Disraeli owning the other third; when he reckoned up their accounts at the end of March 1825, Disraeli found himself worth £1009 and credited Murray with £1650, exclusive of a fresh deposit.[17] In April, Disraeli told Messer that his shares were worth a total of £6000. In addition, he had borrowed £4000 from Messer and his uncle George Basevi, which was invested in a mysterious colonial undertaking.[18]

Not content with making his fortune, Disraeli planned to launch himself into politics. He persuaded Murray to introduce him to Canning. Canning was not only the creator of Anglo-American trade; he was an outsider, like Disraeli – the son of an actress who, since Castlereagh's death in 1822, had achieved a dominating influence in the Tory government of the inactive Lord Liverpool, to the dismay of such Tory insiders as the duke of Wellington or Mrs Arbuthnot, who declared that Canning's 'want of principle or high honourable feeling may be derived from the stock he is sprung from'. In the same breath she pretended to admire 'the institutions of a country where talent and genius can force their possessor into power and opulence in spite of the most adverse circumstances'.[19] Canning was the victim of the double standards Disraeli was soon to encounter as an outsider in politics.

Disraeli dashed off a second pamphlet, entitled 'Lawyers and Legislators or Notes on the American Mining Companies', which he induced Murray to publish on credit, and dedicated ('without permission') to Canning, his would-be patron – a rash presumption, as this pamphlet was even more critical of Canning's cabinet colleague Lord Chancellor Eldon than the first had been.[20]

More daring still, he planned to bring together Murray's publishing and Powles's financial backing to found a daily newspaper, 'which will be under the immediate patronage of Mr Canning'. It would soon become the leading newspaper, an occurrence, wrote Disraeli, 'from which I may obtain not only considerable profit, but which will also materially assist me in gaining the object of my highest ambition': politics. Contemplating the past seven months of unwearied exertion and harrowing care, Disraeli told Messer in April, 'I feel actually dizzy. It is truly work for a life.' And he added: 'On the Mexican mines I rest my sheet anchor.' That was the problem.[21]

Since 1813 *The Times* had been printed by steam; churning out printed sheets at the rate of 1100 per hour, steam presses fed a public hungry for news, and the appetite seemed to grow with the supply. Under Thomas Barnes, who became editor in 1817, *The Times* had displayed an unwelcome and unwonted radicalism, and John Murray, whose Tory *Quarterly Review* (1809) had successfully countered the Whig *Edinburgh Review*, had for some time contemplated founding a Tory rival to *The Times*. Disraeli had little difficulty in talking Murray into his newspaper project, capitalising on the success of the South American speculation. 'Be easy about your mines,' he told Murray in May, 'we were more behind the scenes than I even imagined.' Powles, he reported, 'grows warmer hourly' for the newspaper and is perpetually asking whether things are definitively settled.[22] Three months later, in August, an agreement was drawn up between Disraeli, Murray and Powles to establish a morning paper; Murray was to put up half the capital, and Disraeli and Powles a quarter each. They planned to start publishing in January 1826. But they had no editor. In this emergency, Murray turned to his friend Sir Walter Scott, bestselling author of the day and a Tory who had helped found the *Quarterly*: he was also a friend of Canning. In September Disraeli posted to Scotland on an urgent mission; his destination was Abbotsford, Scott's Border estate, his brief to offer the job of editor to Scott's son-in-law, John Gibson Lockhart.

Disraeli took with him a volume of Froissart's medieval chronicles, but he found little time to read. He had never before ventured north of the Trent; the family spent summers by the seaside at Worthing or Brighton, and the four-day journey by coach from London to Edinburgh was in itself an adventure. He stayed one night at York, where he witnessed the neighbouring gentry pouring in for the annual music festival. 'The four-in-hands of the Yorkshire squires, the splendid rivalry in liveries and outriders, and the immense quantity of gorgeous equipages – numbers with four horses – formed a scene which you can only witness in the mighty and aristocratic county of York.'[23]

In Edinburgh, Disraeli revelled in the delights of a Scotch breakfast (cold grouse and marmalade) and devised an elaborate code for his letters to Murray. Scott was the Chevalier; M (from Melrose) was Lockhart; X was 'a certain personage on whom we called one day, who lives a slight distance from town and who was then unwell' (presumably Canning), while O was 'the political Puck' – Disraeli himself.[24] From Edinburgh he travelled south to Melrose and presented himself at Chiefswood, M's cottage *ornée* on Scott's estate. Lockhart, who was expecting Isaac, was disappointed at seeing the political Puck, and at first 'everything looked as black as possible'. Disraeli described the scene in *Vivian Grey*, where Lockhart (who was strikingly good-looking) becomes Cleveland: 'Mr Cleveland was a tall and elegantly formed man, with a face which might have been a model for manly beauty. He came forward to receive Vivian, with a Newfoundland dog on one side, and a large black greyhound on the other; and the two animals, after having elaborately examined the stranger, divided between them the luxuries of the rug. The reception which Mr Cleveland gave our hero, was cold and constrained in the extreme, but it did not appear to be purposely uncivil.'[25]

Within a few hours, however, the two men 'completely understood each other' and, so Disraeli told Murray, 'were upon the most intimate terms'. Lockhart was reluctant to leave Scotland, and afraid of losing status by accepting the editorship of a newspaper which did not yet exist. The same objection was made more strongly by his father-in-law, Sir Walter, the following day. Disraeli did his persuasive best to convince Lockhart that he was coming to London 'not to be an Editor of a Newspaper, but the Directeur General of an immense organ and at the head of a band of high bred gentlemen and important interests'. All America and the commercial interest is at our beck, he told Lockhart: the church is firm, and the West India interest will pledge themselves. Lockhart must have a seat in parliament – that summer Lockhart had spent two days with Scott's friend the great X (Canning), staying with Southey in the Lake District, and now was surely a favourable time to make a parliamentary arrangement. 'If this point could be arranged,' said the political Puck, 'I have no doubt, that I shall be able to organise, in the interest with which I am now engaged, a most IMMENSE PARTY, & MOST SERVICEABLE ONE.'[26]

Disraeli stayed nearly three weeks with Lockhart. They became friends. He dined at Abbotsford, the Gothic extravaganza which was rapidly devouring Scott's record royalties. They drank whisky in Scott's galleried library, Scott in his armchair surrounded by half-a-dozen Dandie Dinmont terriers; had Disraeli inspected the shelves, he would have found several of Isaac's books – Scott had written notes in his copy of Isaac's *Calamities of Authors* (1812), and the two men had corresponded over Isaac's work on James I, whose reputation Isaac had attempted to rescue from the Whig historians.[27]

Murray forwarded Disraeli's despatches from the Borders to Isaac, who was quite overcome by what his son had achieved – from obscure beginnings, he wrote, the newspaper promised to become 'a new intellectual steam engine'.[28] Murray also wrote a letter of recommendation to Lockhart eulogising Disraeli ('I never met with a young man of greater promise ...') but Scott was not taken in. He cruelly described the dandified Disraeli as 'a sprig of the rod of Aaron ... In point of talents he reminded us of his father for sayth Mungo's garland Crapaud pickanini, Crapaud himself, which means a young coxcomb is like the old one who got him.'[29] William Wright, Lockhart's lawyer friend, however, wrote that Disraeli was a 'sensible clever youth' whose 'judgement however wants sobering down'.[30]

On 7 October Lockhart wrote to Murray declining the post of editor of the newspaper; he was after a higher prize: editorship of the prestigious *Quarterly Review*. With this in view, he agreed to come to London to meet Murray. Lockhart and Disraeli travelled south together and saw Murray on 20 October. Murray, whom Byron described as 'the most timorous of all God's booksellers', was drinking too much, and on this occasion his drunkenness prevented a proper understanding with Lockhart – or so Disraeli thought. He later wrote primly to Lockhart, 'You and he have never rightly understood each other. When such connections were about to be formed between two men, they should have become acquainted not by the stimulus of wine. There should have been some interchange of sentiment and feeling.'[31] Between hiccups, Murray reached an agreement with Lockhart which was witnessed by Disraeli and the lawyer William Wright. Lockhart was to become editor of the *Quarterly*, for which he was to receive £1000 a year; in addition, he was to contribute articles 'consistent with his rank in life' to the newspaper, for which he was to be paid a princely £1500 each year. What Disraeli's role was to be remains a bit of a mystery. A draft letter from Murray to Walter Scott written on 13 October says, 'With regard to our

Great Plan – which really ought not to be designated a newspaper, as that department of literature has hitherto been conducted – Mr Lockhart was never intended to have anything to do as editor: for we have already secured two most efficient and respectable persons to fill that department. I merely wished to receive his general advice and assistance.'[32] That one of the efficient and respectable persons was Disraeli seems more than likely.

In the summer of 1825 Isaac rented Hyde House near Amersham from Robert Plumer Ward, a retired Tory politician, and Disraeli brought Lockhart to stay there. He returned to London to work on the *magnum opus*, as he called the newspaper. Not even the sudden death of his grandmother, Isaac's fierce mother, shook his devotion to the newspaper project. He reported his progress in a series of breathless bulletins dispatched to Lockhart in Scotland during November: he had written to six different correspondents in the Levant and Morea; in Germany, correspondents had been secured in ten cities – a great *coup* in which he was much assisted by Murray's German sister-in-law Mrs William Elliot ('who when devoid of humbug is very clever'); all South America was covered, and all the North American newspapers. As Paris correspondent, Disraeli engaged Dr Maginn, a drunken but talented Irishman, overcoming the doctor's reservations and his tendency to quote Barnes, editor of *The Times*, by giving 'a slight and indefinite sketch of our intentions'. The effect was electric: 'The Dr started from his chair like Giovanni in the Banquet scene, and seemed as astounded, as Attonitus, as Porsenna when Scaevola missed him.' Edward Copleston, provost of Oriel, would cover the universities, and the bishop of Durham and his chaplain, the formidable Henry Philpotts, both staunch opponents of Catholic Emancipation, were to write on religion. As for the mechanical part, Disraeli had engaged his architect cousin, George Basevi, and he could see no reason why publication should not begin on 1 February 1826.[33]

His grandiose claims turn out on inspection to be somewhat exaggerated. True, Maginn went to Paris; and Disraeli wrote to Mr Maas, the hotelier with whom he had stayed in Koblenz, as well as drafting letters in Murray's name to half a dozen correspondents abroad. Philpotts and Copleston, however, and the twenty-seven correspondents Disraeli boasted of in the Levant and the Baltic, belong to the realms of romance. But the rug was pulled from under Disraeli's feet before his claims could be put to the test. He fell victim to a cabal, the double-crossing intrigue so typical of Canning's political era. He was betrayed by Lockhart; but Lockhart was first the target of a cabal from which Disraeli helped to rescue him.

In *Vivian Grey*, someone remarks that Lockhart is 'a man of great power, but I think rather too hot for the Quarterly', and Vivian replies, 'Oh! no, no, no – a little of the Albemarle Anti-attrition will soon cool the fiery wheels of his bounding chariot.'[34] The Albemarle Anti-attrition were the men who advised Murray on the *Quarterly*: 'a *junta* of official scamps', Disraeli called them, the most influential of whom were two Admiralty men – John Barrow, geographer and explorer, and John Wilson Croker. Barrow has often been blamed for plotting against Lockhart, but the plot was probably hatched by the far more sinister figure of J. W. Croker.

Croker was the *éminence grise* of the Tory press. In his notorious 'slashing articles' for the *Quarterly* (anonymous of course and composed in deepest secrecy), Croker gaily 'massacred a she-liberal (it was thought that no one could lash a woman like Croker)' or, as Disraeli wrote in *Coningsby*, 'cut up a rising genius whose politics were different from his own'. The she-liberal whom Croker famously massacred in 1821 was the Irish novelist, Lady Morgan; the rising genius was Keats, whose *Endymion* Croker savaged in 1818 – the review was said (wrongly) to have hastened the poet's death. Croker was anxious lest Lockhart's appointment should undermine his dominance at the *Quarterly*. He was also concerned that Murray's Canningite paper would interfere with his plans to establish a Tory newspaper of his own. Determined to block Lockhart, Croker tried to poison Murray against him by harping on Lockhart's past: as a young man of twenty-three Lockhart had contributed wicked satire to *Blackwood's*, and he was supposed to have written the blasphemous Chaldee MS.[35]

Murray responded to Croker's campaign by sending Disraeli on a second and secret mission to the Borders in November, to ask Scott to write letters of support for Lockhart. This time Disraeli stayed at Abbotsford for only one day. As he came down to dinner, he found Scott 'walking up and down the hall with a very big, stout, florid man, apparently in earnest conversation'. It was Scott's publisher, Archibald Constable, publisher of the *Edinburgh Review*; unknown to Disraeli, Constable was on the point of bankruptcy. In the City, boom was turning to panic: Disraeli's Latin American shares had slumped at the end of October, banks were calling in their bills, and Constable's London agents threatened to foreclose on his account, bringing down not only Constable but Scott, whose affairs were deeply and dangerously involved with his publisher's. Disraeli travelled to London with Constable, who bragged all the way. He was especially proud of an article on Milton in the latest *Edinburgh Review*, which had been much praised at Abbotsford; like all articles in the review it was anonymous, but on the journey south Disraeli ferreted out the secret of its authorship. It was the work of Thomas Babington Macaulay, a lawyer only four years older than Disraeli.[36]

Disraeli was out of his depth. He made a miserable mess of the mission to

Abbotsford. He was supposed not to tell Lockhart what he was up to, but told him everything; he also exceeded his instructions in mentioning the names of Barrow and others to Scott. Back in London, Murray, who had been got at by Barrow, was furious. He accused Disraeli of ruining everything, and made him promise not to write to Lockhart. Disraeli promptly did so, telling Lockhart of the anger of the Emperor (as he and Lockhart called Murray), and ending, 'Consider … this violation of my word is the consequence of my sincere friendship for you, and mention it not to the winds.'[37] Next day, however, Disraeli had a long talk with Murray who, bolstered by Scott's letter of support, now backed Lockhart against Barrow and Croker. Disraeli dashed off a triumphant line to Lockhart, boasting that he had slain the mighty Python of Humbug 'whose vigorous and enormous folds were so fast and fatally encircling us', adding 'You will now come to London *in triumph*'.[38] He wrote daily to Lockhart, reporting fully on events in Albemarle Street, and urging Lockhart to come to London as speedily as possible. He had been mistaken, he told him, in complaining of Murray's inconsistency, vacillation and indecision. Murray was a noble and generous-minded being in thrall to the intrigue of selfish and narrow-minded officials who surrounded him. 'The scales however have at length fallen from our friend's eyes, and the walls of the Admiralty have resounded to his firm and bold but gentlemanly tones … His mind has undergone a revolution which it has taken ten years to bring about.' Lockhart would not know Murray for the same man – 'Thank God I did not postpone my departure to town one other second!'[39]

Though Disraeli was confident he had scotched Croker and the Admiralty gang ('Your fear', he told Lockhart on 25 November, 'that Murray may be endangered by a conference with Croker makes me smile'), he still had nagging doubts about Murray. 'It is *absolutely necessary*', he told Lockhart, 'that you and I should have a conversation before you see Murray. I have no objection to his knowing it, but mind me, it is absolutely necessary.'[40] Lockhart, however, was already writing to Murray. Croker's articles in the *Quarterly*, he wrote, did more harm than good, and his contributions could well be dispensed with – in fact, Croker was banished from the *Quarterly* for six years. Ominously for Disraeli, though, Lockhart also hinted that he thought the *Quarterly* counted for far more than the newspaper: 'It is of the highest importance that in our anxiety about a new affair one should not lose sight of the old and established one.'[41] In all the excitement over Croker and the *Quarterly*, Disraeli had taken his eye off the newspaper; now Lockhart had the job at the *Quarterly*, he wanted little to do with the paper or, for that matter, with Disraeli.

At the end of December, Disraeli suggested a name for the paper: the *Representative*. Then he vanished from the scene.

What happened? For one thing, the City crash of December 1825. A trade deficit caused gold to leave the country, money became scarce, and panic ensued. Disraeli described the sequel in *Vivian Grey*: 'smash went the country banks – consequent runs on the London – a dozen baronets failed in one morning – Portland place deserted – the cause of infant liberty at a terrific discount – the Greek loan disappeared like a vapour in a storm – all the new American stakes refused to pay their dividends – manufactories deserted – the revenue in decline – the country in despair – Orders in Council – meetings of Parliament – change of Ministry – and new loan!'[42] Many of the Latin American mining ventures were sound, but though the mines contained what Disraeli described as veins of immense and incalculable worth, the crash destroyed the economies of the new republics, and the mines were abandoned. Disraeli was ruined, his mining shares worth nothing. He was in no position to put up the quarter share of the newspaper's capital he had undertaken in the agreement he had made with Murray and Powles. Nor was Powles, who had made personal loans to the South American republics totalling £120,000 and lost every penny. Yet Murray, who had also lost a lot of money, went ahead with the newspaper; it began publication at the end of January 1826.

The *Representative* was a short-lived flop. The paper was disastrously dull and shapeless, and lacked a clear editorial policy. Murray, who was said to have hired six editors in seven days, failed to appoint a proper editor. *The Age*, the Tory scandal sheet, printed a story of Murray drunkenly zig-zagging one evening in the neighbourhood of Cavendish Square when someone asked if he wanted a cab. 'No damn me, sir,' hiccupped Murray, 'I want an editor!'[43] He lost £26,000 on the paper, which ceased publication after six months.

Several months later the *Literary Magnet* identified Disraeli as editor of the *Representative* who, 'after a display of puppyism, ignorance, impudence and mendacity, such as have seldom been exhibited under similar circumstances, was deposed amidst the scoffs and jeers of the whole Metropolitan Literary World'. Disraeli always denied that he was the *Representative*'s editor or that he ever wrote a line for the paper. 'All I ever did in connection with the *Representative*,' he told Philip Rose in 1871, 'was at Murray's request to see some persons for him.' The real editor, said Disraeli, was Lockhart. In an autobiographical memorandum of 1860 he recalled that he had hung about Lockhart, 'as boys do about the first distinguished man with whom they become acquainted'; and when Lockhart undertook to edit the paper, 'he often made use of me and I was delighted with his confidence'. When the paper failed, Disraeli alleged that Lockhart, who was 'an expert in all the nebulous chicanery of these literary intrigues', established the myth of Disraeli's editorship to shield himself.[44]

Lockhart's role was probably more damaging than that. In October 1826 Murray wrote that his complaint against Disraeli derived from 'the untruths which he told and for his conduct during (of which in part I made the discovery subsequently) and at the close of our transactions …'.[45] Someone told Murray that Disraeli had deceived and double-crossed him, and it must have been Lockhart. There was a scene with Murray at Albemarle Street, described by Disraeli in *Vivian Grey*.

He raved! he stamped! he blasphemed! but the whole of his abuse was levelled against his former 'monstrous clever' young friend; of whose character he had so often boasted that his own was the prototype, but who was now an adventurer – a swindler – a scoundrel – a liar – a base, deluding, flattering, fawning villain, etc., etc., etc., etc.

'My Lord!' said Vivian.

'I will not hear you – out on your fair words! They have duped me enough already. That I, with my high character and connections! that I … should have been the victim of the arts of a young scoundrel!'[46]

In 1829 Murray told Tom Moore that it was Disraeli who had wheedled him into the ruinous newspaper project and who 'had also been the cause of Lockhart's being brought away from Edinburgh, where … "he was so comfortable," – thereby implying a little that he wished Lockhart back again'.[47] Disraeli had played a crucial part in persuading Murray to appoint Lockhart to the *Quarterly*. Once Lockhart's appointment was secure, he dropped Disraeli, intriguing against him with Murray (and possibly Croker). But Disraeli too had played a double game, siding with Lockhart against Murray. His mistake was to imagine that he could operate as a manipulator; he badly underestimated Lockhart and Croker.

On 21 December 1825 Disraeli was twenty-one. At an age when, as he wrote in *Vivian Grey*, most creatures were moping in halls and colleges, he had quarrelled with John Murray, his only friend in the great world, and he was head over ears in debt. Exactly how much he owed is hard to tell; it always is. By June 1825 he and Evans had together lost £7000 on their mining speculations, about half of which had been paid off by Evans in cash. By the end of December 1825 their joint debt to the moneylender Messer was £2833. Disraeli had also borrowed from his uncle Basevi, and he owed money to Murray, who had published the mining pamphlets on credit. He was probably in debt to Powles, and there were almost certainly others.

Disraeli was not legally answerable for his debts, which were incurred before he was twenty-one. Yet Messer continued to press him and Evans for repayment; he was still pressing Disraeli for £1500 twenty-five years later.[48] Uncle George Basevi probably never saw the thousand pounds he had lent his nephew, which may be one reason why relations with his Basevi cousins began to cool. Yet Disraeli seems to have made no appeal to Isaac to help him out of his scrape, even though Isaac was his sole source of capital funds. Instead, he appeased his creditors through evasions, half-truths, promises. Debt was itself a kind of education; meanwhile he saw a way of turning his recent adventures to good account – he would write a novel about them.

Disraeli always said that he wrote *Vivian Grey* at Hyde House before he was twenty-one, and that he took the idea from the novel, *Tremaine*.[49] *Tremaine, or The Man of Refinement* had been published anonymously in 1825. It was puffed by the publisher, Henry Colburn, as the work of an author famous in political life and brilliant in social circles and became a bestseller largely on account of the mystery surrounding its authorship. 'Who *is* the author of *Tremaine?*' asks a character in *Vivian Grey*, and Vivian teasingly replies, 'It's either Mr Ryder, or Mr Spencer Perceval, or Mr Dyson, or Miss Dyson, or Mr Bowles, or the Duke of Buckingham, or Mr Ward, or a young Officer in the Guards, or an old Clergyman in the North of England, or a Middle-aged Barrister on the Midland Circuit.'[50] Disraeli well knew that the author was Robert Ward (he added Plumer to his name in 1828) from whom Isaac had rented Hyde House: Isaac may have read the novel in manuscript. They met through Ward's solicitor, Benjamin Austen who lived at 33 Guildford Street, close to Bloomsbury Square. Sara, Benjamin Austen's wife, was bright, good-looking and childless; now twenty-nine, she had collected a circle of artists and painters who met in her drawing-room, and, bursting with energy, she started to act as a literary agent. She sold *Tremaine* to Colburn, carefully protecting Ward's anonymity even from his publisher, and she organised publicity for the novel: early in 1825 she wrote asking Isaac to review *Tremaine* for the *Quarterly* – which was how the Austens came to know their neighbours the D'Israelis.

Tremaine is a tedious homily against Voltairean scepticism, preached without humour or sharp dialogue. Ward was a retired party hack of sixty, pompous and a snob – not at all the kind of figure Disraeli admired, but he was impressed by the *Tremaine* formula. It was one of the first 'fashionable novels': silver-fork fiction which promised to divulge the secrets of aristocratic society to a middle-class public hungry for social titillation and gossip. During the crash of 1825–6, when the book trade collapsed, Henry Colburn made record profits by saturating the market with 'fashionable' bestsellers, of which *Tremaine* was one. To Disraeli, who had the adventurer's craving to be on the inside, the formula was irresistible.

Biographers have been rightly dismissive of Disraeli's claim that he wrote

Vivian Grey at Hyde House. He may well have composed the first book there however – a brief and breezy account of Vivian's schooldays. Early in the new year of 1826 Disraeli sat down to finish the novel at Bloomsbury Square. He wrote very fast, crossing out hardly at all: as he recalled in *Contarini Fleming*, page followed scrawled page, tossed on the pile on the floor before the ink was dry, as his mind raced ahead of his pen. It was exhausting, and after several hours his hand hurt and his whole frame ached, but it was exhilarating. Each day, as he reread what he had written, he wrote a little less.[51] By mid-February, he had written more than he could judge for himself; he needed someone to read the manuscript, and he needed a publisher – now Murray was out of the question, who better to arrange things than Isaac's new friend Sara Austen? Though Disraeli barely knew her, he sent her the manuscript. She was prompt and effusive, replying on 25 February: 'I am *quite delighted* with it, and *enter into the spirit of the book entirely* – I have now gone through it twice – and the more I read the better I am pleased.' She breathlessly told him that he had the entrée to her at any time to go through the book together – he must burn her letters, but she had quite forgotten his Christian initial, so directed her letter to Mr D'Israeli Junior.[52]

Sara Austen was willing to sell the book to Henry Colburn, keeping the author's name secret, but the scheme had to be approved by Mr D'Israeli senior. At this stage Isaac's approval probably meant far more to the ambitious Mrs Austen than the friendship of his twenty-one-year-old son – '*I would give the world*', she wrote, '*to know what Mr D'I says of the MS tomorrow* – Cannot you write me a note, or call?' Isaac approved, and Disraeli sat down to finish the book, sending instalments to Mrs Austen, who was copying it out in her own hand – in order, she said, to protect the author's anonymity, and partly no doubt to edit the manuscript, which showed clear signs of hasty composition.[53]

By mid-March he had written enough to publish. Colburn gave £200 for the copyright, and puffed it as the anonymous work of a young man of high life, a 'Don Juan in prose', featuring nearly all those adorning fashionable society. Readers were not disappointed. *Vivian Grey* told the story of 'an elegant, lively lad, with just enough of dandyism to preserve him from committing *gaucheries*, and with a devil of a tongue'. His father, Horace Grey, is a man of distinguished literary abilities and a private income of £2000 a year. The story opens with Vivian's unfortunate experience at private school. At seventeen he is expelled, and spends a year reading the classics in his father's library. Dissuaded by his father from immersing himself in the obscurantist philosophy of the later platonists, Vivian 'stumbled upon a branch of study certainly the most delightful in the world – but, for a boy, as certainly the most pernicious – THE STUDY OF POLITICS'. Bursting with ambition, he was 'a young and tender plant in a moral hot-house'. 'Were I the son of a Millionaire, or a noble, I might have *all*. Curse my lot! that the want of a few rascal counters, and the possession of a little rascal blood, should mar my fortunes!' (This is the only reference to Jewishness in the book.) Vivian makes what he conceives to be the GRAND DISCOVERY. '*Riches are Power*, says the Economist; – and is not *Intellect*? asks the philosopher. And yet, while the influence of the Millionaire is instantly felt in all classes of society, how is it that "Noble Mind" so often leaves us unknown and unhonoured?' Yes, says Vivian to himself, 'we must mix with the herd; Oh, yes! to *rule* men, we must *be* men.'[54]

He plunges into political wire-pulling. His prey is the Marquess of Carabas (from 'Puss in Boots', it is the name given by Puss to the miller's son whose fortune he makes). Disraeli's Carabas is a political *magnifico* who has lost his influence: 'the Marquess's secret applications at the Treasury were no longer listened to; and pert under-secretaries settled their cravats, and whispered "that the Carabas interest was gone by".' When one day the Marquess dines with Vivian's father, Vivian deploys all his arts to fascinate him – 'the flood of anecdotes, and little innocent personalities, and the compliments so exquisitely introduced, that they scarcely appeared to be compliments; and the voice so pleasant, and conciliating, and the quotation from the Marquess's own speech! and the wonderful art of which the Marquess was *not* aware, by which, during all this time, the lively, chattering, amusing, elegant conversationist so full of scandal, politics and cookery, did not so much appear to be Mr Vivian Grey as the Marquess of Carabas himself'. In short, Vivian is a flirt, and the Marquess, who is vain, is taken in.

Vivian/Puss in Boots persuades him that power is within his grasp: 'The peer sat in a musing mood, playing the Devil's tattoo on the library table; at last, he raised his eyes from the French varnish, and said to Vivian, in a low whisper, "Are you so certain that I can command *all and everything*?"' You might be Prime Minister if you wish, says Vivian; you have been betrayed by the party in office, which takes your votes and influence for granted. Give me, says Vivian, taking his lordship's arm – 'give me your Lordship's name, and your Lordship's influence, and I will take upon myself the whole organisation of the CARABAS PARTY.'[55]

At Château Désir, his country mansion, the Marquess gives a dinner for his fellow conspirators Lord Courtown, Sir Berdmore Scrope and Lord Beaconsfield, who makes his first appearance here when someone describes him as 'a very worthy gentleman, but, between ourselves, a damned fool' (the line was cut out of later editions). To Vivian's annoyance, the Marquess gets nervous and drinks too much burgundy before he makes his speech about 'the great business': 'Here the bottle passed and the Marquess took a bumper. "My Lords and Gentlemen, when I take into consideration the nature of the various interests, of which the body politic of this great empire is regulated; (Lord Courtown, the bottle stops with you) when I observe, I repeat, this, I naturally ask myself what right, what claims, what, what, what – I repeat, what right, these governing interests have to the influence which they possess? (Vivian, my boy, you'll find Champagne on the waiter behind you)."[56] The Carabas party has everything but a leader. Vivian is sent on an urgent mission to north Wales to seek out Frederick Cleveland, a political enemy of the Marquess who has left politics in disgust and, sick of the world at twenty-nine, retreated to a remote cottage *ornée* where he is consumed by ennui. Cleveland (who of course is Lockhart; in the manuscript he is Chiefswood, after Lockhart's house) is easily persuaded to lead the Carabas party.

This is, of course, the story of Murray and the *Representative* transposed to politics.[57] *Vivian Grey* is a Canningite novel; not only is it the tale of a Canningite intrigue, but as Elie Halévy shrewdly suggested, its real hero is Canning.[58]

'Oh, Canning! I love the man ...' says Vivian. Disraeli mocks the Tory country gentry who grumble about Canning's liberal policies: men such as Sir Christopher Mowbray, a county member who 'for half a century has supported in the senate, with equal sedulousness and silence, the constitution and the corn laws', and who 'immediately salutes you with a volley of oaths, and damns French wines, Bible societies, and Mr Huskisson'. When the millionaire Mrs Million appears, attended by a train of twelve persons – toad-eaters, physicians, fellow-travellers, secretaries – all bow down before her: gartered peers and starred ambassadors and baronets with titles older than the creation – all yield precedence to Mrs Million. Croker, who hated Canning, appears as the loathsome Stapylton Toad, self-made moneylender, borough monger and toady and factotum to a wealthy peer who holds forth with nauseating insincerity (Croker was an incessant talker and know-all) about the agricultural interest and the English yeoman.[59]

There are hints that one source for the plot was an intrigue orchestrated by Croker: the attempt to block Catholic Emancipation in 1825. Since about 1822 Croker had acted as factotum and man of business to the immensely rich marquess of Hertford. Like Croker, Hertford hated Canning and his liberal Toryism. He opposed Catholic Emancipation, which Canning supported, and when a bill for the Emancipation of the Catholics was introduced in the House of Commons in March 1825, Hertford intrigued with the duke of York to block it. The bill passed the Commons, but the duke of York spoke strongly against it in the House of Lords, where it was defeated. Not content with this, Hertford tried to force a dissolution in the autumn, which would

have proved disastrous to the Canningites: when this failed, Hertford and
Croker turned to the press (in fact, to the *Representative*, which had been
intended as a Canningite paper); an anonymous letter in a female hand was
sent to Canning, warning of Croker's plan to launch an anti-Canningite
paper:

> The Ultra-ultra journal called *Murray's Paper* will be brought out on January 1
> next, in Great George Street, Westminster.
>
> When Lord Hertford's boast (to turn out nineteen of Mr Canning's
> friends), uttered only a few days previous to the late attempt to dissolve
> Parliament, was defeated, the confederates then turned their attention to a
> morning paper, at the suggestion of Street, late of the *Courier*, and this is it!
>
> The bantling will appear under the auspices of the Duke of York, and the
> Marquess.
>
> Thomas George Street, J. Wilson Croker, Lockhart from Edinburgh, and
> Mr Watts, late principal parliamentary reporter to the *Morning Chronicle*, are
> to be joint editors. They intend making a dead set at *The Old Times* (as far as
> reporting goes), and finishing the *New* one. As to the poor *Post*, and the milk
> and water *Herald*, they are also to be annihilated![60]

Disraeli, who was constantly in and out of Albemarle Street at this time, must
have heard something of the Hertford/Croker plot. In *Vivian Grey* the
Carabas cabal to topple the ministry is an echo of Hertford's intrigues –
though as the novel proceeds Carabas becomes less like Hertford (whom
Disraeli had never met) and more like Murray.

Byron is as strong a presence in *Vivian Grey* as Canning. 'We certainly
want a master-spirit to set us right,' says Cleveland/Lockhart. 'We want
Byron.' Disraeli tries to take on the voice of Byron's Don Juan, worldly-wise
and ironic. 'What is this chapter to be about?' he asks chirpily. 'I am sick of
the world.' Not that I am 'a disappointed, moody monster, who lectures the
stars, and fancies himself Rousseau secundus' – no, merely suffering from an
attack of bile. Again, he tells us, 'It's a warm, soft, sunny day in March. I'll lie
down on the lawn and play with my Italian greyhound ... Kiss me, my own
Hyacinth, my dear, dear dog! Oh! you little wretch! you've bit my lip. Get
out!'[61]

Though *Vivian Grey* is the story of an intrigue, it has little plot. Part One
ends in a blast of gothic melodrama, corpses littered everywhere. Disraeli
revenged himself for the *Representative* by killing Lockhart/Cleveland, while
Murray/Carabas dies of a burst blood vessel. Vivian's plans for the Carabas
party are thwarted by a woman of about thirty, Mrs Felix Lorraine, a
German, in whom Vivian meets 'a kind of *double* of myself. The same

wonderful knowledge of the human mind, the same sweetness of voice, the same miraculous management ... yet do I find her the most abandoned of all beings ... And is it possible that I am like her? Oh God! the system of my existence seems to stop: I cannot breathe.'[62] There is self-knowledge here, self-dislike even, which Disraeli, the 'lying puppy' of the *Representative* imbroglio, is not usually credited with. As clever as she is wicked, Mrs Felix Lorraine is more than a match for Vivian, whom she outwits; she resembles Sara Austen in almost every respect except her nationality.

Vivian Grey has sometimes been seen as a moral tale: the struggle between Vivian's selfish ambition and his father's altruism. It is dedicated to Isaac, 'the best and greatest of men', and in the novel the father figure tells Vivian that, though he is a member of *le grand monde*, it is a society based on anti-social principles which Vivian has entered only by artifice. 'Is it not obvious', he asks, 'that true Fame and true Happiness, must rest upon the imperishable social affections?' But Disraeli is ambivalent about ambition. True, in *Vivian Grey* he described its corrupting effects: 'I fear me much', he wrote at the end, 'that Vivian Grey is a lost man.' But he was by no means purged of it; eight years later he wrote in his diary, 'In Vivian Grey [Parts One and Two] I have pourtrayed [*sic*] my active and real ambition.'

Vivian Grey Part I was published on 22 April 1826. Three days before, sandwich men paraded Regent Street bearing giant placards advertising a new sixpenny weekly satirical magazine, the *Star Chamber*. Disraeli always denied any connection with *Star Chamber* – he wrote in 1835 that the charge was 'utterly false'; certainly he was not its editor, who was the Reverend Peter Hall, a clergyman friend of William Meredith's.

'That miserable Peter Hall has not written me a single line concerning the Star Chamber,' wrote Meredith to Disraeli. 'I am dying to know the whole particulars, and how long we are to linger and whether we shall prevail upon Colburn to advertise with us another week.'[63] *Star Chamber* contained a long poem entitled 'The Dunciad of Today', which purported to satirise all living authors and which was probably written by Disraeli. Not only does the 'Dunciad' set to verse literary gossip, much of it obscure, which would have been known to Disraeli through Isaac and the Murray circle, but phrases and *bon mots* from *Vivian Grey* are repeated word for word, and the internal evidence is sufficiently strong to clinch Disraeli's authorship.[64]

Vivian Grey was puffed in Colburn's magazine, the *Literary Gazette*, which carried a three-page review by the editor, William Jerdan. Jerdan predicted great popularity for the book, guessing, though, from Vivian's gossip that the author was not a man of fashion but a literary man. It was a good start. The book sold and people talked – we're all in it, they said; who

can the author be? Plumer Ward told Sara Austen in May, 'All are talking of
Vivian Grey. Its wit, raciness, and boldness are admired; and you would not
have been ill-pleased with the remarks upon particular personages and
characters – the dinner at Château Désir particularly, Mrs Millions, all the
women, the two toadies, and universally, Stapylton.' Sara relayed compliments and gossip to Disraeli, copied out reviews for him and guarded his
anonymity fiercely even from Colburn. 'Don't be *nervous* about V.G.' she
wrote, 'we'll blind them yet – I have never committed you *by even a look*.'[65]
Theodore Hook, editor of the satirical *John Bull*, Croker, Lockhart and Dr
Maginn were all accused of begetting Vivian Grey. In May *Star Chamber*
printed a key, identifying characters such as Brougham (Mr Foaming Fudge)
and Eldon (Lord Past Century) – a clever piece of puffing, because Foaming
Fudge, Charlatan Gas (Canning) etc. are only mentioned once, while the key
suggested a full-blown political satire.

Literary secrets are notoriously leaky, as Disraeli must have known, and by
the middle of May the game was up, and he was revealed as the author of
Vivian Grey. John Murray was one of the first to hear, and was appalled. The
Marquess of Carabas, thought Murray, had to be a caricature of himself:
vain, treacherous as the wind, weak and, worst of all, over-fond of the bottle.
Murray was particularly upset by the drunken dinner scene at Château
Désir. The 'great business' – the Carabas Party – which Vivian Grey set in
motion was clearly the *Representative*; and the Murrays thought that the
wicked Mrs Felix Lorraine was based not (as *Star Chamber* knowingly
suggested) on Lady Caroline Lamb, but on Murray's German sister-in-law,
Mrs William Elliot, who had been active in the setting up of the
Representative. Murray was already angry with Disraeli for duping him;
Vivian Grey added insult to the injury, and he accused Disraeli of breaking
faith and revealing confidences. He ostentatiously cut Isaac and Maria, and
Maria wrote one of her rare letters to him on 21 May asking for an
explanation: how could Isaac's faithful friend John Murray go about blasting
the reputation of Isaac's son when Ben though a *clever boy* was no prodigy but
a 'very very young Man', and the blame for the failure of the *Representative*
lay much more with Murray than it ever did with Benjamin. Benjamin wrote
to Mrs Murray the same day, threatening a duel with her husband.[66]

Isaac, author of *Quarrels of Authors*, was also embroiled. He wrote letters to
Murray, withdrew from a trusteeship he had undertaken on Murray's behalf,
and threatened to write a pamphlet exonerating Benjamin's behaviour over
the *Representative*. He was persuaded to drop this idea by his solicitor friend,
Sharon Turner, Benjamin's godfather, who read the correspondence and
advised that Murray would be driven to answer in a way that could only
damage Benjamin and Isaac. Preoccupied with clearing his son's name over

the *Representative*, Isaac never answered Murray's main charge against him: that he and Maria had read and approved the manuscript of *Vivian Grey*. Perhaps Isaac had nothing to say in his defence; certainly Murray never forgave him. Poor Isaac – his friendship with Murray, who was not only a family friend but gave him the entrée to the literary world he thirsted for, had been blasted by his spoilt prodigy of a son. Never again did he set foot in Murray's Albemarle Street drawing-room and Murray published no more of his books.

Murray was so angry about *Vivian Grey* that he threatened to go to law. Sharon Turner strongly advised against. 'If the author were to swear to me that he meant the Marquess for you,' he wrote, 'I could not believe him: it is in all points so entirely unlike.'[67] Turner was trying to keep the peace between his old friends, but the likeness of the Marquess of Carabas to Murray is by no means exact – for a start, Murray was not a political grandee.

As Disraeli's authorship of *Vivian Grey* became public knowledge, curiosity gave way to annoyance; reviewers kicked themselves for swallowing Colburn's puff and allowing a young unknown Jew to pull the wool over their eyes, and the anti-Colburn press turned spiteful. 'Here is a circumstance for Murray's back shop!' gleefully declared the *London Magazine*, as it broke the secret in June. 'Our cat is wringing her hands. There is much talk about hospitality to servants, and stinging and all that.'[68] In July *Blackwood's Magazine* carried a satirical paragraph, exposing Colburn's much-puffed *Vivian Grey* as the work of 'an obscure person, for whom nobody cares a straw'.[69] Far more vitriolic was the review in the *Literary Magnet*. It alleged that Disraeli had tried to achieve cheap popularity by the meanest and most revolting of artifices: having extracted information by bribing the servants of people of fashion, he had concocted a novel in three weeks which the publisher had then extravagantly and misleadingly puffed. The author, said the *Magnet*, was (in the words of the Marquess of Carabas) 'a swindler – a scoundrel – a liar': he dropped names, he sneered, he talked affectedly of *cuisines superbes* and blackguards, and he kissed greyhounds till they bit his lips – his attempts to be fashionable were ludicrous, exposing him for what he was: an ill-bred outsider. Worse still, 'having heard that several horsewhips were preparing for him, Mr D'Israeli had the meanness to call upon various persons who have been introduced in Vivian Grey, and deny, *upon his honour as a gentleman*, that he was the author of the book'.[70]

A film floated before Disraeli's eyes as he read, his knees trembled and he felt sick at heart: as he recalled in *Contarini Fleming*, he was scalped, sacrificed and ridiculed.[71] It was small comfort that the editor of the *Magnet*, Charles Knight, was a creature of Croker's whom Disraeli had caught trafficking with Croker to block Lockhart's appointment to the *Quarterly* the previous autumn. What stung was the personal abuse – the allegations of meanness and lying and of being a parvenu. Small comfort, too, that Knight's invective masked a thinly-veiled anti-semitism. Ashamed and publicly scorned, Disraeli was powerless to reply.

In June he was ill. Sara Austen was alarmed; dropping her breathless cloak-and-dagger mask, she broke into cypher: 'I cannot continue my note thus coldly,' she wrote. 'My shaking hand will tell that I am nervous with the shock of your illness. *What is the matter?* For God's sake take care of yourself, I dare not say for my sake do so, nor can I scold you for your note now you are ill. So indeed I must pray ... If without risk you can come out tomorrow let me see you at twelve or any hour which will suit you better. I shall not leave the house till I have seen you. I shall be miserably anxious till I do.'[72]

She was more than a little in love with him; and Disraeli – at twenty-one, tall, with large black eyes and black curls brushed forward in the fashion of the day, impudent and witty – well, Disraeli enjoyed flirting with a married woman eight years older. Sara Austen looked rather like his sister Sarah (Daniel Maclise's portraits of both painted a couple of years later show them strikingly alike) and he was attracted by her fast-talking energy and flattered by her admiration for his work. Still worried about money, he also calculated that Sara's prosperous husband could be of use to him.

His doctors ordered rest. Sara Austen, who no doubt felt partly responsible for Disraeli's illness, proposed a tour of Italy. Disraeli jumped at the idea, and wrote waggishly to Benjamin Austen, attempting to laugh off Knight's abuse. 'As for my moral capacities,' said he, 'why I can have a good character from my last place, which I left on account of the disappearance of the silver spoons; I defy also anyone to declare that I am not sober and honest, ex[cep]t when I am entrusted with the key of the wine cellar, when I must candidly confess I have an ugly habit of stealing the Claret, getting drunk and kissing the maids.'[73]

His jauntiness rings hollow. In truth, he was so painfully scarred that to the end of his life he denied any connection with either the *Representative* or *Star Chamber*, as well as suppressing Isaac's friendship with John Murray. *Vivian Grey* he could not repudiate; on the contrary, his immediate reaction was to write a sequel (he had carefully left the ending open) confounding his critics. Later, however, he distanced himself from the novel, denying that the plot and characters were drawn from life. 'Books written by boys', he wrote in the introduction to the new edition of 1853, 'must necessarily be founded on affectation. They can be, at the best, but the results of imagination, acting upon knowledge, not acquired by experience.' The 1853 edition was heavily revised by Sarah Disraeli, who cut out the references to Murray's/Carabas's drunkenness, toned down the excessively frank account of Vivian's middle-class upbringing and pruned the admissions of Vivian's moral depravity.

Disraeli's adventures of 1825–6 strikingly prefigure his later career. The allure of the press; the excitement of the 'great business', of dramatic cloak-and-dagger schemes and behind-the-scenes politico-financial coups; the settling of grudges in print; the cycle of frenetic activity followed by nervous prostration – all these were to recur time and again throughout his mercurial career. *Vivian Grey* is almost prophetic in parts:

> Cleveland's exertions for the party to which Mr Under-Secretary Lorraine belonged were unremitting; and it was mainly through their influence, that a great promotion took place in the official appointments of the party. When the hour of reward came, Mr Lorraine and his friends unfortunately forgot their youthful champion. He remonstrated, and they smiled; he reminded them of private friendship, and they answered him with political expediency. Mr Cleveland went down to the House, and attacked his old co-mates in a spirit of unexampled bitterness.... They trembled on their seats, while they writhed beneath the keenness of his satire: but when the orator came to Mr President Lorraine, he flourished the tomahawk on high like a wild Indian chieftain ...[74]

Substitute Peel and Disraeli for Lorraine and Cleveland, and you have a striking account of the Disraeli–Peel rivalry of the 1840s.

One thing that did change was Disraeli's admiration of Canning. In *Star Chamber*, to which he contributed a series of political fables entitled 'The Modern Aesop', he likened the agricultural interest to a noble oak. 'A rash and revolutionary minister, like the raging north wind, will level it with the ground.' Not until the oak was fallen would we discover how very noble a tree it was, and how many small trees were crushed beneath it. 'Upon the agricultural interest all the other interests of this country depend.'[75] Canning was the rash and revolutionary minister, and on the evidence of 'The Modern Aesop' Disraeli was already doubtful about Canning's Liberal Toryism, which was closer to the Whigs than to the Tory country gentry. His early doubts are echoed in *Endymion*, the last novel he wrote (published in 1880), where Zenobia, the Tory hostess Lady Jersey, asks: 'How can any government go on without the support of the Church and the land? It is quite unnatural.' 'They are trying to introduce here the continental Liberalism,' is the reply. 'Now we know what Liberalism means on the continent. It means the abolition of property and religion.'[76]

THREE

Nervous Breakdown

1826–30

DISRAELI SPENT the summer months of 1826 an invalid lying in darkened rooms in Bloomsbury Square. Doctors diagnosed indigestion but, like Vivian Grey, whose further adventures Disraeli chronicled a few months later, his real illness was depression. Everything seemed worthless. 'His trial had been severe, and because he could no longer interest himself in any of the usual pursuits of men, he believed that he could interest himself in none. But doubting of all things, he doubted of himself ...'[1] At twenty-one, Disraeli was sliding into nervous breakdown. Crushed and wounded by a hostile world, his inflated but fragile sense of self disintegrated.

Early in August he left for Italy with Benjamin and Sara Austen. They travelled in a closed carriage, which was comfortable and convenient. ('No botheration every night unpacking, no fevers in the morning with cording and strapping.') On French soil Ben felt ten thousand times better than he had for the last three years, or so he reported to his dear father. The air and *cuisine* benefited his digestion. In Paris, where they spent five days, waiting for their passports, picaresque Gil Blas doings got him and the Austens the best situated apartment in the 'Hôtel de Terrace' [sic] in the rue de Rivoli. He flourished in an intense heat which seemed to bring everyone out into the open, dancing or sitting in ranks of chairs on the miraculous boulevards.

Revelling in the old city (very like the old town of Edinburgh), and the quais, Nôtre Dame and so on, he went to the Opéra and the Louvre. Paris had undergone an architectural revolution since Isaac's visit during the Peace of Amiens twenty-four years before. The buildings in London's Regent Street were nowhere near as high. Taken as a whole, though, London was preferable because it was a mystery that 'could never be preconceived, and which can never be exhausted'.[2]

From Paris they made for Dijon, where Ben got merrily tipsy ('No man should presume to give an opinion upon burgundy who has not got tipsy at

Dijon'), and on through Burgundy to the Jura Alps. How tense was the atmosphere within that closed carriage as they jolted across France can only be imagined. Austen can hardly have been blind to his wife's *tendresse* for the 'impudent puppy'. But Disraeli, who needed Austen's money, was wise enough not to humiliate him; the triangular relationship, with its possibilities for intrigue and nuance, was one he was fast learning to enjoy and exploit. Sara Austen, Ben told his family, spouted French even more quickly than she did English. She wrote ingratiating letters reassuring dear Mama, as she called Maria, that Ben's indigestion was wonderfully cured ('*indigestion* is become an obsolete term'), thanks partly to some very peculiar pills she bought from Whites (mercury perhaps, which in the form of blue pills was a powerful purgative). Ben, she told his sister, 'has just said high Mass for a *third* bottle of Burgundy'. From Dover, where the D'Israelis had gone for the summer, Sarah wrote of Maria, unwell as ever, sitting by the sea day after day, watching the ships go by while Isaac took daily walks to the pier.[3]

'On the eighteenth day of August [1826] ... standing upon the height of Mount Jura, I beheld the whole range of the High Alps, with Mont Blanc in the centre, without a cloud; a mighty spectacle rarely beheld.' Disraeli penned this sentence five years later in *Contarini Fleming*, but the date and the scene were carefully noted in the diary he kept of his travels and in his letter home.[4]

Geneva was horribly dingy, but it brought him close to Byron. Maurice, Byron's boatman, rowed Disraeli on the lake every night. He was vain, handsome and spoilt by the English visitors and would talk endlessly about Byron at the least sign of interest. The boat was nearly wrecked the night Byron wrote the great storm scene for *Childe Harold*; Byron stripped and folded a great *robe de chambre* around himself in case he had to swim. One day Byron had sent for Maurice and 'sitting down in the boat, he put a pistol on each side (which was his invariable practice) and then gave him 300 Napoleons ordering him to row to Chillon. He then had two torches lighted in the dungeon and wrote for two hours and a half'.[5]

Because there was a chance of a fine storm upon the lake Maurice sent for Disraeli the night before they left Geneva. As he had just dined with Austen they had to take a companion, but fortunately brandy on top of the burgundy they had drunk for dinner kept Austen more or less asleep on Disraeli's cloak in the boat. 'I was soon sobered, not by sleep but by the scene. It was sublime – lightning almost continuous – and sometimes in four places – but as the evening advanced the lake became quite calm and we never had a drop of rain.' He was willing to stay out all night, but they had not yet packed and were due to depart at five in the morning.[6]

Next day he and the Austens travelled along the south side of the lake of

Geneva and entered Savoy. Showers in the early morning produced unforgettable prismatic effects. They soon reached Switzerland and began travelling through the long valley of the Rhône, keeping where possible to little-known tracks to avoid competition with the crowds of English who scoured the usual routes for accommodation. Disraeli's eyes ached as they approached the High Alps. He suffered from the closeness of the air but the scenery was so sublime that they spent several days longer than intended. He got peasants to show him the ravages of past avalanches, ruined villages, former wheat fields as barren and as stony as the shingle.

> The passage of the Simplon is the grand crowning scene to all these horrors. We stayed one day at Brigg where the passage commences on account of the stormy weather, but as it did not abate we set off the next day. Nothing could be more awful than the first part of our passage – the sublimity of the scenery was increased by the partial mists and the gusts of rain. Nothing is more terrific than the near roar of a Cataract which is covered by a mist. It is horrible. When we arrived at the summit of the road, the weather cleared and we found ourselves surrounded by perpetual snow. The scenery here and for a mile or two before was perfect desolation – cataracts coursing down crumbled avalanches whose horrible surface was only varied by the presence of one or two blasted firs. Here in this dreary and desolate scene burst forth a small streak of blue sky, the harbinger of the Italian heaven. During our whole descent down the Italian side which is by far the most splendid we enjoyed the sun. We were for a long time however very cold. I never shall forget the descent – waterfalls are innumerable from the hell of waters to streams finer than gauze – roads cut through solid rock archways and called *grottos* – galleries over precipices whose terminations are invisible – passes in which the descended avalanches of snow are viewed even after their fall with horror – bridges which always span a roaring and rushing torrent – narrow valleys backed with eternal snow peeping over the nearer and blacker background, all combine to produce a succession of scenes which contrasted with the beautiful roads and elegant bridges – the best signs of civilization – cannot surely be paralleled.[7]

As they descended into Italy the height of the mountains moderated and they could see vines and white villages, churches and villas, in the beautiful light. They rode from Arona to Varese through scenery of inconceivable loveliness – purple mountains, glittering lakes, 'cupola'd convents, the many windowed villas crowning luxuriant wooded hills – the undulation of shore – the projecting headland – the receding bay – the roadside uninclosed – yet bounded with walnut and vine and fig and acacia and almond trees bending down under the load of their fruit – the wonderful effect of light and shade – the trunks of every tree looking black as ebony and their thicker foliage from the excessive light – looking quite thin and transparent in the sunshine – the thousand villages – each with a church with a tall thin tower – the large melons trailing over walls and above all the extended prospect ...' For once romance did not exaggerate.

Later, in *Contarini Fleming*, Disraeli reflected that it was in Switzerland that he first began to study nature, looking at it through the eyes of a Romantic. 'It was in Switzerland that I first felt how the constant contemplation of sublime creation develops the poetic power.' His spirits rose as he invented a new persona for himself: the wandering poet, the Romantic man of feelings, his emotions in sublime sympathy with the nature around him. So struck was he by the beauty of Ferney, Voltaire's alpine home, that he reproached Isaac's hero for his lack of sympathy with nature: 'it should have inspired a more Homeric epic than the Henriade, and chastened a more libidinous effusion than the Pucelle'. At Lake Como, they saw the Villa D'Este, famous for the exotic orgies of the late Queen Caroline, estranged wife of George IV. He told his father it was painful to view the indelicate ornaments in the presence of a lady, and he found his Tory prejudices confirmed (Queen Caroline was a Radical heroine). 'Our riots in her favour are the laughing stock of Italy,' he told his father.[8] If Isaac worried about his son slipping the leash and debauching in Italy, he must have taken comfort from the long letters of travelogue Ben sent home. He asked Sarah to preserve his letters as he had kept no journal (though of course he had) and later, he incorporated descriptions from his letters into *Contarini Fleming*.[9]

In Milan, he was impressed by Count Ciconia, the leader of the dandies, a 'genius worthy of Brummell', who managed to make a great figure on a small income. Verona was 'full of pictures which have never been painted ... In the course of a short stroll, you may pass by a Roman amphitheatre – still used – then the castle of some petty prince of the middle ages – and while you are contrasting the sublime elevation of antiquity with the heterogeneous palace of a Scaligeri your eyes light on a gate of oriental appearance and fantastic ornament erected by the Venetians when they were the conquerors of the most fertile district of northern Italy. Memorials of this wonderful people are constantly before you.'[10]

At Vicenza the famous Palladian villas had decayed. Built of red brick, sometimes plastered or whitewashed, the walls 'vied in hideous colour with the ever offensive roof'. The English were fools to envy the Italians their marble. A building of marble or even of stone was rarer here than in England; England's poor building materials were at least kept clean. Italian cornices choked with cobwebs and their saloons stank. Not all the smoke of all the

machines in Manchester and Birmingham could harm a building as much as
the indolence of the Italians. Not a street in all Italy had houses as clean as
London's Regent Street, thought Disraeli, and no palace looked half as white
and imposing as Regent Street's new fire office. The model of Lord
Burlington's Chiswick House was here, dilapidated and roofed with red tiles,
exquisitely proportioned though, with a beautiful interior. The critic
Forsyth claimed that the key to Palladio's work is 'reproducing ancient
beauty in combinations unknown to the ancients themselves'; and he was
quite right, though it was crazy to suggest that the Palladian style suited
windy England.[11]

At last, on 8 September, they reached Venice. They stayed in the Hotel
Danieli, once the proud residence of the Bernadini family. Disraeli paced the
marble floors of their rooms, and admired the hangings of satin and
Tintoretto ceilings depicting Turkish triumphs and trophies. After a hasty
dinner he and the Austens rushed to the mighty crowded square of St Mark.
Ships of war, two Greek and one Turkish, were in port, their crews mingling
with spectators. The Greeks looked magnificent with their high foreheads
and higher caps and elevated brows. Jews were there, too, wearing caps of
black velvet above their beards as an Austrian military band stirred the night
air. Opposite the Church banners fluttered as jugglers and singers celebrated
under a magical silver moon.[12]

They stayed in Venice only five days. Disraeli 'never felt less inclined to
quit a place' which 'quickens the feelings and the fancy, and which enables
the mind to arrive at results with greater facility and rapidity than we do at
home, in our studies'. Sailing down the Grand Canal, his heart thrilled as
they passed palaces belonging to such noble names as Foscarini, Grimani,
Barberigo. Later, in *Contarini Fleming*, he fantasised about a noble Venetian
ancestry, imagining these were the palaces of *his* ancestors. If Disraeli knew of
his old great-aunt, still living in the Ghetto, to whom Isaac may still have sent
money, he did not visit her. The only ghetto he saw was in Ferrara: 'a
tolerably long street enclosed with red wooden gates and holding about 3000
Jews'. One letter to Isaac mentions the neighbouring town of Cento, his
grandfather's birthplace, 'which perhaps you may remember', but Ben did
not trouble to go there. Nor did he visit his Basevi cousins still living in
Verona.[13] It was as if he were deliberately shutting out his Jewish family roots.
The reality was too painful, too much at odds with the figure he wished to
cut; he escaped into a Romantic world of his own making, reliving the history
not of his family but of Lord Byron. At Ferrara he ignored the sufferings of
his ancestors under papal repression, and made for the cell of Tasso, where
Byron had asked to be locked to share the poet's suffering, scratching 'Byron'

with a nail on the brick wall. Beneath it, 'Sam Rogers' (the name of a friend of Isaac and Byron) appeared, printed in pencil in neat bankerly writing.[14]

After Bologna, they headed south to bustling Florence, the cheapest city in all Europe, he claimed. Luxuries were so cheap that an English family like the D'Israelis (two parents and four children) could live with every convenience, including a carriage, for £500 a year. No longer disturbed by the shades of his ancestors, Disraeli abandoned himself to art and tourism. He praised the Great Gallery and the Grand Duke's private collection in the Pitti Palace. Studying fine works of artists of all countries, among which Raphael and other painters of the Roman school were well represented, Disraeli claimed some knowledge of the styles and merits of the four great Italian schools. As a surprise for Isaac, who was writing the life of Charles I, Disraeli commissioned a copyist to make a miniature copy of a magnificent Van Dyck portrait of Charles I which hung in the Pitti Palace. When Signor Carloni, the court painter, missed the likeness, Disraeli made him paint a new one. He gazed at the Venus de Medicis and left it with veneration. He visited Bertolini's studio and had a long talk with a sculptor who was, since the death of Canova, one of the most eminent Italians. Disraeli was particularly fascinated by Saunders, the descendant of a Scotch family who had emigrated to Russia on speculation, and an intimate friend of Tsar Alexander, whom he had assisted in his plans to improve conditions in Russia and promote the fine arts.

'Unless you come to Italy, you can have no idea of what art really is,' he told Isaac. 'I have seen enough in Italy to know that we are not setting about the right way in England to form a national Gallery.' Collections in England were very strong in Flemish and French pictures (Rembrandts and Claudes, for example) but Italian collections had shoals of originals by the first Italian masters. Compared to Italian collections, Lord Grosvenor's was ridiculous. England's National Gallery should keep an agent in Italy and snap up masterpieces which were sold for a song when the owners died in debt. In Florence, as he recalled in *Contarini Fleming*, Disraeli thought only of art and artists. 'I unconsciously adopted their jargon; and began to discourse of copies, and middle tints, and changes of style. I was in great danger of degenerating into an aesthete.' But it was also in Florence that Disraeli recovered the desire to write, and he began to muse on a sequel to *Vivian Grey*.[15]

In October they turned homewards, travelling back through Pisa and the Apennines – 'the Apennines of Romance and Mrs Radcliffe – with streamy blue distances and unfathomable woody dells, and ruined castles, and constant views of the blue Mediterranean, and its thousand bays.' From Turin, he summarised his travels: 'Nature and Art have been tolerably well revealed to me. The Alps, the Apennines and two seas have pretty well done for the first, and tho' I may see more cities I cannot see more varieties of European nature. Five capitals and twelve great cities, innumerable remains of antiquity and the choicest specimens of modern art have told me what man has done and is doing. I feel now that it is not prejudice, when I declare that England with all her imperfections is worth all the world together, and I hope it is not misanthropy when I feel that I love lakes and mountains better than courts and cities, and trees better than men.'[16]

Travel seemed to have mended Disraeli's health. He told his sister that he had been writing hard, though he would gladly throw all his work into the Channel to hear that his father had written fifty pages of his book on Charles I.[17] Back at Bloomsbury Square, he set to work, spurred by the bill for £151 he received from Benjamin Austen, his share of the travel expenses. His plan had been to write a book whose characters embodied philosophical principles (will, materialism etc), but it turned into a very different kind of book – a series of experiments, much of it composed at great speed, some carefully premeditated. Sara Austen acted once more as agent, editor and amanuensis to 'Dis' as she began to call Ben. Ben took walks with her in the afternoons, dined often at Guildford Street, and every few days brought around fresh batches of hastily written manuscript for her to copy; sometimes the writing was so illegible that she was obliged to guess at his meaning.[18] The second part of *Vivian Grey*, which filled three volumes where Part One had filled only two, was completed in three months.

Vivian Grey Part Two is usually dismissed as overlong and tedious. Lady Salisbury, who read it in 1827, thought it 'mad, but clever and interesting'; Sir Walter Scott, reading it on a hot June day, found it 'clever but not so much as to make me in this sultry weather go upstairs to the drawing room to seek the other volumes'. Henry Crabb Robinson, who picked it up in 1839, was unable to finish it, and resolved to read nothing more by the younger Disraeli. Gladstone, who read the whole in 1874, thought the first quarter extremely clever, the rest trash.[19] Disraeli's biographers have been inclined to agree, yet *Vivian Grey* Part Two is an illuminating and revealing biographical document.

Disgraced by his adventures in Part One, Vivian Grey leaves England for Germany, and the novel, which lapses at times into a travelogue based on Disraeli's travels in the Rhineland, tells of his picaresque adventures. It draws heavily on Goethe's *Wilhelm Meister*, which Carlyle had translated in 1824, which also told of the German wanderings of a disillusioned youth. But *Vivian Grey* Part Two is sprawling and shapeless, weighed down with irrelevant digressions, at times incoherent. Even Disraeli admitted that it was uneven and at times unintelligible, and that his mind had teemed with similes as he wrote so that he found himself 'often writing only that they might be accommodated'. Reading *Vivian Grey* was described by Robert Browning in a letter to Elizabeth Barrett in 1845:

> you go breathlessly on with the people of it, page after page, till at last the end *must* come, you feel – and the tangled threads draw to one, and an out-of-door feast in the woods helps you … that is, helps them, the people, wonderfully on, – and, lo, dinner is done, and Vivian Grey is here, and Violet Fane there, and a detachment of the party is drafted off to go catch butterflies, and only two or three stop behind. At this moment, Mr Somebody, a good man and rather the lady's uncle, 'in answer to a question from Violet, drew from his pocket a small neatly written manuscript, and, seating himself on an inverted wine-cooler, proceeded to read the following brief remarks upon the characteristics of the Moeso-Gothic literature' – this ends the page, – which you don't turn at once! But when you *do*, in bitterness of soul, turn it, you read – 'On consideration, I' (Ben, himself) 'shall keep them for Mr Colburn's *New Magazine*' – and deeply you draw thankful breath!

One critic has hailed the book as an early experiment in stream-of-consciousness, a proto-Proustian novel.[20] The very formlessness of Part Two echoes Disraeli's depression, his inability to structure and shape his writing reflecting his lack of control over his life.

Part Two has been disparaged partly because it is usually read in the 1853 edition, which is far duller than the original. The first of the four books, which is strongly autobiographical, was drastically cut in 1853: it starts with a kind of apology, in which Disraeli defiantly declares that he is 'morally ashamed' of none of the personal and political matter contained in the earlier book. As for the charge that he wrote the *Star Chamber* satires, it was a scurrilous lie: 'I never wrote one single line of them,' he insists in the first of many denials.

Vivian, he wrote, was a youth of great talents whose mind had been corrupted by the artificial age he lived in, and Disraeli's purpose had been to punish him for his failings. Yet 'I am blamed for the affectation, the flippancy, the arrogance, the wicked wit of this fictitious character'.[21] Vivian's character was changed by his experiences, as was Disraeli's. He had learned his father's lesson about the social affections, but it cost him his happiness. Vivian is redeemed but, like Disraeli, he is depressed. Wandering aimlessly through the Rhineland, accompanied by a Sancho Panza figure named Essper George, Vivian's character dwindles to insignificance. He no longer dominates the narrative and controls events, as he had done in Part One: he is

passive, someone to whom things happen. The dominant character of the
next two books is not Vivian at all, but the minister, Mr Beckendorff.

Beckendorff is a power-man and a genius; Metternich is his pupil. Unlike
Metternich, Beckendorff is the son of a peasant, an outsider; and as Disraeli
shrewdly observes in a passage weirdly prophetic of his own career: 'A
Minister who has sprung from the people will always conciliate the
aristocracy. Having no family influence of his own, he endeavours to gain the
influence of others; and it often happens that merit is never less considered,
than when merit has made the Minister.'[22] Beckendorff is equally cynical in
his relations with women. As a man he despises them, but as a statesman he
values them as the most precious of political instruments. In appearance he is
remarkable.

> He had very little hair, which was highly powdered, and dressed in a manner
> to render more remarkable the extraordinary elevation of his conical and
> polished forehead. His long piercing black eyes were almost closed, from the
> fullness of their upper lids. His cheeks were sallow, his nose aquiline, his
> mouth compressed. His ears, which were quite uncovered by hair, were so
> wonderfully small that it would be wrong to pass them over unnoticed; as
> indeed were his hands and feet, which in form were quite feminine.

Beckendorff is oriental-looking, perhaps Jewish, and Disraeli stresses his
effeminacy, a characteristic of the 1820s dandy.

> He swung in his right hand the bow of a violin; and in the other, the little
> finger of which was nearly hid by a large antique ring, he held a white
> handkerchief strongly perfumed with violets. Notwithstanding the many
> feminine characteristics which I have noticed, either from the expression of
> the eyes, or the formation of the mouth, the countenance of this individual
> generally conveyed an impression of the greatest firmness and energy.[23]

Vivian visits Beckendorff on his remote estate, where he lives in topsy-turvy
style, working while other men sleep and eating and drinking very little.
Fingering Beckendorff's library shelves, Vivian looks for Machiavelli but
finds only romance and poetry, Scott and Shakespeare. 'No papers, no
despatches, no red tape, no red boxes.' Beckendorff embodies the romance of
power; he is not a self-portrait, but a picture of what Disraeli dreams of
becoming, of his ideal ambition. In Vivian, Disraeli attempts a description of
himself as he is. He confesses to having become a fatalist: 'Within only these
last two years, my career has, in so many instances, indicated that I am not the
master of my own conduct,' Vivian tells Beckendorff; 'I recognise in every

contingency the pre-ordination of my fate.' He speaks with the hopelessness of depression; he cannot plan, let alone control his future. Beckendorff profoundly disagrees with the philosophy. It is, he says, 'A delusion of the brain. Fate, Destiny, Chance, particular and special Providence – idle words! Dismiss them all, Sir! A man's Fate is his own temper.' We are free agents, and circumstances are the creatures of men. Vivian himself once believed this, but he maintains that his temper – his nature – has changed as a result of his experience. No, says Beckendorff, it is a fallacy to believe that temper changes. On the contrary, sooner or later Vivian is bound to revert to his original pursuits; in all probability he will succeed, 'and then I suppose, stretching your legs in your easy-chair, you will at the same moment be convinced of your own genius, and recognise your own Destiny!' Vivian is unconvinced. He is sinking under unparalleled misery. 'I deliver myself up to my remorseless Fate.'[24]

'Apparently, the philosophy on which Beckendorff had regulated his extraordinary career ... was exactly the same with which he himself, Vivian Grey, had started in life.' But though Vivian has renounced his early beliefs, Disraeli has not. His purpose in Part Two was to show how Vivian, once a lost man, is redeemed and changed by his experiences, but his sympathies are clearly with Beckendorff rather than Vivian. Disraeli really believed that man is master of his fate; in *Vivian Grey* Part Two he set out to unlearn his beliefs, and failed. He found it impossible to write convincingly about Vivian, so he invented a new hero in Beckendorff, a fantasy figure who anticipates Sidonia, the idealised self-portrait of the 1840s. Disraeli's lack of interest in Vivian, whose position corresponds far more closely to his own state than Beckendorff's does, is a measure of his despair and self-dislike in 1827: the gulf between ambition and actuality, between Beckendorff and Vivian, must at times have seemed impassable.

Part Two of *Vivian Grey* was published on 23 February 1827. It created far less sensation than its predecessor. Critics attacked an elaborate German drinking scene as extravagant nonsense; this was one of the parts Disraeli had executed with great care, and he leapt to defend it in a learned article on the grotesque in literature, which he wrote in collaboration with Isaac (the manuscript is revised in Isaac's hand) and published in Colburn's *New Monthly Magazine*.[25] Colburn paid £500 for *Vivian Grey* Part Two, and three weeks later Disraeli wrote to John Murray, enclosing £140 owing for the American mining pamphlets. It was a debt of honour: Disraeli was not legally responsible for the debt; as he told Murray, he was paying up on behalf of the bankrupt Powles.[26]

Soon after the publication of *Vivian Grey* Part Two, Disraeli was sitting

alone in his room one evening at about nine o'clock with his watch beside him
on the table when, as he recalled in *Contarini Fleming*, he became disturbed
by the ticking. The noise grew louder, but when he examined the watch he
realised the noise was in his own ears. Next morning he could not write: he
felt languid, indolent, faint. That evening the noise returned. 'From the tick
of a watch it assumed the loud confused moaning of a bell tolling in a storm ...
It was impossible to think. I walked about the room. It became louder and
louder. It seemed to be absolutely deafening. I could compare it to nothing
but the continuous roar of a cataract.' He lay awake all night. In the evenings
he drank wine to escape the noise, but this destroyed his digestion.
Sometimes he fainted as he dressed in the morning. He felt he was losing his
grip on reality. 'I was not always assured of my identity, or even existence; for
I sometimes found it necessary to shout aloud to be sure that I lived; and I was
in the habit, very often at night, of taking down a volume and looking into it
for my name, to be convinced that I had not been dreaming of myself. At
these times there was an incredible acuteness, or intenseness, in my
sensations; every object seemed animated, and, as it were, acting upon me.'
Once he felt something he could only describe as the rushing of blood into his
brain, and he collapsed insensible.[27]

He languished at Bloomsbury Square, doing virtually nothing. He ate
dinners at Lincoln's Inn in 1827 and 1828 (he had also eaten dinners in 1824
and 1825), but he read no law; and he did no writing. 'I continue just "as ill"
as ever,' he told Benjamin Austen in July 1827.[28] In August he went with his
family to Fyfield in Essex, a house which Isaac had rented for the autumn,
and the Austens came too. Here he was seriously ill. Debts crowded in on
him. He and his friend Evans still owed Messer over £1200 from their South
American speculations, and in January 1828 Disraeli wrote wildly to Evans
telling him to keep Messer at bay: 'BE NOT RASH. All is on the dye [*sic*] –
throw it with caution.'[29]

The months crawled by. 'I am at present quite idle,' he told his godfather
Sharon Turner in March 1828. Mindful of Isaac's breakdown thirty years
before, he said he was 'slowly recovering from one of those tremendous
disorganisations which happen to all men at some period of their lives'.[30] To a
neighbour who asked him to an 'assembly' he wrote: 'I am so decidedly an
invalid, that, at present, I am obliged to forego [*sic*] altogether the *deliciae* of
society'.[31]

Ten years later, a doctor described his condition as 'chronic inflammation
of the membranes of the brain'.[32] Looking back in 1846 Disraeli wrote that he
had suffered much and for a long time from 'exhaustion of the nervous
system', for which the only cure was rest, 'and we should guard against the

belief, that there is any cure ... but a gradual one. Repose however is a rare medicine, and impatient suffering is too apt to take refuge in quacks.'[33]

At Bloomsbury Square, doctor followed doctor, each prescribing a different treatment. Disraeli was told to be quiet, to exert himself, to be stimulated, to be soothed, to be on horseback or on a sofa. 'I was bled, blistered, boiled, starved, poisoned, electrified; galvanised; and at the end of a year found myself with exactly the same oppression on my brain.' He was a pathetic creature, never going out of the house, and barely leaving his room. He scarcely spoke and saw no one. He was profoundly depressed. 'I sat in moody silence, revolving in reverie, without the labour of thought, my past life and feelings.'

Nervous breakdown is relatively common among very young men. Nineteenth-century doctors usually attributed it to overwork and worry; in Disraeli's case the stress of writing *Vivian Grey* was the most obvious explanation. But perhaps his collapse was the response of a young man, trapped in the stifling nineteenth-century middle-class family, repressed by a patriarchal father, tortured by conflicting emotions, by resentment, love, guilt and fear, and uncertain of his role; breakdown was a way of dissenting without confrontation, and illness gave the victim a kind of power.[34]

Disraeli rejected the law, the career Isaac had chosen for him ('My father was very warm about this business; the only time in his life in which he exerted authority'); his career as a writer had failed; and day by day his debts testified to his inability to support himself. Buried in *Vivian Grey* Part Two are hints that Disraeli had come to resent Isaac. The character of Mr Sherborne is a thinly disguised portrait of Isaac at his worst: irritable, pedantic and an unpleasant bore, the scourge of young men, whom he calls 'that mass of half-educated, inexperienced, insolent, conceited puppies who think every man's a fool who's older than themselves'.[35] When *Vivian Grey* was revised in 1853 Mr Sherborne was cut out; by then Disraeli had created the myth of Isaac as gentle, scholarly recluse with whom his relations had always been harmonious; anything that contradicted this version was firmly suppressed. In fact, the Governor was a patriarchal figure in the D'Israeli family; Maria D'Israeli took refuge in chronic ill-health, and Ben had a lifelong dislike of confrontation with his father.

What of Disraeli's relationship with Sara Austen? There are signs in *Vivian Grey* Part Two of awakening sexuality. Vivian, who in Part One had shown little interest in women, falls in love. The object of his passion is Violet Fane, young and beautiful with a consumptive's flush. On a picnic, the very food is charged with sexuality. 'The facile knife sank without effort into the plump breast, and the unresisting bird discharged a cargo of rich stuffed balls of the most fascinating flavour.' (This was cut in 1853.) Alone with Violet,

Vivian pours forth words of 'his early follies – his misfortunes – his prospects – his hopes – his happiness – his bliss'. She is silent. Suddenly she clings to him. She is dead.[36]

Violet resembled Sara Austen not at all, but the pattern of flirtation, sexual longing and ultimate frustration perhaps reflects Disraeli's relationship with the older woman. What did he mean when he told his sister on his return from Italy that his companions, the Austens, had been 'uniformly agreeable. Everything that I wished has been realised, and more than I wished granted'? It may not be assuming too much to suggest that he was referring to Sara Austen, and back in England their collaboration on Part Two of *Vivian Grey* brought complex emotions to the surface. But Sara was too conscious of the risks – of the danger of jeopardising her relations with the D'Israeli family, not to mention her marriage – to allow matters to get out of hand. She played an elaborate, teasing game with 'My dear Ben', keeping secrets from his family (when out of London, she wrote to him at her own address at Guildford Street) and especially from his sister Sarah, who was determined not to be left out. 'They [the family] need not know that I have written to you *first*,' she wrote from Lichfield in April 1828 'and I will so manage my letter to Sa that she shall seem to have the preference.' She enjoyed playing the part of elder sister to the family, kind but hearty and rather loud-voiced. 'I take part so much in all that concerns you *all* now, that a great deal of my happiness depends upon the family,' she wrote in 1828.[37] But flirtation over the family dinner table and snatched kisses in Guildford Street did not satisfy Disraeli, and sexual frustration deepened his depression.

He attributed his breakdown to frustrated ambition. 'Whether I shall ever do anything which may mark me out from the crowd I know not,' he told Sharon Turner. 'I am one of those to whom moderate reputation can give no pleasure, and who, in all probability, am incapable of achieving a great one. But how this may be I care not.'[38] He *did* care, though, he cared passionately; and as he endured a twilight existence at Bloomsbury Square he despaired of ever achieving fame. At the root of his misery lay despair at his predicament as a Jew, an outsider, despised by an alien hostile world he yearned to lead. Isaac's solution had been to escape, to retreat into the quiet and safety of his library, but this was not for Ben. Nor was Ben inspired by Isaac's cynical eighteenth-century rationalism. Like John Stuart Mill's mental crisis of 1826 or Thomas Carlyle's protracted depression, Disraeli's breakdown was in part a spiritual crisis: he rejected the rationalist faith in which he had been reared. Mill found salvation in poetry, Carlyle in German Idealist philosophy. Disraeli was later to discover imagination as the antidote to reason, but in 1828 he knew only that reason was not enough.

In the spring of 1828, after over a year of idleness, Disraeli began to write again. Encouraged by Sara Austen, he started work on the satire, *Popanilla*. 'We are very very anxious about you,' Mrs Austen wrote from Lichfield in April. 'I thought of Pop all the way down, and he comes into my head at every interval.' 'Mind you write Pop,' she urged, 'I shall want work when I get home.'[39]

Popanilla is a rearrangement of Papillon, after Aylmer Papillon, the satire Murray had rejected four years before. The two chapters of Aylmer Papillon which survive in Disraeli's papers reflect his studies as a law student, satirising the game laws, Blackstone and Magna Carta.[40] Popanilla, by contrast, is a satire on Utilitarianism, composed almost entirely in 1828.

'There is an island in the Indian Ocean, so unfortunate as not to have been visited either by Discovery Ships or Missionary Societies.' This is the isle of Fantaisie. Popanilla, an islander, is searching for a lock of his mistress's hair, when he comes across a chest of books marked S.D.K. (Society for the Diffusion of Knowledge) washed up on the shore. He reads the books and discovers that he and his fellow islanders are useless savages, desperately in need of civilising. Addressing the king 'in that mild tone of subdued superciliousness with which we should always address kings, and which, while it vindicates our dignity, satisfactorily proves that we are above the vulgar passion of envy', Popanilla 'spoke of man in a savage state, the origins of society, and the elements of the social compact, in sentences which would not have disgraced the mellifluous pen of Bentham. From these he naturally digressed into an agreeable disquisition on the Anglo-Saxons; and, after a little badinage on the Bill of Rights, flew off to an airy *aperçu* of the French Revolution.'

Popanilla demonstrates that the pleasure-loving existence of the islanders is inconsistent with the stern principles of Bentham's Utilitarianism. 'If there were no utility in pleasure,' he tells the king, 'it was quite clear that pleasure could profit no one. If, therefore, it were unprofitable, it was injurious; because that which does not produce a profit is equivalent to a loss; therefore pleasure is a losing business; consequently pleasure is not pleasant.'[41] In true Utilitarian fashion, Popanilla becomes a bore, and the king sends him off to sea; in despair, he tries to decide what useful end would be attained by his death at sea, until 'At length, remembering that fish must be fed, his theory and his desperation were at the same time confirmed.' After three days at sea, he lands on the island of Vraibleusia which is, the natives make haste to tell him, the richest, the most charitable and the freest country in the world (which is of course England). What is freedom? he asks, and a native replies, 'Freedom is, in one word, Liberty: a kind of thing which you foreigners never can understand, and which mere theory can make no man understand.'[42]

Popanilla hears of the centuries-old aboriginal who owns the corn which supplies the whole nation, insisting that his monopoly of corn is the common law of the land. When the islanders grumble, the aboriginal swears there is 'an uninterrupted line of precedents to confirm the claim; and that, if they did not approve of the arrangement, they and their fathers should not have elected to have settled, or presumed to have been spawned, upon his island'. The pale perspiring mechanics complain about the dearness of corn, and the gigantic ruddy-faced aboriginal explains that, thanks to the Corn Laws, 'he and his ancestors, having nothing to do but hunt and shoot, had so preserved their health that, unlike the rest of the human race, they had not degenerated from the original form and nature of man. He showed that it was owing to the vigour of mind and body consequent upon this fine health that Vraibleusia had become the wonder of the world, and that they themselves were so actively employed; and he inferred that they surely could not grudge him the income which he derived, since the income was, in fact, the foundation of their own profits.' He then gives them all a good sound flogging, and departs amid the enthusiastic cheering of those he has lashed.[43]

No wonder radical John Bright was said to admire *Popanilla*. As well as the Corn Laws and the landed gentry, it satirises the duke of Wellington, the constitution and the Church of England. Though it mocks the Benthamites, it shows no signs of Toryism. Nor is Disraeli's criticism of Utilitarianism of the kind he was later to make, attacking their lack of imagination. On the contrary, *Popanilla* criticises Benthamism because it stifles sexuality. The island of Fantaisie has been described as an adult male fantasy, where '"Dance" becomes virtually a euphemism for intercourse ... It is almost as if Disraeli's psyche in 1828 cannot sanction the fusion of the English code of behaviour with his own libidinous, and often licentious, fantasies.'[44] Like *Vivian Grey* Part Two, *Popanilla* is significant less for its substance than for its subtext. The man who fantasised about naked and voluptuous islanders, whose lives consisted of drinking wine and making love, was unlikely to be contented with an elaborate and frustrating parlour game of flirtation with Mrs Austen.

One chapter of *Popanilla* stands out: chapter fourteen is a long and elaborate essay on fruit, an extended metaphor, in which Disraeli likens the taste for fruit to religion. Pineapples represent Roman Catholicism, supplied from abroad; government-grown pineapple suckers are the home-grown religion of Anglicanism, and crabapples are the Puritan sects who preached universal fruit toleration. The metaphor is cleverly developed to explain English history in the seventeenth century, when the acid faction of crabapple eaters abolished the custom of eating foreign pineapples, and when eventually pineapple suckers were restored as the established fruit, and no man could hold office who was not supplied with pineapple from the government depots.

Disraeli's grasp of seventeenth-century history is striking. His tutor was Isaac. In 1828, at around the same time that Disraeli published *Popanilla*, Isaac published the first two volumes of his *Commentaries on the Life and Reign of Charles I*. Though a Tory, Isaac despised history activated by 'mere party spirit'; he might exult, he wrote, 'with the great poet of Reason, that the Whigs have denounced his Toryism, and the Tories have misliked his independence'.[45] In fact, he was a follower of the philosophical historian David Hume. Hume had shed a 'generous tear' for Charles I, and in his *Commentaries* Isaac defended Charles and his apologist Hume from the attacks of the republican Mrs Macauley and the Whig historian Hallam, whose *Constitutional History* had been published in 1827. To this task Isaac brought the fruits of his extensive researches in the manuscript collections of the British Museum. The publisher, Bentley (Isaac was no longer published by John Murray) feared that the tendency of the times, apparently so adverse to Isaac's high Tory views, might prove injurious to the book's reception; but the *Commentaries* was a success. Isaac was awarded an honorary degree by Oxford University, and a further three volumes on Charles I followed (1830–2). To defend Charles I at a moment when the Whig, progressivist tide was about to surge over English history was the action of a King Canute historian, and Isaac's substantial volumes have been neglected by posterity, but his book supplied his son with an invaluable intellectual weapon: a Tory theory of history to counter the Whig orthodoxy.

Popanilla was published by Colburn in June 1828 and dedicated to Plumer Ward. Prompted by Sara Austen, Disraeli had written an elaborate but insincere letter in praise of Ward's latest book in 1827, and Ward returned the compliment. *Popanilla*, he told Disraeli, was 'equal to the Tale of a Tub and Candide, and superior to Zadig and Babouc'. The satire is caustic, and, 'what is best, can offend no one'. Maybe this was why *Popanilla* made so little noise. It received a couple of brief notices, the *Literary Gazette* dismissing it as 'a *jeu d'esprit* of considerable merit, though unequal, and not so racy as Swift of 1828 might have made it'.[46]

Exhausted by writing *Popanilla*, Disraeli became ill again. In July 1828 his family took him to Lyme Regis in search of sea bathing and restorative ozone. 'My dear Ben,' wrote Sara Austen, 'how mortifying to be nearly a month at the sea and only able to bathe once. I know not what to say to comfort you.' Back in London he was no better. 'If I hear from you, let me have better accounts of your head,' wrote William Meredith from Sweden. 'Poor Mrs Austen and Dr Allardyce have conjured up such a phantom between them.'[47] Isaac, who was himself prone to disabling fits of depression, worried not only about Ben, who mooched gloomily about the house, but about the chronic ill-health of Maria. 'My son's life within the last year and a half', Isaac wrote in January 1829, 'has been a blank in his existence. His complaint is one of those perplexing cases which remain uncertain and obscure till they are finally got rid of. Meanwhile, patience and resignation must be his lot.'[48]

In the summer of 1829, prompted by 'the precarious health of several members of my family', Isaac moved his family to Buckinghamshire. Ever since 1825, when they took Plumer Ward's Hyde House, 'their first taste for country life in general, and for Bucks in particular', the D'Israelis had determined to quit London when the opportunity offered.[49]

It was a wrench for Isaac to uproot himself from the scholarly calm of the British Museum and the literary chatter of the Athenaeum Club, but Buckinghamshire brought him closer to the events of the reign of Charles I. Bradenham, the house he took, was (and still is) an elegant wide-fronted red-brick Queen Anne manor house, nestling at the foot of the Chiltern Hills near High Wycombe. In front of the house, grand wrought-iron gates open on to the village green, surrounded by cottages; the parish church stood in the grounds next to the house, and on the other side of the green stood the rectory, then a modern building in the gothic style. Behind the house rose the wooded slopes of the Chilterns – an estate of 1351 acres went with the house, and pigs grew fat beneath the beech trees: Bradenham was famed for its excellent pork and hams, and Isaac took a gluttonous and somewhat perverse delight in his new role of pig farmer.

High Wycombe then was about three hours' journey from London by stage coach, and the D'Israelis' life at Bradenham was isolated in a way hard to imagine only fifteen years later, in the age of railways, penny posts and penny newspapers. The Thame coach came every day from London's Argyll Street through the village, and sometimes left parcels at the gates, containing books and reviews for Isaac; but letter-writing was restricted by the high cost of postage, then payable by the recipient, which Isaac always grudged; the D'Israelis did not live in the franking world of MPs and their correspondents, who enjoyed the much-abused privilege of free postage.[50]

Bradenham House dominates the village and, though Isaac never bought the property – it was the subject of a protracted wrangle in Chancery 1824–54 – he stepped easily into the shoes of squire. He acquired the right to present candidates to the living at Bradenham (the diocese of Oxford made no trouble about his equivocal Jewish status) and the rector and his wife and son became central figures in the D'Israeli family life. Sarah busied herself paying calls, visiting the sick and supervising the garden, and the two younger brothers willingly exchanged Bloomsbury for the bucolic. Jem could never resist buying horses, which more often than not turned out to be lame, and he filled the house with dogs; 'Jem is boisterously zealous,' wrote Isaac, 'and if our nerves can stand him he is an excellent lad.'[51]

Many years later, when he was old and famous, Disraeli walked past Bradenham with Lady Derby. 'It was here that I passed my miserable youth,' he told her. 'Why miserable?' 'I was devoured by ambition I did not see any means of gratifying.'[52] In reality, he loved the place; he loved the trees that grew on the light soils, and in November, when 'the leaf had changed but not fallen, and the vast spiral masses of the dark green juniper effectively contrasted with the rich brown foliage of the beech, varied occasionally by the scarlet leaves of the wild cherry tree', he could imagine, as he recalled in *Endymion*, they were trees in a fairy tale of imprisoned princesses or wandering cavaliers. Soon after the move, his spirits rose.[53]

In the autumn of 1828 Disraeli read a novel entitled *Pelham*, by Edward Lytton Bulwer.* Influenced by *Vivian Grey*, it was the fashionable novel of the year, the story of a dandy whose supercilious and affected comments exposed the social pretension and amorality of Regency society; it created the fashion for black and white evening dress rather than plum or blue. Sara Austen, who read *Pelham* in August, was disappointed. 'His own character is fairly done, but the story ridiculous,' she wrote, and the plagiarisms from Plumer Ward made her cross.[54] Disraeli was struck, however, by the dandyism of *Pelham*. Sublimely selfish, indolent and irresponsible, the dandy stood for everything the Utilitarian middle class despised. This in itself appealed to Disraeli, but in *Pelham* Bulwer gave dandyism a new twist: he made it a cover for ambition, a training for power. Manage yourself and you may manage the world, was the message. Pelham was an MP and a Radical, underlining the ambiguity at the heart of the book: the critic of the social system was himself created by it; the dandy was the quintessential product of rotten Regency society, yet he was sublime.[55]

Early in 1829 Disraeli wrote the author an admiring letter, enclosing a gift of tobacco, but regretting that he was too ill to meet. In reply, Bulwer praised the 'brilliant and unrivalled promise' of *Vivian Grey* and *Popanilla*.[56] Disraeli then contributed four articles to the *Court Journal* (May and June 1829) satirising *Pelham* under the name 'Mivartinos' after Mivart's Hotel, where Bulwer (and Pelham) stayed. Bulwer was convinced the articles were parodies of his style, though he did not know Disraeli wrote them, and he remained friendly towards the invalid writer.[57] 'I cannot express to you how much I was shocked by the melancholy account you give of your health,' he

---

* Edward Lytton Bulwer changed his name to Bulwer-Lytton in 1844. He published either anonymously or under the name of Bulwer-Lytton, but Disraeli referred to him as Bulwer.

told Disraeli, whom he still had not met, in July.[58] A few months later they were close friends.

Bulwer was a butterfly dandy with a head of beautiful curls, a Radical and a friend of J. S. Mill. As Disraeli wrote years later in *Endymion*, 'he combined the Sybarite with the Utilitarian sage, and it secretly delighted him to astonish or embarrass an austere brother republican by the splendour of his family plate or the polished appointments of his household.' He was vain ('his writing desk', says his son, 'stood upon a console in front of a mirror') he was a snob and painfully thin-skinned. Thomas Carlyle, who met him in 1839, described him as 'a high dressed, longfaced, flaccid, yellow-eyed, goose-looking, incoherent figure, with lean body and gaping expression of countenance'. A year older than Disraeli, Bulwer too had been a Byron-crazed youth – as a Cambridge undergraduate, he lay all night on the grave of his newly buried mistress and had an affair with Lady Caroline Lamb; cut off by his rich mother after his rash marriage to the Irish feminist, Rosina Wheeler, Bulwer had plunged savagely into novel-writing to pay for his and Rosina's extravagances.[59]

The winter of 1829–30 is something of a mystery in Disraeli's life. According to Lucien Wolf, he spent a 'roystering winter' in London, experiencing at first hand the dissipation and debauchery he described in his novel *The Young Duke*. He is alleged to have roystered with Bulwer, to have lost more money on the Stock Exchange and landed in a debtors' prison. Monypenny brushed this theory aside in a dismissive footnote; and in old age Disraeli told his secretary, Monty Corry, 'Until my return from the East on the eve of the '32 election, I had lived a very secluded life, and mixed not at all with the world.'[60] But his autobiographical testimony is unreliable, and what little evidence there is seems to support a modified version of the roystering winter theory. For a start, he looked different.

'I am desperately ill,' Disraeli told Benjamin Austen in November 1829, 'and shall be in town in a day or two, *incog.* of course' – incognito because he was hounded by sheriff's officers who hovered at his friends' houses, ready to pounce with writs from his creditors. 'Tell Madam' (that is, Sara Austen) 'I shall call upon her if possible, but I can only call, because I am necessarily betrayed by her, and in consequence *"the heathen rage most furiously"*.'[61] As a boy, Henry Layard, Austen's nephew, remembered his uncle being summoned one evening that winter to rescue Disraeli from a debtors' prison, and perhaps Disraeli really was in trouble with his creditors. But the sheriff's officers also provided him with a convenient excuse. He had no wish to spend time with Sara Austen, of whom he had grown tired, yet he needed Benjamin Austen's help more than ever. Inspired by Bulwer, who planned to enter parliament, Disraeli was in negotiation to become member for the borough of

Hindon in Wiltshire at the cost of £1000 a year. Austen supported his parliamentary ambitions, and they had concocted a plan for Isaac to buy his son an estate – Ben had his eye on a place called Stockton, near Hindon. Not that Disraeli intended to live in a solitary country house, but he needed a property qualification to stand for parliament: the substantial freehold property qualifications for MPs introduced in the reign of Queen Anne (£600 annual value for a county member, £300 for a borough member) were not dropped until 1858, and Isaac did not own Bradenham.[62] Isaac, however, refused to buy land at a time of agricultural distress, and Benjamin, who had more than once interfered in Isaac's affairs 'and never with any particular success', did not press. In any case, the £1000 a year demanded by Hindon was far beyond his means. He did insist, however, on the other, more important plan he made that winter: a grand tour of the Middle East, to Constantinople and Jerusalem.

Between visits to London, Disraeli read voraciously at Bradenham. He plundered the shelves of Isaac's library for books on Judaism and the Jews, on the Middle East and Islam. He made a lot of notes and began to consider a historical novel about Alroy, the twelfth-century Jewish Prince of the Captivity and descendant of Hebrew Kings, who had risen against the Caliphate and for a brief but glorious moment reversed the fortunes of his fallen race, only to be betrayed by his own people. It was an odd story to choose, a story of ambition and hubris and the Jewish predicament, to some degree, Disraeli's own experience; it fed his longing to see the Middle East, and he convinced himself that his recovery depended on his visit. Isaac, however, refused to pay, which meant, Disraeli told Austen, 'I must *hack* for it. A literary prostitute I have never yet been, tho' born in an age of general prostitution, and tho' I have more than once been subject to temptations which might have been the *ruination* of a less virtuous young woman. My muse however is still a virgin, but the mystical flower, I fear, must soon be plucked. Colburn I suppose will be the bawd. Tempting Mother Colburn!' Perhaps Disraeli's language was merely extravagant, but more likely he was writing in a code. In spite of the temptations offered by Sara Austen, Disraeli seems to be saying he had not succumbed. No male prostitute, he. To underline the point he warned Austen to tell no one of the eastern trip, not even his wife, for 'Women are delightful creatures, particularly if they be pretty, which they always are, but then they *chatter* (they can't help it).'[63]

Disraeli put aside his thoughts on Alroy, and settled down at Bradenham to write a money-spinning novel of fashionable life, *The Young Duke*. He wrote at top speed, and as he scribbled life blurred into romance, and he began to act the part and write in the voice of his hero, the satiated man of fashion. 'I am dying,' he drawled in a letter to the fashionable novelist,

Catherine Gore. 'My only chance, and a very forlorn one, of not immediately quitting this life, is immediately quitting this country, almost a greater bore.' 'Youth is a blunder,' he wrote, tossing off an epigram (she had mentioned *Vivian Grey*), 'Manhood a moral, and Old Age a regret.'[64] To Colburn, the bawd, he wrote to say that despite 'being declared to be in a decline, which is all stuff, but really with positive Exile, probable Death, and possible Damnation hanging over me', he was intent on a novel. 'But such a novel! It will astound you, draw tears from Princesses, and grins from printer's devils.'[65] By mid-February 1830 one-and-a-half volumes were written. 'It is a series of scenes,' Disraeli told Meredith, 'every one of which would make the fortune of a fashionable novel: I am confident of its success, and that it will complete the corruption of the public taste.'[66]

While writing *The Young Duke* Disraeli was receiving treatment for his illness from Dr Bolton, a sleek and fashionable St James's physician. Bolton's treatment consisted of blood-letting by cupping-glass, coupled with digitalis, the drug made from powdered foxgloves, usually used to lower the circulation in heart conditions. He was still tormented by the noise in his head, and it would appear that Bolton had diagnosed a heart condition, causing a rushing of blood into the brain. But digitalis, which slows the heart muscle, is a depressant, and Bolton's treatment aggravated the depression which caused the sympton he was trying to cure. Disraeli's mood lurched from jaunty euphoria to melodramatic despair. 'With regard to myself in a word,' he told Sara Austen on 7 March 1830, 'I cannot be worse. With regard to London, it is of all places the one, in my present situation, least suited to me. Solitude and silence do not make my existence easy, but they make it endurable.' He was worried, too, he told her, about his hair, those precious black curls, which grew badly and were going grey which, he declared, flippant once more, 'occasions me more anguish than even the prospect of death'.

Sara Austen could hardly have guessed that his solitude at Bradenham was enlivened and his existence made endurable by the wife of his doctor, Clarissa (Clara) Bolton, whom Disraeli had asked to stay with his family in return for the doctor's attentions. Her stay, Sarah Disraeli recalled, 'proved a little longer than we expected', and perhaps for good reason – Disraeli had begun an affair with her. While Dr Bolton's drugs dragged Disraeli down, Mrs Bolton's attentions catapulted him to an emotional high.[67]

The novel was finished by the end of March. Disraeli brought the manuscript up to London, and dined with William Meredith, who was to accompany him on his journey to the east. The crowds parted, Meredith noted, as Disraeli walked up Regent Street, outlandishly dressed in a blue surtout, military light blue trousers, black stockings with red stripes, and shoes. At dinner with Bulwer a few days later he wore green velvet trousers, shoes with silver buckles, a canary coloured waistcoat and ringlets.[68] (Where did the money come from for his tailor's bills?) Jauntily affected, he might have walked straight out of *Pelham*, and he left the manuscript for Bulwer to read. It was the first book he had written without the help of Sara Austen.

The Young Duke begins:

> George Augustus Frederick, Duke of St James, completed his twenty-first year, an event which created almost as great a sensation among the aristocracy of England as the Norman Conquest. A minority of twenty years had converted a family always amongst the wealthiest of Great Britain into one of the richest in Europe. The Duke of St James possessed estates in the north and in the west of England, besides a whole province in Ireland. In London there were a very handsome square and several streets, all made of bricks, which brought him in yearly more cash than all the palaces of Vicenza are worth in fee-simple, with those of the Grand Canal of Venice to boot. As if this were not enough, he was an hereditary patron of internal navigation; and although perhaps in his two palaces, three castles, four halls, and lodges *ad libitum*, there were more fires burnt than in any other establishment in the empire, this was of no consequence, because the coals were his own. His rent-roll exhibited a sum-total, very neatly written, of two hundred thousand pounds; but this was independent of half a million in the funds, which we had nearly forgotten, and which remained from the accumulation occasioned by the unhappy death of his father.[69]

The young duke at twenty-one is a sublime coxcomb. He returns from the grand tour and determines to conquer society. He makes his début in the Lords and at Almack's, where he gallops with grace and waltzes with vigour, and is caught up in the frantic whirl of the London season.

> Think only of Prime Ministers and Princes, to say nothing of Princesses; nay! think only of managers of operas and French actors, to say nothing of French actresses; think only of jewellers, milliners, artists, horse-dealers, all the shoals who hurried for his sanction; think only of the two or three thousand civilised beings for whom all this population breathed, and who each of them had claims upon our hero's notice! Think of the statesmen, who had so much to ask and so much to give; the dandies to feed with and be fed; the dangerous dowagers and the desperate mothers; the widows, wild as early partridges; the budding virgins, mild as a summer cloud and soft as an opera hat! Think of the drony bores, with their dull hum; think of the chivalric guardsmen, with their

horses to sell and their bills to discount; think of Willis, think of Crockford, think of White's, think of Brooks', and you may form a faint idea of how the young Duke had to talk, and eat, and flirt, and cut, and pet, and patronise![70]

Disraeli is enjoying himself almost as much as his hero, fantasising about showers of diamonds and suppers of ortolans: 'Oh! show me that bosom more delicious even than woman's. Let me die eating ortolans to the sound of soft music!'

But *The Young Duke* is more than a fashionable novel, a brilliant but superficial picture of brilliant manners. In words quoted from Byron's *Don Juan* on the title page, it is 'A moral tale, though gay'; Disraeli himself said the novel was only half fashion and the rest passion. The young duke is spoilt and corrupted by society. He abandons himself to sublime selfishness and is plagued by satiety, the result of too much love of self. Like a wearied hare pursued by the hell-hounds of ennui, he seeks escape in dissipation. 'I am a lost man,' he mourns, echoing the words of Vivian Grey, and there are similarities between the two novels: both Vivian and the duke are corrupted by society, and both suffer and are redeemed.

The young duke's dizzy career of debt, drink, duelling and womanising culminates in a forty-eight hour sitting at cards: 'There they sat, almost breathless, watching every turn with the fell [*sic*] look in their cannibal eyes which showed their total inability to sympathise with their fellow-beings.' (Surely Disraeli must have experienced a gambling hell to describe the gamblers with such conviction. 'The gambling scene lives,' wrote James Clay, his dissipated friend.[71]) The duke loses heavily, but he is shocked, less by his losses than by the faces of his fellow gamblers. 'He looked in the mirror at himself. A blight seemed to have fallen over his beauty, and his presence seemed accursed.'[72] He repents; he has acquired self-knowledge. He seeks the guidance of his guardian, Mr Dacre, a benevolent Roman Catholic aristocrat; and he wins the hand of Dacre's daughter May by making a triumphant speech in the House of Lords in support of Catholic Emancipation.

'What does Ben know of dukes?' Isaac is said to have remarked when he heard of the book, and critics have echoed him down the generations. Disraeli's descriptions of Almack's or horse racing are unblushing pieces of hack work, but his lack of experience of the fashionable world is not fatal to his novel. The novel was not intended to teach the new rich how to behave in society which, as Disraeli explained in *Popanilla*, was the purpose of silver-fork fiction. On the contrary, it is pure fantasy, *Arabian Nights* translated to the world of London society.

As an old man Disraeli disowned *The Young Duke*. It was, he wrote, the only one of his books not written from his own feelings and experience.[73] As so often, he was being disingenuous. In 1846 when Richard Bentley threatened to exploit Disraeli's burgeoning political fame and reissue *The Young Duke*, Disraeli was so anxious to suppress it that he bought back the copyright, and it was not reissued until 1853 when it was significantly revised.[74] The fact was that the original edition gave not too little but too much away; the frivolous fantasy of the young duke is only part of the novel, the other theme is the voice of the narrator who, like the narrator in Byron's *Don Juan*, talks frankly and directly to the reader. Isaac immediately recognised that the narrator was Disraeli himself, who veers between manic exuberance and morbid despair, pouring out his misery in unguarded digressions, most of which were deleted in 1853. In its original edition *The Young Duke* is a key biographical document, revealing Disraeli's abrupt changes of mood: his oscillation between fantasy, arrogance and puppyism on the one hand and self-pitying despair on the other.[75]

'I am one, though young, yet old enough to know, Ambition is a demon,' says the narrator, likening himself to the young Napoleon and to Byron. 'To doubt of the creed in which you have been nurtured is not so terrific as to doubt respecting the intellectual vigour on whose strength you have staked your happiness.'[76] 'My life has been a blunder and a blank, and all ends by my adding one more slight ghost to the shadowy realm of fatal precocity!' 'I have lost the power of conveying what I feel, if indeed that power were ever mine. I write with an aching head and a quivering hand; yet I must write if but to break the solitude.'[77]

In these stream-of-consciousness confessions Disraeli brings us close to the reality of his breakdown, to the agony of self-doubt, self-pity, and loneliness. He is candid too about his Jewishnes: 'The drooping pen falls from my powerless hand, and I feel – I keenly feel myself what indeed I am – far the most prostrate of a fallen race!'[78] In his crisis of identity he clings to two rocks: Isaac ('Oh, my father! ... our friendship is a hallowed joy – it is my pride and let it be thy solace') and England: 'Oh, England! Oh my country – although full many an Eastern clime and Southern race have given me something of their burning blood, it flows for thee! I rejoice that my flying fathers threw their ancient seed on the stern shores which they have not dishonoured – I am proud to be thy child.... if ever the hour shall call, my brain and life are thine.'[79]

It is as if England has become a kind of mother substitute. But though Disraeli identifies with England, he has no loyalty to party. 'Am I a Whig or a Tory? I forget,' he asks in a flippant passage which was also suppressed in 1853 and no wonder; it was not what Tory leaders should be found saying in their youth:

As for the Tories, I admire antiquity, particularly a ruin; even the relics of the Temple of Intolerance have a charm. I think I am a Tory. But then the Whigs give such good dinners, and are the most amusing. I think I am a Whig; but then the Tories are so moral, and morality is my forte; I must be a Tory. But the Whigs dress so much better; and an ill-dressed party, like an ill-dressed man, must be wrong. Yes! I am a decided Whig. And yet – I feel like Garrick between Tragedy and Comedy. I think I will be a Whig and Tory alternate nights, and then both will be pleased; or I have no objection, according to the fashion of the day, to take a place under a Tory ministry, provided I may vote against them.[80]

Probably in 1829 Disraeli was genuinely undecided between Whig and Tory. He hated Benthamism and he had outgrown his early admiration for the liberal Tory Canning, whom he dismissed in *The Young Duke* as 'a consummate rhetorician; but there seemed to me a dash of commonplace in all that he said, and frequent indications of the absence of an original mind'. Bulwer and Byronism pulled Disraeli towards Radicalism, aristocratic and romantic. But Disraeli's instincts were Tory; in *The Young Duke* the narrator's flippancy is contradicted by the morality of the story, which is profoundly conventional and conservative. The duke is redeemed only when he ceases to rebel and conforms to the conventional mores of society, recognising the responsibilities of his position. He is redeemed through love and through politics – his support for Catholic Emancipation. Disraeli, who saw analogies between the positions of Jews and Catholics, sympathised with Catholic Emancipation; and he was aware that though the Whigs preached toleration, Emancipation was carried by a Tory government. If there is a lesson to be learned from the novel, it is that the aristocracy must exert themselves to provide political leadership: a theme Disraeli developed more insistently in *Sybil* fifteen years later. In *The Young Duke* the duties of the aristocracy are underlined in an encounter with a Utilitarian, roughly based on James Mill, whom the young duke meets on a coach journey, and who tells him in a menacing tone that men are opening their eyes and beginning to question the use of an aristocracy.

Bulwer read the first book of the manuscript and was not very impressed. He had not liked *Vivian Grey*, and he now told Disraeli that the judgement of the new book was flawed – it was too indulgent to flippancies. He advised Disraeli to look again at 'the antithetical neatnesses of style which make the great feature of your composition. Whenever they attain a witticism or a new truth (which is nine times out of ten) don't alter a syllable. But whenever you see that form of words which aims at a point and does not acquire it, be remorseless.' By flippancies, said Bulwer, he meant 'an ornate and showy effeminacy, which I think you should lop off on the same principle as Lord Ellenborough should cut off his hair'. In a mere fashionable novel, or to a mere dandy, the flippancies and the hair might be left: 'But I do not think the one suits a man who is capable of great things, nor the other a man who occupies great places.' The critics, warned Bulwer, would be hostile: 'I fear you are likely to be attacked and vituperated to a degree which fame can scarcely recompense. Recollect that you have written a book [*Vivian Grey*] of wonderful promise, but which got you enemies. You have therefore to meet, in *this* book, a very severe ordeal, both of expectation and malice.'[81] These were fair criticisms. Where Disraeli's epigrams came off, they sparkled; when he tried for an epigram and failed, the result was bathos.

He was so stung by Bulwer's criticism that he contemplated suppressing the book. In London he was cupped (or bled) and retreated to Bradenham, where he spent some days in a trance from digitalis, sleeping sixteen out of twenty-four hours. Reassured by Bulwer that *The Young Duke* needed only polishing, he revised the manuscript and brought it up to London early in May.[82] Without telling Isaac, he offered it first to John Murray – he still hoped to regain Murray's friendship; Murray declined Disraeli's request for an interview, whereupon the book was sold to Colburn for £500 in post-dated bills. He needed to sell it quickly to pay for his travels, and it was far more suited to Colburn's market than Murray's; but his approach to Murray gave him an opening which he hoped to use in the future, and he wrote fulsomely to Murray, praising his honour and impartiality – 'the first I have never doubted, and the second it is your interest to exercise.'[83]

Benjamin Austen had made Disraeli's trip to the Middle East possible by lending him £500, and he planned to leave England with Meredith at the end of May. News of his departure alarmed his creditors. Robert Messer was pressing for about £1500, and Disraeli wrote to Thomas Evans, whom he left to fend off Messer single-handed, to explain that he had been ordered abroad because of his health. 'For the last three years – I will not talk of enjoyment – Life has not afforded me a moment's ease; and after having lived in perfect solitude for nearly eighteen months, I am about to be shipped off for the last resource of a warmer climate. To leave England at all is to me most distressing; to leave it without finally arranging my distracted affairs, costs me a pang, which is indeed bitter.' Then he added, 'I assure you, dear Evans, that it would be very difficult to find one, who is really more interested in the welfare of another, than I am in yours, and although you may perhaps doubt the sincerity of this declaration, I nevertheless make it.'

As insincere as it was egotistical, Disraeli's letter can have given small comfort to the unfortunate Evans, but there was nothing he could do. Rather more shrewd was Thomas Jones, the surgeon who had delivered Sarah Disraeli and whose son had been at school with Ben. Disraeli owed him £3000 plus interest in arrears (£175), and on the morning of his departure Benjamin signed an undertaking that in event of his death the debt should be repaid.[84]

FOUR

The Great Asian Mystery

1830–1

DISRAELI AND Meredith reached Falmouth on England's south-west coast after a very rough passage on a steamer, *The Shannon*. The wind had been ahead the whole time and Benjamin assured 'My Dear Sa' on Tuesday 1 June that he had not been sick and never felt a qualm. Shortly before they left Meredith had become engaged to marry Sarah after a secret engagement lasting nearly ten years. The Merediths were rich, but William's marriage had been delayed by his even richer uncle, a contractor, whose heir he was, and whose objections to Jewish Sarah had been withdrawn only on the eve of departure.[1]

After about a week HMS *Messenger* arrived. She was a 'beastly uncomfortable steamer, lacking decency and refinement', but she survived the Bay of Biscay and landed the two most important young men in Sarah's life on the Rock of Gibraltar, in a country where great hedges of aloes sixteen feet high and occasional palms and woods of olives, and myrtles and orange bowers provided an exotic contrast to 'beloved and beechy Bucks'. Jews with gaberdines and skull caps and Moors in radiant costume were on the Rock, as were Spaniards and Genoese and Scottish Highlanders. An English assistant inspector of health, to whom Disraeli had a letter of introduction, introduced them to the governor of the Rock, Sir George Don, 'a General and GCB, a very fine old gentleman, of the Windsor Terrace school, courtly almost regal in his manner'. Disraeli assured Bradenham that all Isaac's works were in the public Garrison and Merchants' Libraries. *Vivian Grey* was also there, 'looked upon at Gibraltar as one of the masterpieces of the 19th century. You may feel their intellectual pulse from this. At first I apologised and talked of youthful blunders and all that, really being ashamed, but finding them to my astonishment sincere, and fearing they were stupid enough to adopt my last opinion, I shifted my position just in time, looked very grand, and pass myself off for a child of the sun, like the Spaniards in Peru.'

The governor asked them to dine, lent them one of his servants, a man named Brunet, and even gave them a route to the savage mountain district in Spain, the Sierra da Ronda. Brunet was fifty, 'light as a butterfly', an excellent shot and a gifted cook in a country where cooking was usually an abomination. Keeping their luggage to a minimum – Disraeli used the red bag his mother had made him for his pistols – they travelled for a week, rising at four in the morning, and riding till ten, when they stopped because of the heat. By five in the afternoon it was cool enough to ride for another three hours or so, picking their way over terrain like the 'steep bed of an exhausted cataract'. There were plenty of robbers, no roads, and Disraeli had never been more exhausted, but Meredith was as good a man to travel with as he had been in Germany six years ago, and the air of the savage mountains, the rising sun and rising appetite, the picaresque people and the impending danger would have had an excellent effect had it not been for 'the old enemy'.

'I sometimes think it lighter about the head,' Disraeli wrote, 'but the palpitation about the heart greatly increases, otherwise my health is wonderful. Never have I been better, but what use is this, when the end of all existence is debarred me. I say no more upon this melancholy subject by which I am ever, and infinitely depressed, and often most so when the world least imagines it – but to complain is useless, and to endure almost impossible, but existence is certainly less irksome than the mild distraction of this various life.'[2]

'You never *before* mentioned palpitations of the *heart* – should we read head?' wrote Isaac in alarm. Nor is it clear what he meant by being debarred the end of existence – possibly a doctor had warned him not to marry on account of his mental instability.[3] He was still in the mood of *The Young Duke*, swinging between jaunty euphoria and self-dramatised despair. He complained that his hair was coming out, all of it, just after it had been so perfect that women had tugged what they thought was a wig. A real wig was out of the question. Coconut oil was readily available, but what if it made his hair turn grey or green?

News reached Gibraltar of the death of King George IV. Isaac, a staunch Tory, complained of a 'thick cloud' cast over monarchy, and Sarah deplored the new democratic days which, she said, meant that Colburn had tired of Disraeli's aristocratic young duke – 'in this our mobbing and huzzaing age, Colburn deems us too vulgar'. Disraeli's response was flippant. The king's death, he said, 'is the destruction of my dress waistcoats. I truly grieve.'[4]

In Gibraltar he found plenty of opportunity to Pelhamise or play the dandy. He was insufferably affected, amazing the officers on the Rock by carrying *two* canes, a morning and an evening cane, which were changed as the gun fired. 'I owe to them even more attentions than to being the supposed author of – what is it – I forget.' Gibraltar's judge advocate, Baron Field, a friend of Wordsworth's and a vulgar bore, pounced on Disraeli saying he had seen Isaac at Murray's, 'first man of the day, and all that'. Disraeli 'gave him a lecture on canes, which made him stare and he has avoided me ever since'. He made himself agreeable where it mattered, to Sir George Don and his wife, an old woman of seventy, who presided over a scene resembling a small German court. Too ill to entertain when Disraeli first arrived, Lady Don told him he was the cause of her exertions – a lie, but flattering nevertheless, and Disraeli was captivated. 'To listen to her, you would think you were charming away the hours with a blooming beauty in May Fair': she was the only person he knew who gave him the least idea of the *brillantes*, who chatted with Montesquieu and corresponded with Horace Walpole.[5]

Disraeli and Meredith had originally planned to travel straight to Malta, but they explored the south of Spain, Andalusia, the once famous kingdom of the Moors. Two days on horseback took them to Cadiz, white houses and green jalousies sparkling in the sun: 'Figaro is in every street, Rosina in every balcony.' Brackenbury, the English consul, was grand enough for an ambassador and he introduced Disraeli to Fleuritz, the rudely silent Spanish governor of Cadiz, as 'the son of the greatest author in England'. Disraeli played the dandy with the Spaniard, who was quite unable to understand badinage. Six Miss Brackenburys took Disraeli's side: Fleuritz 'gives a Mashalla look of pious resignation and has bowed to the ground every night since that he has met me'. The beauty of Cadiz, wrote Disraeli, was artificial – it was 'without an association, not a church, a picture, or a palace'. His letters show no glimmer of the sense of identity which later led him to locate his ancestors in thirteenth-century Cadiz; and though they passed Medina Sidonia, which was to lend its name to his greatest fictional character, he seems not to have visited it.[6]

Seville he also found disappointing – its reputation, he thought, must precede the Moors – and from Seville he began to write a series of long, careful letters home, rather like those he wrote from Italy in 1826, recording his impressions in a series of literary set-pieces, many of which he incorporated wholesale into *Contarini Fleming*. In Seville he discovered Murillo, whom he thought the most original of artists: 'No man has painted more, or oftener reached the ideal. He never fails. Where can his bad pictures be?' Fifty years later, as fallen prime minister, Disraeli addressed a party meeting in London standing beneath a painting of a Madonna by Murillo. 'The colouring both of painted effigy and living figure was of the same tone,' wrote an observer; 'the sallow flesh tints, black hair and clothing were almost identical in both.'[7]

At Cordova a grand and charming young woman from Madrid, travelling with her imposing husband and a supercilious duenna, pressed the two travellers to accompany her on the long and bandit-infested drive to Granada, having more confidence in two armed Englishmen than in her twenty-four soldiers of the once famous Spanish infantry. They refused, and hurried ahead, hoping to avoid the bandits lying in wait for her. The moon rose and they covered two leagues before their guide reported the sound of distant horse. Disraeli and Meredith drew up in fear, with their purses ready, but it was only a company of actors on mules and donkeys, and women on side-saddles chanting 'ave', their waists encircled by the brawny arms of their admirers, a scene worthy of Cervantes. In *Contarini Fleming* he added a sequel, in which he bravely rescued the good young woman from an attack by the bandits. Spain was the country for a national novelist, he told Sarah. 'The alfresco life of the inhabitants induces a variety of the most picturesque manners, their savageness makes each district retain with barbarous jealousy their own customs and their own costumes. A weak government resolves society into its original elements and robbery becomes much more honourable than war, inasmuch as the robber is paid, and the soldier in arrear.'[8]

At Granada, he raved over the Alhambra. 'Description is always a bore,' he told Isaac, and embarked on a lengthy account of Spain's Saracenic architecture and the Alhambra in particular. 'Conceive it in the times of the Boabdils [Moors] – conceive it with all its costly decoration, all the gilding, all the imperial purple, all the violet relief, all the scarlet borders, all the glittering inscriptions, and costly mosaics burnished, bright and fresh – conceive it full of still greater ornaments, the living groups with their rich and vivid and picturesque costume, and above all, their shining arms, some standing conversing in groups, some smoking in sedate silence, some telling their beads, some squatting round a Storier. Then the bustle and rush, and the arriving horsemen all in motion, and all glancing at the most brilliant Sun.'[9]

From Granada he wrote his mother a letter on an elephantine sheet, 'all about Spanish Ladies and Tomata [*sic*] Sauce'. Almost every day he dined on an Olio, he told her, a plateful of boiled beef and sausage and french beans and melons and peas drowned in thin piquant tomato sauce, and he gave her a receipt for a dish which might charm Isaac: fry four pounds of tomatoes very small with onions, add four eggs, mix well and serve up like a dry soup. After dinner, he told her, you take your siesta – he usually slept for two hours – and then it was time to call upon any agreeable family and take tea or chocolate with them, often under the piazza or colonnade of the patio. When the hot scented air is cool enough for the public walk, all is liveliness – bowing, kissing, gentle criticism of friends and, above all, the fluttering and tapping and poking of eloquent fans. 'A Spanish lady with her fan might shame the tactics of a troop of horse. Now she unfurls it with the slow pomp and conscious elegance of a peacock, now she flutters it with all the languor of a listless beauty, now with all the liveliness of a vivacious one. Now, in the midst of a very Tornado, she closes it with a whirr which makes you start – Pop!' His dear mother knew he was rather an admirer of the blonde, and he had been captivated by two Englishwomen in Spain, but the Spanish women interested him greatly. 'Their charm consists in their sensibility. Each incident, every person, every word, touches the fancy of a Spanish lady and her features are constantly confuting the creed of Mahomet, and proving she has a soul: but there is nothing quick, harsh, or forced about her.'

He warned his mother that 'the least exertion of mind instantly aggravates all my symptoms, and even this letter is an exertion which you would hardly credit'.

But to exist, and to feel existence more tolerable, to observe, and to remember, to record a thought that suddenly starts up, or to catch a new image which glances over the surface of my mind – this is still left me. But the moment I attempt to meditate or combine, to ascertain a question that is doubtful or in any way to call the greater powers of the intellect into play, that moment I feel am a lost man. The palpitation in my heart and head increases in violence, an indescribable feeling of idiocy comes over me, and for hours I am plunged in a state of the darkest despair ... I pursue this life only for a year; if at the end of that period I find no relief, I resign myself to my fate. Were I a catholic without the ties of life which alone reconcile me to my bitter existence I would then enter a Convent, but as I am a member of a family to which I am devotedly attached, and a good Protestant, I shall return to them and to my country, but to a solitary room which I shall never leave. I see no one, and speak with no one. I am serious. Prepare yourself for this, but hope better things.[10]

'Your account of the Spanish dames is very charming,' wrote Sarah tartly, 'but you do not tell us what would be still more interesting, the names of the English who could captivate you.'[11] Maria was anguished by Disraeli's account of his health, but he was being theatrical, in part at least. To Benjamin Austen Disraeli used his health as an excuse for not joining the Austens in Italy, but the truth is that he was beginning to recover. Spain, he told Sarah, had awakened an enthusiasm within him which he had thought dead.[12] It was a country of which he had read little and thought nothing; he was ignorant of its politics and history but felt, as he had in Venice, that he belonged. His letters home are silent on an incident in the Alhambra recorded by Meredith in his diary, when Disraeli was taken for a Moor. ('Es mi Casa' –

this is my palace – he said.) Nor did he tell his family of the notice his coat of arms attracted from the Spaniards. 'I was not then aware', he wrote in 1845, 'that I bore the quarterings ... of Castille and Leon – i.e. the shield of the House of Lara.'[13]

'Ever since you left,' wrote Sarah, 'accessions, elections and revolutions have followed one another so rapidly that we have not had breathing time.' The August elections had boosted the Whigs, and though England still had a Tory government, the 'thick and thin principles' of the *Quarterly* now 'seem quite out of fashion'. Isaac had not written a single page of his Tory *Commentaries on Charles I* for two months, so disturbed was he by 'this new Revolution which seemed to turn the whole system of one's thoughts – who now would care for Charles I?'[14]

Turning his back on England, revolution and Tory gloom, Disraeli steamed east in search of sun, health and adventure. From Gibraltar, he and Meredith endured a rough and disagreeable voyage to Malta, where they arrived in mid-August. After a week in quarantine in the Lanzaretto (where Byron had been), Disraeli stepped out into Byron's 'little military hothouse'.

James Clay was at large, already out of quarantine. A year younger than Disraeli, Clay had known Ralph at Winchester and Meredith at Oxford. Rich, cocky and handsome, he was the son of a city merchant and, according to Disraeli, was a hero on the island. He had beaten the whole garrison at billiards, rackets and other wicked games, given lessons to their prima donna and annoyed 'the primo tenore'. Now he offered to race their horses on foot, given a one hundred yards' start. And in Italy, where Clay had just been, he had 'diddled the Russian Legation at Ecarte, dished Prince Pignatelli at billiards, and been the inspiration for Lord Burghesh's Opera and Lady Normanby's Farce'.

Disraeli needed no letters of introduction to the agreeable officers at Malta because officers on HMS *Messenger* had long been expecting 'your worship's offspring'. His stories had beaten him to Malta. 'The Messiah-ship has been answered, and I am received with branches of palm. Here the younkers do nothing but play rackets, billiards and cards, race and smoke. To govern men you must either excel in their accomplishments – or despise them. Clay does one; I do the other, and we are equally popular.' He claimed affectation told even better than wit. When a rackets ball came to rest in the gallery where Disraeli was sitting among strangers, he handed it to a young rifleman and humbly asked him to forward its passage into the rackets court as he had never thrown a ball in his life. He boasted that this incident was talked about in all the messes.

He called on Sir Frederick Ponsonby, the notoriously exclusive governor of Malta, and made him roll on his sofa with laughter. Making it a rule 'always to leave with a good impression', after quarter of an hour Disraeli jumped up and apologised for breaking into Ponsonby's morning. He sauntered down the Strada Reale, nearly as good as London's Regent Street, and got five invitations to dinner. By the time he arrived home, after a session in the palatial and exclusive Union Club where he was an honorary member, he found an invitation from Lady Emily and Sir Frederick Ponsonby. Clay, who was very grand after the company of princes in Italy, and who as a fellow rackets player expected recognition from Ponsonby, was so annoyed at not being asked to dine immediately that he had refused an invitation and gone into opposition.[15]

'To govern men you must either excel in their accomplishments – or despise them' was the philosophy Disraeli had learned from Bulwer's *Pelham*, and in Malta he used dandyism and affectation for all he was worth. Sir Frederick Ponsonby, a brother of Lady Caroline Lamb, perhaps appreciated his exhibitionism; not so the red-faced horsy officers of the Royal Fusiliers. In Gibraltar the officers had ceased to invite 'that damned bumptious Jew boy' to their messes, and there is something pathetic about Disraeli's claim that he was as popular as Clay in Malta. He compensated by despising them. 'By heavens,' he told Ralph, 'I believe these fellows are boys till they are Majors, and sometimes don't even stop then. Their ignorance often is astounding.' Clay later recalled that in Malta he got to know two Benjamin Disraelis – a fine, unaffected companion when you were alone with him, who became an intolerable coxcomb the moment he entered society. His extreme, attention-seeking behaviour masked a sense that he neither belonged nor was liked; his affectation was to pass through many styles, but it was rooted in the uneasiness of the outsider.[16]

'You and William are both equally uncommunicative respecting each other,' wrote Sarah; 'if you have not *separated* do occasionally condescend to notice each other's existence.' Even before Malta Disraeli was tiring of Meredith, and his friendship with Clay, whom Meredith disliked, made matters worse. Disraeli spent most of his time with Clay, and he began to smoke. 'Conceive me with a Turkish pipe seven foot long puffing on a sofa.'[17] He found smoking relieved his head and made him feel more of a Turk. 'Tobacco', he remarked in *Sybil*, 'is the tomb of love', but in Malta and the Turkish empire this was not his experience. Clay shone as an athlete and a whist player, but another activity in which he excelled, as Robert Blake wrote, was sexual intercourse.[18] Clay's promiscuity accounts for the horror with which Bradenham viewed him, but it also explains the fascination he held for Disraeli, who enjoyed the company of philanderers and welcomed Clay's guidance to the fleshpots of Malta.

By the third week of September Disraeli at last knew how he would travel to Cyprus, their next port of call. Clay had hired a yacht of fifty-five tons with a crew of seven, and since Meredith was unwilling to take the yacht jointly with Clay, it was agreed that they would pay Clay a fair rate and get dropped where and when they liked. 'You should see me', Disraeli told Ralph, 'in the costume of a Greek pirate. A blood red shirt with silver studs as big as shillings, an immense scarf for girdle full of pistols and daggers, a red cap, red slippers, blue broad striped jacket and trousers. Excessively wicked!' They had painted out the yacht's unromantic name 'Susan', and were taking on board one of Byron's former servants as Clay's valet. Dagger-carrying Tita was mild as a lamb despite mustachios that touched the earth. Byron had died in his arms.[19]

Late in September 1830 Disraeli and Tita and Meredith and Clay set sail for Corfu, one of the seven Ionian Islands which since 1815 had been under British protection. Their passage was stormy, but Disraeli liked the sailor's life even though it made him dirty and destroyed his careful get-up. Although Corfu was a poor village, the lovely island offered him everything he expected from Grecian scenery: 'gleaming waters, woody isles, olive, vine, a clear sky, and a warm sun'. Zante, with its remnants of a decent Venetian town, was said to be even more beautiful. Byron had visited Yanina, the capital of nearby Albania, and Disraeli was keen to do the same, but he told his father that the whole country was in insurrection.

'Do not be surprised', Disraeli told Benjamin Austen from Malta, 'if you hear something very strange indeed.'[20] Dressed like a Greek pirate and accompanied by Byron's valet, he had a plan to fight in the Albanian war. He did not tell his family, but he intended to volunteer for the Turkish army. Since 1821 Turks and Greeks had been locked in a savage war. In England it was seen as the Greeks' struggle for independence of the Porte, and Whigs and Liberals sympathised with the Greeks while Tories backed the Turks ('give my love to the Turks', wrote the crusty Tory, Benjamin Austen). Byron died in the Greek cause at Missolonghi in 1824, since when the Turks had ravaged Greece. But at Navarino in 1827, Admiral Codrington, who had been sent on a peacekeeping expedition, led the combined British, French and Russian fleets to smash the Turkish-Egyptian navy. Capitalising on Turkey's weakness, Russia invaded in 1829, and the defeated Sultan Mahmoud II was forced to cede the independence of Greece. To add to the Sultan's difficulties, Mehemet Ali, the Albanian adventurer who ruled Egypt, had instigated a rebellion in Albania. Disraeli was fiercely pro-Turk, in spite of his admiration for Byron. In *Popanilla* he had satirised Navarino

('Codrington's bloody blunder', he called it in a letter to Benjamin Austen), and in Spain and Malta his Turkish sympathies grew daily more intense.[21]

When he reached Corfu, he found the Albanian insurrection had been crushed. 'I am glad to say the Porte every where triumphant,' he told Isaac. In *Contarini Fleming* Disraeli imagined himself riding in a cavalry charge with the Turkish army: in real life, he 'turned his intended campaign into a visit of congratulation to headquarters'. Sir Frederick Adam, lord high commissioner of the Ionian Isles (a friend of Walter Scott and a Peninsula veteran) entrusted Disraeli with a letter to be delivered to the grand vizier, who was thought to be with the Turkish army on the west coast of Greece, near Preseva. 'For once in my life I am to be an ambassador,' wrote Disraeli, who firmly took the leading role, appointing Meredith and Clay his aides-de-camp.[22]

They sailed from Corfu to Preseva. Disraeli told his father he was 'still infirm but no longer destitute of hope'. The Ambracian Sea stirred him to memories of Homer and the wanderings of the cunning Ulysses. 'I wander in pursuit of health like the immortal exile in pursuit of that lost shore which is now almost glittering in my sight. Five years of my life have been already wasted, and sometimes I think my pilgrimage may be as long as that of Ulysses.'[23] At Preseva, on a promontory looking over the Ambracian Gulf, they met Meyer the British consul general, to whom Sir Frederick had given Disraeli a 'very warm' letter of recommendation. Dining at Meyer's astonishingly well-stocked table, Disraeli was shocked to learn that the Albanian beys had been slaughtered at a banquet given by the grand vizier. Meyer assured him that the beys would never have trusted the grand vizier's pledge of safety; they would have done the killing if the vizier had not. 'The practice of politics in the East may be defined by one word, dissimulation. The most wary dissembler is the consummate statesman.'[24] Meyer taught Disraeli a lesson he never forgot; not only, as prime minister, was he unmoved by the Bulgarian atrocities nearly forty years later, but in English politics Disraeli, who had already shown a talent for deceit over the *Representative*, became a skilled practitioner of dissimulation.

The savage vizier had now moved north, and Disraeli, Meredith, Clay and Tita set off after him, carrying Sir Frederick Adam's letter. They sailed up to Salora in mid-October and with an armed company of six horsemen reached Arta in Albania. Except for the British consulate, Arta was in ruins, whole streets razed to the ground. Disraeli rested on a divan for the first time, and for the first time heard the muezzin from the minaret. He was highly affected by the experience.

Next morning he paid a visit to Kalio Bey, governor of Arta, who had remained loyal to the Porte during the aristocracy's insurrection. Once the wealthiest, now one of the most powerful Albanian notables, he kept his state in the midst of desolation. 'I cannot describe to you the awe with which I first entered the divan of a Great Turk, or the curious feelings with which for the first time in my life I found myself squatting on the right hand of a Bey smoking an amber-mouthed chibouque, drinking coffee, and paying him compliments through an Interpreter.'[25] The handsome bey, who had been well treated as a prisoner in Russia, was remarkably bland and Disraeli was transfixed by him; it was his first encounter with an eastern potentate.

Kalio Bey lent them an Albanian of his guard, completely armed with daggers and pistols, and their procession, including three Bayasdeers Ingleses (sons of English beys), journeyed over a wild mountain pass towards Yanina, slowed by a boy carrying a gazelle. For all their efforts they got nowhere near Yanina by sunset and were forced to spend a night at a vast and dilapidated khan, built by the Albanian chief Ali Pacha when 'his long sagacious, and unmolested reign had permitted him to turn this unrivalled country which combines all the excellences of Southern Europe and Western Asia to some of the purposes for which it is fitted'.

Kalio Bey had given them a letter for the Turkish colonel at the Khan, a young bey who tried, without success, to understand Tita's Greek. There was no interpreter and the three Englishmen resorted to sign language, smoking, exchanging pipes by way of compliment and pressing their hands to their hearts to show thanks as they sat on the same divan. They were too well bred to have more than an occasional joke. Clay with grave face suggested playing écarté, but they were all so ravenous that they offered their host a glass of brandy, hoping he would feed them. 'Mashallah! had the effect only taken place 1830 years ago, instead of in the present age of scepticism, it would have been instantly voted a first rate miracle.' Meredith went outside, pretending to go shooting. By the time he returned, Clay, Disraeli and the bey had finished a bottle of brandy. Dry unsugary figs came. Pistols were inspected in a graceful pantomime. Tita at last asked for bread, and a capital supper was produced, complete with wine which they would have had to drink even if it had been poison, it was such a compliment. They ate with their fingers. More brandy was drunk, the room turned round. The bey merrily shook hands with Disraeli and shouted English picked up from them. The bey roared, Disraeli smacked him on the back and woke in the middle of the night sleeping on the divan rolled in its sacred carpet. He found Abraham's bosom in a large flagon of water and as he looked at the wood fire and thought of the blazing blocks of wood in the hall at Bradenham he asked himself whether he was really in the mountain of an Albanian chief, then shrugged his shoulders and slept and woke without a headache, giving their host a pipe as a memorial to getting tipsy together.[26]

Next day they crossed another steep mountain pass, then descended into a vast ruined plain where olive woods had been burnt and villages, fortresses and khan were deserted. Lofty mountains backed the city of Yanina, once one of the most prosperous and brilliant of cities in the Turkish dominions. Ruined houses, mosques with just their towers standing, streets razed – these were as nothing. An area of a square mile looked as if locusts had raided, 'desolating the works of man as well as those of God'. Bazaars had been destroyed a few months previously when furious Albanian soldiers heard of the massacre of their chiefs by the grand vizier, yet the fancifully dressed people of this city were anything but sad. Many of them looked at Disraeli, Meredith and Clay and took them for 'mylords Inglese', perhaps the first in these parts since Byron and Hobhouse had come nine years before.

Disraeli forgot this was an extraordinary scene even for the east, the result of the grand vizier's presence at Yanina, and he enjoyed 'the now obsolete magnificence of Oriental life'. 'Military chieftains in the most brilliant colours and most showy furs, and attended by a cortège of officers equally splendid, continuously passed us – now for the first time a Dervish saluted me and now a Delhi with his high cap reined in his desperate steed as the suite of some Pacha blocked up the turning of the street – the Albanian costume is inexhaustible in its combinations, and Jews and Greek priests must not be forgotten.' A Turkish sheik in entirely green clothes, a scribe with his writing materials in his girdle, a little old Greek physician who could count to nine on his fingers. A kettle drum banged by a slave on a camel made a wild unearthly din. Here, on his first day in Turkey, Disraeli saw all the characteristics of which he had read (far better prepared for Turkey than for Spain, he was soaked in Gibbon and Thomas Hope's *Anastasius*). 'I longed to write an Eastern tale,' he recalled in *Contarini Fleming*; the bazaar scenes were stored up for *Alroy*.[27]

He delivered his letter for the grand vizier to an official, the kelmya bey, and an hour was fixed for their audience with Redschid. They entered the gates of Yanina's battered fortress palace and 'hurried through courts and corridors all full of guards and pages and attendant chiefs and in fact every species of Turkish population, for in these countries one head does everything and we with our subdivisions of labour have no idea of the labour of a Turkish Premier'. At length they reached the antechamber, a vast room full of picturesque oriental groups. Here they waited ten minutes: 'I never thought that I could have lived to have wished to have kicked my heels in a minister's antechamber', when suddenly they were summoned to 'the awful presence of the pillar of the Turkish Empire, the man who has the reputation of being the main spring of the new system of regeneration, the renowned Redschid, an approved warrior, a consummate politician, unrivalled as a dissembler in a country where dissimulation is the principal portion of their moral culture'.

> Here squatted up in a corner of the large divan I bowed with all the nonchalance of St James Street, to a little, ferocious-looking, shrivelled, care worn man, plainly dressed with a brow covered with wrinkles, and a countenance clouded with anxiety and thought. I entered the shedlike Divan of the kind and comparatively insignificant Kalio Bey with a feeling of awe, I seated myself on the Divan of the Grand Vizier, who as the Austrian Consul observed, had destroyed, in the course of the last three months, NOT in war, 'upwards of four thousand of his acquaintance', with the self-possession of a morning call.... Some compliments now passed between us, and pipes and coffee were then brought by four of these lacqueys – then His Highness waved his hand and in an instant the chamber was cleared. Our conversation I need not repeat. We congratulated him on the pacification of Albania. He rejoined that the peace of the world was his only object and that the happiness of mankind his only wish – this went on for the usual time. He asked us no questions about ourselves or our country as other Turks did, but seemed quite overwhelmed with business, moody and anxious, while we were with him three separate Tartars arrived with dispatches. What a life![28]

Redschid had suppressed the Albanian rebellion with a duplicity and a ruthlessness remarkable even for a Turk. Yet Disraeli was not repelled; on the contrary, when he wrote to Benjamin Austen of 'the delight of being made much of by a man who was daily decapitating half the province', he meant what he said. To moral indignation, to the Christian sense of sin, Disraeli was a stranger; he revelled in the intrigue and duplicity of the east.[29]

Writing home from Preseva, where he returned in late October, having stayed a week at Yanina, 'lionising and being a lion', amazing the Turks with his fancy costumes, and being entertained each evening by the singers and dancing girls sent by the vizier, he gazed out over the Ambracian Gulf, the scene of the Battle of Actium, where Octavian defeated Cleopatra; beyond lay the islands of Ulysses and Sappho. 'When I gaze upon this scene,' he wrote, 'I remember the barbaric splendour and turbulent existence, which I have just quitted, with disgust. I recur to the feelings, in the indulgence of which I can alone find happiness, and from which an inexorable destiny seems resolved to shut me out.'[30]

He was being self-pitying but perverse. No doubt the Turks were barbaric, but the Middle East offered an alternative to the feelings from which he was shut out, to marriage and middle-class uxoriousness. Among the warlike

Turks, Disraeli was free to indulge his sexual fantasies without guilt or responsibility.

'I am sure James Clay must be very much improved for you to make such a friend of him,' wrote Sarah. 'How you come to be in a boat sailing with him on the Aegean Sea I cannot understand.'[31] For about a fortnight Disraeli, Clay and Meredith sailed through the Ionian Islands, staying within a couple of miles of the coast, keeping look-out for warlike pirates but touching at every inviting island or harbour, enjoying sunsets 'like the neck of a dove'. Musket practice by the crew sustained their courage; the Englishmen banged away with their pistols. Disraeli assured Benjamin Austen that the Greeks were convinced they had come about the vacant throne of Greece. Leopold of Saxe-Coburg had refused the crown that summer; he told Austen that if he had £25,000 to throw away, 'I might increase my headache by wearing a crown.'[32]

On their arrival at Piraeus, Disraeli climbed a small hill forming the side of the harbour and, screwing up his eyes, gazed short-sightedly upon an immense plain covered with olive woods and skirted by mountains. Some isolated hills rose at a distance from the bounding ridge. At the foot of the hill, six miles or so from him, was a considerable walled city and in front of it he could make out the blur of a Doric temple in the violet sunset. The city was Athens; Disraeli told his father, 'I never witnessed anything so truly beautiful, and I have seen a great deal.' Athens was still under the Turks, but the Grecian Commission had just arrived, and Disraeli told Bradenham they were the first Englishmen to see the Acropolis, which had been shut for the past nine years. They found almost every house roofless, but the ancient remains had been respected. Minor injury to the Parthenon and other temples inside the Acropolis during the siege had marred details but not the general effect. They walked among hundreds of military shells and cannon balls, and the Temple of Theseus, seen clearly at a short distance, looked as though it had just been finished by Pericles.[33]

Disraeli was moved by Athens, but no more than that: he was an indifferent classicist and Athens did not appeal to his imagination in the way that Venice did. Nor did he sympathise with the Greeks' current struggle for independence: 'I detest the Greeks more than ever,' he told Benjamin Austen, and in *Contarini Fleming* the contrast between the beauty of the Parthenon and the condition of the modern Greeks, 'unlettered slaves in barbarous lands', prompted reflection on the inevitable decline of races.[34] Travelling inside the country, to Marathon for instance, was exceptionally unpleasant. If you were lucky enough to find a shed to shelter in at night, you could be sure that vermin had found it too. He and Clay suffered severely, but for some reason the vermin left Meredith alone. All three were short of sleep and survived as best they could on a diet of honey and wild boar, which he reported was not as good as Bradenham pork. He consoled himself with his pipe.

At the end of November, after two days in Aegina, a favourable wind arose, and they were off for Constantinople. Sixteen islands came in sight, the clustering Cyclades, and they sailed east among the very heart of them, and reached the Dardanelles. 'What a road to a great city – narrower and much longer than the straits of Gibraltar, but not with such sublime shores. Asia and Europe look more kindly on each other, than Europe and her more sultry sister.' Near sunset, as the city came in sight, Disraeli again felt an excitement which he had thought dead.[35] Three years later, he recalled the approach to Constantinople as the moment when he thought that he should write an epic poem which, like Homer's *Iliad*, would celebrate the spirit of his time.[36]

Disraeli found no letters waiting in Constantinople; they had been sent on to Alexandria. Hungry for news, he plunged into a pile of *Galignani's Messengers*, the Paris-printed English language newspaper that circulated among the English abroad. He learned of the Whig government, formed in November, of political confusion which he itched to dramatise as a pantomime, 'Lord Mayor's Day or Harlequin Brougham', after the cancellation of the king's visit to the City on account of unrest and Brougham's appointment as lord chancellor.[37] He must have read too of the agricultural incendiarism, the Swing riots, which were alarming his family – at Wycombe a crowd of between 500 and 2000 demolished the paper mills where machinery was employed, distracting Sarah from her work with Isaac on the fifth volume of his *Commentaries*.[38]

Disraeli's travelogue from Constantinople described the cypress groves and mosque domes, the minarets and boats, the Bosphorus and, best of all, the bazaar.

The Bazaar would delight you however more than the Bosphorus. Fancy the Burlington Arcade or some of the Parisian passages and panoramas, fancy perhaps a square mile of the ground covered with these arcades intersecting each other in all directions, and full of every product of the Empire from diamonds to dates. The magnificence, novelty and variety of the goods on sale, the whole nation of shopkeepers all in different dress, the crowd of buyers from all parts of the world – are just to be hinted at. Here every people have a characteristic costume. Turks Greeks Jews and Armenians are the staple population – the latter seem to predominate. The Armenians wear round and very unbecoming black caps and robes – the Jews a black hat wreathed with a white handkerchief – the Greeks black turbans – the Turks indulge in all

combinations of costume. The meanest merchant in the Bazaar looks like a
Sultan in an Eastern fairy tale. This is mainly to be ascribed to the marvellous
brilliancy of their dyes, which is one of the most remarkable circumstances in
their social life, and which has never been explained to me. A common pair of
slippers that you can purchase in the street is tinged of a vermilion or lake so
extraordinary, that I can compare their costume to nothing but the warmest
beam of a southern sunset.

He saw the Sultan Mahmoud II several times, though he was not presented
(Contarini Fleming has an audience with him). Mahmoud's westernising,
modernising rule impressed Disraeli, who saw little to convince him that
Turkey was the sick man of Europe; on the contrary, he was struck by the
youthful Turks in their European uniforms, 'lounging with all the
listlessness of royal illegitimates. It is on the rising generation that the Sultan
depends, and if one may form an opinion, not in vain.' Sir Robert Gordon,
the ambassador, a younger brother of Lord Aberdeen, befriended Disraeli
and Clay, introducing them among the Franks, as Disraeli called the
Europeans, and entertaining them to 'a rollicking week at the Palace, with
romping of the most horrible description, and things called "games of
forfeits"'. When the weather grew rough, they abandoned the yacht and took
lodgings at Pera, a Frankish settlement.[39]

Writing to Bulwer six days after his twenty-sixth birthday, Disraeli
confessed that his Turkish prejudices were confirmed. 'The life of this
people greatly accords with my taste, which is naturally somewhat indolent
and melancholy, and I do not think would disgust you. To repose on
voluptuous ottomans, and smoke superb pipes, daily to indulge in the
luxuries of a bath which requires half a dozen attendants for its perfection, to
court the air in a carved caique by shores which are a continual scene and to
find no exercise greater than a canter on a barb, is I think a far more sensible
life than all the bustle of clubs, and all the boring of saloons.'[40]

It was a hint, the closest Disraeli came to admitting to the forays he and
Clay were making into the famous brothels of Constantinople. Sarah had few
illusions about Disraeli's new friend. It is confidently reported, she told Ben,
that Clay 'has married a fair dame of tarnished reputation in every town he
has visited'.[41] Her marriage was much on her mind. At Bradenham the
Merediths gathered for Christmas; William's father suffered a stroke and his
rich uncle was seriously ill. In Constantinople, William, the only one of the
trio who was returning to marry, tired of Clay and Disraeli, and at the end of
December left Constantinople to explore the Bithynian mountains which,
wrote Disraeli, 'are remarkable for being more devoid of interest than any
hills in existence'. Sarah understood. 'All the united families, except me', she

wrote, 'are in consternation at the separation which has taken place between you and William.'[42]

Disraeli assured his family he planned to sail from Constantinople to Egypt, returning in time for Bradenham races in the spring. In *Contarini Fleming*, however, he wrote that though his health improved in Constantinople, his desire for wandering increased. 'I began to think that I should now never be able to settle in life. The desire of fame did not revive. I felt no intellectual energy; I required nothing more than to be amused.'[43] Jerusalem, his original destination, still beckoned. By mid-January he and Clay were keen to leave Constantinople. Sir Robert Gordon did everything to keep them, offering them rooms at the palace, but they escaped, leaving Gordon in ill humour and with a flashing breeze sailed down the Dardanelles, eager to reach Smyrna, where Meredith was.

Wintry gales and violent rains set in, pinning them there for about ten days, but Disraeli and Meredith had so much to say to one another that they got over the affair better than expected. He thought Meredith's exploration of Asia Minor quite mad – it was a country 'equally unsatisfactory to the topographer, the antiquarian, and the man of taste'. Meredith had got hold of some Egyptian books, and was astonished to learn that there were more remains in Egypt than in all the rest of the globe put together, but he was still intent on going his own way; intent on 'the unseen relics of some cock and bull city' in Asia Minor. Disraeli tried in vain to dissuade him and again they parted.

Clay and Disraeli found themselves in an archipelago, the Sporades, and a contrary wind kept them off Rhodes. But they spent a day on Cyprus, which, wrote Disraeli, was 'more delightful to me as the residence of Fortunatus [a Turkish magician], than as the rosy realm of Venus, or the romantic Kingdom of the Crusaders'. Nearly fifty years later Disraeli was to acquire Cyprus for the British Empire. A pilot took them from Cyprus to Jaffa, and one morning, under a clear blue sky and intense sun, they saw the entire coast of Syria, high and mountainous, with snow on the loftiest ranges. They passed Beirut, the ancient Tyre, Acre, and eventually cast anchor in the roads of Jaffa. A descendant of an old Venetian family Disraeli had read about gave them rice, spices, pistachio nuts, perfumed *roti*, and dazzling confectionery.[44]

From Jaffa to Jerusalem was a gruelling two days' journey on horseback across the boulder-strewn Syrian desert. Most travellers found it unpleasant and dangerous, but Disraeli delighted in the poetry of the desert and discovered a bond with the Bedouin Arabs, proud and warlike horsemen, who combined primitive simplicity with civilisation. 'Truly may I say', he wrote in *Contarini Fleming*, 'that on the plains of Syria I parted for ever with my ambition. The calm enjoyment of existence appeared to me, as it now does, the highest attainable felicity.'[45]

In a letter to Sarah, he described the first sight of Jerusalem from the Mount of Olives:

Jerusalem is entirely surrounded by an old feudal wall with towers and gates of the times of the crusaders and in perfect preservation; as the town is built upon a hill, you can from the opposite height discern the roof of almost every house. In the front is the magnificent mosque built upon the site of the Temple, with its beautiful garden and fantastic gates – a variety of domes and towers arise in all directions, the houses are of a bright stone. I was thunderstruck. I saw before me apparently a gorgeous city. Nothing can be conceived more wild and terrible and barren than the surrounding scenery ... dark, stony, and severe, but the ground is thrown about in such picturesque undulations, that the mind is full of the sublime, not the beautiful, and rich and waving woods, and sparkling cultivation would be misplaced. The city on the other side is in the plain, the ravine not being all round. It is, as it were, in a bowl of mountains ... except Athens, I never saw anything more essentially striking – no city, except that, whose site was so pre-eminently impressive.[46]

His description is perfunctory, his language conventional (magnificent, beautiful, fantastic, gorgeous ...). 'I have dotted down materials for descriptions,' he told Sarah, 'I leave it to your lively imagination to fill up the rest.' He was wrong, too, in attributing the city walls to the Crusaders; they were built much later in the sixteenth century by the Turks.

He and Clay spent a week in Jerusalem. In his letter home he gave a brief and unsatisfactory account: 'Weather delicious – mild summer heat – made an immense sensation – received visits from the Vicar General of the Pope, the Spanish Prior etc. Never more delighted in my life.' During the second half of his sixteen months spent travelling Disraeli's letters home slowed to a trickle. Of the seventeen letters to Bradenham, only three were written after Constantinople. That he kept a journal is suggested by his novels, *Contarini Fleming* and *Alroy*, which give more detailed accounts of Jerusalem, of the Church of the Holy Sepulchre and of the Mosque of Omar which, Disraeli relates in a footnote to *Alroy*, he endeavoured to enter at hazard to his life. 'I was detected, and surrounded by a crowd of turbanned fanatics, and escaped with difficulty,' but not before he had 'caught a glimpse of splendid courts, and light airy gates of Saracenic triumph, flights of noble steps, long arcades, and interior gardens, where silver fountains spouted their tall streams amid the taller cypresses.'[47]

Jerusalem in 1831 was ruled from Constantinople, a remote, crumbling outpost of the Ottoman empire, dirty and dilapidated. In 1840 it had a population of 13,000 – 4500 Muslims, 3500 Christians and 5000 Jews. The Jews lived in the poorest quarter, but there is no record that Disraeli went there; in *Contarini Fleming* he idealised the city, describing it as hilly and clean.

Partly perhaps because his letters home reveal little about Jerusalem, biographers have been slow to realise the significance of Disraeli's visit. Not until 1982, sixteen years after the appearance of his biography, did Robert Blake attempt a reassessment. 'There can be no doubt', he wrote, 'that of all his many experiences on his tour the one that left the greatest and most lasting impression upon him was the visit to Jerusalem.'[48] Like Venice and Andalusia, Jerusalem left traces and sparked associations which his letters home do not convey. In *The Young Duke* he had described himself as 'the most prostrate of a fallen race'. Jerusalem seems to have changed that view. The preface to the *Revolutionary Epick* (1834) described the novel *Alroy* as 'the celebration of a gorgeous incident in that sacred and romantic people from whom I derive my blood and name'. The city of Jerusalem, with its Jewish and Christian holy places thronged with thousands of pilgrims, was the physical embodiment of the eccentric view he later developed of Christianity as the completion of Judaism. And he discovered a romantic race, not in the poor Jewish quarter of Jerusalem, but among the Bedouin Arabs – 'the Arabs', he wrote in *Tancred*, 'are only Jews upon horseback.'[49] Yet if Jerusalem gave him a sense of identity, its effects were slow to emerge. Not until fifteen years later did Disraeli develop his full-blown theory of the Jewish race and concoct a Venetian-Spanish Sephardic ancestry for himself.

He complained in March 1831 of a wretched journey from Jaffa to Alexandria. At Alexandria, however, things improved because the great Egyptian merchant Mr Briggs, agent of Mehemet Ali and an old connection of Disraeli's from the time of the *Representative*, had written from England instructing his partner to pay Disraeli great attention as the son of the celebrated author.

He was very surprised when Meredith arrived after a very hard passage on a Turkish ship. Meredith sent him a note, asking him to come alongside as he was threatened with a month's quarantine. He would go mad, Disraeli thought, and told Sarah he was going to the Governor General, who was a good fellow, to see what could be done. 'God bless you all. I am afraid you will never get this, as I am out of the lands of regular posts, ambassadors, and public offices.'[50]

From Alexandria he crossed the desert to Rosetta, a twelve-hour journey, throughout which he was perpetually deceived by a mirage, and thought he would ride into the sea. At Rosetta he first saw the mighty Nile, its banks covered with palm groves, and from there the consul's grand cabined boat took them to Cairo, through the famous delta, the soil rich and flat, reminding him of the plains of Pays Bas. Villages of mud studded the river, clustered in palm trees. The moonlit Nile was indescribably charming, the palms magical and Cairo swarmed with rich costumes, its houses of unbaked brick looking very dilapidated. For about three weeks he and Clay continued in the luxurious boat down the Nile, to Thebes. There Egypt became a valley formed by a river running through a desert; beyond the rich soil you could see deserts on each side for several miles. He wrote that, whereas the Libyan desert on the Africa side was interminable burning sands, the Arabian and Syrian deserts were what the English called downs.

One night they landed on the African side, where the desert stretched to the very banks of the Nile, and saw pilgrims who had been to Mecca, in picturesque groups, some boiling coffee, others squatting with their pipes and some performing their devotions. As Disraeli walked about a mile from the shore the air became dark and the heat was stifling. He rushed back to the boat as a terrifying column of sand, a simoom, bore down: 'The wind was the most awful sound I ever heard. Five columns of sand taller than the monument emptied themselves on our party. Every sail was rent to pieces, men buried in the earth.' Three sailing boats capsized, the crew swimming to shore. 'The wind, the screaming, the shouting, the driving of the sand were enough to make you mad.' They shut all the windows of the cabin and jumped into bed, but the sand still came in as hot as fire.

Denders and Thebes and the remains in upper Egypt made Italy and Greece mere toys. 'Conceive a feverish and tumultuous dream full of triumphal gates, processions of paintings, interminable walls of heroic sculpture, granite colossi of Gods and Kings, prodigious obelisks, avenues of Sphynxes and a hall of a thousand columns, thirty feet in girth and of a proportionate height. My mind and eyes ache with a grandeur so little in unison with our own littleness – there the landscape too was quite characteristic, mountains of burning sand, vegetation unnaturally vivid, groves of cocoa trees, groups of crocodile and an ebony population in a state of nudity armed with spears of reeds.'[51]

After a tedious return voyage down the Nile, Disraeli was glad to settle in Cairo at the end of May. From the *Galignani's Messengers* he saw on his return he read of the Reform Bill, which had passed its second reading by a majority of one on 23 March. Isaac grumbled about the revolution sweeping across Europe, and worried that no one would read the new volume of his history of Charles I – 'when the storm is up who listens to the Singing Bird?' (the book earned him an honorary degree from Oxford University in 1832). But Disraeli hailed the Bill as 'wonderful news'. Anticipating the Whig government's defeat and an election, he was keen to return home at once – he told his family he planned to sail for Malta and home in three or four weeks. *The Young Duke* was published at last in April, and Disraeli announced that he cared not a jot about it. 'I meant the hero to be a model for our youth, but after two years confinement in these revolutionary times I fear he will prove old fashioned.'[52]

In Cairo Clay was ill with intermittent fever, probably malaria, and Tita was ill too, with dysentery. 'I who am an invalid am firm on my legs ... I being somewhat indolent and feeble, live *à la Turque* while Clay and Giovanni [Tita] are always in action and have done nothing but shoot and swim from morning to night.' Disraeli's pipe was cooled in a wet silk bag, his coffee boiled with spices and he finished his last chibouque with a sherbet of pomegranate.

Wandering in the gardens of the palace of Mehemet Ali, Disraeli 'suddenly came across him one afternoon surrounded by his Court, a very brilliant circle, in most gorgeous dresses, particularly the black eunuchs in scarlet and gold, and who ride white horses'. He was taken by his arm and led to the circle. Quarter of an hour later, before his highness finished playing chess with his fool, Disraeli made his bow and departed. Had he stayed, Mehemet Ali would have spoken to him as he was exceedingly fond of the English, but as Disraeli had no interpreter and nor did the pacha, he thought it best to leave. His presentation was delayed by Clay's illness; it was more a bore than anything else, as the pacha received you alone and cross-examined you to death. He did eventually gain an audience with Mehemet Ali, which he described in *Vindication of the English Constitution* (1835). According to this account, Mehemet Ali cross-questioned him about the English parliament, which he saw as the key to England's greatness and which he was naively eager to copy in Egypt. 'See here!' said the notoriously despotic Mehemet Ali, producing a list, 'here are my Parliaments; but I have made up my mind, to prevent inconvenience, to elect them myself.'[53] Disraeli was no admirer of Mehemet Ali, who was to challenge the sultan in 1833 by invading Syria, and he later applauded Palmerston's handling of the Eastern Crisis (1839–40), when Mehemet Ali was expelled from Syria and the authority of the sultan upheld.

Meredith was away searching for ruins (he was writing a book about Egyptian architecture) and in Cairo Disraeli discovered a new friend, Paul Emile Botta. The son of an Italian historian, Botta was a physician and an archaeologist. In 1842 he became French consul at Mosul and excavated Khorsabad; by an odd twist he was beaten in the race to discover Nineveh by

Henry Layard, nephew of Benjamin and Sara Austen, whose interest in the east had been partly fired by Disraeli.[54] Botta and Disraeli talked late into the night, smoking their pipes. In *Contarini Fleming* Botta is Marigny, a sceptic and absolute materialist, and a few years later Disraeli described Botta as 'the most philosophic mind that I ever came in contact with ... My mind made a jump in these high discourses.' Botta was fashionably bored – tired of himself, he told Disraeli, and 'disgusted with the world where nothing is certain but misery and longing after what cannot be obtained'.[55] He spent his nights smoking opium (probably he and Disraeli smoked it together); a letter he wrote a year later from Senaar gives a taste of their Cairo conversations:

[the women here] have an artificial quality which, pour un homme blasé, gives them all the charms of novelty. When young they shut them (don't blush I shall be as chaste as possible) by a surgical operation ... which insures their virginity against the most rash attempts. They remain so until the day or rather night of their wedding which to be completed requires the aid of the knife with which a way is made exactly as we cut a piece of melon to know if the inside is good. The happy husband ascends then the breach and gets in through blood and shrieks.[56]

Disraeli wrote that he longed to be fleshing quills with Isaac, 'now that I have got the use of my brain for the first time in my life'. In *Contarini Fleming* he explained that it was while riding in the Cairo desert that he felt once again the desire for composition. 'I found myself perpetually indulging in audible soliloquy ... I felt no inclination to return to Europe.'[57] His desire to write had reawakened at precisely the moment the Reform Bill had revived his political ambitions, and the conflict between literature and politics formed the theme of the novel he was composing, in his head if not yet on paper, *Contarini Fleming*, which opens with a description of the Egyptian simoom.

He lingered in Cairo, smoking with Botta and waiting for Meredith. At Bradenham, Sarah was longing desperately for their return. She ached for Ben even more than William, breaking out of her habitual dry detachment. 'Where you are, what you are doing, when you will be here, are our unending speculations, the dogs never bark at an unusual hour but our hearts palpitate.' When Ralph came in late and unexpected one evening, he made Isaac so nervous that he could not finish his rubber. 'The only wonder is how we have existed so long without you.'[58] No news came during that hot sultry summer ('which we Anti-Reformers look upon as a punishment for the sins of the Majority') and, as cholera swept England, Sarah imagined plague and pestilence in Egypt. William's sick father was now blind and his rich uncle dead, but no one knew the contents of the will. 'We want you terribly – we are *all* too nervous to enjoy ourselves which makes the time seem longer.'[59]

After two months' silence, Disraeli wrote with trembling pen to Isaac on 20 July. 'Read this alone,' he wrote. 'Our William is lost to us.' On the eve of their departure from Cairo, Meredith had felt unwell and called in the best European physician, who said there was an inflammation in the bowels, bled him in the arms and applied leeches. The pain went away and slight fever remained. Clay went to Alexandria to see about a ship while Disraeli looked after 'our friend'. On the third day smallpox erupted, but there were no dangerous symptoms; the doctor ordered some squills and went away confident. A week later, one of Meredith's attendants ran in to the adjoining room, where Disraeli was talking to Botta. The servant said Meredith had fainted. The body was warm and blood flowed when Botta opened a vein; everyone but Disraeli saw the terrible truth. Only that morning the doctor had congratulated William on his recovery, and Disraeli was utterly unprepared for the death. In *Contarini Fleming* he described his shock and disbelief as he staggered about the room wringing his hands. 'I seized the corpse in my arms and fiercely embraced it. I thought I could re-animate it.'

Botta sat up all night with him as he 'could not sleep and dared not be alone'. Through that night of horror, he told Isaac he thought only of Sarah. 'Our innocent lamb, our angel is stricken. The joy of our eyes and hearts. Save her! Save her! I will come home directly.' He would willingly give his own life for William's.[60] His letters glossed over the horrifying medical details of William's illness, recorded in the doctor's report.[61]

Disraeli enclosed a letter for Sarah in his letter to Isaac. William was, in this world, lost for ever. But Sarah was still needed – 'if you are lost to me,' he wrote, 'where, where am I to fly for refuge! I have no wife, I have no betrothed, nor since I have been better acquainted with my own mind and temper, and situation, have I sought them. Live then my heart's treasure for one who has loved you with a surpassing love, and who would cheerfully have yielded his own existence to have saved you the bitterness of reading this. Yes! my beloved! be my genius, my solace, my companion, my joy! We will never part, and if I cannot be to you all of our lost friend, at least we will feel, that Life can never be a blank while illuminated by the pure and perfect love of a Sister and a Brother!'[62]

His appeal to Sarah to dedicate herself to him seems astoundingly egotistical, but it was realistic. Nearing thirty, Sarah's chances of finding a husband after an engagement of ten years were slim. She was devastated by William's death, but her feelings for her brother were more intense, more possessive and more passionate than those for William had been. Ben's proposal was finely judged.

FIVE

'I am for myself'

1831–2

'YOU CANNOT conceive the state I am in,' Disraeli wrote to Isaac from HMS *Hermes* on the voyage home; 'literally not a shirt to my back – and nothing but Turkish Slippers and a single coat.... If the Reform Bill pass, I intend to offer myself for Wycomb.'

In the meantime, he was hard at work on the novel he had begun in Egypt. You will be astounded, he told Isaac, at the quantity I have planned and written – 'constant intellectual exertion is now my only resource'. The fatal event (Disraeli still could not bring himself to mention William's name) had 'entirely changed my character, or rather forced me to recur to my original one'. Marriage was no longer his ambition: 'I wish no more to increase the circle of domestic sympathies, since they lead to such misery'; in any case, the east had taught him that there were alternatives.[1]

He reached Falmouth on 23 October 1831 to find England rain sodden and on the brink of revolution. The House of Lords had thrown out the Reform Bill on 8 October, Parliament had been prorogued on 20 October, and a week later in Bristol the reform mob sacked the Mansion House and the Bishop's Palace. Delayed in Exeter (or so he said) by a feverish cold and inflammation on the chest, Disraeli apparently took a week to reach London, travelling by stage through pouring rain; still shivering, he hastened on to Bradenham, dreading his first meeting with his sister since William's death.

His homecoming heartened Sarah at first, but she was very unwell the next day. He busied himself writing to William's sister, sending on the dead man's belongings, and choosing a classical volume for himself from William's library. 'Unfortunately,' he wrote, 'we possess none of his hair.' Sarah could barely keep her self-control when William's name was mentioned: the following February the Merediths sent her a diamond ring as a memorial, and she gave way to 'the wildest and most ungovernable grief'.[2]

'Live then, my heart's treasure, for one who has ever loved you with a

surpassing love,' Disraeli had written to Sarah the day after Meredith died –
'We will never part.' Love between brother and sister made emotional and
practical sense in a world of late-marrying men, spinster sisters and virgin
brides: Romanticism embraced it and added an edge of sexual daring – incest
was the fashionable Romantic vice. Disraeli's Romanticism taught him to
hallow 'the pure and perfect love of a Sister and a Brother', and in some ways
he really did make Sarah his wife, as he had promised. Affection, intellectual
affinity, understanding, an audience, just *being* there: the kind of love he
craved from Maria and which she never gave him, Sarah lavished upon him.
Disraeli responded by writing to her the best letters he ever wrote, allowing
her to live his London life vicariously. In *Alroy*, dedicated to her, he
celebrated the relationship between Alroy (Disraeli) and his sister Miriam: 'I
know not love,' says Alroy, 'save that pure affection which doth subsist
between me and … my sister.' Disraeli liked to picture himself like Alroy,
returning fresh from his triumphs on the field of battle (in Disraeli's case,
London) to stroll in the garden at Bradenham with Sarah, one arm 'wound
round her delicate waist, and with the other he clasped her soft and graceful
hand'.[3]

After ten days at Bradenham, Disraeli was back in London, plunged into
the affair of Henry Stanley. Henry Stanley was a son of Lord Derby and the
younger brother of Edward Stanley, the rising young Whig Irish Chief
Secretary; Disraeli met Henry on the return voyage aboard HMS *Hermes*,
and they travelled up to London together. Stanley was deeply in debt and,
Disraeli told Sarah, 'lost his good genius when I left London, and instead of
having the courage to go to his father, is playing hide and seek and can
nowhere be heard of'. His father opened a letter of Disraeli's addressed to
Knowsley, his Lancashire home – fortunately it contained good advice – and
Lord Derby 'looks entirely to me for succour, and I am surrounded by
Stanleys, all day long, full of despair, making researches and following clues'.
With Henry Stanley's uncle, Colonel Long, Disraeli searched the London
underworld – 'you cannot imagine what curious characters I am obliged to
see.'[4] On 14 November, Stanley was still missing, but Disraeli had traced him
to 'the new exclusive Hell in St James St and after a mixture of diplomacy and
courage, which I trust were worthy of Mr Pelham, or any other hero of three
volumes post 8vo, I made the leg, who keeps it, make me strange and sad
disclosures'. Tipped off by the leg, Effie Bond, the owner of the St James's
gambling hell, Disraeli advised the Stanleys to send the police after the
missing Henry, but his brothers were reluctant to call in the Bow Street
Runners. Next day, Disraeli heard that Henry had been seen in Manchester
the previous week, supposedly on his way home to Knowsley, where he
turned up soon afterwards.[5]

After Disraeli died, his solicitor and executor Sir Philip Rose set aside a bundle of letters which referred to the Henry Stanley affair. According to Rose's note, Disraeli was accused by Henry Stanley's older brother Edward of playing a double game: Edward Stanley alleged that 'while Disraeli was working day and night to discover his missing relative, he was, all the time, party to a conspiracy to entangle him, and in league with the Bonds'. Though Henry's father was grateful to Disraeli and believed he had acted in good faith, Edward was unconvinced.[6]

Rose heard the story from Disraeli's brother Ralph, who was in London at the time of the search. The evidence has been destroyed, but Edward Stanley probably had reason to be suspicious. Effie Bond was a low-life acquaintance of Disraeli's, to whom he owed money. Very likely, Disraeli introduced Henry Stanley to Effie Bond when he arrived back in London, and probably knew all along that Stanley had gone to ground at Bond's. Though anxious to please Stanley's grand relations, he also wanted to protect Bond, and waited until Henry was safely away before telling the Stanleys about Bond. It was hardly a conspiracy, but Disraeli was less than honest with Henry Stanley's relations.

Disraeli needed Bond's goodwill (he wrote a lot of letters to Bond which have disappeared) and he may have felt a sneaking sympathy for him: in *Henrietta Temple* he painted a flattering portrait of the owner of a St James's Street hell, Mr Bond Sharpe, based partly on Crockford, the king of London gambling, but owing his name at least to Effie Bond. For Henry Stanley, Disraeli had scant respect. 'Henry Stanley is in town,' he told Sarah the following April, 'and a great bore. He asked me to go with him to Newmarket to the Craven, but I refused.'

The Henry Stanley affair probably damaged Disraeli. It added the name of Edward Stanley to his enemies. Like his offhand treatment of Sir Robert Gordon in Constantinople, his duplicity over Stanley shows his naivety and ineptitude as a social climber – his failure to realise the importance of family ties (even where black sheep were concerned) to the British aristocracy.

In London in November Disraeli also saw his doctor, Bolton, who prescribed a six weeks' course of mercury, standard treatment for venereal disease. That this was Disraeli's complaint is confirmed by a letter from James Clay, who wrote a birthday letter from Venice on 21 December 1831 (he was twenty-seven): 'Between us we have contrived to stumble on all the thorns with which (as Mr Dickens, the Winchester Porter, was wont poetically to observe) Venus guards her roses; for while you were cursing the greater evils I contrived to secure the minor viz a gleet from over exertion and crabs. The former I richly earned, and it wore itself out, the latter was quickly cured and I am in high cue for a real debauch in Venice.' Clay went on to relate how he had got drunk *solus cum solo* the night before: 'I drank and drank again and read and re-read my letters until it became impossible to distinguish one correspondent from another. On reading what I thought was your handwriting I found an exhortation to marry and settle, and when I took up, as I believed, a letter from my mother I read that "Mercury had succeeded to Venus" – a most extraordinary letter from an elderly gentlewoman.'[7]

Disraeli retired to Bradenham to recuperate. Six weeks or so later he reported to Benjamin Austen that, though pulled down by mercury, his head was not troubling him, and he was working like a tiger on his immortal work: *Contarini Fleming* or the Psychological Romance, which he had brought back half-finished from his travels.

'I have observed that, after writing a book, my mind always makes a great spring,' Disraeli wrote, and *Contarini Fleming* is indeed a very different sort of book from *The Young Duke*. It was just as well; *The Young Duke* had been roundly condemned by the critics. The book is read, and hated, wrote Albany Fonblanque in the *Examiner*; it is trash, the kind of book men read when they have fevers or broken legs. Radical critics were predictably hostile; most virulent was the Benthamite *Westminster Review*, which attacked the book's excessive and revolting toadyism towards the aristocracy. This is no butterfly to break on a wheel, wrote the critic (whom Disraeli believed to be Dr Bowring): it is a bug, an unwholesome production. 'I hear I am praised in it,' wrote Macaulay to his sister. 'On this the rascal may rely, that, when I take him and his tribe of slanderers in hand, as I shall do one of these days, I will not bate him one lash for all his panegyric.'[8] Disraeli was deaf to the critics and shrugged off the abuse – *The Young Duke*, he wrote, was 'a singing bird in a storm, and the thunder crushed his chirp'; but this kind of criticism was not calculated to advance his own career as a reformer.[9]

In *Contarini Fleming*, Disraeli abandoned the fashionable novel for *Bildungsroman*: he called it the psychological romance, a description of the development of the poetic character. H. H. Milman, the publisher's reader, described it as 'very wild, very extravagant, very German, very powerful, very poetical. It will I think be much read ... It is much more in the Macaulay than in the Croker line, and the former is evidently in the ascendant.'[10] *Contarini Fleming* was not only a work of serious literary ambition; it had a political purpose – to distance Disraeli from the frivolous Toryism of *The Young Duke* and identify him with the reformers; with Macaulay, the leading orator for reform, as against the Tory Croker, who meditated retirement from parliament if the Reform Bill passed.

Disraeli claimed that he composed his novels in his head before he began to write. For months he mused over his creation without writing a word. 'I do not think that meditation can be too long, or execution too rapid.... It is not merely characters and the general conduct of the story that I thus prepare, but the connection of every incident, often whole conversations, sometimes even slight phrases.'[11] *Contarini Fleming* was composed in Cairo, and on the long voyage home Disraeli began to write, scribbling through the dull weeks of quarantine in Malta. How much he had written before his return can only be conjectured – possibly the first two parts of the novel, roughly 60,000 words, taking the story up to 1826; after this point the novel incorporates material from his letters home.

The Psychological Romance is the fictional autobiography of Contarini Fleming, the son of a northern baron and a noble Venetian who dies when he is born; it is the thinly masked story of Disraeli's life. Rejected by his mother (who is Maria), Contarini endures a miserable childhood; he is trained for politics by his father, a minister at a northern court, but disgraces himself by writing a scandalous novel (a *Vivian Grey*) entitled Manstein; he escapes to Italy, and in Venice meets and falls in love with Alcesté, his cousin, the last of the Contarini family, whom he marries. After her death in childbirth, Contarini travels to Athens, Jerusalem and Constantinople, and the novel degenerates into travelogue, incorporating chunks from Disraeli's letters. Contarini is struggling to find his vocation, torn between politics and literature, and the conflict within him is encapsulated in his name: in the novel the north stands for politics and power, and the south for literature and romance. News of the death of his father returns him to a sense of his political vocation, and the novel ends with him settled in Italy and contemplating political reform.

As literature, *Contarini Fleming* is flawed by Disraeli's inability to distance himself – it is too subjective, too autobiographical; but this gives the book biographical value.[12] Not only is it the indispensable text on Disraeli's childhood, documenting the difficult relationship with Maria; it reveals much about his relationship with Isaac. The most striking character in the book is Baron Fleming, Contarini's father. One source for the baron is Disraeli himself: the baron is an idealised portrait of Disraeli's political ambition, while Contarini embodies his literary ambition. The baron *looks* like Disraeli, for example. At thirty-four, he has risen entirely through his own talents to be secretary of state for Foreign Affairs in a country where he has no interests and no connexions.

> The minister of a free people, he was the personal as well as the political pupil of Metternich. Yet he respected the institutions of his country, because

they existed, and because experience proved that under their influence the natives had become more powerful machines.

His practice of politics was compressed in two words, subtlety and force. The minister of an emperor, he would have maintained his system by armies; in the cabinet of a small kingdom, he compensated for his deficiency by intrigue.

His perfection of human nature was a practical man. He looked upon a theorist either with alarm or with contempt. Proud in his own energies, and conscious that he owed everything to his own dexterity, he believed all to depend upon the influence of individual character. He required men not to think but to act, not to examine but to obey; and, animating their brute force with his own intelligence, he found the success, which he believed could never be attained by the rational conduct of an enlightened people.[13]

Distrustful of theory and rational argument, skilled in intrigue and manipulation, an admirer of Metternich: this is a profile of a High Tory. Disraeli's purpose in *Contarini*, however, is to reinvent himself as a reformer and repudiate his earlier Toryism. The young Contarini embarks on a precocious political career under the tutelage of his father, but his initial frenzy of ambition gives way to disgust at his own worldliness and narrow 'selfism'.

The father also incorporates elements of Isaac, and Isaac recommended the bookish Crabb Robinson, a crony at the Athenaeum Club, to read *Contarini Fleming* as a portrait of himself. Though a clever man, Isaac was a poor talker, and his sagging lower jaw gave an impression of near-idiocy. 'There is a man', said Samuel Rogers, 'with only half an intellect; and yet he makes books that can't help living.'[14] It was a failing that made Isaac intensely aware of the importance of cultivating an intelligent manner, and the advice Baron Fleming gives the young Contarini surely echoes Isaac's words to his son:

Read French authors. Read Rochefoucault. The French writers are the finest in the world, for they clear our heads of all ridiculous ideas. Study precision.

Do not talk too much at present; do not *try* to talk. But whenever you speak, speak with self-possession. Speak in a subdued tone, and always look at the person whom you are addressing.... Never argue. In society nothing must be discussed; give only results. If any person differ from you, bow and turn the conversation. In society never think; always be on the watch or you will miss many opportunities and say many disagreeable things.

Talk to women, talk to women as much as you can. This is the best school.[15]

Baron Fleming discourages Contarini's literary ambitions. 'Mix in society,' he tells him, 'and I will answer that you will lose your poetic feeling; for in you ... it is not a creative faculty originating in a peculiar organisation, but simply the consequence of a nervous susceptibility that is common to all.' If this was Isaac's advice to his son, it was frank and perceptive. But perhaps the father's most memorable utterance is, 'My son, you will be Prime Minister of ...; perhaps something greater.'[16]

The death of Meredith casts long shadows over the novel. Disraeli's description of the sudden death of Alcesté, Contarini's wife, is very reminiscent and produces the same shock, fear and disbelief. But Alcesté's death has a wider significance as well. It represents the death of a dream – the dream of marriage which not only Sarah but Disraeli entertained before his departure for the east in 1830. That Alcesté dies while giving birth to a stillborn son is surely significant. One of the psychological puzzles about Disraeli is his apparent lack of desire for children despite his pride of family and race; buried in *Contarini Fleming* is the hint that this was a deliberate decision. A voluntary exile from the bourgeois family, Disraeli recognised that conventional marriage was inconsistent with his ambitions for fame.

Alcesté's death affects Contarini in the way Meredith's did Disraeli: it forces him to return to his original character. After travelling to Constantinople and Jerusalem, he recognises that action or politics, rather than literature, is his vocation. As Winter, the wisdom figure in the novel, says: 'Action is now your part. Meditation is culture. It is well to think until a man has discovered his genius, and developed his faculties, but then let him put his intelligence in motion. Act, act, act ...' The Reform crisis gives Contarini his opportunity. 'Perchance ... the political regeneration of the country to which I am devoted may not be distant, and in that great work I am resolved to participate.' The death of Alcesté has purged Contarini of his narrow selfism, of his High Tory worldliness, and the novel ends on a note of radical exhortation: 'If I am to be remembered, let me be remembered as one who, in a sad night of gloomy ignorance and savage bigotry was prescient of the flaming morning-break of bright philosophy, as one who deeply sympathised with his fellow-men, and felt a proud and profound conviction of their perfectibility; as one who devoted himself to the amelioration of his kind, by the destruction of error and the propagation of truth.'[17]

The novel is a portrait, of both the artist and the prime minister as a young man. It heralds the triumph of politics over literature, of Radicalism over Toryism; it may have been Disraeli's bid for literary fame, but its message is unequivocally political.

Disraeli moved up to London from Bradenham in February 1832, bringing

with him the completed manuscript of *Contarini Fleming*. Turning his back
on middle-class Bloomsbury, he took furnished lodgings at No. 35 Duke
Street, St James's. It was a slightly seedy street in the heart of fashionable
civilisation as Disraeli then saw it – a civilisation whose twin poles were
Almack's in nearby King Street, where the miscellaneous world of fashion
assembled under the patronage of Lady Jersey, and Crockford's in St James's
Street, where 'Crocky' presided over the gambling 'slaves' who packed his
splendid salons. Despite the February fogs, Disraeli felt wonderfully well –
he was in real fine feather, he told Sarah, sustained by a healthy diet of roast
meat and brandy and water.

Determined to make a serious bid for literary fame, Disraeli offered his
novel not to Colburn, who had published *Vivian Grey* and *The Young Duke*,
but to John Murray, and a week later was pressing Murray for an answer. 'I
have an impending election in the county,' he wrote, underlining the novel's
political significance. 'It is a great object with me, that my work should be
published before that election.'[18] Murray was in no position to give an
answer. He sent the manuscript to Lockhart who, knowing it was Disraeli's,
found it full of interest but, venomous as ever, considered it flawed by
affectations and absurdities. Murray next sent it to the ecclesiastical historian
H. H. Milman without revealing the author's name and, though Disraeli
huffed and puffed, bombarding Murray with importunate letters written at 2
a. m., Milman, who was suffering from an eye disorder, did not reply until 5
March. His report was enthusiastic; he insisted only on a change of title
(Disraeli wanted to call in The Psychological Romance) – 'It is a rapid volume
of travels, a "Childe Harold" in prose; therefore do not let it be called "a
Romance" on any account.'[19]

Disraeli's impatience with Murray was due partly to his chronic need for
money. Creditors and tradesmen crowded in upon his return from abroad;
Messer still pressed for repayment of £1500. Disraeli's decision to leave
Colburn meant that he was unable to borrow against the security of his new
novel, and this threw him back on the resources of Benjamin Austen. Disraeli
had repaid the £500 lent by Austen to finance his travels with the money he
received on publication of *The Young Duke* but, rather than mortgage his new
work to Colburn, he was obliged to borrow more from Austen, running up
fresh debts of £315 by January 1832. Unfortunately, Murray's agreement to
publish did little to ease these problems. Murray refused both to pay a sum
for the copyright, or to give an allowance against profits (Disraeli asked for a
modest £200); instead he proposed to divide the profits on an edition, a much
more hazardous and less lucrative arrangement. Far from solving his
financial problems, *Contarini Fleming* forced Disraeli into dependence on
Benjamin Austen; his response was to manipulate Austen for all he was

worth. Austen, hinted Disraeli, was patron to a genius (*Contarini Fleming* was in no way inferior to Byron's *Childe Harold*) and sponsor to a future Tory member; his help came at a crucial moment in Disraeli's career; of course, repayment was possible, but the political situation meant in some obscure way that repayment *now* was out of the question – unless, that is, Austen chose to bring Disraeli's brilliant career down in ruins.[20]

His treatment of Sara Austen was even more cold-blooded. 'I have hitherto avoided dining with the Austens,' he told Sarah, 'but am at last ticketted for Saturday.' Sara Austen, prattling and over-protective, bored him ('these domestic engagements destroy me'), and he no longer needed or wanted her as a confidante. But if he was to borrow from Austen he had to humour Mrs Austen – to sit listening to her dull gossip in her dull Bloomsbury drawing-room: perhaps he also called on her one dark afternoon and unwillingly made love to her behind drawn curtains. Resentful and neglected, Sara Austen was quick to take offence; when Disraeli failed to appear at a dinner she had arranged in his honour, she sent her spies to ascertain that he was indeed at home at Duke Street and wrote to Bradenham complaining bitterly.[21]

Disraeli was ruthless, elbowing and pushing his way into the great world. Not that his social climbing was very successful. In the winter of 1831 Isaac, goaded by Sarah, had nobbled his acquaintance Lord Eliot, who agreed to propose Benjamin for election to the exclusive Travellers' Club.[22] Though Disraeli easily met the formal entry requirement of having travelled 500 miles out of London in a straight line, he did not know Lord Auckland, the Whig peer who ran the club; no one joined the Travellers' without Auckland's say so, and Disraeli was blackballed. He was unabashed. 'There is no disgrace in being blackballed,' he told Sarah, 'as these things happen every night and to the first people.' Ever sanguine, he canvassed men on the committee, and was sure he would be a Travellers' Club member by the election.[23] (He wasn't.)

'We must make a push at the Committee of the Athenaeum,' Disraeli wrote after he was blackballed by the Travellers'. The Athenaeum was Isaac's club, and Disraeli assumed his election would be a matter of course. At the end of March, before he heard from the Athenaeum, he was invited to join the new 'Conservative Club' – the 'Anti-Brooke's [*sic*] club', he called it, then in Charles Street, soon to become the Carlton. He thought it expedient to refuse, perhaps because membership would identify him too closely with the Tories: none but the thoroughgoing chose to belong to the Charles Street gang, as it was then known.[24] Two weeks later, Disraeli heard he had been blackballed at the Athenaeum. Perhaps he earned this snub by walking upstairs, in defiance of club rules, and talking to Isaac in the library, or perhaps, as Bulwer warned, the 'ninnies' worried that he would clap them into a book; but the D'Israeli family were convinced that Croker, who had virtually founded the Athenaeum, was behind it. Isaac was bitterly offended, but Disraeli pretended to be indifferent. 'I do not care about the Ath which must be left to chance but certainly I cannot belong to the Conservative *now*.'[25] Not until 1866 was he elected to the Athenaeum.

Crokerland – all-male, subfusc – was an alien world to Disraeli; anti-semitism was never far below the surface – Isaac, Disraeli noted, had been profiled in *Fraser's Magazine* as *Israel* D'Israeli 'which leads to an observation or two'. He was more at home in drawing-rooms than clubs, and his letters to Sarah sparkle with brilliant soirées and reunions, with lords and 'blues' and dandies. But in 1832 he was still on the outer fringes of London society; true, he knew a couple of lords – Lord Eliot, a Tory MP, and Lord Strangford, a literary ex-diplomat, ('there is no calling on Ben without finding him engaged with Lords,' gloated Isaac), but Disraeli's only real friend in the society world was Bulwer.

At Bulwer's lavish Hertford Street parties, his wife Rosina was 'a blaze of jewels, and looked like Juno, only instead of a peacock, she had a dog in her lap called Fairy, not bigger than a bird of Paradise and quite as brilliant'. At another 'brilliant reunion', Bulwer came up to Disraeli and said there was one blue who insisted upon an introduction. 'Oh! my dear fellow, I cannot – really – the power of repartee has deserted me.' Bulwer led him up to 'a very sumptuous personage, looking like a full rich blown rose' – the novelist Catherine Gore: 'I never rec'd. so cordial a reception in my life.' Letitia Landon, the poetess L.E.L., who may or may not have been having an affair with Bulwer, he avoided – she 'looked the very personification of Brompton – pink satin dress and white satin shoes, red cheeks snub nose, and her hair a la [*sic*] Sappho.'[26] L.E.L. was at another soirée a week later, but quite changed: 'she had thrown off her Greco Bromptonian costume and was perfectly *a la française* [*sic*] and really looked pretty.' At the end of the evening, Disraeli addressed a few words to her, 'of the value of which she seemed sensible'. And he was introduced to Mary Anne Wyndham Lewis, a friend of Rosina's and wife of the Tory member for Maidstone, 'a pretty little woman, a flirt and a rattle' he told Sarah; 'indeed gifted with a volubility I shd think unequalled, and of which I can convey no idea. She told me that she liked silent melancholy men. I answered that I had no doubt of it.'[27]

'For silent read stupid,' retorted Sarah, who had heard gossip about Mrs Wyndham Lewis's empty-headed admirers. A day or two later he wrote Mrs Wyndham Lewis a note:

I have read your tale which I admire exceedingly. It is very poetic and

Provencale, and worthy of a Troubadour. I have found out the writer, and will
tell you when we meet.

    I hope *la belle du monde* is quite well this morn!
      Your true knight
      Raymond de Toulouse.[28]

Mary Anne treasured 'The first note I ever received from dear Dizzy'. Others
at Bulwer's parties were less friendly. When Disraeli rose from a cane chair,
its marks visible on the seat of his green velvet trousers as he walked with his
coat-tails over each arm, Sam Rogers, Isaac's friend, asked, 'Who's that?'
'Oh! young Disraeli, the Jew,' said Rosina. 'Rather the wandering Jew, with
the brand of *Cane* on him,' said Rogers. Of all the 'zoological' collection of
monstrosities gathered at Mrs Bulwer's, wrote the poet Thomas Moore, the
most conspicuous was the young D'Israeli, 'in velvet trousers, and [quoting
Milton] his hair "dropping odours, dropping" – God knows what else
besides'.[29]

In his Duke Street rooms, Disraeli was hard at work. The previous
November, at dinner with Dr Bolton, Disraeli had met a mysterious baron,
Haber, a noble spy in the interest of Charles X, the Bourbon king of France,
deposed in the Revolution of July 1830. The son of a German Jewish banker
from Baden, Moritz von Haber spent a fortune financing legitimist causes,
the Carlists in Spain and the Bourbons in France; the liberal foreign policy of
Britain's Whig government was anathema to him, as was the proposal to
create an independent Belgian state in alliance with France, and he was in
London intriguing to prevent an Anglo-French entente.[30]

    Haber's talk of spies and secret societies captivated Disraeli. In February
Haber and his associate Baron de Haussez, minister of marine under Charles
X and now a legitimist exile, plied Disraeli with documents: the cabinet
papers of Charles X, the despatches of the Dutch ambassador, a secret
correspondence with the most eminent opposition member in France. Such
secrets! 'I am writing a book which will electrify all Europe,' he told Sarah. 'I
am perfectly uncontrolled, and, if I have time enough, I hope to produce
something which will not only ensure my election, but produce me a political
reputation, which is the foundation of everything, second to none.'[31]

    Isaac was sceptical. 'Beware, my dear, of secret agents,' he warned, 'beware
of forgeries and delusions.' Disraeli did not listen. 'I am writing a very John
Bull book,' he told Sarah, 'which will quite delight you and my mother. I am
still a Reformer, but I shall destroy the foreign policy of the Grey faction.'
That, in a nutshell, was the dilemma created by the Haberian book: how to
reconcile an attack on Whig foreign policy with support for the Reform Bill.

Disraeli tried to sidestep it by claiming to be independent: 'as for parties,' he wrote, '*I am for myself.*'[32]

The book, or pamphlet, was finished by the end of March. More than half was written by Disraeli, the rest by Haber. Capitalising on the opening created by *Contarini Fleming*, Disraeli persuaded Murray to publish. As a title he proposed *Gallomania* (*or Mania for What is French*); when Murray ('that blockhead') objected that this was too obscure, Disraeli reluctantly agreed to a modified version – *England and France; or a Cure for the Ministerial Gallomania.*

The meaning of the term Gallomania was made abundantly clear by the book's dedication to the prime minister, Lord Grey. 'My Lord,' Disraeli impudently declared, 'it has ever been considered an indubitable characteristic of insanity in men to mistake their friends for their enemies.' A man who persistently injured our ancient ally the Netherlands and assisted our hereditary foe the French, as Grey did, must be insane. 'To your Lordship, therefore, as the most eminent Gallomaniac of the day, I dedicate this volume.'

Gallomania is a legitimist text, an attack on the liberal view, promoted by men like Macaulay, that France's July Revolution of 1830 represented the triumph of civil and religious liberty – France's Revolution of 1688, with Louis Philippe as the French equivalent of William of Orange. Louis Philippe, wrote Disraeli, was an unprincipled adventurer who depended on military success for his survival. 'In France,' he wrote, 'there is no real middle party between the old Bourbons – the party of peace and order – and the *Mouvement* – the party of revolution and war; whether that party delight in the name of Liberal, Napoleonist or Republican.' Louis Philippe, who was of neither party and had both against him, was unlikely to survive. The Bourbons, however, 'backed by the royalists, and by the indirect support of all the European governments, might balance and baffle the *Mouvement*; and it is for this reason', claimed Disraeli, 'that I should wish to see those Bourbons again upon the throne.'[33]

Liberty, said he, was alien to the French, they could not comprehend it; they were subversives, who sent their agents to spread disaffection over Europe and, 'the great majority of the continental countries being absolute, the French immediately became *liberal*' – hence the superficial prattle about liberty in France. After the July Revolution Louis Philippe's first object was to gain recognition from the European powers by any means, and his instrument to achieve this was 'Propagandism': emissaries were sent all over Europe, to England, to Ireland and even to Egypt (where Disraeli himself had spotted a French agent soliciting secret interviews with the pacha), to assist

French agents there in stirring the people to revolt – hence the revolutions of 1830 in Belgium, Poland, Germany and Italy.[34]

This was the kind of conspiracy theory beloved of High Tories, men whose instinct for control and manipulation rather than reasoned argument led them to perceive in foreign affairs a web of intrigue, of secret agents and secret societies. But though Disraeli echoed the paranoia of Metternich and the restoration generation of 1815, he disclaimed any connexion with the Tories. 'I am neither Whig nor Tory,' he declared. 'My politics are described by one word, and that word is ENGLAND.'[35]

The case against Whig foreign policy was that it was dictated not by a proper judgement of national interest but by a morbid appetite for popularity. In England, propagandism took the form of a mania for obtruding our political institutions upon other countries – hence the misguided attempts to introduce representative government in Ireland, in Bavaria and Württemberg, in Portugal and even in France, where Louis XVIII had sacrificed his dynasty to 'his ignorant admiration of the English constitution, and to his blind confidence in the glowing superficialities of M. Delolme'. Disasters like this were allowed to happen because English politicians were profoundly ignorant of foreign policy. Anyone, said Disraeli, could be a political economist: 'he reads a few articles in a Review, and immediately babbles about the currency, jests at our colonies, and sneers at the balance of trade.' Anyone could be a political philosopher too: 'let him read but a few more articles and the title pages of Jeremy Bentham – who ever read further? – and he is prepared to destroy every institution in the country.' Foreign policy was a different matter; it required deeper study, personal acquaintance with European states and statesmen, and above all, a philosophic mind above prejudice or passion – in fact it was such a difficult subject that it had lately been voted of subordinate importance. 'To my mind,' declared Disraeli, 'it is of primary, of paramount importance.'[36]

Gallomania, commented *The Times*, was 'coloured with absolutism from beginning to end'. When Disraeli later became a partisan of Louis Philippe's, he saw *Gallomania* as an embarrassing youthful folly; in 1842 Mary Anne wrote from Paris, where Disraeli was paying court to Louis Philippe, that 'M Buchon a literary friend of ours, tells us as a great secret that the Gallomania was written by Scott'.[37] But though Disraeli wrote *Gallomania* at Haber's dictation, it was not hack work; secret societies held an enduring fascination for him and as an enthusiast for the Ottoman empire it was consistent that he should dismiss revolutionary movements as conspiracies by French agents.

In spite of his Tory analysis of foreign affairs, Disraeli refused to mention the Reform Bill in *Gallomania*. The inconsistency of attacking the Whigs' foreign policy without demonstrating its connection with Reform was pointed out by J. W. Croker, the critic to whom Murray sent the proofs. But Disraeli was adamant: 'It is quite impossible that anything adverse to the general measure of Reform can issue from my pen.' He refused to meet Croker: 'More than once I have had an opportunity to form that acquaintance and more than once I have declined it,' but he wrote him a note, arguing that passing over Reform in silence would give the book a broader appeal and strengthen the case against the Whig government. 'It is important that this work should be a work not of *party* but of national interest, and ... a large class ... who think themselves bound to support the present administration from superficial sympathy with their domestic measures, have long viewed their foreign policy with distrust and alarm.'[38]

Disraeli was playing a double game, trying to hedge his bets. In *Contarini Fleming* he aligned himself with the Reformers; a month later, with *Gallomania*, he wrote a High Tory tract. In the spring of 1832, as the Reform Bill reached the House of Lords once more, it was uncertain (to Disraeli at least) whether the bill would be destroyed and the Whigs go, or whether the king would agree to create peers to pass the bill. 'I care very little, whatever may be the result,' he told Sarah in March, 'as, under all circumstances, I hope to float uppermost.'[39] On 14 April, the day the bill passed its Second Reading in the Lords, he told Sarah he was 'sure of a Boro' if the Tories ultimately succeed, which I doubt, and have a fair chance the other way', adding somewhat unconvincingly, 'And really do not care about it, as I am more desirous of writing than ever.'[40] Banking on the victory of the Reformers, Disraeli kept his authorship of *Gallomania* a secret and, to protect himself further, refused to mention Reform.

Haber, on the other hand, was betting on the defeat of the bill in the Lords. Though the diplomatic Conference of London had resolved to create an independent Belgium the previous year, Haber still clung to the forlorn hope of aborting the new state. If the Whigs fell, he calculated, the Russians might refuse to ratify the treaty establishing Belgium's frontiers, encouraging the prince of Orange to invade from Holland. Disraeli urged Murray to rush *Gallomania* out in time for the Second Reading debate in the Lords (9 April); publication was in fact a week later, but Disraeli succeeded in putting proofs into the hands of Wellington and Aberdeen before the debate.

The Reform Bill passed its Second Reading, but the Whigs were defeated in the House of Lords on 7 May and Lord Grey resigned two days later. The political agitation which for a year and a half had shaken England to its centre, increased, as Disraeli recalled in *Coningsby*, in its intensity and virulence. *Gallomania*, which had been well reviewed in *The Times* (20 April), was overtaken by events; a promised review in the *Edinburgh* was spiked, and it failed to sell its edition. The crisis Disraeli had been waiting for had come at last and, from the eye of the storm, he scribbled bulletins (often inaccurate) to Sarah at Bradenham.

On 15 May he wrote: 'I very much fear that the Whigs are again in, and on their own terms.' *Contarini Fleming* was published the same day. A worse moment could hardly have been chosen and Disraeli later recalled that the book was almost stillborn.[41] It was reviewed by L.E.L. in the *Literary Gazette* (those few words Disraeli had condescended to address to her paid dividends): 'We know of no writer of the present day,' she wrote, 'to whom the word "genius" may be more truly applied.' Disraeli was not at all pleased when Sarah dismissed L.E.L.'s review as 'sentimental Brompton slip-slop'. Who but L.E.L., asked Sarah, would call Contarini and Alcesté a 'young couple' as if they had just married at Kensington and Chelsea?[42] Bulwer gave *Contarini* generous praise in his journal, *New Monthly Magazine*, in July, but puffs from friends failed to sell copies in a country in the midst of a revolution. Murray sold about half the edition of 1250 (the remainder were sold off cheaply) and he and Disraeli each received a profit of £18.[43] Disraeli was cheered by Tom Campbell, the poet, who told him, 'Don't be nervous about the sale, that's nothing. Nothing sells, but this will *last*. It's a philosophical work Sir!' Disraeli himself thought it 'the perfection of English Prose and a chef d'ouvre [*sic*]', but complained that no critic had the slightest idea of its purpose. One of its few admirers was William Beckford, the author of *Vathek*, to whom Disraeli sent a copy; he replied with four exclamations – 'How wildly original! How full of intense thought! How awakening! How delightful!' The novel was also admired by Mary Shelley. 'Who is the Author?' she asked John Murray. 'I like parts of it excessively – especially the first volume.'[44]

Contarini Fleming deserved more attention than it received. That Disraeli would have devoted himself to literature if the book had succeeded seems unlikely, but its failure helped to confirm him in his choice of politics over literature, which was after all the message of the book.

As the Whigs resumed office, and the passage of the Reform Bill seemed certain, Disraeli identified himself more closely with the Radicals. His Radicalism was romantic and aristocratic. He met a deputation of Birmingham Radicals at a dinner in May and found them 'poor things'; even Thomas Attwood, the leader, was a third-rate man with a vicious Warwickshire accent, he told Sarah, though he had about him a pleasing simplicity. Disraeli could afford to be condescending. Only the day before (23 May) he had dined with the Tory MP Lord Eliot and sat next to the distinguished personage himself – Peel. Disraeli watched fascinated as the great man – then Tory leader in the Commons – lustily attacked his turbot; he was too absorbed to catch the names of the other guests. They all seemed afraid of Peel, he noted; 'I can easily conceive that he could be very disagreeable but yesterday he was in a most condescending mood and unbent with becoming haughtiness.' Disraeli was pleased with his own performance. 'I reminded him by my dignified familiarity both, that he was an Ex-minister, and I a present Radical.' Eliot recalled, however, that Peel took an intuitive dislike to Disraeli, prompted by his brashly asking for a loan of some papers to illustrate a work he was writing. Peel buried his head in his neckcloth and did not address another word to Disraeli all evening.[45]

His political ambitions were nursed by his confidante, Clara Bolton. Dr Bolton, fat and fashionable, rather resembled the late king, George IV; he was physician to many politicians, and his wife Clara befriended his patients, establishing a kind of salon. Baron Haber, Charles Gore, private secretary to Lord John Russell, and the Whig MP Marcus Hill were regulars at her evening reunions which, said Disraeli, all agreed were better than a club. Clara was a rather vulgar, blowsy woman, an adventuress and a meddler, with a passion for controlling other people's relationships; she had begun a flirtation with Disraeli before his journey to the east, and on his return she played the role of 'puffer general', parading rich heiresses before him. Her plan to marry Disraeli off to Margaret Trotter, daughter of a partner in Coutts's Bank, came to nothing: 'as I understand from another more accurate source, that the lady has *down* only 20,000£,' Disraeli told Sarah, 'why, I am in no hurry.' In any case, Isaac had other ideas: he projected a double marriage between Benjamin, Ralph and the two Meredith sisters, neatly tying up the loose ends and large fortune left by William Meredith's death. This drove Clara Bolton to frantic despair: 'Pray do not wed one of them you must have a brilliant star like yourself Keep your heart quiet. I do not like *those girls from what I hear the person* who told me made use of these words they are half city half [illegible] half clever half fools ... do not fall in love I am nervous about you.'[46] Disraeli, who had no intention of marrying anyone, consoled Clara by making her his mistress, or so his family believed, and so, much later, did Sir Philip Rose. In the summer of 1832 Disraeli asked his sister Sarah to invite Mrs Bolton ('if you do not *disapprove*') to Bradenham, 'first because I don't think it possible for her to come, 2ndly because she is of great service to me and I know she would highly prize the attention and 3rdly, because if she do come she would not bore you, as you would rather like her. She is so very much improved.'[47] Wisely, perhaps, after much shilly-shallying, Mrs Bolton decided not to come.

The Reform Bill received the royal assent on 7 June. The week before, a vacancy had been created at Wycombe by the resignation of Sir Thomas

Baring, one of the two Whig members. Wycombe was a two-member closed borough dominated by the corporation and had about fifty voters in 1832. The Reform Bill did not come into effect until the next dissolution, and the by-election was among the last in England to be fought on the unreformed franchise.

It was the opportunity Disraeli had been waiting for. In January he had made a canvass of the borough, staking his claim to succeed Baring. 'Whigs, Tories, and Radicals, Quakers and Evangelicals, Abolition of Slavery, Reform, Conservation, Corn-laws, here is hard work, for one, who is to please all parties,' he told Benjamin Austen. In March, Isaac bought a small farm at Hambleton in Buckinghamshire, providing Disraeli with a property qualification, and from London Disraeli issued lordly instructions to Sarah and Jem to cultivate 'my constituents' with jars of oriental tobacco and pigeon-shooting matches.[48] By declaring himself a Radical and publishing *Contarini Fleming*, Disraeli hoped to capitalise on the popularity of the Reform Act and gain Whig votes. He even wrote to Robert Smith, son of Lord Carrington, the second Whig member for the borough, asking for his support. But there was a Tory subtext to Disraeli's Radicalism. The plan was to regenerate the Wycombe Whigs and turn them all into Tories. No doubt it was partly inspired by Disraeli's agent, John Nash, a Tory solicitor and agent to the marquess of Chandos, the leader of the Bucks Tories. 'I hate to hear *you* called a radical,' wrote Clara Bolton, who was herself a Tory. 'Thou art thyself;' and she explained confusingly that 'it was as easy for a radical without infringing his integrity, to unite with the Tories, who admit of no change, as for him to unite with the Whigs, who are for *all change*'. Nudged by his wife, Dr Bolton stood surety for a loan of £2500 from a certain Mash to pay Disraeli's election expenses.[49]

'I start in the high Radical interest,' Disraeli declared to Austen on 2 June. 'Toryism is worn out, and I cannot condescend to be a Whig.'[50] Even if he could condescend, the Whigs did not want him; that was the trouble.

Disraeli knew that his only real chance of winning Wycombe was an uncontested election; if he was to prevent a Whig candidate from standing, he needed the confidence of the Wycombe Whigs. Lacking local influence, he turned to Bulwer, who wrote to the Wycombe Whigs, asking them to support Disraeli, and to the Radicals Joseph Hume and Daniel O'Connell, asking them to send letters of support. O'Connell refused to write a letter, Hume wrote a letter which he withdrew four days later when he heard Disraeli was standing against supporters of reform – but not before Disraeli had printed his letter as a handbill which he was forced publicly and embarrassingly to recall; a separate approach to Sir Francis Burdett came to nothing.

On 9 June the Whigs produced a candidate, none other than the prime minister's son, Colonel Charles Grey. Grey, who was Disraeli's age, had never made a speech in his life; nor for that matter had Disraeli, but as a thoroughbred Whig Grey was ideally placed to win the pro-Reform votes Disraeli had been angling for.

Disraeli's authorship of *Gallomania*, with its impudent attack on Lord Grey, certainly did not endear him to the Wycombe Whigs, but his failure to obtain their support was due largely to his ignorance and mismanagement of local politics. Sarah and Jem, who ran the campaign while their brother lorded it in London, were innocents in the jungle of small-town politics. They enlisted a retired naval officer named Huffam, who turned out to be an alcoholic, and, inside the borough, gained the support of the mayor, a Tory named John Carter; they appointed John Nash as Disraeli's agent. What the Disraeli family seems not to have appreciated was that fifteen years earlier Nash had led an attack on the borough corporation which, after a prolonged and bitter legal battle, the corporation won. By appointing Nash as his agent Disraeli forfeited any chance of obtaining the backing of the corporation, by far the most powerful entity in the borough. Sir Thomas Baring, whom Disraeli hoped to succeed, had been the corporation member – in fact, he had paid their legal costs, and the corporation supported Reform largely out of gratitude to Baring. Colonel Grey was brought in as the corporation candidate by Robert Wheeler, an old enemy of Nash's.[51]

Grey arrived in Wycombe on the evening of 9 June; attended by two Treasury lords and accompanied by a hired mob and a band, he paraded the town, and then made a stammering ten-minute speech from his phaeton in support of Reform. All Wycombe was assembled and Disraeli, feeling it was the crisis, jumped up on the portico of the Red Lion. As he recalled in *A Year at Hartlebury*, he took off his hat – passed his hand through his curls, paused a moment – and then spoke. One hand on the larger-than-life red lion on the portico, he gave it to them for an hour and a quarter, attacking Treasury influence and claiming to stand for the freedom and independence of the electors of Wycombe. 'When the poll is declared,' he announced, pointing to the head of the lion, 'I shall be there, and', pointing to the tail, 'my opponent shall be there.' 'I made them all mad,' he wrote. 'A great many absolutely *cried*. I never made so many friends in my life or converted so many enemies. All the women are on my side – and wear my colours, pink and white.'[52]

On 13 June Disraeli made his own formal entry into the town, his carriage adorned with pink and white, blowing kisses to the women, conspicuous in a black velvet coat with white satin lining, embroidered waistcoat criss-crossed with heavy chains, white kid gloves with black silk fringes at the wrist. The *Bucks Gazette* mocked him as an Adonis of the sable cheek, adored by women who were 'easy' in their politics.[53] His 'oriental' appearance excited comment,

Disraeli before his tour to the Middle East. By Maclise, 1828.

Benjamin D'Israeli, Disraeli's
grandfather, who came to England from
Italy in about 1748.

Sarah Syprut de Gabay Villareal, second
wife of old Benjamin D'Israeli and
Disraeli's grandmother. She died in
1825. By F. Ferriere.

Isaac D'Israeli in 1832. By Maclise.

Maria Basevi, Disraeli's mother. Disraeli
inherited her looks. After J. Downman.

Sarah Disraeli, Disraeli's sister, in 1828. By Maclise.

6 Bloomsbury Square, the D'Israeli family home, 1817–1829.

James Clay, Disraeli's
dissipated travelling
companion in the Middle
East; 'a handsome
youth with the complexion
of a ripe peach' (Blake).

The Author of *Alroy*. Disraeli *à la
Turque*, by Maclise for *Fraser's
Magazine*, 1833.

Bulwer, the butterfly dandy, by
Maclise, 1832. His writing desk
stood in front of a mirror.

Lady Blessington in middle age by
Maclise. She is mocked by Lawrence's
portrait of her as a beauty.

Lady Caroline Maxse. By Rochard.

Alfred D'Orsay, prince of the
dandies. By Maclise.

Henrietta Sykes by Chalon. Disraeli thought this portrait marvellous.

Lyndhurst by Maclise, 1836. 'The lower part of his countenance betrayed the deficiencies of his character; a want of high purpose and some sensual attributes.'

Bradenham House, High Wycombe. The D'Israeli family home, 1829–1849.

above left Mary Anne Disraeli
by Chalon, 1840. Mutton
dressed as lamb.

above right Jew d'Esprit.
Disraeli's marriage portrait by
Chalon, looking a youthful
thirty-four.

1 Grosvenor Gate (today 93
Park Lane). Disraeli's London
house after his marriage.

JUDGEMENTS
AGAINST
B. D'ISRAELI, Esq.

IN THE QUEEN'S BENCH.

AT THE SUIT OF	DEBT,			COSTS		
Kensington Lewis	158	0	0	3	0	0
Thomas Ward	3000	0	0	3	10	0
Charles Waller	7000	0	0	3	10	0
John Barton	20	0	0	29	2	0
Sir Benjamin Smith	505	16	11			
R. K. Lane	500	0	0			
Mary Ann Marsh	5000	0	0			
Same	2300	0	0			

IN THE COMMON PLEAS.

Beale	19	17	0
Low	754	18	0
Weston	267	13	6

IN THE EXCHEQUER.

	£.	s	D.	£.	s.	D.
J. W. Edwards	200	0	0	15	13	0
Charles Lewis	308	0	6			
James Whitcombe	760	12	0	23	9	0
Henry Harris	200	0	0			

Making a total of Twenty-two Thousand and Thirty-six Pounds, Two Shillings, and Eleven Pence of Judgment

Debts against MR. B. D'ISRAELI WITHIN THREE YEARS.! which are still unsatisfied, and which the said BENJAMIN well knew at the time of Contracting the same he had no means of satisfying. In this list are included the names of unhappy Tailors, Hosiers, Upholsterers, Jew Money Lenders (for this Child of Israel was not satisfied with merely spoiling the Egyptians), Spunging Housekeepers, and, in short, persons of every denomination who were foolish enough to Trust him,

HONEST ELECTORS OF SHREWSBURY!

Will you be represented by such a man? Can you confide in his pledges? Take warning by your brethren at Maidstone, whom Benjamin cannot face again. He seeks a place in Parliament merely for the purpose of avoiding the necessity of a Prison, or the benefit of the Insolvent Debtors Act

Challenge him to deny either the truth or accuracy of the above list, which has been carefully extracted from the Judgement Rolls of the several Courts of Law.

Shrewsbury Election Broadsheet, 1841, listing judgements against Disraeli for debts.

his ambivalence over Reform caused confusion. His slogan, 'Grey and Reform; Disraeli and the People', appeared to imply, as Bulwer anxiously pointed out, not only that the cause of Reform was opposed to the people, but that Disraeli was against Reform.[54] It did, however, reflect the reality of Disraeli's campaign: trying to pick up Tory anti-Reform votes while aligning himself with the popular anti-corporation party in the borough.

The election combined the customs of the old closed borough with the new practices introduced by the Reform Act; polling, which had always taken place behind closed doors in a snug room in the town hall, was held on a hustings erected outside, amid the cheers and hooting of the mob. At the close of poll the result was: Grey 23; Disraeli 12.

Disraeli leapt to his feet and angrily harangued the crowd for an hour and a half. He attacked Thomas Baring for voting against him, and he defended himself against the charge of being a closet Tory. 'The nearest thing to a Tory in disguise is a Whig in office,' he jeered, pointing at Lord Nugent, a Treasury lord and supporter of Grey's; Nugent, a historian, who was still smarting from Isaac's hostile review of his Whiggish *Memorials* of Hampden a few months earlier, challenged Disraeli to a duel, later withdrawing, much to the disappointment of Disraeli, who would have relished the publicity. But the crux of his speech was bitterness towards the Whigs. 'The Whigs have cast me off and they shall repent it,' was Grey's recollection of what Disraeli said; in a letter to *The Times* Disraeli claimed that his words were, 'The Whigs have opposed me, not I them, and they shall repent it.'[55] It was a subtle but significant distinction. Disraeli was already claiming that he had desired no connexion with the Whigs, but if the Whigs had offered their backing, he would willingly have accepted it. Had it not been for Charles Grey, Disraeli might well have sat as Radical–Whig member for Wycombe. Grey's intervention acted as a catalyst, driving Disraeli to play two sides against the centre, developing the Tory Radicalism already inherent in his thinking.

The June election at Wycombe was the preliminary to the real struggle: the general election in December, the first under the terms of the Reform Act. Wycombe retained its two members, and the enfranchisement of the £10 householder increased the borough electorate from about 50 to about 300; Disraeli pinned his hopes of victory on the new voters.

He stood once more as a Radical and Independent. James Clay, who stayed at Bradenham that autumn, stood surety for a new loan of £1000 from the moneylender Mash, and on 1 October Disraeli at last responded to Whig taunts that he lacked a policy by issuing an address. He stood, he declared, as an Independent, pledged to oppose the disgusting system of nomination under which Colonel Grey, a stranger, had obtained election merely because he was the son of the prime minister. Though he wore the badge of no party and the livery of no faction, he pledged himself to Radical measures: the secret ballot, triennial parliaments, and repeal of the newspaper stamp duty, known as the tax on knowledge. When Radicalism threatened to attack Tory interests, however, Disraeli trod very carefully. Abolition of slavery, a strong Radical cause, was potentially embarrassing personally, as his Lindo cousins had interests in the West Indies; 'I have already explained', he airily remarked in his address, 'how I think the abolition of slavery may be safely and speedily effected.' On the Corn Laws, he wanted to have it both ways, supporting any change which relieved the consumer without injuring the farmer; and though he supported the Radical demand for the commutation of tithes, he nimbly avoided attacking the church. Not that he identified himself with the Tories; on the contrary, he wound up with a stirring appeal to the independent electors of Wycombe to 'rid yourselves of all that political jargon and factious slang of Whig and Tory, two names with one meaning, used only to delude you, and unite in forming a great national party which can alone save the country from impending destruction'.[56]

As the only opponent of the two sitting Whigs, Robert Smith and Charles Grey, he hoped to gain sufficent Radical and Tory votes to beat Grey into third place. 'The general opinion here, is that I have the best of it,' he told Benjamin Austen on 6 October, assuring him that 'I really am most active, and I believe work harder at this moment than any man in the kingdom'.[57] The revising barrister appointed under the Reform Act completed his list of voters by the end of October, but when canvassing began Disraeli's hopes began to fade.

Hartlebury (1834), the novel Disraeli wrote jointly with Sarah, contains an account of the Wycombe election of December 1832. The hero of the novel, Aubrey Bohun (based on Disraeli) is a Radical, who wins his election through making an alliance with the Tories. This was Disraeli's tactic at Wycombe in December, but there was a difference. In the novel, the Tories form the nucleus of the corporation; in real life the corporation was dominated by the Whigs. In spite of the Reform Act, the corporation continued to exercise a controlling influence on the politics of the borough. Nor did Disraeli pick up the votes of the newly enfranchised £10 householders, many of whom voted for Grey out of gratitude for the Reform Act. A significant proportion of the new voters at Wycombe were Methodists, and for them opposition to the payment of church tithes was one of the leading issues at the election. Disraeli's attempt to fudge on the issue of tithe commutation did not deceive the Methodists, nor did they welcome the prospect of an alliance with the Tory Anglican clergy who backed Disraeli.[58] Opposition between church and dissent was a basic obstacle in the way of a Tory–Radical alliance; as Disraeli wrote in *Hartlebury*, the dissenters of Wycombe High Street formed a 'low Whig' oligarchy of sleek sectarians, who 'under the pretence of anti-slavery meetings, bible societies, and missions "to the heathen", were in fact always sapping the foundations of that church which was the only barrier against their barbarising creeds'; they were full of what they called gratitude to Lord Grey for Reform and, though not numerous, were powerful in the town. As the town's principal employers of labour in lace-making and chair-making, they tyrannised over their 'inferiors', many of whom were bound to them by mortgages and loans at hard interest and short dates. Narrow-minded and cold-hearted, the low Whigs of country towns like Wycombe were, wrote Disraeli, the real cause of Manchester massacres, the incitement to revolution: 'these are the men who, though they think they are only snuffing the candle in their own miserable hard-hearted parlours, are in fact lighting the torch of every incendiary in the kingdom.' The low Whigs hated Disraeli because he was not snub-nosed like them, because he was a gentleman and a dandy; they hated him with that intense enmity which 'cold-blooded, calculating, unsympathetic, selfish mortals always innately feel for a man of genius, a man whose generous and lively spirit always makes them ashamed of their dead, dunghill-like existence'.[59]

No chance of Disraeli making conversions here, and his failure to recruit among the Radicals drove him to attempt to appeal to the Whigs' enemies on the High Street, the Tories. At a Tory dinner at the end of November, he made a speech denying the Whig charge that he was a destructive Radical. Triennial parliaments, he reassured them, had existed in the days of Queen Anne, the most glorious epoch in England's history; when the Whigs took power under the Hanoverians they had passed the Septennial Act, the basis of Walpole's grinding oppression and corruption, and Sir William Wyndham the Tory leader had called for triennial parliaments. 'Now I,' claimed Disraeli, 'who am cried down and branded as a destructive Radical, only advocate what Sir William Wyndham sought to recover as an act of justice to the people.'[60] Disraeli's speech echoed Sir Francis Burdett, the patrician Radical MP for Westminster, who described himself as a Tory of the reign of Queen Anne; Disraeli had praised Burdett in *The Young Duke* and unsuccessfully sought his backing at Wycombe in June 1832. Whatever the merits of Disraeli's historical argument, however, it offered little comfort to the worried Tories of Wycombe.

Disraeli was happiest orating to the mob. The mob hated the low Whigs of the High Street, who dined in their back parlours for fear of having their windows broken during the election, and though the mob liked the Reform Act, they roared and cheered when Disraeli championed popular rights and poured scorn and invective on the pseudo-popular Whigs. 'The fact is,'

wrote Disraeli, 'no people relish eloquence of the highest order so much as
the lowest mob.' They understood everything: 'Allusion to History which
they have never read, metaphorical expression drawn from sources of which
they have no experience – with all they sympathise.' In *Hartlebury*, he tried to
convey the excitement of the campaign; he liked electioneering better than
hunting, second only to war, he wrote, and it reminded him of the politics of
the Greek republics – 'I suppose I am as much like Alcibiades as [Wycombe]
is like Athens.'[61]

The final state of the poll was: Smith 170; Grey 140; Disraeli 119.[62] It was
an honourable defeat, and it taught Disraeli a crucial lesson. December 1832
was the last election he fought as a Radical. When he next stood at Wycombe
in 1834 it was as an Independent. Radical Tories, Disraeli saw, stood little
chance of winning on the borough franchise of 1832. The £10 householders
of Wycombe were nonconformists and low Whigs who hated the Tories and
the church. The natural allies of the Tories were the people – not the ten
pounders but the mob, denied the vote in 1832, whom Disraeli delighted to
set alight with his fiery oratory.

The poll was declared at Wycombe on 12 December, but nominations for
the Bucks county elections were still open, and Disraeli, by now in the grip of
electioneering mania, spotted a vacancy. He dashed off an address,
responding to a requisition signed by over 500 freeholders. He appealed for
the farmers' vote, but though he vilified the rapacious, tyrannical Whigs he
carefully avoided naming the Tories. 'I came forward', he declared, 'as the
supporter of that great interest which is the only solid basis of the social
fabric, and convinced that the sound prosperity of this country depends upon
the protected industry of the farmer.'[63] He was too late. By the time he arrived
at Aylesbury on 13 December, Mr Scott Murray, an amiable local landowner,
had come forward as a Tory candidate; and, after talking to Lord Chandos,
leader of the Bucks Tories, Disraeli withdrew.

He announced his withdrawal at the nomination meeting in Aylesbury
town hall on 17 December before a hostile audience of 2000. Scott Murray
failed to speak altogether; Disraeli was greeted with catcalls and yells of 'Tory
Radical', 'Radical Tory', 'Mountebank Orator', and though he enraged the
crowd by turning on them and calling them cowardly, he made himself
heard. It was a nightmare ordeal, an experience which Disraeli was later to
remember with a shudder; it was eclipsed only by the barracking he received
during his maiden speech in 1837. No doubt his transformation from Radical
at Wycombe to Tory in Bucks looked like opportunism, but there was logic in
it. His public argument was that Radicalism was a close relation to
eighteenth-century Toryism. They were *against* the same things: office-
holders, organised parties and oligarchs, whether Whig or Tory. Disraeli

attacked the Whig and Tory parties as being as bad as each other, because both were bloated with the spoils of office. Radicals and *true* Tories were 'outs' in permanent opposition to the 'ins'; both were populists, and both hated the Whig aristocracy, the proud oligarchs who stifled and strangled small towns like Wycombe. 'Independence' was the cry of Radicals and Tories alike.

The rhetoric did not convince. Disraeli was both a romantic Radical and an instinctive Tory, two qualities which the Whig 'revolution' of the 1830s made it hard to reconcile. 'What is he?' was a question Disraeli still could not answer convincingly in 1832.

SIX

Henrietta

1832–4

UNDAUNTED BY his defeat at Wycombe, Disraeli plunged back into literary life. He wrote to Lockhart, vindictive editor of the Tory *Quarterly Review*, complaining about a 'sidewind sneer' in Lockhart's review of *Zohrab the Hostage* which put words out of *Vivian Grey* into the mouth of the Young Duke. ('Young Dukes will not again be caught inviting Marchionesses of Bucklersbury to "wine" with them.') 'I have long been aware', Disraeli wrote, 'of the hostile influence (to use no harsher term) which you have exercised over my literary career'; perhaps he was still sore about Lockhart's treacherous treatment of him over the *Representative* six years before, and he was stung too by his offensive criticism of Bulwer's novels in the same review. Lockhart's attack was the start of a vendetta in which Disraeli naturally took Bulwer's side – a month or so later he wrote to the editor of the *Edinburgh Review*, Whig rival of the *Quarterly*, proposing a review of *Zohrab* which would 'show the public the consequence of having a tenth rate novelist at the head of a great critical journal'.[1]

Lockhart's hostility partly explains why Disraeli did not write for the powerful periodical press; the columns of the *Quarterly*, to which Isaac had regularly contributed, were firmly closed to him, and for years afterwards Lockhart pursued him with poison darts of malignancy. As late as 1844, when *Coningsby* appeared, Lockhart told his son, 'Ben Disraeli, the Jew scamp, has published a very blackguard novel ... Awful vanity of the Hebrew!'[2]

In January 1833 Disraeli was back in London, seeking a publisher for *Alroy*, his new novel, the story of a twelfth-century Jewish rebel against Moslem rule. Like *Contarini*, *Alroy* was largely the product of Disraeli's eastern tour. His notes for the book dated back to the winter of 1829–30 at Bradenham when, ill and depressed, he had begun to read the history of the Jews. He pored over the Talmud and plundered Isaac's library, immersing himself in the voluminous tomes of early eighteenth-century French *érudits*: Basnage's *History of the Jews* and Calmet's *Great Dictionary of the Holy Bible*; he took extracts from Enfield's *Philosophy of the Jews* and Lightfoot's *Hebrew and Talmudical Exercitations* (1658).

Disraeli later maintained that he was inspired to write *Alroy* by his visit to Jerusalem in 1831.[3] But though he thought about the story on his travels, he probably put very little on paper; the novel opens with a description of Alroy's relationship with his sister which could not have been written until Disraeli's return from Egypt after Meredith's death, and it seems unlikely that he began to write until the summer of 1832, after the Wycombe by-election. 'Alroy', he told Sarah in August, 'flourishes like a young cedar of Lebanon.'[4]

Alroy is among the least accessible of Disraeli's novels. The first chapter makes equal sense read backwards or forwards. To convey a sense of the orient, Disraeli developed a style which he called verse prose. It abounds in sentences like this: 'Pallid and mad, he swift upsprang, and he tore up a tree by its lusty roots, and down the declivity, dashing with rapid leaps, he struck the ravisher on the temple with the mighty pine.' *Alroy* is important, however, partly because of its Jewishness. Disraeli called it the third novel in his autobiographical trilogy; in *Alroy* he described his 'ideal ambition'.[5]

At first sight, this seems puzzling. David Alroy, the thirteenth-century Jewish Prince of the Captivity, rebels against the rule of the Persian caliphate and restores the fortunes of his fallen race, only to be destroyed by his marriage to the caliph's daughter. It is hard to see what relevance this story could conceivably have had to Disraeli in 1832. However, wrapped up in layers of orientalism, in deserts and bazaars, in Persian palaces and shrieking prophetesses, there is a very modern problem. Alroy is prompted to rebel by a sense of his own worthlessness as a Jew; at times he makes speeches which could have come out of the mouth of Disraeli at the time of his depression:

if thou didst rise each morning only to feel existence to be dishonour, and to find thyself marked out among surrounding men as something foul and fatal; if it were thy lot, like theirs, at best to drag on a mean and dull career, hopeless and aimless, or with no other hope or aim but that which is degrading, and all this too with a keen sense of thy intrinsic worth, and a deep conviction of superior race; why then, perchance, [thou] might even discover 'twere worth a struggle to be free and honoured.[6]

Alroy's problems begin once he has conquered the caliphate. He is torn between two choices – toleration and latitudinarianism on the one hand, and orthodoxy on the other. It is a choice between Jerusalem, rocky, barren and orthodox, and silkily seductive Babylon. Should Jews assimilate, grow rich and powerful, gain acceptance, but lose their faith, identity and dynamism? Or should they keep their separate identity, but languish in the ghetto? It was a topical issue in 1832: toleration for Jews was in the air, the first Jewish Emancipation bill was introduced in 1833; and though in *Alroy* the Jews are granting not receiving toleration, Disraeli has one ear on the public debate and the other on the dining-room at Bradenham, where Isaac urged assimilation.

At first, Alroy inclines towards latitudinarianism. 'Shall this quick blaze of empire sink to a glimmering and twilight sway over some petty province, the decent patriarch of a pastoral horde?' No, says Alroy, 'universal empire must not be founded on sectarian prejudices and exclusive rights.'[7] By marrying the daughter of the Persian caliph, Alroy capitulates to Babylon.

His latitudinarianism exemplifies the argument advanced by Isaac in the *Genius of Judaism*, published soon after *Alroy*, in which he argued for the abandonment of Jewish dietary laws, and the absorption of the Jewish genius into the majority religion. Isaac was a humanist; as Crabb Robinson wrote, after a long talk with him at the Athenaeum in 1833, he 'is more of a philosopher than I had any idea – it seems an anti-supernaturalist – at least not alarmed at any freedom of speculation'. The young J. H. Newman could hardly bear to mention Isaac's name, so lax and offensive did he find his religious views.[8] But Disraeli did not endorse his father's humanism; in *Alroy* the hero's downfall comes about because he abandons his Jewish faith and marries a non-Jewess. He is defeated and taken prisoner, and deep in the dungeon of Baghdad he repents of his false notions of toleration: 'Babylon has vanished and Jerusalem remains, and what are the waters of the Euphrates to the brook of Kedron!' Alroy is redeemed by suffering; he refuses an offer to save his life if he abandons his Jewish faith, and as he dies, his head sabred off by the king of Karasmé, 'a smile of triumphant derision seemed to play upon his dying features'.[9]

Alroy, in other words, is not a liberal text; far from it. It affirms the virtues of orthodoxy, and reveals Disraeli's rejection of Isaac's liberal humanism. *Alroy* also contradicts the liberalism of *Contarini Fleming*; it confirms Disraeli's essential Toryism, or rather his belief in such anti-liberal, Romantic values as race and faith. Nor is it fanciful to see Alroy as Disraeli's ideal ambition. True, Disraeli did not see himself as a defender of Jewish orthodoxy, nor did he at this stage cherish Zionist ambitions to reconquer Jerusalem for the Jews. But the novel expressed Disraeli's dreams of achieving leadership and power in an alien English culture; it confirmed his new-found confidence about his race and his determination to conquer England as a Jew, rather than abandoning his Jewishness and becoming assimilated. In its pride of race, in that final sneer of defiance, *Alroy* encapsulates Disraeli's solution to the sense of worthlessness which had plunged him into such profound depression only five years before.[10]

Alroy, as one critic has observed, is a moral tale; the moral health of the hero determines the action of the novel. But at the time it was read and caused a minor sensation not because of its morality or because of the Jewish issue, but because of the eastern eroticism which bubbles up through Disraeli's stilted verse prose. 'I do observe the influence of women very potent over me,' says Alroy; yet he finds the daughters of his tribe please him not, and he yearns to 'pillow this moody brow upon some snowy bosom'. Babylon becomes a metaphor for sex and snowy bosoms. 'It is the tender twilight hour, when maidens in their lonely bower, sigh softer than the eve! The languid rose her head upraises, and listens with a blush.' Everything about the caliph's daughter Schirene is drenched with sexuality; even her pet gazelle has warm voluptuous lips and 'large and lustrous eyes more eloquent than many a tongue'. Most explicit is the description of the day after her wedding to Alroy. 'My plaintive nightingale, shall we hunt today?' says Schirene. 'Alas! my rose, I would rather lie upon this lazy couch, and gaze upon thy beauty!' After discussing their plans in this fashion, 'She threw her arms around his neck and covered his face with kisses.' The next thing we know, 'Sunset sounded from the minarets'; making it plain what the day's occupation has been.[11]

Murray, who had made very little on *Contarini* and had lost money on *Gallomania*, refused to publish *Alroy*, but Saunders and Otley snapped it up – Disraeli wrote to Sarah to say that he had made an excellent arrangement. In spite of the slump which hit novel publishing around the time of the Reform Bill, Saunders and Otley made an offer of £300 on an edition of a thousand. Though they would barely make a profit on the edition, they seemed overwhelmed with the connection; when Disraeli said he would give up literature unless he could earn £3000 a year, Mr Saunders had replied, 'Well, Sir, let us hope'. This was all nonsense, to be sure, but Saunders and Otley put Disraeli in high spirits: 'my return to the next Parliament may be considered certain,' he wrote. 'In the meantime, make money, make money.'[12]

Saunders and Otley wanted a short tale to pad *Alroy* to fill three volumes at a guinea-and-a-half, and in the middle of January 1833 Disraeli departed for Bath to write with Bulwer. They took unfashionable lodgings at £2 a week with no servant – 'we do everything but cook our own dinners. We have two sitting rooms and scribble in solitude in the morning until two.'[13] Disraeli's tale was called *Iskander*; he described it as a fine contrast to *Alroy*, but the theme was much the same: the revolt against Ottoman rule of a prince whose faith and country had been suppressed, only this time, perhaps at his publisher's request, the hero, Iskander, was not a Jew but a Greek Christian. Written fast, even by his standards – he wrote 120 pages in Bath – *Iskander* is a melodrama which capitalises on Disraeli's reputation as an orientalist. The plot revolves round the friendship between two men, Iskander and Nicaeus, prince of Athens; this was a new theme for Disraeli, and it may have been sparked by his intimacy with Bulwer.

'We are great lions here as you may suspect,' Disraeli told Sarah: at a public ball Bulwer and he went in late and were 'mobbed'. Most evenings they stayed in, 'preferring the relaxation of our own society and smoking Latakia', a Turkish tobacco. Bulwer was writing *England and the English*, a grave and philosophical work which he dedicated to Isaac, and between puffs of late-night Latakia he deplored England's money-worshipping society which held literary men in such low esteem and arranged marriages for money not love; according to Disraeli, many a hint from their colloquies was poured into the book.

'Bulwer is getting on immensely,' Disraeli said; though only a year older than him, Bulwer was already an active MP and the editor of a monthly journal as well as an established writer; Disraeli seemed to have achieved little by comparison. In the coach on the journey back to London he confessed to Bulwer that he was naturally indolent. People said he was ambitious, but it was pride not ambition that prompted him. 'They shall not say I have failed.' Bulwer turned round, pressed his arm and replied, 'We are sacrificing our youth ... but we are bound to go on. How our enemies would triumph were we to retire from the stage. And yet I have more than once been tempted to throw it all up.'[14]

Back in London, he dined with Bulwer *en famille* and sat next to Rosina's mother, Mrs Wheeler, the Irish feminist, 'not so pleasant, something between Jeremy Bentham and Meg Merrilies, very clever but awfully revolutionary'; while she poured the rights of women into Disraeli's ear, 'Bulwer abused system mongers and the sex, and Rosina played with her dog'. He went to hear Bulwer speak in the House, and saw at once that Bulwer would never succeed as a speaker. It was a good debate, Macaulay was admirable, but, 'between ourselves,' he told Sarah, 'I could floor them all. I was never more confident of anything than that I could carry everything before me in that House. The time will come.'[15]

Alroy appeared on 5 March. Half the edition of a thousand was subscribed before publication, 'in these times very good'. It was 'a great hit', selling better than anything he had published since *Vivian Grey*; and this despite being well received by the critics. Not that the critics were ecstatic. They admired the wildness of *Alroy* and its Hebrew spirit; some hailed Disraeli as a genius, but a wasted genius, and the new style of Arabian prose poetry did not find favour. 'O Reader dear! do pray look here,' rhymed the waspish Dr Maginn in a parody of the new style, 'and you will spy the curly hair, and forehead fair, and nose so high, and gleaming eye of Benjamin D'Is-ra-e-li.' (Disraeli was often wrongly pronounced with four syllables.)[16] His claim, many years later, that Lord Grey's Reform Bill prevented him from making a literary revolution, seems hard to credit, but though the critics complained about the style, 'the common readers seem to like the poetry and the excitement'.[17]

Most gratifying was the praise showered on *Alroy* by Beckford, Caliph Vathek himself. Beckford refused to meet Disraeli, communicating through his bookseller and agent, George Clarke, who was authorised to let Disraeli copy a series of letters praising *Alroy*. 'What appears to be *hauteur* and extreme conceit in Disraeli,' wrote Beckford, 'is consciousness, uncontrollable *consciousness* of superior power.' Clarke reported that when he visited Disraeli he found him in his sitting-room with his father and brother, scarcely visible for smoke from his pipe; Beckford, who thought smoking a filthy habit, deplored that the fire of such genius should evaporate in smoke.[18]

Disraeli, meanwhile, was indolent; a butterfly living on his wits and his oriental reputation, dining out nightly and concocting light literary soufflés like 'Ixion in Heaven' for Bulwer's *New Monthly Magazine*. Mrs Caroline Norton, then at the height of her influence as a Whig hostess, asked him to her house in Storey's Gate, near St James's Park. In her tiny first-floor sitting-room, painted white and nearly filled by a vast blue couch, he met her sisters, Georgy (Lady Seymour) and Helen (Mrs Blackwood, later Lady Dufferin): granddaughters of Richard Brinsley Sheridan, the three sisters were handsome, bright and, said Disraeli, 'very Sheridanic'. 'You see Georgy's the beauty,' explained Helen with a pout, 'and Carry's the wit, and I ought to be the good one, but then I am such a liar.' Disraeli, gaudily over-dressed in black velvet coat, gold-braided purple trousers and scarlet waistcoat, flirted with Helen, flashing the rings he wore outside his white gloves; she told him that she knew all his books by heart, and could spout whole pages of *Vivian Grey* and *Contarini Fleming*.[19] He stayed until 3 a. m., and two days later wrote her a note: 'I hope you are as well as you are witty, and as happy as you are beautiful.' Soon he was sending her advance proofs of *Alroy* – 'I am not very sanguine as to the work which I think is too strange for the million' – and writing to her in the style of the *Arabian Nights*: 'When I am a Despot ... I shall decapitate you and place your head upon Storey's Gate.'[20]

He played the eastern lover, long black ringlets curling down his shoulders; Helen was his slave – at least that was the idea, but very soon the roles were reversed. She too complained about his smoking, objecting to the smell of the amber-mouthed chibouque; and though she signed herself 'Schirene', she responded to Disraeli's growing dependence with a teasing irony which left him bemused and floundering. 'You are irresistible,' he wrote, '... I have often told you so, you cannot complain that you are resisted. At least it appears to me that I am docile and devoted enough, although you sometimes indeed call me despotic.' When Helen was away he missed her. 'I am overwhelmed', he wrote, 'with a deep, a terrific and invincible melancholy (I see as usual that you laugh – some day or other, you will find that all this is not affectation) – your continued absence, the conviction that if even in town, I could only by wretched fits and starts, enjoy your inspiring presence, fill me with uncontrollable sadness ... Enough of this, as I cannot bear being ridiculed.'[21]

Caroline Norton, unhappily married to the lumpish and embittered George Norton, who beat her, was the intimate friend of Lord Melbourne, then home secretary; Disraeli called her Aspasia, after Pericles's mistress, charming, talented but loose and a trouble-maker. There was something wild, Irish and dangerous about the Sheridan sisters; they were witty, affected, and compulsive flirts, and women disliked them. 'Mrs Norton is so nice,' said Harriet Granville, 'it is a pity she is not quite nice, for if she were quite nice she would be so very nice.' Caroline Norton danced too near the fire – her husband brought a suit against Melbourne in 1836, though the prime minister was acquitted of adultery and it seems unlikely that he and Caroline were lovers.[22]

At dinner at Storey's Gate in February Disraeli met Melbourne, and the story goes that Melbourne asked what his ambition was. 'To be prime minister,' said Disraeli. Impossible, replied Melbourne with a sigh, 'It is all arranged and settled.' Stanley, he gravely explained, would be the next Prime Minister. Perhaps it was on another occasion that Disraeli flung a letter from Botta detailing Arab sexual practices across the table to Melbourne. Benjamin Haydon the painter was there, and was shocked. Disraeli, he wrote in his diary, 'talked much of the East, and seemed tinged with a disposition to palliate its infamous vices ... I meant to ask him if he preferred Aegypt, where Sodomy was *preferment*, to England, where it very properly was Death.' A week later, Haydon learned that a certain Baring Wall had been charged with indecency with a policeman the very night of Disraeli's extraordinary behaviour at Mrs Norton's. 'I think no man would go on in that odd manner,' he wrote of Disraeli, 'wear green velvet trousers and ruffles, without having odd feelings. He ought to be kicked. I hate the look of the fellow.'[23]

Perhaps Haydon overreacted; dandies were notoriously effeminate. But

Haydon had put his painter's finger on a distinctive strain in Disraeli's nature: his latent homosexuality. Like his political Radicalism, it was an attitude Disraeli found no difficulty in reconciling with the more conventional frameworks of Toryism or heterosexuality; bisexuality came as naturally to Disraeli as did Tory Radicalism.

In March 1833 a vacancy occurred in the borough of Marylebone when one of the two Whig members resigned, and Disraeli offered himself as a candidate. This time he came forward as a Radical. In his address, published in *The Times* on 9 March, he declared himself against the government but a supporter of 'that great system of amelioration which all honest men must desire'. Three days later, he withdrew, his ambition dampened, he told Helen Blackwood, by a poetical fit and a cutting easterly wind – he had a lifelong horror of the east wind, which blighted his spirits and blasted his health. More to the point, his election looked uncertain, and 'I would not go to the poll without a certainty'. He made a virtue of withdrawing; he announced that his aim of opposing the conspiracy to convert Marylebone into 'a nomination borough of the present arbitrary Administration' could only be secured by concentrating the forces of opposition, which won him the gratitude of the Tory press.[24]

Radical at Wycombe, Tory in Bucks, now a Radical again – what was he? At Wycombe George Dashwood, Whig MP for Bucks, made very pointed remarks about the political prostitution of character by a person whose sole object in seeking a seat in parliament was self-aggrandisement, and who swallowed pledges like a cormorant swallowed fish. Disraeli was stung to reply. 'I am writing a very odd book in one vol,' he told Sarah on 14 March.[25] *What Is He?* By The Author of *Vivian Grey* was not a book at all; it was a brief pamphlet. It rattles along like a fusillade of pistol shots, the argument marching through terse theses and logical false antitheses. Government before the Reform Act, asserts Disraeli, was based on aristocratic principle. That principle was abandoned in 1832, and no new principle adopted. Hence the deplorable weakness of the Whig government, and the consequent danger of revolution. To be strong, government must be founded on principle – we had either to revert to the *aristocratic* principle or advance to the *democratic*.

True, concedes Disraeli, the House of Commons *looks* aristocratic in 1833, and true too, the Reform Act was a law to destroy not aristocracy but Toryism – everywhere the Tories' closed boroughs were sacrificed and those of the Whigs preserved (like Wycombe). But the aristocratic principle was destroyed, not by the Reform Act itself but by the means by which it was passed: the intimidation of the House of Lords. The moment the peers passed the bill, the House of Lords was 'as completely abrogated and extinguished as if its Members had torn off their robes and coronets, and flung them into the river, and, stalking in silence to their palaces, had never returned to that Chamber, which every Peer must now enter with a blush or with a pang'. The only way to prevent the complete breakdown of government was to advance the democratic principle. 'A Tory and a Radical, I understand; a Whig, a democratic aristocrat, I cannot comprehend.' Once the Tories recognised that the aristocratic principle could not be restored, it was 'their duty to coalesce with the Radicals, and permit both political nicknames to merge in the common, the intelligible, and the dignified title of a National Party'.

How was the democratic principle to be advanced? Through the measures he had urged at Wycombe: the ballot and the repeal of the Septennial Act. He gave one further reason why the restoration of aristocratic government was impossible: for the last three centuries Europe had been in a state of transition from feudal to federal principles. He had said much the same at the end of *Contarini Fleming* and, drawing again on *Contarini*, he declared that we might yet be rescued by a proud spirit, whose destiny it would be to maintain the glory of the empire and secure the happiness of the people. 'Who will be the proud spirit?' was Isaac's question when he read the pamphlet.[26]

Early in April an election petition was threatened at Marylebone, and *What Is He?* was rushed out in anticipation of another contest. The petition was dismissed, but not before rumours of Disraeli's fighting Marylebone had reached Grub Street. On what does he intend to *stand*? asked *The Town*. 'On my head,' was the reply given in the journal.[27] But the pamphlet helped to make Disraeli's position clearer. After his prevarication over the Reform Act and flirtation with the Whigs in 1832, *What Is He?* established one point firmly: Disraeli was not a Whig. He had met and befriended Colonel Grey, his Whig opponent, in the House of Commons ('we are more than friendly,' he told Sarah in August 1832) but he was still sore over his defeat at Wycombe, and in the pamphlet he began to develop the critique of Whiggery as a pseudo-democratic oligarchy which was to become a central element in his thought. As the Tory journalist Maginn, a friend from the *Representative*, wrote in a profile of Disraeli in *Fraser's* in May, handsomely illustrated by the artist Maclise, 'There is one good thing about him, viz., that he can never be a Whig.'[28]

'I can give you no idea of the success of *What Is He?*' Disraeli told Sarah; it was 'as much a favourite with the Tories as the Rads'. It sold, which pamphlets rarely did, going into three editions. People said it was very clever, which it was, in a knuckle-cracking, continental way – too clever for many Tories still swallowing hard to digest 1832, whose classical education had left them with a pious horror of democracy. Radicals, on the other hand, could not bring themselves to believe in him – he was too flashy. 'The great obstacle to your success', wrote W. J. Fox, a Radical Unitarian minister whom Disraeli had met with Bulwer, 'is that, if not your sincerity, certainly your earnestness, is doubted by very many persons.'[29]

'What can possess so bright a genius to dabble again and again in such a muddy horsepond?' wondered Beckford, who admired *What Is He?* for its terseness and energy. Helen Blackwood, too, regretted Disraeli's politics. 'I see your existence *must* be a political one,' she wrote ruefully, on hearing of the pamphlet; but she feared that 'if you don't end by being *all* you wish (and moderate success would not content you), you are the sort of man to sit down with your hands in your pockets, and be good for nothing all the days of your life.' Disraeli's reply was the last thing Helen expected – a cruel snub. 'I do not send you my pamphlet,' he wrote, 'because the politics will not please you, altho' I am not a Tory, and never intended to be one.... I have a melancholy presentiment that horrible politics will ultimately, if not very soon, dissolve that agreeable acquaintance which has been the consolation of my life.'[30]

Horrible politics indeed! Disraeli had a far more compelling reason for snubbing Helen Blackwood; her name was Henrietta Sykes. Shall I ever be forgiven, mused Disraeli six months later, 'Methinks the fair Helen would be merciful if – but never! never!'[31] Never, never would he abandon Henrietta Sykes ...

'How came you to be such great friends with Lady Sykes?' asked Sarah at the end of April. 'Is she agreeable?' Henrietta was the daughter of Henry Villebois, a wealthy, sporting Norfolk squire and a partner in the brewers' firm of Truman and Hanbury, but her background was tainted by scandal. Her father had not been married to her mother, the daughter of a horse dealer named Elmore and a 'bad set'; after bearing Villebois a family, she left him for his best friend, who made her an offer of marriage. Unlike Helen Blackwood, Henrietta was older than Disraeli; she had been married for eleven years to Sir Francis Sykes, and had four children – the youngest, Eva, was born in 1830. Sir Francis Sykes was the third baronet, the grandson of another Francis Sykes, a vastly wealthy East India Company nabob and friend of Warren Hastings. He suffered from poor health, the legacy of scarlet fever in childhood, made worse by money worries – his father had been a wastrel, and the nabob's fortune, now depleted, was barely sufficient to maintain Basildon Park, the 'Palladian palace' as Disraeli called it, which the nabob had built in the valley of the Thames, and a town house in Upper Grosvenor Street, Mayfair.[32]

Henrietta was bored; her portrait, made by Chalon in 1834, shows a bare-shouldered, rather heavy woman, ripe and expensive; her wide, long-lashed eyes glance sideways, but modest she is not; an English Madame Bovary, she is tempestuous, moody, voluptuous. It is an extraordinarily sensual image; Disraeli thought it marvellous, the most exquisite portrait he had ever seen, no doubt because it captured what attracted him about Henrietta.[33]

Henrietta introduced him to the formidable Lady Cork, who took him up. At eighty-eight Lady Cork (a connection of Sir Francis's) was the last remaining link, as Disraeli wrote, between the two centuries; she had been the confidante of the young Fox, but her appetite for society was as voracious as ever, and she still held court in her house in New Burlington Street. Disraeli described her in *Henrietta Temple*, where she features as Lady Bellair (Dickens made her Mrs Leo Hunter). Lady Cork always said she paid her first homage to talent, her second to beauty, and her third to blood: 'As for mere wealth, she really despised it, though she liked her favourites to be rich.' She could be very impertinent, but Disraeli quickly realised that she loathed being treated with servility, and he tried to convey to Sarah an idea of the old lion huntress's singular mixture of sarcasm and benevolence. He met Lady Cork at a dinner party, and when he announced that he was going to the weekly ball at the Sykes's after dinner she replied: '[Henrietta] is my favourite of all the young women in London and I have left her my china. I have left it to her because she has got a heart, and she is very beautiful too. I would not if I were you leave this house too soon. Here you have *bon société*, there you have only amusement.' Disraeli: 'I detest amusement.' 'I am glad to hear it. I can't understand why you go to Lady Sykes then. I have done all I could to put her in *bon société*, but she will not. She lets her sisters lead her away. Nothing but dancing, dancing, dancing. Do you dance?' 'Never.' 'I am glad to hear it. Now mind, never go out of *bon société*.'[34]

Disraeli's lodgings filled with invitations, some from people he did not know – he kept them all for Sarah to see. In society, he was as outrageous as before: Lady Morgan, the Irish novelist, who met him at the Countess Montalembert's, thought him an 'egregious coxcomb ... outraging the privilege a young man has of being absurd'.[35] Yet, as Disraeli confided to Benjamin Austen, he was 'only *nominally in town*. The engrossing nature of my pursuits I leave to your imagination.' Henrietta whisked him off on roving expeditions, or took him down with her to Basildon. His letters home dried up, and his family fretted at his silence. Odd, rhapsodical scraps got through to Sarah: 'We did nothing but catch trout, and wander in beautiful woods, eat cold pasties, and drink iced champagne. The only books taken were my works.'[36]

It was a grand passion, an affair such as he had scripted for himself in

Contarini Fleming and *Alroy*, and he threw himself into it obsessively. Nothing mattered but Henrietta; his passion for her scorched his soul, as he tried to describe in *Henrietta Temple*: 'An immortal flame burns in the breast of that man who adores and is adored. He is an ethereal being. The accidents of earth touch him not. Revolutions of empire, changes of creed, mutations of opinion, are to him but the clouds and meteors of a stormy sky ... Nothing can subdue him. He laughs alike at loss or failure, loss of friends, loss of character.'[37]

He did little writing that summer, abandoning himself to a present of lounging and pleasure. In May he was dropped by Ellen Meredith, William's sister, whom his family wished him to marry. He cold-bloodedly proposed and Ellen refused him; Disraeli was hurt, and became icy and cutting towards Ellen and her mother; when Sarah, who had acted as go-between, explained that Mrs Meredith objected, reasonably enough, that Disraeli was not in love with Ellen, he retorted, 'As for "Love", all my friends who married for Love and beauty either beat their wives or live apart from them. This is literally the case. I may commit many follies in life, but I never intend to marry for "love", which I am sure is a guarantee of infelicity.'[38]

A man besotted by a married woman whom he could never marry might well write like this. He was seen everywhere with Henrietta – at the theatre, at Mrs Wyndham Lewis's parties, at Henrietta's dinners; it was a very public affair. He went to the opera with her (she adored music) and at Rossini's *Tancredi* he sat in Henrietta's box with Lady Charlotte Bertie, twenty-one-year-old daughter of the Earl of Lindsey. 'Bye the bye,' he asked Sarah, 'would you like her for a sister in law? Very clever, £25,000 and domestic. It is feasible.' Sarah took fright: beware, she wrote, of £25,000 which belongs to a young lady who can spend it herself, and remember that improvident blood half fills her veins. If Sarah had only known, it was Disraeli not Lady Charlotte who was improvident. With Henrietta beside him, he had flirted energetically with Lady Charlotte, who was set alight by his fast-talking brilliancy. 'He is wild, enthusiastic and very poetical,' she wrote in her diary. Nonetheless, she was puzzled by his inconsistencies. He told her that repose is the great thing and nothing repays exertion; yet he dreamed of noise and light, and swore that nothing could compensate him for an obscure youth. Why, she wondered, echoing Helen Blackwood, did such a brilliant creature want to get into parliament? Disraeli brought her flowers a few days later, this time making less effort to impress, and she liked him better. 'He is a follower of Beethoven in taste though not musical,' she wrote. Lady Charlotte had refused the sixty-seven-year-old Plumer Ward the previous year, and in July 1833 she married the forty-eight-year-old J. J. Guest, a 'Croesus of the forge' and very vulgar, Disraeli told Sarah; the match was arranged by Mrs

Wyndham Lewis, whose husband was Guest's partner, and who was 'as proud as Punch, or rather Judy – So much for a romantic lady'.[39]

One day in June, Disraeli announced that he was bringing Lady Sykes down to Bradenham at the end of the week. Sarah was thrown into a panic: the cook was a problem, there was no wine, and what if it rained? Lady Sykes would die of ennui, and then she would hate us. 'Be not alarmed about amusement,' Disraeli wrote back; 'our guests are indolent and loungy.' Small comfort for Sarah; but though it poured with rain and Sarah lost her spaniel, Pop (named after Popanilla), the visit was a success. Henrietta brought her own carriage, page, maid and three-year-old Eva and, Sarah noticed, instantly transformed her room into a modern apartment, perfuming the air with scented sachets which overpowered the housekeeper's dried roses, and heaping the furniture with piles of the latest novels. No wonder Sir Francis's finances were under strain.[40]

In August, as the season ended, Disraeli returned to Bradenham in search of solitude and meditation. 'I am dying to write,' he told Sarah. 'I look forward to six months of constant composition.' He left Henrietta alone in London – Sir Francis was away shooting grouse – and she wrote to him at midnight: 'It is the night Dearest the night that we used to pass so happily together.... The dear head is it better? That it were pillowed on my bosom for ever. I would be such an affectionate old Nurse to my child ...' And she signed herself 'your Mother'. More often she called him Amin, after the handsome seducer of slave girls and concubines in the *Arabian Nights*.[41]

Disraeli's letters to Henrietta have disappeared, so we have only hers, preserved despite Sir Philip Rose's strict instruction that they should be at once destroyed. Her letters make plain the physical side of their relationship, artlessly effusing about sleeping in his arms or 'ten happy minutes on the sopha' (sofas feature often, presumably because in crinoline and stays they were easier than beds); occasionally she was stricken not by conscience but by panic: 'Do you think any misery can occur to us *now* from all the loved embraces? I fear we are very rash people, and when I think I shake.'[42] Not that their affair was beset by the more usual hazards: she had no child by Disraeli, and, despite the fact that she already had four children, she seems to have had none by any of her many lovers. She was, however, vulnerable to the threat of publicity, and Henrietta and Disraeli soon became tangled up in the knots and loose ends of his messy *amours* and her adulterous marriage. Sir Francis had taken up with Clara Bolton, with the connivance of her husband, Dr Bolton, who, according to Sir Philip Rose, was 'said to derive a pecuniary benefit from the connection', hiring out the decoy duck, as Disraeli called Clara. He had treated Mrs Bolton badly, dropping her when she was no longer useful to him, and, still smarting, she tried to stir up Sir Francis against Disraeli's liaison with Henrietta.

Soon after he left London, Mrs Bolton called on Henrietta, who had had a sleepless night and refused to see her – she was looking too awful, she told Disraeli: 'such eyes, red, yellow, anything but blue'. Suspecting Disraeli was still in the house, Mrs Bolton summoned Sir Francis back from the grouse moor; a few days later he descended on Henrietta and forbade her to see Disraeli. Next morning, having heard that Sir Francis had been sighted with Mrs Bolton, Henrietta walked to Mrs Bolton's house in Park Lane – and what was outside the door but Sir Francis's cab? Bracing herself for a scene (she was enjoying herself) Henrietta, 'stiff as a poker and perfectly cool', marched into the drawing-room without being announced and took the lovers by surprise. Mrs Bolton, said she, you and Sir Francis are 'aware of my more than intimacy with Disraeli. It has suited all parties to be a great deal together, not certainly from the intimacy of the ladies, for I have never expressed a friendship for you. I have never been even commonly ladylike in my conduct to you and when together Disraeli and I Francis and you formed to [*sic*] distinct parties ...' Consequently, she refused to meet Mrs Bolton in Sir Francis's absence; she agreed to meet her with Sir Francis, but only on condition that he recognised *her* intimacy with Disraeli: 'Before I leave this house the solemn promise must be given *never* to mention Disraeli's name as a bug bear.'

Mrs Bolton, taken by surprise (Sir Francis wisely stayed silent), replied that she had complained about Disraeli not from malice but because he was 'a heartless wretch. I have stuck up for him for years. Our acquaintance has been of nine years' standing,' she said, brandishing his letters. 'Disraeli has influenced his *dear* family to desert me, witness his Father never having called upon me, and through him your character is gone – I heard from good authority ... no one would visit you next year on his account and he will leave you, he has left you, I know him well – he is everywhere despised.' Henrietta stood her ground, undaunted. Mrs Bolton cried, Sir Francis cried and, she triumphantly reported, 'I did *not cry* and had apologies from both.'[43]

Henrietta departed on a trip to Calais with Sir Francis, summoning Disraeli from Bradenham to say goodbye. It was the end of the first act of a sexual comedy which might have been sordid had it not been farcical.

Disraeli's official biographer, Monypenny, observed a discreet silence about Henrietta, and the affair was disinterred only in the 1960s by the American scholar B. R. Jerman. Robert Blake added significantly to the story, but perhaps no biographer has equalled Maurice Edelman's account in *Disraeli in Love*, the novel he wrote about the affair.

The affair with Henrietta was probably the only occasion when Disraeli abandoned himself to a grand passion; a true Romantic, he was in love with the idea of being in love. Nevertheless, there were strong similarities with his earlier relationships with Sara Austen and Clara Bolton. True, Henrietta was no intellectual, nor was she a political schemer; Disraeli was not a literary or political protégé but a lover. Like Sara and Clara, however, Henrietta was older than he was; a woman who signed herself 'your mother' was hardly a conventional mistress. The need for a woman to mother him ran deep in Disraeli, whose nature had been shaped by Maria's rejection. As with Sara and Clara, the relationship depended on the husband's compliance – Disraeli had no intention of running off with Henrietta, and in an age when divorce was taboo the licensed lover played a necessary role; by seeking to poison Sir Francis Sykes against him, Clara Bolton was acting destructively. Like the women he was involved with earlier, Henrietta was useful to Disraeli: she validated him socially; as her lover he acquired contacts, invitations; for once he became an insider, and if the price was notoriety, Disraeli was not one to complain.

At Bradenham in September Disraeli started a diary, writing in the back of his travel journal of 1826. 'I have passed the whole of this year ... in uninterrupted lounging and pleasure,' he began. Henrietta had made this year the happiest of his life, but how long would these feelings last? His life had not been happy. 'Nature has given me an awful ambition and fiery passions. My life has been a struggle with moments of rapture – a storm with dashes of moonlight. Love, Poetry ...' he turned the page and scribbled over a couple of pages which were later torn out, when or by whom is not known; so much has been torn or crossed out that the notebook has become known to researchers as the 'Mutilated Diary'.

'My disposition', he went on, 'is now *indolent*.' True, his career would probably be more energetic than ever – 'the world will wonder at my ambition. Alas, I struggle from Pride. It is Pride that now prompts me, not Ambition. They shall not say I have failed. It is not Love that makes me say this.' In spite of Henrietta, Disraeli revealed himself as more self-absorbed than ever, untouched by pangs of separation or the tortures of jealousy. Shutting his mind to the sexual comedy enacted in London, Disraeli brooded on his destiny.

My mind is a continental mind. It is a revolutionary mind. I am only truly great in action.... I co[ul]d rule the House of Commons, altho' there would be great prejudice against me at first. It is the most jealous assembly in the world. The fixed character of our English society, the consequence of our aristocratic institutions, renders a *career* difficult. Poetry is the safety valve of my passions, but I wish to *act* what I *write*. My works are the *embodification* [*sic*] of my feelings. In Vivian Grey I have poortrayed [*sic*] my active and real ambition. In Alroy, my ideal ambition. The P.R. [Psychological Romance] is a developm'. of my poetic character. This Trilogy is the secret history of my feelings. I shall write no more about myself. [He ended abruptly:] The Utilitarians in Politics are like the Unitarians in Religion. Both omit Imagination in their systems, and Imagination governs Mankind.[44]

Imagination governs mankind. In that remarkable passage of self-analysis, Disraeli encapsulated his critique of rationalistic systems; in a brilliant flash, the Mutilated Diary illuminates the working of his mind.

That autumn at Bradenham he was moody, poetical, self-absorbed – in short, impossible. How much his family knew about Henrietta is uncertain, but the bowers of Bradenham were far from serene. Isaac worried that his genius son was going to waste, and when at the end of September Disraeli left for London without telling anyone (summoned once more by Henrietta) Isaac sent an anxious letter after him, imploring him to discipline his mind, 'too long the creature of imagination'.[45]

'Seven weeks and not a line in my book,' Disraeli wrote in his diary at the end of October. Not that he had been idle; the researchers of the Disraeli Project revealed in 1979 that he was at work on the novel he was writing jointly with Sarah: *A Year at Hartlebury or the Election*. It is a thinly masked account of the Wycombe election of 1832, and most of it – the descriptions of Bradenham (Hartlebury), of the country neighbours – was written by Sarah. Disraeli wrote the parts describing the election and added a portrait of the hero, Aubrey Bohun, recently returned to Bohun Castle (Lord Carrington's Wycombe Abbey) from his travels abroad: 'Aubrey Bohun combined a fine poetical temperament, with a great love of action. The combination is rare. He was a man of genius. But with great powers he possessed what does not always fall to the lot of their possessors – a great destiny.'[46]

This is a self-portrait of course, echoing the Mutilated Diary, and in *Hartlebury* Disraeli created an idealised character from the sketch in the diary. Bohun, he wrote, was drawn back to England by the Reform Bill which he imagined was about to plunge England into revolution: 'At the prospect of insurrection, he turned with more affection towards a country which he had hitherto condemned as too uneventful for a man of genius.'

'My mind ... is a revolutionary mind,' Disraeli had written in his diary, and in *Hartlebury* he enlarged on the theme. Bohun, he wrote, 'had too great a stake in the existing order of society to precipitate a revolution, though he intended to ride the storm, if the hurricane did occur. And this I think was his duty. It is the fashion now "to go along with the people", but I think the people ought to be led, ought to have ideas given them by those whom nature and education have qualified to govern states and regulate the conduct of mankind.' Bohun's/Disraeli's support for the Reform Bill evaporated, wrote Disraeli, inventing a new past for himself, when he returned home and realised that the bill was a Whig measure and not a democratic one, entrenching in power the Whig party, who were pledged to an anti-national foreign policy. This had been the argument of *Gallomania*, and in *Hartlebury* Disraeli pushed it to radical conclusions:

> [Bohun/Disraeli] was desirous of seeing a new party formed, which while it granted those alterations in our domestic policy which the spirit of the age required, should maintain and prosecute the ancient external policy by which the empire had been founded, and of this party he wished to place himself at the head – a position which his high lineage – his splendid fortune – and his superior talents, justified him in contemplating. Deeming the dismemberment of the empire the necessary consequence of the Whigs long remaining in office, Mr Bohun was of opinion that we should get rid of the Whigs at any price, and as he considered that that result was impossible, according to the new constitution, he was the advocate of movement. Perceiving that the nomination of representatives, in the vast majority of the towns, was in the hands of the Sectarian Low Whig Oligarchy, he thought that the only mode by which this barbarising power could be destroyed was to expand the Whig constituency into a national constituency.[47]

Rightly has *Hartlebury* been described as Disraeli's *Mein Kampf*. True, the agenda he sketched was a response to his experience at Wycombe, where he failed to win the votes of the new £10 householders; and in 1833 it looked as though the Tories were smashed, incapable of ever again achieving a majority. Nonetheless, Disraeli's thinking in *Hartlebury* anticipates his politics in the 1860s and 1870s: a nationalistic foreign policy; confounding Whigs by enfranchising the urban working class; 'movement' or reform in domestic policy ... The outlines of his 'Tory Democracy' of the 1860s can be clearly perceived in the self-made Tory Radicalism of the 1830s.[48]

There is a darker side to *Hartlebury*, however. If, on the one hand, it is Disraeli's idealised self-portrait, on the other it depicts him through the critical eyes of his sister Sarah. It was published under a pseudonym, Cherry and Fair Star, the heroes of a popular melodrama of that name staged in 1822. The names are from a fairy tale about two royal children, first cousins, who were cast adrift and eventually married. One theory is that Disraeli wrote the 1822 melodrama, but this seems rather far-fetched; it is more likely that

Sarah chose the name because she wanted to suggest that the authors were husband and wife.[49] Even odder was her introduction to the novel: 'Our honeymoon being over, we have amused ourselves during the autumn by writing a novel. All we hope is that the Public will deem our literary union as felicitous as we find our personal one.'

Some idea of what Sarah meant by saying that their honeymoon was over can be deduced from the parts of the novel which she wrote. The heroine, whom she created, is a younger version of herself: Helen Molesworth, an alert nineteen-year-old, the daughter of the squire of Bradenham/Hartlebury, who enjoys doing good, visiting the poor and the sick – almshouses, we are told, are her favourite destination. Helen's life at Hartlebury is secluded, domestic and uneventful. It is a village world, seen through a woman's eye. Children and flowers are closely observed (Sarah was the knowledgeable mistress of the garden at Bradenham); the progress of families up and down the social ladder is logged more precisely and acidly than it ever was by Disraeli. But Helen's world is not serene; it seems threatened by the upheaval and violence of the world outside, and the threat comes closer with the arrival of the electric Bohun/Disraeli.

Bohun resolves to win the heart of Helen Molesworth. As the novel proceeds, however, it emerges that far from seeing Bohun as a genius Sarah is repelled by him: a man with a dark secret in his past, a heartless libertine, tainted by his experiences in the east. Bohun's idea of love is a European adaptation of Turkish fashion – instead of imprisoning the body, Bohun/Disraeli wants bondage of the soul: Helen must yield herself up to him absolutely. When Bohun wins his election, Helen shudders at the thought that she has been dazzled by his meretricious brilliancy. 'Hartlebury at peace – Mr Bohun in London' is the title of one chapter, aptly capturing Sarah's relief at her brother's return to town. Disraeli/Bohun is blithely unaware of Sarah/Helen's doubts; in London he is a sensation, courted and sought out everywhere. When Sarah/Helen discovers that Bohun is already married, her fear turns to horror. He proposes; she refuses and, as he turns away, a terrible demonic scowl comes over his face. Sarah's evil Bohun is hardly the same character as Disraeli's conquering hero; the book ends oddly, abruptly and violently, when Bohun is shot and murdered by someone he has been blackmailing.

Even Sarah felt she had gone too far by killing off Disraeli. She read the end of the book to the family as soon as she had written it; 'unanimous the cry for justice on [Bohun's murderer] ... they are very urgent with you to make him commit suicide.' Disraeli replied tartly, 'Do what you like with the end. I will have nothing to do with the suicide or anything else. Poetical justice is all stuff. I think you will spoil the book, but you are Lady Paramount.'[50] He had good reason to be annoyed. Sarah's demonic Bohun was hardly a flattering picture; this was probably one reason why he never acknowledged the novel as his progeny. The violence of Sarah's feelings is intriguing, if only because it seems so out of character. Perhaps it reflected her suppressed anger at William Meredith's death, for which she may have blamed her brother. More likely, she resented the one-sidedness of her relationship with Ben. It was all very well for him to tell her to 'Live only for me', keeping her in the country while he enjoyed London society; and when he became involved in a passionate affair with Lady Sykes his promises to Sarah must have seemed dismayingly empty. She felt betrayed.

Hartlebury, wrote Disraeli in late November, was 'already far advanced', and a month later he sent the manuscript to a publisher, though it was still unfinished; the last chapters were written by Sarah in January 1834. It was very short; Ralph, who copied it out, wrote small, but Sarah confessed it was 'a very little book indeed'. Disraeli made a virtue of its brevity, likening it to the two volumes of *Vivian Grey*.[51]

At the end of January Saunders and Otley agreed to take the novel, but Disraeli was enraged, not only by their offer of a mere £20 – £10 each – small beer after the £300 they had paid for *Alroy*, but by their low opinion of the work, especially his part. 'All the Election part they think most weak. I longed to tell them that I wrote it.'[52]

Hartlebury meant very little to Disraeli; he wrote it effortlessly. Far more important was the epic poem he had been brooding on since the summer. Tension and rows at Bradenham made composition impossible, and the poem remained mostly unwritten. In November Sir Francis Sykes asked Disraeli to stay with him and Henrietta in Essex near Southend, and Disraeli snatched at the chance, bringing the epic with him. The Sykeses had taken a comfortable old grange, and Sir Francis sailed his yacht and shot snipe and wildfowl. Disraeli rose each morning between seven and eight, very early for him, tumbled into his sitting-room and worked on the epic until one; Sir Francis was painting his portrait and, Disraeli told Sarah, 'if he can be induced to finish it, which is not his forte, Lady S intends to give it to my father, and it is to be hung up where the cross is'. Also at Southend were the Boltons, both of them: 'the *damnable* Boltons', wrote Henrietta, 'they poison even my sweetest source of enjoyment', and she complained of being 'every minute annoyed by the coarse vulgarity of the one, and the hypocrisy, the low cunning of the other'. In spite of Clara's machinations, Sir Francis continued cordial towards Disraeli, though Henrietta suffered agonies when Clara threatened to expose her at Bradenham and when Bolton hinted that he had tipped off Westmacott, editor of the scandal sheet, *The Age*.[53]

Only now, it seems, did Bradenham become aware of the full extent of Disraeli's involvement with Henrietta, and after a fortnight at Southend he returned to face an unhappy Sarah and an irate Isaac. His debts too were becoming unmanageable once more. Since selling *Alroy* in January for £300 he had earned very little, and creditors pressed for at least £1200. Though he planned to act on what he called a screw system while writing the epic, and give up his rooms in Duke Street, he desperately needed money, and he applied to his old source, Benjamin Austen. Austen lent him £300, but insisted on prompt repayment, whereupon Disraeli brazenly asked for another £1200 in exchange for the formal assignment of the copyrights on his works. He stood to make £1000 on *Hartlebury* and the epic, he blithely assured Austen, as well as £1500 on a complete edition of his romances; doubtless he could raise the money if he came up to London, but it would take time and occasion anxiety, and in the meanwhile the epic, 'the child of my fancy from which I cannot spare an hour, night or day, would receive a fatal blow, yet write I cannot in the present state of things – therefore I appeal to you, a friend often tried and never found wanting'.[54]

Austen was unmoved. Disraeli had tried him too often, he wrote, and 'I have felt for some time past that your Recollections of it ceased with the Necessity.' Disraeli, who was well aware that the way to Austen's purse was through his wife, meanwhile wrote flatteringly to Sara Austen. 'You appear to be the only person in the world, except myself, who have any energy': would she please find out whether the Empress Josephine, who was a Creole, was dark – he needed to know for the epic. Undaunted by Austen's refusal, Disraeli appealed to their friendship. 'I awoke from a dream,' he wrote. 'For these eight years I have considered you my friend, with me no idle word, whatever you may think.' Last season, perhaps, Austen might have found fault with his conduct; but 'I was so circumstanced last year that my acquaintance I utterly neglected, [my] relations ... I never went near, and I disregarded an entrance which offered itself to me to the most brilliant society of the metropolis.' This is hard to believe, and so is his assurance that his debts were '*entirely* and *altogether* electioneering debts'. 'Friends', he told Austen, 'are not made every day.... It is in youth only that these connections are formed, and yours was my last. Had the friend [William Meredith] who in his gloomier hours never found me wanting, been spared to me, I should not have been forced to write this humiliating letter! Farewell!'[55]

It was shameless, but it worked. Disraeli called on the Austens after Christmas, and Austen lent him £1200 at $2\frac{1}{2}$ per cent. It was just as well; his relations with Isaac were worse than ever; no hope of help from that quarter. 'Papa's letter was certainly most furious,' he told Sarah, 'but I am used to them. Such an abuse of the meaning of words has seldom been met with –

"your strange and dead silence has filled us with the most heartrending affliction.'" Disraeli sneered, but he and Sarah worried that Isaac, now sixty-eight, was growing blind; and S. P. Denning, who made a portrait of Isaac, noticed at once the '*great defect*', Sarah reported to her brother – 'a manner of dropping the underjaw which entirely destroys every ray of intelligence in the face.'[56]

Early in January 1834 Disraeli escaped again to Southend and Henrietta, where he planned to spend the two serene months he needed to finish the epic. Sir Francis's health broke down, and Henrietta was obliged to take him away, leaving Disraeli alone with three-year-old Eva, a golden-haired, rosy-cheeked child who prattled unceasingly. 'I pass my days in constant composition,' Disraeli told Sarah. 'I live solely on snipes and ride a good deal. You could not have a softer climate or sunnier skies than this much abused Southend.' Once he hunted with Sir Henry Smythe's hounds. He had probably never hunted before; nevertheless he boasted that although not in scarlet he was the best mounted man in the field, 'riding Lady Sykes' arabian mare which I nearly killed, a run of thirty miles and I stopped at nothing'.[57] He was not exaggerating. The diary of the Master of the East Essex Hunt confirms that the day Disraeli hunted, they did indeed have a record run of thirty miles.[58]

Disraeli wrote the *Revolutionary Epick* mostly at Southend. Three books, roughly 3000 lines of blank verse, were written and published – a fragment of the whole, which Disraeli reckoned could not be completed in under 30,000 lines. The first two books had been sketched out by November 1833, when he first arrived at Southend, where he composed Book Three, which 'goes on with a giants pace'. In December he told Mrs Austen that he had finished the first three books, and in January and February 1834 he reworked and revised the manuscript, making considerable additions. 'The poem rather expands,' he reported to Sarah, 'but I have much enriched many parts.' Poetry was a struggle: 'although I have written 800 lines here what with additions and alterations the affair is so transmogrified that I calculate I have something like 1,500 lines yet to write. If blotting will make a perfect poem, mine ought to be eternal.'[59] Book One of the epic, comprising 1500 lines and fifty quarto pages, was published in March; Books Two and Three, which together were another 1500 lines, followed as Part Two in June.

Disraeli explained the purpose of the epic in a letter to Sara Austen, repeated in the preface to the poem. 'It appears to me', he wrote, 'that all great works that have formed an epoch in the history of the human intellect have been an embodification [*sic*] of the spirit of their age.' The heroic age produced *The Iliad*, a heroic poem; the Roman Empire produced a political poem, *The Aeneid*; the revival of letters produced a national poem, the *Divine*

Comedy, and the Reformation produced a religious poem in *Paradise Lost*. 'Since the revolt of America a new principle has been at work in the world to which I trace all that occurs. This is the *Revolutionary* principle, and this is what I wish to embody in '*The Revolutionary Epick*'. It was an astounding claim: Disraeli seriously proposed himself as the successor to Homer, as a member of the glorious company.[60]

In the preface, he claimed that the epic was conceived on the plains of Troy. 'Standing upon Asia, and gazing upon Europe, with the broad Hellespont alone between us, and the shadow of Night descending on the mountains, these mighty continents appeared to me, as it were, the Rival Principles of Government that, at present contend for the mastery of the world.' The theme of the poem was the struggle between the principles of Feudalism and Federalism. 'I imagine the Genius of *Feudalism*, and the Genius of *Federalism* appearing before the almighty throne, and pleading their respective and antagonist causes. The pleading of the Feudal Genius, in which I can say all that can be urged in favour of the aristocratic system of society, forms the first book: the pleading of the Federal, the second.' In *What Is He?* he had predicted a 'proud spirit' who was to resolve the conflict; in the epic he made the Omnipotent declare 'that a man is born of supernatural energies, and that whichever side he embraces will succeed ... The man is Napoleon just about to conquer Italy. The spirits descend to earth to join him. He adopts the Federal or Democratic side. The Feudal stirs up the Kings against him. Hence my machinery!'[61]

'The conception', wrote Disraeli, 'seems to me sublime. All depends on the execution.' It did indeed; and the breathtaking arrogance of his purpose together with his blindness to his own limitations exposed him to ridicule and ill-natured criticism. In January he gave a recitation of his work at the Austens': dressed in velvet coat, shirt collar turned down à la Byron, elaborately embroidered waistcoat spewing voluminous frills, heavily scented and his black hair pomaded and curled, he stood with his back to the fire and solemnly announced himself as the Homer or Dante of his age. The scene, according to Henry Layard, Mrs Austen's nephew, was irresistibly comic; after Disraeli had left the room someone declaimed an impromptu burlesque of the opening lines, and the party dissolved into laughter.[62]

Bathos, bombast and pretentiousness are the weaknesses of the epic, and not even the conception was original. Shelley had written two epic poems about the French Revolution, and the machinery and ideas of Disraeli's epic owe much to him; even the names are borrowed from Shelley – Demogorgon, Magros and Lyridon. His epic is easily dismissed as the deplorable product of an overheated ambition and a wanton lack of taste.

The epic develops the theme which had been absorbing Disraeli's mind

since he wrote *What Is He?*: the conflict between aristocracy and democracy –
where did he stand? and was it possible to reconcile the two? The epic adds
little to the argument of the pamphlet, though Disraeli now shows greater
sympathy towards aristocracy, which he describes thus:

> He who is bred
> Within an honoured place,
> And from his mother womb unto his grave
> Nought low, nought sordid, views; but early taught
> By all the glories of his ancestors,
> Them to remember, doth himself respect:
> Around whose infant image, all men's thoughts
> Cluster, like bees, to gather sweetest hopes;
> And, as he mixes with the multitude,
> Feels like a trophy in the market-place.[63]

The argument summarised in the table of contents sounds promising
enough: Man governed by his Imagination, not by his Reason – The state
sacred: even its faults to be viewed with reverence – Forms of government of
little importance. But he lacked the power to translate these concepts into
verse and the interest of the epic lies not in the substance but in the subtext.
At Southend Disraeli's mind had not been on politics ('Any place but
Parliamt. at present', he told Sarah): his overwhelming preoccupation, his
obsession, was Henrietta. He could not resist bringing the story of himself
and Henrietta into the poem:

> in that fell hour,
> Too oft the dooming of the child of song,
> And those quick spirits, whose creative brain
> Raise up the Daemon they cannot control,
> In that fell hour of agony and hate,
> When men are wolves, and the wild earth a waste,
> And our names Execration ...
> then most fair!
> Most beautiful! For when all desert us,
> Art thou most faithful, and calumnious tongues
> But make thine own sweet lips more firm and fond![64]

In the revised 1864 edition of the *Epick*, Disraeli cut this, and another canto
which he pruned very severely was also surely inspired by Henrietta:

But gorgeous ASIA, on her golden throne
The Cleopatra of man's destiny;
Brilliant and dusky as a summer night
Lo! on her couch of mad voluptuousness
The Capitolian hero wildly thrown,
Pouring the passion of his eager soul.[65]

The verse is impregnated with passion. This passage is a metaphor inspired by the sea which introduces the proud spirit, Napoleon:

Man must rise:
And as upon the breast of slumbering ocean
The wind descends, unseen, unrecognised,
A dusky spot that practised mariner
Can scarce detect, but soon the billows swell,
Then rise and foam, against the adverse shore,
Dashing with thunderous charge; their sprayey crests
Glancing and gleaming like the tossing plumes
Of hostile armies …
thus, in human life
Upon the mass the man of genius breathes
His spell creative, thus their swelling hearts
Rise to his charm![66]

Man, rise, breast, slumbering, dusky, swell, rise, foam, thunderous, charge, tossing, swelling, hearts, rise … Thus Disraeli, genius and proud spirit, bleary-eyed at his writing table, still warm from Henrietta's embraces.

SEVEN

Lord Lyndhurst's Friend

1834–6

DISRAELI RETURNED to London in March 1834. He told the Austens he lived like a poet in a garret; his mornings were sacred to the epic, he never went out until three, and though he was naturally too busy with the poem to visit Austen and discuss his debts, he assured 'my dear Austen, that every morning that I rise to my great work, I feel more sensible of the invaluable friendship that has permitted me to prosecute it'.[1]

He took lodgings at No. 31A Park Street, just round the corner from the Sykeses' town house at No. 34 Grosvenor Street. When Sir Francis left in March for an indefinite stay abroad, Disraeli was openly installed as Henrietta's lover; he gave directions for his letters to be forwarded to her house and even Sir Francis wrote to him there. 'What a happy or rather amusing society Henrietta and myself commanded this year,' he recalled in August at the season's end. 'What Delicious little suppers after the Opera!'[2]

1834 was a season of 'unparalleled success and gaiety'. Last season he had been Lady Cork's protégé; this season he was taken up by Lady Blessington. Now in her mid-forties, Lady Blessington was still beautiful but like an overblown rose and growing stout. Benjamin Haydon described her lounging in a soft chair, 'her beautiful complexion engoldened by the luxurious light of an amorous sleepy lamp, her whole air melting, voluptuous, intellectual and overwhelming!' But Lady Blessington was not quite respectable. Ever since she had been sold in marriage at fourteen by her brutal drunken Irish father, scandal had dogged her. Marriage to the fabulously rich Earl of Blessington had not redeemed her. Lawrence's portrait of her took London by storm – a beauty in full bloom, and she herself outshone it; but, like her rival, the divorced Lady Holland, she was shunned by respectable women. The Blessingtons escaped to Italy, taking with them the exquisite Alfred D'Orsay, a Peter Pan figure with whom Blessington, who was bisexual, was probably infatuated. Though eleven years Lady Blessington's junior, D'Orsay's quick-witted good humour amused her, and he became part of the household. Blessington made a foolish will, leaving his vast Irish estates to D'Orsay on condition he married one of his two daughters, and he duly married the fifteen-year-old Lady Harriet Gardiner. After Blessington's death in 1829 Lady Blessington returned to London and moved in to a house in Seamore Place, Park Lane, with D'Orsay and Harriet, and gossips murmured that the marriage was a blind for Lady Blessington's liaison with D'Orsay, and a scheme for getting hold of the Blessington fortune. The marriage, they said, was unconsummated, and when Harriet fled from Seamore Place, in 1831 taking her fortune with her, tongues wagged even more. Though she banished D'Orsay briefly from the house, Lady Blessington's reputation was in tatters. Speculation about her relationship with D'Orsay has gone on ever since, but it seems unlikely that they were lovers; D'Orsay was rumoured to be impotent, and years later, as he lay dying in Paris, he sobbed 'she was to me a mother! a dear, dear mother'. According to Bulwer, who knew Lady Blessington better than anyone, there had been no 'criminal connection' between her and D'Orsay, 'nor indeed any love of that kind'.[3]

Blessington left her poorly provided for, but despite growing money worries Lady Blessington held court at Seamore Place, cultivating literary lions and aristocratic Radicals, and writing ten hours a day to support herself and D'Orsay. D'Orsay reigned as king of the dandies, a gorgeous dragonfly, recklessly extravagant and speaking the broken English of a stage Frenchman. Disraeli was introduced by Bulwer. D'Orsay took a fancy to him, and Lady Blessington declared violently in his favour. At dinner in her octagonal dining-room, where she sat bare-armed in the candlelight, her jewel-encircled hands reflected in the mirrors lining the walls, the only woman at a table of men, Disraeli met Lord Durham. The American journalist N. P. Willis recorded the brilliance of Disraeli's conversation, 'satirical, contemptuous, pathetic, humorous, everything in a moment'; Durham was a man Disraeli wanted to impress.[4]

'Radical Jack' Durham, the spoiled child of the Whigs, had withdrawn from Grey's government in 1833 in protest at its moderation. In June 1834, after the right-wing Whigs Stanley and Graham resigned over the Irish church, it seemed to Disraeli that the Whigs had either to leave office and let in the Tories, or bring Durham back on his own terms. Disraeli identified strongly with Durham and the 'Ultra-Liberal party', who gathered at Lady Blessington's. 'I hope', he told Sarah, 'that a Conservative Government may be formed for a short time, as *we* [author's emphasis] are certainly not matured sufficiently, tho' gaining gigantic strength every hour. But the Tories give up the game in despair.' Excitedly, he reported that Durham 'becomes every day more violent in his demands'. Triennial parliaments, extension of the franchise, the ballot – Durham's demands were very similar to the programme he had canvassed at Wycombe and in *What Is He*? 'In short,' wrote Disraeli, 'a revolution, for this must lead to a fatal collision with the House of Lords.'[5]

Disraeli dined with O'Connell, the Irish leader whose demands were splitting the Whigs. They talked for three hours, and Disraeli found him 'as agreeable as I had often previously heard'. He admired the position O'Connell had made for himself and noted the risks he had taken in raising himself from the son of a gentleman farmer to *'une des puissances du monde* (his very words)'. 'I am not in his toils,' he told Sarah, 'and wish I were, for everyone seems to lean to him in this storm'.[6]

Disraeli was enjoying himself, talking politics with Henrietta on his arm at Thomas Hope's ball – 'the finest thing this year ... They supped off gold and dined in the Sculpture Gallery' – or conning the duke of Wellington at Lady Cork's, wearing the blue Garter ribbon ('He always wears the blue ribbon when mischief is going on.') It was *The Young Duke* come true. He made his début at Almack's with a subscription from Lady Tankerville, D'Orsay's niece, and ate whitebait with D'Orsay and the dandies at Blackwall. He went every day to fêtes and water-parties, and though the rain spoilt most nights in July, Henrietta's grand water-party, where all the ladies were beauties and all the men wits, and they drank champagne and sang to the music of guitars, was 'the most delightful I ever was at'.[7]

'I have had great success in society this year in every respect,' Disraeli reported to Sarah, 'I am as popular with the Dandies as I was hated by the second rate men. I make my way easily in the highest set, where there is no envy, malice etc., and where they like to admire and be amused. Yest[erda]y Lord Durham called upon me, being the first day he has been in town since we met. I was not at home; but this Lady Bless[ington] told me. I am also right in pol[itics] as well as society, being now backed by a very powerful party; and I think the winning one.'[8]

But Disraeli had backed the wrong horse: Durham stayed out of the government, Grey resigned as prime minister, and under Melbourne, his successor, the Whigs limped on; but there was no denying Disraeli's social success. It was just as well; his literary career was a fiasco. The *Revolutionary Epick*, published under the name of D'Israeli the Younger, was a flop. Even Isaac was dubious; though he told Disraeli that he had revived a mode of writing which had become obsolete, and that the epic was 'pregnant with sublime matters', Isaac was not sanguine for its success, dryly noting that he 'did not despair of its attraction for the few'. Lady Cork laid out seventeen shillings in crimson velvet, and got her maid to bind the volume. But the critics were unimpressed; irritated by the arrogance of Disraeli's preface, they condemned the verse, criticising the 'mistaken use of odd expressions for poetry and strong epithets for power'. Disraeli, who found poetry 'a terrible labour', took the hint and (thankfully perhaps) hurled his lyre into limbo.[9]

Nathaniel Willis was wrong to claim in February 1835 that Disraeli was unable to sell a book *at all*;[10] his lighter skits and journalism sold well. In May 1834 he had made an agreement with Colburn to supply articles for the *New Monthly Magazine* for £100, and in July appeared the first of four articles entitled 'The Infernal Marriage'.

'The Infernal Marriage' is a satire on manners and society cleverly transposed into classical myth. It is the story of Proserpine, daughter of Jupiter and Ceres, who was abducted by Pluto, king of Hell and god of the infernal regions. Proserpine arrives in Hell, a breathless newly-wed, and is duly horrified by Cerberus, her husband's monstrous dog, and by the Furies, his hideous attendants, who hate her. Proserpine is a liberal, and she refuses to believe in predestination and free will: 'It appears', says one of the Fates, with a glance of contempt, 'that your Majesty, though a Goddess, is an Atheist.' Back at Olympus, Ceres is distraught at Proserpine's marriage, and Jupiter, who is supposed to be George IV, tries to persuade her that Pluto is a brilliant match, far preferable to Apollo. 'I have no opinion of a literary son-in-law,' says he. 'These scribblers are at present the fashion, and are very well to ask to dinner; but I confess a more intimate connection with them is not at all to my taste.' Pluto may be old, ugly and ill-tempered, but, says Jupiter, 'He has a splendid income, a magnificent estate; his settlements are worthy of his means. This ought to satisfy a mother; and his political influence is necessary to me, and this satisfies a father.'[11]

Like *Popanilla* six years earlier, 'The Infernal Marriage' is playful and light-hearted, neither savage nor malicious – that is, until the fourth article in October, which describes the Elysian Fields, alias London society. The Elysians, says Disraeli, are highly bred, with a peculiar calmness, which comes from carefully avoiding passion or intense emotion; and they are eminently a moral people. If a lady commits herself and gives preference to an admirer, 'the Elysian world immediately begin to look unutterable things, shrug its moral shoulders, and elevate its charitable eye-brows'. Then it was that the Elysian 'moral police' came into play:

Immediately that it was clearly ascertained that two persons of different sexes took an irrational interest in each other's society, all the world instantly went about, actuated by a purely charitable sentiment, telling the most extraordinary falsehoods concerning them that they could devise. Thus it was the fashion to call at one house and announce that you had detected the unhappy pair at a private box at the theatre, and immediately to pay your respects at another mansion and declare that you had observed them on the very same day, and at the very same hour, in a boat on the river.[12]

This, says Disraeli, is the process known in Elysium as 'being talked about', a process with which he and Henrietta were only too familiar. His purpose was to expose the double standards of society; love, he claimed defiantly, counted for more than the approval of the moral police. 'To wander in the green shade of secret woods and whisper our affection; to float on the sunny waters of some gentle stream, and listen to a serenade; to canter with a light-hearted cavalcade over breezy downs, or cool our panting chargers in the summer stillness of winding and woody lanes; to banquet with the beautiful and the witty; to send care to the devil, and indulge the whim of the moment; the priest, the warrior, and the statesman may frown and struggle as they like; but this is existence, and this, this is Elysium!'[13] He meant every word he wrote. One of the many contradicitions of his complex nature was the combination of indolence with a craving for action. Woods and secret summer shade mattered as much to him as dazzling salons; with Henrietta he could abandon himself utterly to a continual present of romance.

Disraeli told Sarah that 'The Infernal Marriage' was 'the most successful thing I ever wrote – I hear something of it every day'. He was as usual over-sanguine, but the story was a success. Isaac thought it his most original composition, and Beckford admired its originality as well as its 'sly, dry humour'. Disraeli nonetheless left the story unfinished. Why it stops so abruptly is a mystery; years later he claimed that he had written further instalments, but that the manuscript had been stolen from his rooms.[14]

As usual Disraeli retreated to Bradenham at the end of the 1834 season leaving Henrietta in London. Parting was painful: he told Lady Blessington, who had become his confidante (he had contributed a story for her annual *Book of Beauty*) that separation was 'more irksome than even my bitterest imagination predicted ... I feel as desolate as a ghost, and I do not think I shall ever be able to settle to anything again.' He was very idle, sitting outside in the August heat, smoking his Turkish pipes under a sycamore, 'solemn as a Pacha'. Lady Blessington urged him to write down his feelings before his passion was blunted; Disraeli balefully replied that he had a horror of journalising and had never kept a diary in his life.[15]

It wasn't true of course. Not only was he taking stock of the past season in the notebook known as the Mutilated Diary; he was working on a novel, *Henrietta Temple*, a love story inspired by his affair with Henrietta, which was to mend their broken fortunes. His progress was slow that golden autumn at Bradenham – he wrote only one volume. He told Benjamin Austen in October that he had been prevented from bringing the novel out in November by a strange illness – on mounting his horse one day he had a determination of blood to the head, and was obliged to throw himself on the floor of the hall, since when he had kept to his sofa for two months, dosing himself with Ammonia, '(heavenly maid!)'. Disraeli naturally feared a recurrence of his noises in the head, but his dizziness was probably caused by smoking too many Turkish pipes. He himself blamed the enforced idleness at Bradenham: 'I am never well save in action,' he told Lady Blessington, 'and then I feel immortal.... Dyspepsia always makes me wish for a civil war.... I am dying for action, and rust like a Damascus sabre in the sheath of a poltroon,' he wrote.[16]

Back in London in late October, he found not only action but a patron: not Durham, but the Tory Lord Lyndhurst, ex-lord chancellor, a magnifico to play Marquess of Carabas to Disraeli's Vivian Grey. He met Lyndhurst at dinner with Henrietta at the end of the summer, and they took to each other instantly. Disraeli was struck by Lyndhurst's advice that 'if he were to choose a career *now*, it would to be at once editor and proprietor of a first rate newspaper'.[17]

Lyndhurst was then over sixty, a self-made political lawyer. Like Disraeli, he was an outsider, the son of an American painter, J. S. Copley; his sympathies were initially Radical, some said Jacobin, but he had now climbed to the top of Tory politics. Silky-mannered and still young-looking beneath his brown wig, Lyndhurst resembled a high-bred falcon – 'nothing could be finer than the upper part of his countenance,' Disraeli later wrote. However, 'the lower part of his countenance betrayed the deficiencies of his character; a want of high purpose, and some sensual attributes.' Disraeli added in pencil, 'Gleams of want of refinement from early associations, when the females were not ladies, and having entered polished society late. Nearer 50 than 40.'[18] Like Vivian Grey's marquess, Lyndhurst had a weakness: women. Disraeli exploited it.

Henrietta was the link. According to Philip Rose, she was the mistress of both Lyndhurst and Disraeli. 'The allegation, at the time, was that Disraeli introduced her to Lord L. and made use of the influence she acquired over Lord L., to forward his own advancement.' In fact, it was Henrietta who brought Lyndhurst and Disraeli together; but she certainly used her influence with Lyndhurst to help Disraeli. 'I can will him in everything,' she told Disraeli, 'and where women are concerned never was there a greater fool.' Lyndhurst's wife died early in 1834: 'He swallowed a large quantity of laudanum and set off to see her remains,' wrote Campbell, his malicious biographer. Henrietta, who was incurably extravagant and had been left on a short allowance by Sir Francis, was heavily in debt, and Lyndhurst came to the rescue. In September he took her to France with his family, paying for everything. His generosity was doubtless not disinterested, but Henrietta at first believed she could manage him. 'Ld Lyndhurst is anxious you should be in Parlt.,' she told Disraeli. 'Seriously he is a most excellent being and I am sure I can make him do what I please – even the Durhamites – he is a grt. friend of Brougham.'[19]

When Disraeli became jealous, Henrietta reassured him that Lyndhurst 'never glances at love and seriously I do not think he cares for anything beyond killing reflection'. That this remained the case seems unlikely; at some point in 1834–5 Henrietta became Lyndhurst's mistress. Certainly the gossips thought so. In December 1834 Lady Blessington, who was probably well informed, had a long conversation with Crabb Robinson: 'of Lord Lyndhurst and Lady Sykes and young Disraeli she related strange stories. But she declared her conviction that Lord Lyndhurst was privy to nothing dishonourable on the part of his wife, and cited him as an instance of the facility with which great men may be deceived by women.'[20]

In London in October Lyndhurst took Disraeli into his confidence, telling him that the end of Whiggism was at hand: 'the time had arrived when the movement might be stopped'. Lyndhurst was looking for a way of bringing the government down, and he settled on an agricultural amendment. Disraeli posted off to Bucks on 11 November to see Lord Chandos, the Ultra Tory leader, who agreed to organise a revolt of the country party and petition for the repeal of the Malt Tax, in exchange for office in a Tory government. The following morning, as Disraeli was leaving Wotton, Chandos's house, his foot on the carriage step, Chandos called him back and told him that Lord Spencer was dead. It was the last blow to the Whig government, removing Althorp, chancellor of the exchequer, to the Lords. No need now for a country party revolt; though Lyndhurst saw the duke of Wellington and told him the Chandos plan, the duke 'threw cold water upon it'. The following day the king dismissed the Whigs, and sent for the duke, who advised him to send for Peel, then wintering in Italy; meanwhile Wellington and Lyndhurst carried on the government of the country between them.[21]

'Great was the suspense until Peel arrived.' The excitement of the three weeks' waiting while Peel hastened across Europe reverberates in the pages of *Coningsby* and *Endymion*. The clubs filled as Tory hopefuls swarmed into town; halls and staircases buzzed with rumour – what kind of Tory government was Peel's to be? The duke would not be pumped. 'All that he knew, which he told in his curt, husky manner, was, that he had to carry on the King's government.' As for Lyndhurst, 'he listened and smiled, and then in his musical voice asked them questions in return, which is the best possible mode of avoiding awkward inquiries'.[22] Only one thing was certain: an election, and Disraeli, who was fidgeting over his uncertain election prospects, worried that he could get nothing definite out of Lyndhurst.

Failing the Tories, he tried the Radicals, approaching Durham. 'My electioneering prospects look gloomy,' he wrote on 17 November. Would Durham use his influence to persuade Hobhouse, Whig candidate for Aylesbury, to stand down in Disraeli's favour? As for the Tories forming a provisional government, it was a case, said he, of Wellington playing Baptist to Peel's Messiah! Disraeli's disloyalty to the Tories failed to win him Durham's support; he politely declined to help at Aylesbury. Two weeks later Disraeli wrote to Lyndhurst, announcing that he had 'just received a communication from Lord Durham which imperatively commands my decision'. Durham, he said, had offered him a seat for the mere legal expenses. 'How then, my dear Lord, am I to act?'[23]

Durham's letter has disappeared, but from a copy of Disraeli's reply it appears that, far from offering a seat, Durham was complaining that Disraeli had joined the Tories.[24] His ultimatum to Lyndhurst did the trick, however. Lyndhurst spoke to the duke of Wellington, and the duke wrote to Lord Granville Somerset, chairman of the Tories' election committee; Lyndhurst also approached Greville, Whig gossip and clerk to the Privy Council, about putting Disraeli in for Lynn. Greville was not impressed by what he heard about Disraeli. 'His political principles must ... be in abeyance,' he wrote in his diary on 6 December, 'for he said that Durham was doing all he could to get him by the offer of a seat, and so forth; if, therefore, he is undecided and wavering between Chandos and Durham, he must be a mighty impartial personage. I don't think', he wrote, pursing his lips, 'that such a man will do, though just such as Lyndhurst would be connected with.'[25]

The mighty impartial personage stood at Wycombe in December as an Independent. Lyndhurst, however, procured £500 for him out of Tory party funds, and in his election address of 16 December, issued as a pamphlet called *The Crisis Examined*, Disraeli declared himself a follower of the duke of Wellington. 'I unwillingly came forward here again,' he grandly wrote to a Wycombe elector, 'but felt it a point of duty to yield to the solicitations of that great man, who has delivered Europe and saved England.' He was silent on the ballot and triennial parliaments, and stood on a stoutly Tory platform, rather to the right of Peel. In defiance of Peel, he called for repeal of the Malt Tax, Chandos's cry, and declared himself against municipal reform, which Peel favoured. Lyndhurst brought the pamphlet to a dinner of cabinet ministers – 'there was nothing else mentioned,' Disraeli told Sarah, and Wellington ordered fifty copies.[26]

Though he stood at Wycombe as a Tory in all but name, he was not supported by the local Tory potentate, Lord Carrington, 'the Abbot', as Disraeli called him, of Wycombe Abbey. Not only was Carrington unwilling to campaign against his son, Robert Smith, who sat as a Whig for Wycombe; he was healthily suspicious of Disraeli, whom he thought 'a very extraordinary sort of person' and a Radical agitator. Back in the summer Lady Cork had called Carrington an old fool for failing to appreciate Disraeli's qualities: 'He would not dine at your house if you were to ask him,' she crowed, which probably did not help; and in December, Carrington intrigued with Wycombe Tories to block Disraeli's candidature. Disraeli was leaked a letter incriminating Carrington, which he showed to Lyndhurst, who showed it to Wellington, who wrote Carrington an angry letter. Carrington nevertheless refused to declare for Disraeli, remaining stubbornly and sullenly neutral, 'a neutrality so strict,' Disraeli wrote, 'that it amounted to a blockade'. The poll was declared on 7 January 1835: Smith 289; Grey 147; Disraeli 128. Disraeli wrote to Wellington that night, blaming Carrington for his defeat and fulsomely avowing his support: 'if the devotion of my energies to your cause, IN or OUT, can ever avail you, your Grace may count upon one, who seeks no greater satisfaction than that of serving a really great man.'[27]

It was later alleged that Disraeli joined the Tories on the advice of Lord Lyndhurst, who told him that the party lacked brains, as all the clever young men were Radicals.[28] Lyndhurst's advice was sound, but Disraeli's mind was already more than half made up; there was no future for a Radical who opposed both the Whigs and the Utilitarians, as he did. As his overtures to Durham showed, Disraeli in some moods still saw himself as Radical, and he became a Radical Tory. Disraeli's connexion with Lyndhurst did mean, however, that he was linked with the right of the party – with the duke of Wellington and the High Tories. At the 1834 election Peel had issued the Tamworth Manifesto, calling for a Conservative party of moderate reform. Old Toryism, the wily Lyndhurst saw, was no answer to Peel's new Conservatism, and Disraeli's brief as Lyndhurst's friend was to modernise and revivify the thinking of the Tory right. Disraeli was not Lyndhurst's secretary, he seems to have received no payment; but he gained the backing of an influential patron and a political education.

In London after the election, Disraeli nursed a sore leg, telling Benjamin Austen he had a broken shin (he was late paying a bill): 'I would attempt to express my bitter mortification but I am really TOO ILL.' He cut old friends with the ruthlessness of an *arriviste*, and was, he said, forced to run away from a dull domestic dinner at the Merediths: 'the idea of the hot coffee and the cold women was so dreadful. I sat next to Miss B. whose conversation was monosyllabic, like the sharp curt snarl of a papier maché poodle.'[29]

He was now protégé and factotum to Lyndhurst, lord chancellor in Peel's government. He made an application for a job for Ralph, and he helped Lyndhurst entertain, and at a dinner in January, given to Lord Abinger and the barons of the Exchequer, Disraeli met Gladstone, already in parliament though five years his junior. The dinner was 'rather dull, but we had a swan, very white and tender and stuffed with truffles, the best company there'. Gladstone, his eyes fixed not on the swan but on the eminent judges, did not even mention Disraeli in his diary.[30]

Disraeli still kept communications open to the Radicals, however, and at the end of January 1835 joined a new Radical club, the Westminster, later the Reform; he was introduced by Bulwer's brother Henry, and the club's members included O'Connell and Joseph Hume. The Tories were strengthened by the election but still a minority, and in February Whigs, Radicals and O'Connell agreed to act together to bring the government down. Parliament met on 18 February, sitting in buildings gutted by the great fire of October; Peel's government proposed such admirable measures of reform that, Disraeli recalled, 'Lord L. became sanguine, and thought that they had weathered the storm'. Lyndhurst's optimism was infections and on 8 March Disraeli withdrew from the Westminster Club. He told Sarah that 'nobody, not even the Whigs, now even dreams of the Tories ever going out again. What a revolution!' He was cock-a-hoop, assuring Sarah, 'As for Lyndhurst, he is safe for life, and as he maintains for me a warm friendship, I need not say to you that I rejoice.' He spoke too soon. Just over two weeks later, on 8 April, Peel resigned.[31]

Ten years later, in *Coningsby*, Disraeli attacked Peel's government of 1834–5 as misguided and premature. Peel, he wrote, was summoned to govern, by a 'perplexed, ill-informed, jaded, shallow generation, repeating cries which they did not comprehend', a generation 'largely acred, consoled up to their chins, but without knowledge, genius, thought, truth or faith'; a government so ill-conceived was bound to crash.[32] This was wisdom after the event; in 1835 he believed that the Tories would be in power for a generation, and after their fall he intrigued to bring Peel back.

On 15 April Mrs Caroline Norton sent for Disraeli, and they were closeted together for two hours on the blue sofa in Storey's Gate. She told him that Melbourne and the old constitutional, aristocratic Whigs wished to form a coalition with Peel and Lyndhurst; 'Melbourne was her prompter and he and she wished the affair to be arranged by Lord L'. Melbourne, according to her, expressed 'an absolute horror of O'Connell with whom he said nothing should induce him to form a connection'; nor was he prepared to make

Brougham lord chancellor again. From Mrs Norton, Disraeli went straight to Lyndhurst, with whom he remained in close conference until half past seven. Disraeli and Caroline Norton were an improbable pair of cabinet-makers, but Disraeli was sanguine of success. Not immediately: 'There seem great, I fear insuperable difficulties in the way of an immediate coalition,' he told Isaac on 17 April, 'tho' eventually it must take place.' A Whig government could not survive more than a few months, when Peel would be recalled; meanwhile, 'we are all in the highest spirits, and ... the excitement is unparalleled'.[33]

Next day, while Melbourne formed a Whig government, Disraeli was summoned by Lord Granville Somerset, the Tory organiser, who said the Tories were willing to start him at a by-election occasioned by the formation of the new government. 'I was astonished at his courtesy, and strong expressions of desire to see me in,' Disraeli wrote to Isaac. Somerset had his own reasons for wanting Disraeli in; he was the son-in-law of Lord Carrington, and anxious to get Disraeli out of the way at Wycombe.[34]

A week later, Disraeli was in Taunton, contesting the re-election of Henry Labouchère. He stood for the first time as an official Tory; and, thanks to Henrietta, who had used her influence with Lyndhurst, he was endorsed by Bonham, the party's election organiser, and carried £300 from party funds in his pocket.[35] Dressed, to the astonishment of the people of Taunton, in bottle-green frock coat, waistcoat criss-crossed with chains, and fancy pantaloons, he wore his glossy black curls brushed away from his right temple and falling luxuriantly over his left ear; when he began to speak he minced and lisped affectedly, fiddling with his hands to show off his rings. According to Sydney Smith, the boys called out 'Old clothes!' and offered to sell him sealing-wax and slippers. His Radical past was an added hazard, and the *Morning Chronicle* attacked him as an ex-Radical and opportunist. In his speech on nomination day (27 April) Disraeli defended his consistency: his aim in political life had always been to break the Whigs, he claimed, hence his earlier support for triennial parliaments and the ballot; but now that the balance of parties was restored, these measures were no longer necessary. He won on the show of hands on the hustings, 'which no blue candidate ever did before', he told Sarah – no idle ceremony, he assured her, 'for the potwallopers of Taunton are as eloquent as those of Athens'. Next day he scribbled: 'I live in a rage of enthusiasm; even my opponents promise to vote for me *next time*. The fatigue is awful. Two long speeches today and nine hours' canvass on foot in a blaze of repartee. I am quite exhausted and can scarcely see to write.'[36]

He was beaten, as he knew he would be, 452 to 282. Nevertheless, he claimed a moral victory: 'I have risen 100% since the Taunton election and there seems a determination among the Tories to get me in *coute qui coute* [*sic*].' Chandos started a subscription at the Carlton, which he headed with £50, and Isaac sent a contribution of £400 towards the campaign costs.[37]

His reincarnation as a Tory did not go unnoticed on the left. The first to pounce was O'Connell. According to *The Times* report of his Taunton speech, which was probably inaccurate, Disraeli had described O'Connell as an incendiary and a traitor – harsh words from one who, only months before, had sought O'Connell out and cultivated his political acquaintance.[38] O'Connell replied in a speech at Dublin on 2 May: Disraeli, who now described him as a traitor, had asked for a letter of support when he stood as a Radical at Wycombe in 1832. Disraeli was a blackguard, a liar, a living lie, a reptile and a Jew – a Jew of 'the lowest and most disgusting grade of moral turpitude…. He has just the qualities of the impenitent thief on the Cross, and I verily believe, if Mr Disraeli's family herald were to be examined, and his genealogy traced, the same person would be discovered to be the heir at law of the exalted individual to whom I allude.'

The ostensible issue at Taunton had been Disraeli's change of party, but underlying this was a tide of anti-semitic abuse which O'Connell's attack brought to the surface. Rather than merely deny the accuracy of *The Times* report of his Taunton speech, Disraeli resolved to treat O'Connell's attack as an affair of honour and issue a challenge. It was a deliberate tactic. O'Connell, as was well known, would never fight; his excuse was that he had once killed a man, but his refusal to fight was considered a blot on his honour because he need never accept responsibility for his words, and it was this weakness Disraeli resolved to exploit.[39]

After reading O'Connell's speech in *The Times*, Disraeli hurried round to D'Orsay. O'Connell's son Morgan had fought a duel the day before on his father's behalf, and Disraeli accordingly sent Morgan a challenge. D'Orsay made the necessary arrangements, sending for Henry Baillie as Disraeli's second; wisely perhaps, D'Orsay refused to act for Disraeli 'as he thought a foreigner should not interfere in a political duel'. When Morgan declined to fight, Disraeli responded by publishing his challenge, together with a long letter to Daniel O'Connell. 'Although you have long placed yourself out of the pale of civilization,' he began, 'still I am one who will not be insulted, even by a yahoo, without chastising it.' He conceded that he had switched from Radical to Tory, but claimed his aim had always been to break the Whigs, unlike O'Connell, who until recently had vilified the Whigs and now professed himself 'devoted' to them. Which of us is the more consistent? asked Disraeli – or D'Israeli, as he signed himself; and he ended by declaring 'We shall meet at Philippi'.[40]

Disraeli and D'Orsay were closeted until ten o'clock, when they dressed to go to Rossini's *Otello*. 'There is but one opinion among *all parties*,' Disraeli told Sarah the next day, when the letters appeared in *The Times*, 'vizt. that I have *squabashed* them.... I believe an affair was never better managed.' On second thoughts, though, he doubted whether his *Times* letter had been strong enough; on 6 May he wrote again to Morgan, telling him that if he had failed to convey his feelings to O'Connell, it had been his intention to insult him, 'And I fervently pray that you, or some one of his blood, may attempt to avenge the inextinguishable hatred with which I shall pursue his existence.'[41]

On the morning of 9 May, as Disraeli lay in bed, 'thankful that I had kicked all the O'Connells and that I was at length to have a quiet morning', the police officer of Marylebone rushed into his room and took him into custody. At the instance of the O'Connells, Disraeli was bound to keep the peace with two sureties for £250 each; he thought this a most unnecessary precaution by the O'Connells, but it was justified by his violent language to Morgan. Even Isaac objected to the letter of 6 May; Disraeli replied irritably that it was all very well to criticise from Bradenham but before the letter to Morgan, 'the affair was nothing; it was only clever and pamphleteering, now the O'Connells are kicked into a gutter, and pinned up to the wall, like rats with a sword through them'.[42]

'Row with O'Connell in which I greatly distinguish myself,' Disraeli wrote in his diary a year later. O'Connell was the scapegoat of the Tories in 1835, and quarrelling with him was a cheap way of gaining notoriety, as Disraeli's critics were quick to point out.[43] Though he hated the Irish, Disraeli liked and rather admired O'Connell, but it took some courage to rise in his own defence, not only over his political consistency but also over his Jewishness. The O'Connell quarrel was the first occasion when Disraeli tried to gain notoriety by publishing violent abuse.

The row with O'Connell did not silence Disraeli's critics. On 29 May an anonymous pamphlet appeared, addressed to the electors of Taunton, accusing him of gross political apostasy, charging him with ungrateful and dishonest behaviour towards O'Connell, and revealing his membership of the Radical Westminster Club. Disraeli replied at length in a printed address, but in June and July two more anonymous broadsides appeared. The author was Edward Cox, a twenty-six-year-old Taunton solicitor and Liberal, who compiled a long list of charges. He found plenty of evidence: letters of support from Hume and O'Connell in 1832, as well as *What Is He?* and Wycombe addresses; inquiries at Wycombe revealed unpaid election debts and, going back to the *Vivian Grey* days, Cox charged him with editing the *Representative* and founding the satirical *Star Chamber*.[44]

Disraeli replied in two long open letters addressed to Edwards Beadon, his agent at Taunton, which were printed as pamphlets. On points of fact, he was as slippery as an eel. To the charge that he had been a member of the Radical Westminster Reform Club, he returned a variety of answers, none convincing. As for his election debts at Wycombe, he claimed to have paid all his bills instantly; but when Cox produced fresh evidence of money owing to the mayor of Wycombe, Disraeli brushed it aside as a matter for his agent. He ducked and weaved around the truth, flatly denying that he was editor of the *Representative* or was ever involved with *Star Chamber*.

But the nub of the argument was the charge of apostasy. Why, asked Cox, did Disraeli not admit that he had been a Radical, but had changed his opinions – why persist in denying the fact? Because, replied Disraeli, I have not changed my opinions; it is the Tories who have changed, not me. In 1832 he thought Radical measures the only way to stop the Whigs, as a Tory government could not maintain itself; now it could. He denied that he had deceived the electors of Wycombe by pretending to be a Radical when in fact he was a Tory; on the contrary, he had deliberately formed a coalition of Radicals and Tories, and 'This was not done in a corner'. So how did he explain his support for triennial parliaments and the ballot? Triennial parliaments had been the cry of the eighteenth-century Country Party; but Disraeli claimed he had urged the ballot as a security against the unprincipled 'system of Terrorism' exercised at Wycombe by 'a small knot of wealthy and tyrannical sectarians always stimulating their inferior townsmen against the county gentlemen or avenging the disobedience of those townsmen to their commands by every species of legal persecution'. These were the low Whigs, the nonconformist shopkeeper oligarchy of Wycombe High Street, and Disraeli hated them – his dislike of these men led him to repudiate the Reform Act of 1832: 'I ... could not comprehend how the conduct of the government which had just formed a new constituency, in which a preponderating influence was given to a sectarian minority, could be in harmony with the feelings of the people.'[45]

The country or the people, as opposed to the constituency: it was a vital distinction. It provided a bridge across which Disraeli nimbly hopped from Radicalism to Toryism; a way of reconciling antipathy to 1832 with being on the side of the people. It led him to make the astounding claim that 'the Tory party is the real democratic party of this country'. For one thing, the Tories maintained national institutions, the objects of which were 'the protection, the maintenance, the moral, civil and religious education of the great mass of the English people: institutions which whether they assume the form of churches, or universities, or societies of men to protect the helpless ... alike flourish for the advantage and happiness of the multitude'. For another, it was the Tories who introduced the Chandos clause in 1832, giving the vote to the £50 tenant, '*a most democratic measure*'. And the Tories opposed short parliaments and the ballot for democratic reasons, not because 'they will give too much power to *the people*: it is because they will give too much power to *the constituency*; a shrewd and vast difference. The more popular the constituency, the stronger the Tories will become, but why they are now in danger, and why the constitution of England is in danger is that for party purposes the power of the state has been thrown into the hands of a sectarian oligarchy.' Not the aristocratic Whigs but their allies in the constituency, the disaffected dissenting low Whigs.[46]

Disraeli did not deny that he had supported reform in 1832. But he now said that he had given the bill his 'frigid approbation' merely because 'I had no wish to have my head broken' – a claim as plausible as it was untrue. As for his former allies, the Radicals, they had turned out to be 'nothing more than a parcel of place hunters or revolutionists in disguise'. Either, like Hume, they wanted to frighten the Whigs into giving them office, or, like O'Connell and the Irish, 'they wished to destroy the Institutions of the Country established for the benefit of the people, and this section are now avowed or implied Republicans'.[47]

In becoming a Tory, Disraeli did not slough off his Radicalism and leave it behind like an old skin. Quite the contrary, he remained a Radical in many respects – in his belief in change and 'democracy', in his faith in the People and his hatred of oligarchy. For him, the tension between Radicalism and Toryism was a creative one; after 1834 he evolved a synthesis between the conflicting principles of democracy and aristocracy: a new creed of Tory Radicalism. It could hardly have been further removed from Peel's Conservatism, with its cautious acceptance of 1832 and appeal to the urban middle class.

In May 1835 Sir Francis Sykes returned unexpectedly after more than a year abroad. Prompted by Disraeli, he had agreed in February to pay an allowance of £1800 to Henrietta, whom he had left penniless; and, far from making trouble on his return, Sykes was pathetically grateful when Disraeli introduced him to his new friends, Lyndhurst and D'Orsay. Sykes's mental state was noticeably unstable; Disraeli described him as 'in a state of excitement which young Rapid never attained. He now does nothing but dance.' Sir Francis agreed to Lyndhurst's formalising his relationship with Henrietta by paying for her keep. Sykes now proposed to allow her £500 a year, and Lyndhurst was to pay for various things on top, but he found Sykes hard to deal with: 'the truth is,' he wrote, 'Sir Francis is rather a queer person.'[48]

The climax of the season that summer was a masked ball at Hanover Square. Henrietta wore powder in her hair and dressed as a picture by

Reynolds, and Lyndhurst was a French marshal: at half-past two Lyndhurst gave a supper 'of the supremest ton and beauty ... everyone looked blue who was not going to Lyndhurst's'. At the ball, Disraeli met Frances Anne, Lady Londonderry, who was Cleopatra, 'in a dress literally embroidered with emeralds and diamonds from top to toe. It looked like armour, and she like a Rhinoceros.' The following week he dined with the Londonderrys at Rosebank, their summer retreat on the Thames: 'Tis the prettiest babyhouse in the world; a pavilion rather than a villa, all green paint, white chintz and looking-glass.'[49] Only four years older than Disraeli, she was heiress to the coal-rich Vane-Tempest estates in County Durham; she married Castlerengh's half-brother and heir, who was twice her age, and poured unlimited wealth and considerable cleverness into the conquest of Tory society, challenging the rule of Lady Jersey. She and Disraeli became intimate, though she remained somehow icy, as if still encrusted in her diamonds.

In July Disraeli descended on Bradenham, bringing with him Lord Lyndhurst; Henrietta came too. County neighbours gasped; fifty years later Sir Philip Rose vividly remembered the scandal caused by Disraeli having 'introduced his reputed mistress, and her Paramour, to his *home*, and made them the associates of his *Sister*, as well as his Father and Mother'. Heedless of local gossip, Disraeli told Sarah that the visit was 'most successful' and Lyndhurst was '*quite delighted*' with it – Maria's food would have done honour to any establishment.[50] Frankly, Disraeli now cared more for Lyndhurst's friendship and patronage than he did for Henrietta.

Lyndhurst had formed another plan to stop the 'movement' and bring the government down. This time it was the Whigs' Municipal Corporations Bill he planned to throw out; the bill would sweep away closed corporations many of which (though not Wycombe) were bastions of Toryism and Anglicanism, replacing them by elected town councils in which the nonconformist low Whigs were bound to dominate. Lyndhurst was inspired by the king, or so Disraeli alleged in a note he wrote a year later: 'Jealousy of Peel. Lyndhurst determines to accept the Premiership if offered, having recd. hints from Windsor.'[51] Lyndhurst talked of demanding ten seats in the Commons, which were to be given to ten young men whom he would select. Disraeli was one.

Disraeli was beside himself with excitement. 'I cannot trust myself to write about politics,' he told Sarah. 'I cannot think of the hot weather or anything else. There is too much at stake.' Peel had accepted the principle of municipal reform in the Commons, and Wellington, leader of the Tory peers, wished the Lords to pass the bill, but at a meeting on 3 August at Apsley House Lyndhurst persuaded the peers to wreck it. On 11 August, the day before the bill went into committee in the House of Lords, Disraeli reported that

Lyndhurst had taken over the leadership of the peers from the duke, 'and there is every probability of his being Prime Minister. Indeed his own disinclination alone stands in the way'. Lyndhurst's revolt was a slap in the face for Peel, who retreated to Drayton in a sulk; Disraeli complained angrily that Peel's admission of the bill's principle had thrown away one of the best cards the Tories ever played, and so completely trammelled his party, that 'but for the boldness of one man, nothing would have been done'. When Sir John Campbell, the Whig attorney general, twitted Lyndhurst with striking out clauses of the bill which Peel had approved in the Commons, Lyndhurst replied: 'Peel! what is Peel to me? D–n Peel!!!'[52]

Lyndhurst promised Disraeli a seat – 'He says *he has arranged it*,' he assured his sister (who had heard this so many times that she must by now have been somewhat sceptical). Disraeli was not to get his seat for nothing, though; Lyndhurst, who was keenly aware of the newspapers' growing influence, wanted him to defend the peers in the Tory press. During August, as Lyndhurst mangled the bill in committee, Disraeli wrote daily leaders for the Tory *Morning Post*. Read the *Morning Post*, Disraeli urged Sarah, 'in whose columns some great unknown has suddenly risen, whose exploits form almost the sole staple of political conversation'.[53]

The *Morning Post* articles were his first essays in political journalism. Initially they strain for effect, shrilly prophesying crisis and the collapse of Melbourne's government. The early articles are remarkable for their buttering and puffing of Lord Lyndhurst, as lavish as the abuse of his opponents is vitriolic. Campbell, the attorney general, who had criticised Lyndhurst and the Lords, is described as 'an orang-outang of unusual magnitude dancing under a banana tree and licking its hairy chops, and winking with exultation its cunning eyes as it beholds the delicious and impending fruit'.[54]

Buried beneath the abuse is a defence of the Lords. The House of Commons, claimed Disraeli, which affected to be the representative of the people, was no such thing: 'It is the representative of a section, and a limited and varying section of the people, called THE CONSTITUENCY – a body certainly more numerous, but as conventional, as privileged, and as irresponsible as the House of Lords itself.'[55] The question at issue, he declared, was 'will the people of England be governed by the Commons alone? ... Will the people of England permit the whole power of the state to be monopolised by one favoured class?' Disraeli did not push this argument to its conclusion and claim that the Lords was just as representative of the *people* as the Commons; rather, he argued that the *constituency* was no more responsible than the peers. Irresponsible power was no more tolerable, he claimed, whether it was exercised by the 300,000 men who had voted at the last election, or by 300 peers. If anything, the peers were preferable to the constituency: 'the three hundred are known, and therefore much more under the influence of public opinion than the 300,000 who pervade society like a favoured sect, and in some degree, like the Jesuits, form a secret order.'

As for the Municipal Corporations Bill, he allowed not a hint of criticism of Peel to show in his articles. He claimed that the peers had accepted the principle of the bill – the substitution of self-election in municipal bodies by free election by a popular constituency. They objected to the detail. 'The principle of the Corporation Bill advances the popular cause with which the Tories sympathise; the details of the Corporation Bill only promote and confirm Whig power, and that the Tories oppose, because they believe that power by the Whigs will ever be employed for anti-national purposes.'[56]

Peel, watching the peers angrily from Drayton, determined to best Lyndhurst; on 31 August, when the bill returned to the Commons, Peel appeared unexpectedly and spoke against the most controversial of Lyndhurst's amendments, which appointed aldermen who, like peers, were to hold office for life. This was the signal the waverers in the Lords had been waiting for; as Disraeli wrote, 'a part of the Lords, led by Wharncliffe, frightened at not being supported in the Commons, seceded from their engagement at a meeting at Apsley House' (3 September). Lyndhurst gave way, the peers climbed down, and the bill passed.

In the last of his *Morning Post* articles (7 September), Disraeli claimed that the principles of the constitution had not only rallied but triumphed: certainly the House of Lords had reasserted itself after the humiliation of 1832 when, as Disraeli wrote in *What Is He?*, the peers might as well have thrown their coronets into the Thames. Nevertheless, thanks to Peel, the peers had failed to wreck the bill. 'The consequence of P's [Peel's] conduct', Disraeli wrote in his note of 1836, 'was the inevitable demonstration apparently in favour of the Whigs by the Corporation Elections in Novr. This alone saved the Cabinet. They had become so unpopular in the Country.'[57] Lyndhurst had been right, Disraeli believed, but had crumbled at the first sign of trouble from Peel, who was jealous and ruthless. Disraeli now began to doubt the extent of Lyndhurst's ambition.

In August the Sykeses took a villa in Richmond, where Disraeli lived with them until December. Lyndhurst was installed nearby at the Star and Garter. Sir Francis was very ill once more. Disraeli rode up to town in the mornings on Henrietta's mare, returning in the evening for a late dinner 'in just that state of exhaustion which makes a capital repast and fine wine a source of health as well as pleasure'.[58]

Creditors buzzed around him like wasps. He was pestered by his tailor, Mr

Culverwell. He not only borrowed money from Culverwell but used him as an agent; Culverwell was the spider at the centre of a tangled web of debts, bills and creditors. Disraeli could barely keep pace with the interest payments, and he fobbed Culverwell off with excuse after excuse: he was confined at Richmond with a broken shin, or detained at Bradenham by Isaac's illness; he was 'engaged *in the most important public business*, and [did] not wish to be troubled with any commonplace business whatever', so please could he renew the bill from Mr Reynolds, husband of his cousin Maria Basevi, from whom he had borrowed two or three thousand pounds. In September Lyndhurst stayed at Bradenham for a fortnight, and Henrietta came too; Disraeli was distracted by dunning letters, anxiously scanning each morning's post before his guests came down, and he implored Culverwell to hold his creditors at bay. 'Pray prevent anything unpleasant,' he wrote, 'as, for obvious reasons, on account of the company now staying here, it would be most inconvenient for me to come to town.'[59]

At Richmond, working closely with Lyndhurst, Disraeli wrote a political tract, picking up where the *Morning Post* articles left off and by mid-November had written enough to approach publishers. He had been earnestly requested by the most eminent members of the Tory party, he alleged, to publish his 'Vindication of the English Constitution' immediately, 'in order that it may operate as a manifesto before the meeting of Parliament'; he claimed there was also another work in progress, a history of the reform of the House of Commons, which was 'founded on material accessible only to himself'.[60] The 'History of the Reform' probably existed only in Disraeli's head, though Lyndhurst may have given him inside information; the events of 1828–32 fascinated him, and he returned to them again and again in his novels. But *The Vindication of the English Constitution in a Letter to a Noble and Learned Lord* by Disraeli the Younger was published by Saunders and Otley on 16 December 1835.

Lyndhurst's defeat over the Municipal Corporations Bill had plunged him into a state of reactionary gloom; he told Greville in September that 'there was no chance of the House of Lords surviving ten years, that power must reside in the House of Commons ... and that the House of Commons would not endure the independent authority of the other House'.[61] Part of Disraeli's purpose in the *Vindication* was to defend the House of Lords against Radical attacks and to provide arguments in support of Lyndhurst and the Tory peers; the book's style is influenced by Disraeli's exposure to the Lords. He peppered his paper liberally with 'your Lordships' and 'my Lords', writing in the first person as though he were addressing the peers. The argument of the *Vindication*, however, owed little to Lyndhurst.

This was Disraeli's first and only attempt to write a treatise defining his philosophy of politics, and it is an uneven mixture of plagiarism and originality, of commonplaces and insight. On what basis should political institutions be founded, was the question he set out to answer. Not, as the Utilitarians argued, on the basis of abstract right. The doctrine of Utilitarianism, he claimed, was philosophically flawed. Utility, which had never been properly defined, was 'a mere phrase, to which any man may ascribe any meaning that his interests prompt or his passions dictate'. 'To say that when a man acts he acts from self-interest is only to announce that when a man does act he acts.' This was neatly put but unoriginal; Macaulay had said much the same in his essay on Mill in 1829.[62] Utilitarians failed to realise that institutions in England were the slow growth of ages, founded on precedent and prescription. Magna Carta, at which they sneered, and the Petition of Right were claimed not as abstract right but as inheritance. 'In short, all our struggles for freedom smack of law ... arbitrary monarchs and rebellious Parliaments alike cloak their encroachments under the sacred veil of right, alike quote precedent and cling to prescription.' That the English constitution was planted in history was proved by the failure of attempts to export it to France, Naples and Spain after 1815 – the system of propagandism, which Disraeli first exposed in *Gallomania*.

Contrary to the Utilitarians, he claimed to prove that 'political institutions, founded on abstract rights and principles, are mere nullities; that the only certain and legitimate foundation of liberty is law; that if there be no privity between the old legal Constitution of a country and the new legislature, the latter must fall; and that a free government on a great scale of national representation is the very gradual work of time, and especially of preparatory institutions.' '"Privity"', Disraeli explained to a baffled reader, 'in the sense of *connection* is a technical term of law.'[63]

Lord Eliot, to whom Disraeli sent a copy of the *Vindication*, claimed that there had been nothing like it since Burke – 'Indeed, many passages forcibly recall to my mind parts of the Essay on the French Revolution.' He was right: the arguments about precedent are derived from Burke, and the passages on Magna Carta and the Petition of Right come straight out of Burke's *Reflections on the Revolution in France*; hostile critics charged Disraeli with transcribing Burke and imitating his style.[64]

The second step in his argument was to refute the Utilitarians' claim that the House of Commons represented the people. 'My Lord,' declares Disraeli, 'I do not believe that the House of Commons is the House of the People, or that the members of the House of Commons are the representatives of the People.' Rather than state that the House of Commons represented the constituency, Disraeli now claimed that it represented an estate of the realm, the Commons or Third Estate. Historically, the House of

Commons had represented the privileged order of knights and burgesses, and the Commons were still an estate of the realm. 'For although their representatives may be chosen by three hundred thousand men instead of one hundred thousand, they are still only the representatives of a limited and favoured class of the kingdom.'[65]

This constitutional medievalism was a mistake. To substantiate the point that the Commons was an estate, he needed to prove that the constitution had not changed in essentials since the middle ages. Under the Plantagenets, he claimed, 'the present constitution was amply, if not perfectly, developed'. The reign of Charles I saw 'a struggle to restore the ancient liberties of the nation, and to regain and complete the constitution of the Plantagenets'. Disraeli wrote crude, outdated Whig history: the theory of an ancient medieval constitution, passed down from generation to generation, defended by parliament against the aggressions of the Stuart kings. Not even Whigs believed this any more, let alone Isaac, who had written a subtle Tory reappraisal of Charles I.[66]

Nor did Disraeli's historicism cloak the essential Radicalism of his argument. Lord Eliot, whose nose was highly attuned to any whiff of Radical, pounced at once: 'If I took exception to any part of your book it would be to that in which you separate the Electoral body from the people. All that you say is perfectly true, but your argument goes to universal suffrage.' It did indeed; the implication is surely that the House of Commons *should* represent the people, not merely a favoured estate.[67]

But Disraeli's brief was to defend the House of Lords which, like the Commons, formed an estate of the realm. In the Lords, he claimed, there was 'representation without election'; indeed, in some ways, the House of Lords was more responsible than the House of Commons, as the three hundred thousand electors were far less accountable to the general body of the people than the three hundred peers, always in the public eye. Radicals attacked the hereditary character of the upper house, but it was precisely because the peers were hereditary that they were so well suited to act as a senate. Paraphrasing his words in the *Revolutionary Epick*, he described them as 'an order of men who are born honoured, and taught to respect themselves by the good fame and glory of their ancestors; who from the womb to the grave are trained to loathe and recoil from everything that is mean and sordid, and whose honour is a more precious possession than their parks and palaces'.[68]

As he was struggling to finish the *Vindication*, Disraeli wrote to Isaac, 'Lord L.... thinks the Vindication admirable, but it is difficult writing, and the part on the Whigs and Tories has cost me dear.'[69] The part on the Whigs and Tories comes at the end of the book, and it is plain why Disraeli found it hard. Since the controversy with Cox six months before, he had argued that the Tories were the party of the people, the truly national party; in the *Vindication* he attempted to base this claim on a theory of history. Abandoning the platitudinous Whig history he had written earlier, he proposed a revisionist Tory view. Here, for the first time, is the theory of the Venetian Oligarchy.

He began by stating a paradox. The Whigs claimed to be the party of civil and religious liberty. Yet in the reign of George I they were the supporters of the court, maintaining their doctrines in defiance of the people. The Tories, on the other hand, professed the doctrines of the Divine Right of Kings, passive obedience and non-resistance. Yet the Tories upheld this servile creed in defiance of the court, and were supported by nine-tenths of the nation. How did this confusion come about?

In 1714, declared Disraeli, the Whig magnificoes foisted the Hanoverian succession upon the nation, and reduced George I to the situation of a Venetian Doge. They established the Cabinet, from which the king was excluded; they 'swamped' the House of Commons with the Septennial Act of 1716; they even tried to deprive the king of the power of creating peers by introducing the Peerage Bill of 1718, which destroyed equality of civil rights and concentrated the whole powers of the state in the House of Lords, but which was thrown out by the Tories in the House of Commons. The Whigs were not 'a national party, influenced by any great and avowed principles of public policy and conduct, but a small knot of great families who have no other object but their own aggrandisement, and who seek to gratify it by all possible means'. Themselves hostile to the crown, they formed a powerful alliance with nonconformists hostile to the church; 'but the republican model of the House of Russell was Venice; of their plebeian allies, Geneva'. Their cry of civil and religious freedom merely meant 'a Doge and no Bishops: advocating the liberty of the subject, the Peers would have established an oligarchy; upholding toleration, the Puritans aimed at supremacy'. After 1714, the Whigs acquired a second ally, the money interest – 'the fungus spawn of public loans, who began to elbow the country gentlemen, and beat them out of the representation of their boroughs by the long purses of a Plutocracy'.[70]

The Whig party formed a permanent minority, according to Disraeli; even now, after the *coup d'état* of 1832, they were only maintained in power by Irish and Scottish votes. 'The rest of the nation – that is to say, nine-tenths of the people of England – formed the Tory party, the landed proprietors and peasantry of the kingdom, headed by a spirited and popular Church, and looking to the kingly power in the abstract, though not to the reigning King, as their only protection from an impending oligarchy.'

The Whigs were odious to the English people because they were anti-national. To establish an oligarchical republic, they declared war against the great national institutions which stood in their way. Yet it was these institutions which made us a nation. The crown, the church, the universities, the municipal corporations, the magistracy – without them, the English people, 'instead of being a nation, would present only a mass of individuals governed by a metropolis'. The English would become a prey to equality, the Gallic, grovelling kind of equality which levels, not the sublime, English equality which elevates, investing all Englishmen with equality of civil rights and making them like the Hebrews in religion, 'a favoured and peculiar people'. Without its national institutions, England would become like France – a despotism. The Tory party, which supports the country's institutions because they secure equality of civil rights, 'is the national party; it is the really democratic party of England'.[71]

The first man to seize this truth and seek to rid the Tory party of its obnoxious and servile doctrine of divine right, claimed Disraeli, was Lord Bolingbroke.

Opposed to the Whigs from principle, for an oligarchy is hostile to genius, and recoiling from the Tory tenets, which his unprejudiced and vigorous mind taught him at the same time to dread and to condemn, Lord Bolingbroke, at the outset of his career, incurred the commonplace imputation of insincerity and inconsistency, because, in an age of unsettled parties with professions contradictory of their conduct, he maintained that vigilant and meditative independence which is the privilege of an original and determined spirit. It is probable that in the earlier years of his career he meditated over the formation of a new party, that dream of youthful ambition in a perplexed and discordant age, but destined in English politics to be never more substantial than a vision. More experienced in political life, he became aware that he had only to choose between the Whigs and the Tories, and his sagacious intellect, not satisfied with the superficial character of these celebrated divisions, penetrated their interior and essential qualities, and discovered, in spite of all the affectation of popular sympathy on one side, and of admiration of arbitrary power on the other, that this choice was in fact a choice between oligarchy and democracy.[72]

It sounds familiar. 'In reading your sketch of Bolingbroke,' commented Lord Eliot, 'I could not help thinking that if opportunities are not withheld, you may become what he might have been.' Much the same thought occurred to Philip Guedalla, reading this passage nearly a century later. 'Cf. self,' he pencilled in the margin. 'Identification with Bolingbroke. D. cannot resist the autobiography still.' Quite so; the sketch of Bolingbroke is a self-portrait of Disraeli. Bolingbroke certainly did not recoil from Toryism at the outset of his career; on the contrary, he was secretary of state under Tory Queen Anne at thirty-two, and joined the Pretender in 1715. He did not as a young man contemplate forming a new party, nor did he think in terms of oligarchy and democracy. That this was how Disraeli saw himself is made abundantly clear in a letter he wrote to *The Times*, defending himself once again against attacks on his consistency. On his return to England in the midst of the crisis over the Reform Bill, he recalled: 'I found the nation in terror of a rampant democracy. I saw only an impending oligarchy. I found the House of Commons packed, and the independence of the House of Lords announced as terminated. I recognised a repetition of the same oligarchical *coups d'état* from which we had escaped by a miracle little more than a century before; therefore I determined to the utmost of my power to oppose the Whigs.'[73]

Disraeli's aspirations to be the Bolingbroke, the proud spirit, of his age must have looked absurdly inflated and egotistical in 1835. But his claim that the Tories were the truly national democratic party against the oligarchical Whigs was clever and commanded respect. Thomas Moore recorded a conversation with the Whig Lord Lansdowne (December 1835), 'Speaking of D'Israeli "the younger's" view of the political character of the Whigs and Tories, in his late pamphlets, Lord Lansdowne remarked that there was a good deal of truth in what he said as to the Tories having taken a more democratic line in general, than the Whigs, their political position since the Revolution having led them to court the alliance of the people against the aristocracy.'[74] The idea of the Tory party as an alliance of people and establishment institutions against oligarchy was too radical for the country gentlemen of 1835, but it foreshadows the Young England novels of the 1840s and the Tory Democracy of 1867. With the *Vindication*, Disraeli at last resolved the tension between Radicalism and Toryism to create a new political synthesis.

Isaac was delighted with the *Vindication*. 'Your vulgar birthday was, it seems, last Monday,' he wrote on 23 December (Disraeli was thirty-one) 'but your nobler political birth has occurred this week.' After the epic, the *Vindication* came as a relief; Isaac felt his son was at last realising his potential: 'I never doubted your powers, they were not latent to me. With more management on your side they would have been acknowledged long ere now – universally. You never wanted for genius, but it was apt in its fullness to run over. You have now acquired, what many a great genius never could, *a perfect style* ...' Not many fathers write to their sons like that. Isaac saw that Disraeli would never succeed as a mere creature of imagination; in politics, however, his 'perfect style' gave him a unique advantage. 'Should you ever succeed in getting into Parliament I will know that your moral intrepidity and your rapid combinations of ideas will throw out many "a Vindication".'[75]

The *Vindication*, Lord Strangford told Disraeli, is making a very great noise: 'there has been nothing since Burke like it.' 'London Review on D'Israeli and Aristocracy', Gladstone noted in his diary (5 February 1836). The twenty-page piece in John Stuart Mill's Radical *London Review* was predictably hostile: while exposing Disraeli's plagiarism and solecisms, it sneered sarcastically at his ambition to emulate Bolingbroke and teach the Tories Torism, riding to power on the shoulders of the mob.[76] Old enemies took the opportunity of pay off scores – Lockhart, for example, whom Lyndhurst asked to a party in the hopes he would review the *Vindication*. 'Chance!' wrote Disraeli. 'He never spoke a word. He is known in society by the name of "The Viper"; but if he tries to sting me, he will find my heel of iron.' Another creature from Disraeli's past who did sting him was Joseph Hume, who wrote to the *Globe* alleging that Disraeli had called on him to ask for his support as a Radical in 1832. Disraeli's scorching reply in *The Times* denied that he had ever been to Hume's house (which was true), accused Hume of lying and ignored altogether the charge of Radicalism. He prided himself on having worsted Hume, who, 'according to his custom ... had lied terribly,' he told Sarah. 'No one can stand better with his party than I do.'[77]

He sent a copy of the *Vindication* to Peel, with a 'cold, dry note', expecting to hear nothing, Peel being 'the most jealous, frigid and haughty of men; and as I had reason to believe anything but friendly to me'. To his surprise, Peel replied that he had already bought a copy, and was gratified to find a topic apparently so exhausted treated with so much originality – seemingly faint praise, but Lyndhurst told Disraeli, 'It is MUCH, considering the writer, under any circumstances'. Always ready to plot and complain when Peel's back was turned, Disraeli jumped at the smallest crumbs of encouragement.[78]

In December 1835 Disraeli quit Richmond and moved to London, lodging in Long's Hotel on New Bond Street. 'I like this hotel,' he told Isaac. ''Tis gay and good rooms, and so central as to command everybody in a minute.' Influenza, his old enemy, kept him prisoner in his room, and he entertained from his hotel bed; Lyndhurst sat with him a great deal. He stayed in London over Christmas, kept from Bradenham and his family by an affair which he described with an air of important mystery as 'the great business'. Which all went back to his financial situation. Trapped by snowballing debt, nagging creditors, badly-paid writing and dandy extravagance, Disraeli could only see one way out – a dramatic financial *coup*. Where else to look but the exotic world of secret diplomacy, a world largely controlled by the fabulously powerful Jewish financiers who manipulated the Great Powers behind the scenes? His link was the Jewish Baron Haber, the cloak-and-dagger reactionary who appears to have turned up again in 1835.

The evidence is fragmentary and hard to piece together, but it seems to have been through Haber that Disraeli became a kind of agent, negotiating a loan for the Swedish government which was raised on the London money market. In January 1836, when Benjamin Austen pressed for repayment of a loan, Disraeli told him that though his debts were £1300, his estate was solvent, as his assets included £1000 due in April, 'the result of a piece of business which has engaged my attention during the last five months, and respecting which I have twice visited the Hague'. Haber's headquarters were at the Hague; Disraeli goes on to mention 'the Solicitor of the Legation by whom I was employed', and we know from internal evidence that the solicitor to the Swedish legation in London was a new and important connexion of Disraeli's – William Pyne.[79]

Pyne was a City solicitor of the firm of Pyne and Richards. His clients included Sir Francis Sykes, which was probably how Disraeli came to know him. In September 1835 Pyne patched up an agreement with a creditor named Mash, who threatened to go to law to recover the £3500 Disraeli had borrowed to pay for the Wycombe elections of 1832.[80] Pyne was useful; not only did he offer the moral support and financial security which Benjamin Austen had once provided, but he turned out to be a valuable ally against Austen. It was probably through Disraeli that Pyne was appointed solicitor to the Swedish legation.

Benjamin Austen, chasing overdue debts, grew impatient. Rumours had reached him, he wrote in March, that Disraeli was on the verge of bankruptcy, yet Disraeli merely made allusion to some 'mysterious Source of Wealth', and refused as ever to apply to Isaac. 'Do pray put an end to this correspondence by removing the cause of it,' he snapped. Disraeli's reply was to suggest Austen see Pyne, the solicitor to the legation; when, a month later, the money had still not arrived, he told Austen that 'there are no causes of delay but those of form, and which the next despatches from the Court in question may entirely remove'. Small wonder Austen's temper was wearing thin. In fact, the business of the Swedish loan came to nothing, as Austen predicted: it was floated in July, but Disraeli was not involved.[81]

'Haber again,' reads Disraeli's cryptic note in the Mutilated Diary for the spring of 1836. The 'great business' was not the Swedish loan, but a grand politico-financial scheme of the sort that fired Disraeli's imagination (he had used the same phrase to describe the affair of the *Representative* ten years before): the Carlist loan. Haber was a devoted admirer and backer of Don Carlos, the reactionary Spanish pretender, who in 1833 had rebelled against the Spanish Queen Isabella (daughter of Don Carlos's brother King Ferdinand) and her mother, Queen Regent Christina, plunging Spain into civil war. Palmerston was sympathetic to the queen. Britain did not intervene formally but Rothschild lent substantial sums, and in the summer of 1835 Palmerston sent the British Legion of over 8000 mercenary troops to fight for the queen of Spain. Metternich, on the other hand, sympathised with the Carlists; Austria was too poor to give much help, but Metternich put pressure on the Legitimist powers to subscribe to Don Carlos.

This was where Haber came into the picture, as a Carlist fundraiser. Disraeli acted (or purported to act) as Haber's English agent, negotiating with London financiers such as Sir Charles Cockerell. 'There is every prospect of my completing the great business in the course of the week with the house of Sir Chas. Cockerell and Co,' he wrote to Isaac, whom he had let into the secret at an early stage. He was unable to join Haber on a mission to Naples, but he had 'displayed so much ability in these affairs, that I am permitted to retain my original advantage subject to securing the results of the mission by my own means. All this can be done and a proper deputy properly remunerated for £1500 or £2000.'[82]

How much, if anything, Disraeli pocketed as a result of these obscure and involved transactions is not known; like most such schemes it was probably more talk than cash. Nevertheless, the fact remains that Disraeli was actively backing the enemies not only of the Whig government but of Peel, whose brief ministry of 1834–5 had broadly followed Palmerston's policy in Spain. Don Carlos was the focus of Legitimist feeling in England, and Disraeli had written a Legitimist tract in *Gallomania*. But his support for the Carlists was not ideological; he wanted a Carlist victory because it would humiliate and possibly wreck the Whig government. On 26 March, when the queen of Spain seemed on the brink of bankruptcy, Disraeli wrote triumphantly to Sarah:

> I think a catastrophe in foreign politics is impending, and after all, these may turn out the Whigs. In my strange life nothing is more remarkable than to find myself in the situation of being the focus of the most important information. See *The Times* of today. My accidental connection with that paper has led to great results. I think it is all up with the Queen of Spain. If things turn out as they promise, you will never regret my long visit to London, and I can assure you, I shall enjoy the day when I may come and have a quiet smoke at Bradenham, first embracing you all, before my lips are tainted with the fumes of Gibel [Latakian tobacco].[83]

Of course, the queen of Spain did not go under – Palmerston intervened with naval support, and though the Carlists gained the upper hand, their success did not turn out the Whigs. But the 'great business' was not the only reason for Disraeli's prolonged stay in London; there was also his connection with

The Times. Between 18 January and 14 May 1836, he contributed a series of nineteen anonymous open letters signed Runnymede, addressed mainly to members of the Whig government.

'The Letters of Runnymede are the only things talked of in London,' Disraeli told Isaac. 'The author is unknown, and will probably remain.' Runnymede was Disraeli's first contribution to *The Times*: a deliberate exercise in political abuse of the most extravagant and scabrous kind. Disraeli likened the government to 'the Swalbach swine in the Brunnen bubbles, guzzling and grunting in a bed of mire, fouling themselves and bedaubing every luckless passenger with their contaminating filth'. Spring Rice, the chancellor of the exchequer, was an 'industrious flea'; Lord Glenelg, colonial secretary, 'stretched on an easy couch in luxurious listlessness, with all the prim voluptuousness of a puritanical Sardanapalus'; Lord John Russell, leader of the House, was like the god worshipped by the Egyptians, treasured in the inmost recess of the political temple, who turns out to be – an insect! Palmerston was 'the great Apollo of aspiring understrappers', the 'Lord Fanny of diplomacy'.[84]

Runnymede succeeded in creating a sensation. Lyndhurst was delighted. 'Barnes will worship you,' he wrote. Barnes, editor of *The Times*, was nervous, however. 'You have a surprising disdain for the law of libel,' he told Disraeli, and insisted a reference be cut to Melbourne's Siren Desidia which seemed to refer to Caroline Norton, 'a very substantial Siren whose fleshly attractions are supposed to be as agreeable to Lord Melbourne as the last patent easy chair'.[85] Runnymede praised Peel, however: 'In your chivalry alone is our hope. Clad in the panoply of your splendid talents and your spotless character ...'. Peel is a knight in armour, about to slay the dragon of Radicalism. Never, writes the oily Runnymede, not even under Pitt, has the Tory party been so united as it is now under Peel.[86]

'Establish my character as a great political writer by the "Letters of Runnymede",' wrote Disraeli in his diary. There was talk, there always was, of getting into parliament, this time for St Ives: 'I hope before eight and forty hours have passed', he wrote to Sarah, 'that it may be in my power to tell you the astounding intelligence that I am an MP.' He wasn't; the Tory member for St Ives did not give up his seat. In March, however, he was elected to the Carlton on the second attempt; it was 'a great lounge ... I write in this room where are some 80 persons all of the first importance.' All seemed set fair for the Bolingbroke of his generation to leap to the centre of the political stage.[87]

EIGHT

Scrapes with Count D'Orsay

1836–7

'WE ARE now busy night and day preparing for the H. of Lords,' Disraeli told Sarah in April 1836. The session had started in the Lords, and Lyndhurst was once more plotting to stop the 'Movement'. Egged on by Ernest, duke of Cumberland, a reactionary mischiefmaker, Lyndhurst planned to destroy one of the Whigs' chief measures: the Irish Municipal Corporations Bill.

In 1835 his plan to stop the Movement and destroy the English Municipal Corporations Bill had turned into a revolt against Peel; now, however, he gained Peel's support. In the narrative he wrote of these events in September 1836, Disraeli criticised Peel as 'timid and always acting on the defensive'. He failed to see that Peel, who recoiled with priggish distaste from the backstairs intrigues of royal dukes, did not want to bring the government down until he could form one of his own. Irish municipal reform was hardly likely to destroy the government, however; and Peel, who had supported the principle of English municipal reform, heartily disliked the Irish bill, which seemed calculated to deliver Irish town councils into the hands of O'Connell's Catholic party.

Disraeli's role was to defend Lyndhurst and the Lords in the press. The Irish Municipal Bill reached the House of Lords on 18 April, and he addressed a couple of Runnymede Letters to the peers. Disraeli hated the Irish, and Runnymede excelled himself in shrill racial abuse. The Irish were a 'wild, reckless, indolent, uncertain and superstitious race' – a savage population under the influence of the papacy, whose history was 'an unbroken circle of bigotry and blood'. 'There is not a man in Britain', thundered Runnymede, 'who at the bottom of his heart is not proud of our Empire, and who does not despise the inferior race who dare to menace its integrity.'[1]

The peers amended the bill, extinguishing the Irish corporations altogether, as Peel wished; it returned to the Commons in May, where it was amended back to its original form, and in June, when it reached the Lords once more, the battle really began. Lyndhurst made a speech on 27 June which Disraeli said was a masterpiece: 'Since Canning, there has been nothing like it.' He had good reason to be enthusiastic – Lyndhurst used arguments from the *Vindication*, and Disraeli's contribution was spotted in the press: according to the *Morning Chronicle*, 'both L. and Sir R. P. are said to have adopted Mr Disraeli's view of the constitution'. Disraeli spelled out his views in a new series of Runnymede letters for *The Times*, entitled The Spirit of Whiggism; he denied the Radical charge of a collision between the Lords and the people, arguing as before that the House of Lords was, in its way, just as representative as the House of Commons. The Runnymede letters were republished in July under the title *Whigs and Whiggism*, and in his dedication to Peel Disraeli underscored the point. The constitution, he claimed, had triumphed during the present session because, thanks to Runnymede, the public mind had been cleared of a vast amount of error. No one would now claim a collision between Peers and People. 'We know very well that the House of Commons is not the House of "the People"; we know very well the "the People" is a body not intelligible in a political sense; we know very well that the Lords and the Commons are both sections of the Nation, and both alike and equally representative of that great community.'[2]

The Whigs dropped the Irish Municipal Bill, and Disraeli claimed a triumph for Lyndhurst – according to his September narrative, Lyndhurst became virtual leader of the Upper House, bowling down Whig bills like ninepins. 'Rage of the Irish party,' scrawled Disraeli. 'The country rally round Lyndhurst.' At the session's end, on 18 August, Lyndhurst delivered a set speech, reviewing the session; he and Disraeli concocted the speech in the coach returning from a visit to Henrietta at Basildon. Lyndhurst's speech 'really has made everyone quite mad', Disraeli wrote; the following day, he worked until nine o'clock preparing it as a pamphlet, which reprinted and circulated through the country in innumerable editions. In September Lyndhurst's stock was so high that Disraeli found the Carlton buzzing with rumours about the king's desire to make him premier.[3]

Disraeli was pleased with his own advance that session. 'Resume my acquaintance with Sir Robt. Peel,' he jotted in his diary in September. 'My influence greatly increased from the perfect confidence of L. and my success as a political writer.' The meeting with Peel took place at a dinner held by Chandos at Greenwich on 18 July. 'I was the only person there not a member of Parliament,' Disraeli told Sarah; Peel 'came up to me and resumed our acquaintance most flatteringly'. But for every rung of the ladder he climbed, a viper was ready to sting his heel. Later that week, Peel asked him to dine with a party of the late government at the Carlton. 'Is it safe?' he whispered in a note to Pyne. 'I fear not.' He lived in fear of being publicly exposed by his creditor Mash, a money-lending courtier; back in March, when it had been rumoured at the Carlton that Disraeli's return to parliament was imminent, Mash had closed in, fearful that MPs' immunity from arrest would place Disraeli beyond his clutches.[4]

Parliamentary immunity was much needed; his income had dwindled to nothing. Isaac made regular payments to Ralph and Jem, but his bank books show no allowance to Benjamin; presumably Benjamin had spent the principal on his early South American speculations. For his political journalism, which was prolific in 1835–6, he received nothing; he wrote, as he later explained, to connect himself with Lyndhurst, and to establish a claim upon him which might some day be useful. When Haber's schemes failed to turn to gold, Disraeli was driven back to novel writing. In June he made an agreement with Colburn to deliver a novel in the autumn, 'for a greater sum than I have ever yet received'. Isaac, intent on a political career for his son, was dismayed. 'How', he asked, 'will the fictionist assort with the politician? Most deeply am I regretting that you find it necessary to return to drink of the old waters.' Isaac was living in an unreal world; he had not an inkling of the scale of his son's debts.[5]

The novel was *Henrietta Temple*. One volume was already finished, written at Bradenham during the lovesick autumn of 1834, at the start of the affair with Henrietta. When Disraeli returned to the manuscript and picked up the strings of the story two years later, his affair was running aground.

In the spring of 1836 she moved into a house in Park Lane, which she furnished, Disraeli wrote, with 'lavish and enchanting taste'. She was more extravagant than ever, taking an opera box 'in the best situation', and 'Miladi is having her portrait taken by Maclise'.[6] Daniel Maclise was a handsome, lusty Irishman and notorious philanderer. His medievalist watercolour of the Sykes family depicts Henrietta in full sail and gorgeous; very soon she became the painter's lover. Her involvement with Maclise is usually blamed for the break-up of her relationship with Disraeli but the truth may have been more complicated. According to Rosina, Bulwer's wife, writing in 1855, '[Maclise's] and Disraeli's intriguing *en partie carrée* [party of four] with Lady Sykes at the same time as Lord Lyndhurst, was the first honourable stepping-stone of the be-puffed artist's and the trading politician's fortunes'. That Disraeli connived at Henrietta's intimacy with Maclise in the summer of 1836 is conceivable: 'Maclise, a painter' is the cryptic entry in his diary in September, giving little away. Maclise was an old friend; the Disraeli family had been among the first to spot the painter's talent on his arrival from

Ireland and he had drawn Disraeli's portrait in 1828 and again for *Fraser's* in 1833.[7]

In August 1836 Disraeli and Lyndhurst stayed at Basildon on a 'visit of charity' – Sir Francis had returned unexpectedly from abroad, descending with 'a train of savage men', Disraeli told Sarah, 'three or four foreign servants, and all his hangers on and toadeys [*sic*] – dreadful'. Sykes suffered from an eye disorder, and one of his attendants was an eye specialist; but Disraeli thought Sykes crazed. Not knowing what to do with himself, he had tossed a ducat as to whether he should return home – 'It unfortunately came down heads and here he is – ill, I think dying and very frenzied'.[8] Nor was he harmless. He could be cruel to Henrietta; in Maclise's family group, Sykes stands in the rear, a vengeful and oddly menacing figure, eyes closed, brandishing over his wife's head a weapon which looks like nothing so much as a gigantic phallus.

Henrietta's fecklessness, her husband's insanity – the Sykes ménage was becoming a nightmare, hurtling dizzily towards disaster. Disraeli wanted to escape, and at the end of August he retreated to Bradenham. He had been writing hard since June, when he stayed with Bulwer, and at Bradenham he shut himself in his room and wrote unceasingly. On 25 September he told Pyne, 'I have no pecuniary cares for the next three months, and I wish if possible to reap a great harvest in this serene interval, and finish, or nearly so, a second novel for Jany., getting the forthcoming one out in the very early part of Novr.' He was still troubled by Mash – was it safe, he asked Pyne, to go up to London? 'Shall I go to Paris?', but his finances had become suddenly stable.[9]

The clue to Disraeli's unwonted calm is given by a puzzling entry in the Mutilated Diary for September 1836: 'the singular good services of Pyne to me'. Pyne seems to have evolved a complex, subtle 'system', as Disraeli called it, for keeping Disraeli afloat. He juggled with debts and creditors, put his name to Disraeli's bills, renewed old bills, often at exorbitant rates of interest – 40% was quite usual – and plugged the holes in Disraeli's leaking credit-worthiness. The 'system' was a knotted tangle of bills, debts and moneys accounted for several times over, which defies unravelling. Taking advantage of the respite provided, Disraeli scribbled novels for Colburn. He anticipated between £3000 and £4000 being poured into his coffers by May, he told Pyne in November, 'but the ships, though built and building, are not yet launched, and ... I doubt whether on our present system I can hope effectively to assist you before the Spring. Do you think the present system can be maintained?'[10]

The system evidently depended on money, several thousand pounds, advanced by Pyne against the security of Disraeli's novels; given the extraordinarily precarious state of Disraeli's finances, it is hard to see where

Pyne could have raised this sum. One suggestion is that he syphoned the money out of the account of another of his clients: Sir Francis Sykes. In 1835, at Disraeli's instance, Sir Francis had authorised Pyne to pay Henrietta an allowance of £1800 during his absence abroad; in 1838 Sir Francis claimed that Pyne and Richards had paid out £2000 in excess of Henrietta's allowance during 1836–7 and, though there is no direct proof, it seems probable that this money went to Disraeli.[11] Not only did Disraeli cuckold Sir Francis; he stole his money.

Henrietta Temple. A Love Story is the story of Disraeli's affair with Henrietta Sykes. Ferdinand Armine, the hero, is the only child of a proud, depressed Catholic aristocrat and heir to an estate crippled by mortgages. He has a duty to restore the Armine family fortunes, but he betrays his parents by running deeply into debt; in an attempt to redeem himself, he becomes dutifully engaged to his cousin Katharine, an heiress, only to fall in love at first sight with Henrietta Temple. The plot hinges on Ferdinand's double engagement: Henrietta is devastated when she discovers that Ferdinand is betrothed and she is rescued by the princely Lord Montfort, to whom she becomes engaged, while Ferdinand is engulfed by debt and misery. He is extricated by the splendid Count Mirabel, a figure closely based on Count D'Orsay; in the end Ferdinand is reunited with Henrietta and Katharine marries Montfort.

Ferdinand Armine is not the Disraelian autobiographical fantasy figure we have come to expect. He is not a genius. In politics he is a Whig. But his name, Armine, is derived from Amin, Henrietta's pet name for Disraeli, and Ferdinand is a portrait of the side of Disraeli which Henrietta evoked – indolent and loungy, abandoning himself to a perpetual present. In the first volume (Books I and II), written in the autumn of 1834, he described the raptures of that summer with Henrietta, wandering in the June heat through the gardens of her home, a Palladian pavilion which is evidently Basildon. ('A façade of four Ionic columns fronted an octagon hall, adorned with statues, which led into a saloon of considerable size and fine proportion ... The lofty walls were covered with an Indian paper of vivid fancy, and adorned with several pictures which his practised eye assured him were of great merit.')[12]

Monypenny comments that the main interest of the novel lies in the first volume, which vividly describes first love at the height of its spiritual ardour and intensity.[13] Yet this first part is full of foreboding. Ferdinand's love is tainted by guilt, debt and deception, and it is hard to see how it can end other than in disaster. Already in 1834, at the height of the affair with Henrietta, Disraeli was guilty and ashamed. It is a picture not of first love but of adulterous love.

Two years later, when Disraeli took the manuscript out of its drawer, he wrote more directly about his affair. Nothing very explicit is said, but to readers of the second volume it must have been plain that Ferdinand and Henrietta have become lovers. Darlings and darling darlings clog the pages; ridiculed by critics, many were pruned by the prudent blue pencil of Sarah, when she edited the novel for a new edition in 1853. 'It is the habit of lovers', explains Disraeli, no doubt remembering Henrietta's visits to his parents' home, 'to grow every day less discreet; for every day their almost constant companionship becomes more a necessity.'[14]

'O Ferdinand!' exclaims Henrietta. 'You reason, I only feel.' Such an observation from one's mistress, comments Disraeli, is rather a reproach than a compliment. To Ferdinand, 'the prospect of separation from Henrietta, for however short a period, was absolute agony'. This was how he felt in August 1834, when he left Henrietta for Bradenham, and the letters from Henrietta to Ferdinand are so similar to Henrietta Sykes's that there can be little doubt that her letters were by him as he wrote. 'Mine own, own love! I have not laid down the whole night,' she writes. 'Write me one line, only one line, to tell me you are well. I shall be in despair until I hear from you.' Another passage pruned by Sarah from the first edition: 'My tears are too evident. See, they fall upon the page. It is stained. Kiss it, Ferdinand, just here. I will press my lips just here; do you also press yours…. I cannot write, darling. I cannot restrain my tears.'[15] Monckton Milnes, writing in 1844, singled out Henrietta's letters as 'the best we have met with in modern fiction' – high praise for Lady Sykes.[16]

Henrietta Temple is really two books. Once Disraeli has poured out the story of his affair, it turns into a fashionable novel. As Henrietta Temple is made to say, 'In a fine novel, manners should be observed, and morals should be sustained; we require thought and passion, as well as costume and the lively representation of conventional arrangements; and the thought and passion will be the better for these accessories.' The novel is still strongly autobiographical, however. Henrietta Temple is no shrinking romantic heroine; she does not stay faithful to her Ferdinand and pine away for love. True to the life of Henrietta Sykes, she becomes betrothed to someone else: Lord Montfort, 'a man of as romantic a temperament as Ferdinand; but with Lord Montfort, life was the romance of reason; with Ferdinand, the romance of imagination'.[17] Ferdinand is enraged at Henrietta's betrayal:

When he recollected how he had loved this woman, what he had sacrificed for her, and what misery he had in consequence entailed upon himself and all those dear to him; when he contrasted his present perilous situation with her triumphant prosperity, and remembered that while he had devoted himself to a love which proved false, she who had deserted him was, by a caprice of

fortune, absolutely rewarded for her fickleness; he was enraged, he was
disgusted, he despised himself for having been her slave; he began even to hate
her. Terrible moment when we first dare to view with feelings of repugnance
the being that our soul has long idolised! It is the most awful of revelations. We
start back in horror, as if in the act of profanation.[18]

On the evidence of *Henrietta Temple*, Disraeli was no longer in love with
Henrietta Sykes in the autumn of 1836. Ferdinand's attention shifts from his
love to his debts, and the last books of the novel are dominated not by
Henrietta but by Count D'Orsay/Mirabel. We leave Henrietta's world of
soft bowers and summer shade for D'Orsay's male world of debts and
'scrapes' – scrapes, it has been rightly pointed out, is the key word of the later
chapters.[19] Disraeli/Ferdinand is glimpsed in a gloomy quarter off Regent
Street called Golden Square, in the dingy, ugly and overfurnished office of
Mr Levison, a money lender. Mr Levison is Jewish, but he is a screw and
Disraeli has no sympathy for him. 'No fellow is ever dished who has any
connection,' says someone. 'So long as a man bustles about and is in a good
set, something always turns up.' The good set is to be found at Crockford's,
where the genial Mr Bond Sharpe presides over a society of waggish good
fellows, whose leader is the glamorous Count Mirabel/D'Orsay. 'Capital',
observes Disraeli, 'is a wonderful thing. But we are scarcely aware of this fact
until we are past thirty; and then, by some singular process, which we will not
now stop to analyse, one's capital is in general sensibly diminished. As men
advance in life, all passions resolve themselves into money. Love, ambition,
even poetry, end in this.' Debt is not disgrace, it is a way of life, an
adventure.[20]

One morning, as Ferdinand is lying in bed in his hotel, the door bursts
open, and he is arrested by the bailiffs, and taken to a sponging house or
debtors' prison. Count Mirabel appears, regales Ferdinand with champagne,
and pays off his debts. Whether Disraeli himself had ever been committed to
the type of sponging house he described so authentically is debatable. Henry
Baillie later claimed that he witnessed the scene described in the novel, when
Disraeli was rescued by D'Orsay; the incident remembered was probably
Disraeli's arrest during the quarrel with the O'Connells in 1835, when Baillie
acted as his second.[21]

As Professor Vincent wrote, 'For a love story, there is a great deal of male
bonding going on. We feel that the author, if asked to choose between perfect
passion and having Count Mirabel as a chum, might be hard put to it.'
D'Orsay over Henrietta; perhaps it was a choice Disraeli had already made.
Henrietta Temple was dedicated to D'Orsay, the real hero of the book. 'Je

regrette seulement que Mirabel ait fait connaissance avec Armine dans un Hell,' was D'Orsay's comment.[22]

Henrietta Temple was published on 1 December. Reviewers called it clever but affected, high-flown but foolish; the *Literary Gazette* found the love-making overstrained and exaggerated; *The Times* thought the love scenes too detailed and balked at Henrietta's love letters. The severest critics were Disraeli's friends. The novel disappointed Lady Blessington and D'Orsay, both of whom judged it not 'worthy' of Disraeli: 'If I thought less highly of your Genius I dare not risk telling you this,' wrote Lady Blessington, painfully candid despite the novel being dedicated to D'Orsay. Disraeli was slightly ashamed of it; though he 'boldly defended it' to Bulwer, he told Beckford, whose critical opinion he valued highly, that it was not worth reading. It was too popular, too commonplace, too uncritically and soppily sentimental. It was pap. For these very reasons, it was a commercial success.[23]

'Tears, tears, tears!' was the one report on *Henrietta Temple* Bulwer heard at Lady Charlotte Bury's. At Strathfieldsaye Lady Wilton said the book had made her cry so much that she excited everyone's curiosity. It sold. Colburn met Disraeli with a smiling face. 'He says he shall not be content unless he works it up like [Bulwer's] "Pelham",' Disraeli told Sarah. By February 1250 copies had been sold – his briskest sale since *Vivian Grey*. Colburn said (Disraeli told Sarah on 19 December), 'if I can only manage to get out another book this season, of a deep and high interest, he thinks I shall have regained at a bound all the lost ground of the last 3 years in this sort of work'.[24]

During the writing of *Henrietta Temple*, Disraeli still found time for politics, despite his debts and the pressures of Pyne's system. In August 1836 he became a justice of the peace for Bucks and made occasional sallies from Bradenham to take part in county business. Lyndhurst spent the autumn in Paris, and Disraeli's political stage shifted to the county of Bucks, with the magnifico Lord Chandos playing the role of Carabas to his Vivian Grey. All over the country that autumn the Conservatives were feasting and spouting, and in Bucks they were rallied by Chandos. Though he had given up hope of winning Wycombe, Disraeli valued his patronage; in wilder moments he even dreamed of buying an estate and sitting for the county.

Chandos was the head of the agricultural interest: his influence at Westminster depended on the name he had made for himself as the Farmers' Friend, the leader of the jolly Bucks yeomen. Having gained the vote for the farmer with the Chandos Clause, he founded a Bucks Agricultural Association which agitated for the repeal of the Malt Tax and agricultural protection.[25] That autumn Disraeli spoke at a dinner of the South Bucks Agricultural Association at Salthill, and denied that the meeting was nothing to do with politics. This touched a raw nerve with the Bucks farmers, who felt uneasy at the implication that they were engaging in the unrespectable and subversive business of extra-parliamentary politics. Disraeli was obliged to issue an address explaining his speech. 'Conscious that a party feeling, neither impelled, nor ought to impel, our conduct,' he wrote, 'we have of late fallen into the fatal error of declaring that our purposes are not *political*.' Political action on the part of the farmers was imperative, he claimed. 'There are I think more than intimations of an impending and very hostile attack upon the agricultural interest of this country.... I have long perceived that it is the intention of a certain party in the State, to resolve all political differences into one great contention between TOWN and COUNTRY.'[26]

His address prefigures quite strikingly the politics of the 1840s, which hinged on the conflict of town and country. In Bucks, the agricultural campaign continued with a grand Conservative dinner of the whole county at Aylesbury on 9 December, where Disraeli was to propose a toast to Lyndhurst and the House of Lords. 'It will be a grand and interesting spectacle,' Disraeli told D'Orsay, whom he pressed to come, 'and one to which you are perhaps strange.' He wrote to Pyne a few days before, 'I trust there is no danger of my being nabbed by Mash, as this would be a fatal contretemps, inasmuch as in all probability, I am addressing my future constituents.' Prompted by Disraeli, Barnes of *The Times* sent reporters and the dinner gained wide publicity. According to the *Spectator*, 'the speaking, as a whole, was as stupid as usual, except Mr Disraeli, who, after a little of his usual rhodomontade about the Peers being the founders of liberty, grew abusive and amusing.' His most virulent abuse was reserved as usual for O'Connell, a safe target, against whom he quoted Dean Swift. 'These are the last howls of a dog dissected alive –' delighting his audience.[27]

This speech was a hit. Up in London soon afterwards, it earned Disraeli a place at an exclusive members' dinner at the Carlton. Chandos was generous with his praise; standing with his back to the fire in a room full of men, he declared, 'Although Disraeli is here and I flatter no man, I say that that I have been in the House of Commons 20 years and never heard a speech like it.'[28] Disraeli ran into Lord Strangford, a toady of the duke of Wellington, who reported from Strathfieldsaye that the duke had grunted at dinner, 'It was the most manly thing done yet; when will he come into Parliament?' Lyndhurst wrote warmly from Paris: it would be infamous if the speech were not followed by an effort to get Disraeli into parliament, and as for Chandos, 'he is become a very important person. His hold on the country is most powerful and extensive'. Disraeli dined tête-à-tête with Bulwer, who told him his speech was the finest in the world and his novel *Henrietta Temple* the very worst.[29]

'There is no news,' Disraeli ended his letter to Sarah on 19 December. He was less than frank: only days before he had broken with Henrietta – 'Parted for ever with Henrietta', is the bleak entry in the Mutilated Diary.

There was a row, a truly terrible row. It was about Maclise. Disraeli described it euphemistically in a letter to Bulwer a few days later: 'certain domestic annoyances that had been long menacing me, and which I trusted I might at least prevent from terminating in a disgraceful catastrophe ... burst upon my head with triple thunder.' Bulwer annotated this letter years later, 'I believe this refers to Lady Sykes who exercised an influence over him – and was implicated in an affair with David [*sic*] Maclise – then his friend.'[30]

From Henrietta, Disraeli fled to the Carlton. There he ran into Bulwer who, tactless as ever, made ill-natured remarks about Henrietta's affairs. Disraeli flared up, hotly defending her – 'I could not bear to hear a person spoken lightly of to whom I am indebted for the happiest years of my life and whom I have ever found a faithful friend,' he told D'Orsay. 'It seemed to me', he explained later to Bulwer, 'that all the barriers of my life were simultaneously failing, and that not only Love was vanishing but Friendship also.' Very soon after he quarrelled with Bulwer, he wrote to D'Orsay, confessing what he could not tell Bulwer, 'that I am overwhelmed with some domestic vexations which it is out of the power even of your friendship to soothe. Your quick, but delicate, mind will make you comprehend what I cannot venture to express.' He was fearful that D'Orsay might laugh at him for caring, 'when perhaps I ought to congratulate myself that an intimacy which must have, I suppose, sooner or later concluded, has terminated in a manner which may cost my heart a pang but certainly not my conscience'. Echoing the words of *Henrietta Temple*, he added, 'it is in vain to reason with those who feel. In calmer moments, I may be of your opinion; at present I am wretched.'[31]

The Maclise episode had at least the merit that he could end the affair – as end it he must – without treating her badly. Disraeli possessed what he described as a warm heart. It was his most attractive quality. He knew how to love. D'Orsay was the friend who saw him through. He sat up late with Disraeli, who described himself as being 'in a state of great excitement', administering much champagne and some philosophy – so much champagne that Disraeli 'did not sleep a single wink and heard every hour strike'.[32] It was *Henrietta Temple* come true.

Cutting Henrietta out of his life left many loose ends. There was the delicate matter of Lyndhurst. Disraeli still needed Lyndhurst's friendship and, as Lady Blessington advised, a breach was to be avoided at all costs: 'nothing could have a worse appearance upon the public or be more likely to give rise to reports injurious to you both.' Keeping in with Lyndhurst meant telling him about Maclise, and Disraeli wrote several letters to Paris, where Lyndhurst was enjoying himself dining out, intriguing against the government of Count Molé and making himself ridiculous by being 'married', as Disraeli put it, to four or five persons. Henrietta said that she had received several letters from Lord L., 'but I have refrained from answering them as I felt convinced by your manner he had said something of me, and to no one will I stoop. I am aware of your correspondence with him and I hear of you from Miss Copley [Lyndhurst's daughter].' But Lyndhurst needed no prompting from Disraeli to break with Henrietta. In Paris he had taken up with a Miss G, Georgiana, daughter of Lewis Goldsmith, a Jewess over thirty years younger than him, whom he was to marry in August.[33]

Disraeli left London on Christmas Eve, arriving at Bradenham just before a fall of snow blocked the road with drifts as high as a man's breast. 'This really is Xmas,' he wrote to Pyne on 26 December. 'I assure you when I reached the old hall and found the beech blocks crackling and blazing I felt no common sentiments of gratitude to that kind friend whose never tired zeal allowed me to reach my home, and is some consolation for the plague [of] women, the wear and tear of politics and the dunning of creditors. We are now howr. comparatively in still waters, thanks to your pilotage ...' Disraeli evidently assumed that the system could and would continue; despite the break with Henrietta, he still depended on Sir Francis's money. 'Let me know', he told Pyne, 'if anything occurs in Park Lane. I shall write from here to Sir F. perhaps today.'[34]

He was in a very odd state. 'I am on the whole savagely gay,' he told Pyne on 8 January, 'and sincerely glad that I am freer of encumbrances, in every sense of the word, than I was this time last year.' He was neither bitter nor angry towards Henrietta, he merely wanted her to drop into oblivion. Henrietta was not bitter either. 'What can I say sufficient to convey to you my deep admiration of your book and the extreme pleasure I felt in reading it,' she wrote of *Henrietta Temple*; she could hardly fail to be pleased with the portrait Disraeli had painted and the compliment of printing her letters. 'Your complete triumph is echoed by everyone I come near.' As for Sir Francis, of whom she was not afraid despite his mad bouts, he 'is perfectly recovered and *tolerably* kind to me – he is not in the slightest degree aware but that the sole reason for your absence from London is your application to your books and frightened me by projecting a trip to Bradenham'. She feared telling her husband about Maclise, and with good reason – she had seemingly destroyed a carefully constructed arrangement, beneficial to all parties, for the mere gratification of wantonness. Disraeli/Lyndhurst was one thing, Maclise was quite another. Even Lady Blessington, whose suffering at the hands of society and whose loyalty to her sex had led her to take Henrietta's side in the past, admitted that she had changed her mind, 'which change took place from the reports continually in circulation relatively to her forming *her* attachments'.[35]

Yet Disraeli owed much to Henrietta. True, she was possessive, gushing and demanding, but it was she, more than anyone, who cured Disraeli of the coxcombry, the affectation, conceit and superciliousness which had made him so many enemies. Benjamin Haydon, who hated Disraeli when he first met him in 1833, found him 'much improved and not so effeminate' in 1835. At Lady Blessington's, early in 1837, Crabb Robinson encountered 'a stranger whose conversation interested and even pleased me till I knew he was young Disraeli'; though prepared to dislike Disraeli, he was forced to admit himself amused.[36]

In place of Henrietta, Disraeli had D'Orsay's friendship. At six-foot-three, an intrepid horseman and foxhunter, D'Orsay was famed for his manliness, but he left no trail of women behind him. Jane Carlyle, Thomas's wife, who met D'Orsay in 1839 wrote that 'at first sight his beauty is of that rather disgusting sort which seems to be like genius, "of no sex". And this impression is greatly helped by the fantastical finery of his dress: sky-blue satin cravat, yards of gold chain, white French gloves, light drab great-coat lined with velvet of the same colour ...'[37] How emotional the relationship was between D'Orsay and Disraeli can only be guessed, but Disraeli certainly became dependent on D'Orsay's support.

Disraeli was still the prisoner of Pyne's system, and at Bradenham over Christmas he threw himself into a new novel. Another woman's name: *Venetia*. But this time Colburn wanted something 'serious and pathetic'. Not autobiography, nor politics. The new novel, he told Lady Blessington, was 'in a higher vein' than *Henrietta Temple*; 'what you and E.L.B. [Bulwer] would call "worthy of me", alias unpopular'.[38] Disraeli's novel was a study of Byron and Shelley; he was intrigued by the story of Byron's daughter, Ada, brought up by his estranged wife, Lady Annabella, in ignorance of her father.

In the snow at Bradenham Disraeli tried to imagine Ada's childhood, isolated, solitary, in an ancient hall like Bradenham itself. Taking liberties with chronology, he described the childhood of Byron too, growing up at the same time in a neighbouring gothic abbey. He wrote furiously, filling the emptiness left by Henrietta as he pictured the two children, snowed up at Christmas in the ancient hall, playing at the history of Rome – 'and now that we have conquered every place we do not know what to do'. 'The quantity I have written, and am pouring forth', he told Pyne in January 1837, 'is something monstrous. I find it a relief, and now that I have nothing else to distract my thoughts, I am resolved to ruin Colburn.' He was in treaty for Bulwer's London rooms in the Albany, which had once been Byron's: 'a

curious co-incidence of Successive Scribblers', he told Pyne; 'the spell I
suppose growing weaker every degree, and the inspiration less genuine; but I
may flare up yet and surprise you all.' He was 'bobbish', he wrote a few days
later – so much so that he was thinking of buying the neighbouring estate of
Chequers which was for sale. Not for under £40,000, he thought, more like
£50,000 because there is timber, 'but at any rate I should like to leave half the
purchase money in mortgage, if practicable'. He added a P.S. '*I enclose the
blasted bills.*'[39]

Lyndhurst's imminent return from Paris brought Disraeli up to London
in mid-January, ready, he told Pyne, to settle the affairs of the nation over
copious libations of claret. Politics resumed with Peel's speech at Glasgow on
13 January to an audience of nearly 2500 – 'indeed it is wonderful', Disraeli
wrote to Sarah, 'that the greatest conservative assembly that has yet occurred
should take place in the Manufacturing and Radical capital of Scotland.' Very
timely too was Peel's defence, not only of the Protestant churches but also of
the House of Lords, the latter cribbed, Disraeli claimed, from the
Vindication. Yet Disraeli was nonetheless critical. Peel's speech did good, he
thought, from its firm and uncompromising tone, but 'as a composition it
appears to me both solemn and tawdry; he cannot soar, and his attempts to be
imaginative and sentimental must be offensive to every man of taste and
refined feeling'. Gratifyingly, the Radical press spotted Peel's debt, if not to
Disraeli at any rate to Lyndhurst, and called him Lyndhurst's slave.[40]

Lyndhurst returned at the end of January, full of his Parisian adventures.
'He has seen everyone of note of every party and class,' Disraeli wrote,
'literary and political, Carlist, Constitutional, Republican.' Yet Lyndhurst
was less active in the House of Lords this session. He told Greville that
politics had earned him little but abuse in 1836, and he did not intend to take
so active a part; from the Whig benches, it seemed to Campbell that he
pretended to abdicate the lead in the Lords to Brougham, who was
disaffected with the Whigs, and over whom Lyndhurst acquired a complete
ascendancy. Lyndhurst was too 'amiable', too easy, and too fond of Paris; he
returned there in the early spring. There was no breach between him and
Disraeli, but Disraeli's respect for him was gone, and he gossiped maliciously
about the older man's womanising. Early in 1837 the government seemed on
the brink of resignation – 'The Whigs and Tories watch each other like a cat
and a dog, and neither will make the first move,' but Disraeli did not seek to
become involved – 'with the exception of seeing L. occasionally, I shall
devote myself to the fair Venetia.'[41]

Venetia was taking shape at Kensington Gore, in the tree-lined suburb of
Knightsbridge, where Disraeli was the guest of Count D'Orsay. Lady
Blessington had moved the year before in the name of economy to Gore

House, once Wilberforce's, which she had sumptuously furnished on credit: 'a palace it is,' wrote Disraeli, 'long galleries, crimson saloons, libraries green as spring, boudoirs blazing with reflected lights, cabinets without end, and colossal tripods'. D'Orsay lived in a perfectly appointed bachelor establishment adjoining 'Miladi', and here Disraeli stayed, fleeing London's impenetrable January fog, all-day gloom and killer influenza – 'people die here by dozens', he told Sarah, gleefully and inaccurately listing the victims. Life with Mirabel/D'Orsay suited him exactly. His own room, luxuriously equipped with writing materials – though the winter mornings were so dark he was obliged to call for candles; a long morning's writing, helped along by tea and D'Orsay's admirable pipes; dejeuner a lá fourchette [the accents are Disraeli's] at half-past one; dinner, when D'Orsay did not dine out, which was generally every other night, either tete á trois [*sic*] with Miladi, or with one or two guests such as Bulwer. To defy the influenza D'Orsay and Disraeli took medicated air baths which he claimed rendered exercise unnecessary and did his head much good.[42]

The Blessington–D'Orsay menage was very conducive to writing *Venetia*. Disraeli contributed a series of soft satirical pieces called 'A New Voyage of Sindbad the Sailor' to *The Times*, which flopped; he explained to Sarah on 3 February that 'I can think only of my new book, which entirely engrosses my mind'. A few days later, he reported that his hero Cadurcis/Byron had gone to Eton (why not Harrow?), and 'I am in the middle of the second and the most difficult book, but it is very good indeed, and I think I have overcome all difficulties'.[43]

Not that his stay at Kensington Gore was altogether free of strains. 'Miladi here writes ten hours a day; and makes 2000£ pr. ann.' Lady Blessington laboured at her novels, her poetry and her annual *Book of Beauty* (to which Disraeli was a regular contributor), harassed by decorators' bills, by the cost of maintaining her Irish poor relations, and, worst of all, by the debts of D'Orsay, incurable spendthrift and gambler. Late at night she confided bitter, pinched epigrams in her Night Thoughts Book; a bandage around her head supported her sagging chin. 'She is not entirely free from the irritability of genius,' wrote Disraeli, 'but what can be expected from such severe labour.' If Disraeli did experience the sharp side of her tongue, it was hardly surprising; his finances were leaky and rickety as ever, and he easily persuaded the pathologically generous D'Orsay to renew his bills, thus committing the already overstretched finances of Kensington Gore to the quagmire of his debts. A debtor by profession, Disraeli was a leech, borrowing unscrupulously from his friends; driven by urgent need, he was like a drug addict, blind to the moral consequences of his behaviour. When D'Orsay became cold and angry at the abuse of his hospitality, Disraeli was pathetically anxious to retain his friendship. 'Pray, my dear, dear D'Orsay,' he pleaded, 'do not quarrel with me, for if you do, I shall feel very much like a chilly person when a cloud steals over the Sun, and begin to shiver.'[44]

Debt taught Disraeli to treat his friends ruthlessly, and to lie plausibly. It was an invaluable education for parliamentary politics.

In February he was invited by Chandos to go down to Aylesbury to vote in the by-election caused by the death of James Praed, one of the members for Bucks county. At the last minute George Dashwood, a Whig, decided to contest the seat against Harcourt, the Tory candidate, throwing the Bucks Tories into a panic. At 4 p.m. on 15 February, the day before polling began, a dispatch arrived from Bucks, summoning Chandos urgently. 'Our party, tho' much the strongest, are taken by surprise and have lost their wits in the absence of their leaders,' Disraeli explained to William Pyne; 'it became absolutely necessary that Lord Chandos and myself shd. immediately proceed to Aylesbury, not only to vote the first day, but to restore order to our ranks.'[45]

Disraeli was writing to Pyne from Chandos's town house, Buckingham House, in Pall Mall. It was 3.30 a.m. on Thursday 16 February. He had not been to bed, and the carriage was at the door, he was in a state of feverish agitation. He had received a distressed letter from Pyne, urgently asking him to call that day, and he wrote to reassure Pyne that only the paramount importance of the political business on which he was engaged prevented him from attending. 'Our defeat at this moment would be a fatal blow to the Tory party,' he wrote. 'I am trying to keep my head cool, being already jaded by want of sleep.' He told Pyne he would reach him on Friday morning, trusting 'that will not be too late for your purposes, which I try to believe at this moment are not so painful as I fear they are'.[46]

That evening, Disraeli collapsed outside the George Inn, Aylesbury. He was bled with leeches and taken to Bradenham to recover, where he stayed ten days, Harcourt having meanwhile soundly defeated Dashwood, in spite of the panic of his supporters. Disraeli's family feared his collapse was epilepsy, but a London doctor assured him that it was not a fit at all, but a 'bilious swoon'. Years later a doctor told Mary Anne that his fainting was caused entirely by his smoking. *The Times* reported dramatically that Disraeli had fallen down in a fit, and his creditors, smelling death, closed in. Back in London on 27 February, Disraeli appeared in the Carlton, where he received a levée of sympathetic MPs – 'Apparently the hare had many friends,' was his grim comment to Sarah.[47]

London was not a safe place for the hare to be. In any case, it seemed unlikely that the government would arrange for any business of importance to occur before Easter, and on 4 March he returned to Bradenham. Urged by D'Orsay, Lady Blessington and Pyne, he at length resolved to do what he had avoided for so long, and make application to Isaac. Why was he so reluctant to seek Isaac's help? Benjamin Austen, who knew the family's finances, grew impatient with his endless procrastination, yet his reluctance to apply to his father was genuine. Isaac was, as Disraeli wrote, 'one of the old school', living off prudently husbanded family capital, safely invested in 3 per cent Consols.[48] He had a morbid horror of debt; socially insecure, he dreaded being disgraced in the country of his adoption and clung to solvency and capital as his son clung to his pride of race.

Isaac, who seems to have been forewarned by a letter from Lady Blessington, raised the subject on Saturday night. Disraeli could not bring himself to tell anything like the whole truth, and assured him blithely that everything was settled. Except, said Isaac, this annuity. How much, he demanded. At length Disraeli ventured to say £2000. Isaac 'looked blue, but said it must be settled'. His son, relieved, assured him that it did not press; Isaac must consult his own convenience.[49]

In plays and novels, as Disraeli told D'Orsay, the curtain descends or the volume closes at this point, and all is well; 'but in real life there is a degrading detail, that keeps the wound open'. Isaac, mortified at his son's disgrace, lectured and scolded – 'Jaw succeeds jaw with never-ending row,' wrote Disraeli, paraphrasing Horace; the scenes were the harder to endure because he had disclosed only a fraction of his indebtedness. On the very day after the talk with Isaac, the post brought a 'fatal letter' from Pyne, enclosing one from a London wine merchant, Davis and Son, threatening arrest in respect of a bill for £200 or £300 which had been dishonoured. Davis was a business connection of Pyne's, who held several of Disraeli's bills, many of which had been discounted, which meant that Disraeli did not know his creditors. In this case it was a man named Collins, whom he sought to mollify in a desperate attempt to gain time. 'I *must* be at the Assizes tomorrow, and therefore it is not wilful neglect of his business that I do not comply with his request (Sunday being a completely blank day here) ...' Meanwhile, he wrote to Archibald White, a Wycombe solicitor, once his agent, but with 'no great hopes of immediate succour', as he was already in White's debt. 'Of all things in the world,' Disraeli implored Pyne, 'pray preserve me from a Sheriff's Officer in my own county.'[50]

He tried to settle to *Venetia*. His publisher's deadline loomed in May; he had reckoned too rashly, he told Pyne after an exceptionally harassing fortnight, on the calm March and April which he needed to come up to scratch with Colburn. He felt bereft, shunned in his disgrace by his London friends, all except Chandos, who 'though stern and reserved, has a kind heart'. Much was going on, he was sure of it, but 'I have no share in it'.[51]

A disgraceful catastrophe seemed impossible to prevent. On 23 March a writ from Davis reached the Wycombe sheriff's officer, followed soon after on the London coach by young Davis himself, whose scheme it was to nab Disraeli as he sat on the magistrate's bench. Fortunately, though Market Day it was not magistrate's day; and the sheriff's officer was a partisan of Disraeli's – not only was he a creditor, but he seems to have accepted 'secret service' money from Disraeli in exchange for delivering writs in private; and 'by the energy of White and the kindness of my younger brother, who was at Market and who signed a bail bond for me, not a little astonished, as you may suppose, at the application, I still have the pleasure of dating from Bradenham House; but what tomorrow may bring I can't say, for I know nothing of the bills, when they are due or who holds them'. This was not paranoia. The arrangement whereby Davis held Disraeli's bills was part of Pyne's system, of which Disraeli was genuinely ignorant; now that Davis had lost confidence, there was no telling when the next writ would come or who would issue it. Disraeli's frantic bulletins to Pyne, carefully suppressed by Monypenny in his official biography, show how close he came to arrest, disgrace and ruin.[52]

'Now, my dear friend, what is to be done?' Disraeli asked Pyne on 23 March. He had a month to finish *Venetia* but to write the quantity required a composed mind was imperative. An application to Isaac to rescue him from Davis was out of the question. 'I really believe he would never forgive me. Indeed I do not think my family could hold up their heads under the infliction. They are so simple and unused so utterly to anything of the kind. A sacrifice of property to maintain character would be intelligible, but a sacrifice of property and character and credit first destroyed, my father would indeed have every cause to view me with bitterness.' Davis and his tribe of creditors must be kept quiet until Isaac went to London in a few weeks' time to settle the £2000. Disraeli managed to raise some money locally – bills from White, for instance, and £100 from John Nash, Isaac's Wycombe solicitor who had also acted as Disraeli's election agent. On 2 April, just as he had scrounged and scraped together enough to pay off Collins's £300, he heard that a writ had arrived, this time for £800–900, from another unknown creditor named Green, whom Disraeli, scenting a conspiracy, believed to be Davis in disguise. Davis, wrote Disraeli, was playing a deep game, deceiving Pyne, with whom he had intimate relations; convinced of Isaac's munificence, Davis had written secretly to the sheriff's officer, telling him to deliver the writ to Isaac and bully him for the money. Thank God for the friendship of the sheriff's officer; but even he was growing nervous lest his kindness brought him into a scrape. The worst of this new writ, Disraeli told Pyne, 'is that it shakes even my hold on White, even on my brother. It is such an immediate and flagrant contradiction of all my representations and most recent statements.'[53]

By now, Disraeli was on the run. Fearful of being nabbed if his whereabouts became known, he shuttled to and from London by stage coach almost daily. Having spent thirty guineas of ready money on bribes to the sheriff's officer – money well spent – he was unable to afford even his Carlton Club subscription of ten guineas; desperate to retain his last precious toehold in London, he begged Pyne to pay the bill. Chandos needed him at the Quarter Sessions at Aylesbury on 6 April, where there was talk of a writ being served – dare he show his face? 'I must be taken ill at the last minute,' he told Pyne. Reassured by Pyne, he not only attended but foolishly made a speech, which was reported in *The Times*, thus signalling his whereabouts to Davis.[54]

Since *The Times* report of his collapse in February, every possible claim had poured in. Old acquaintances such as Wycombe election bills reappeared, pressing for payment; and Benjamin Austen's familiar handwriting made its predictable appearance. In fact, Disraeli had already paid off most of the £1200 he borrowed from Austen at 2.5 per cent in January 1834. By October 1836 half the principal had been cancelled, and the interest paid. Austen continued to worry and growl and Disraeli was unable to wriggle out of a promise to pay him some of the money he received in December for *Henrietta Temple*, though he managed to delay payment to January. There was still a balance of £500 owing, and after some prevarication – the excuse this time was that the bank had stopped payment – Disraeli told Austen on 4 February 1837 that he had written to Isaac, 'a very good letter without anything disagreeable in it, mentioning no names and merely saying how I was situated with an obligation of honour as well as law'. It seems highly unlikely that this letter was ever written; after holding out for so long against Austen's insistence that he apply to Isaac, he would surely not have given in so easily, nor is there evidence that he approached Isaac before his collapse at Aylesbury. More likely, Disraeli said he had written and that Isaac was willing to help, as an inducement and guarantee, to persuade Austen to take a doubtful bill for £500. Austen seems to have succeeded in discounting the bill at over five per cent, leaving £30 owing, and it was this that he nagged Disraeli to pay. Irritated, Disraeli replied on 9 April that, having paid off £1500 of debts since December, he had never been so distressed; Austen's £30 was 'only one of a host', and he must wait for the new novel in May.[55]

It was the last dealing he had with Benjamin Austen. Mrs Austen received a copy of each of his works on publication, but Disraeli's perfunctory promises to call remained unfulfilled. Sir Philip Rose was probably understating the case when he wrote that 'after Disraeli became a great man, and especially after his marriage, both Mr Austen and his wife seemed to be suffering under a morbid feeling of slight and neglect, and were in the habit of charging him with forgetfulness of his early friends'.[56]

In April 1837 Disraeli had far more to worry about; alerted by *The Times* report of his Quarter Sessions speech, Green, impelled by Davis, issued a writ to take the person on 11 April. Imprisonment for debt was serious; it meant disgrace, not only with his family but in the eyes of the world, putting parliament out of his reach. Perhaps it was on this occasion that, forewarned by the family doctor, Dr Rose, father of Sir Philip, Disraeli jumped into a well at Wycombe to evade the sheriff's officer. The bullying Davis plainly believed, as Disraeli told Pyne, 'that my father will pay instantly writs are issued'; the opposite was the case: 'The more cause there is for alarm, the more slowly and suspiciously he would act.' The worst of it was that Disraeli could no longer rely on the support of his family: 'I have put myself in such a false position, that I can scarcely believe that my father will ever be induced to look upon it with the charity he might otherwise have done, since I have contrived to realize all those results, which he has long taught me to look upon with the greatest apprehension and mortification.'[57]

Despite the pain and anxiety, Disraeli continued to write. Only 150 pages of *Venetia* remained to be written, he told Pyne on 15 April, which he should canter through by the end of the month, 'but I find it difficult to command the Muse amid all these vexations. The form of Davis, or the unknown visage of Green, mix themselves up, by some damnable process, with the radiant countenance of my heroine, and tho' visions of spunging houses and KB [King's Bench] might have been in keeping with the last vol. of Henrietta Temple, they do not accord quite so well with the more ethereal scenes of the fair Venetia.'

Nervous about his book, he itched to be in town. Lyndhurst, about to return from Paris, seemed to think he would be lord chancellor before he reached Dover – 'I think there is something in the wind,' worried Disraeli. He was anxious too about D'Orsay, who was understandably angry that a writ had been issued against him for guaranteeing one of Disraeli's bills: 'I fear there will be some alienation of feeling,' he told Pyne on 19 April, 'as he seems vastly vexed; but God is great!' Then, a few days later he wrote to Pyne in despair, 'I conclude from your silence, that the game is up, and that our system has failed.' Only one question remained. '*Can I remain here for one week with safety and propriety?* By safety, I mean freedom from arrest; by propriety, I allude to my position with Count D'Orsay. I have not replied to his letter, because from your silence it was not in my power.'[58]

For over two months Disraeli had endured torture; isolated from his family by his debts (even Sarah knew very little), estranged from D'Orsay, his closest friend. Pyne was his only confidant, to whom he clung for salvation, and Pyne's failure to write threw him into a panic. The system still held, however; Davis was silenced, and Disraeli gained the week he needed at Bradenham to finish the book. Not the least remarkable part of the story was Disraeli's ability to write the greater part of *Venetia* under these conditions.

A week later he was in London. Isaac was there too, gouty and grumpy; too unwell to go out at night, he sat at home, Disraeli told D'Orsay, 'reading the Pickwick papers and bullying his sons'. Isaac evidently settled his son's affairs, though it is not clear how much Disraeli received, or whether he dared to ask for more than £2000. The crisis suddenly dissolves, Disraeli sends no more distress signals to Pyne, and nothing more is heard of the dastardly Davis. *Venetia* was due to come out on 11 May, almost before Disraeli's ink was dry, let alone the printer's. 'Colburn', Disraeli told Sarah, 'seems very sanguine and determined to omit no step that will ensure success.'[59]

Venetia was dedicated to Lord Lyndhurst, whose daughter Susan died in Paris two days before the book came out. The 'godmother' of *Venetia*, however, was Lady Blessington, who had taken a motherly interest in it when Disraeli stayed at Kensington Gore: 'I do not think that you will find any golden hint of our musing strolls has been thrown away upon me,' Disraeli wrote in March 1837, 'and I should not be surprised, if in six weeks, she may ring the bell at your hall door, and request admittance, where I know she will find at least one sympathising friend.'[60]

A book of 'a deep and high interest', was what Colburn had asked for in December 1836. In Byron and Shelley, Disraeli chose a subject which was apparently entirely outside his experience. Venetia, the poet's daughter of the title, is a fatherless child brought up by her mother Lady Annabel in isolation in an ancient hall. In a nearby abbey is the little Lord Cadurcis, another fatherless child. Cadurcis is Byron; Venetia's absent father (Marmion Herbert) Shelley. Shelley, or rather the *idea* of Shelley, dominates the book. Venetia is obsessed with the mystery of her missing father. Shelley's poetry inspires Cadurcis/Byron, who takes London by storm, wins Lady Caroline Lamb, fights a duel, is disgraced. In Italy he meets Shelley, now older and mellowed; here Venetia is reunited with her father, and Lady Annabel with her husband, but the idyll is shattered when the two poets are drowned sailing off Spezia.

The events Disraeli described were very recent; Byron had died only thirteen years before, and many of the characters were still alive. Disraeli's solution was to set his story fifty years back, at the time of the American War of Independence, and to conflate the two poets' lives. To Shelley, who is made a generation older than Byron, is given Byron's wife of one year, Lady Annabella, and Byron's daughter Ada; while Byron is given Shelley's death by drowning at sea. The Whig *Edinburgh Review* nevertheless refused to discuss the novel in detail on the grounds of its intrusiveness; though Lady Caroline Lamb was no longer living, she had been the wife of the ruling Whig prime minister, Melbourne.[61]

The lives of Byron and Shelley was a strange subject to choose. No doubt Disraeli reckoned that the poets' glamour would sell the book. He had access, too, to inside information. Lady Blessington, who had known Byron in Italy (she published her *Journal of the Conversations of Lord Byron* in 1834) primed Disraeli with stories about the real Byron behind the public mask; and at Gore House Disraeli met Trelawney, who had been present at Shelley's death. On the face of it, however, *Venetia* is out of character for Disraeli; a novel with no autobiography, no politics, no agenda.

Cadurcis, it is true, bears a slight resemblance to Disraeli. The poet's childhood – his boyhood rages, his quarrels with his mother – is described with an empathy and psychological insight unusual in Disraeli. Consciously or not, he seems to be evoking his own experience. Like Contarini or Alroy, Cadurcis broods in secret about his destiny, and he is fiercely proud of his race. 'Power and pomp, ancestral fame, the legendary respect of ages, all that was great, exciting, and heroic, all that was marked out from the commonplace current of human events ...' His ancestors had conquered in France and Palestine, and Cadurcis feels the power of emulating them; but, 'What career was open in this mechanical age to the chivalric genius of his race?'[62] Like Vivian Grey, Contarini and Alroy, Cadurcis achieves fame at a precociously early age and impetuously throws it all away, as Disraeli had done.

Yet Cadurcis/Byron does not engage Disraeli's sympathies; not once are we told that he is a genius or a man of imagination. A hearty ex-Etonian of robustly orthodox opinions, he boasts, 'I have not a grain of poetry in my composition.' At Cambridge he discovers Shelley's poetry; it is a revelation. Cad, as Disraeli referred to his hero in his letters, takes the London of 1784 by storm, and, soon forgetting Herbert's philosophy, delivers himself up to 'the absorbing egotism which had ever been latent in his passionate and ambitious mind'. Disraeli repeatedly stresses Byron's egotism and vanity; he makes a critic describe Byron's verse as 'Exaggerated passion, bombastic language, egotism to excess, and, which perhaps is the only portion that is genuine, mixed with common-place scepticism and impossible morals, and a sort of vague, dreamy philosophy, which, if it mean anything, means atheism, borrowed from his idol, Herbert, and which he himself evidently does not comprehend'. The jaunty, swaggering dandy of Don Juan, the Byron whom Disraeli had admired so much ten years before, is exposed as a spoiled and petted darling, dining affectedly on biscuits and soda water. Disraeli has come a long way since *The Young Duke*.[63]

In *Venetia*, Shelley's sun dulls Byron's flame. Antichrist or angel? Which is the true Shelley, Disraeli soon reveals. 'Young, irresistibly prepossessing in his appearance, with great eloquence ... an ardent imagination and a subtle mind', he is both philosopher and poet. No mere sceptic, Disraeli's Shelley is a visionary with a faith of his own; a utopian and an idealist, a genius. Even his higher nonsense is sympathetically described:

> In politics a violent republican, and an advocate, certainly a disinterested one, of a complete equality of property and conditions, utterly objecting to the very foundation of our moral system, and especially a strenuous antagonist of marriage, which he taught himself to esteem not only as an unnatural tie, but as eminently unjust towards that softer sex, who had been so long the victims of man; discarding as a mockery the received revelations of the divine will; and, if no longer an atheist, substituting merely for such an outrageous dogma a subtle and shadowy Platonism ...[64]

Disraeli's admiration for Shelley has perhaps been underestimated. The *Revolutionary Epick* was inspired by Shelley, or rather cribbed from him. It was brave of Disraeli to portray Shelley so sympathetically at a time when his reputation was in eclipse, darkened by scandal. Yet this only makes *Venetia* the more puzzling. Why risk a sympathetic portrait of a libertine at a time when his entry into parliament as a Tory was far from certain? Perhaps Disraeli's revolutionary mind still pulled him; perhaps *Venetia* was the last protest of Disraeli the subversive before orthodoxy engulfed him. But this is not really a novel of protest, nor is Disraeli writing primarily about politics. The most engrossing part of the novel is the beginning, the first two books, written at Christmas 1836 after the break with Henrietta, describing the childhoods of Cadurcis and Venetia and her mother Lady Annabel. 'There are three characters in whom one has an interest at once,' wrote Crabb Robinson. As Professor Schwarz has argued, *Venetia* is really about family ties, about childhood and the relations between parents and children.[65] A parent's friendship, says Disraeli, is the only one that can be depended upon:

> All other intimacies, however ardent, are liable to cool; all other confidence, however unlimited, to be violated.... As for women, as for the mistress of our hearts, who has not learnt that the bosom on which we have reposed with idolatry all our secret sorrows and sanguine hopes, eventually becomes the

very heart that exults in our misery and baffles our welfare? ... Love is a
dream, and friendship a delusion. No wonder we grow callous; for how few
have the opportunity of returning to the hearth which they quitted in levity or
thoughtless weariness, yet which alone is faithful to them; whose sweet
affections require not the stimulus of prosperity or fame, the lure of
accomplishments, or the tribute of flattery; but which are constant to us in
distress, and console us even in disgrace![66]

Breaking with Henrietta left Disraeli more than ever appreciative of the
family he had spurned, wistfully nostalgic for the lost security of childhood.
To the world he was savagely gay, but *Venetia* gives glimpses of a domestic
tenderness which he normally kept well hidden. Perhaps, as one critic
suggested, 'It may not be too much to see both Cadurcis's intellectual
recognition of Marmion's worth and Venetia's emotional reconciliation with
her father as indications of Disraeli's own increasing appreciation of his
father.'[67] But the true significance of *Venetia* lies in Disraeli's recognition that
he has changed. In a sense, it is a work of exorcism. The critical portrait of
Byron signals his repudiation of his Byronic youth. The Shelley whom he
idealises is not the youthful libertine but the older, mellowed Shelley who
exists only in Disraeli's imagination, a family man, saintlike father and
wisdom figure. 'Once I sacrificed my happiness to my philosophy, and now I
have sacrificed my philosophy to my happiness.' There was hope even for a
libertine and a revolutionary, an Alcibiades like Disraeli himself.[68]

   Venetia is the most literary of his novels, scattered with classical allusions.
But his ambitious intentions are frustrated by the execution, which is hasty
and slipshod; he described the book to Lady Blessington as one of his 'plaster
of Paris casts, or rather statues of snow that melt as soon as they are
fashioned'. By the time he neared the end of the novel, he was worn to a
ravelling, at times near-hysterical about his debts, and *Venetia* suffered. 'I
hope my inspiration has not been much diluted by these distractions,'
Disraeli told Pyne, 'but I am a little nervous.'[69] He plagiarised, borrowing a
celebrated passage from Macaulay's 'Essay on Byron' ('no spectacle [is] so
ridiculous as the British public in one of its periodical fits of morality'). 'The
fellow has plundered me impudently,' wrote Macaulay when the plagiarism
was exposed in 1852; but to be fair to Disraeli he did preface his borrowing
with the words, 'It has been well observed that ...' Towards the end, as his
deadline loomed, Disraeli lumped in a slab of Cervantes and pages of
dialogue lifted from Shelley's little-known *Discourse on the Manners of the
Ancients.*[70]

   Disraeli told Beckford that *Venetia* was 'more in our way' than *Henrietta
Temple*, 'tho' adulterated enough with commonplace, I hope, to be popular'.

To Sara Austen he wrote, 'I am very glad you like "Venetia"; but for myself I have not had time to look her over since her appearance, or even to glance at a single review.' Of course he scanned the reviews, telling his sister that there had been several, 'all very laudatory', taking their tone from *Fraser's Magazine*, which had eulogised the book. Bending over backwards to discover in *Venetia* a Conservative text, *Fraser's* reviewer turned a blind eye to Disraeli's sympathy for Shelley's revolutionary creed, pointing instead to the resignation and religious spirit of his female characters which, thought the reviewer, was well calculated to strengthen and confirm the wives and daughters of the middle class in those principles of morality and religion essential to permanent happiness.[71]

In October the *Edinburgh Review* advertised a lengthy notice of both *Venetia* and *Henrietta Temple*. 'Very kind of the Whigs,' wrote Disraeli, bracing himself for a savage assault – 'I am howr. perfectly callous.' The reviewer attacked the two works as crudely and hastily executed, and criticised Disraeli's extravagance of feeling, his falsetto straining for effect, his plunges into wild passion too early in the book. Disraeli expressed himself surprised to find 'a mild, and even laudatory criticism; considering the quarter, a very favourable one'. But the *Edinburgh* reviewer did ask a pertinent question: whether 'Mr D'Israeli' was capable of producing a really good work of fiction. Being a Whig, the reviewer naturally thought not – 'He appears to us to want some of the most essential elements of a great novelist.' He had failed to fulfil the early promise of *Vivian Grey*.

Many disinterested critics would have agreed.[72]

Disraeli frankly did not care. His debts behind him, he set his sights on politics. In London he found the Carlton humming with the Westminster election. In a move that echoed Disraeli's change of party, Sir Francis Burdett, the patrician Radical member for Westminster, had resigned his seat and was seeking re-election as a Tory. Bonham, the Conservative organiser, set up a committee, and Disraeli volunteered to canvass. He was given the district of Mayfair, which included one street entirely filled with cooks, chiefly foreigners; he later described this genteel colony of servants in the opening pages of *Tancred*. 'I have been very successful in my canvass,' he told Sarah, 'but I cannot judge of the result from that, as mine was an aristocratic division. I have gained great credit as a canvasser; when the gentlemen are out, I always ask for the ladies.' Bonham, he reported, had told the Committee that 'if all had exerted themselves like Cecil Forester and Disraeli, we shd have beat in a canter'. Burdett's victory on 11 May was a triumph for the Tories and, writing in his diary that autumn, Disraeli claimed the credit – 'distinguished myself very much in the election of

Burdett for Westminster ... the success mainly attributable to myself, proposed and organised the youth of the Carlton including all the nobility, fashion and influence of our party to canvass'.[73]

The London season rolled on. Disraeli partied, picked up gossip at the Carlton, canvassed MPs' support for George Stephenson in the hotly contested battle over the London to Brighton railway, and dreamed again of becoming a country gentleman. 'Have the kindness to let me know about the estate,' he wrote grandly to Pyne, 'so that I may write into Bucks ...' This from a man who had narrowly escaped debtors' prison a few weeks before. Lord Francis Egerton, millionaire son of the duke of Bridgewater, invited him to the best assembly of the season, a grand concert at Bridgewater House, a thousand persons and the picture gallery illuminated – 'I enjoyed myself excessively,' he told Sarah.[74]

At Windsor, King William IV lay dying, and a general election loomed. 'The King dies like an old lion,' Disraeli said. William IV died early in the morning of 20 June, and a few hours later the young queen met the Privy Council at Kensington Palace. Lyndhurst attended and Disraeli accompanied him; as they drove from the Palace, Lyndhurst told Disraeli how he kissed the queen's hand which was 'remarkably sweet and soft. She read her address well and was perfectly composed tho' alone in the council chamber and attended by no woman.' Though Disraeli later romanticised the scene of Victoria's Privy Council in *Sybil*, at the time he grudged admiration for the young queen. She was after all the friend of the Whigs: 'I fear the prestige in favour of royalty is confined now to the possessors of property,' he wrote after attending the prorogation on 17 July, when he noted the crowd remained sourly silent.[75]

The new reign threw politics into a tumult. 'I write in the midst of 3 or 400 persons and in a scene of great excitement,' Disraeli scribbled from the Carlton on 20 June. 'The battle now approaches; what will be my fate I pretend not to foresee.' The dissolution was expected in mid-July, yet he had no seat. Barnstaple, where he was negotiating to succeed his friend Major Fancourt, who was retiring, was a possibility, but nothing was settled. He hung around the Carlton, which was full until long past midnight – 'deputations from the country, permanent committees, places that want candidates and candidates that want places'.[76] Ten days went by with no seat, the dissolution drew nearer, and Disraeli's excitement turned to an agony of suspense, so tormenting that he could barely write to Sarah. He penned a brief and anxious note to her early on 30 June, then a few hours later wrote: 'My darling, The clouds have at length dispelled, and my prospects seem as bright as the day. At 6 o'clock this evening I start for Maidstone with Wyndham Lewis, who tells me that he can command 750 plumpers alone out of the 1400 votes. I suppose by Wednesday I shall have completed my canvass. I write in greatest haste and with my love to all. I am, yr D'[77]

Wyndham Lewis was the husband of Mary Anne, 'a pretty little woman, a flirt and a rattle', whom Disraeli had met in 1832; elderly and wealthy, he was a partner in the Guests' Dowlais ironworks at Merthyr, and had sat for Maidstone since 1835. Maidstone was a two-member borough, and it was rumoured that the second member, a Whig named Robarts, was not standing. An early canvass convinced Wyndham Lewis that there was a chance for a second Tory; a deputation was sent to the Carlton, Disraeli's name was mentioned among the candidates wanting places, and Wyndham Lewis, prompted by his wife, snapped him up.

Maidstone was notoriously corrupt. In 1835 Greville, the diarist, noted a conversation with Robarts, who told him that 'the one prevailing object among the whole community is to make money out of their votes'. Such boroughs were predisposed towards the Whigs and reform because of the envy, sour dissatisfaction and resentment of the electorate: 'When they contrast their own life of labour and privation with the wealth and splendour which they see around them, there is little difficulty in persuading them that they are grievously wronged, and that the wrong is in the nature of the institutions themselves.'[78] The Tories' chances depended on paying more for votes than the Whigs, which Wyndham Lewis was wealthy enough to do; there were hints too that the Tories might counter the Whiggism of envy by attacking the Whig Poor Law of 1834, which pressed hard upon the borough's poor.

Disraeli arrived in Maidstone as Wyndham Lewis's candidate, and for the first two days he canvassed 'on the strength of WL's personal influence which from his influence and munificence is very great'. On 3 July he spoke at a public meeting in the evening, writing nervously to Pyne minutes before his speech to stymie an angry creditor. 'For God's sake take care no writ comes down from him. I was glad to find the Sheriff's Officer here among my staunch supporters; I suppose gratitude.' In his speech he denounced the Poor Law. Peel and the Tories had supported the bill in parliament, but Disraeli claimed to have been the first county magistrate to raise his voice against it after John Walter, the owner of *The Times*, who began the anti-Poor Law campaign. The bill, declared Disraeli, was founded on a moral error – 'it went on the principle that relief to the poor is a *charity*. I maintain that it is a *right!*' By cancelling outdoor relief and immuring the poor man in the workhouse as in a prison, it deprived him (said Disraeli, evoking a scene from George Morland) of the consolation of witnessing the games of his grandchildren and viewing the tombs of his forefathers. He spoke for an hour; it was, he told Sarah unblushingly, 'the best speech I ever made yet';

thereafter he canvassed on his own influence. 'It seems to me', he wrote, 'that all the strength and property of the Boro' are on our side, and opposition to the Poor Law makes us popular with the multitude.' On 8 July, having completed their canvass, he and Wyndham Lewis issued an address, coupling opposition to the Poor Law with defence of the Protestant constitution (Maidstone had numerous Dissenters): 'It will be our object to resist that Liberalism in politics, which it seems, is only another phrase for an attack upon the Protestant Religion and the English Poor.' By 5.30 that afternoon he was back in London. 'I have JUST returned,' he scrawled to Sarah, 'having completed a most TRIUMPHANT CANVASS.'[79]

The queen dissolved parliament on 18 July, and Disraeli stayed in London for another week before returning to Maidstone, where the nomination meeting was held on 26 July. The Whig Robarts finally retired and several of his supporters seceded to Disraeli – presumably not without payment. Confident of an uncontested election, Disraeli became bullish. 'It was thought impossible in these times that a man cd enter Pt for the first time for a Boro' in such a manner ... So much for the "maddest of all mad acts", my uncle G's [George Basevi's] prescience, and B.E.L.'s [Lindo's] unrivalled powers of Encouragement,' he wrote, referring to his latest unsuccessful attempt to persuade his Basevi relations to pay his election expenses.[80]

Three days before nomination day, however, there appeared in Maidstone, having lost his seat in Hull, Colonel Perronet Thompson, owner of the *Westminster Review*, who stood as a Radical, making a contest inevitable and apparently justifying the Basevis' scepticism. Disraeli's dandified appearance on the hustings on 26 July astonished the people of Maidstone, as was no doubt his intention; the mob howled abuse, and his speech on the hustings was punctuated with cries of 'Shylock', 'Old Clothes', and offers of ham and bacon. 'Mr Disraeli – I hope I pronounce his name right,' declared Perronet Thompson's proposer, sarcastically referring to his rival's origins; 'Colonel Perronet Thompson – I hope I pronounce his name aright,' retorted Disraeli in a speech the next day. For the first time in his electioneering career, he lost on the show of hands; Wyndham Lewis's generosity, however, guaranteed his return in the contest that ensued – as carpers were quick to point out, his seat was bought by Wyndham Lewis, and had little to do with his merits as a candidate. He spent polling day whirling round the borough with the Lewises, he and Mary Anne screaming with laughter as the women clasped the struggling Wyndham in their arms and kissed him again and again. At eleven o'clock he reported the state of the poll to Sarah: Lewis 707; Disraeli 616; Colonel Thompson 412; and he signed himself, DIZZY. The final state of the poll was: Wyndham Lewis 782; Disraeli 668; Perronet Thompson 559; Perry 25.[81]

Parliament at last! He hastened to Bradenham to celebrate, astonished and proud to find Wycombe plastered with placards proclaiming his victory, the news having been celebrated the day before with bell-ringing, illuminations and a band, which paraded till long after midnight. Yet his triumph was threatened by scandal. 'During the election', he wrote in his diary, 'occurred the terrible catastrophe of Henrietta, exactly one year after we had parted.' She was discovered by Sir Francis in bed with Maclise in her house in Park Lane. Poor, foolish Henrietta; she was disgraced. Sir Francis, cruelly vindictive, removed her children, shut her out of the house late at night, confiscated her clothes and jewels; not content with this, he placed an advertisement, broadcasting her adultery, and instituted proceedings against Maclise. It was a wretched, sordid business, potentially damaging to Disraeli on account of a 'monstrous story' circulating: that £2000 which Sir Francis alleged was paid to Henrietta by Pyne and Richards in excess of her allowance had found its way into Disraeli's pocket.[82]

Henrietta did not vanish altogether. She reappears under the protection of an unnamed baronet, 'remarkable for his wealth and the cultivation of such branches of the arts as a lavish expenditure of money amongst upholsterers, picture dealers, and dealers in virtu can command'. Both rich and extravagant, the baronet sounds almost too good to be true. Intriguingly, Henrietta entered Gladstone's life in 1845, when he called to see her magnificent Raphael, which he thought eclipsed all her pictures and nearly every other.[83]

Disraeli survived the Henrietta scandal, his hand held by yet another older woman: Mary Anne Lewis. She called him her Parliamentary Protégé – 'Mark what I say,' she told her brother after the election, '... mark what I prophesy – Mr Disraeli will, in a very few years be one of the greatest men of his day.' Equally telling was the verdict of another woman Disraeli met that July: Lady Salisbury, effortlessly intelligent wife of the second marquess, mother of one Conservative prime minister and grandmother of another. Disraeli, she thought, bore the mark of the Jew very strongly about him, and his way of speaking reminded her so much of Lord Lyndhurst that she almost thought he was in the room. 'He is evidently very clever, but superlatively vulgar,' was her damning comment. It was a verdict the Cecil dynasty never saw cause to change.[84]

NINE

Mary Anne

1837–9

'I FIND that it makes a sensible difference in the opinion of one's friends,' Disraeli wrote to Sarah of his election. 'I can scarcely keep my countenance.' At the end of August he left London for Bradenham, 'ill, hot and pressed to death by my family'.[1] He kept up a stream of arch and flowery notes to the flirtatious Mrs Wyndham Lewis, confiding in her his anxieties about Henrietta's catastrophe. 'All here is very quiet and happy,' he wrote from Bradenham. 'Not a word about the painful subject, which, it is tacitly agreed, shall be consigned to oblivion.' Tactful indeed, as gossip about Henrietta and Maclise was rife that autumn; even the queen knew, from Melbourne, who told her, 'They're a bad set; they're grand daughters of Elmore, the horse dealer; old Elmore trafficked with his daughters as much as he did with his horses.'

Mary Anne came to stay, bringing with her Wyndham Lewis, whom Disraeli described as 'one of the oddest men that ever lived, but I like him very much'.[2] 'After you went,' Disraeli told Mary Anne, 'everything and everybody were most dull and *triste*.' Nothing ever happened, he grumbled, except the occasional capture of a poacher. Jem rose at six to shoot partridges and worried that the September rain would spoil his harvest, while Disraeli kept to his rooms, did some desultory political reading, and complained that the changeable atmosphere made him languid and ill. The family doctor, Dr Rose of Wycombe, was at length called in; he treated Disraeli for gout and, strengthened by a course of Guinness advised by Mary Anne, his health soon recovered. October brought a brisk campaign of Bucks county politics – after-dinner speeches at farmers' dinners, Conservative dinners, Quarter Sessions at Aylesbury and a visit to Chandos at Wotton. Then he went to Woolbeding in Sussex, to stay with Lady Caroline Maxse. Shooting-dandies and endless horses, guns and dogs threatened to bore him; but because he did not shoot, he was very popular with the ladies and stayed indoors gossiping with the amiable Lady Caroline. He intended to marry, he told her, very soon; now that he was an MP he needed a home, and he was tired of intrigue and other men's wives.[3]

Back at Bradenham, he spent ten quiet days before parliament met. In November, on the eve of his departure for London, he wrote a final entry in his diary. 'I am now as one leaving a secure home for an unknown sea. What will the next twelve months produce?' It was not going to be easy. As an ex-Radical who had entered parliament as a Conservative, he had some explaining to do. 'This evidence of somewhat fickle principles will not, I should fear, much assist his *debut* in the House,' wrote William Archer Shee, noting that Disraeli's self-conceit might lead him to make the mistake of trying to take the House by storm. Shee was a contemporary of Ralph's and Jem's, who remembered Disraeli from children's parties at Bloomsbury Square; now, he noted, he and his family never saw Disraeli, who preferred his own coterie of flatterers.[4] Plenty of people would have enjoyed seeing him fail.

Yet he entered parliament with an agenda, already outlined in his *Vindication* of 1835. His politics had been analysed in a long review of the *Vindication*, published in J. S. Mill's short-lived *London Review* in 1836. 'One day a Jacobin, and another an Ultra Tory,' wrote the reviewer, but rather than attacking Disraeli's inconsistency the reviewer conceded that his aim was to blend the two. 'A great intrigue has been fermenting in his mind, the end of which is to be that the Tories are to ride into power on the shoulders of the mob.' This, the reviewer scoffed, was an impossible task. Not only did it run counter to the creed and sentiments of the Tory party and the Carlton Club, but the projected alliance of Tories and democracy never could succeed in reversing the trend towards conflict between aristocracy and democracy.

> As a portion of an aristocratic party, formed by the fusion of Whigs and Tories into one mass, the Tories may again perchance for awhile maintain their political existence. But that they can ever again cajole a majority of the nation into the support of a ministry composed of Tory leaders, or professing Tory principles – that they can successfully resist the advancing power of democracy – or that they will direct its progress, and share its triumph – are fancies that none but such a dreamer of dreams as D'Israeli the Younger can mistake for realities.[5]

Visionary though it seemed, in the long term Disraeli's alliance of Tories and people was to prove equally as accurate a reading of historical forces as the Radicals' prognosis of conflict between aristocracy and democracy. In the short term, however, his scheme merely earned him the suspicion of the Tories and the resentment of the Radicals.

The result of the 1837 election was to make the Conservatives the largest and most powerful Opposition yet, with 309 seats to the Whigs' 349. In England, the Conservatives held a majority of seats (239: 232 Whig); the Whigs depended for their majority on the Celtic fringe, particularly on the 73 Irish members. Their survival, as Disraeli wrote, was a matter of playing Irish boroughs against the English counties; in *Coningsby* he said, 'The Reform Bill did not do more injury to the Tories, than the attempt to govern this country without a decided Parliamentary majority did the Whigs.'[6]

Disraeli took his seat on 15 November 1837. When he went down to the House with Wyndham at two o'clock the large chamber which, until the fire three years before had been the House of Lords, was full of members, standing in groups and chatting. 'Order, order,' came a cry, and members took their seats, Disraeli on the second bench behind Peel. Looking to Disraeli's short-sighted and jaundiced eye like an old laundress, Abercromby, the Whig speaker, 'mumbled and moaned some dullness before being carried to the speaker's chair'. Next day, Disraeli dined with Peel at the Carlton, a House dinner of fourteen men; Peel's show of favour had 'created some jealousy and surprise', he told Sarah, and he reported that 'Peel took wine with me and with no one else.'[7]

Members poured into town all Sunday, and by 4.30 the Carlton was full; on Monday morning as many as 300 members turned up at a meeting at Peel's. Thence to the House, and at two o'clock the Commons were summoned to the Lords as the queen opened her first parliament. The rush was terrific: Abercromby was nearly thrown down and trampled, and his mace-bearer banged members' heads with his weapon. Even Disraeli conceded that the queen looked admirable beneath her diamond tiara: 'the peers in robes, the peeresses, and the sumptuous groups of courtiers rendered the affair most glittering and imposing.' Escaping to the Carlton after the queen's speech, he was nearly crushed by the mob; his hat was squashed and covered with mud, and several times he called upon the police and military who roared the magical words 'Member of Parliament', whereupon the crowds parted, and 'the mobocracy envying us our privileges, [called out] "Jim Crow" ' as the MPs stalked through the envious files. After snatching half a sandwich and trying to scribble to Sarah, he was back in the House for the debate on the address. The House was again crammed, with members sitting on the stairs and on chairs and benches behind the speaker's chair. He left at ten, after the division, and supped at the Carlton off oysters, Guinness, and broiled bones. It had been the most remarkable day of his life.[8]

Benjamin Hawes, a Whig MP who remembered him as an eight-year-old at Potticary's School, told him 'we are all expecting to hear *you lash us*', but even Disraeli was intimidated at first. When a debate on Municipal Officers' Oaths, which was listened to by Montefiore the sheriff of London ('Sir Moses and no mistake'), turned out to be 'the Jew Question by a sidewind' (4 December), Disraeli sat tight and voted with his party against relieving the Jews. 'Nobody looked at me, and I was not at all uncomfortable, but voted in the majority of only 12 with the utmost sangfroid.'[9] Perhaps he had been cowed by the majesty of parliament, but his loyalties on the Jewish question were not yet fixed. Only two years earlier he had boasted to Isaac about ridiculing the distinguished Ashkenazi Jew Isaac Goldsmith and his barrister son, Francis. 'I asked the son, if he were a Jew, why he called himself Francis Henry; and I quizzed and mystified them in every possible manner.'[10]

He did not remain silent for long. On 6 December the rowdy and unruly debate on the Tories' Spottiswoode subscription for presenting petitions against Irish election returns and unseating the O'Connellites, reminded him, he told Lady Caroline Maxse, of the earlier legislative scenes of the French Revolution – 'A spirit of almost sanguinary hostility pervaded our riotous discussions'.[11] It was hard, he said, to keep a bridle on one's tongue in these high-pressure debates – the more so for a man who had for so long imagined himself taking the House by storm, like Bohun, his hero in *Hartlebury* who, scorning advice to wait until he has caught the tone of the House, makes the most successful début ever. On the second day of the debate O'Connell spoke, and Disraeli who, ever since his challenge to O'Connell in 1835, had fantasised about worsting him in a debate ('We shall meet at Philippi'), could no longer contain himself. While O'Connell was speaking he went over to Stanley, who was due to answer O'Connell, and asked his permission to speak first.

At midnight he was on his feet, begging the House's indulgence as a maiden speaker, crossing swords at last with O'Connell. No, the Spottis-woode subscription was not a Protestant fund, as O'Connell had alleged ... He had barely begun before thirty or forty Radicals and Irish started to jeer, hiss and groan. 'I shall be very glad to receive indulgence even from the hon. members opposite. If, however, hon. gentlemen do not wish to hear me, I will sit down without a murmur.' Growing plainly nervous, he blundered on. Since the Reform Bill borough-mongering in Ireland had assumed a deeper and darker hue, seats were openly bought and sold, a system of intimidation ... The catcalls grew louder, the Irish drummed their feet; five minutes more, he pleaded. I stand here as the virtual representative of the new members – scornful, scoffing laughter burst out on both sides of the House. 'Now, why smile? Why envy me? Why should not I, too, have a tail, if it be only for a single night?' Tumult drowned him out, but he refused to sit down, spouting his carefully memorised peroration, which degenerated into gobbledegook. There was something about the 'amatory eclogue' between the noble Tityrus [Virgilian shepherd] of the Treasury Bench [Lord John Russell] and the learned Daphne [? Daphnis, another shepherd] of Liskeard [Charles Buller] which, notwithstanding the *amantium ira* had resulted in the *amoris integratio*. Next came a picture of Lord John Russell holding in one hand the keys of St Peter and in the other ... but the row was too loud for him to go on. He had endured twenty minutes – 'I have begun several things many times, and I have often succeeded at the last. I will sit down now but', he screamed, clearly audible above the din, 'the time will come when you will hear me!'[12]

Sir John Campbell, the attorney general, whom Disraeli had never spoken to before, came up to him in the lobby and asked, 'Now, Mr Disraeli, could you just tell me how you finished one sentence in your speech, we are anxious to know – "In one hand the keys of St Peter, and in the other ...?" ' 'In the other the cap of liberty, Sir John.' Disraeli thought it a friendly gesture, perhaps it was; but Monckton Milnes, another new member, thought Disraeli's leg was being pulled – it was Campbell whom Disraeli had called an orang-outang.[13]

'Failure!' groaned Disraeli in the lobby afterwards when Chandos, his ever-loyal patron, came up to congratulate him. No such thing, said Chandos, and told him that Peel had said, 'He did all he could under the circumstances. I say anything but failure; he must make his way.' Disraeli blamed his failure not on his own performance but on the Radicals and Irish. It was as painful as his first speech at Aylesbury in 1832; nevertheless Peel had cheered him repeatedly. Others, though, had spotted Peel laughing; and the cold-blooded aristocrat, Stanley, who spoke next cruelly ignored his speech. None of the courtesy customarily accorded a maiden speech was extended to Disraeli; it was like a primitive sacrifice, a ritual murder, his own side looking on as he was torn to pieces by the Irish. Perhaps Monckton Milnes's friend MacCarthy summed it up in the comment, 'Disraeli is of the *Junge Judentum*, not the young England, and so may be damned.'[14]

The speech made a sensation nonetheless. 'Next to undoubted success the best thing is to make a great noise,' he told Sarah, 'and the many articles that are daily written to announce my failure only prove that I have not failed.' The barracking of the Irish and the Radicals probably saved him from making a fool of himself; certainly this was the opinion of the veteran Irish member, Richard Sheil: 'if there had not been this interruption, Mr Disraeli might have made a failure – I don't call this a failure, it is a crash.' At dinner with Bulwer, Sheil took Disraeli aside. 'Now get rid of your genius for a session,' he advised. 'Speak often, for you must not show yourself cowed, but speak shortly. Be very quiet, try to be dull ... Astonish them by speaking on subjects of detail. Quote figures, dates, calculations.' Isaac, meekly wise, considered his son's performance had been too theatrical. 'Whether any display of that nature you have indulged in, I know not,' he wrote, telling home truths in his quaint foreigner's English.[15]

A week later, acting on Sheil's advice, Disraeli spoke again. This time the debate was on Talfourd's Copyright Bill, and he rose not to make a speech, but to say something pointed and to the purpose: could some redress be found against literary piracy? A few brief sentences delivered, he told Sarah (though this escaped the ears of *Hansard's* reporter), to a steady chorus of 'hear, hear'. The House was not full, but the Cabinet and Tory leaders were present, and Disraeli was confident he had earned their approval.

As parliament adjourned for Christmas, the French rebelled in Lower Canada, led by Papineau; ministers panicked and cut short the holidays. Disraeli did not reach Bradenham until soon after Christmas; Mary Anne stayed for New Year, while Wyndham was in Wales. On New Year's day Disraeli sent a note to her room, 'Mrs Wyndham, It comes in with rain; I hope it will end with sunshine.'[16]

About this time D'Orsay is said to have told him, 'You will not make love! You will not intrigue! You have your seat: do not risk anything! If a widow, then marry!'[17] It was good advice. He needed Wyndham Lewis's goodwill and generosity, yet he used Mary Anne for cynical, worldly ends, in the same way as he had used Sara Austen and Henrietta. In July Wyndham had advanced Disraeli's share of their joint election expenses, which came to a total of £4559 – more or less what was to be expected for a venal two-member borough like Maidstone; Disraeli promised to pay £500 by the end of 1837, and the balance (though how much this amounted to is unclear) soon afterwards.[18]

Over Christmas, he nerved himself to apply to Isaac; though the squire was 'very cantankerous *de rebus pecuniariis*', as he was apt to be at Christmas, he regarded elections as a legitimate expense, and the appeal succeeded. It did not solve all Disraeli's problems, though; he was haunted about his debt to a mysterious 'Mr B.', who may well have been the banker and Tory MP Thomas Baring. 'He is so stern, so inflexible in matters of business,' Disraeli told Pyne, 'that his friendship is gone for ever if, after what occurred between us, I am not strictly punctual and correct.'[19]

Wyndham Lewis pressed him to come up to town to settle his election debts early in January, but Disraeli insisted on staying at Bradenham until parliament met. He was engaged, he said, on business – one must imagine him enunciating every syllable precisely, bus-i-ness – '*from the highest quarter*, which must be attended to. A day, an hour is of importance to me in this affair, which concerns our party, and a day or so in the other business can be nothing.' He told Pyne on 3 January 1838 that he had received that morning a letter from the highest quarter, 'probably the most important I have ever received', and to comply with it he must shut himself in his room until parliament met.[20]

Between 3 and 15 January he contributed ten daily articles to *The Times*. Signed 'Cœur de Lion' and headed Old England, they are a bold imitation of Carlyle. 'How is the King's Government to be carried on?' says Cœur de Lion, was the question asked by the duke of Wellington in 1831. 'Great question of a great man! True hero-question, prescient, far-seeing, not easily answered by common men.' Linking the Reform crisis of 1831 to the French Canadian Papineau revolt of 1838, Cœur de Lion asks a second question, how is the Queen's Empire to be maintained? 'Reformed Parliament has not answered them; Reform Ministry has not answered them; town-councils have not answered them; New Poor Law has not answered them; justice to Ireland has not answered them; colonial conciliation has not answered them ... Yet answers must be found to both – to hero question and national question.' Carlyle laughed aloud when he discovered the articles, taking the imitation as a compliment, though at first he suspected Thackeray of being the author.[21]

Whether Disraeli was referring to *The Times* articles when he talked about the 'highest quarter' is obscure. The articles are clever but repetitive, and Disraeli evidently knew very little about Canada; he could conceivably have been working on something else while he wrote them. One possibility is suggested by an item in the *Satirist* at the end of January, gloating over the loss of a bundle of 'D'I's' manuscript letters to *The Times*; there are also hints that Disraeli was composing a party manifesto or pamphlet. Judging from Cœur de Lion's hero-worship of the duke, Disraeli was commissioned, if not by Wellington himself, by someone close to him, possibly Lyndhurst. 'On Sunday morning', Disraeli told Mary Anne on 9 January, 'I had another packet of papers, and have scarcely been out of my robe de chambre since, working night and day.'[22]

Back in London on 16 January, Disraeli listened to dull speeches in a thin, cold House. 'The genius of Canada seemed to pervade our deliberations,' he told Mary Anne; 'even Sir Robert seemed to sink under its frigid influence.' 'Town is very dull; everybody is frozen to death,' he told Sarah, and in the Lords the duke of Wellington spoilt all with his damned generosity, announcing his support for the Whigs' Canada policy: 'Great disgust in Tory ranks, even among the highest; Duke supposed to be passeé [*sic*] and to like being buttered with Whig laudation.' To Disraeli's delight, however, Peel appeared to break ranks with the duke and attacked the bill granting extraordinary powers to Lord Durham, whom the Whigs sent out to crush the French-Canadian rebels and prevent a war of independence in British North America. Disraeli thought Peel was impelled by his party's disgust at the Duke's 'betisé' [*sic*] and his realisation that without action the party could not be held together, but Peel was genuinely critical of the government's policy and distrustful of the Radical maverick Durham. One speaker who impressed Disraeli was Gladstone, who 'spoke very well, tho' with the unavoidable want of interest which accompanies elaborate speeches which you know are to lead to no result, i.e. no division'.[23]

With Mrs Wyndham Lewis he saw *Hamlet*, played by Charles Kean, son of the great Edmund Kean; she took a snug box with a capital fire and an amusing party, but Disraeli was dismissive of young Kean: 'mediocrity'. In mid-February, London's powerful hostesses threw open their gilded salons, and the season began. At a brilliant concert, among the Lansdownes and the Salisburys, he spotted Mrs Wyndham Lewis, 'who was very proud, evidently, of being there'. He was most struck by the Rothschilds, particularly the young wife from Frankfurt, 'tall, graceful, dark, and clear, picturesquely dressed, a robe of yellow silk, a hat and feathers, with a sort of *Sevigné* [bandeau] beneath of magnificent pearls'; she was, 'quite a Murillo' – a beautiful Jewess. A few days later to Salisbury House, through streets half a foot deep in snow and slush; he was presented to Lyndhurst's new, much younger and much talked about wife, also Jewish. Disraeli was agreeably surprised: 'She is not at all national in the vulgar sense, her features being very small.' Lady Salisbury received him with cordiality, he reported, and talked to him a great deal, but he owed his invitation to Lady Londonderry, his stalwart ally among the Tory hostesses.[24]

'Politics are critical,' he told Sarah on 19 February, 'and will remain so probably for the next fortnight.' Durham's appointment failed to mollify the Radicals, who rebelled against the government's repressive policy in Canada, and the Radical Sir William Molesworth gave notice of a motion of no confidence in Lord Glenelg, the colonial secretary. Many Tories, not least Disraeli, saw a chance of bringing the government down; for a fortnight he laboured, a wire-puller at the Carlton, canvassing support for Molesworth's motion. By 2 March he was so confident of success that he wrote to Peel, offering to write a Conservative party manifesto – perhaps he already had the draft in his drawer, written at Bradenham at the instance of the 'highest quarter'. Peel replied dismissively the same day: 'Any manifestation of opinion on public matters … can be made in Parliament while Parliament is sitting.' Molesworth's motion was a damp squib; at the last minute, Peel deflected his party from destroying the government.[25]

Disraeli blamed Stanley ('that harebrained Hotspur'), who had, he thought, dissuaded Peel from backing Molesworth; he little realised the depth of Peel's aversion to the Molesworth plot. Peel wished neither to beat the government nor to collaborate with the Radicals. He tucked his chin deep into his high, white neckcloth at the very idea; a Tory-Radical alliance, however fleeting, ran clean counter to his design of building a party of official men, dominated by the ex-Whigs Stanley and Graham. Corn Laws (15 March) gave Disraeli his next opportunity. Since January he had been preparing himself, at Chandos's suggestion, for the debate on the motion moved annually by the aristocratic Radical, Charles Villiers, for Corn Law repeal. Finding a thin House about six o'clock, he determined to make a speech merely for the press, but though he moved on to the front benches, empty except for Chandos, who advised him to speak boldly from the floor, he failed to catch the speaker's eye. After dinner the benches filled up – Disraeli reckoned there were 400 members in the House – and he was obliged to shift his place until at last he had no seat, but stood behind the speaker's chair. About ten o'clock he was beckoned to the front bench (Hardinge wanted to ask him something) and he sat down, though he ought not to have done, next to Graham, who advised him not to speak – the House was noisy and tired; but as he rose to go, the speaker called his name. 'I was in for it, put my hat down, advanced to the table, and dashed along.'

Much had been said, he declared, about the advantages British manufacturers would derive from the Corn Laws' abolition; but it was a delusion to suppose that the Corn Laws injured the demand for British manufactures abroad. True, the demand was declining in the Levant, but you need only ask the mercantile houses of Constantinople and Smyrna to learn that this was in no degree owing to the Corn Laws, but to the inferiority of British manufactures. How then had the cry against the Corn Laws been raised? 'It was the interest solely of the manufacturing capitalist, who had contrived to raise a large party in favour of that repeal, by the specious pretext, that it would lead to a reduction of rents, and by obtaining the co-operation of a section in this country, who were hostile to a political system based on the preponderance of the landed interest.'[26]

Lord John Russell sat, arms folded, watching intently throughout his speech: Disraeli, too short-sighted to see the expressions on the faces opposite, thought he detected a malignant smile, but learned afterwards that Russell was impressed. Peel was sitting too far away to shake Disraeli's hand when he sat down, but Disraeli heard him cheer. In the lobby the squires came up to shake hands – 'They were so grateful, and well they might be, for certainly they had nothing to say for themselves.'[27]

'To complete my vexations, my colleague has just fallen down in a fit and died!' he wrote to Pyne. The sudden death of Wyndham Lewis, delivering his affairs into the hands of the lawyers, tightened the pressure on Disraeli to repay his share of the Maidstone expenses; he had so far paid £500 and procrastinated over the balance, keeping up a flow of excuses and good intentions. Nursing an influenza, he waited until the next day before he saw Mary Anne, who was overcome. She had been in the room when Wyndham died: he was sitting writing when he fell from his chair. There was a coroners' inquest. Mary Anne was left a life interest in his property, yielding an income of between and four and five thousand pounds. Wyndham's one-fifth share in the Dowlais ironworks was left to his brother.[28]

Mary Anne was forty-six, though few would have guessed it. Still girlish, she was childless, uneducated and in her way an adventuress. Parish records reveal that she was born Marianne Evans in Exeter in 1792. She used to say that her parents ran away together, and it is certainly true that her mother's family was richer and grander than her father's. Her father, John Evans, was a penniless naval lieutenant, whose family had farmed for generations at the village of Brampford Speke, near Exeter. Her mother was Eleanor Viney, daughter of a Wiltshire landowning family; she was cousin to various county families, including the Scropes of Castle Combe, and brought a fortune of £5300 and a promise of great expectations from her aunt, Mary Anne Viney of Gloucester.

Mary Anne barely knew her father, who died in the West Indies, probably of fever, when she was two. She and her adored, weak-willed brother John were brought up by their mother, living first with their Evans grandparents at Brampford Speke, then briefly in Gloucester with their distinguished soldier uncle Sir James Viney at Cathedral House, on the Taylor of Gloucester's College Green, which the Viney family had occupied for over a century. When Mary Anne was eighteen, her mother made a shadowy second marriage to Thomas Yate, an unsatisfactory character who was master of ceremonies at the Clifton Assembly Rooms, and they moved to Bristol. Here Little Whizzy, as John called his sister, may have worked in a milliner's shop, though in her Cinderella moods she claimed that the shop was in Exeter. Certainly she thrived in Clifton society, cheerfully breaking hearts, and there she met and bewitched Wyndham Lewis. He was twelve years older and a wealthy ironmaster, but Augustus Hare's story that Wyndham spotted her as a factory girl walking barefoot to work is spurious. They married in 1815, and went to live at Greenmeadow, Wyndham's house near Cardiff. His share in Dowlais ironworks brought windfall profits, but he was often away on business; no babies came, and though Mary Anne consoled herself with flirtations, coy scuffles behind bedroom doors and kisses snatched in conservatories, she soon tired of Cardiff.[29]

In 1820 Wyndham became member for Cardiff, propelled into the great world by Mary Anne. The Lewises moved permanently to London in 1827, buying the lease of No. 1 Grosvenor Gate (now 93 Park Lane), a new sparkling white stucco house on the marquess of Westminster's recently developed Grosvenor Estate, its curved balconies overlooking Hyde Park. Mary Anne launched herself into society, her breathless, giddy chatter masking shrewd common sense. She was a compulsive flirt with an unquenchable thirst for admiration; the empty carriages of men callers stood waiting for hours outside Grosvenor Gate, and when she died she left bundles of notes from mysterious gentlemen who enjoyed the lover's privilege of calling her Rose. In her thirties she hovered on the fringes of Lord Worcester's disreputable set, which included courtesans like Hariette Wilson. In the last years of her marriage to Lewis she probably had an affair with George Beauclerk. But she was friends too with Peel's eminently respectable sister, Mrs Dawson, and with the ill-natured blue, Rosina Bulwer, who mocked her. 'Who is this Dr Swift, Rosina?' asked Mary Anne, at a dinner at Bulwer's, 'that they have been talking about? Can I ask him to my parties?' (Dean Swift died in 1745.) When, in about 1832, Rosina asked Disraeli to take Mary Anne in to dinner, he allegedly replied, 'Oh anything rather than that insufferable woman, but Allah is great.'[30] Mary Anne was a loyal friend, and took Rosina's side over the separation with Bulwer, which perhaps explains why Disraeli saw less of her after 1832–3.

Rosina later alleged that Disraeli proposed to Mary Anne while the coroners were tramping up the stairs. Rosina had an axe to grind; instead of commiserating with Mary Anne on Wyndham's death, she lamented the death of her own darling dog Fairy. Mary Anne's scurrilous tongue made Rosina's self-obsession the gossip of the town, causing recriminations and a quarrel between the two women, in which Rosina came out worst.[31] Disraeli could not abide Rosina; she epitomised all he most hated about the Irish. Himself the butt of racial hatred, Disraeli had no compunction about venting his spleen against Irish blood: 'I never see her', he wrote, 'without thinking of a hod of mortar and a potato. Nature certainly intended that she should console her sorrows in Potheen.'[32]

His intimacy with Mary Anne rapidly intensified. Two weeks after Wyndham's death, he was writing 'My dearest Mrs Wyndham'. 'The babbling world already gives you to the Tory novelist,' wrote Augustus Berkeley, a balding and envious beau of Mary Anne's, one of many jackals who prowled around Grosvenor Gate after Wyndham's death; another was George Beauclerk.[33] Disraeli, as he later admitted, was influenced by no romantic feelings; marriage to a wealthy merry widow had much to recommend it. He was tiring of bachelor life, and Mary Anne enticed him to Grosvenor Gate with sea-coal fires, cosy luncheons and confidential chat.

He spent Easter at Bradenham. Mary Anne was in Wales, arranging Wyndham's property with his brother, and Disraeli bombarded her with fatherly advice, warning her not to sign anything ('you are a lone lamb in this world'), little knowing how shrewd a manager she was. He was anxious, he told her, about Isaac's health. Isaac was now virtually blind and complained of strange symptoms in his head; the doctors prescribed cupping in the hope that lowering his blood pressure would reduce the damage to the optic nerve – a treatment of which Disraeli was rightly sceptical. Though an eldest son, as he reminded Mary Anne, he dreaded his father's death. 'The first wish of my life has ever been, that after all his kindness to me, and all the anxiety which I have cost him, he should live to see me settled and steady, and successful to his hearts content.' Leaving Bradenham, he told her, was always a wrench. After a week or so there, he got used to quiet habits and felt 'the charm of domestic bliss'; he never left home without feeling as he did when he went to school, but 'after all, like the shower bath, it needs only a plunge'.[34]

Mary Anne touched him with her grief. At times, when she had nothing to do, she was almost destroyed by misery, she wrote. No one, not even her brother John, could love her as Wyndham had – his perfect sweetness of temper, never an impatient word. She was not too miserable to flirt, however. 'I am glad you pass so much of your time with Lady Lny,' she wrote from Clifton, where she was staying with her mother. 'I do not know what you mean by passing "*so much*" of my time with Lady Londonderry,' Disraeli rejoined, adding, 'I hope you are amused at Clifton. You do not appear to have any time to write; at least not to me.' 'You hope I am AMUSED at Clifton,' came back the blistering reply. 'I have passed all my mornings ... overwhelmed with business papers ... In fact turning Mamma's little property here into money.' As for Lady L., she told him, she did not disapprove: on the contrary, the more you go there, the less likely you are to marry yourself to some odious woman – 'I hate married men.'[35] She sent him Wyndham's watchchains, which he wore criss-crossing his waistcoat at a banquet given by Chandos to Peel. 'I wore *your chains*. I hope you are not ashamed of your slave,' he wrote, and ended, 'I am happy if you are.'[36]

'I am now apt to forget all business,' Disraeli told her on 31 May. But one piece of business he could not ignore: the Maidstone election petition, brought against Fector, the Tory who won the by-election consequent on Wyndham's death. At the election committee, Charles Austin, the counsel, alleged that in July 1837 Disraeli had promised bribes to the electors which he had not paid. This was probably true, but Disraeli saw Austin's statement as an attack on his honour. The charge of corruption was bad enough; and a man who was known to be poor could not allow talk of unpaid election debts to jeopardise his chances of re-election. He sat up late one night composing a letter to the *Morning Post*. Austin's statement, he declared, was utterly false; he had never made any pecuniary promises to the electors of Maidstone. All his expenses were paid by Wyndham Lewis, to whom he had discharged his share. It was too neat, and the lack of detail was suspicious; conscious perhaps of the shakiness of his defence, Disraeli poured invective on Austin and the legal profession as a whole. Austin's statement was 'but the blustering artifice of a rhetorical hireling, availing himself of the vile license of a loose-tongued lawyer, not only to make a statement which was false, but to make it with a consciousness of its falsehood'.[37]

This was an attack which Austin could not ignore, and Disraeli knew it. Anything is better than submitting to an insult, he told Mary Anne; 'if I did, you would be ashamed of me, and I should be unworthy of your love'. It was his first avowal of love, and it was fashionably romantic – he was a knight in armour, ready to die defending his honour and Mary Anne's against the slurs of a loose-tongued lawyer. 'But I fear there is no chivalry nowadays, and I dare say the fellow will not do what he ought. I repeat, my sweetest love, be calm.'[38]

Austin did not do what Disraeli thought he ought. He did not issue a challenge to a duel; he applied in the Court of Queen's Bench for leave to bring an action for libel. The case was heard on 14 June. Austin denied the accuracy of the newspaper reports stating that he had made personal attacks on Disraeli. Disraeli, who had not been present at the election committee, admitted that he had not checked the newspaper reports before writing his letter; he had consulted a member of the committee, Lord Ernest Bruce, who was not only deaf but mischievous. Though Disraeli's counsel regretted that he had accused Austin if Austin did not say what he was reported to have said, the libel was proved. But Disraeli had skilfully shifted the issue; the court did not concern itself with the question of his unpaid bills.

Disraeli was summoned for judgement in November. For three hours successive lawyers, led by Sir John Campbell the attorney general, pressed him to write a letter of apology. Disraeli drafted the first few lines, but his pen veered away from contrition. He had prepared an elaborate speech, which he was at last allowed to deliver under the guise of a plea in mitigation. He regretted, he said, what he had done. He was sorry he had injured any man who had not attempted to injure him, or annoyed a gentleman of the highest honour and integrity. Neither of these descriptions fitted Austin, to whom Disraeli carefully avoided apologising, and his speech was calculated to annoy the court. He was brought there, he went on, by a fiction of the law, by an offence not against the law but against lawyers. When he attacked the privilege of lawyers to make false, unsubstantiated statements, he had in mind the description of an advocate's duty given by a great authority, a lord chancellor no less. He read out a passage about the advocate's overriding duty to his client; he paused for effect. The passage was taken from Brougham, and Brougham's ideas of honour were notoriously elastic.

It was a queer apology, but Campbell had the good sense to accept it as such, and the case was dismissed. 'I think I have gained great *kudos* by the affair,' Disraeli told Sarah. He had succeeded in turning a potentially harmful issue to his advantage. As for Mary Anne, she was saved from tearful hand-wringing as the shots rang out at dawn. But someone had to pay the lawyer's bill; that was the trouble with having a man of imagination as your lover.[39]

London teemed with foreigners in the summer of 1838. The hotels were packed with the flotsam and jetsam of the Holy Roman Empire; two Italian princes, for example, visible each night in brilliant uniforms and sparkling stars, retired to a filthy third-floor crib in a hotel in Leicester Square, as if their carriage turned into a pumpkin at break of dawn. D'Orsay was in his element vying with Eurodandies like the turquoise-jacketed Hungarian Count Zichy, teasing the duke of Ossuna, only living descendant of the Borgias, and beguiling the 'offs and ons', Kissiloffs and Strogonoffs.[40]

Disraeli, whose wardrobe did not include court dress, resolved not to attend the coronation, consoling himself with the reflection that 'to get up very early (8 o'c): to sit dressed like a flunky in the Abbey for seven or eight hours and to listen to a sermon by the Bp. of London can be no great enjoyment'. But in the end he could not resist it; persuaded by Ralph, he borrowed court dress at 2.30 a.m. on the day of the coronation ('It turned out that I have a very fine leg, which I never knew before!'). It was the first coronation in which the Commons were given a part, cheering the queen nine times, and Disraeli had one of the best seats. The queen, he reported, performed her part with grace and completeness, but the others were painfully unrehearsed. There were few moist eyes at the coronation; Disraeli sneered sardonically at Melbourne, who wore his coronet cocked over his nose and held the sword of state like a butcher. Lyndhurst paid his homage with dignity, but then blundered by not backing from the throne. Lord Rolle, aged eighty-two and a friend of Mary Anne's, caught his foot and rolled down the steps of the throne, whereupon the queen advanced and held out her hand. Foreigners, Disraeli told Sarah, thought Lord Rolle's tumble was a tenure by which he held his barony.[41]

The people – the surging, cheering crowds who thronged the benches lining the procession from Buckingham Palace to the Abbey – the Other

Nation over whom the queen reigned, and who struck the diarist Greville, no democrat, as the thing best worth seeing about the whole coronation, barely impinged on Disraeli, so dazzled was he by the glittering rich.[42]

Mary Anne, swathed in black crape, stayed at Grosvenor Gate. Two items in her account book (a pair of black lace gloves for £1 8s 6d and a parasol for £1 2s 0d) tell of the entertainment she gave to watch the military review in Hyde Park. No one was allowed on the drawing-room floor, lest there be an appearance of a party. Lord Rolle sat in solitary state on the balcony, a footman on each side 'as is his custom'.[43]

From Grosvenor Gate, Disraeli proceeded (alone, naturally) to the Londonderry banquet at Holdernesse House. Only 150 invited, and all sat down to luncheon in the gallery of sculpture, which was so magnificent that 'everybody lost their presence of mind'. 'It was the kindest thing possible of Fanny asking me,' Disraeli told Sarah, 'as it was not to be expected in any way.'[44] Fanny – Frances Anne, marchioness of Londonderry – was indeed faithful that summer, showering him with invitations. In *Sybil*, she is Lady Deloraine (as so often with Disraeli the fictional name is part anagram), 'the only good woman the Tories have', brilliantly skilled in the subtle social arts of keeping the party together; but her interest in Disraeli was more than political, and Mary Anne was right to see her as a rival.

By now he saw Mary Anne every day. He sent notes around to her from his bed when he woke. 'How is my sweet one? A good night?', and as soon as he was dressed called at Grosvenor Gate 'at our usual hour of happy meeting', about twelve, before going on to the House. He was rarely at the Carlton; 'of late,' he confessed, 'I have become terribly backward in political gossip.'[45]

In the House, the debates on Irish Municipal Corporations meandered aimlessly, as the bill was carved up again by the Lords and shelved once more by the government; on 10 August Disraeli rose after O'Connell at the end of a debate and spoke for ten minutes. The House, he declared, had been sitting for nine months, wasting time on Irish measures, which were called for not by the necessities of Ireland but for the purpose of keeping the Whigs in power. Nine months' sitting, 'the ordinary period of gestation, had produced nothing but this abortion, this strangled offspring of the noble lord'. Though there were only eight Tories in the House, the speech was a success. 'I thought it as well', he wrote to Sarah, 'that my voice should be heard at the end of the Session and especially on an Irish subject.'[46]

Nine months before, in December 1837, Disraeli had written to Lady Caroline Maxse: 'I am not married, but any old, ugly and ill-tempered woman may have me tomorrow. I care for no other qualifications. A wretched home makes us enjoy the world, and is the only certain source of general happiness.'[47] What he left unsaid was that the old woman had to be rich. He needed to marry money if he were to survive in parliament. Though he pushed Peel to bring down the Whigs, he had every cause to dread a dissolution. Unpaid bills and election expenses, unfortunately publicised by the Austin case, meant that Maidstone was unlikely to re-elect him, even if he could afford it. He had no wealthy patron, and without money there was no chance of another seat. Loss of parliamentary privilege, disgrace and bankruptcy loomed. He was hardly an eligible suitor. Not only was he a financial liability, but he hovered equivocally between Jewry and Anglicanism. His Christian baptism ruled out marriage with an orthodox Jew, though it was Murillo-like Jewish beauties like the young Rothschild wife that he admired. His Jewish name and blood disqualified him from marrying into a conventional Anglican family.

Mary Anne seemed a practical solution. True, she was twelve years older, but Disraeli was always vague about age, and Mary Anne was skilful at adapting hers – the inscription she composed for Wyndham's tomb recorded that she was his wife for seventeen years of unbroken happiness, not twenty-three. Disraeli probably thought she was forty-two. In any case, he liked older women. Marriage to Mary Anne would probably mean no children, a matter on which Disraeli was strangely silent. Despite his pride of race (or perhaps because of it), he had no ambition to found a dynasty; he was a prophet, a teacher, a genius – not a bearded patriarch. Childlessness he could accept. And Mary Anne cared little about his Jewishness. She brought Grosvenor Gate for her lifetime, her widow's jointure, and the prospect of cancelling the debt to Wyndham still outstanding from the Maidstone election. Moreover, Isaac had often talked of making a settlement on his son when he married.

But Disraeli was also a warm-hearted romantic, and almost in spite of his cynical self he found himself falling in love with her. She came down to Bradenham at the end of August and stayed six weeks. He sent notes in the mornings to her room (a compulsive magpie, she treasured every scrap of paper ever sent to her), they strolled together through the September beeches; unable to sleep, he paced his room in the small hours, composing poetry. Amongst the sonnets to 'her who is the solace of my life', the hymns to 'Thick tresses, Nature's auburn boon' (for Nature read Art) and 'White shoulders, rounder than the moon', there is a scrap of verse that she could hardly fail to smile at:

> Would I were that flea
> That is biting your knee
> Or at least a young fly

That is near your bright eye
Or were I a dove
This, I tell you, my love,
That I should make my nest
In that exquisite breast.

Or were I even Pol
As proud as the Sol
I think I should tip
A kiss on that lip.

But I am poor Dis
With a secondrate phiz
and all I can do
Is to love you most true.[48]

At the end of September he proposed, and she accepted him. The very next day he wrote to Pyne, 'It is settled that the business is to come off on the turn of the year.' Isaac intended making a satisfactory settlement. But an earlier date could not possibly be fixed, on account of Mary Anne's mourning, and meanwhile 'the system' must be ended. 'I am resolved, D.V., not to renew another bill.' A sum of money must be raised to pay off bills as they became due, perhaps on the security of Disraeli's farmer brother James. 'Don't let this letter be lying about your table,' he wrote.[49]

Disraeli's haste was cold-blooded, calculating, and unseemly, and Mary Anne resented it. She had paid the lawyer's fee for the Austin case, accepting a postdated bill from Disraeli; she had been moved to generosity by his tears, but now she regretted it. They quarrelled, and Mary Anne angrily insisted on returning to London on 6 October. A string of imploring messages to her room failed to change her mind. 'Pray let us meet and look happy, even if we be not,' ended the last of these. For three days after she left he was in a state of gloomy stupefaction and self-pity: spiritless and apathetic, he scarcely left his room. He signed himself with the 'mystical mark', a squiggle of a rose or a heart which sometimes resembles a turnip, their code for an embrace. Mary Anne wrote from London, brisk and bracing. Do not be idle, she told him; take a walk each day with your sister (advice he most certainly ignored) and remember the Tragedy – 'let this be one of the many proofs of your love, dearest.'[50]

The 'tragedy' was *Count Alarcos*, the verse drama which Disraeli had begun to write while Mary Anne was at Bradenham. Based on a Spanish ballad translated by Lockhart, it is the story, set by Disraeli in thirteenth-century Castile, of a Spanish noble, Alarcos, who murders his wife in order to marry the Infanta. *Alarcos* is violent in parts, strongly reminiscent of *Macbeth*, a very odd story for an aspiring Victorian husband to write. Yet it was his impending marriage to Mary Anne which inspired the drama. On 18 October, after writing all day without ceasing, not going down to dinner and staying in his room until evening, he told her: 'I poured into the fictitious scene my actual sensations, and the pages teem with passages which you will not read without emotion, for they come from my heart, and they commemorate my love, my doubt, my misery. Your name was before me … my inspiration, my hope, perhaps my despair.'[51]

Alarcos is the husband of Florimonde, the gentle, domestic mother of his children, who prefers her quiet home to the tumult of the court. Alarcos, however, recently returned to Castile from exile, hankers after the court. He is an eagle to her dove (Disraeli and Mary Anne wrote to each other as eagle and dove – Mary Anne kept a dove in a cage at Grosvenor Gate) and Alarcos sighs:

> Ah, Florimonde! thou art too pure;
> Unsoiled in the rough and miry paths
> Of this same trampling world …
> > … There's a rapture
> In the strife of factions, that a woman's soul
> Can never reach.[52]

Not all women are as pure as Florimonde. Solisa, daughter of the king, the infanta whom Alarcos once loved, wants to marry him. She scorns the suggestion that she should become his mistress – 'to act a toy/For his loose hours':

> > … not to dare to show
> Before the world my homage; when he's ill
> To be away, and only share his gay
> And lusty pillow; to be shut out from all
> That multitude of cares and charms that waits
> But on companionship; and then to feel
> These joys another shares, another hand
> These delicate rites performs …
> > … this is not love;
> This is pollution.[53]

Wicked Solisa seeks to persuade Alarcos to murder his wife. In a mock confession scene before the high altar in the cathedral, Alarcos confesses the

crime he has not yet committed, and tells the prior that he murdered his wife
for love of another whom he always loved. Cross-questioned by the prior, he
admits that love was not his only motive:

> A breath,
> A shadow, essence subtler far than love:
> And yet I loved her, and for love had dared
> All that I ventured for this twin-born lure
> Cradled with love, for which I soiled my soul.
> O, father, it was Power.[54]

Few men contemplating marriage write violent tragedies about uxoricide.
The murder of Florimonde is symbolic: it stands for the death of
conventional patriarchal marriage and family life – the kind of marriage that
his union with Mary Anne put out of his reach for ever. The tragedy pivots
on the question of Alarcos's motivation – whether he murdered his wife for
love of Solisa or to gratify his lust for power; and through Alarcos, Disraeli
explored and tested his motives for making what was, on the face of it, a
worldly marriage.

As he wrote at Bradenham, he tortured himself with imagined woes. 'Dark
doubt my breast invades,' he apostrophised Mary Anne, 'Parted, can Love
remain?' 'I send you the mystical mark,' he told her, sketching the turnip
shape, 'but my hand trembles as I sketch it, and my lips grow pale.'[55] Mary
Anne refused to see him until the tragedy was finished; she had plenty to do at
Grosvenor Gate, arranging her affairs. In the evenings she sang Disraeli's
song, The Yeoman of Bucks,* with Eliza, whom she had brought with her
as a child from Cardiff; now twenty, Eliza watched her with disapproving and
resentful eyes, gathering evidence of her mistress's immoral behaviour. On
17 October, Mary Anne wrote, 'I started at 12 for the City, received my
dividend and lodged 1000 in the 3 p.c. Consols took a walk in the park with
Eliza, met Captn & Mrs Neale in their cab and asked them – he takes *snuff*,
how I hate it – to take tea with me.' Neale was one of her admirers, but she
was careful to explain that it was another suitor, Augustus Berkeley, who took

---

* Ah! land of the Chilterns! Ah! land of the Vale!
Will the sons of thy soil from their faith ever fail?
No! if Chandos' green banner wave high in the wind,
There are some gallant spirits will ne'er lag behind.
  The yeomen of Bucks!
And if the dark cloud that now over us lours,
Bring revolt to the state, and bear gloom to our bow'rs,
We know a brave band that right soon will be seen
Astir in their saddles to guard their young Queen.
  The yeomen of Bucks!

snuff. 'When the eagle leaves you, the vultures return,' responded Disraeli, swallowing his jealousy.[56] Writing each day from nine until two, and taking cayenne prescribed by Mary Anne to improve his circulation, he reported great and brilliant progress, and pressed her to reward him with a visit to Bradenham. Impossible, she replied, until the play is finished and, tattooing her letter with secret pin marks, she taunted him with yet another beau, Mr Stapleton, who (as it happened) was also writing a tragedy. Disraeli, by now in a frenzy of jealousy, pictured the toad Stapleton (by a strange coincidence, he shared his name with the Croker character in *Vivian Grey*) reading his tragedy to her, like the serpent in paradise, and wrote gloomily about fading emotions and final estrangement. To which Mary Anne replied, 'I cannot ... say I do not feel angry, for I do very.' Simply because she did not instantly obey his wishes, he had lost all confidence in 'your poor little Dove'.[57]

Disraeli abandoned himself to an orgy of despair and longing. His nights, he told her, were horrible, or rather of 'fatal bliss', and he woke with shattered nerves; he no longer cared for politics, and he had lost all heart for his tragedy: writing tragedies was no use unless they were as fine as Shakespeare's, and that was impossible. This separation was unendurable. 'My ideas of Love are the perpetual enjoyment of the society of the sweet being to whom I am devoted.' Yet when he came up to London in November for his speech in court over the Austin case they quarrelled; she scolded him for being too confident of her love, and they parted with ruffled feelings.[58] He returned to Bradenham on the Western Railroad. The North Star, a new engine of enormous and unprecedented power, reached Maidenhead in 42 minutes, a rate of 36 miles an hour – 'the only satisfactory piece of railroad travelling I ever performed'. He took to his bed with influenza, and Maria, his mother, nursed him. He wrote her a poem for her birthday: 'As becomes a faithful wife,/Act thou a nursing parent.' The tragedy depressed him. He burnt more than he wrote. 'If mine ever appear, it shall be a masterpiece; but that appearance is very doubtful.'[59] Three political sonnets by Disraeli appeared in *The Times*; flat, feeble, and banal, they were called a halt to by the editor. Disraeli in love was hardly an inspired poet.

'I have been obliged to betake myself to bed again, and wish you were with me there,' Disraeli wrote on 5 December. Mary Anne stayed a week in December, and soon after she left who should ride up to Bradenham but D'Orsay, staying at Wycombe Abbey with Robert Smith, now Lord Carrington, once Disraeli's Whig opponent at Wycombe. Disraeli, who had not been inside Wycombe Abbey since 1832, at first refused their invitation to dine; at length he allowed D'Orsay to persuade him, ending his feud – it was a noisy party and he did not reach home until nearly one. It was fortunate that he had mended his fences. Carrington was soon to be appointed Lord Lieutenant of Bucks, and he turned out to be a Tory in all but name.

Mary Anne no longer tortured him with jealousy. 'ON MY WORD Dizzy,' she had written from Norfolk, where she had been staying with the Milner Gibsons the previous month, 'not a word or look of love to me from anyone', and she squiggled a turnip shape. But now, staying at Chastleton for Christmas, she did not write, and Disraeli was mortified by her silence. It was unaccountable, he raged, in a person who had no doubt found time to write to 'her lawyer or trustee, and probably to many a corpulent beau, or seedy second-rate dandy'. Mary Anne was unrepentant. Disraeli had never expressed any desire to hear from her, had never appreciated her letters, and 'I do not like to send coals to Newcastle'. A woman, she told him, should never be fonder of a man than he is of her, 'except when he is *ill* or *lonely*. And *then* you will find me devoted and affectionate.'[60]

A week of sleepless nights and tortured days left Disraeli prostrate. His constitution, severely tried by the agitation and excitement of the past six months, quite gave way; he excused himself from visits to Chandos and Carrington (he must have been truly wretched), and sank groaning on his sofa, whence he wrote to Mary Anne. 'I am so nervous I can ...,' he ended, his writing trailing into a wavering line.[61] 'I am mad with Love,' he told her next day. 'My passion is frenzy.' Mary Anne came to Bradenham for the New Year with her mother, Mrs Yate, her brother and Eliza, and Disraeli begged her to 'take care to have your hand *ungloved*, when you arrive, so that you may stand by me, and I may hold and clasp and feel your soft delicious hand, as I help your mother out of the carriage'.[62]

Alone once more at Bradenham in January, he told Mary Anne in London he worked like a bee on *Alarcos* and slept like a top. When he confessed to a bad night as a result of drinking wine, she was pitiless. 'Shame, shame Dizzy,' she wrote. 'If you only drank 4 glasses and 2 were enough, it is equally unworthy and what is worse silly. No better than a poor animal.'[63] Drinking too deep in Isaac's well-stocked cellar did not help the emotional *crises* and sleepless nights to which Disraeli was so distressingly prone at Bradenham.

Tragedy Disraeli found the most difficult of all forms of composition. News from the Cape of the mysterious and macabre murder of the newly married L.E.L. (Letitia Landon), perhaps by her husband's mistress, gave him cheer – it 'will at least prove', he told Mary Anne, 'that my tragedy is not unnatural'. By dint of shutting himself up in his room, and remembering that 'Every line brings me nearer to my charmer', *Alarcos* was finished by the end of January. He hastened up to London through snow, the horrors of the coach ride relieved by a foot muff. Winter had arrived, and 'I want to nestle with my dove to keep me warm'.[64]

A letter from Lady Londonderry lay unanswered on his table. Disraeli wrote at length after five months' silence, 'her son Lord Seaham having made a successful debut at a political dinner, I thought a congratulation would get me out of a scrape,' he told Mary Anne. 'You approve?'[65]

'When I read in the beginning of your letter, The Tragedy is finished', wrote D'Orsay, 'I thought that you were married, but on reflection I supposed that if it was so, you would have said, The Comedy.'[66] Disraeli arrived in London more than ever determined to rip apart the tangled web of delays, excuses, evasions and silence Mary Anne had woven around the subject of their marriage. On 6 February, the day after the queen opened parliament, there was a great meeting at Peel's, and later Disraeli went on to Grosvenor Gate. Mary Anne accused him of allowing D'Orsay to influence him. She was frightened of what her enemies would say – Rosina, she knew, was spreading gossip that she planned to marry as soon as her widow's weeds were thrown off. The moment he rose the following morning Disraeli sent a note. 'My friends do not influence my conduct, and I cannot believe that you have really any enemies.' He ended, 'I write this utterly hopeless and seeing no future but one of impenetrable gloom.' Mary Anne, who had spent the morning paying her clockmaker's and upholsterer's bills, and buying waxlights, anchovy paste, raspberry jam and currant jelly, was shocked and upset. When Disraeli appeared at Grosvenor Gate, she called him a selfish bully and, he thought, told him to quit her house for ever. He walked out.[67] She had not yet learned how greatly Dizzy disliked scenes, and sent to his Park Street rooms, asking why he was angry. Disraeli replied at five o'clock, formal and cold – My dear Mrs Wyndham, he began. He had quit her house, he assured her, not in anger, but in sorrow and mortification; he was at last convinced that their intimacy must terminate.[68]

But he was still dissatisfied; so much that he wanted to say remained unsaid. He pulled out a sheet of paper and began to write. 'I write, as if it were the night before my execution.' Anger poured on to the paper, a letter of nearly 2000 words in an hour or so. 'Every hour of my life,' he told her, 'I hear of our approaching union from all lips except your own.' Her earlier talk of marriage, he now realised with bitterness, was merely a ruse to stimulate and secure his affection. She talked of her reputation: was she not aware that the continuance of the present state of affairs, which could only render her *disreputable*, must render him *infamous*. 'There is only one construction which Society, and justly, puts upon a connection between a woman, who is supposed to be rich, and a man whom she avowedly loves, and does not marry. In England especially there is no stigma more damning.' At present he was like an insolvent whose credit was not suspected: within a few weeks he must choose between being ridiculous or being contemptible. Either he must be jilted by her or, worse, sink into ignominy as 'what your friend Lady Morgan has already styled me "*Mrs Wyndham Lewis's De* [*sic*] *Novo*" '. It was a cruel cut: Di Novo was a male prostitute currently shocking London society with his extortionate demands on the English-born and immensely fat duchess of Cannizzaro.

He had already covered five pages; there was worse to come. 'When I first made my advances to you, I was influenced by no romantic feelings,' he declared. 'My father had long wished me to marry; my settling in life was the implied, tho' not stipulated, condition of a disposition of his property, which would have been convenient to me. I myself, about to commence a practical career, wished for the solace of a home, and shrunk from all the torturing passions of intrigue. I was not blind to worldly advantages in such an alliance, but I had already proved, that my heart was not to be purchased. I found you in sorrow, and that heart was touched.'

As for her fortune, he wrote, ruthlessly candid, it proved much less than he imagined – merely a jointure, sufficient to maintain her establishment. 'To eat and to sleep in that house, and nominally to call it mine; these could be only objects for a penniless adventurer.' No, this was no inducement for him to sacrifice his sweet liberty: 'when months ago I told you one day that there was only one link between us, I felt that my heart was inextricably engaged to you and but for that I would have terminated our acquainted [*sic*]. From that moment I devoted to you all the passion of my being. Alas! It has been poured upon the Sand!' Had they married, he declared, not one shilling of her income would have been seen by him. No paid husband he. 'By heavens, as far as worldly interests are concerned, your alliance could not benefit me.' Mindful of Lady Londonderry and his social currency as single man and MP, he rubbed it in: 'All that society can offer is at my command; it is not the apparent possession of a jointure that ever elevates position. I can live,' he wrote, reminding her of his expectations as an eldest son, 'as I live, witht. disgrace, until the inevitable progress of events gives me that independence wh. is all I require.'

No, 'not all the gold of Ophir shd ever lead me to the altar. Far different are the qualities which I require ... My nature –' he wrote 'requires' and crossed it out – 'demands that my life should be perpetual love.'

As for *her* conduct, all his friends had warned him, eager to save him from perdition; he had only himself to blame. 'Coxcomb to suppose that you wd. conduct yourself to me in a manner different to that in which you have behaved to fifty others!' How, he demanded, could she find the heart to do this to *him*: 'Was there no ignoble prey at hand, that you must degrade a bird of heaven? Why not have let your Captain Neil have been the minion of your gamesome house, witht. humiliating and debasing me? Nature never intended me for a toy and a dupe.' He was becoming theatrical. These were the very words he had put into the mouths of characters in *Alarcos*. Triumph, he told her, you have broken my spirit. And then a last, savage cut, 'For a few years you may flutter in some frivolous circle, and trifle with some spirits perhaps as false and selfish as your own. But the time will come when you will sigh for any heart that could be fond … then you will recall to your memory the passionate heart that you have forfeited, and the genius you have betrayed.'[69]

Impulsively, he dispatched this twenty-page screed to Grosvenor Gate after barely reading it through, something a more prudent and less romantic Englishman would never have done, though who knows which was right. A note came winging back – his letter was cruel. He scrawled over another sheet of paper, his fourth letter to her that day, 'and is not your conduct "cruel"? It has cut me to the very heart's core.' He never meant to write a cruel letter, he told her, but he wrote a true one. 'I wrote what I felt.' There are barriers between us, he told her, to that unlimited confidence and trust which love requires. 'If you think', he ended, 'that I have expressed the truth, shun that Disraeli whom you perhaps still love.'[70]

No doubt his extraordinary outburst was true to his feelings when he wrote it; but that is only one kind of truth. Contrary to his proud assurances, he was indeed a penniless adventurer, desperately in need of her widow's jointure for his political survival. Though he was brutally frank about her finances, he was disingenuously silent about his own. There *were* still barriers, and they were largely of Disraeli's making.

Mary Anne's response to this emotional bombardment was direct, intuitive, and in a way magnificent. Late that evening she wrote, 'For Gods sake come to me. I am ill and almost distracted. I will answer all you wish. I never desird [*sic*] you to leave the house or implied or thought a word about money. I recd a most distressing letter and you left me at the moment not knowing from the house. I have not been a widow a year and the world know not how I was situated with him … I often feel [shame] at the *apparent* impropriety of my present position. I am devoted to you.'[71]

It was a cry from the heart few could resist, least of all Disraeli. He wrote a little stiffly the next morning (he had after all jilted her the night before) to say that, though he preferred communicating by writing, he would call at two o'clock, and her note had cost him many tears. She sent back a single line: 'I am too ill to see any one but yourself today, oh come.' He melted. 'My darling and my life, I will come to you *immediately* I am dressed. I found her dear note of yesterday and kissed it very much. She is the joy of my life and I wish to be her solace. Dis.'[72]

By six that evening he was in the House, telling Sarah the political gossip he had heard from Chandos, now the duke of Buckingham ('nothing can be kinder than he is'). The corner was turned. But it was Mary Anne who gave herself to Dizzy Dearest; he was not the giver. Mary Anne dismissed the corpulent beaux and seedy second-rate dandies from Grosvenor Gate; Disraeli did not admit to his debts.

The Whig government stumbled on, though Disraeli and the Tories anticipated a speedy break-up. From Manchester, the Anti-Corn Law Parliament converged on London, and on 14 February Disraeli accompanied the duke of Buckingham, the Bucks Tory gentry and 'a host of Horwoods, Brickhills etc' on a deputation to Melbourne, whom they petitioned to maintain the Corn Law. Though the government was rumoured to favour abolition, they found Melbourne 'frank and rollicking, evidently in his heart a thoro' Tory and agriculturist; he rubbed his hands and laughed, and when the evil consequences were insisted on, he agreed to everything: "and my Lord," said some Horwood from Ely, "Will not the fundholder be endangered?" "Oh of course," said Melbourne.'

A week later the Anti-Corn Law Parliament returned to their constituencies, having failed to gain a hearing at the bar of the House. 'Who'd have supposed,' Disraeli wrote to Sarah, 'after all their meetings and menaces, that the mountain shd not have produced even a mouse, and that they should cut and run without even a debate on the question?'[73] The debate on Villiers's annual anti-Corn Law motion came on 12 March and lasted five days. Disraeli was anxious to speak (he had collected new and curious information), and from two p.m. to two a.m. he was in the House, 'watching the chances, a wild and almost desperate process, of catching the speaker's eye'. The debate closed without a word from him, leaving him mortified, as he had spent seven weeks of thought and research on the subject, and he was 'at a loss to foresee any other great question of which I should have so thoro' a knowledge'. Villiers's motion, however, was soundly beaten and the ministerialists split; the division, thought Disraeli, was a *real blow* to the Whigs. 'It shows that as the House of Commons is now constituted, no further organic change can be carried.'[74]

He dined once again with Peel, arriving late to find twenty-five gentlemen 'grubbing in solemn silence' – a sumptuous dinner, third course of dried salmon, olives, caviare, woodcock pie, foie gras. 'I threw a shot over the table,' he told Sarah, 'and set them going, and in time they became even noisy.' Peel, he thought, was pleased that he broke the awful stillness, and talked to him a great deal, though sitting far removed. Disraeli watched Peel closely, reading signs of favour into his words and smiles as avidly as a courtier at Versailles, but he was coy about allowing himself to be caught. 'As regards the trammels of party,' he told David Urquhart, the maverick eastern expert, 'I believe there is not a man in the house whose seat renders him more independent of them, than my own – as regards my own views, I have no other impulse than a fair love of fame, and a deep interest in the glory of my country.'[75]

He was one of a handful of Tories who voted in favour of the Radical Tom Duncombe's motion to remove the restrictions on Westminster theatres during Lent on Wednesdays and Fridays. Not that he meant to attack the church. He charged Sarah to research the history of theatre under Elizabeth and James I: was the Lenten restriction 'ecclesiastical polity', he asked her, 'or is it a puritanic innovation? If the latter I could justify my vote.' Primed by her ('you are a library and a librarian both'), he made a learned speech, demonstrating that Protestantism had brought a relaxation in popish Lenten observances. Though he voted with the Radicals, he was anxious to prove his respect for the established religion, and noted with relief that Dungannon, an ultra churchman, took the same side.[76]

He took an independent line too on the Irish Municipal Corporations Bill, which made its annual parliamentary appearance in March. Speaking against Peel, who this session declared himself in favour of the bill, Disraeli attacked Irish Municipal reform on the grounds that it undermined the system of centralisation which had been the principle of Irish government under both parties for forty years. 'In England, where society was strong, they tolerated a weak government; but in Ireland, where society was weak, the policy should be to have the government strong.' It was a sound Tory argument; and Peel, sore though he was at the Conservative schism, complimented Disraeli on his speech, telling him he took the only proper line of opposition to the bill.[77]

By the end of March the government was tottering. The young queen, whose popularity had boosted the government over the past year, besmirched herself and her ministers over the affair of Lady Flora Hastings, the lady of the bedchamber whom she falsely accused of being pregnant – 'a *really* vile slander', wrote Disraeli, noting the thin attendance at the queen's drawing-rooms. 'The Palace scandal is more than a blow to Ld Melbourne,' he told Sarah; 'I fear it is to the Queenly office.' From the north came ominous rumblings of Chartism. 'We are all talking of the making of pikes here and the arming of the Chartists,' but he had not yet discovered the Other Nation, and for him the real drama was staged at Westminster in the world of high politics. 'There is some screw loose,' he wrote on 26 March, '(but where I know not) as many Whigs and Radicals confess it.'[78]

By now Disraeli spent most days at Grosvenor Gate. Arguments raged between Mary Anne, her mother and her brother John. 'I of course never open my mouth and am always scrupulously polite,' he told Sarah, somewhat disloyally, 'but what avails the utmost frigidity of civilisation against a brother in hysterics and a mother who menaces with a prayer-book!' – particularly so, when his own constant presence, as he well knew, was at the bottom of it.[79]

Mid-April found Westminster in the grip of a crisis, and Disraeli was exultant. He drank in the bustle and excitement, walking proudly down Parliament Street as strangers appealed to him for news, and jostling to find a seat in the chamber among the 500 members who attended prayers. 'This is just one of those occasions in old days when I used to feel so mortified at not being an M.P.,' he told Sarah. Peel had the game in his hands, but stubbornly refused to turn the ministers out, preferring that they should resign. Disraeli sat through a week of long and languid Irish debates, anticipating a division daily. 'Nothing can be conceived more wearisome than each night has been,' he wrote; but the division, when eventually it came on 19 April, was bathos: a government majority of twenty-two.[80]

Lord John Russell published his letter to his constituents, attacking the government, on 3 May. 'The fate of the Whigs is sealed,' wrote Disraeli: in an open letter to *The Times* signed Laelius, he rubbed in the significance of what he ironically described as Russell's Conservative manifesto.[81]

'Social London is rather dull,' Disraeli told Sarah; 'indeed no one thinks of anything but politics.' Peel had at length decided to plunge the stiletto, opposing the ministers' decision to suspend the Jamaica parliament: the only good speech in the Jamaica debate, according to Disraeli, was Peel's, 'the rest very dull. I did not rise, as Peel had touched upon most of my business points' – he had obtained an interview with Peel the previous afternoon, doubtless for the purpose of briefing him. When the Jamaica division took place, very late on the night of 6 May, the Radicals threw the government over, and the ministerial majority fell to five; when Disraeli left the House at 2 a.m. to spend a wretched night – he did not rise until two the following afternoon – he knew that the government would resign.[82]

At noon on 8 May, the queen, who was much upset at Melbourne's resignation, sent for the duke of Wellington, who advised her to send for Peel. At two Disraeli, who was in the Carlton, saw Peel wearing full court dress pass in his carriage down Pall Mall to the palace. About four, Peel left the palace and went to the duke of Wellington, having expressed his willingness to take office. Nothing more had transpired at six o'clock, when Disraeli wrote to Mary Anne. Two days rolled by, the Carlton thronged with expectant Tories hungry for office and thirsty for honours, and still nothing happened. There had been a hitch. On Friday about midday, as Disraeli was turning the corner of Park Street on his way to Grosvenor Gate, a messenger summoned him to Lyndhurst's. From there he scribbled to Mary Anne,

'Peel is out and given up the Government already in consequence of Whig intrigues about the Household. I have not the slightest doubt that her Majesty will be obliged to surrender.' This was the Bedchamber Crisis, and Lyndhurst wanted him to write a Laelius letter for *The Times* addressed to the queen, imploring her to change her mind and dismiss her Whig ladies, giving Peel the mark of confidence he demanded as a condition of taking office. Next morning Disraeli was up early (for him) at eight o'clock, and at work in the Carlton by ten; the letter was finished that night when, exhausted, he copied and dispatched it.[83]

'You are a queen,' he wrote; 'but you are a human being and a woman.' Laelius sought to mollify the queen by explaining the reasonableness of Peel's demands; of course, said he, he realised her affection for her ladies; but even mistresses of the robes and ladies of the bedchamber, 'though angelic, are human', and they could hardly be expected to stand aside while their Whig relatives were nightly arrayed in attempts to destroy your majesty's government. It was the language Melbourne might have used – almost instinctively Disraeli knew how to manage his sovereign; but even as he wrote Melbourne was back in office.

'Was Conservatism,' asked Disraeli in *Sybil*, 'that mighty mystery of the nineteenth century – was it after all to be brained by a fan!' In *Sybil*, he criticised Peel for crossing the queen, and with the advantage of hindsight, argued that Peel *should* have taken office and grasped the opportunity of identifying the Tory party with the revival of the royal prerogative, made possible by the accession of a youthful queen whose appearance touched the imagination. At the time, however, he blamed the Whigs not Peel; it was Peel not the queen who touched his imagination, and in the third Laelius letter, to Melbourne (28 May), he penned a flattering sketch of Peel, whom he eulogised as

one of long official practice, of greater political experience; of that happy age when vigour of manhood is not impaired, and when men have attained as much experience as, without over-refining action, is compatible with practical wisdom; when an elevated and thoughtful ambition is, not eager, yet prepared, for power, free from both the restlessness of youth and the discontent of declining age – epochs that alike deem life too short for delay. Add to this a temperament essentially national, and a habit of life pleasing to the manners and prejudices of his countrymen, with many of the virtues of the English character and some of its peculiarities; confident, rather than sanguine; guided by principles, yet not despising expedients; fearful to commit himself, yet never shrinking from responsibility; proud, yet free from vanity, and reserved rather from disposition than from an ungenerous prudence; most courageous when in peril; most cautious in prosperity.[84]

Peel was too great a man to seek to obtain office by artifice, or accept it on sufferance.

Alarcos was published in June. Disraeli had originally hoped to put it on the stage. Encouraged by Lady Blessington, who read the manuscript and declared it a real tragedy not a dramatic poem, he sent it to Macready, who was staging Bulwer's successful play, *Richelieu*. Macready rejected *Alarcos*, noting in his diary that it would never come to any good, and Disraeli decided to publish. He dedicated it to Lord Francis Egerton, the immensely wealthy heir to the Bridgewater millions. Like Disraeli, a poet and politician, Egerton was ungainly, grave and lugubrious; finding him once in jocular vein late at night in the House was 'rare and peculiar – very queer indeed – like a Turk who had worked himself up with opium to be funny'.

The tragedy created a ripple of sensation because of its wickedness; Lady Anna Grenville, Buckingham's nineteen-year-old daughter and a favourite of Disraeli's, was not allowed to read it. Lord Strangford admired it, and so did Sidney Herbert, who quoted a passage; Lord Powerscourt raved about it and Monckton Milnes was astonished the author did not give it to Macready, whose fortune it would have made – to which Disraeli, one imagines, said nothing. 'Strange', he told Sarah, 'that I never yet wrote anything that was more talked off in society, and yet it has never been noticed by the scribbling critics.' The reviews when they came compared *Alarcos* favourably with Bulwer's *Richelieu* which, Disraeli wrote, was poor stuff as a composition, but more attuned to theatre: his tragedy neglected altogether the dramatic requirements of the stage.[85]

There was theatre enough in the House. Melbourne's government was weaker than ever after the Bedchamber Crisis, encouraging the Chartists to redouble their efforts. Their monster petition, signed by well over a million, was presented in June. Disraeli was racked by headaches and 'megrim' brought on by the stifling June heat; the London air was heavy with 'vapour' and the fetid stink of rotting food and sewage. Mary Anne prescribed abstinence from wine and flesh, but despite his good resolutions Disraeli was unable to resist dining with the duke of Buckingham to eat venison.

At the close of the session and in languid summer heat, the Whigs gave birth to an education scheme. The scheme proposed an increase in the government grant to schools, first introduced in 1833; at the same time reducing the share received by church schools and imposing central control in the form of schools inspectors. Education was a battleground between

Church and Dissent, and from the Tory benches the scheme was savaged by the high churchmen Sir Robert Inglis and Gladstone and the evangelical Lord Ashley; it was an unlikely subject for Disraeli, who was certainly no churchman. But the scheme raised the issue of state control, and on 20 June, having risen twice before on previous nights and given up in despair, Disraeli found himself on his legs. England's happy system of self-government depended on the notion 'that the individual should be strong, and the Government weak, and that to diminish the duties of the citizen was to peril the rights of the subject'; state education was a return to a barbarous age, to the system of paternal government obtaining in Prussia or Austria. The speech was charged with a new awareness of the Condition of the People – of Manchester cellars and wild woodland districts of Kent peopled by inhabitants in the rudest state of ignorance and semi-barbarity. And he ended by rebuking the government for allowing so grave an issue to degenerate into a mere party squabble – the government had placed the country in a state of provisional insurrection; let them remember that they were deciding on the education of those by whom the Chartist Petition had been signed.[86]

'I have just made a brilliant and effective speech,' Disraeli scribbled to Mary Anne and to Sarah as he sat listening to Ewart replying. At the Carlton congratulations 'came thick as the autumnal leaves of Vallombrosa', he told Sarah, quoting Milton, and two old foes, Lords Ashley and Lincoln, tendered their congratulations with hands extended: 'How strange that nearly in despair at the end of the session I should have made by universal consent the best speech on our side on the most important party question.'[87]

A week later, he gave Bradenham formal written notice of his approaching union with Mary Anne; by now he was living at Grosvenor Gate. Isaac, the dear papa, whom Mary Anne had already captivated, was overjoyed. 'My dear daughter! for I fully respond to the endearing title you have invested me with,' he wrote, ponderously fond. 'You make me feel quite in love with you.'[88] Dizzy's nuptials were eclipsed by the illness of Mary Anne's brother John, who arrived unexpectedly at Grosvenor Gate with 'a brain fever', possibly a type of malaria contracted on service in Mauritius. Mary Anne took the extraordinary step of concealing his presence and his illness from her mother, who was living in the house; and as his fever grew dangerously worse, and the doctor paid daily visits, Mary Anne suffered agonies of suspense and sleeplessness in keeping everything from her mother. At Grosvenor Gate, Disraeli had not a moment to himself, as Mary Anne was greatly affected, and he did not like to leave her. After a week's illness, John expired, fortunately without a murmur, as his mother still did not know that her son was in the house.[89]

Unable to face the funeral and dreading breaking John's death to her mother, Mary Anne whirled the old lady off to stay with a clergyman cousin near Biggleswade. Disraeli was left at Grosvenor Gate to announce John's death to his brother officers of the 29th Regiment of Infantry and to deal with the body. He sorted the dead man's clothes and his few possessions; ne'er-do-well John left no will and no money. Alone, Disraeli attended the funeral at Kensal Green, where John was buried next to Wyndham Lewis. Mary Anne's inscription on his grave shortened his life by four years to forty-four.

Disraeli nursed a deranged liver. He was under doctor's orders to rest, but the brightest parties of the season were in that week, and as the Chartists rioted in Birmingham (4–6 July), Disraeli hesitated in a state of painful indecision, refusing Buckingham's dinner at Greenwich one moment and sneaking back in the next. The dinner was sumptuous, and Brougham's speeches set them roaring, but there were too many clodhopping Bucks squires: 'animals called Chetwodes, Pauncefote, Duncombes, strange existences styled Christophers and an entity of the name of Lucas!!' Next day was Lyndhurst's banquet, and Disraeli was easily persuaded to defy his doctor and reverse his refusal; while a violent thunderstorm raged outside, reminding guests of a scene from *Alarcos*, Disraeli met Webster, the American senator, said to be a refined and spiritual Yankee, though to Disraeli he seemed a Brother Jonathan, complete with twang.[90] No doubt to spare her concern, Disraeli did not tell Mary Anne he had been at the banquet, but even he did not have the stomach next day for Lady Londonderry's three fêtes in one day: breakfast at Rosebank, dinner at Greenwich and a ball at Holdernesse House. He spent it quietly in the little library at Grosvenor Gate with books and papers, preparing for the debate on the Prussian League, and dined at five on plain boiled chicken. On 9 July the Prussian debate was counted out, and Disraeli lost the chance of speaking, for which he had forfeited dinner with Lord (Vesey) Fitzgerald, the most difficult man to dine with in London, his invitation a measure of Disraeli's rise on the parliamentary barometer.

'Never mind dear about the Prussian question,' wrote Mary Anne from Biggleswade. Closeted in the little library, Disraeli prepared for the last great blaze of the season, the debate on the Chartists' National Petition. 'I have no time to write,' he told Sarah on the day of the debate, 'as I am full of Chartism.'[91] Very few Tories were in the House; Chartism was billed as a squabble between Whigs and Radicals, and the ministerial benches were crowded.

Disraeli's speech was hardly a conventional or predictable Tory response. He began by diagnosing the cause of Chartism. It was not economical, for such causes led to tumult but not organisation. Nor was it political; popular movements were not inspired by abstract political rights. 'But there was something between an economical and a political cause, which might be the spring of this great movement ... an apprehension on the part of the people, that their civil rights were invaded.' The movement for the Charter dated back to the Reform Bill. Before 1832 a small class was invested with political rights, on condition that they guarded the civil rights of the multitude. In 1832 power was transferred to a new class, who were not invested with public duties. The administration of justice, the command of the militia, the distribution of relief – none of these social duties was performed by the new political class. Willing to sacrifice neither time nor expense, the new class called for government that was both cheap and centralised. Hence the New Poor Law, an invasion of the civil rights of the people, which, Disraeli claimed, was the real cause of Chartism. Boldly independent, he blamed the Tories for consenting to the Poor Law. They had acted contrary to principle: 'the principle of opposing everything like central government, and favouring in every possible degree the distribution of power'. In England, claimed Disraeli, the exercise of political power must be associated with great public duties. If the Whigs supposed that they could establish a permanent government on a monarchy of the middle classes, they 'would be indulging a great delusion, which, if persisted in, must shake our institutions and endanger the Throne'. It was this government by the middle classes that the Chartists were protesting against, not the aristocracy, not the Corn Laws. Though I disapprove of the Charter declared Disraeli, I sympathise with the Chartists.[92]

Peel was in the House, and as Disraeli spoke he felt unsure of his audience, aware that the few Tories behind him liked what he said as little as the ministerialists packing the benches opposite. In *Sybil* he imagined the bewilderment his speech produced at Brooks's Club.

'I think he must be going to turn Radical,' said the Warwickshire peer.

'Why, the whole speech was against Radicalism,' said Mr Egerton.

'Ah, then he is going to turn Whig, I suppose.'

'He is ultra anti-Whig,' said Egerton.

'Then what the deuce is he?' said Mr Berners.

'Not a Conservative certainly, for Lady St Julians [Jersey] does nothing but abuse him.'

'I suppose he is crotchety,' suggested the Warwickshire noble.

'That speech of Egremont [Disraeli] was the most really democratic speech that I ever read,' said the grey-headed gentleman.[93]

The speech has been oddly neglected by some biographers. Disraeli saw it as a landmark, so much so, that in *Sybil*, where he put it into the mouth of his hero, Egremont, it provides the crisis of the book, the point where the two nations, aristocracy and Chartists, converge. Like Egremont, Disraeli was crotchety about the people. True, he had barely seen, far less spoken to, a Chartist; he had never visited Birmingham or Manchester; and he applauded a 'fine old cock' such as Watkins Wynn who placed himself at the head of the yeomanry to put down a Chartist revolt in Montgomeryshire. But Disraeli did not declare for the Chartists merely for effect. For one thing, Peel, as he well knew, did not like men who thought for themselves, and liked Radical Tories still less – Disraeli had much to lose. For another, the argument of his speech was consistent with his evolution since 1832. It has been suggested that Disraeli's support for the Chartists echoed the Tory Radical Richard Oastler, but ever since 1832 he had inveighed against the cold-hearted, tight-fisted low Whigs and called for an alliance of Tories and people.[94] Now it was the low Whigs and their Poor Law whom he blamed for Chartism; and he warned the aristocracy that unless they restored the civil rights of the people, they could not expect to keep their power.

Birmingham rioted upon parliament's rejection of the Chartist Petition, and the government rushed through police bills and extraordinary measures. 'I have made up my mind to oppose,' Disraeli told Sarah, 'even if I stand alone on our side, every anti-insurrectionary Measure which the government announce they will bring forward. They may be necessary, and much more, but the Whigs are not the people who ought to have recourse to them – they ought to resign.'[95] He had voted with the ministers and Peel against the Chartist Petition, but on 23 July he voted in a minority of three against a Birmingham Police Bill. Next day, he accused Lord John Russell of declaring war on Birmingham. Russell had no right, he declared, to come down at the eleventh hour of the session to call for extraordinary confidence and extraordinary powers, without giving a detailed account of the state of the country.[96]

The session dragged on through August, and as a thin House wearily nodded through police bills and reporters dozed in the gallery, Disraeli fought his lonely quixotic battles against the Whigs' anti-insurrectionary measures. He was encouraged by the Tory Radical Sir Francis Burdett, who also wished for a debate on the state of the nation. On 8 August he dined with Burdett – 'everything stately and old fashioned but agreeable'; full of Burdett's good claret, he went down to the House, where he spoke against the Rural Police Bill, taking his analysis from *Tait's Magazine*. 'It made great effect, quoting all the pages and names without any documents.' Next day he spoke again, reviewing the session. 'The complete command of the house I now have is remarkable. The moment I rose perfect silence, O'Connell particularly attentive, members running from the library and all hurrying to their seats.'[97]

John's death plunged Mary Anne into blackest mourning, from which she had only recently (and some thought prematurely) emerged. Nonetheless, the marriage was agreed for the end of the session, though Mary Anne was shy about naming a date and Disraeli, engrossed with Chartism, did not press. 'I don't much like leaving England in the present state of the country,' he confessed, and as the rain poured down relentlessly throughout August, drenching the harvest, he bleakly contemplated the prospect of revolution.[98] He and Mary Anne stayed a couple of nights at Bradenham (20–22 August), where they fixed on the following Wednesday, 28 August. On Saturday the ring was bought, the licence obtained, the clergyman appointed for half-past ten at St George's, Hanover Square.

Disraeli was very nervous – he had not slept. He spent the day before the wedding in a fruitless search first for Pyne and then for his partner Mr Richards, to whom he wrote in the small hours of Wednesday, 'You are aware that I have written to Mr B [Baring]? I am exceedingly anxious to speak to you on his affairs and to assist him to the utmost of my power – but it is IMPOSSIBLE for me not to quit London today, indeed I shd. say England.' After a few hours' rest, tossing and panicking about his debts, he wrote to Pyne on his wedding morning: 'During the honeymoon and travel, it is possible that letters may be occasionally *read*. I think it right to say that Mrs D. is aware that I am about raising a sum of money, but is ignorant of the method.' Would Pyne therefore write to Disraeli on the subject *generally*, avoiding details as to the method of security?[99]

Lyndhurst drove Disraeli to the church and acted as best man. Mary Anne, who had also passed a sleepless night, 'blazed in a travelling dress of exotic brilliancy'; she was given away by her blue-blooded cousin, William Scrope. No one else was there, and the ceremony was very short. Disraeli almost put the ring on the wrong finger, until corrected by Mary Anne. Mindful of the mock-feudal Eglinton Tournament, which was staged the same wet August day, he told his mother, 'Scrope was a very gallant father, and as for Lyndhurst, he made the most accomplished squire that ever tended a knight. If any in the Tournament obtain as good a one, I make no doubt that like myself, he will gain the Meed from the Queen of Beauty.'[100]

On 28 August Mary Anne wrote in her account book, 'Dear Dizzy became my husband'. Little did she know how inauspicious a beginning it was.

TEN

No Office from Peel

1839–42

THE HONEYMOON was spent in Baden, Munich and Paris, and exactly three months after the wedding, Disraeli and Mary Anne were back at Grosvenor Gate. London in December was foggy, flat and barren of gossip, but they were overwhelmed with business. Mary Anne was gratified by a magnificent forty-four-piece breakfast service of Worcester china, the generous gift of the Merediths. Disraeli drove her out to Highgate, to visit his cousin Nathaniel Basevi; the Basevis had little cause to love Disraeli, who had borrowed shamelessly from them, and the visit was not a success. 'It was a cold brisk day. Louisa was out, we were shown into a drawing room without a fire, and Nat, shorter than I could conceive humanity, with a mackintosh, a spade, an odd cap and singular spectacles, rushed in to greet us, supposing it was my mother and father; altogether a most chilly visit and a great failure.'[1]

About this time, Mary Anne jotted down a list, comparing their characters. She began with a couplet, 'His eyes they are as black as sloes, But oh! so beautiful his nose,' and then wrote her list, him on the left, her on the right:

Very calm	Very effervescent
Manners grave and almost sad	Gay and happy looking when speaking
Never irritable	Very irritable
Bad-humoured	Good-humoured
Warm in love but cold in friendship	Cold in love but warm in friendship
Very patient	No patience
Very studious	Very idle
Very generous	Only generous to those she loves
Often says what he does not think	Never says anything she does not think

It is impossible to find out who he likes or dislikes from his manner He does not show his feelings	Her manner is quite different, and to those she likes she show her feelings
No vanity	Much vanity
Conceited	No conceit
No self-love	Much self-love
He is seldom amused	Everything amuses her
He is a genius	She is a dunce
He is to be depended on to a certain degree	She is not to be depended on
His whole soul is devoted to politics and ambition	She has no ambition and hates politics

So it is evident they sympathise only on one subject: Maidstone, like most husbands and wives about their Children.[2]

At Grosvenor Gate, Disraeli lived like a guest in his wife's house. True, he was obliged to put up with his mother-in-law, Mrs Yate. But Mary Anne was in sole command of the household, which consisted of between six and eight indoor servants as well as a coachman. Even when she was away, he seldom spoke to the servants and they never spoke to him. He paid for nothing. Mary Anne financed the house out of her jointure, drawing money regularly from Drummond's Bank; it was she who bought the wine and supervised the stables, methodically balancing all receipts and outgoings in her account book. Everything was costed down to the last cup of tea: half a pound of black tea, she calculated, ought to last eleven days, and 'one pound of sugar ought to last five days for Mama and Dizzy not allowing for extras (or nearly 50 cups)'. Grosvenor Gate was truly a house of separate spheres, Mary Anne's businesslike efficiency complementing Dizzy's airy disregard for practicalities.

For the first time in his life, Disraeli could entertain; Grosvenor Gate was virtually designed for the purpose. It still stands today, much as it was. The front door on the wide south front opens on to a marble hall and a spectacular oval staircase, spiralling up four floors to a glass dome, and illuminated at night by brass chandeliers suspended from the dome. A mansion, you think, rather French, but the architect has played a trick, setting the staircase against the back north wall of the house; wide but shallow, Grosvenor Gate is the front slice of a grand town house with nothing behind and few bedrooms. Designed to impress, it is a stage set, glitzy and showy, rather than a solid Victorian family house. Snobbish visitors sniffed at the decoration, which was thoroughly conventional, the kind of effect an upholsterer might have contrived. The large downstairs dining-room was painted a dull brown, and hung with conventional paintings – the statutory Dead Game, and a bad copy of a Murillo. Upstairs, the huge L-shaped drawing-room was a blaze of splendour, crimson Wilton carpets, gold silk damask curtains and heavy gilt-framed mirrors. But the furniture was covered in dated yellow damask, and the rooms were bare of the fashionable clutter of Victoriana, stuffed birds and beadwork.[3] To the Victorian eye, Grosvenor Gate was distinctly old-fashioned, and a touch vulgar, the gilded cage of a Regency rentier; but Disraeli, short-sighted and almost devoid of taste, was oblivious. Nor did he object to Mary Anne's bright brown servants' livery, though the coats were badly made and brown was a colour unknown to heraldry.[4]

He held his first men's dinner on 19 January at two days' notice; scouring the House of Lords, and succeeding in collecting four – Lyndhurst, Strangford, Powerscourt, Ossulton – as well as D'Orsay and Bulwer; the men between them consumed eight bottles, carefully detailed by Mary Anne in her account book: three claret, three sherry, one champaign [sic], one port. The duke of Buckingham condescended to dine in February – a coup, but a worrying one, as 'society bores him and the farm is his only interest'; fortunately, the duke was amused, 'examined the tables, vowed he had never drunk such champaigne, and lauded the china'. Altogether Disraeli invited sixty MPs, and forty came. 'I shall now rest upon my oars,' he told Sarah, ignoring the anti-semitic jibes of the *Satirist*, which mocked his 'mansion' ('We trust the police will keep an eye on him.'). 'There is scarcely anyone of station in the House or society that I have not paid this attention to, which was most politic, and would not have created such sensation at any other time of the year.'[5]

No invitations came that summer from Lady Londonderry, whose reaction to the marriage was distinctly frosty. But though marriage barred him from the glittering salons, Mary Anne was a capable hostess. A great many lords and ladies called on her, Dizzy reported, and she was happy in her successes. At a supper of Lyndhurst's, she wore the brilliant diamonds which Wyndham Lewis had given her (valued at 3500 guineas); she yielded, said Disraeli, only to Lady Londonderry, who wore her Eglinton tournament dress, which was correct but not becoming. Mary Anne was painted by Chalon in bare shoulders and ribbons, her hair in spaniel-like bunches, and Disraeli published the portrait in Lady Blessington's *Book of Beauty*, inviting more cruel jibes from the *Satirist*, which sneered at Disraeli's attempt to pass off his rubicund, middle-aged wife as being of youth and beauty.[6]

Isaac was delighted by the marriage, and gave Mary Anne a new carriage as a wedding present. Both Dizzy and Mary Anne worried over Isaac's sight, which failed alarmingly at the end of 1839: when he looked at a blank sheet of paper it swarmed with black print. Disraeli ordered his father to Grosvenor Gate, and summoned the royal surgeon oculist, who pronounced a heartening diagnosis: the spectres were caused not by an organic defect of the eye but by the morbid state of the system. Isaac was living too high, drinking too much sherry and soda. Abstinence, the doctors insisted, would cure his sight. They were living in a learned fools' paradise. Isaac's sight never recovered; he had suffered what Disraeli later realised was a 'paralysis of the optic nerve', which his biographer translates to mean myopic retinal degeneration. Though unable to read or write, Isaac's spirits were not crushed: he and Sarah embarked together on another book, the *Amenities of Literature*, three volumes of fragments from his manuscripts, which they compiled closeted in the library at Bradenham – an odd couple, the gouty old *philosophe*, whose silky manners and easy morals jarred the earnestness of the new age, and his straight-backed sharp-eyed daughter.[7]

Sarah, who never went out, and who lived vicariously through Dizzy's success, took less kindly to his marriage than Isaac did; Mary Anne, who was barely educated, could never take Sarah's place as Dizzy's quick-witted audience and well-read critic. Mary Anne was soon jealous of Sarah's intimacy with her brother, and although his daily letters to Sarah continued, he wrote secretly from the Carlton, where Sarah's letters were kept by a friendly porter. He told her occasionally to write to Grosvenor Gate, or 'the sudden ceasing of the correspondence may produce surprise'.[8] The introduction of the penny post in January 1840 brought an end to his treasured privilege of franking; he had now to catch the hateful new post, which closed at five or six, before any news was heard and far too early in the day. Disraeli was by then barely out of Grosvenor Gate, often rising as late as midday or one.

As a married woman Mary Anne could not own property, but under the marriage settlement her property and capital were held in trust for her exclusive use by George Dawson and Sir John Guest. Disraeli could not get his hands on her money without her agreement, and he still kept her in ignorance of his debts. So he was forced to carry on another clandestine correspondence – with William Pyne. He was dissatisfied with Pyne, who had become invisible when most needed and dilatory about answering letters. In January 1840 Disraeli told him, '*I wish everything to be left to me at this moment.*' His plan to end the system and pay off his debts had been wishful thinking; he lived still in fear of irate creditors presenting themselves at Grosvenor Gate in the hopes of extracting money from his rich wife. An officer serving a writ in July 'deported himself so vulgarly and violently', he told Pyne, 'that I was obliged to order the servants to turn him out'.[9]

Parliament reassembled in January 1840 in fear and trembling of a Chartist rising – 'the troops ordered to be ready, the police in all directions, and the fiire engines all full'.[10] Disraeli sat listening impatiently while the House became every hour more deeply embroiled in the issues of parliamentary privilege raised by the case of Stockdale *v*. Hansard. Stockdale had sued Hansard for printing a libel about him in a parliamentary paper; the law courts upheld Stockdale, but the government came to Hansard's rescue, claiming that he was protected by parliamentary privilege. Any chance of defeating the government was crushed by Peel, who championed the privileges of the House against the courts, aligning himself with Russell. Like most of the Tories, however, Disraeli took the side of the law; he made a speech (21 January) likening the ministry's claims for parliamentary privilege to the grasping spirit of the Commons in the reign of Charles I.

In his pocket as he spoke was a note from Peel, inviting him to a meeting of sixteen MPs the following day; it was proudly preserved by Mary Anne, who wrote on it, 'Dizzy was the only one who had not been in office'. The meeting was hardly a Shadow Cabinet as Monypenny suggests, but Disraeli's invitation was certainly a mark of Peel's favour.[11] He was not asked again, and it is easy to see why. '[They] say that I am trying to form a new party, and acknowledge that I have partizans ... Fas est ab hoste,' he commented, quoting Ovid (It is fair to learn from your enemy). He was sitting in the House, listening to a Tory baronet, Sir John Yarde Buller, moving the opposition motion of no confidence in the government, and 'if possible speaking worse than his colleague Sir Tom [Acland] did last year – Sir Tom only stuttered, this here Baronet sticks'. Disraeli was put up early in the debate to answer a government speaker who broke down, landing him with 'a lame bird to kill or rather a dying one – and though I made a somewhat brilliant Guerilla operation, there was not that solid tactical movement that I had originally contemplated'.[12] He had no party yet, but his speech made plain his independence from the Tories, who censured the government for failing to put down the Chartists. 'I am not afraid or ashamed to say', he declared, 'that I wish more sympathy had been shown on both sides towards the Chartists.'[13]

The defeat of Buller's motion by a disappointing majority of twenty-one decided the fate of the session, confirming the Whigs in office. 'Everything is very dull,' he told Sarah on 7 February, 'nothing is thought of but the Queen's marriage, and nobody ever mentions it.' Victoria married Albert on 10 February, and Disraeli spent all day 'prince hunting', at length spotting the royal couple as they processed through Kensington – 'he is a very good looking fellow.' A week later, he joined the procession of members to Buckingham Palace to tender congratulations; he wore court dress ('it is generally agreed', he told Sarah, 'that *I* am never to wear any other but a Court costume; being, according to Ossulton, a very Charles 2'), and he found the royal presence 'altogether effective', the prince leaning on the queen's left 'in high military fig very handsome'; even Buckingham Palace, which he had never entered before, impressed him, always having heard it abused – though it was nothing beside the Bavarian palaces he and Mary Anne saw on honeymoon.[14]

Disraeli had no plans for a monarchical revival, but he was strongly drawn to the idea of a new party. Charles Attwood, Newcastle Radical and brother of Thomas Attwood of the Birmingham Political Union, wrote in June, calling for a new party of Conservatives, '*which shall* embrace the Radical masses, Sir, and no mistake'. I entirely agree with you, Disraeli promptly replied, about a union of the Conservative party and the Radical Masses. 'Their interests are identical; united they form the Nation; and their division has only permitted a miserable minority, under the specious name of the People, to spoil all rights of property and person.' Since entering public life in 1832, he claimed, 'I have worked for no other object, and no other end, than to aid the formation of a National Party' – hence his satisfaction at Attwood's report that such a union was progressing in Northumberland, 'long the sacred refuge of Saxon liberty'.[15] He developed the line of thought in a speech on the Chartists the following month. The aristocracy, he declared, were the natural leaders of the people; 'for the aristocracy and the labouring population formed the nation, and it was only when gross misconception ... prevailed, that a miserable minority, under the specious designation of popular advocates, was able to pervert the nation's order'.[16]

Not that he trusted the people he aspired to lead. Mary Anne's investments included Welsh railway shares, and Disraeli wrote anxiously to ascertain whether there were many Chartists in the neighbourhood, lest they affect the share value.[17]

On 6 August 1840 Louis Napoleon Bonaparte landed at Boulogne with fifty-six men, in a harebrained attempt to dethrone King Louis Philippe by inciting rebellion in the local garrison. 'Never was anyone so rash and crude to all appearances as this "monsieur",' Disraeli wrote scathingly, 'for he was joined by no one. A fine house in Carlton Gardens, his Arabian horses, and excellent cook was hardly worse than his present situation.' He had met Louis Napoleon the previous summer at Lady Blessington's. D'Orsay had befriended the prince, banished by Louis Philippe after an earlier attempt; grand society, however, kept aloof: 'the Tories did not love revolutionary dynasties, and the Whigs being in office could not sanction a pretender'. At a water-party at Bulwer's Craven Cottage on the Thames, Disraeli and Mary Anne arrived late, and Louis Napoleon, who was even later, offered to row them to meet the other guests. He rowed straight into a mudbank, the boat stuck, and Mary Anne berated him: 'You should not undertake things which you cannot accomplish. You are always, Sir, too adventurous.' Disraeli of course remained silent.[18]

Forty years later, in *Endymion*, Disraeli sketched Louis Napoleon as the mysterious Colonel Albert, a foreign gentleman whose links with secret societies and alliance with Rothschild place him at the centre of the real powers behind the scenes of European diplomacy. *Endymion* was written with the advantage of hindsight. In 1840 Disraeli could only wonder at Louis Napoleon's foolhardiness, never for one moment suspecting that within a decade he would become president of France. Nor did Disraeli appreciate the similarities between his own Radical Toryism and the mélange of Socialism and Bonapartism which the prince had concocted in *Idées Napoléoniennes*, written in London in 1839.

The social sensation of the summer of 1840 was the duke of Buckingham's ball at Stowe, in honour of Queen Adelaide, widow of William IV. Disraeli grumbled at the bore; a queen dowager, 'seems to me as uninteresting a personage as can well be imagined – no power, and, in the present instance, no society, for she has not a court, although we pay for it'. They travelled by rail to Wolverton, bringing their carriage with them, themselves in the first class, the two servants third, and posted on to Buckingham, where they stayed; no doubt Dizzy was silent and yawning with anticipatory and affected disgust, while Mary Anne supervised the arrangements, totting up the cost of the expedition, which came to precisely £11 19s 1d – virtually half the yearly wage of her maid, Collings. Mary Anne wore her diamonds, and the duke gave her his arm and took her up to the duchess in grandiose style; but Lyndhurst, whom they met, shook his head with an expression which spoke volumes. Not only had Buckingham erected a temporary room for the ball – 'in itself a blunder, as anyone can guingettise,' wrote Disraeli, coining a word, 'and princes give balls because they have palaces'. But the space was colossal, capable of holding 2000 people, and not 600 were there, including the scrapings of the county, and 'so many priests that it had the character of the Archbishop's levée'. Nothing could be more dull, or more completely a failure, he wrote savagely; it was 'the greatest failure of the ducal house of failures'. Perhaps he already knew that Buckingham was living beyond his means, and, like Disraeli though on a princely scale, borrowing to pay interest on his debts. Mary Anne, however, was gratified by her visit to Stowe and, Disraeli told Sarah disloyally, 'the Morning Post having noticed Mrs Disraeli "among the brilliant assemblage" we are repayed for the bore'.[19]

Isaac, Maria and Sarah spent the autumn of 1840 touring north Wales; Disraeli and his wife stayed in London. It was the third bad harvest in succession, but in London Disraeli lost touch with feeling in the country; he did not attend the Bucks Quarter Sessions in October and hear the grumbling of the country gentry; nor did he visit his Maidstone constituency, which he had virtually ceased to represent, having quarrelled with his greedy constituents over money. London in the autumn was a desert, he complained, and empty of men, who had flocked north to shoot, leaving the petticoats in an immense majority. He and Mary Anne were kept alive by Lord Walpole, their elegant and fantastical new friend whom Disraeli called the Horace Walpole of the nineteenth century; Walpole stayed at Grosvenor Gate, and his rivalry with Monckton Milnes for the hand of the fabulously wealthy Angela Burdett-Coutts formed the autumn's topic of gossip, which Dizzy and Mary Anne worried like dogs with a bone. (Miss Burdett-Coutts remained unmarried for another forty years.) Disraeli had met Monckton Milnes, the poet and MP, the previous year, when he was asked to one of Milnes's celebrated breakfast parties. Carlyle described Milnes as 'a most bland-smiling, semi-quizzical, affectionate, highbred, Italianized little man of five feet, who has long olive-blond hair, a dimple next to no chin, and flings his arm round your neck when he addresses you in public society'. Disraeli found him fussy and somewhat absurd, cruelly describing his face as 'like a Herculaneum masque, or a countenance cut out of an orange'.[20]

That autumn, he made two valuable new political friendships. One was with Henry Hope, a Tory MP and the eldest of three brothers, the quarrelling heirs to a Dutch banking fortune; though no longer as wealthy as the Rothschilds, Henry Hope was a very rich man. In October, Disraeli and Mary Anne stayed with Hope at Deepdene, near Dorking, where in the midst of romantic grounds and steeply sloping glades of rhododendrons, they found 'the most perfect Italian palace you can conceive – full of balconies, adorned on the outside with busts and crowned with terraced towers'. Hope, who was four years younger than Disraeli, possessed, Disraeli later wrote, 'a penetrating judgement and an inflexible will'. Though unmarried, he was a princely host, and he hankered, not exactly after power but after the political influence that his own vast fortune together with Deepdene made possible. He was a natural political patron, and in *Coningsby*, which was dedicated to him, Disraeli paid tribute to his contribution to the Young England movement.[21]

The second new friendship that autumn was with George Smythe, whom he encountered through the contest for the high stewardship of Cambridge, which fell vacant in October. The Tories nominated Lyndhurst, who was abroad taking the waters in Marienbad and visiting Metternich, and Lyndhurst was opposed by the twenty-three-year-old Lord Lyttelton, whose campaign was organised by Lord John Manners, second son of the duke of Rutland. Disraeli, a warm partisan of Lyndhurst's, blamed

Lyttelton's candidature on the greed of the fellows of Trinity, who were tired of waiting for loaves and fishes, and sought to establish a claim on the government. This was too cynical: Lyttelton claimed to stand on non-political grounds and opposed Lyndhurst's candidature as a mere political job. For Manners, the election was a struggle of principle versus politics: 'Hurrah for the former!' It was a clash of generations. Not only was Lyndhurst unacceptable as a place-hunter and party hack (he was backed by Peel, and the duke of Wellington canvassed for him); he was too 'easy', too comfortable for young men like Manners who had been fired by the new moral earnestness, and the election developed into a whispering campaign against Lyndhurst's immoral past. Disraeli scoffed at 'moral' Lyttelton who, he was told, was one of the greatest rakes at Cambridge, and he crowed when Lyndhurst romped home with twice as many votes as Lyttelton. 'It is considered one of the greatest triumphs on record. The other side are in despair.'[22]

Manners's greatest friend at Cambridge was George Smythe, and Manners was bitterly disappointed when, at the bidding of his father Lord Strangford, Smythe reneged on a promise to vote for Lyttelton and voted for Lyndhurst instead. Strangford was a friend of Disraeli's, an impoverished peer, once a diplomat, now a waspish drawing-room reactionary; he had scraped together sufficient pennies to buy back part of the family estate in Kent, and on their honeymoon Disraeli and Mary Anne had visited the chapel full of family tombs which Strangford had restored in Ashford church. His son George was extraordinarily attractive, though not really good-looking – spoilt, precocious but brilliant. In *Endymion*, where he features as Waldershare, Disraeli described him as 'profligate, but sentimental; unprincipled, but romantic; the child of whim, and the slave of an imagination so freakish and deceptive, that it was always impossible to foretell his course'.[23] Written forty years after, Disraeli's flat, colourless prose gives little idea of Smythe's vivid magnetism. Disraeli enlisted his support for Lyndhurst's campaign, and Smythe was present at the small dinner held at Grosvenor Gate to celebrate Lyndhurst's election. A large silver flagon was filled with mulled wine, and Lord Forester drank Lyndhurst's health, three times three.[24] Smythe's sister married Disraeli's friend Henry Baillie, another tie linking the politician and young George.

At Grosvenor Gate Disraeli was harassed by creditors. On 1 November a writ, delivered to Mary Anne while Disraeli was out, produced 'a terrible domestic crisis'. Perhaps an explanation followed. Certainly, the verse he addressed to Mary Anne on her birthday (11 November) suggests that harmony was restored:

With airy fancy and with spirits light
　　Breaking the dense
Cloud of ill-omened thoughts that hover round
　　The ambitious breast,
That restless chases Reputation's sound,
　　And finds no rest.
But on her bosom and her gentle heart,
　　There is yet peace.[25]

Christmas 1840 was spent at Deepdene – a large and merry party with Henry Hope. The *Satirist* sneered at the 'Jew and genteel', and pictured Mary Anne showing off her whitewashed neck and face, and Disraeli calculating how much he could borrow from his host; did they see it, one wonders. After a visit to Bradenham, they were back in London at the end of January 1841, ready for the reassembly of parliament. The dwindling of the Whigs' majority to single figures meant that by-elections were critical, and George Smythe was fighting Canterbury. On 30 January Disraeli told Sarah, 'Forester, Loftus, Ld John Manners, and a large party of "Young England" have gone down today. I was asked but declined.'[26]

　　The phrase Young England jumps out; it is Disraeli's first use of the name, perhaps its first recorded use to describe the group of George Smythe, Lord John Manners and their friends. It all began in the summer vacation of 1838, which Smythe and Manners spent in the Lake District, where they heard Frederick Faber preach. Faber was a disciple of Newman and the Oxford Movement, and his preaching came as a revelation to the two Cambridge undergraduates. 'We have now virtually pledged ourselves', Manners wrote in his journal, 'to attempt to restore what? I hardly know – but still it is a glorious attempt ... I think a change is working for the better, and all, or nearly all, the enthusiasm of the young spirits of Britain is with us.' Faber talked wildly about separating church and state, 'and then for a crash to end in the supremacy of the Church'. Smythe and Manners, on the other hand, were convinced that their mission lay in politics.[27]

　　The religious inspiration of Young England meant little to Disraeli, who was impervious to the spiritual fervour generated by Newman. Nor, at this point, did Manners and Smythe see Disraeli as a possible leader. On the contrary, Manners, who met him at the end of January 1841, was distinctly suspicious; he wrote in his diary, 'D'Israeli talked well, but a little too well.'[28] Yet Disraeli's sympathy for the Chartists chimed with Young England, as did his opposition to the New Poor Law. On 8 February he moved the postponement of a Poor Law Amendment Bill; the Poor Law, he claimed, was an affront against Tory principle, an unnecessary and illegitimate piece of government interference. Government had achieved nothing of great benefit in domestic policy: 'Government did not institute the system of national education – did not institute the universities – it did not create our colonial empire – it did not conquer India – it did not make our roads or build our bridges.' Interference over the Poor Law had brought a political revolution, destroying the old parochial constitution of the country by grouping parishes into Poor Law unions. In the name of economy, the poor were immured in workhouses like prisons and treated like criminals; yet expenditure was not diminished, and an immense mass of disaffection had resulted.[29]

Greville grumbled at Tory critics of the Poor Law, whom he accused of currying favour with their constituencies by attacking an unpopular measure which they were anxious to pass. Disraeli, however, had little contact with his constituents, and his opposition was sincere – he voted against the Poor Law in defiance of his party four times during the 1841 session.[30] Despite this independence, he hoped for notice from Peel.

The first battle of the session came at the end of February over Morpeth's Irish Registration Bill, reducing the qualification for the Irish county franchise. Never were four such nights, Disraeli told Sarah, and on 25 February the government majority dropped to five. Disraeli dined at home each day, dressed, and returned to the House at ten; after the House was up he supped at Crockford's, to which he had just been elected and which was 'like a French palace and very different to any club' – the splendours of its glittering golden saloon are lovingly described in the opening chapter of *Sybil*.[31]

Mindful of the division over Morpeth's bill, Disraeli wrote an article for *The Times*, signed Atticus, addressed as an open letter to the duke of Wellington whom he had met the previous year ('he accorded me a most gracious and friendly reception and looked right hearty').[32] 'Your Grace', began Atticus, oily but ironic, 'has performed a greater number of great exploits than any living man; but you never achieved a deed more remarkable or more difficult than keeping the Whigs in office.' Ministers, he argued, carry on the government of the country by two methods: 'first, practically, by a Conservative majority, and secondly, theoretically, by a revolutionary majority'. As long as anything is to be done – a tax raised, the national honour vindicated, an armament equipped – a successful appeal is made to the loyal support of the Conservative party, 'but the moment that party evinces any ambition to possess itself of the forms as well as the spirit of power ... the theoretical method is forthwith recurred to'. Some abstract declaration about ecclesiastical property or the franchise is pompously announced; and, as in the case of Morpeth's Bill, the revolutionary majority is produced to demonstrate that the Conservatives are disqualified for office.[33]

It was a clever analysis, encapsulating the situation in a nutshell, and the article was a success – 'Atticus an IMMENSE hit,' he told Sarah, as usual exaggerating. He and Mary Anne dined out so often that season that she did not hire a box at the opera; 'this seems like gaiety,' Disraeli told Sarah, 'but people complain that London is very dull.' It was as flat as the end of the session – the Carlton in March was 'a *tableau vivant* and the few men lingering about it really corpses'. Prince Esterhazy gave a recherché party, where were the duke, Peel and Stanley, and Mary Anne had a long conversation with Sir Robert – she was very friendly with his sister, Mrs Dawson. Disraeli attended a dinner at Peel's which was, like all male gatherings, dull enough. 'I had hopes of at least eating a good dinner, for our host entertains well; but that chatterbox [Monckton] Milnes would sit next to me, and I had not even the consolation of a silent stuff.' But he was in raptures at a party at Lady Blessington's when D'Orsay introduced him as 'one of the next Ministers'.[34]

Dissolution loomed, and Disraeli grew uneasy about his debts. Mash, to whom he still owed £5000, had died, and his executors threatened to bring an action, Pyne having failed to arrange a settlement with them. A bill of D'Orsay's for £754 which Disraeli had endorsed, returning one of D'Orsay's many favours to him, became due; it was in the hands of 'a great ruffian', and Disraeli was obliged to borrow to pay it. G. S. Ford, whose writ in November had precipitated the domestic crisis, lent him the money at 40 per cent. Despairing of Pyne, whom he described as 'done up', Disraeli authorised Ford to silence his creditors, tidying his judgement debts before the election.[35]

Faced with bad harvests, a declining revenue and a disintegrating majority, the Whigs proposed a radical new financial policy. '"Lord Roehampton [Palmerston] thinks that something must be done about the corn laws," murmured Berengaria one day to Endymion, rather crestfallen; "but they will try sugar and timber first."' So, in *Endymion*, Disraeli imagined the first stirrings and whispering of the Whig budget of 1841, 'which led to such vast consequences, and which, directly or indirectly, gave such a new form and colour to English politics'. On 30 April Russell announced a change in the Corn Laws, and in the budget which followed Baring proposed reductions in the duties on timber and sugar. 'We are here in the midst of a revolution ... and it is utterly impossible to say what turn affairs will take. I can't help thinking the Whigs, tho' they have shown their utter desperation and recklessness, have overshot the mark.' The Whigs were doomed; their attempt to rally the Radicals by lashing the great monopolies –

West Indian planters, Canadian timber merchants and squires and farmers – created instead a clamour in favour of Conservative principles.[36]

Political crisis pumped Disraeli's adrenalin: 'our party are in high spirits, and full of confidence – but the excitement is very great and the Whigs are evidently desperate.' The present of a peafowl from Bradenham gave him an excuse to make up a dinner at forty-eight hours' notice: the duke of Buckingham, Lord Salisbury, Lord Francis Egerton, and 'some others as great, perhaps at this moment more influential' – to wit, Goulburn, a member of Peel's inner group. In the House, Peel attacked the government over sugar, and Disraeli intervened in the debate; his speech, refuting the argument that reduced duties on West Indian sugar would open new markets to the British manufacturer, drew 'iron tears down Pluto's cheek', in the form of praise and applause from Peel.[37]

The government was soundly beaten over sugar, but still they clung to office. On 27 May Peel moved a resolution of no confidence, and Disraeli spoke again, prefacing his speech with a fulsome eulogy of Peel, whom he absolved from the charge of faction:

> Placed in an age of rapid civilisation and rapid transition, he had adapted the practical character of his measures to the condition of the times. When in power, he had never proposed a change which he did not carry, and when in Opposition he never forgot that he was at the head of the Conservative party. He had never employed his influence for factious purposes, and had never been stimulated in his exertions by a disordered desire of obtaining office. ... Whether in or out of office he had done his best to make the settlement of the new constitution of England work for the benefit of the present time and of posterity.[38]

This was the case for Peel's defence; Professor Gash, Peel's admiring biographer, could hardly have done better. Not a hint of the bitter criticism Disraeli was later to voice in *Coningsby*, where he savaged Peel for his betrayal of Tory principle.

In 1841 Peel was the man the country wanted. The Whigs were beaten in the no confidence motion by a majority of one; still refusing to resign, they announced a dissolution on 9 June.

Disraeli was ready for the dissolution. He and Mary Anne had broken with Maidstone very soon after their marriage, and since December 1839 his friend Lord Forester had been searching for a seat for him. His reputation as a critic of the Poor Law brought an invitation to stand for Leicester, but on Forester's advice he opted for Shrewsbury, where expenses were lower and where Forester's Shropshire estate gave him local influence. Not that his return was a certainty: it was a two-member borough with a strong Liberal tradition, and in 1837 representation was divided between a Conservative and a Liberal. Anxious to keep expenses to a minimum, Disraeli proposed joining forces with George Tomline, his Tory running mate, and employing a single agent. On 8 June he and Tomline issued their address. It made no mention of the Poor Law, but stressed the Whigs' attack on the great monopolies; their attempt to promote factitious hostility between the interests of the agriculturist, the manufacturer and the merchant was condemned, and so was their mismanagement of the nation's finances.[39] Disraeli saw Tomline on 12 June, and found him 'frigid, *jealous*, and impracticable'; suspecting Tomline of plotting to steal a march and arrive in Shrewsbury first, Disraeli made hurried preparations for the journey. 'I must now into the city,' he told Mary Anne, 'and get the *argent* and lodge it at Drummonds. Thank God and you, 'tis all ready.' The *argent* or pocket money included £500 Disraeli raised from Pyne a few weeks earlier; Mary Anne also contributed. 'Tomline says', Disraeli told her, 'he understands the Salopians don't like *speaking*. We shall see. George Smythe quizzes all this; I have told *him*.'[40]

Shrewsbury was a gruelling twelve hours' journey from London, six hours by rail to Wolverhampton and a further six hours by road; Disraeli and Mary Anne arrived on 14 June, travelling in their own carriage, bringing with them £180, and put up at the Lion Inn. Canvassing was wearying, from eight in the morning until sunset, 'scarcely with ½ hour's bait', and he met with even more anti-Jewish abuse than usual: pieces of pork on sticks waved in his face, and a man driving up to the hustings in a cart drawn by an ass, or 'Jerusalem pony', announcing 'I come here to take you back to Jerusalem'. Undaunted by the cries of Jew and Judas, after a week's canvassing he felt that 'all looks very well indeed – all I fear is overconfidence'.[41]

He was right. On 24 June, the day after the dissolution of parliament deprived him of the privilege of immunity from arrest, a handbill was plastered over the town, listing the judgement debts against him during the past three years, which totalled over £21,000. He seeks a place in parliament merely for the purpose of avoiding prison or bankruptcy, shouted the poster. Peering through his eyeglass at the familiar names, Disraeli coolly remarked, 'How accurate they are! Now let us go on.'[42] Most of the debts were in fact settled – not paid exactly, but subject to holding arrangements which squared them for the time being, and Disraeli wrote anxiously to Pyne's partner to settle with the few creditors still outstanding. 'Affairs are *urgent*.' To Mary Anne, the poster was probably a revelation: Disraeli had concealed the extent of his debts, refusing to name a figure. On 25 June he issued an address, explaining that many of the judgements of recent date were collaterals for a noble friend (D'Orsay) who had since settled his affairs, relieving Disraeli of all liability. 'I should not have solicited your Suffrages,' he declared, gilding the lily, 'had I not been in possession of that ample Independence which renders the attainment of any Office in the State, except as the recognition of Public Service, to me a matter of complete indifference.'[43]

In the long run, Disraeli believed, the attack did him good, but he was saved by Mary Anne. The notes she kept reveal the thoroughness of her canvass, and her skill and success in eliciting promises. Galvanised by what the local Liberal paper enviously described as the energy of despair, she beguiled and flattered the shopkeepers – 'Such a gay lady, Sir!' they told Disraeli, 'You never can have a dull moment, Sir' – gaining the votes of the £10 householders to whom he had nothing to say, but whom he could not afford to ignore. 'Mary Anne has done wonders'; and he told his mother that Mary Anne alone had succeeded in making him 'from a somewhat unpopular, to one of the most popular candidates in her Majesty's dominions'.[44]

The poll was declared on 30 June, with Disraeli a close second to Tomline, and comfortably ahead of his Liberal opponents.[45] He and Mary Anne were chaired, and made a triumphal procession around the town, quaffing the triumph cup at forty different spots, which made both of them tipsy but Disraeli claimed that he came admirably to time to a dinner and a speech. Then to nearby Loton Park, where they stayed with Sir Baldwin Leighton, whom he described as a complete old English gentleman – sentiments not reciprocated by Sir Baldwin, who in his diary described Disraeli as clever, but 'devoid of any principle except that of getting himself on in the world'.[46]

'Here I am again,' Disraeli wrote to Sarah on 7 July, 'having been only five days out of Parliament!' Only days before on the verge of disgrace and prison, he was now jubilant, gloating at the Carlton as news came in of Conservative gains and Peel's majority climbed from 60 to more like 80. 'Never was anything like it,' he wrote, 'since the India Bill', when Fox was dismissed by George III and beaten by Pitt at the 1784 election; in fact, it was without precedent: the first time an opposition had beaten in an election a majority in office. The Whigs, however, were still in office, and the meeting of parliament was not until the end of August. Meanwhile, as the rain poured down, presaging yet another disastrous harvest ('We are frightened out of our wits'), the press abounded with rumours – Disraeli was billed by the *Herald* as Paymaster of the Forces, and by the *Satirist* as '*Jew*-nior' Lord at the Admiralty. He affected unconcern: 'all will remain in obscurity until partridge shooting' (1 September), he wrote portentously.[47]

Not that he was idle. On 2 August *The Times* published a letter signed by Pittacus calling for the removal of the speaker, Shaw-Lefevre, who was accused of partisanship in the choice of election committees. Shaw-Lefevre, though Whig, was an able speaker, and the campaign against him, backed by the Ultra wing of the party, stank of the kind of intrigue Peel was determined to avoid. Bonham, Peel's henchman, told his chief that Disraeli was Pittacus, and that he had been spreading bitter abuse; Stanley also blamed Disraeli. On his return to London from Bradenham, Disraeli met Bonham, who informed him, 'with that morose jocularity which he sometimes affects, that the party was flourishing, notwithstanding my attempts "to stir up dissension on the Speakership"'. Disraeli instantly composed an aggrieved letter to Peel, registering surprise that Bonham should accuse him of the Pittacus letter. 'I confess my mortification,' he wrote, 'that after having occasionally, for nearly ten years, exercised my pen, when I thought it could serve the interests of our party, I should be esteemed the author of a paper which I remember as absolutely deficient in the commonest rules of composition.' Surely Peel, who had recognised him as the author of the Laelius letter of 1839, did not suppose that anything so ill-written as the Pittacus letter came from Disraeli's pen?[48]

His arrogant letter did not actually deny the charge of authorship; he was silent too on the substantive issue of the speakership, and with good reason: he was up to his neck in the plot to oust Shaw-Lefevre. But it is unlikely that he was so rash as to publish such a letter when Peel was about to form his government; Pittacus was probably Sir Richard Vyvyan, an Ultra MP and open malcontent, whom Disraeli met in July and described as 'a man of great abilities and richly cultivated'.[49]

Parliament met on 19 August and unanimously re-elected the speaker. Still hopeful of office, Disraeli wrote to Sarah: 'All is blank but in a few days …? …'[50] On 24 August, Peel moved a motion of no confidence, and Disraeli rose to speak. He accused the government of clinging to office unconstitutionally: when defeated in June, they had claimed the support of the crown, dragging the queen into the faction fight; now they held office in defiance of parliament, where they were a minority, and they must resign forthwith. That a government beaten at the polls should resign before meeting parliament was a novel constitutional doctrine, and his speech met with an ominous and conspicuous shake of the head from his enemy Stanley. The government fell in the early morning of 28 August, beaten by a majority of 91. 'We have beat the enemy to pieces,' Disraeli scribbled to Mary Anne '– not only turned out but *no one* can do anything of the kind in future.'[51]

Peel kissed hands on Monday 30 August, and the list of Cabinet ministers appeared in *The Times* on Wednesday. The junior appointments followed.

No letter came from Peel. 'I can't stay at this infernal club,' Disraeli wrote from the Carlton, and walked to Crockford's for a change of scene.[52] Still nothing the next day or the next, when the first list of junior ministers trickled into the newspapers.

On Saturday night, 4 September, Mary Anne wrote to Sir Robert, imploring him to recognise Mr Disraeli's exertions. 'Literature he has abandoned for politics,' she wrote. 'Do not destroy his hopes and make him feel his life has been a mistake.' She told Peel of her past exertions for his splendid self, of the more than £40,000 spent at Maidstone through her influence alone; one seat, she pledged, should always be at his command. It was a begging letter: 'My husband's political career is for ever crushed, if you do not appreciate him' could hardly be construed as anything but a request for office. Tradition alleges that Mary Anne wrote without Dizzy's knowledge, but there is no evidence for this; the story seems a later invention, intended to shield him from the charge of soliciting office.[53]

Disraeli himself wrote to Peel on the Sunday. He disdained, he said, to press his obvious claim – the elections he had fought, the sums expended, the seat at his command – in short, all the points which Mary Anne had covered. He stressed instead the peculiarity of his case: 'I have had to struggle against a storm of political hate and malice, which few men ever experienced, from the moment, at the instigation of a member of your cabinet [Lyndhurst], I enrolled myself under your banner.' He told Peel he had been sustained by the conviction that recognition would come; to be unrecognised was overwhelming – save me, he begged, from an intolerable humiliation.

Peel's reply was a big dog barking at a little dog: no member of the Cabinet ever received the slightest authority from me, he said, to make to you the communication you mention. Wilfully misunderstanding Disraeli's letter, Peel pompously demonstrated that members of the Cabinet were not empowered to make offers of office. This was not what Disraeli had said, and he wrote at once to correct Peel: there had been no pledge of office from a member of the Cabinet. If Peel had made such a pledge and not redeemed it, he would not have written. 'Not to be appreciated may be a mortification; to be baulked of a promised reward is only a vulgar accident of life, to be borne without a murmur.'[54]

What a crash, after all that work, all that expense. There have been many attempts to explain Peel's failure to give Disraeli office. According to one theory, published by George Smythe in a newspaper article of 1854, Peel was dissuaded by the parasites who surrounded him, the Crokers and Bonhams, upon whom Disraeli took his revenge in *Coningsby*. Certainly Croker had little love for him, and Bonham, who drew up the working lists for Peel, even less; with the Pittacus affair fresh in his mind, he saw Disraeli as nothing but a troublemaker. A second theory, proposed by Sir Philip Rose, blames Stanley, who nursed a grudge stretching back ten years to Disraeli's involvement in the disgrace and disappearance of his gambler brother Henry. Too bad that an upstart Jew should know his family secrets! In the House, Stanley did his formidable best to trip Disraeli up, and in 1841 is said to have told Peel, who was prepared to pay heavily to secure Stanley's inclusion in the Cabinet, that 'if that scoundrel were taken in he would not remain himself'. Another theory Rose reported ascribes Peel's coolness to the Henrietta Sykes-Lyndhurst scandal, which still cast its shadow over Disraeli.[55]

These theories, which float down to us smelling faintly of the Carlton's leather armchairs and cigar smoke, share a common assumption: that Peel wanted to give Disraeli office. There is not a scrap of evidence that Peel ever intended any such thing; his name does not appear on any of the lists Peel used in constructing his government.[56]

Disraeli's only real hope lay in a powerful patron pushing his claims. Two of his patrons held Cabinet office: the duke of Buckingham as lord privy seal, and Lyndhurst who, notwithstanding the Henrietta scandal, was once again lord chancellor. But Buckingham, for whom Peel had scant respect, was appointed as a sop to please the farmers. Disraeli was well aware that his friend Richard Plantagenet was a duke of little brain – 'After all,' he wrote on one occasion, 'I suppose he is as clever as Lord Rockingham, but then I don't think he ever read a book in his life, on any subject.'[57] He pinned his hopes on Lyndhurst; during the anxious days of Cabinet-making he hung around Lyndhurst's house, and he told Sarah afterwards that Lyndhurst was 'stupified [sic] at the catastrophe and at all times expected more than I ever anticipated'.[58] To his credit, he was not bitter; a lesser man might have charged Lyndhurst with betrayal.

Failing a patron, his claims were slight. His relations with Peel were hardly intimate or warm; in fact, he was the kind of party man Peel most abhorred – a Radical Tory, whose wild speeches about Chartism or the Poor Law defied the party line and courted cheap popularity. He was clever, but neither sound nor loyal. Everything about him smacked of the outsider. This was not a simple matter of birth, though Disraeli's lack of aristocratic connexions was a serious handicap – virtually all Peel's appointments were titled or aristocratic.[59] But Peel was no aristocrat, nor was his protégé Gladstone, five years Disraeli's junior, to whom he gave office as vice-president of the Board of Trade. Since 1832 Peel had laboured to rebuild the Tory party as a credible party of government; himself the archetypal official politician, he had no place in his new ministry for an exotic like Disraeli.

The chief claim Disraeli pressed was a surprisingly revealing one: the storm of political malice and hate which he had endured. He was referring

partly to the attacks on his apostasy (his desertion of the Radicals), but more
to the hate he aroused as a Jew. An outsider in the deepest sense, an alien, he
idealised the society he lived in; he wanted not only to be accepted by it but to
dominate and lead it. As a young man he had forged an identity as a
flamboyant literary dandy, but literature could never give him the power he
craved, even if his novels had been more successful. Since entering
parliament, not only had he written no novels, he had shed his literary
persona; as Mary Anne told Peel, he had abandoned literature for politics. He
wore his hair short, saw little of D'Orsay and Bulwer, and no more is heard of
the famous rings.

Rejection by Peel showed that this was perhaps not enough. To dominate
in English aristocratic society, he must, as Isaiah Berlin perceived, invent a
new identity, an identity which would appeal to people's imaginations.[60] The
key lay in his Jewishness. As a dandy, he had dressed the Jew, but in
parliament he played it down, hoping no one noticed him when the Jewish
issue came up, biting his lip when the mob hurled pork in his face and
ignoring the jibes of the *Satirist*. After 1841 he became far more positive
about his Jewishness. The pride of race, first expressed in *Alroy* and more
than hinted at in *Contarini Fleming*, but oddly dormant after 1837, developed
into a theory of Jewish superiority, turning his chief political liability into an
asset. At the same time, he concocted a romantic and aristocratic Sephardic
ancestry for himself, claiming descent from Spanish Jews who emigrated to
Italy during the Inquisition. There are hints of this in *Alarcos* (1839), set in
thirteenth-century Castile; one character in the play, the Count of Sidonia
(the name reappears in *Coningsby*), woos 'the haughty Lara', and it was from
the Lara family that Disraeli claimed descent. He boasted that his crest, the
castle of Castile, was shared with the house of Lara, and he first displayed it at
the 1841 election.

On 7 September, the day Peel refused him office, an election petition was
presented against Disraeli and Tomline at Shrewsbury. If Disraeli were
unseated for corruption, he could be arrested for debt, and the news brought
swarms of creditors, like sharks smelling blood. He and Mary Anne made
hurried plans to flee the country; parliament was not due to meet until
January, and they proposed to go vagabonding in France. Disraeli spent a
harassed week battling with his creditors, and on the eve of departure he
wrote to Sarah from Pyne's office that he was 'almost glad that there was any
political disappointment which might account for what must otherwise have
created great uneasiness'. In other words, Mary Anne, who had just paid the
Shrewsbury election expenses, knew nothing of Disraeli's financial crisis;
ascribing his preoccupied manner to the snub from Peel, she was unaware

that creditors were threatening to seize the contents of her house. Somehow, the bailiffs were kept out of Grosvenor Gate: 'my household Gods have not been desecrated,' he told Sarah, in whom he now confided his debts, 'and I have the consolation to leave England with the conviction that the catastrophe can't happen in my absence.' He left one piece of unfinished business for Sarah to attend to: a law appointment for Ralph, which Lyndhurst had as good as promised, but which required a letter from Sarah asking the favour. She wrote, and Ralph was rewarded with a comfortable clerkship in Chancery.[61]

Disraeli and his wife left for Normandy on 15 September, and stayed mainly in Caen. Mary Anne enjoyed herself; they lived very well for an extremely reasonable sum – their three months' stay cost a total of £103 18s 6d; they saw no company, and she described Caen as a second honeymoon. Disraeli, melancholy and bruised, found consolation in her devotion, and on her birthday he placed grateful verses on the breakfast table:

> My broken lyre
> Shall still resound a strain. To thee, sweet wife –
> O! would I could call back its ancient fire!
> Then might I do some justice to thy charms,
> And quick devotion, that surround my days
> With joy and safety. Shielded from all harms,
> By thy fond watchfulness, I sing thy praise,
> My stay in woe, my councillor in care!
> O! mayst thou only joy in future share![62]

Drumming his fingers in the quiet of a French country town, he gloomily contemplated the worst – what to do if he were unseated on petition. Abroad, he would be safe from his creditors, and the consular service was a possibility, or maybe diplomacy ... Soon his brain was racing, hatching plans which revolved round a mysterious 'principal personage', probably the Russian diplomat Count Matuszewic. It was another 'great business', and he wrote a fluent cloak-and-dagger letter to Pyne, enthusing about prospects of great magnitude involving a conference in Paris which was rendered abortive by the illness of the principal personage, who was in England. Procrastination in great affairs is bad, he told Pyne; but it would not do to return to England and find himself in a nest of hornets, and 'of the two evils postponement of the great business would be preferable'. Would Pyne let him know how the land lay: there was Ford's loan at 40 per cent and several bills now due, in all about £2000, requiring 'a price of £1000 to operate on the enemy's line, and keep them in check'. What progress, he asked, on 'the great project regarding a certain hereditary title' – apparently a dramatic plan to clear his debts at one stroke, which would permit undivided attention to the great business. 'I invite a dispatch from you upon this important matter,' he wrote, like Metternich to a secret agent, instructing Pyne to reply under cover to the British consul in Caen ('Don't say you have heard from me to anyone').[63]

They returned to Grosvenor Gate on 6 December. Creditors pounced, catching Mary Anne unaware when Dizzy was out: 'My darling Mary Anne,' he wrote from Pyne's office, 'Mr Gibbs is an infuriate usurer, and can do nothing. I defy him.' Mrs Yate, Mary Anne's mother, was ill at Bradenham, and when news came of another attack they hastened down. His wife, Disraeli wrote to D'Orsay, 'says nothing in the world would delight her more than to extricate us both from all our Scrapes. She is, as you know, a heroine, and as I have ceased to be a hero, it is fortunate that one of us has some great qualities.'[64]

After Christmas at Bradenham and a visit to Shrewsbury, they returned to Grosvenor Gate in time for the opening of Peel's first parliament on 5 February, leaving Mrs Yate ill at Bradenham. Back in London, Disraeli felt acutely his exclusion from office. He wrote forlornly to Sarah: 'I can tell you nothing for we live more alone than we did at Caen, and tho' I date this from the Carlton, 'tis only from the Library, being obliged to come here for books.'[65]

Not that he was drifting. For one thing, he was resolved not to oppose Peel's measures. There were already signs of trouble over the Corn Laws: in February Peel announced his plan to modify the sliding scale, reducing the level of protection, and the duke of Buckingham resigned from the Cabinet. 'If he had only brains eno' he might be Premier,' Disraeli told Sarah, but Richard Plantagenet hanged himself politically by accepting the Garter from Peel, aborting a possible farmers' revolt. Peel's sliding scale seemed to please no party, wrote Disraeli; nevertheless, he neither spoke nor voted against it. The Shrewsbury election petition still hung over him, and both from Mrs Dawson, who was 'most friendly and particularly disagreeable [sic]', and from Bonham he heard 'goodnatured rumours': the goodwill of the party wire-pullers over his petition was to be bought only by supporting Peel's Corn Law.[66]

As Disraeli remembered in *Endymion*, 1842 was a 'political economy' parliament. 'Finance and commerce are everybody's subjects, and are most convenient to make speeches about for men who cannot speak French, and who have had no education.' Disraeli's French was execrable, and political economy had never been his strength; the 'great business' he had dreamed up in Caen had revived his interest in foreign affairs – why not make this his subject in the new parliament? He would have few rivals; and by attacking Palmerston, one of the Whig leaders, he would gain recognition, much as he had earlier gained notoriety by his antagonism to O'Connell. Unlike political economy, which you gleaned from books, foreign affairs would enable him to make use of his rare and curious sources of information and his knowledge of the east. As for his French, he tried to improve it by keeping a daily diary of affairs and thoughts in French which, he told Mary Anne, exaggerating wildly, 'I now write with great ease and some elegance'.[67]

He put down a motion calling for the absorption of the consular service into the diplomatic, and by 21 February he had mastered his subject and his speech was prepared. He rehearsed it without reference to a single paper; packed with rich and novel detail, it took three hours to go through. 'I have at last a great opportunity, and I have carved it out myself,' he told Mary Anne. In the House the Corn Laws dragged on, and Disraeli sat silently through the debate, praying for time for his motion. George Smythe's maiden speech, defending the Corn Laws, was a failure: 'very radical indeed and unprincipled as his little agreeable self but too elaborate – his manner affected and his tone artificial and pronunciation too – but still ability – tho' puerile'. Granby, elder brother of Lord John Manners, also made a protectionist speech, and Disraeli watched as the Radicals, 'awestruck at a future Duke ... listened with open mouths to his high Castilian emptiness'. On 25 February, when the House divided over Peel's Corn Law resolutions, Sir Richard Vyvyan and Lord Ossulton rose to leave, determined no longer to support Peel. 'The *general rumor* was that I had done the same,' wrote Disraeli, 'and several men expressed their surprise, when they saw me in the Lobby; I believe these rumors have been intentionally circulated.' For the previous week, however, he had had an understanding with the Whips, and the government themselves had not *now* the slightest doubt of his support – 'my presence at the late divisions has been most *politic and necessary*.'[68]

'You cannot conceive how solitary I feel,' Disraeli wrote despondently on 24 February, 'utterly isolated. Before the change of Government, political party was a tie among men, but now it is only a tie among the men who are in office. The supporter of administration, who is not in place and power himself, is a solitary animal. He has neither hope, nor fear.'[69]

The consular motion changed all that. It was appointed for 8 March, and for several days before, Disraeli cosseted himself. Edmund Kean, the great actor whom Disraeli was supposed to resemble (some thought his style modelled on Kean) can hardly have taken so much care of himself before a first night. He stayed home each evening, for fear of catching cold at the House and losing his voice; he nursed his digestion with a diet of excellent roast mutton and a nightly glass of Mary Anne's best claret, and he doctored his voice with ammonia. His mornings were spent in recitation; the day before the speech his hair was dressed by his wife's hairdresser, Brieden-bach.[70]

At five o'clock on the afternoon of 8 March, he rose to an exceptionally disagreeable audience: 'Everyone seemed to affect not to be aware of my existence, and there was a general buzz and chatter.'[71] Feeling cold and faint, he began in a voice so low that the reporters barely heard: it was surprising, he remarked, that the first commercial nation in the world should entrust superintendence of its commercial interests to the consular service, which was avowedly inferior to the diplomatic service. The distinction between the two was impossible to maintain. He cited the case of the Turkish empire, mentioning the consuls by name; primed with material from Powles, his old associate of the South American mining bubble, he detailed the situation in the South American republics, where the diplomatic service had taken over commercial questions, and Mexican mining companies applied not to the consul but to diplomats. After quarter of an hour the audience was attentive; armed with Egyptian matter supplied by Lord Claud Hamilton, who seconded his motion, Disraeli attacked Palmerston's policy. In Egypt, he explained, there was no diplomatic agency, only a consul, who was a Levantine, and in 1831, when Mehemet Ali invaded Syria, no representations to the pacha were made by the consul on behalf of the British government. If Palmerston had paid more attention to the Levant, and representations had been made, the invasion might not have happened; Britain would have kept its alliance with France and the Eastern Crisis of 1840 would have been avoided. So useless was the consular service that when the Whig government required statistical reports on foreign trade they ignored the consuls and engaged expensive special envoys, such as the unfortunate Dr Bowring, whose report Disraeli had massacred in a speech in July 1840. 'Though not an aristocrat, I would be the last person to indulge in anti-aristocratic invectives,' declared Disraeli, and proceeded to do exactly that, denouncing the consular service as a haven for aristocratic jobbers, a refuge for the destitute.[72]

When he sat down, after two hours and twenty minutes, you could have heard a pin fall, or so he told Mary Anne; probably his usual exaggeration. Palmerston in his reply loftily brushed Disraeli aside like a tiresome wasp, criticised his ignorance of the subject and his want of taste in making personal attacks, and expressed the sarcastic hope that he might obtain office. Disraeli replied:

I must ... return my thanks to the noble Lord for his warm aspirations for my political preferment. Coming from such a quarter, I consider them auspicious.

The noble Viscount is a consummate master of the subject, and if to assist my advancement, he will only impart to me the secret of his own unprecedented rise, and by what means he has continued to enjoy power under seven successive administrations, I shall have at least gained a valuable result by this discussion.[73]

The wasp knew how to sting; it was Palmerston whom he had castigated in a Runnymede letter as the Lord Fanny of diplomacy.

Disraeli's consular speech was a stylish performance. He spoke with no notes, ranging over countries from the Nile to the Elbe. Particularly striking was his manner, and he was delighted when George Smythe told him it was exactly as he talked at the Carlton or at his own table: conversational, colloquial, a little nonchalant and, above all, sarcastic. His attack on aristocratic jobbery drew praise from his Radical friend Tom Duncombe, and from 'the mighty Mister Cobden'. But his warmest admirers were on his own side: 'all young England, the new members etc, were deeply impressed'. George Smythe was ecstatic, Lord John Manners came and sat next to him in the House, and Henry Baillie, who walked with him to the Carlton afterwards, told him in his cold quiet way, 'Upon my soul, I am not sure, it was not the best speech I ever heard.'[74]

'I already find myself without effort the leader of a party – chiefly of the youth, and new members,' he said a few days later. 'I find my position changed.' This was premature, but the speech certainly raised his stock. No more did he complain of loneliness; on the contrary, the wicked Richard Vyvyan was always whispering in his ear, begging him to speak against Peel's Corn Bill. This was precisely what Disraeli was resolved not to do, and, like Talleyrand, who 'when he did not clearly see his way, always took to his bed', Disraeli kept away from the House, going down to Bradenham to join Mary Anne.[75]

Mary Anne spent more than a month at Bradenham that spring, nursing her dying mother, and Disraeli missed her sorely. It was the first separation since their marriage, and he found himself wandering round the empty rooms at Grosvenor Gate speaking her name out loud and breaking into exclamations of affection. Worst of all was waking alone in his 'widowed bed', when he spoke and received no answer, 'and no welcome from that hand, which is so tenderly vigilant not to rouse me'.[76] (Mary Anne, unlike Dizzy, did not stay in bed until midday.)

At Bradenham, Mary Anne became overwrought, nervous and tearful; she was enraged when she discovered Sarah secretly forwarding letters to Grosvenor Gate: 'All this cheapens me so, Dizzy,' she stormed. Disraeli pretended innocence, protesting, quite untruthfully, that he no longer wrote to Sarah and he was reproachful: 'Nothing can remove the perverted view in which you persist to consider my relations with my family. My correspondence, almost my cordial intercourse, with them has ceased; and as for Bradenham, I can truly say, that after all that has occurred there, I never go there but with disgust and apprehension.'[77] These were bitter words written in anger; almost certainly they exaggerate. Yet his relationship with Sarah, which had been almost abnormally close, was poisoned by his wife's jealousy; and for the time being, Mary Anne's insistence that Sarah correspond with her and not with Dizzy was to deprive him of a valued confidante and posterity of the continuance of a sparkling political correspondence.

Of course Dizzy was no angel. His debts, multiplying at giddy and inexorable rates of compound interest, drove him to ever more tortuous and devious expedients. In 1842 claims and bills totalling at least £23,000 became due, and he came to an arrangement with Ford, who undertook to clear his embarrassments and especially his judgement debts ('always the *great point* with me') in exchange for Disraeli's making him his family solicitor, giving Ford formal management of his affairs and introducing him to his wife. Ford, whose apparent openness masked blood-sucking cunning, had at last succeeded in getting his teeth into Mary Anne's wealth. He made an initial loan of £5000 at 5 per cent, and she rashly agreed to sign any papers he wished. Unknown to her, Disraeli borrowed at least a further £5000 from Ford. Nor, it seems, did she know that while she was at Bradenham Ford's agents tramped over Grosvenor Gate from attic to cellar, compiling an inventory of the contents, which Disraeli mortgaged as security for a further loan, solemnly handing over one chair as symbol of the change of title. When Mary Anne's mother died in May, the £5000 she left to her daughter was instantly swallowed up by Ford.[78]

'The Shrewsbury Petition is withdrawn,' Disraeli triumphantly announced to Sarah in April. This 'great *coup*, almost in the present circumstances as great as my return', was effected by Bailey, a Gloucester solicitor and Mrs Yate's agent for the property she owned in Gloucester. Bailey arranged a swap: the Shrewsbury Whigs agreed not to proceed against Disraeli and Tomline, and in exchange a petition was dropped against the Whig members for Gloucester, where Disraeli's friends Henry Hope and Lord Loftus had been defeated, the Gloucester Whigs prevailing upon the Shrewsbury Whigs to sacrifice themselves to extricate their neighbours. Under the new strict system of election committees introduced in 1841, corruption was far easier to prove; without a compromise, Disraeli had good reason to despair about keeping his seat. Not that the Shrewsbury–Gloucester swap was innocent and straightforward; there was a hidden agenda. In

February 1841 Disraeli had assigned Bailey a debt worth £2500 which became due that August; he renewed it and made payments of over £1000 to Bailey: on the same day that the petition was withdrawn, Bailey transferred the debt of £2500 to the Gloucester under-sheriff, who was a key player in the business of the petition. Debts were a useful form of currency.[79]

The withdrawal of the Shrewsbury petition broke Disraeli's chains. No longer need he court the smiles of the party managers. Peel introduced his historic budget on 11 March, reintroducing income tax – 'a thunderbolt,' wrote Disraeli, 'but Peel can do anything at this minute'. In *Sybil* he satirised 'the gentleman in Downing Street', whose glib arguments magically demonstrate that income tax in fact *increases* income, and whose 'frank and explicit' manner conceals his own mind and confuses the minds of others. In 1842, however, Disraeli showed no signs of opposing Peel's financial edicts. On the contrary, he made a speech defending Peel against the charge of inconsistency over free trade, giving a history lecture to prove that free trade was first promulgated not by the Whigs but by Pitt and Shelburne.[80] When Tom Duncombe presented the Chartists' monster petition, six miles long, on 2 May, Disraeli took no part in the debate; he neither sympathised with the Chartists nor criticised the Poor Law, and Ashley and the agitation for Factory Reform left him unmoved. Disraeli, in short, had abandoned the Tory Radicalism of his first parliament. Now the Tories had gained a majority on the 1832 franchise, there was less to be gained from courting the people; Tory Radicalism was a cry of opposition, not government.

He focused instead on foreign affairs. 'The deep gloom and mortification that pervades all classes and circles about India is the feature of the day,' he told Mary Anne as news reached London of the disastrous invasion of Afghanistan.[81] In a speech on income tax he pointed out that though all parties agreed to its odious necessity, no one inquired into its causes: the war in India, and in June he seconded Henry Baillie's motion for an inquiry into the war. In these hard, dry, matter-of-fact, income-tax days, claimed he, war must be subject to parliamentary control. But the Whigs had never once explained the purpose of the war: under Palmerston foreign policy had been concealed from the public.[82] He developed the case against Palmerston in a debate on the commercial distress, when he declared that the cause of distress was not, as Radicals argued, the Corn Laws but the anti-commercial foreign policy of Palmerston. Liverpool and Huskisson had pursued free trade in the 1820s, returning to the policies of Pitt and Shelburne, but after 1830 Palmerston's diplomacy had closed European markets to British commerce – France, Germany and Spain were all estranged. 'What the cause [of distress] is, the Minister, who for ten years exercised a power never criticised, who, in a period of domestic turbulence conducted public affairs and was never called to account, is the prime witness.'[83]

There is a dramatic scene in *Coningsby* when the youthful hero shelters from a storm in a humble inn, where he is joined by a stranger. 'He was above the middle height, and of a distinguished air and figure; pale, with an impressive brow, and dark eyes of great intelligence.' Coningsby had never met anyone like him before.

> His sentences were so short, his language so racy, his voice rang so clear, his elocution was so complete. On all subjects his mind seemed to be instructed, and his opinions formed. He flung out a result in a few words; he solved with a phrase some deep problems that men muse over for years. He said many things that were strange, yet they immediately appeared to be true. Then, without the slightest air of pretension or parade, he seemed to know everybody as well as everything. Monarchs, statesmen, authors, adventurers ... All this, too, without any excitement of manner; on the contrary, with repose amounting almost to nonchalance. If his address had any fault in it, it was rather a deficiency of earnestness. A slight spirit of mockery played over his speech even when you deemed him most serious; you were startled by his sudden transitions from profound thought to poignant sarcasm. A very singular freedom from passion and prejudice on every subject which they treated, might be some compensation for this want of earnestness, perhaps was its consequence.[84]

The stranger, Sidonia, is of course Disraeli – Disraeli in the part he had invented for himself since his rejection by Peel. Cosmopolitan, mysterious, eastern, a man of secrets and conspiracies and a master of foreign affairs, Sidonia is Jewish, 'of the faith that the Apostles professed before they followed their master', excluded by his faith from action but proud of his Sephardic descent. Sidonia/Disraeli (note the partial anagram) existed side by side with his earlier political persona of Radical Tory, enlightened aristocratic leader of the people. In 1842 Sidonia/Disraeli was in the ascendant, but Radical Tory was by no means dead; he was to re-emerge in *Sybil* as Charles Egremont, and in 1867, when he piloted the Tories' leap in the dark over the Second Reform Bill.

Sidonia is no longer young; he is a leader and teacher of youth. In 1842 Disraeli was thirty-seven (fatal thirty-seven, the age at which Byron died). Already he saw himself as a leader of a party of youth – in July he told Lord John Manners that he wished to form a party with certain general principles, not to interfere with acceptance of office – even six men acting together would have great weight, he urged.[85] The outlines of the Young England party were formed; its driving impulse the intimacy which had grown up between Disraeli and George Smythe.

By 1842 Smythe had come to fill the part in his life formerly occupied by D'Orsay or Bulwer. Since his marriage Disraeli's relations with D'Orsay had cooled; he told Mary Anne how much he disliked visiting Gore House, now threatened with bankruptcy by D'Orsay's debts. D'Orsay was unchanged and in high spirits, but Lady Blessington was silent, subdued and broken. Another year, she told Disraeli, would kill her, and she complained bitterly that having fought against so much prejudice and made a position for herself, she was to see it all shattered. 'I think it is horrid,' wrote Disraeli.[86]

George Smythe was a famous Lothario, apparently as irresistible to women as he was capricious and remorseless. There are, however, hints of sexual ambiguity, as there are with D'Orsay. One observer wrote of the contrast between the masculine vigour of Smythe's physique and the 'effeminacy' of his mind. Frederick Faber, who inspired Smythe's political mission, had a homosexual infatuation for him in 1838–9; repressed homosexuality was a powerful undercurrent of the Oxford Movement. Whether Smythe, like Byron, was active homosexually is not known; in an age when sodomy was a capital offence, homosexual acts were buried in a conspiracy of silence, and the scraps and hints that survive do not amount to very much. Undoubtedly Smythe, whose mother had died when he was eight, felt an emotional need for the guidance, perhaps the love, of an older man; in 1842 that older man was Disraeli.[87]

Disraeli's first loyalty, however, was to Mary Anne. Smythe and his young friends were baffled by his devotion to his middle-aged wife. Sir William Gregory, a Tory MP and contemporary of Smythe's, found her repulsive – 'flat, angular, under-bred, with a harsh, grating voice'; he and Smythe called her Marianne behind her back, and laughed at her gauche and foolish sayings, such as her remark about a man's complexion: 'Ah, I wish you could only see Dizzy in his bath, then you would know what white skin is.' Once Smythe overstepped the mark, and asked Disraeli what he saw in her. 'George,' said Disraeli, looking him straight in the eye, 'there is one word in the English language of which you are ignorant.' 'What is that?' asked Smythe, somewhat taken aback. 'Gratitude, George,' responded Disraeli. It was a sharpish snub, and Smythe never mentioned the subject again.[88]

Disraeli had good cause to be grateful. At last, sometime in 1841 or 1842, he had confessed his debts to her, and she responded magnificently. He and Mary Anne spent the autumn of 1842 in Paris, and before they left Disraeli placed a note in a sealed envelope, to be opened by Isaac in the event of Disraeli's dying before him. Thanks to the unexampled devotion of his beloved wife, wrote Disraeli, he was now entering upon an era of worldly prosperity and mental satisfaction. Since their marriage, he wished Isaac to know, Mary Anne had spent more than £13,000 on his debts and elections, 'and is prepared to grapple with claims and incumbrances to an amount not inferior'.[89]

'He is a genius, she is a dunce,' Mary Anne wrote light-heartedly at the time of their marriage, and historians, mostly male and academic, have taken her at this valuation. True, she was no intellectual – according to Dizzy, she did not know whether the Greeks or the Romans came first.[90] It was partly because of his need for intellectual companionship that he sought the company of clever young men like Smythe. But for all her gaucheness and embarrassing remarks, Mary Anne had a shrewdness and intuitive judgement which Disraeli lacked. On their third wedding anniversary in 1842 Disraeli addressed to her a progress report in verse on the past twelve months.

> But the black forms that sound my fate,
>   Then felt their coming prey,
> Spirits of envy, strife and hate,
>   Whose pinions dimmed our day;
> Have baffled fled, and we remain,
>   Like pilgrims near a sunny fane.
> 'Tis woman's mind these marvels worked,
>   Heroic, wise and fond;
> Beneath whose smile no treachery lurked,
>   When altars blessed the bond,
> That chased the sorrows of my life,
> And gave to me a matchless Wife![91]

It was bad verse, but it was true. Mary Anne gave him the kind of love his mother had denied him: unquestioning, adoring devotion. (She always cut his hair, and he discovered after her death that she had kept every lock.) Far more than her money, her devotion gave him the emotional anchor essential to his success; without her support, he might well have been the brilliant, unbalanced failure in politics that he was in literature. He was a genius, but he owed his success to Mary Anne.

ELEVEN

Sidonia and Young England

1842-4

IN THE late summer of 1842, soon after the session had ended, Disraeli jotted down some thoughts in a commonplace book. His notes are cryptic and disjointed but revealing. 'Similarity of characters in different ages,' he wrote. 'Augustus – Pompeius – Peel –' That the great characters of antiquity were reproduced in modern times was a favourite theory of his and of George Smythe's; likening Peel to two worthy but unimaginative Roman emperors encapsulated his criticism of his leader. On another page he wrote: 'The Influence of Individual Character', which he illustrated by the story of Marcus Aurelius, whose influence alone had preserved the morality of the empire. Frederick of Prussia was another example of Disraeli's philosophy (first expressed in *Vivian Grey* Part Two) of the individual's power to triumph over society and shape his own success.

A few pages later he wrote, 'Eunuchs', and a list of names – Abelard, Photius, Origen. 'Heroes, impotent or averse to women', came next: Mars. de Gassion, Tilli, Turenne, Battori the Invincible. 'Private Life more important than public leading to greater results,' he wrote a few pages later, but his jottings returned to the familiar theme of worldly success. 'Spirit of the Times. To know it and oneself the secret of success.' On one page, he listed men who had achieved youthful success, ranging from Hannibal, who was twenty-six when he invaded Italy, through Luther and John of Austria, who at twenty-five won the battle of Lepanto, to Napoleon, Bolingbroke, Nelson. On another page, he wrote the names of some famous Jews – Mendelssohn, Heine, Spinoza; next to them he listed the names of Mendizabel, the Spanish minister; Cancrin, the Russian minister of finance; Count Arnim, the Prussian ambassador in Paris; Soult and Massena, Napoleon's marshals: all these he seemed to believe were Jews.[1]

The lists of youthful heroes and Jewish notables reappear in *Coningsby*, where they are put into the mouth of Sidonia. The novel was not yet written, but the character of Sidonia – exotic, cosmopolitan and 'averse to women' – was already taking shape, a Disraeli fantasy, an escape from the reality of his blocked political career.

Late in September 1842 Disraeli and Mary Anne crossed to Paris, where they stayed until parliament reassembled in January. Shutting Grosvenor Gate was an economy measure; Mary Anne left the servants on board wages with twelve pieces of soap and seven pounds of candles to last the autumn. Installed in a sunny suite in the rue de Rivoli overlooking the Tuileries, with three servants including a cook, she kept expenses down to £84 a month. Disraeli basked in the warm October sun, windows open and the glass at seventy in the shade, and his mind teemed with fresh and vast political combinations.

Paris was empty of celebrities, but the few who were there could be found in the salon of the duchess of Grammont, D'Orsay's sister and 'like him in petticoats', who received every other night in her little house in the Faubourg St Honoré, crammed with 'pretty furniture, old cabinets and pictures of the de Grammonts'. Old Lewis Goldsmith, Lady Lyndhurst's father, who had been an agent of Napoleon's, gave the Disraelis a grand banquet of diplomats and foreign ministers: 'they all talked at the same time, shouted and gesticulated, the noise Neapolitan, and the salle à manger being very small, and there being fourteen bougies alit [sic] on the table ... the effect was overwhelming.' Disraeli sent Sarah glittering lists of names: Princes de Beaufremont, Counts de Chambellan, Duchesses de Marmier. 'What names!' he wrote. 'But where are the territories? There are only 100 men in France who have 10,000£ per ann.: Henry Hope and de Rothschild cd. buy them all.'[2]

Hope and Anthony de Rothschild as it happened were both in Paris; so were George Smythe and his Young England friend Alexander Baillie Cochrane. Strolling through the sunny boulevards, Disraeli loftily unfolded the possibilities for a new party to Smythe, who had arrived in Paris fresh from talks in Geneva with John Manners, with *carte blanche* to arrange matters with Disraeli. Smythe and Cochrane dined with the Disraelis, and though 'Kok' was suspicious of Disraeli, whom he barely knew and whose jokes he dreaded, they agreed to form an esoteric party. '*We have settled*,' Smythe reported to Manners, '*subject to your approval, to sit together, and to vote together, the majority deciding.*'[3] Less easily resolved was the question of office: Disraeli urged that the party should undertake to refuse all offers, but Smythe objected, and it was left to the individual to refuse or accept.

Disraeli's Paris talks with Smythe and Cochrane launched Young England as a parliamentary movement; it could hardly be described as a party – no attempt was made to agree principles, for instance. 'This, then is the germ of our party,' Manners wrote in his diary, '– no particular principles, but a hotch-potch, each surrendering his own to the majority.' Young England has sometimes been described as a political expression of the Oxford Movement; Manners was a true follower of the Movement, sceptical about political solutions and, like the High Tory Gladstone, looking to the church for salvation. To please Manners, Disraeli agreed that Young England's standard of Christianity should be 'the moderate Oxford principles'. But Disraeli rarely set foot in a church, and as Smythe acutely pointed out, 'Dizzy's attachment to moderate Oxfordism is something like Bonaparte's to moderate Mahomedanism.' 'I have already christened us the Diz-Union,' Smythe told Disraeli on 20 October 1842.[4]

Disraeli's ambition was another source of friction. Smythe told Manners in awestruck tones that 'Dizzy has much more parliamentary power than I had any notion of. The two Hodgsons are his, and Quintin Dick. He has a great hold on Walter, and "The Times". Henry Hope (who will come in soon) is entirely in his hands.' In Paris, after Smythe's departure for London, Disraeli speculated to Cochrane about forming a party of sixty. Cochrane, who had never really wanted Disraeli at all, preferring to fight with Manners and Smythe as three musketeers, was appalled: 'D'I's head', he wrote, 'is full of great movements, vast combinations, the importance of numbers, cabinet dinners, the practice of dissimulation! in fact of the vaguest speculations, the mere phantasmagoria of politique legerdemain.'[5]

Disraeli, meanwhile, set about securing an audience with the French king, Louis Philippe. The court was in mourning owing to the death of the prince royal, but he gained an entrée through his friend Henry Bulwer, *chargé d'affaires* at the British embassy, who introduced him to General Baudrand, an aide-de-camp to Louis Philippe. Disraeli sketched his purpose in a remarkable memorandum he addressed to the king. Attacking Palmerston for repudiating the French alliance, Disraeli proclaimed himself dedicated to restoring the understanding between the two countries. *Gallomania*, Disraeli's anti-Orleanist polemic of ten years before, was forgotten.

A party should be organised in parliament to press for the French alliance. Peel's majority of ninety, Disraeli told the king, included forty or fifty agricultural malcontents, 'It is obvious therefore that another section of conservative members full of youth –' (he wrote 'ambition' and crossed it out) 'and energy ... must exercise an irresistible control over the tone of the Minister. Sympathising in general with his domestic policy, they may dictate the character of his foreign.' Disraeli confided to the king that he had 'already been solicited to place himself at the head of a parliamentary party which there is every reason to believe would adopt his views on ... Foreign Policy ... a party of the youth of England, influenced by the noblest views and partaking in nothing of the character of a parliamentary intrigue'. Disraeli also proposed organising the press in favour of the alliance. This was not a mere matter of buying an outlet; far more could be achieved by a single man (Disraeli) speaking in the journals of every school of politics, whose ideas would soon become the voice of the nation.[6]

It is a revealing document, indicating how far Disraeli's priorities had shifted since 1841. Since Peel's refusal of office, Disraeli had shed his youthful Radical Toryism. Sympathising, as he wrote, with Peel's domestic policy, he turned his energies to foreign affairs. Yet it was his sympathy with the Chartists and his attack on the Poor Law, which attracted the Young England group.

Louis Philippe was always willing to see English MPs, and Disraeli's audience took place on 21 November. Speaking perfect English, the king held forth (according to Disraeli's later recollection) about the security of his dynasty, likening himself to William III. He had no need of Disraeli's help; as Disraeli must have known, both Peel and his foreign minister, Aberdeen, were committed to restoring the French alliance. Perhaps Disraeli hoped for secret service payments from the king; if so, he was almost certainly disappointed. Disraeli's startlingly frank memorandum is testimony to his delusions of grandeur, which Louis Philippe was quick to exploit; as Baillie Cochrane sneered, 'the great man himself is closeted with Louis Philippe at St Cloud, and already pictures himself the founder of some new dynasty with his Manfred love-locks stamped on the current coin of the realm.'[7]

The royal audience propelled Disraeli and Mary Anne into the giddy heights of Paris society. They dined with Guizot, to whom Disraeli was commended by the king, 'his first dinner for the season, and given only to the great personages, even the Cabinet Ministers only appeared at the soirée'. Naturally, 'all was sumptuous, servants in rich liveries and guests with every ribbon of the rainbow'. Among them was Baron James de Rothschild, uncle of Disraeli's friend Anthony, who was 'a happy mixture of the French Dandy and the orange boy'.[8] Thiers, Tocqueville, Lamartine, Odilon-Barrot, the Duc Decazes and Count Molé – Disraeli revelled in his social triumphs. 'We are both *in high health*,' he told Sarah. Mary Anne went to the opera in Rothschild's box, lined with crimson velvet, and wore mourning for the prince royal; she was greatly admired, Disraeli reported, in black crape with tucks and deep fringes of bugles.

Disraeli was presented to the queen: 'I passed for the first time in my life an evening in the domesticity of a Court.' His letters glow with triumph, proudly detailing each mark of royal favour: a royal conducted tour round the Tuileries ('It is rare to make the tour of a palace with a King for the Cicerone'); private talks with Louis Philippe and invitations to attend at court. 'You must understand that I am the only stranger who has been received at Court. It causes a great sensation here.' (He was referring to the royal mourning.) He drank tea *alone* with the queen and was summoned to the king's cabinet. 'I am in personal as well as political favour there.' The grandest spectacle of all, however, was a ball given by Baron Solomon de Rothschild, brother of James – 'an hôtel in decoration surpassing all the palaces of Munich – a greater retinue of servants and liveries more gorgeous than the Thuilleries [*sic*] – and pineapples plentiful as blackberries.'⁹

London in February was a dreary anti-climax. How could it be otherwise? 'All at present uncertain and unsatisfactory,' Disraeli told Sarah from the Carlton on 4 February 1843. 'Peel feeble and frigid I think – and general grumbling.'

Back in London he was confronted by judgement debts totalling £30,000. Ford, his agent for the past two years, was himself in trouble and had obtained a judgement against Disraeli for £10,000. Disraeli replaced Ford with a solicitor named Wright, who made an arrangement with Lord Exmouth, another debtor whose affairs were already entangled with Disraeli's own. It took all his diplomatic skill to manipulate the good-natured Exmouth ('I never knew a more honest and more honourable man') into entrusting his affairs to Wright, and agreeing to mortgage his estates, jeopardising his prospects of marrying an heiress, in exchange for an insurance on Disraeli's life. By April the money was raised, and he boldly but prematurely claimed that, thanks to the 'co-operation' of Lord Exmouth, 'I have effected the entire satisfaction of every judgement which exists against me.' No sooner were his debts patched up than a fresh crisis occurred – the bankruptcy of Mrs Edmonds, listed in Disraeli's commonplace book as 'the female usurer'; she also kept a gaming house. Disraeli and D'Orsay had borrowed heavily from her, and *The Times* alleged that she had like 'a second Venus thrown a cloud of protection around them, and had by their misconduct been the sufferer'. Disraeli managed to prevent his name appearing in the press report of the bankruptcy proceedings; as he told Wright, 'any connection with such proceedings and persons ever carries a taint'.¹⁰

When creditors continued to nag, he instructed Wright to 'take care that no PUBLICITY as regards Ld E or myself, occur', but Disraeli no longer lived on the brink of bankruptcy. Mary Anne's income from property and investments was between £5500 and £6000 in 1843; the cost of running Grosvenor Gate was no more than £1400 a year, leaving a clear margin for election expenses and emergency payments.¹¹ Mary Anne's housekeeping was ruthlessly and obsessively parsimonious: pity the housemaid who hoped to grow fat on leftovers. Servants came and went with distressing frequency, though Dizzy, who rarely spoke to them, was no doubt oblivious. Whenever parliament was not sitting, the house was shut and the servants put on board wages, while the Disraelis fled to a cheap hotel in France or cheaper still, to Bradenham, where they lived for almost nothing.

In parliament that session (1843) Young England was slow to emerge. Smythe and Manners dined often at Grosvenor Gate, and at Easter the Disraelis and Young England stayed at Deepdene with Henry Hope. Lord John Manners wrote in his diary (18 April): 'Our *partie carrée* [party of four] is still in existence after many dangers. Disraeli is a very easy man to get on with, and incomparably clever.' In parliament, however, Young England did not act as a group, and Disraeli's first two speeches of the session were on foreign policy topics he had discussed with Louis Philippe: the alliance with France (14 February) and the Webster-Ashburton Boundary Treaty with the United States (22 March). 'I have at last made a great speech,' he told Sarah after the first, but complained (as usual) that he was never worse reported, and the speech made little impact.[12] Peel's prestige declined in 1843 as his government appeared powerless in the face of economic distress, but it was not Young England but Cobden who emerged as Peel's most damaging critic, storming the country in a campaign of stirring public meetings.

The Anti-Corn Law League alarmed the Tories of Shrewsbury, and early in May Disraeli was obliged to make an unexpected visit to his constituency ('very inconvenient to me in the midst of the settlement of my affairs'). It coincided with Shrewsbury races – Mary Anne was the grand lady at the ball, in white with a dark wreath, velvet flowers twined with diamonds – and Disraeli saw a horse race. His speech was a robust defence of Corn Laws as protection to native industry. 'I take the only broad and safe line – namely, that what we ought to uphold is the preponderance of the landed interest; that the preponderance of the landed interest has made England; that it is an immense element of political power and stability.' For the first time, he spoke the language of Young England; he praised the feudal principle and blamed the distress not on the labouring class but on the deterioration of the aristocracy. Finally, he pledged himself to oppose the government if it abandoned the Corn Laws.

'Nothing could equal the enthusiasm of my auditors; or be stronger than my position here,' he told Sarah.[13] He and Mary Anne hastened back to London, completing the 160-mile journey in a record ten hours. A fortnight later, in the division on the Canadian Corn Bill, admitting Canadian corn at a preferential duty which was seen by protectionists as free trade by the back door, Disraeli voted against the government (26 May). 'I had not the moral courage nor the immoral audacity to say one thing to my constituents, and within 24 hours [*sic*] vote diametrically opposite,' he told his constituents the following year. His real motive, however, was to oppose Peel. In July, when Londonderry switched his influence at Durham to let in the Anti-Corn Law campaigner John Bright, Disraeli applauded. 'Londonderry's flare up has cut the government in the wind. They could not believe it possible,' he told Sarah. 'Oh! for 50 Durhams!'[14]

Young England made its mark over Ireland, which, Disraeli wrote, was now 'the only thought and word'. Since 1842 the Young Ireland movement had stirred Irish nationalism, echoing Mazzini's Young Italy, and both Smythe and Manners (but not Disraeli) visited Ireland in the summer of 1843. In July Smythe and Manners attacked the government's policy of coercion, contending that Ireland should be governed according to the policy of Charles I and not of Cromwell; Disraeli did not vote but on 12 July Smythe, Manners, Ferrand and Cochrane voted against the government. From the opposition benches Macaulay noted that the Tories were broken into 'three or more factions which hate each other more than they hate the Whigs. I mean the faction which stands by Peel, the faction which is represented by Vivian and the Morning Post, and the faction of Smythe and Cochrane.'[15]

'Mary Anne', Disraeli wrote on 7 August, 'is very tired of town, and wants much to come down to Bradenham, but I am cruising for two subjects on which I wish to speak, Ireland and Servia.' His speech on Ireland (9 August) was his first open attack on Peel. He charged Peel with abandoning the old Tory doctrines and principles and governing Ireland on the principles of the Roundheads: hostility towards the people, and lack of sympathy towards the Catholics. Peel, he claimed, had left his party in the lurch; 'at a time like this it was necessary to recur to the principles which were the foundation of the party, when those who had been its leaders no longer led it, and they found themselves sinking into a faction, degenerating into the lowest position in which a public man could be placed – when, in fact, they were supporting a Ministry without knowing what principles they were maintaining.' Towards O'Connell and the repeal agitation, Peel's policy was to do nothing, and the government's Irish Arms bill (which the House was debating) was so contemptible a measure that Disraeli pledged himself to abstain. Ireland, he pregnantly declared, 'had arrived at that pitch which required a great man, to have recourse to great remedial measures'.

Peel, who industriously rubbed his nose throughout the speech, avoided exposing Disraeli's weak point – his sympathy with the Irish Catholics. Who, he sarcastically asked, was the great man who was to arise? Clearly not the Honourable Gentleman, whose opinion over the Arms Bill was that on the whole it was better not to vote at all.[16] But Peel's heavy-footed wit was lost on

Disraeli, who had already left the House; Peel grimly told the queen that Disraeli and Smythe had made speeches indicating their future opposition to the government. 'D'Israeli and Smythe,' wrote Greville, 'who are the principal characters (together with John Manners) of the little squad called "Young England", were abusive and impertinent.' Such was the resentment occasioned that Disraeli's speech on the Servian revolt (15 August), criticising the government's inactivity and imploring them to support the integrity of Turkey against Russia, brought a sharp rebuke from Lord Sandon, a supporter of Peel's, who accused him of heaping the grossest terms of contumely and opprobrium on his own front bench. This was unfair. Disraeli was sarcastic, but not abusive, and Palmerston rose to his defence.[17]

By the end of the 1843 session the newspapers were full of Young England: 'if I were to give you a report of all that has been written on this fruitful topic,' Disraeli told Sarah, 'it would be a volume.' The group of four rarely voted together, and Manners and Cochrane spoke more often and attended more assiduously than Disraeli, who made only seven speeches in 1843. Yet he was recognised as its leader; as Sir James Graham told Croker, 'the puppets are moved by Disraeli, who is the ablest man among them: I consider him unprincipled and disappointed, and in despair he has tried the effect of bullying.... Disraeli alone is mischievous; and with him I have no desire to keep terms.'[18]

At the end of the session Disraeli, Mary Anne and Smythe stayed nearly a month at Deepdene with Henry Hope. It was a blazing hot September, and Hope's neo-classical villa stood sharply silhouetted against a blue Italian sky. Mary Anne played with the two young bears Hope kept chained to trees, prompting Isaac to remark that 'young bears turn on a sudden into old Bears, and that though they may appear now "amiable and elegant" they have deep-seated within them ... the toryism of their forefathers.'[19]

Disraeli paced the cool marble galleries or strolled among the steep glades of rhododendrons, talking with Hope who, he told Sarah, 'is all kindness – both *politically and domestically*'. Perhaps Hope had lent Disraeli money; certainly Disraeli went out of his way to charm his host. Smythe looked on sardonically as 'gloomy Dis' tried to explain Puseyism to Hope, 'who hates it, first, because he is a "Philosopher" and hates all religion, and secondly, because his brother likes it. Dizzy attempts to rob it of all its religion, and to assure Hope that his brother does not understand the real and genuine and esoteric principle. This to me ... is irresistibly droll.'[20]

Disraeli had brought notebooks and paper; he wanted to write. He owed Lady Blessington a piece for her *Keepsake* and (possibly in collaboration with Smythe) he dashed off a literary arabesque which he called 'Fantasia'. A strange, dream-like piece, it tells of moonlit gardens, of statues which leap from their pedestals and make love to nymphs, of a maiden who removes her mask to reveal the head of a splendid serpent. 'Yours is the common lot of premature passion,' the serpent tells the hero, 'you have fallen in love with a masque, and obtained a monster.'

Erotic fantasy was a distraction. Encouraged by Hope and Smythe, he planned a novel about Young England, and scribbled stray thoughts in a notebook. Names of people, adventurers, eccentric characters, dandies, usurers, prime ministers – 'with all of these I have held long repeated and confidential conversation'; 'mere men in office' such as Goulburn, 'literary-political' (Macaulay, Bulwer, Milnes), Young England – a very odd page, excluding Cochrane. Two pages were filled with names of women (though not Henrietta's), but there were only two in the list of churchmen. Listing those of the great world made him feel he belonged, but when he read the notebook again in 1860 he noted wryly, 'I thought then I had seen a great deal of the world – after what has occurred since it appears to me to be a nursery dream.'

On one page he wrote, 'Statistics – effect of. For the middle class marriage often the only adventure of life.' There in a nutshell was why he could not write a Victorian domestic novel: his indifference towards domestic realism and contempt for the middle class. On the next page he wrote, 'St James' St described/The projected swamping of the house of Lords in 1832/Prospect of being among the new peers: social effect/An Election before and after the Reform: the same place'.[21]

1832 – that was where the story should begin. The *Bildungsroman* of a Young Englander, his political education over the past twelve years. A book about Smythe – an orphan, naturally, the youthful Smythe, whom Disraeli called Coningsby, had first to be exposed to illegitimate and corrupt political influences. Disraeli's answer was to give Smythe/Coningsby a guardian, Rigby, closely based on J. W. Croker. It was a savage portrait; Rigby was described as a man 'destitute of all imagination and noble sentiment ... blessed with a vigorous, mendacious fancy, fruitful in small expedients, and never happier than when devising shifts for great men's scruples'. Campbell admired the portrait of Croker as 'the most malignant and masterly libel I have ever met with'.

What Croker had done to deserve this is a puzzle. He was a friend and literary ally of Isaac, who paid fulsome tribute to him in his *Charles I*; and though Croker had been instrumental in sabotaging the *Representative* newspaper and in blackballing Disraeli from the Athenaeum Club, Disraeli had revenged himself in *Vivian Grey*, where Croker is caricatured as Stapylton Toad. No doubt he was annoyed by Croker's 'slashing article' in the *Quarterly Review*, which referred dismissively to Young England: 'Their number is so small, their views so vague, and their influence so slight, that it may seem superfluous to allude to them,' were it not for their impolicy in creating distrust of Peel, 'the only statesman in whom the great Conservative body has any confidence'. But the reason for Rigby *was* revenge. Rightly or wrongly, Disraeli seems to have blamed his exclusion from office in 1841 on Croker and Bonham. George Smythe certainly believed this was the reason, and he added in an article written in 1854 that 'we owe to this circumstance those immortal sketches of the Rigbys, the Tadpoles and the Tapers'.[22]

Croker had been man of business to the marquess of Hertford, the magnificent voluptuary whose death eighteen months before had scandalised London. Disraeli had relayed gossip to Mary Anne, detailing the scandal of Hertford's will and his characteristic death. 'The ruling passion; Pope cd. do it justice,' he wrote. Hertford had gone to Richmond to give dinner to three French prostitutes, and they got so tipsy with champagne, 'that they were sick coming home and would have all the windows open, and the marquess caught a cold and died'.[23]

Disraeli began writing at Deepdene, and during his stay there he sketched in Croker and Lord Hertford, easily recognisable as Lord Monmouth, who became Smythe's grandfather. The schoolboy Coningsby, innocent yet serious, resembling Smythe with his chestnut curls and irregular features, went to meet his grandfather; when Lord Monmouth, that superb and icy being, bows like Louis Quatorze and asks, 'How do you like Eton?' Coningsby bursts into tears.

If he were to tell Smythe's story properly, Disraeli realised he had to see Eton, as the friendship formed there between Smythe and Manners was the germ of Young England. He also needed to see Manchester, which he described in the novel as the new Athens. 'The Age of Ruins is past. Have you seen Manchester?' Disraeli and Mary Anne travelled to Manchester early in October. Cobden heard of his visit and invited him to speak at a literary meeting at the Free Trade Hall, with Dickens in the chair. In his speech, said by Mary Anne to be by far the finest (naturally), he likened the merchants of Manchester to the merchant patriciate of Venice or Florence in their patronage of the arts. He was not flattering his audience; the impression Manchester made on him can be gauged from *Coningsby*, where he wrote of passing over 'plains where iron and coal supersede turf and corn, dingy as the entrance of Hades, and flaming with furnaces', reaching 'illumined factories, with more windows than Italian palaces, and smoking chimneys taller than Egyptian obelisks'. Like Coningsby, Disraeli found himself in a new world, pregnant with new ideas, an unprecedented partnership of capital and science, and a great source of wealth; 'and he perceived that this wealth was rapidly developing classes whose power was imperfectly recognised in the constitutional scheme, and whose duties in the social system seemed altogether omitted'.[24] After ten days in the north, they travelled down to Bradenham, visiting Eton on the way. 'I am writing and want a workroom,' Disraeli warned Sarah; 'let me have my old writing-room next to your room.'

In *Sybil*, and again in the General Preface to the 1870 edition of his novels, Disraeli says that the topic of *Coningsby* was 'the state of our political parties; their origin, their history, their present position'.[25] Certainly the novel investigates the character of the Tory party. But the question at the heart of the book is, who should rule? That was why the story begins in May 1832, with the duke of Wellington's abortive attempt to form an Anti-Reform Ministry, which, said Disraeli, marked the end of old-style aristocratic power. 'Nothing in parliamentary history so humiliating as the funeral oration delivered … by the Duke of Wellington over the old constitution, that, modelled on the Venetian, had governed England since the accession of the House of Hanover.' Ten years earlier, in *What Is He?* and then in *Vindication of the English Constitution*, he had made the same point about the end of oligarchy; but where in 1833 he urged democracy and in 1835 a revival of the Lords, in *Coningsby* he hinted at a monarchical revival. 'But if the peers have ceased to be magnificoes,' he asked, 'may it not also happen that the Sovereign may cease to be a Doge? It is not impossible that the political movements of our time, which seem on the surface to have a tendency to democracy, may have in reality a monarchical basis.'[26]

Lord Monmouth, stately yet venal, symbolises the old aristocratic order; after the passing of the Reform Bill in 1832 he leaves England for abroad – 'I am unable to remain in this Radical-ridden country,' he tells Coningsby. 'I fear these are evil days for the NEW GENERATION!' At Eton, which Disraeli prettily describes in Book One, Coningsby, the hero of the school, is loved by Millbank, the son of a manufacturer, a stern and priggish boy, sometimes wrongly thought to be based on Gladstone (the model was John Walter junior of *The Times*, a Young England sympathiser). Millbank's schoolboy passion symbolises the middle-class/aristocratic alliance of the new generation.

Coningsby is questing for political faith, asking himself 'why governments were hated and religions despised. Why loyalty was dead, and reverence only a galvanised corpse?' He asks Rigby, who delivers a lecture on Schedule A of the Reform Bill, the shortage of churches and the *Quarterly Review*. By satirising the barrenness of Peel's Conservatism and presenting Peel's party as a perversion of true Toryism, Disraeli sought to prove the legitimacy of Young England. The chapters of political narrative are clogged with detailed references to recent events, but the central argument is clear enough. It was

Peel's misfortune, claimed Disraeli, that he entered politics at a time when
the Tory party 'pursued a policy which was either founded on no principle
whatever, or on principles exactly contrary to those which had always guided
the conduct of the great Tory leaders'. During the war years there had
shuffled into power a generation of pseudo-Tories, so-called practical men,
led by Liverpool, the arch-mediocrity. The true Tory principles of Pitt and
Shelburne had been abandoned; instead of the widening of the electorate,
freedom of commerce and the rescue of the Catholics from the Puritanic
yoke, the pseudo-Tories practised exclusive principles in the constitution
and restriction in commerce. Only Canning had attempted to restore true
Toryism.

Peel's Tamworth Manifesto of 1834 'was an attempt to construct a party
without principles; its basis therefore was necessarily Latitudinarianism; and
its inevitable consequence has been Political Infidelity'. Peel's new doctrine
of Conservatism was 'an attempt to carry on affairs by substituting the
fulfilment of the duties of office for the performance of the functions of
government; and to maintain this negative system by the mere influence of
property, reputable private conduct, and what are called good connections'.
The wire-puller Tadpole put it in a nutshell. 'A sound Conservative
government', said he, musingly, 'I understand: Tory men and Whig
measures.'[27]

Disraeli's criticism of Peel's Convervatism was vigorous and hard-hitting,
and so was his satire of the hacks and party managers – the Rigbys, the
Tadpoles and the Tapers; far less clear is what he believed the solution to be.
One possibility was clearly Young England. Lord John Manners is
introduced as Lord Henry Sydney who, like Manners in his pamphlet, *A
Plea for National Holy-Days* (1843), urges dancing round a maypole on the
village green and the restoration of the ancient order of the peasantry.
Manners's friend, the Roman Catholic Ambrose Lyle Phillipps, is there too,
thinly disguised as Eustace Lyle. At St Geneviève, Lyle presides over an
idealised Catholic community, inspired by his Cavalier ancestors; he gives
alms to the poor, and at Christmas the yule logs blaze and the buttery hatch is
open to all from noon to sunset. 'For a Christian gentleman of high degree
was Eustace Lyle.' But Disraeli did not really sympathise with this pseudo-
medievalism and Cavalier paternalism. Manners wrote in his journal about
this time, 'Could I only satisfy myself that D'Israeli believed all that he said, I
should be more satisfied: his historical views are quite mine, but does he
believe them?'[28] Nor did Disraeli share Manners's concern for the poor.
Quite the contrary, *Coningsby* has very little to say about the Condition of
England question which Carlyle had broadcast so trenchantly in *Past and
Present*, published earlier that year.

The market place, Shrewsbury. Disraeli's constituency, 1841–1847.

Rebuilding the House of Commons. The new committee rooms, 1845.

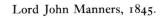
Lord John Manners, 1845.

below left George Smythe. Idealised portrait for Disraeli's Gallery of Friendship, which he collected in old age at Hughenden.

below right Young England's Old Habits. Disraeli as a (Jewish) old-clothes merchant. *Punch*, 1845.

YOUNG ENGLAND'S LAMENT.

[YOUNG ENGLAND *discovered sitting dolorously before his parlour-fire: he grievously waileth as follows :—*]

I REALLY can't imagine why,
　　With my confess'd ability—
From the ungrateful Tories, I
　　Get nothing——but civility.

The " independent " dodge I 've tried,
　　I 've also tried servility ;—
It 's all the same,—they *won't* provide,—
　　I only get——civility.

I 've flattered PEEL ; he smiles back thanks
　　With Belial's own tranquillity ;
But still he keeps me in " the ranks,"
　　And pays me——with civility.

I 've worried him, I 've sneered at him,
　　I 've threatened bold hostility,—
But no—he still preserves his im-
　　perturbable civility.

If not the birth, at least I 've now
　　The *manners* of nobility ;
But yet SIR ROBERT scorns to bow
　　With more than mere civility.

Well, I 've been pretty mild as yet,
　　But now I 'll try scurrility ;
It 's very hard if *that* don't get
　　Me more than mere civility.

Young England's Lament. *Punch*, 1845.

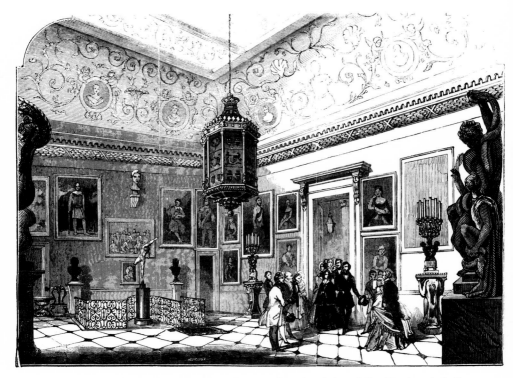

Queen Victoria's departure from Stowe after the duke of Buckingham's ball, January 1845. Disraeli and Mary Anne queued here for an hour on the evening of the ball, 'half lit up, and no seats or fire, only a little hot air and a great deal of cold wind'.

Lord George Bentinck, 1846.

The Speaking Machine. Disraeli and Bentinck, *Punch*, 1846.

Peel speaking in the House of Commons on 27 January 1846, introducing his proposals to repeal the Corn Laws. *Illustrated London News.*

Disraeli harassing Peel. *Punch*, 1846.

Punch, 1846.

POOR ROBIN Premier's
Curfew Bill did fail,
By the country party's head,
And the Irish party's tail.

Here sits SIR ROBIN,
Sad and sold :
His fate this rhyme
Will soon unfold.

This is ROBIN Premier,
So proud and cold, but good,
Who carried through the Bill for
Giving us cheap food.

Who floor'd SIR ROBIN ?
"I," said BEN DIZZY,
"With my speeches so fizzy ;
And I floor'd SIR ROBIN."

Here is BEN DIZZY,
With his speeches so fizzy.

Who howl'd him out ?
"We," said the Rout,
"With a scoff and a shout ;
And we howl'd him out."

Here is the Rout
Howling him out.

Actaeon worried by his own Dogs. *Punch*, 1846.

Young Gulliver and the Brobdinage Minister. *Punch*, 1844.

MANAGER PEEL TAKING HIS FAREWELL BENEFIT.

Manager Peel Taking his Farewell Benefit. *Punch*, 1846.

Disraeli by Francis Grant, 1852. Grant, who normally charged 300 guineas, painted Disraeli for nothing. Disraeli was then in his mid-forties, but Grant made him look fifteen years younger. Note the kiss curl.

Coningsby has been described, and with good reason, as 'first and foremost an anti-Tory novel'.[29] Take away Peel and Tadpole and Taper and the twelve-hundred-a-year official men whom Disraeli so despised, and what are you left with? A party of squires and churchmen; yet neither of these appear in the pages of *Coningsby*. Nothing is said of the soil or the country. The three men who influence Coningsby in his search for faith are Eustace Lyle, a Roman Catholic, Millbank senior, a Lancashire manufacturer and Sidonia, a Jewish financier. Hardly a typical Tory trio. If Peel was guilty of building a party without principles, Disraeli was building a party without Tories.

He wrote *Coningsby* in the same year that Engels compiled his horrifying account of the *Condition of the Working Class in England*, which focuses on Manchester, but Disraeli saw Manchester through very different eyes; it is glowingly described as the city which embodies the spirit of the age. 'What Art was to the Ancient world, Science is to the Modern.' Mr Millbank, the millowner, expresses Lancashire's criticism of the hereditary aristocracy: 'I have yet to learn that they are richer than we are, better informed, wiser, or more distinguished for public or private virtue.' This is an echo of the criticism of the idle aristocracy propounded by Carlyle in *Past and Present*, but Disraeli's prime criticism concerns their legitimacy. The so-called aristocracy, Millbank tells Coningsby, boast their Norman ancestry, but their families are built on the dissolution of the monasteries, and Millbank, as a descendant of Saxon industry, claims a far more ancient lineage.

Millbank may have been a portrait (and a flattering one) of Cobden; certainly Cobden thought so and thanked Disraeli for the compliment, but the author had an ulterior motive. The hidden agenda of *Coningsby* is Disraeli's immediate political ambitions and manoeuvring. Cobden occupied a pivotal position in 1843–4, and was potentially a key agent of Peel's destruction. Louis Philippe also figured in Disraeli's calculations, and is flatteringly described as Ulysses. ('The tendency of advanced civilisation is in truth to pure Monarchy.') And only his aspirations to form an anti-Peel bloc can explain the lavish praise he heaped upon the Whig leader, Lord John Russell.[30] Hence the paradox that *Coningsby*, which purports to be a Tory novel, has only criticism for the Tory leaders and only praise for their opponents.

Thirty-five years later, in *Endymion*, Disraeli returned to the events he described in *Coningsby*, reintroducing many of the same characters, including Cobden. The story is told, however, from a Liberal angle, the hero is a Liberal MP, and the historical Toryism of Young England is ridiculed and belittled. *Endymion* is the book inside *Coningsby* which is struggling to get out; taken to its anti-Tory extreme, it turns into a Liberal novel.

Most compelling of the portraits in *Coningsby* is Sidonia, whom many contemporaries recognised as Lionel de Rothschild (he too reappears in *Endymion*). Like Rothschild, Sidonia's father 'staked all that he was worth on the Waterloo loan; and the event made him one of the richest capitalists in Europe'. His credit keeps governments afloat, yet as a Jew he is excluded from parliament. 'Can anything be more absurd than that a nation should apply to an individual to maintain its credit, and, with its credit, its existence as an empire, and its comfort as a people; and that individual one to whom its laws deny the proudest rights of citizenship, the privilege of sitting in its senate and holding land?'[31]

Disraeli had good reason to flatter Rothschild. He had recently entered the Rothschild orbit, introduced in 1839 when Anthony, Lionel's younger brother, married Louisa Montefiore, a cousin of Dizzy's through Maria. The Rothschild connexion had been critical to his Paris success, and with Sidonia Disraeli sought to woo Lionel de Rothschild.[32] But Sidonia is only part Rothschild. To a large extent he is a self-portrait. Sidonia even shares the ancestry which Disraeli had invented, and which he elaborated in the Memoir he wrote of Isaac in 1849. He is a Marrano Jew whose ancestors were expelled from Spain at the time of the Inquisition.[33] Disraeli/Sidonia can look the grandest of English dukes in the eye; he boasts a lineage far prouder than the oldest English strawberry leaf.

Yet there is a side to Sidonia which is neither Rothschild nor Disraeli: his heartlessness. Rothschild was a family man, and Disraeli did not deny his debt to Mary Anne; Sidonia, by contrast, 'was not a marrying man'. Not only does he refuse to marry outside his race, but he has no heart, no affections. 'Woman was to him a toy, man a machine.' His attitude towards women was Oriental. He liked chorus girls and clever women: 'He liked the drawing-room, and he liked the Desert, but he would not consent that either should trench on their mutual privileges.' Sidonia cannot be redeemed through love. 'The lot most precious to man ... to find in another heart a perfect and profound sympathy ... all this Nature had denied to Sidonia.' Doomed to solitariness, he worships intellect. He is a connoisseur of knowledge, whose penetrative intellect was 'matured by long meditation, and assisted by that absolute freedom from prejudice, which was the compensatory possession of a man without a country'. Sidonia 'held relations with all the clever outcasts of the world ... The secret history of the world was his pastime. His great pleasure was to contrast the hidden motive, with the public pretext, of transactions.'[34]

Sidonia's scepticism, and his inability to achieve redemption through love point to a source not in life but in legend, the Wandering Jew. The Wandering Jew, cursed by Christ and doomed to wander perpetually in search of redemption he can never achieve, was a popular Romantic theme, usually presented unsympathetically, as a metaphor for the fate of the Jews, destined to wander for ever. By the 1840s an alternative, sympathetic version had emerged: the Wandering Jew as symbol of scepticism, intellect and sometimes of the aspirations of the Jewish people.[35] Sidonia fits this version, nor is it stretching belief too far to suggest that the Wandering Jew formed part of Disraeli's autobiographical fantasy. It is appropriate that Sidonia should be the mouthpiece of his views about the racial superiority of the Jews.

Disraeli's theory of race is first expressed in *Coningsby*. Following Blumenbach, the German Enlightenment theorist ('the Newton of physiology'), Disraeli proposed a theory of five races, the Caucasian, the Mongolian, the Malayan, the American, the Ethiopian. The Caucasian race is the superior, and it includes not only Saxons, Normans and Greeks but Arabs and Jews; an unorthodox classification. Of the Caucasian races, claimed Disraeli (and here he was entirely on his own), the Jews were superior, because they were 'the only Caucasian race that has remained pure and unmixed'. Sidonia remarks, 'The fact is, you cannot destroy a pure race of the Caucasian organisation.' In spite of centuries of persecution, the Jewish mind still shapes the affairs of Europe. 'I speak not of their laws, which you still obey; of their literature, with which your minds are saturated; but of the living Hebrew intellect.' Sidonia relates how he raised a loan for Russia and encountered Count Cancrin, a Lithuanian Jew, the minister of Finance; the loan took him to Spain, where he met Mendizabel; to France and Marshal Soult; to Prussia and Count Arnim: all were Jews. According to Sidonia, the first Jesuits were Jews, and the mighty German intellectual revolution – a second Reformation – is driven by Jews who monopolise the professorial chairs of Germany. Music, according to Disraeli, is also a Jewish monopoly – Rossini, Meyerbeer, Mendelssohn.[36]

Sidonia is the vehicle for Disraeli's theory of a Jewish world conspiracy. 'So you see', says Sidonia, 'that the world is governed by very different personages from what is imagined by those who are not behind the scenes.' The idea of a secret conspiracy of Jews is as old as Christianity, but the modern anti-semitic myth of a Jewish world conspiracy was formulated at the time of the French Revolution by the French Jesuit Barruel. In *Coningsby* Disraeli turned anti-semitic demonology on its head. Not only did he argue that the Jewish world conspiracy was a fact; he cited it as evidence of the power and centrality of the Jews. Many of those he listed were not Jews at all. Soult was not a Jew, nor was Arnim; it is doubtful whether Cancrin was. Yet he was not joking; when challenged about Cancrin's descent, Disraeli responded that he was convinced of his Jewishness. 'I had it, ten years ago, from a secret agent of the Counts, who also knew his father: my informant himself a Hebrew, and one so accurate, that tho' he has imparted to me much secret intelligence, I have never found him tripping.'[37] For Disraeli the Jewish conspiracy was a reality, and he was a member of the elect, a belief crucial to his self-esteem. A Jew and a convert, Disraeli was never truly at ease in the company of men. As his biographer André Maurois perceived, 'To feel himself their equal, he needed to be their Chief.'[38] His claim to be their chief rested not only on his genius but on his innate racial superiority and power as a Jew. Hence Sidonia.

Sidonia is leader and teacher of the Young Englanders, yet he shares few of the ideas associated with Young England. Nor does he advocate the Radical Toryism Disraeli had urged before 1841. Riding to power on the shoulders of the mob is not Sidonia's idea of politics; politics is about *control*, manipulating governments behind the scenes, secrecy and conspiracies. Manipulation and control were characteristics of High Toryism; and as Sidonia explains to Coningsby, the Jews are essentially Tories. Restriction has forced them to become revolutionaries against their nature:

> The Jews ... are a race essentially monarchical, deeply religious, and shrinking themselves from converts as from a calamity, are ever anxious to see the religious systems of the countries in which they live flourish; yet, since your society has become agitated in England, and powerful combinations menace your institutions, you find the once loyal Hebrew invariably arrayed in the same ranks as the leveller and the latitudinarian, and prepared to support the policy which may even endanger his life and property, rather than tamely continue under a system which seeks to degrade them.... Yet the Jews, Coningsby, are essentially Tories. Toryism, indeed, is but copied from the mighty prototype which has fashioned Europe.[39]

'Rely upon it', Sidonia says, 'that England should think more of the community and less of the government.' He teaches Coningsby to question the value of parliamentary government and to prefer enlightened monarchy. He is sceptical about reason, condemning the misguided attempts of the Utilitarians to reconstruct society on a rational basis. 'Man is only truly great when he acts from the passions; never irresistible but when he appeals to the imagination.... Man is made to adore and to obey: but if you will not command him, if you give him nothing to worship, he will fashion his own divinities, and find a chieftain in his own passions.'[40] Sidonia/Disraeli encapsulated the nightmare haunting politics in the 1840s.

With Sidonia, Disraeli invented a new persona for himself – Jewish, High Tory and a leader, completing the metamorphosis begun when Peel denied Disraeli office in 1841. Yet his evolution from Radical via Radical Tory to High Tory was not without a certain inner logic. For Disraeli the real division in politics was between reason and imagination. As a Radical he had opposed Utilitarianism; as a Tory he opposed Peel's Conservatism or Liberal Toryism: based on reason and argument, Conservatism was fatally lacking in imagination. 'If Democracy be combated only by Conservatism, Democracy must triumph, and at no distant date.'[41]

Coningsby is only partly based on George Smythe; he is also reminiscent of Disraeli's earlier fictional heroes. Like Contarini Fleming or Ferdinand Armine (*Henrietta Temple*) he is heir to an ancient house.[42] The relationship between the young Coningsby, searching for faith, and the wisdom figure Sidonia, dramatises Disraeli's own evolution from Radical Tory to High Tory. *Coningsby* is not so much a political manifesto as an autobiography, a dialogue between Disraeli's young self and his mature self.

At Bradenham in the autumn of 1843 the writing came easily. Closeted in his writing room next to Sarah, Disraeli scrawled to Mary Anne, 'My dearest, it is impossible to get on better. I have already written ten pages and have never stopped. Send me half a glass of wine and a crust of bread.' He was dependent on her advice, even in his writing. 'Darling, I wish you would come up and talk over a little point, if you are not particularly engaged.'[43]

At the same time that he was digging his pen into Peel in *Coningsby*, he was addressing begging letters to the home secretary, Graham, Peel's close political ally, asking for a job for his brother Jem. Jem, now thirty, was an engagingly unsuccessful farmer who could not pronounce his 'r's: Disraeli had written to Graham the previous year ('Jem if he have occasion to *express* his thanks to Sir James, must recollect that express is spelt with an R'), and now, like an impudent schoolboy, he returned to taunt his masters. He was, he told Graham, exempt from 'those obsolete notions ... that a member of a party, who had done that party some service, has any claims upon their consideration'. Nonetheless, if Graham refused, Jem 'will at least, by the attempt have acquired a more correct conception of the nature of party connections, and the value of party services'. Naturally Graham refused; how could he do otherwise? As for Peel, he was if anything gratified by Disraeli's impudence in asking for favours. 'It is a good thing', he told Graham, 'when such a man puts his shabbiness on record.'[44]

Late in January 1844 Disraeli and Mary Anne left Bradenham for Grosvenor Gate, with the still unfinished manuscript of *Coningsby*. Parliament met on 1 February, and only then did Disraeli realise that he had been struck off Peel's circular at the start of the session. He promptly wrote to Peel to complain. No doubt his speeches on Ireland and Servia had been deficient in 'hearty goodwill' towards his political chief; 'but pardon me, if I now observe ... that you might have found some reason for this ... in the want of courtesy in debate, which I have had the frequent mortification of experiencing from you, since your accession to Power.'[45] Peel, who in private expressed deep distrust of Disraeli, was icily polite, accepting his explanation. Though the rift was temporarily healed, there is a dreadful inevitability about Disraeli's quarrel with Peel; like a rebellious son, he was driven by the need to destroy a leader who refused to recognise his abilities.

To mark the reconciliation, Disraeli spoke in the Irish debate (16 February 1844). He painted a golden picture of the state of Ireland under Strafford, and he called, as he had done the previous August, for a return to the true Tory principles and the Irish policy of Charles I. Ireland's ills he blamed on Cromwell and the Puritans, not the Protestants, provoking Macaulay to deliver a history lecture on Ireland, and he summed up the Irish question in an epigram which would be turned against him a quarter of a century later during the debate on the Irish Church: 'a starving population, an absentee aristocracy, and an alien Church, and in addition the weakest executive in the world. That is the Irish question.' Rather than blame Peel for deserting Tory principles, he gently mocked him. All that was required in Ireland was the removal of prejudices, much as had been required when Peel reconstructed the Tory party after 1832. 'There sits the right honourable baronet at this moment,' he declared, turning to the Treasury bench where Peel was sandwiched between Graham and Stanley, 'with a Secretary of State on each side of him, whose prejudices he has succeeded most effectually in removing.' Even Peel laughed. It was, as the diarist Greville wrote, 'a very clever speech, not *saying* so much, but implying it, and under the guise of compliment making an ingenious and amusing attack on Peel, Stanley and Graham'.[46]

Greville thought Disraeli's speech the most striking of the debate; at last he had caught the ear of the House. No one was more aware of this than Disraeli. Two days later, on the Sunday night after dinner, he and Mary Anne sat alone in the Little Library at Grosvenor Gate, hugging themselves over Dizzy's success; at Mary Anne's command, Dizzy wrote down the compliments he had received. A report from Manners of breakfast with Monckton Milnes, where nothing was spoken of but the speech, or Bernal's remark to Smythe that if Disraeli was 'a Lord Tom Noddy, that man would revolutionise the nation'. Smythe, reported Disraeli, is all for Tom Noddyism.[47]

Coningsby was finished in March, when Disraeli signed a contract with Colburn the publisher. Within days he was revising the first proofs, and the novel appeared on 11 May. The first to read it were Young England, and they cheered wildly. Hope, reported Disraeli, was 'enchanted', Cochrane 'raving' (this despite being described in the novel, where he appears as Buckhurst, as 'absurd, extravagant, grotesque, noisy ...'), Manners 'full of mild rapture'. Smythe, whose book it was, was intoxicated – 'dazzled, bewildered, tipsy with admiration the most passionate and wild.... Thank God,' he wrote, 'I have a faith at last!'[48]

A political novel, *Coningsby* naturally received political reviews. Disraeli was well aware of this; when it received an inadequate notice in *The Times* which, thanks to his friendship with John Walter junior, was an ally of Young England, he wrote to complain that, 'considering the influence of *The Times*, and the generally understood sympathy of its columns with many of the topics treated in *Coningsby*, the review is one calculated to do the work very great injury'.[49]

One of the shrewdest critics was Thackeray, writing in the Whig *Morning Chronicle*. *Coningsby*, he wrote, was the fashionable novel, pushed to its extreme – 'dandy-social, dandy-political, dandy-religious'. Dandies are even made to regenerate the world, and this strained credulity: 'Fancy a prostrate world kissing the feet of a reformer – in patent blacking; fancy a prophet delivering heavenly messages – with his hair in papers.' Though a dandy, wrote Thackeray, Disraeli was a genius. Disraeli responded by asking Thackeray to dinner. (In 1847, however, Thackeray ridiculed Disraeli's dandyism and his belief in Jewish superiority in 'Codlingsby', an extravagantly anti-semitic skit on *Coningsby* and *Tancred* for *Punch* which, since 1844, had annoyed Disraeli with anti-Jewish jibes. Yet Thackeray was not above providing his own version of the marquess of Hertford in *Vanity Fair*, where he is Lord Steyne. Disraeli revenged himself in *Endymion*, where Thackeray is portrayed as St Barbe, vain, snobbish and self-obsessed.)[50]

Thackeray's ambivalence was typical of the Victorian intellectual aristocracy, the George Eliots, Anthony Trollopes and Thomas Carlyles. Grudgingly, they admitted Disraeli's cleverness, but they disliked his flashiness, and they were repelled by his theory of Jewish racial superiority. Harriet Martineau, whom Disraeli had savaged in a *Times* review of her *Society in America* in 1837, could not even bring herself to read *Coningsby*. 'D's vulgar charlatanerie offends me so,' she told Monckton Milnes, 'and so destroys trust in his sayings, that I had rather avoid the provocation of reading him. I never could respect or like a man who feels no pain in making himself ridiculous, with and by personal pretension; and the more genius he may have, the worse the case.'[51]

Monckton Milnes reviewed *Coningsby* for *Hood's Magazine*. He found much to praise, particularly Disraeli's bold avowal of faith in his race which, however fanciful, was 'deeply interesting, in our cold sceptical days'. But Milnes disliked Disraeli's practice of introducing real people; he thought the book smart and fashionable, and he doubted whether it would last.[52] Disraeli thanked him, adding that Mrs Disraeli 'has several puissant arguments for you in store'; privately, he consoled himself with the thought that Milnes, who considered himself a Young Englander, resented that he did not appear in the novel. Milnes's criticism was fair, though. As the intellectual socialite Lady Harriet Baring remarked, the characters in *Coningsby* were 'envelopes of men', not real men at all.[53] Milnes had good reason to be annoyed by Disraeli's success. His own Young England group, which included high churchmen such as Gladstone, had met in 1838 or earlier, two years before Disraeli's first use of the word.[54]

Even admirers of *Coningsby* were annoyed by Disraeli's descriptions of Eton, which were peppered with inaccuracies insiders delight in finding. Disraeli shrugged their criticisms aside. When Lord Lyttelton, a pious Etonian, wrote a five-page letter, listing Disraeli's solecisms and complaining about the inaccuracy of the schoolboy slang, Disraeli replied that it had been suggested to him by Cookesley, the Eton master who had advised him on the proofs.[55] No doubt Disraeli was equally unimpressed by hunting men who objected to his ignorance and effrontery in making Sidonia win a steeplechase on an Arab horse rather than an English thoroughbred.

Coningsby sold. Its publication was superbly well timed; stimulated by the public's curiosity about Young England, it went through three editions in three months. 'Coningsby keeps moving about 40 a day on average,' Disraeli reported in June; in July he told Sarah that 'Its success has exceeded all my hopes'.[56] Keys to the principal characters were supplied to simple folk in the country, at the rate of a shilling including the postage stamp. English-language editions were published in Paris and Leipzig. Disraeli told the cultivated American minister, Edward Everett, with whom he breakfasted that July, that he 'wanted *fame*, and nothing else'. In 1845 Everett sent him a copy of a cheap pirate American edition; Disraeli did not grumble at the lack of royalties, but he complained about the proliferation of misprints. 'Every misprint in your editions is an injury to my fame.'[57]

Coningsby launched Disraeli on a career of fame in the summer of 1844. 'Every day, every hour, something is said, or heard, or written.' The book, he told Sarah, was 'wonderfully popular with the ladies'. Sydney Smith asked to meet him; at dinner he talked of nothing but Croker/Rigby, afterwards dubbing the Disraelis Dizzy and Quizzy.[58] The compliments aimed at Lionel de Rothschild achieved their purpose. Mary Anne made sure that they did; she visited Mrs Montefiore, Louisa de Rothschild's mother, in a fever about the book, urging them all to read it. Lord Ponsonby was 'so "enchanted with Sidonia" that we are all to dine together at the Lionels *en petit comité* on Sunday'.[59] Triumph!

Disraeli spoke only four times during the session of 1844, though Mary

Anne noted in her account book that 'Dizzy dined much at the House'. Sitting in his place, silent and impassive, he watched as Peel's credit slipped away. Feeling on the backbenches boiled up in May, when Lord Ashley introduced a ten-hour amendment to Graham's Factory Bill, reducing the hours worked by women from the twelve hours proposed by the government to ten. Disraeli voted in favour of Ashley's amendment, as did the other Young Englanders, except for Smythe. Unlike Manners and Cochrane, however, Disraeli remained silent; he later claimed that he tried to speak but failed. He did not make a speech supporting factory reform until 1850; it may well be that the reason why he did not join what Cobden called 'the Socialist fools behind Peel' was because he did not want to alienate Cobden, whose support he was clearly seeking in *Coningsby*.[60]

The government was defeated over Ashley's amendment and, in an astounding act of prime ministerial arrogance, Peel forced the House to rescind its vote. On 14 June, a Friday, the government was defeated again, this time over the Protectionist Miles's amendment to a bill reducing sugar duties. Disraeli, who paired against the government, was absent from the House, chained to Grosvenor Gate by Mary Anne's summer entertainment, a grand dinner followed by an evening party for two hundred. The guests of honour were the Lionel de Rothschilds, and, as the party thinned and the men left to vote, Dizzy no doubt talked high politics to Baron Lionel.[61] The result was a dinner two days later given by Rothschild for the Whig leaders, Lords John Russell and Lansdowne, and the Disraelis. It was a bizarre combination, and Hobhouse, who sat next to Disraeli, thought the party was intended to bring Disraeli into contact with the Whigs. Hobhouse, who happened to be reading *Coningsby*, found Disraeli communicative: he 'spoke with that sort of confidence which sometimes belongs to men of genius, and sometimes to very impudent pretenders'. Disraeli assured him Peel would be turned out the very next day. When Hobhouse objected that the Whigs could not form a government, Disraeli replied that Russell might '*easily*, but not if they tried to govern on the old Whig scheme … He said that Ireland was no obstacle; we could govern it, although the Tories could not. The Corn-laws might be settled as well by us as by Peel, and as to the Poor-laws, some modification must be made by any one who would govern.' Hobhouse shook his head; Disraeli declared that 'Peel had completely failed to keep together his party and must *go*, if not now at least very speedily. He said Russell was one of the very few men in the House of Commons who had a *strong will*, and was fit to govern. He thought nothing of Stanley; Graham he admired for his capacity.'[62]

The anti-Peel bloc of Rothschild and Russell which formed the hidden agenda of *Coningsby* seemed to be taking shape. Yet we know of Disraeli's

intrigues only because Hobhouse kept a diary. Who knows what conversations Disraeli held with the Whigs or with Rothschild? and one can only
guess at his relations with Cobden. In June 1844, however, Russell was not
ready to form a government. He took no notice of Disraeli's remarks to
Hobhouse and made no preparations to defeat Peel.

On 17 June Disraeli attended a meeting of two hundred Tory MPs at the
Carlton. A resolution of support for Peel was passed, but Disraeli was among
the handful of MPs who spoke against him. That evening in the House, Peel
made an offensive, dictatorial speech, rebuking his followers for deserting
him over sugar duties. Disraeli saw his chance; in a short, mocking speech, he
lashed Peel for bullying his supporters into rescinding yet another vote. Peel
claimed a horror of slavery and slave-grown sugar, jeered Disraeli, but his
horror extended everywhere except to the benches behind him. 'There the
gang is still assembled, and there the thong of the whip still sounds.'
Hobhouse noted the tremendous cheer that greeted Disraeli's sally; Peel,
Stanley and Graham sat in painful silence amid the applause of many of their
own side and all those opposite. 'I never saw them look so wretched.' Disraeli
came up and told Hobhouse that he expected Peel to lose, but the
government survived by a majority of twenty-two. Peel had been saved by
Russell.[63]

Queen Victoria, eight months pregnant and distraught at the prospect of
losing her and Albert's dear Sir Robert, blamed the government's crisis on
'the recklessness of a handful of foolish half "Puseyite", half "Young
England" people'. But far more to blame was Peel himself; his frigid
arrogance undermined his position, and his credibility was irreparably
damaged by the Sugar Duties crisis. Never again, wrote Greville, will Peel be
considered a great minister. 'He is at the head of a weak, discontented Party.'
Even Gladstone, his devoted disciple, who was reading *Coningsby* at the time
of the crisis, confessed that listening to Peel's speech gave him what in
Gladstone/Glynn family language was called 'a creep': a deep wound had
been inflicted on the party's spirit, and 'a great man had committed a great
error'.[64]

Since his breach with Peel in 1843, Disraeli had neglected his constituency. His position at Shrewsbury was worryingly unsafe, and at the end of
August he made his third visit since the election. He travelled alone, leaving
Mary Anne in London, and in Shrewsbury he made the most of it: it was
their wedding anniversary, and (so he said) they were parted for the first time.
'The women shed tears, which indeed I can barely myself restrain.' He was
aware of the political appeal of this mawkish uxoriousness, which astutely
exploited Mary Anne's popularity in the constituency. The agent, he told
Mary Anne, says '*my domestic character does me a great deal of good at*

Shrewsbury'. But Mary Anne's cosseting, her magic draughts for sleeping, her mothering, had become necessary to him, and he missed her. The hot bottle was in constant use and a great comfort, but he said he felt very lonely at night (he was only away for three) and could not keep his spirits up.

'The only thing that consoles me for our separation,' wrote Dizzy, 'is my strong conviction that my presence here was absolutely necessary. What might have injured me, I have now turned to good account.' He paid calls on the tradesmen, making a canvass of his chief supporters. 'It is understood that I am *the tradesmen's member* – so I don't trouble myself much about the pseudo aristocracy, and less about the real.' He discovered his supporters quite approved the attack on the government, but 'a little alarmed in some quarters I find about Popery, Monasteries and John Manners. This I shall quietly soften down.'[65]

His chance came with a speech to his constituents, but to his annoyance he learned that reporters were engaged from the London papers 'and I must be careful'. He was silent on the Church and Ireland, concentrating instead on the Condition of England question, on which he claimed to have written long before it was discussed in parliament. 'I had long been aware', he told the four hundred Salopians crowded into the Lion Inn, 'that there was something rotten in the core of our social system.' While immense fortunes accumulated, and Britain became the most prosperous nation in the world, the working classes, the creators of wealth, were sinking into poverty and degradation. As for Peel, Disraeli's independence from the government was welcomed in Shrewsbury. He denied asking Peel for a place, disingenuously adding 'let Sir Robert Peel ... say that I asked for a place, and I will undertake to give them an answer which shall be perfectly satisfactory.' No, he declared, he cared not for office but for fame. 'I love to live in the eyes of the country; and it is a glorious thing for a man to do who has had my difficulties to contend against.' He ended with a sally against Peel. 'Remember the end,' he prompted a local newspaper editor next day, 'In his adversity I was his supporter, in his prosperity I will not be his slave.'[66]

Young England reached its apogee in 1844, sending ripples into the worlds of literature and politics. Smythe, Manners and Cochrane became celebrated for their white waistcoats; at Grosvenor Gate they concocted speeches and articles under Disraeli's supervision. Peter Borthwick, owner of the *Morning Post* and a friend of Disraeli, lent them the columns of his paper. At *The Times* John Walter junior even provided a small room which, Baillie Cochrane recalled, brought the advantages of early information and competent advisers.[67]

In *Anti-Coningsby* (1844), a two-volume skit, William North imagined the scenario where Peel resigned and the Coningsby cabinet was formed. 'Ben Sidonia' is identified as Disraeli: 'a man of a peculiarly good-looking countenance, corkscrew curls and a sarcastic curl of lip'. It is an anti-semitic fantasy, informed by sources like *Punch*, which specialised in coarse and virulent anti-Jewish 'humour', and the novels of Rosina Bulwer Lytton, Disraeli's pet hate and a sour anti-semite: from Rosina was taken the story of Disraeli in velvet trousers rising from a cane chair with the brand of Cain upon him. Young England, claims *Anti-Coningsby*, has no policy but the Sidonian Manifesto of 1844. The Jewish Emancipation Bill is the chief measure of the Coningsby government. The House of Commons is filled with Jews; Ben Sidonia proposes the abolition of elective representation and is crowned Emperor. *Anti-Coningsby* was unusual in its emphasis on the Jewish theme in Young England; most critics focused on its social policies.

> Give us our old nobility,
> And feudal glories past,
> Unbelieving politicians
> Be from our Senate cast.
> Emancipate the Hebrews
> Conciliate the Pope
> Found mechanic institutions
> And learn to trust in HOPE.[68]

Poring over the newspapers for his study of the *Condition of the Working Class in England in 1844*, twenty-three-year-old Friedrich Engels applauded Young England for being opposed to the class interests of the bourgeoisie. 'The hope of Young England is a restoration of the old "Merrie England" with its brilliant features and its romantic feudalism.' Of course, he wrote in a condescending footnote, its aim was ridiculous, a satire upon all historic development. In the *Communist Manifesto* (1848), Karl Marx was bitingly sarcastic about Young England, which he saw as feudal socialism: 'half lamentation, half lampoon; half echo of the past, half menace of the future; at times, by its bitter, witty and incisive criticism, striking the bourgeoisie to the very heart's core; but always ludicrous in its effect, through total incapacity to comprehend the march of modern history.' The aristocracy, said Marx, waved alms bags before the proletariat, but people saw the old feudal coats of arms on their hind legs, and deserted with loud and irreverent laughter.[69]

Marx's and Engels's views of Young England as feudal socialism owes more to John Manners than Disraeli. *Coningsby* was silent on the Condition of England, and Disraeli barely spoke on the issue in 1844. Young England's aristocratic socialism did not really convince. It was, as George Eliot sharply remarked, 'the aristocratic dilettantism which attempts to restore the "good old times" by a sort of idyllic masquerading, and to grow fidelity and veneration as we grow turnips, by an artificial system of manure'.[70] Her criticism ignored the religious side to Manners's thought; like Gladstone he was a Puseyite in politics, inspired by an idealistic 'high' view of state and church. But Puseyism was an electoral liability, as Disraeli discovered at Shrewsbury; in parliament it cost Young England the sympathy of the evangelicals like Ashley, whose social views were broadly similar to theirs. As Thomas Carlyle explained to Monckton Milnes, '*if* Young England would altogether fling its shovel-hat into the lumber-room, much more cast its purple stockings to the nettles; and honestly recognising what was dead, and leaving the dead to bury that, address itself frankly to the magnificent but as yet chaotic and appalling Future, in the *spirit* of the Past and Present; telling men at every turn that it knew and saw forever clearly the *body* of the Past to be dead ... what achievements might not Young England perhaps manage for us! Whatsoever was noble and manful among us, in terrible want of a rallying-point at present, might rally there, and march. But alas, alas!'[71]

That Young England failed to act as rallying-point was not Disraeli's fault; the purple stockings and shovel hat were not his doing. For him, Young England was about the regeneration of aristocratic leadership, which Carlyle too had diagnosed in *Past and Present* as the fundamental need of the times. Young England succeeded because it acted as a focus for the growing but unarticulated resentment and disillusion with Peel's liberal, unimaginative Conservatism both inside and outside parliament; a case of brilliant timing. For Disraeli, to whom intrigue was vitally necessary, Young England was invaluable political cover. It flagged his credentials as party loyalist, the guardian of the Tory faith, while in private, he plotted with Liberals and Radicals to bring down Peel's government. If he was consistent in anything after 1841, it was in his campaign against Peel.

His relationship with Smythe was Young England's emotional dynamic. Disraeli prompted Smythe's speeches and journalism, and helped write his book, *Historic Fancies* (1844), a collection of sketches and verse on the French Revolution. Smythe's views were so chaotic that some regarded him as 'a staunch Russian; others as a ferocious Jacobin'. But, as *Anti-Coningsby* pointed out, he was 'neither one nor the other but ... a sort of cross between the two'.[72] In this he resembled Disraeli in his Tory Radical days. Smythe was self-indulgent and utterly unreliable, but Disraeli relished his quick wit, his conversational brilliance and his animal magnetism. He was as promiscuous sexually as Disraeli was politically, and Disraeli derived a vicarious excitement from his many affairs.

In the novel *Coningsby*, Disraeli had Smythe/Coningsby marry an heiress,

Edith Millbank. One critic has suggested that his intention was to make the purity of Coningsby's love for Edith mirror his discovery of uncorrupted political faith.[73] Perhaps so, but it was also his intention to control Smythe's life as he did Coningsby's, to arrange a marriage with an heiress. At the time Disraeli was writing *Coningsby*, Smythe was involved in a messy affair with Eugénie Mayer – he got her pregnant and fled to Paris. *Coningsby*, however, raised Smythe's stock, and he was worshipped as a romantic hero which, as his sister-in-law tartly noted, was 'very unwholesome to a mind that required bracing rather than humouring and panegyrising'. In August 1844 Disraeli packed him off to Germany, in pursuit of the wily millionairess, Angela Burdett-Coutts, four years his senior and a seasoned practitioner in playing hard to get. 'You are like the Good Genie one reads of in your own Oriental tales,' wrote Smythe to his 'Cid and Captain', 'and I am very like some of their madder heroes.' The Genie was frustrated, however, by Smythe's frivolity, and his compulsive womanising. Casanova-like, he catalogued his amorous adventures in illegible letters to Disraeli; dallying with married women, with actresses and someone called 'Cochranes Green Gage', Smythe allowed himself to be endlessly sidetracked from Coutts and her millions. He 'seems to have made a complete failure', Disraeli wrote irritably. Thirty-five years later, in *Endymion*, Disraeli regained control, when he made Smythe/Waldershare marry Angela, who is Adriana Neuchâtel in the novel.[74]

TWELVE

'The Great Object
of my Political Life'

1844–5

YOUNG ENGLAND was the fashion in 1844. In October the merchants of Manchester invited Disraeli, Smythe and Manners to address the meeting of their Athenaeum. The duke of Rutland and Lord Strangford, who deplored Disraeli's influence over his sons, objected. 'I do not know Mr Disraeli by sight,' wrote the duke, 'but I have respect only for his talents, which I think he sadly misuses.' Only when it was agreed that the occasion should not be political but a strictly literary tea did the two fathers relent, and the meeting was triumphantly successful. It was scripted by Disraeli, who wrote most of the speeches. The Young Englanders flattered their audience of three thousand, appealing for a marriage between manufacturing and art and, more specifically, calling for a liberal education for the working class.[1]

Manchester is usually seen as the climax of Young England. *The Times* gave it six columns and printed a leader endorsing the call for working-class education. About this time Disraeli was writing to Manners about 'the great financial principle', possibly differentiation between taxation on earned and unearned income: 'It seems to me that it may remedy most ills, and reconcile all interests, and that a more comprehensive and secure basis for a rising school of statesmen and a new scheme of politics, cannot be devised.'[2] Presumably the great financial principle was linked in Disraeli's scheme to education for the working class – an interventionist policy financed by progressive taxation.

Young England's Manchester speeches produced mixed reactions. Monckton Milnes was irritated by the praise they received for talking education and liberality, 'the very things for which the Radicals have been called all possible blackguards and atheists'. Gladstone felt impelled to write to his fellow Tractarian, Manners, rebuking Young England for its false and exaggerated view of the capacities of government:

It is most easy to complain as you do of '*laissez-faire*' and '*laissez-aller*': nor do I in word or in heart presume to blame you: but I should sorely blame myself if with my experience and convictions of *the growing impotence of government for its highest functions,* I were either to recommend attempts beyond its powers, which would react unfavourably upon its remaining capabilities, or to be a party to proposed substitutes for its true moral and paternal work which appear to me mere counterfeits.[3]

Gladstone's stern and priggish letter points to the dilemma facing Young England: how to draw up a policy of social reform without compromising the movement's Tractarianism, which implied a deep-rooted distrust of the state as an agent of improvement. Disraeli was not convinced that legislation was the solution; he placed no faith in legislative panaceas, but in a change of heart and mind on the part of the governors.

The Manchester triumph was followed by a tour of country houses, culminating in the Disraelis' visit to Fryston, the Yorkshire home of Monckton Milnes. Their host was not Dicky but his father, old Mr Milnes, who took a malicious delight in annoying his son, affecting unbounded admiration for Dizzy in order to vex Dicky. Old Mr Milnes made lavish preparations for the Disraelis, borrowed a chef, laid on sumptuous food, turtle soup, salmon, woodcocks, and assembled eighteen or twenty guests. Gathorne Hardy, a young lawyer who was there, heartily disliked Disraeli, finding him clever but vain, egotistical and afraid of talking freely lest he lose ground. Another guest who was prepared to dislike the Disraelis was Lady Elizabeth Spencer-Stanhope, a woman about the same age as Mary Anne, well-bred, conventional and rather grand. She was disarmed by Disraeli at dinner, by his soft voice, and his attentive, half-foreign manner. Mary Anne was ridiculous in a wreath and lace dress looped up on either side over pink satin (she was fifty-two), but Lady Elizabeth was won over by her warmth and spontaneity, by her touching devotion to Dizzy and her abundant supply of gossip.[4]

Disraeli planned another novel, a companion to *Coningsby*. *Coningsby* had dealt with the state of political parties, but was silent on the Condition of England, the phrase on everyone's lips in 1844. This was the theme he planned to treat in his new novel, using what he described as the same agency as *Coningsby*, namely 'it is the past alone that can explain the present, and it is youth alone that can mould the remedial future'. THE TWO NATIONS occurs as an entry in Disraeli's commonplace book in 1842, but not until 1844 did he link the phrase to the Condition of England question. 'How are the two Nations?' asked Smythe in a letter in August 1844.[5]

In that month Disraeli's friend, the Radical Tom Duncombe, a protagonist of the Chartists who had presented their petition in 1842, sent Disraeli a packet of letters belonging to the Chartist leader, Feargus O'Connor. Disraeli later claimed that the O'Connor documents inspired his novel. Another source was the visit he and Mary Anne paid that autumn, after the Manchester speech, to Lord Francis Egerton. Egerton was heir to the millions of the Canal Duke of Bridgewater, but nonetheless he chose to live at Worsley, his industrial estate in the wet, flat Staffordshire coalfield, the air murky with fire and smoke vomiting from furnaces and chimneys, where he had built churches, schools and reading rooms, sparing neither pains nor money to educate and improve the people.[6] Disraeli was impressed, less by Egerton's industrial feudalism than by the dreary, desolate mining landscape: it was a glimpse of hell, and Egerton's story of the Plug Plot of 1842, when he succeeded in dissuading his miners from joining the rebellion, was a startling reminder of the revolutionary energies simmering beneath the crust of capitalism.

After their visit to Egerton, Disraeli and Mary Anne stayed at Bingley with W. B. Ferrand, a paternalistic squire and Tory Radical MP sympathetic to Young England. Disraeli spoke at the dinner (11 October) held to celebrate Ferrand's introduction of allotments for the factory workers of Bingley. Standing beneath a flag inscribed 'The Throne and the Cottage', Disraeli stirred his audience of manufacturers, mechanics and farmers with an exciting speech about Young England's aspirations to end social exclusiveness and make England once more a nation instead of a mere collection of classes.

Bingley was a rapidly growing industrial village, its tall mill chimneys rising out of picturesque countryside; nearby were the ruins of Fountains Abbey, which Disraeli visited with John Manners. Manners no longer distrusted Disraeli, and Disraeli warmed to his boyish enthusiasm as they struggled through the brambles and rank vegetation which covered the ruined abbey to reach the great church. On the moor, Manners climbed a large stone known as the Druids' Altar, to the alarm of Mary Anne; the novel, mused Disraeli, should be Manners's, much as *Coningsby* had been Smythe's. Popery, monasteries and John Manners might be anathema to the voters of Shrewsbury, but they were compelling topics for a novelist.[7]

At the end of October, Disraeli retreated to Bradenham, and he and Manners agreed to make no more Young England speeches. 'We have carried to a happy conclusion a highly successful campaign, unquestionably raised our names in the country, ascertained that the feeling of the nation is with us, and having supplied the world with sufficient suggestions, the wisest thing we can do, is to leave them to chew the cud.' Disraeli had a great deal to do.

His constituency took little of his time: a visit once a year, very little correspondence. But preparing himself for the session, briefing Manners and Smythe, proposing their policy and writing their speeches was a time-consuming business. He was an omnivorous reader, devouring blue books of parliamentary papers, volumes of state papers on foreign policy, pamphlets and periodicals (in 1845–6 he bought 283 lbs. of blue books which retailed at 3d a pound). Making a parliamentary reputation, let alone a new party, was hard work.[8]

Sybil, as the novel was entitled, opens with a famous description of jaded, gilded youth in the glittering salons of Crockford's Club on the eve of the Derby of 1837. For all the sparkling epigrams ('I rather like bad wine,' said Mr Mountchesney; 'one gets so bored with good wine'), the first chapter is not inviting. The incomprehensible talk of betting odds, the confusing surfeit of titles, the forced cleverness and artificial lightness repel, in the same way that Disraeli's conversation repelled Gathorne Hardy at Fryston.

Sybil is the story of Egremont, younger brother of the earl of Marney and a rather priggish young man, the unthinking product of Eton and Oxford, who has reached the age of twenty-seven and learned nothing until he enters parliament in 1837, when, through a series of unbelievable coincidences, he achieves his real education at the hands of the People. Unlike *Coningsby*, *Sybil* is not informed by a Disraelian autobiographical fantasy. Sidonia does not reappear. The plot is weak, many of the characters fail to convince, and the novel ranges over an unwieldy canvas, from London drawing-rooms to Manchester slums. What holds all this together is the narrator's voice.[9] *Sybil* succeeds (and it does succeed triumphantly) because it is a vehicle for Disraeli's parliamentary voice, for the men's gossip of the lobby or the club, for his reading of blue books. It is resonant with echoes; Disraeli's rich political experience during the 1844 session is crammed into its pages. *Sybil* is sometimes described as an 'objective' rather than an autobiographical novel, but Disraeli is the most important character in the book, though he does not actually appear.

The past alone can explain the present, claimed Disraeli, and *Sybil* begins with a dissertation on the history of England. The third chapter is a remarkable polemic against the Whig interpretation of history. Echoing Macaulay's essay of 1828 on Hallam's *Constitutional History*, Disraeli satirises 'the cause for which Hampden died in the field and Russell on the scaffold' – the cause of civil and religious liberty which the Whigs maintain was promoted by parliament against the Stuarts, by the Glorious Revolution of 1688 and the Reform Act of 1832. This, says Disraeli, is a great mystification; propaganda made by the Whig oligarchy to convince the people it crippled that it stood for the cause of freedom. If the true history of England were ever written, declares Disraeli, 'the world would be more astonished than when reading the Roman annals by Niebuhr' (the German historian whose work on Latin texts had revolutionised Roman history).

Disraeli's Tory theory claims: At the Reformation, the Whig aristocracy built their estates on the ruins of the monasteries, which were really the property of the people. This gave the Whigs a vested interest in the Reformation which they dignified with the name of civil and religious liberty. When James II threatened to restore their lands to the people, the Whigs promptly issued the invitation to William of Orange; in 1688, on the plea of civil and religious liberty, the Whigs changed the dynasty to gain the power of the crown. William III invaded for financial reasons, to mobilise England's credit in his war against France. Not only did William plunge England into war with France but he brought 'Dutch finance' (the National Debt) which, said Disraeli, mortgaged industry to protect property – that is, industry was taxed to meet interest on the debt which kept the Whig oligarchy in power. Disraeli maintained that 1688 was a mistake: James II did not intend to destroy the Church of England, merely to blend it with the Catholic Church, and his rule would have saved England from the triple curse of Venetian politics, Dutch finance, and French wars. 1714 entrenched the Venetian oligarchy, the king became a doge, and the people were hoodwinked that Whig rule meant freedom.

The Tory hero Bolingbroke, on the other hand, urged a strong king, a permanent alliance with France and commercial freedom. The Whigs shut him out, but Bolingbroke's system was kept alive by a Tory apostolic succession of 'suppressed characters'. From Bolingbroke it passed to Carteret, Walpole's opponent, who transmitted it to his son-in-law, Shelburne, according to Disraeli the ablest minister of the eighteenth century, though utterly suppressed. Shelburne it was who anticipated the importance of the rising middle class as an ally for the crown against the Great Revolution families, and the younger Pitt was his pupil. Pitt not only relaxed commercial restrictions but under Shelburne's influence proposed parliamentary reform; when this failed, he attempted to baffle the patrician oligarchy by creating a plebeian aristocracy. 'He made peers of second-rate squires and fat graziers. He caught them in the alleys of Lombard Street and clutched them from the counting-houses of Cornhill.' The French war, however, was Pitt's evil demon. He fell back on the policies of oligarchy, and, with the exception of the brief ascendancy of Canning ('long kept down by the plebeian aristocracy of Mr Pitt as an adventurer'), the Tory idea had ever since been in eclipse.

Robert Blake has written that 'Disraeli had no real historical sense; he wrote propaganda, not history'.[10] Disraeli did little research; he wrote to Lord Lansdowne, to check Shelburne's connection with Carteret and with Pitt, but little else. And his notion of an apostolic succession keeping the Tory idea alive down the ages is merely a Tory version of the Whig idea of liberty broadening from precedent to precedent. Disraeli knew it was claptrap, and in *Endymion* he satirised it, ridiculing Smythe/Waldershare for his idea of a succession of Tory heroic spirits. But his theory that Whig history was a great mystification, propaganda in the interests of the ruling class, was new for his time and in some ways it anticipates Marxist history. Marxists would agree that the Whig oligarchy blotted the people out from history, though not with his view that the crown was blotted out too. The historical theory of *Sybil* represents a real advance on the early chapters of the *Vindication of the English Constitution*, where he had merely rehashed conventional Whig views. No longer did Disraeli believe in the Whig idea of progress; on the contrary, he now claimed that since the dissolution of the monasteries English history had been a story of decline.

In *Sybil*, he said that he had first expounded his theory of the mighty Whig mystery at Wycombe in 1832. The Reform Act made the theory credible: 'insensibly it created and prepared a popular intelligence to which one can appeal, no longer hopelessly, in an attempt to dispel the mysteries with which for nearly three centuries it has been the labour of party writers to involve a national history.'[11] The theory exposed the inadequacy of all aristocrats, Whig and Tory; birth, says Disraeli, is no claim to leadership. In England, even the most ancient genealogies are spurious, and the aristocracy must learn the rules if they are to survive. Egremont's tight-fisted brother Lord Marney is a Tory, but he eulogises the Poor Law, is fierce against allotments, agrees with the doctrines of the political economists (except of course in the case of land) and abhors the influence of the church. Meanwhile, the pauperised labourers on his estate burn ricks.

Egremont's education begins amid the ruins of his brother's Marney Abbey, once a hospital and centre of alms for the poor, now a place where cattle graze. Here, in a scene surely inspired by Carlyle's *Past and Present*, which had evoked an idealised pre-Reformation monastic world, Egremont broods on the Condition of England. The abbey is modelled on Fountains; here Egremont is joined by two strangers, and they talk of the people. Our queen, says Egremont, reigns over the greatest nation that ever existed.

'Which nation?' asked the younger stranger, 'for she reigns over two.'
The stranger paused; Egremont was silent, but looked inquiringly.
'Yes,' resumed the younger stranger, after a moment's interval. 'Two nations; between whom there is no intercourse and no sympathy; who are as

ignorant of each other's habits, thoughts, and feelings, as if they were dwellers in different zones, or inhabitants of different planets; who are formed by a different breeding, are fed by a different food, are ordered by different manners, and are not governed by the same laws.'

'You speak of –' said Egremont, hesitatingly.

'THE RICH AND THE POOR.'

At this moment a sudden flush of rosy light, suffusing the grey ruins, indicated that the sun had just fallen ... when from the Lady's chapel there rose the evening hymn to the Virgin. A single voice; but tones of almost supernatural sweetness; tender and solemn yet flexible and thrilling.[12]

It is the voice of Sybil, a Catholic and the daughter of the People; but a timeless moment, as one critic has written, is no remedy for social ills.[13]

The abbey proclaims a religious solution. Though a Roman Catholic, Sybil is assisted in relieving the poor by the vicar of Mowbray, Aubrey St Lys. St Lys is a Tractarian, and in two chapters closely read by Gladstone in the notes on *Sybil* preserved among his papers, Disraeli explored the Oxford Movement.[14] 'For all that has occurred,' says St Lys, 'I blame only the church. The church deserted the people; and from that moment the church has been in danger, and the people degraded.'

To criticise the Reformation was one thing, but Disraeli linked his nostalgia for the pre-Reformation church to a theological argument which is eccentric to say the least. 'The Church of Rome', declares St Lys, 'is to be respected as the only Hebraeo–Christian church extant' – a phrase extracted by Gladstone in his notes. 'Christianity is completed Judaism, or it is nothing. Christianity is incomprehensible without Judaism, as Judaism is incomplete without Christianity.'[15]

St Lys has sometimes been identified as Faber, the Tractarian inspirer of Manners and Smythe. But St Lys is evidently no orthodox Tractarian. His name is meant to be pronounced Sin-less, as in St John, one of Disraeli's Tory heroes. He is a spiritual version of Sidonia, and, like Sidonia, St Lys is a Disraeli self-portrait who speaks Disraeli's words. The idea of Christianity as completed Judaism was one he was to develop as an argument for the removal of Jewish disabilities in 1847.[16] Years later, Disraeli described himself as the blank page between the Old Testament and the New.

In the advertisement to *Sybil* Disraeli claimed that the descriptions of the Condition of the People were written from his own observation, but many were derived from blue books or printed sources. The rural hovels of Marney, for instance, with their stagnant drains, streaming walls, flooded floors and reeking dunghills, are borrowed from Edwin Chadwick's sensational *Report on the Sanitary Condition of the Labouring Population*

(1842). The descriptions of working-class life in Manchester (Mowbray in the novel) have been traced to the work of William Dodd, the factory cripple. The mining landscape, a wilderness of scattered cottages interspersed with blazing furnaces, a country like a rabbit warren, and the iniquitous tommy shop – these were drawn from the *First Report from the Midland Mining Commissioners, South Staffs* (1843).[17]

Disraeli's use of the blue books is selective. Chadwick's *Report* bristles with moral outrage at the vice caused by overcrowding and squalor, the Mining Commissioners detailed the miners' sexual misconduct, and William Dodd enlarged on the moral depravity of the factory workers. None of this material was used by Disraeli, who quietly purified his sources. The People of his Other Nation do not smell or swear; they are disembodied expressions of ideas.

His other main source was parliamentary debates – dull debates where, as he wrote in *Sybil*, 'the facts are only a repetition of the blue books you have already read', or those charged with emotion, such as the Ten Hours' debates of 1844, echoed in *Sybil*. It was through the reformed House of Commons that Disraeli discovered the People, just as he discovered that Whig history was a great mystification. But his skilful borrowing does not invalidate the novel: his descriptions of the People achieved their purpose, described by an appreciative reader from Sheffield as 'calling public attention to the "People" as a distinct Nation'. 'The scenes of low life are admirable,' wrote Manners, 'the dialogue true (so far as I know) to a letter.' Lady Blessington agreed: Disraeli, she wrote, 'will be repaid by the gratitude of those whose interest he has so eloquently espoused as well as by those who are glad to be instructed in that of which we are but too ignorant, the wants of, and injustice rendered to the poor'. Lady Blessington's remarks found support in the response of a woman from the opposite end of the social scale, a mechanic's wife from Camden, who told Disraeli that, unlike his earlier books, *Sybil* was a work the People could feel and understand. 'Now you have given us something for which we can thank you, something which will live in our hearts, something we can teach to our children.'[18]

Writing with the blue book open in front of him, deftly transforming the official evidence into novelist's prose, Disraeli sketched the nightmare Black Country iron town of Wodgate (Willenhall), a hell where there are no churches, no schools, no masters; no one to preach or control. 'It is not that the people are immoral, for immorality implies some forethought; or ignorant, for ignorance is relative; and their worst actions only the impulse of a gross or savage instinct.' In fact, the blue book showed churches in Willenhall, but Disraeli's picture of Wodgate, with its labour aristocracy of master workmen, brutal, violent tyrants like Bishop Hatton, threw into relief the novel's central question: who should lead the People?[19]

Disraeli has often been criticised for failing to offer solutions to problems he identifies in *Sybil*. True, he proposed no legislation for the poor, in spite of his trenchant criticism of the Poor Law Amendment Act, but his lack of faith in legislative panaceas is one of the novel's strengths. He was concerned less with material and moral problems than with wider issues such as leadership, and no one could legislate for that. On the other hand, speeches in parliament could change things, or so he believed, by dispelling the great Whig mystery. Egremont makes a beautiful speech (the speech Disraeli made), sympathising with the Chartists in 1839. A truly democratic speech, the gist of it was 'that if you [the aristocracy] wished for time to retain your political power, you could only effect your purpose by securing for the people greater social felicity'. Egremont, however, is 'crotchety'; his speech baffles his party, and no wonder, because the Tory party, which believed that power had only one duty, to secure the social welfare of the People, no longer exists. 'But we forget, Sir Robert Peel is not the leader of the tory party,' Disraeli declares in the sarcastic tones of parliamentary debate.

The romance between Sybil and Egremont is Disraeli's solution to the two nations. Critics mocked the marriage as unrealistic, flawed in that Sybil turns out not to be the daughter of the People at all but an heiress and an aristocrat. For Disraeli, the marriage of an aristocrat to a working-class woman was unthinkable, and the significance of Sybil's marriage to Egremont is allegorical rather than social. Sybil dominates the last two books which comprise one third of the novel; Disraeli, who began by writing a social Condition of England novel, ended by writing an allegorical romance.[20]

The allegory begins in Westminster Abbey. It was here one hot July day in 1844 that Disraeli, Macaulay, Hobhouse and a crowd of others had angrily waited, stifling in their black suits, squeezed and elbowed backwards and forwards, unable to gain entry to the funeral of the poet Tom Campbell.[21] Remembering his annoyance, Disraeli railed against the mean and sordid arrangements which shut the People out from the church of the Blessed Martyr Charles I – 'But the British public will bear anything; they are so busy in speculating in railway shares.' In the novel an organ bursts forth, and Egremont chances upon Sybil, a meeting which mirrors the meeting at Fountains/Marney Abbey where Egremont's journey began. Sybil, the daughter of the People, still believes that the People can rule themselves, and that Chartism is a sacred cause. Egremont tries to teach her that the People can never lead themselves. The natural leaders of the People are the new generation of the aristocracy, 'believe me they are the only ones'.[22]

Of course it is possible to argue that Disraeli's paternalism is stifling and condescending, and so it is by modern standards. The last two books of *Sybil*, however, which are often dismissed as pot-boiling romance written under pressure, give a startling glimpse of the nightmare fear that prompted Disraeli's call for aristocratic leadership. Sybil, who believed that the world was divided into the two nations of privileged oppressors and the miserable but innocent oppressed, learns that the world is more complex than she supposed. 'The people, she found, was not that pure embodiment of unity of feeling, of interest, and of purpose, which she had pictured in her abstractions. The people had enemies among the people; their own passions; which made them often sympathise, often combine, with the privileged.'[23] It is a crucial discovery. The idea of the two nations, proposed to Egremont by Stephen Morley amid the ruins of Fountains, is an over-simplification; the People are more complex. Stephen Morley is a socialist, dedicated to moral force and the ideal of community of the People; he loves Sybil, and her rejection of him symbolises her repudiation of his ideas.

The novel is profoundly, despairingly anti-democratic. How vivid are Disraeli's fears becomes plain when Sybil makes a desperate journey alone across London to Seven Dials, in a vain attempt to save her Chartist father from arrest. Her journey has rightly been likened to a descent into hell; unlike the industrial north, the East End of London was a hell Disraeli knew, and his slums are alive with market-places of entrails and carrion, gutters running gore, the multitude blaspheming, bargaining, drinking, wrangling, and a brothel which Sybil narrowly escapes. Hell, for Disraeli, is the other nation. Hell is when the People rule themselves, hell is violence and revolution. The last Book (VI), based on the Plug Plot of 1842, describes the invasion of Manchester/Mowbray by the ironworkers of Willenhall/Wodgate, who stop the mills by removing the plugs from the boilers. Known as the Hell-cats, the barbarians are led by Bishop Hatton, mounted on a white mule, wall-eyed and hideous of form, a latter-day Pilgrimage of Grace. Religious imagery abounds; blazing furnaces and hellfire are everywhere; issuing 'shrieks of wild passion which announce that men have discarded all the trammels of civilisation', the Hell-cats set fire to the tommy shop, which is consumed by flames like the tongues of wild beasts.

Disraeli's aristocratic paternalism is driven by fear, sheer terror at the prospect of the People ruling themselves. Violence and savage animal passion seethe beneath the thin, fragile crust of civilisation. Aristocratic leadership is the only alternative to revolution. Disraeli, who as a young man had advocated democracy, has developed the instinctive Toryism of an old bear. *Sybil* has less to say than *Coningsby* about party politics, but it is profoundly a more Tory book.

'I get on to my satisfaction,' Disraeli told John Manners in November 1844, 'but authors are not the best critics of their own productions; I am more anxious about your opinion than my own.' The sustained labour of writing *Sybil* was painful ('I am daily more convinced, that there is no *toil* like literature'); he wrote as few letters as possible that autumn, and no notes to Mary Anne survive. By Christmas 1844 only two books (300 manuscript pages) had been written, but Disraeli and Mary Anne were tiring of Bradenham and its silent beeches. 'Two months of absolute loneliness here make us feel the necessity of repairing to the haunts of men and women,' Disraeli told Monckton Milnes on 24 December, and in early January 1845 they were back at Grosvenor Gate.[24]

At the last minute, Disraeli accepted an invitation to Stowe, where the duke of Buckingham outdid himself with a sumptuous ball for the queen and Albert, Peel and Aberdeen. Mary Anne wore black velvet, Dizzy 'shorts' (knee breeches) and white waistcoat, and for an hour they queued, Mary Anne told Bradenham, cross and shivering, waiting to be presented to the queen, like a flock of sheep in the vestibule, which was 'half lit up, and no seats or fire, only a little hot air and a great deal of cold wind; a marble floor'. After the queen retired at eleven, all became joy and triumph to Mary Anne and Dizzy. Peel shook hands 'most cordially', and remained talking some time. The duke of Buckingham took Mary Anne by the arm, and the duchess sat with her on the sofa and told her that the queen had pointed Dizzy out, saying *'There's Mr Disraeli'*. Do you call all this nothing? asked Mary Anne. Next morning, she toured the royal apartment, quizzing the royal bed (they slept 'without pillows or *bolster'*) and prying into their lavatory arrangements. In another room, Peel was closeted with Graham and Aberdeen; according to Buckingham, he was discussing a startling change to the Corn Laws. Disraeli little knew how soon was to be tested his definition of treason (in *Sybil*) as 'voting against a Minister, who, though he may have changed all the policy which you have been elected to support, expects your vote and confidence all the same'.[25]

The Stowe Ball was a brief distraction from *Sybil*, which flowed on through January. By the beginning of the session in February two-thirds of the book was ready: Disraeli told Sarah he had written 600 pages, reaching the end of Book Four, and only 300 remained to write.[26]

By 1845 Disraeli was in open revolt against Peel. Manners and Smythe, on the other hand, who were both under pressure to cut their connection with Disraeli, dared not follow him; they were still his closest political allies, but their fathers had effectively wrecked Young England, which no longer functioned as a group. Disraeli's prospects looked bleak enough at the beginning of the 1845 session; Peel seemed set to govern for a generation.

When the Whig Lord Campbell congratulated Disraeli on the spread of Young England, he replied, 'we were in the third year of the Walpole administration'.[27] No chance of political combinations succeeding against so impregnable a minister; literature held out more hopeful prospects and, meanwhile, he tried to enhance his position by pursuing a vendetta against Peel.

His first opportunity came during the debate (20 February) on Tom Duncombe's demand for an inquiry into the opening of letters by the post office, which was in fact a personal attack on Graham, the home secretary. Disraeli's speech, Peel told the queen, was flippant and hostile.[28] He mocked Peel for simulating anger ('some of the younger members were much frightened, but I advised them not to be terrified. I told them that the right honourable baronet would not eat them up, would not even resign; the very worst thing he would do would be to tell them to rescind a vote'). They were in the third year of a Walpolian administration, declared Disraeli again, party feeling was extinct, and he hoped that without offence he might give an independent vote.

In the same speech, he alleged that Francis Bonham, the party agent and Peel's intimate friend, had been a plotter in the Despard conspiracy of 1802. Peel crushingly explained that Disraeli had confused Francis Bonham with his elder brother Philip,[29] and capped his snub by quoting some lines of Canning's:

> Give me the avowed, the erect, the manly foe;
> Bold I can meet, perhaps may turn, the blow;
> But of all plagues, good Heaven, Thy wrath can send,
> Save, save, O save me, from the candid friend!

It was a rash choice of verse. Disraeli apologised the following day, but Peel's treatment of Canning was still fresh in men's minds and gave Disraeli a new opportunity. Smythe checked the source: 'It is in the Antijacobin, dear Cid and Captain – in a poem of Canning's yclept New Morality.'[30] A week later, in a second debate on Duncombe's Post Office charges, Disraeli seized his chance. Carelessly, superciliously, as if by accident, he glided towards the issue of Peel's leadership, describing the tyranny brought into play when a member on the government side made a speech portending a disagreeable division for the government. Irritability on the Treasury bench; a secret supporter of the government put up to impute mean motives, and finally a passionate appeal from Peel as if the government's survival were threatened. Yet Peel seemed to forget that his supporters were elected on the hustings under very different circumstances. 'I was sent here to sit on this side,' declared Disraeli, 'to support a Tory Ministry. Whether a Tory Ministry exists or not I do not pretend to decide; but I am bound to believe that the Tory majority still remains, and therefore I do not think it is the majority that should cross the House but only the Ministry.' Taking his stand on the ground of *Coningsby* and *Sybil* ('But we forget,' he had written only the other week, 'Sir Robert Peel is not the leader of the tory party ...'), Disraeli fired a quiverful of carefully rehearsed sarcasms. Peel, said he, had no need for a coalition with the Whigs. 'The right honourable gentleman caught the Whigs bathing and walked away with their clothes. He has left them in the full enjoyment of their liberal position, and he is himself a strict conservative of their garments.' Peel had tamed the Shrew of Liberalism, he was the political Petruchio. As for Canning, whom Peel had quoted (and here Disraeli reached a climax of sarcastic irony), 'The theme – the poet – the speaker – what a felicitous combination!'[31]

'There never was an instance of a trip being succeeded by such a leap,' Disraeli triumphantly wrote to Bradenham. He sat down to thunders of cheers which, Smythe told Mary Anne, would have made her cry with delight. Peel was left floundering, 'stunned and stupid' as Disraeli said; sarcasm and irony were weapons which left him defenceless, and his reply was feeble and too long. In the library at Bradenham, Isaac, now totally blind, murmured over and again, 'The theme – the poet – the speaker'.[32]

Rarely had Disraeli sustained such pressure of work as he did in February and March 1845, dividing his time between feverish writing of *Sybil* and vigilant attendance at the House. Sitting behind Peel hour after hour, watching his leader nervously rearrange his coat-tails or beat the red box on the green table as he spoke. No company came to Grosvenor Gate, Mary Anne consoling herself for Dizzy's absorption by keeping strict control on fuel consumption, noting in her account book that only six coal fires (each costing 5s. a week) burned in the cold and muffled house.

Peel features less in *Sybil* than in *Coningsby*, perhaps because politics gave Disraeli an outlet for his spleen. In one chapter, however, he satirises the gentleman in Downing Street, who says one thing to a deputation of country members and tenant farmers complaining about high income tax and low corn prices and exactly the reverse to a deputation of Manchester manufacturers, who are told that the cure for the depression of trade is cheap food, which will enable them to compete with the foreigner. ('Capital passage,' wrote Gladstone in his notes on *Sybil*.) Peel tacitly acknowledged his inability to satisfy both farmers and manufacturers in March, when Cobden made a powerful attack on the Corn Laws and Peel remained silent, murmuring to Sidney Herbert, who sat next to him, 'You must answer this for I cannot.' Disraeli listened as Herbert bungled his reply, ineptly referring to the agriculturists whining to parliament.[33]

Herbert's blunder gave Disraeli his chance. A few days later, in a speech in support of a motion for relief for agriculture, he charged Peel with deserting the Gentlemen of England, sending down his valet, who says in the genteelest manner, 'We can have no whining here'. Protection, he declared, 'appears to be in about the same condition that Protestantism was in in 1828. The country will draw its moral. For my part, if we are to have free trade, I, who honour genius, prefer that such measures should be proposed by the honourable Member for Stockport [Cobden] than by one, who through skilful parliamentary manoeuvres, has tampered with the generous confidence of a great people and of a great party.' A Conservative government, he declared, pausing dramatically for effect, is an Organised Hyprocrisy.[34]

Peel sat, twitching nervously, vainly endeavouring to control his annoyance, while the House filled with delirious laughter. But the tumultuous cheers were furnished, as Disraeli recalled a few years later, by the voices opposite, 'and the tory gentlemen beneath the gangway who swelled the chorus did so with downcast eyes, as if they yet hesitated to give utterance to feelings too long and too painfully suppressed'.[35] His attacks were tolerated because he expressed what the majority felt, but none dared say. 'Were not Peel the most unpopular head of a party that ever existed,' wrote Lord Ashley, who admired Disraeli's speech, which he thought clever and biting, 'these things would be put down by rebuke in public, and by frowns in private society.'[36] Some said, as Monckton Milnes noted in March, that Disraeli injured only himself by his philippics against Peel. Certainly, he was freely accused of malice and of seeking revenge for his exclusion from office. Yet it is hard not to admire Disraeli's defiance of the unwritten rule, the code of so-called honour which enjoined silence on backbenchers passed over for office, empowering the Whips to punish independence. 'I am so angry with Peel for passing over out-and-out the best speaker among us younger men for a pack of illiterate lordlings,' wrote Monckton Milnes (who had himself also been denied office), 'that I am not sorry to see the consequences.' Only a Jew, thought Milnes, could break the rules as Disraeli did; he 'has no Christian sentimentalities about him; none of your forgiveness of injuries; he is a son of the old jealous implacable Jehovah'.[37] *Forte nihil difficile* was the motto Disraeli adopted, lovingly copied by Mary Anne into her account book: nothing is difficult to the brave.

The leading issue of the 1845 session was Ireland, where Peel proposed to increase the government grant to the Roman Catholic seminary of Maynooth. It marked his conversion to the so-called Cavalier policy for

Ireland urged by Disraeli and Young England the previous session – that of allying with Irish Catholics. But Maynooth enraged Protestant and dissenting feeling in England. From Shrewsbury, Disraeli's agent Ouseley wrote that the most popular step Disraeli could take would be to oppose it.[38] Peel's announcement of the Maynooth grant (3 April) was greeted by a series of savagely malicious leaders in *The Times*, denouncing his inconsistency, his lack of principle, the reign of terror he exercised over his followers. Both Hobhouse and Monckton Milnes believed the writer was Disraeli.[39] Certainly, the articles are consistent with his speech on Maynooth (11 April), his third philippic against Peel.

Disraeli rose after Gladstone, who made a lengthy and involved speech explaining why he supported the Maynooth grant, even though he had resigned from the government over the issue because it contradicted his book on *The State in its Relation with the Church* (1838). Disraeli, unlike most members, had actually read the book and put his finger on Gladstone's weak point: 'subtle casuist as he may be', Gladstone had failed in his book to supply the new principle of government he promised. Brazenly ignoring his own change of front over Ireland, Disraeli professed himself disappointed that Gladstone of all men, 'the last paladin of principle, the very chivalry of abstraction', should have abandoned his principles. It was Disraeli's first brush with Gladstone, who was exposed for the first time to Disraeli's sarcasm. Two months before, he had listened to Gladstone's obscure resignation speech, and remarked that his career was finished. As Peel's difficulties multiplied, however, Gladstone came to be seen as a potential leader, and Disraeli, well aware of Gladstone's rising stock, described him (to King Louis Philippe) as 'quite equal to Peel with the advantage of youth'.[40]

But the real target of Disraeli's Maynooth speech was, of course, Peel, who, said Disraeli, had referred to the three courses open to him, and indeed he was right. 'There is the course that the right honourable Gentleman has left. There is the course that the right honourable Gentleman is following; and there is usually the course which the right honourable Gentleman ought to follow.' Amid guffaws of laughter, Disraeli proceeded to lambast Peel for his change of course. He opposed Maynooth, he declared, because 'the government were not morally entitled to bring such a measure forward'. It was the reverse of the measures Peel had professed in opposition. Peel had 'destroyed party, and abandoned Parliamentary government'. Instead, 'We have a great Parliamentary middleman,' who 'bamboozles one party, and plunders the other (great laughter) till, having obtained a position to which he is not entitled, he cries out, "Let us have no party questions, but fixity of tenure." (Cheers) I want to have a Commission issued to inquire into the tenure by which Downing-street is held. (Laughter and cheers).'[41]

All eyes turned to Peel, who hung his head, changed colour and drew his hat over his eyes while, as Hobhouse noted, Graham wore a forced smile. Disraeli's philippics were superb parliamentary theatre. 'Disraeli does the showman,' noted *The Times* in a eulogistic leader which surely even Disraeli did not write (though perhaps Smythe did). 'He expatiates, moralises, gossips and cracks his jokes with as sublime an indifference as if the object were utterly brute and unintelligent; and always ends with a barbarous valedictory poke, that we may have at least one good roar.' Peel was pitilessly flayed; he stands before us, wrote *The Times*, 'glaring, enormous and grotesque'. Disraeli was Van Dyck to Peel's Charles I; it was through his portraits of Peel that he made his parliamentary reputation.[42]

More than 150 Conservatives voted against Peel over Maynooth, and he owed his survival to Whig votes. In a speech which made Peel's face go white, Macaulay supported Disraeli's criticisms, charging Peel with betraying the men and the passions he had used to gain power in opposition. 'Did you think,' he asked, 'when you went on session after session, thwarting and reviling those whom you knew to be in the right, and flattering all the worst passions of those whom you knew to be in the wrong, that the day of reckoning would never come? It has come. There you sit, doing penance for the disingenuousness of years.'

'I am glad Macaulay has taken up my line,' Disraeli told Hobhouse. Exactly what Disraeli's line was, however, was by no means clear. In the two previous sessions, 1844 and 1843, he had achieved notoriety by attacking Peel for governing Ireland according to the policy of Cromwell rather than Charles I, and aligning his government with the Protestant minority against the Roman Catholics. Now Peel had adopted the Young England policy of sending messages of peace to Ireland, but, rather than welcome the convert, Disraeli attacked Peel's inconsistency and declared that the Irish should not accept conciliation from such polluted hands. Both Smythe and Manners supported the Maynooth grant, which led to the break-up of Young England, but Disraeli was in danger of losing his seat at Protestant Shrewsbury if he supported Peel and, besides, he had set his eyes on a higher game. The country gentlemen who cheered his Corn Law speech with downcast eyes were staunch Protestants to a man, and Disraeli saw a chance of leading a backbench revolt. He had accused Peel of a Machiavellian system, but it was he, not Peel, who was Machiavellian, abandoning his principles and throwing over Young England for the opportunity of personal advantage. His reward was the handsome red coat of deputy lieutenant, which he promptly obtained from Lord Carrington, lord lieutenant of Buckinghamshire.[43]

Protestant sectarians eagerly seized on Disraeli as a convert to their cause. In 1846 the Reverend Tresham Gregg, a militant Irish Protestant, insisted on dedicating a furious Protestant volume to him.[44] Disraeli affected embarrassment, but over Maynooth he shamelessly cultivated Protestant support. He approached Lord Ashley, the leading voice of Protestantism, breaking the ice by complimenting him on his speech: 'great conciliation with *steady and full assertion of Protestantism*', he told Ashley, 'approved by all from the violent to the lukewarm.'[45]

Throughout April Disraeli laboured to finish *Sybil*. Hounded by the printers, he crowded catastrophes into the last chapters, killing off his protagonists, while composing invective against Peel and in *The Times* fulminating against Maynooth. The apocalyptic last book of *Sybil*, with its nightmare vision of revolution, was written in the weeks that Disraeli knifed the prime minister in the House. Yet it was plain that Peel's fall would spell the exclusion from power of the Tory aristocracy whose leadership Disraeli saw as the key to avoiding revolution. 'The country gentlemen cannot be more ready to give us the death-blow than we are prepared to receive it,' wrote Graham in March 1845. 'If they will rush on to their own destruction, they must have their way: we have endeavoured to save them, and they regard us as enemies for so doing.'[46]

'Sybil was finished yesterday,' Disraeli triumphantly told Sarah on 1 May. 'I have never been thro' such a four months, and hope never again.'[47] Colburn rushed the book out and it sold briskly, going through three editions (2500 copies) during the summer. Isaac, up in London for his seventy-ninth birthday (he and Sarah dined at Grosvenor Gate) was immersed in it, read aloud to him by Sarah. A day or two after publication, Disraeli met the Chartist, Thomas Cooper, newly released from prison, bearing a note from Tom Duncombe. Cooper wanted an introduction to a publisher, which Disraeli supplied, finding him, 'In appearance, Morley to the life!'[48]

Not all readers were enthusiastic. Henry Crabb Robinson, who had admired *Coningsby*, found *Sybil* unsatisfactory, exhibiting the two nations in coarse contrast. W. R. Greg, writing in the Radical *Westminster Review*, thought *Sybil* no improvement on *Coningsby*, deploring its coarseness and lack of real feeling for the poor. Thackeray, too, preferred *Coningsby*. The success of *Coningsby*, he wrote, was due not to the Jewish theory, nor to the Tory history, but to the satire, the sketches of Rigby and Tadpole and Taper, which were equalled only by Disraeli's recent parliamentary sketches of Peel. Satire was Disraeli's strength, but *Sybil* contained no personalities; instead it was filled with heavy undigested chunks of Tory history. Country readers, sneered Thackeray, who had required keys to the personalities in *Coningsby*, would need keys to British history since 1688 to understand *Sybil*.[49]

Yet *Sybil*'s claim to greatness, to timelessness, depends partly on the absence of caricature. Even Thackeray conceded that Disraeli's descriptions of the people, though amateurish, pioneered a magnificent and untrodden field; Carlyle had discussed the Condition of England in *Past and Present*, but Disraeli was one of the first to realise its fictional potential. The attempt to combine the Condition of England with Tory high politics and history was no doubt flawed – 'Charles the First's head!' scoffed Thackeray. 'Mr Gunter [the fashionable pastrycook] might just as well serve it up in sugar on a supper-table between a Charlotte Russe and a trifle'; but *Sybil* was certainly ambitious, a heartfelt attempt by Disraeli to distance himself from the smart, slick, dandy world of his earlier fiction and to penetrate underlying social realities.

After the crisis of Maynooth, politics cooled, and Disraeli and Mary Anne plunged into social life. Mary Anne's account book records a sequence of gatherings at Grosvenor Gate – *déjeuners* and breakfast parties – this in spite of Disraeli's insistence that he hated breakfasting out and never ate in public in the morning. 'Men who breakfast out are generally liberals,' tut-tutted the Tory hostesses in *Sybil*. 'It shows a restless, revolutionary mind.' *Sybil* itself was a fruitful source of social success. Not only did Disraeli follow up his praise of Lord Shelburne, until then truly a suppressed figure of history, by sending a copy to Lord Lansdowne, who approved Disraeli's treatment of his father, and responded with the hoped-for invitation to Lansdowne House. 'Nothing can be conceived more splendid, or more courteous to us, than the son of Shelburne.'[50] *Sybil* also restored relations with Lady Londonderry, flatteringly painted in the novel as Lady Deloraine. Not that *Sybil* is altogether approving of the great society hostesses; their world is satirised as fiercely as the party hacks are in *Coningsby*. But Disraeli was careful to distinguish between Lady St Julians, who is Lady Jersey, the tyrannical ruler of society, and Lady Deloraine, Egremont's mother. Snobbish and arrogant, Lady St Julians is snubbed by Egremont, who tells her she is a fine lady trying to govern the world by social influences: 'asking people once or twice a year to an inconvenient crowd in your house; now haughtily smirking and now impertinently staring at them.'[51]

Egremont's speech, thought Lord John Manners, was rather too rude.[52] So it was, but that was the intention, to point the contrast between Lady Deloraine and her odious rival, Lady Jersey. Flattery, Disraeli had learned, usually gets you where you want to be. He sent a copy of *Sybil* to Lady Londonderry, and then wrote regretting his separation from 'the person to whose condescending kindness I am most indebted, and that too, at a period of my life when it was doubly precious'. Mary Anne was holding a *déjeuner*, but 'We will not presume to ask you to honour us by visiting us tomorrow, tho' the gratification would be deep, and my wife would esteem it the highest possible distinction, because all this, even to decline, might trouble you.'[53] Self-abasement could hardly get much lower. Fanny relented, Disraeli was reinstated and, best of all, Mary Anne gained the coveted privilege of inclusion on her published lists of guests. 'Fanny most friendly to me, and sufficiently courteous to MA,' Disraeli proudly confided to Sarah. It was 'a great social revolution', and what with a ball at Lord Salisbury's and an assembly at Lady Palmerston's, 'MA suddenly finds herself floating in the highest circles and much fêted. She is of course delighted. Lady Jersey, who meets us everywhere, in a stupor of malice and astonishment!'[54]

The session ended in early August, leaving Peel, whose fall had seemed imminent in April, quite as powerful as he had been at its beginning. 'Practically speaking,' recalled Disraeli, 'the conservative government at the end of the session of '45, was far stronger than even at the commencement of '42. If they had forfeited the hearts of their adherents, they had not lost their votes, while both in parliament and in the country, they had succeeded in appropriating a mass of loose, superficial opinion not trammelled by party ties.'[55]

Young England, meanwhile, was breaking up. *The Times*, which had given it the oxygen of publicity, turned against the movement, probably under the influence of John Walter senior, who had never been a supporter. Disraeli turned his attention to a new journal, *The Oxford and Cambridge Review*. Manners wrote a puffing review of *Sybil* in the first number in July, and Smythe contributed an article on Earl Grey in the second which, said Disraeli, 'made a great noise and quite established the Review' (in fact, he wrote it himself); but in August, Manners and Smythe having gone abroad, Disraeli told Sarah 'I am afraid the following Nos. will knock it up. So much for Dandies being Critics.'[56]

Disraeli was tiring of Smythe. His place at Grosvenor Gate parties that summer was taken by his *bête noire*, Monckton Milnes. Piqued at his exclusion from *Sybil*, Smythe told Disraeli that he preferred *Coningsby*. Disraeli was hurt and got Mary Anne to write a letter to Smythe saying their friendship was over. Smythe wrote from Paris to make amends in September: 'Carissimo mio, as I must call you, despite all you say vicariously about my professions being belied by my practice … I … shall probably disgust you of a friendship you have often forsworn, but which will never die.' But Disraeli *was* disgusted and certainly bored. Young England had served its purpose, and he had less need of Smythe, who began to drift out of his orbit.[57]

After two years' relative peace, Disraeli found himself once more on the brink of financial crisis in the summer of 1845. His income, or rather Mary Anne's, from land and securities he estimated in 1845 at £6375. Mary Anne reckoned her expenditure over the nine months to September at £1385;

much of the remainder of her income – well over £4000 – had gone, as it regularly did, to paying Disraeli's creditors. Despite the success of *Sybil*, for which he was paid £800, he urgently needed an additional £5000.[58]

One source of credit would be a new edition of his works, and Disraeli persuaded Colburn to republish *Alroy* and *Contarini Fleming*. He had bought back the copyright of *Vivian Grey* from Colburn, but on rereading it he decided that reissue was impossible without substantial revisions.[59] No new edition of *Vivian Grey* appeared until 1853, when the book was pruned of embarrassing evidence of middle-class origins belying the exotic aristocratic Jewish ancestry he had invented for himself. Colburn insisted on new prefaces to *Alroy* and *Contarini*, but Disraeli was so distracted by his debts that he could barely command his mind to write them. He was harassed to death, he told Sarah.[60] For a fortnight he called daily at the Carlton, in hourly expectation of being called upon to insure his life, concealing his purpose from Mary Anne, to whom he addressed lines on their sixth wedding anniversary (28 August). '"Henceforth confide in me," she smiling said', he wrote, (did he intend the irony?) 'Be still thy plea, fair Prophetess of bliss! My trust is perfect.'

Mary Anne was in an even worse state than Dizzy – fretful, sleepless, tearful, hysterical. 'She is very low and shattered,' Disraeli told Sarah, sneaking out of Grosvenor Gate to write secretly from the Carlton, as usual confiding in Sarah at the least hint of trouble at home.[61] At Grosvenor Gate Mary Anne packed frenetically, desperate to leave London for abroad; kept in the dark about Dizzy's finances, she was unable to understand his reasons for procrastination. Her friend Baroness Lionel de Rothschild described a bizarre visit from Mary Anne, who rushed into her arms, unannounced and out of breath: 'I have been running so fast, we have no horses, no carriage, no servants, we are going abroad, I have been so busy correcting proof-sheets, the publishers are so tiresome, we ought to have been gone a month ago; I should have called upon you long ere now, I have been so nervous, so excited, so agitated, poor Dis has been sitting up the whole night writing.' Never logical at the best of times, Mary Anne was wild, excitable and very hard to follow: 'besides my adored husband I care for no one on earth, but I love your glorious race, I am rich, I am prosperous, I think it right to entertain serious thoughts, to look calmly upon one's end.' It was a farewell visit, she said; she was convinced that she and Dizzy would be blown up on the railroad or the steamer, she talked of her diamond butterfly and her emerald tiara, and at length produced a paper leaving all her personal property in the event of Dizzy dying before her, to Evelina, Baroness Lionel's six-year-old daughter. 'I love the Jews – I have attached myself to your children and she is my favourite, she shall, she must wear the butterfly.'

Baroness Lionel returned the will next day after a miserable night, and there was a scene, a very disagreeable one. But Mary Anne's love of the Jews did not extend to Dizzy's sister; rather than leave her diamonds to Sarah she made another will which was wilder still, leaving everything to Robert Peel Dawson, nephew of the prime minister and ironically named son of her friend Mrs Dawson.[62]

The story of the will as told by Baroness Lionel suggests that Mary Anne was in a nervous, hysterical state, with little hold on reality. Conceivably, however, there was a characteristically shrewd method in Mary Anne's madness. The will was made (in Disraeli's hand) on 5 September. On the same day he wrote cryptically to Sarah that 'the clouds are dispelling'. His debts miraculously mended; his affairs had turned out better than he could have expected, 'and on the whole the financial future is more promising than I can remember it'.[63] What had happened? Disraeli gave no clues, but it is not impossible that (though the baroness did not know it) Baron Lionel de Rothschild had come to the rescue, and Disraeli's optimism about the future suggests that Rothschild had put up substantially more than the £5000 he urgently needed. Mary Anne's will was perhaps her and Disraeli's attempt to recompense Rothschild for a gift they could not repay.

Early in September the Disraelis crossed to Boulogne, heading vaguely for Germany. They took no carriage but a quantity of baggage; no itinerary, but a need for rest and economy. In spite of the mysterious improvement in Disraeli's finances ('I think it *quite impossible* that any unpleasant letters can arrive,' he told Sarah) retrenchment was imperative. In Boulogne, where they found *Sybil* advertised as 'Disraeli's new novel' in every window, he hired an ancient landau drawn by two very small horses which took their luggage in a basket top, and they jolted slowly to St Omer and next day to Cassel in the depths of rural Flanders. There they stayed, renting a house for 16s. a week, and Mary Anne thrived on the cheapness of Flanders: six fowls, bought live in the market, cost five francs and meat was 6d a pound. Mary Anne hired a Flemish cook who stewed pigeons in the fashion of the sixteenth-century duke of Alba – a rich red-brown sauce of eggs, cloves and onions, and she tried vainly to tame the fat young pigeons that fluttered about the breakfast table.

Cassel was savage, primitive and isolated – no library, no bookshop, Sir Robert Peel unheard of. The people talked Flemish not French, carillons sounded perpetually and the country was sunk deep in Catholicism. Each day they walked through the meadows, among red cows and milkmaids, Mary Anne scaling stiles and leaping ditches. After four weeks Disraeli reported her recovered; after two months they had walked a total of 300 miles and

Mary Anne was plump as a partridge. Disraeli leaping stiles in his London clothes was surely a strange sight, but his letters to Bradenham breathe health and contentment. He began work on a new novel, *Tancred*, the third part of the Young England trilogy. Each morning they rose at 5.30, and Disraeli was in his room by six. 'I have been able to write very regularly,' he reported on 26 October, 'and made better progress than usual which is encouraging.'[64]

The novel is the story of Tancred, twenty-one-year-old son of the duke of Bellamont, whose search to discover 'What is DUTY, and what is FAITH? What ought I to DO, and what ought I to BELIEVE?' takes him to the Holy Land and the Church of the Holy Sepulchre. Disraeli wrote the first two books of *Tancred* in Cassel, the rest was written a year later. The first part is social comedy set in London, the second Asian romance, and biographically there is a case for treating the two parts separately. In the General Preface he wrote in 1870, Disraeli said that the aim of *Tancred* was to treat of 'the duties of the Church as a main remedial agency in our present state'. But this was written twenty-five years later, after Disraeli had become absorbed in church affairs. *Tancred* satirises a handful of churchmen – Blomfield, bishop of London, the ecclesiastical Peel, is clearly recognisable – but it is not a church novel. The news that 'Mr Newman is at last *really* gone over to the Romish church' reached Disraeli in Flanders, but the crisis in the Oxford Movement did not interest him. Not until he wrote the General Preface did Disraeli reflect that the religious design of *Tancred* had been aborted by Newman's secession. By taking refuge in the medieval superstition of Rome, Newman damaged the Anglican church which, 'Resting on the Church of Jerusalem, modified by the divine school of Galilee ... would have formed the rock of truth which Providence, by the instrumentality of the Semitic race, had promised to St Peter.' In 1845 Disraeli's concern was less with the church than with race and the need for faith in politics.[65]

'*I* love your glorious race ... I love the Jews.' Mary Anne's outburst to Baroness Lionel gives a hint of the raised emotional temperature of the Disraeli marriage, the cloud of adoring, uncritical worship of genius and race which enveloped Disraeli and which, at dawn that Flanders autumn, he distilled into his novel. *Sybil* had been dedicated to Mary Anne, 'The most severe of critics – but a perfect Wife!', but it is *Tancred* that is really Mary Anne's. The first two books, which chronicle Tancred's adventures in society before his journey to Jerusalem, are rooted in the season of 1845, beginning with the Stowe ball, which is his coming-of-age. Like *Sybil*, *Tancred* is resonant with echoes, but what brings the first part alive is not Disraeli's public, parliamentary voice, but he and Mary Anne talking, the gossip of husband and wife. 'As some men keep up their Greek by reading every day a chapter in the New Testament,' he wrote in *Tancred*, 'so Coningsby [but

Disraeli was speaking for himself] kept up his knowledge of the world, by always, once at least in the four and twenty hours, having a delightful conversation with his wife ... there was not an anecdote, a trait, a good thing said, or a bad thing, which did not reach him by a fine critic and a lively narrator.[66]

Mary Anne appears in *Tancred*, good-naturedly satirised as Mrs Guy Flouncey, a character who had featured in *Coningsby* merely as a type, a social climber. Mrs Guy Flouncey, who was nobody in 1837, has conquered society by 1845. Like Mary Anne, she is pretty and a flirt, born with strong social instincts. In 1837 she was 'a rattle', with a too-startling laugh, a trifle vulgar, and (like Mary Anne) popular with men, which 'necessarily made her unfashionable among women who, if they did not absolutely hate her, which they would have done had she had a noble lover, were determined not to help her up the social ladder'. To conquer society, Mrs Guy Flouncey had to gain a friend among the women. 'She knew that the fine ladies, among whom, from the first, she had determined to place herself, were moral martinets with respect to anyone not born among themselves.'[67] Her invasion of society dramatises the Disraelis' 'social revolution' of 1845, and Disraeli acknowledged Mary Anne's contribution to *Tancred* in the verses he wrote on her birthday (11 November).

> Partner of all my thoughts, whose vivid brain,
> Rich with suggestive sympathy, can aid
> My struggling fancy! Friend that never failed!
> And sweet companion of secluded days!

Politically, *Tancred* testifies to Disraeli's disillusion with Young England. True, Henry Sidney/Lord John Manners is eulogised for his hard work, his devotion to improving the condition of the people. But Monckton Milnes, who had complained at his exclusion from *Coningsby* and *Sybil*, is cattily portrayed as Vavassour, giver of famous breakfasts, a socialite and a snob, pompous, greedy and self-important; certainly not the serious political or literary figure he considered himself to be. The heroes of the two earlier novels fail to fulfil the expectations created for them. Egremont, now Lord Marney, is dismissed as a 'man of fine mind rather than of brilliant talents'. Coningsby is even more disappointing; a complacently successful member of parliament in whom prosperity has developed 'a native vein of sauciness', he has grown coarse and commonplace. If Smythe was hurt by *Sybil*, *Tancred* must surely have enraged him, cruelly reflecting as it does Disraeli's disenchantment. Nor is the disillusion merely personal; it is significant that

Tancred declares against a parliamentary career which he says can no longer save the country, at the very moment he meets Smythe and Manners.[68]

Parliament, says Disraeli, has become insignificant. 'O'Connell has taken a good share of its power; Cobden has taken another; and ... if our order [the aristocracy] had any spirit or prescience, they would put themselves at the head of the people and take the rest.'[69] Representative government is 'a fatal drollery' which never existed in the east. The progress of civilisation too is an illusion. England's advance is not an affair of progress, but of race – the Anglo-Saxon race. 'And when a superior race, with a superior idea to Work and Order, advances, its state will be progressive.' 'All is race; there is no other truth.' However, 'the decay of a race is an inevitable necessity, unless it lives in deserts and never mixes its blood.'[70] Only the Jews are immune from decline. Their very antiquity gives them a spirituality which Anglo-Saxons cannot approach. A few centuries before, says Sidonia, who reappears in *Tancred*, your bishops were tattooed savages. 'This is the advantage which Rome has over you, and which you never can understand. That Church was founded by a Hebrew, and the magnetic influence still lingers ... Theology requires an apprenticeship of some thousand years at least; to say nothing of clime and race.'[71] Individualism is brushed aside. 'What is individual character but the personification of race, its perfection and choice exemplar?' The individual who personified the virtues of a superior race was bound to triumph.

Parliamentary government, progress, individualism: the shibboleths of nineteenth-century liberalism are bowled over like ninepins. As Robert Blake has written, 'if we take him literally Disraeli does appear to be arguing against the Parliamentary system, against self-government, against "progress", against "reason".'[72] Almost certainly we *should* take him literally; *Tancred* deserves to be read as an attack on nineteenth-century liberalism. It reveals Disraeli as being fundamentally at odds with Peel's liberal Toryism. If in *Coningsby* Disraeli failed to provide a clear alternative to Peel's Conservatism, he supplied it in *Tancred*: not an historic doctrine of Toryism, not a nationalistic creed, but a deterministic theory of race; an aristocratic clerisy in place of parliament, and in place of reason, faith.

In his forties, Disraeli showed a new openness to religion. The last part of *Sybil*, with its apocalyptic vision of hell, is more religious than anything he had written before. The godless universe of the new science of evolution also disturbed him. In January 1845 when he read Chambers's *Vestiges of Natural History of Creation* (1844), he instantly realised its implications. As a fashionable woman remarks in *Tancred*, 'It is impossible to contradict anything in it. You understand, it is all science ... Everything is proved: by geology, you know ... We are a link in the chain, as inferior animals were that preceded us: we in turn shall be inferior; all that will remain of us will be some relics in a new red sandstone. This is development. We had fins; we may have wings.' Tancred is repelled. His response is not to argue, but to flee; to quit London and its corruption as quickly as possible.[73]

As Monypenny perceptively pointed out, 'Sidonia is indeed a god, and perhaps as near to the deity of Disraeli's religion as we are ever likely to get.'[74] But Sidonia was also Disraeli's idealised view of himself. One is left with the mildly disturbing reflection that the god whom he adored was not the Supreme Being but himself.

God was not an easy person to live with. Lady de Rothschild (Anthony's wife), who saw a lot of him at this time and who disliked him, found Disraeli grand and condescending. He made her feel '*lamentably stupid*', although he was trying to please. He was intolerably affected with the children, and she noticed wryly how he became grave, moody and Tancredian when he was not the centre of attention. All the same, she could not help but feel 'a sort of pride in the thought that he belongs to us – that he is one of Israel's sons'.[75]

In late November 1845, as winter came to Cassel, Disraeli and Mary Anne prepared to leave. News had reached them from Sarah of the wet English autumn, the fields of blighted, sodden corn and, worse still, the Irish potato famine. Disraeli was also badly shaken by the tragic death of his cousin the architect George Basevi, who was killed falling from the belfry of Ely Cathedral. Despite the gathering gloom and confusion in England, they resolved to travel to Paris, which they reached on 29 November after a gruelling three-day coach journey.

Disraeli plunged into a political atmosphere of fever heat. Lord John Russell's 'Edinburgh Letter' (22 November), condemning Peel's inaction over the famine in Ireland and calling for the repeal of the Corn Laws, had ignited a political crisis. Despite having spent the last three months in a Flemish wilderness where he had not seen *The Times* let alone talked to a politician, Disraeli knew exactly what to do. Tancred and his eastern wanderings were forgotten. Out came his scarlet deputy lieutenant's uniform, and on Tuesday he was at St Cloud. When he entered the palace the twenty courtiers playing billiards put down their cues and stared; one rushed out to read the name inscribed in the antechamber, and the room rang with 'Disraeli, Disraeli'. Fame! The king beckoned him into another room, and they spoke for half an hour. He found Louis Philippe alarmed and excited about English politics – 'Whether the Government could stand?'[76] After his interview with Louis Philippe, Disraeli lived in a heady whirl of ministers and ambassadors. On 12 December the news reached Paris that Peel had resigned, and Russell was attempting to form a Whig government pledged to

Corn Law repeal. Disraeli seized the opportunity to work for Peel's destruction by strengthening the Whigs' position in Paris, and began to intrigue on Palmerston's behalf. Palmerston's foreign policy had antagonised France in 1841, and the prospect of his return to the Foreign Office filled the Tuileries with dismay.

On the evening of 12 December Disraeli saw Guizot, and told him that Peel's return to office was highly improbable. Next day he saw Louis Philippe, who was alarmed about Palmerston; Disraeli tried to reassure him. As he put it in the account he wrote in his *Life of Lord George Bentinck*, 'One, to whom the King had disburthened his mind in an hour of intolerable anxiety and from whom his majesty asked that counsel which circumstances permitted to be given, tried to relieve him from these bugbears of state in a truer appreciation of the position than those around him cared to encourage.' Louis Philippe confided his fears of a vast revolutionary movement in central Europe, and Disraeli assured him of the Whigs' cordiality. 'It was suggested to the king that through the medium of some private friend, it might be wise to ... seek for some frank explanation of [Palmerston's] feelings with respect to France.'[77] The private friend was of course Disraeli, who wrote to Palmerston on 14 December, giving a lengthy report of his interview with the king, and suggesting Palmerston signal his friendliness towards France, possibly by a speech in parliament. Disraeli would willingly assist, he wrote, but for his reluctance to quit Paris, 'especially as the great object of my political life is now achieved'.[78]

'The great object of my political life ...' To secure Peel's fall Disraeli would stop at nothing; even a Whig government pledged to free trade in corn was preferable to Peel. So much for the Corn Laws, which he was to champion so vigorously in the New Year. Still more significant is his relationship with Palmerston. Only three years before, Disraeli had tried to distinguish himself in parliament with an elaborate attack on Palmerston's foreign policy. Now, in Paris Disraeli was acting as Palmerston's intermediary with the French court, an odd role for the guardian of the Tory party's conscience. His connection with Palmerston probably went deeper than the surviving evidence suggests, and it was crucial to his calculations in 1846. In *Tancred*, he later likened Palmerston to the elder Pitt; higher praise he could hardly give, and he never gave a compliment without good reason.[79]

Russell's attempt to form a Whig minority government was doomed, as Disraeli well knew. 'What exciting times!' he told Sarah. 'All agree that tho' Peel may return, he has lost his prestige – Cobden and 'The Times' will alone triumph.'[80]

The twenty-first of December was Disraeli's forty-first birthday, and he had much to celebrate. Peel had returned to office (20 December), committed to repeal the Corn Laws, and Disraeli rejoiced in the weakness of his position. He wrote to Lord John Manners, 'Peel is so vain, that he wants to figure in history as the settler of all the great questions, but a parliamentary constitution is not favourable to such ambitions; things must be done by parties, not by persons using parties as tools; especially men without imagination or any inspiring qualities, or who rather offer you duplicity instead of inspiration.'[81]

THIRTEEN

The Breaking of Peel

1846

DISRAELI AND Mary Anne reached London on 18 January 1846, to find politics 'more wild and confused than ever'. Disraeli thought Peel's difficulties were insurmountable, but though the squires grumbled over their Christmas hearths and damned Peel on the hunting field, the Protectionists were barely organised – a rump of angry but inarticulate agriculturists. Peel had returned to office a man in a dream, convinced of the righteousness of his mission to repeal the Corn Laws, and confident that he could hold his party together. Gladstone recorded that when he accepted Peel's offer of a seat in the Cabinet, 'We *held* hands instinctively, and I could not but reciprocate with emphasis his "God bless you".'

Disraeli returned to London to find a letter from Smythe announcing his acceptance of office from Peel as under secretary at the Foreign Office. 'I shall ever feel to you as to a man of genius who succoured and solaced and strengthened me when I was deserted even by myself,' wrote Smythe, in a vain attempt to soften the blow. Disraeli was mortified. He saw Smythe's defection as betrayal, and this redoubled his anger with Peel. 'I think [Smythe's] loss rather sharpened my lance,' he drily told Prince Metternich two years later.[1]

Parliament met on 22 January, and the House listened tensely as Peel explained how his opinions on protection had changed. It was not what the Tory gentry wanted to hear. Lucid narratives demonstrating that the level of wages did not fluctuate with the price of corn gave no comfort to them. Nor did Peel's vindication of Conservatism win the hearts of men who suspected the doctrine as new-fangled claptrap. 'I have thought it consistent with true Conservative policy', Peel claimed in a peroration which has become famous, 'to promote so much of happiness and contentment among the people that the voice of disaffection should be no longer heard, and that thoughts of the dissolution of our institutions should be forgotten in the midst of physical enjoyment.' Not a single cheer came from the benches behind him, and during Russell's speech which followed the House became tame and dispirited; it seemed that the debate was about to end – to the minister's advantage.[2]

Suddenly Disraeli was on his feet. Only Peel's peculiar tone, he claimed, had persuaded him to speak, and in 'an hour of jibes and bitterness' he ridiculed the speech. Listening to Disraeli for the first time, Greville thought 'his fluency wonderful, his cleverness great, and his mode of speaking certainly effective, though there is something monotonous in it'.[3] Amid roars of laughter, Disraeli likened Peel to the Turkish admiral who steered his fleet into the enemy's port or, more violently, to a nurse who, entrusted with the care of the infant Protection, dashed its brains out, and had come to give master and mistress an account of the murder. As for Peel's claim that he had put down agitation, he surely could not deny that he was legislating with reference to the agitation of Cobden. 'What other excuses has he, for even his mouldy potatoes have failed him, even the reports of his vagrant professors have failed him.' To deny the seriousness of the Irish famine was central to Disraeli's strategy; the real issue, claimed Disraeli, was one of principle – Peel had pledged himself to protection, and having changed his mind he had no right to turn round and upbraid his party, encouraging them to betray their constituencies. 'Let men stand by the principle by which they rise – right or wrong ... If they be in the wrong, they must retire to that shade of private life with which our present rulers have often threatened us. ... It is not a legitimate trial of the principles of free trade against the principle of protection if a Parliament, the majority of which are elected to support protection, be gained over to free trade by the arts of the very individual whom they were elected to support in an opposite career. It is not fair to the people of England.'[4]

'D'Israeli amused us so much,' wrote Lady Stanley of Alderley to her daughter-in-law, 'but *poor* Peel – he was really quite *touching* – I wonder if he whimpered in one part – really D'Is was *almost* too hard upon him.'[5] It was a savage personal attack, bearing no reference to the principle of Protection, much of it crude knockabout stuff. But Disraeli's gibes and hits masked a serious argument.

Peel insisted that neither his party nor the electorate was competent to decide the Corn Laws; the issue must be decided by parliament. Disraeli, on the other hand, argued, as he had done over Maynooth, that Peel was bound by pledges to the electorate and to his party: a Minister who changed his mind should resign or dissolve.[6] The constitutional argument reflected a wider division. Disraeli charged Peel with introducing free trade into politics and destroying the independence of party. As a Liberal Tory or Conservative, however, Peel believed in removing fetters and controls both in the economy and in politics; parliamentary politics for him was a matter of informed debate in which the best argument won, and his speeches were closely reasoned, dense with figures, lucid lectures on political economy. Disraeli, by contrast, did not really believe that politics should be decided by reasoned argument. His instincts were High Tory; he believed in the management both of opinion and of the economy and, indeed, of 'the People'. For him, party performed a rather similar function to economic protection: a device for exercising control.[7]

More was at stake in 1846 than methods of government; at issue was the future of the landed aristocracy. Should they, as Peel argued, endeavour to save their political power by yielding to opposition, as they had done in 1832, or should they cling to the economic privilege which was the basis of their political power, as Disraeli urged? Both were right. For a generation after 1846, high wheat prices, economic prosperity and political stability appeared to vindicate Peel. After 1875 free trade allowed the influx of cheap American wheat, causing agricultural depression and the collapse of aristocratic power, as the Protentionists had predicted.

Disraeli, the Jewish mountebank, was an incongruous leader for the party of soil and horseflesh, but he had one key qualification: a belief, articulated frequently in his novels, in aristocratic government. The paradox was that in 1846 he took his stand on grounds of lofty constitutional principle, charging Peel with breaking faith with his party; yet in his writings Disraeli disputed the value of parliamentary government, arguing for the despotism of which he now accused Peel.

Disraeli's speech of 22 January 1846 was one of the most important he ever made. Though he claimed to speak impromptu, much of it reads as if it were elaborately rehearsed beforehand; he was still stinging from the loss of Smythe, but it took considerable courage to speak from the backbenches in the formal debate on the Address. The risk came off. The frequent laughter and cheers which punctuated Disraeli's speech came from the Tory benches – sullenly silent while Peel spoke. Disraeli probably knew that the Protectionists already claimed the support of 140 members; by striking immediately the session opened, he made an effective bid for their support.

That Disraeli was accepted as spokesman of the country party in 1846 was largely owing to the man who emerged as their leader: Lord George Bentinck. After Bentinck's premature death in 1848, Disraeli wrote his biography. *Lord George Bentinck*, published in 1852, is still the indispensable account of the crisis of 1846, but it is a strange book. It tells the story of the years Disraeli later saw as the three most memorable of his own life (1846–8), yet he never mentions himself by name. None of his diatribes against Peel is noticed, nor are the extraordinary scenes which they occasioned.[8] Lord George himself is repeatedly eulogised, yet he remains somehow hollow and unreal. There is much, however, that needs to be explained about Lord George Bentinck.

Bentinck was the second surviving son of the 4th duke of Portland, and only two years Disraeli's senior. Disraeli described him rather fancifully as a Whig of 1688, but in reality he was a follower of Canning, whose nephew he was and whom he had briefly served as private secretary. A supporter of Catholic Emancipation, he refused office under Grey in 1830, and in 1834 followed his friend Lord Stanley on to the Conservative benches. High Tory he was not: as Disraeli wrote, 'he was for the established church, but for nothing more, and very repugnant to priestly domination'. During twenty years in parliament, he never once spoke in an important debate. Occasionally, after hunting all day with Mr Assheton Smith, he was to be seen entering the House at a late hour clad, in Disraeli's romantic phrase, 'in a white great-coat which softened, but did not conceal, the scarlet hunting-coat'; more prosaically, it was his habit after dining at White's to come down to the House and slumber on the back benches. Tall, good-looking and auburn-haired, he devoted his energies to racing; with sixty or seventy horses kept in training at Goodwood with his friend the Protectionist duke of Richmond, in the 1840s he emerged as the purifier of the sport, the scourge of vice in a world rife with corruption, and in 1844 he exposed the fraudulent Running Rein Derby. It was on grounds of honour that he opposed Peel over the Corn Laws in the winter of 1845–6. 'I keep horses in three counties,' he said, 'and they tell me that I shall save some fifteen hundred a year by free trade. I don't care for that; what I cannot bear is being sold.'[9] He was vulnerable to the charge of double standards. The purifier of the turf was himself a massive and unscrupulous gambler. He had to be; the costs of his inflated and extravagant stud far outweighed his income and winnings and he met the gap by betting, which for him was a profession demanding vigilant and systematic attention to form and odds. Greville, his cousin, who hated him, accused him of every type of malpractice, of falsely representing his horses as unsound or instructing his jockeys to pull them. But Greville was only one of many enemies; Bentinck's career was littered with quarrels which he pursued with vindictiveness and rancour. 'A strong difference from his views', wrote William Gregory, 'was tantamount to a moral offence.' He was an obsessive, a man who threw himself into a mission with tireless zeal, a man who *needed* enemies to validate his self-image and accused his enemies of sins, often grossly exaggerated, which he was only too willing to overlook in himself; it may be significant that his brother, the 5th duke, ended his life a strange recluse, building miles of tunnels beneath his Welbeck estate.[10]

In 1846 Bentinck plunged into the Protectionist cause, driven by a grinding hatred of Peel, and talking wildly of honour and betrayal. 'My sole ambition', he wrote in 1847, 'was to rally the broken and dispirited forces of a betrayed and insulted party, and to avenge the country gentlemen and landed aristocracy of England upon the Minister who, presuming upon their weakness, falsely flattered himself that they could be trampled upon with impunity.'[11] He brought social and moral authority with the country squires as well as titanic powers of work, but he suffered from a crucial handicap: virtually uneducated, he was a poor speaker, long-winded, with a high, weak voice. Disraeli, deeply distrusted by the squires, represented the asset Bentinck needed. Yet though Disraeli had vilified Peel, he did not hate him as Bentinck did. In *Lord George Bentinck* it is Peel, rather than the unreal Bentinck, who engages Disraeli's sympathy and imagination.[12] During the 1846 session, as Peel's frigid arrogance and smug superiority dissolved, his feelings about his enemy became more ambivalent.

Disraeli is often accused of caring not a jot for the issue of Protection, but this is not quite fair. True, he intrigued in December 1845 to replace Peel by a pro-Repeal Whig government. But his record on the Corn Laws was consistent; even in his Radical days at Wycombe he had campaigned for the Corn Law, prompted by Chandos and his farmers. At Shrewsbury, where his seat was uncomfortably unsafe, he was under pressure to support the Corn Law and in 1843 he had pledged himself to support it if Peel abandoned it. Though the Shrewsbury Tories were divided over Repeal in 1846, Disraeli was assured by his agent that as a Protectionist he could be sure of re-election – in February the Tories of Shrewsbury sent him a brawned boar's head as a token of their esteem.[13] Disraeli was a stranger to the country gentlemen's feeling of betrayal. Yet his opposition to Repeal was perhaps the more effective because Protection was negotiable, a means to an end; as a pragmatic Protectionist he was able to save the country party from retreating into a self-destructive Great Sulk after 1846.

He and Bentinck barely knew each other before 1846. Not until many years later did Disraeli discover that Bentinck had kept him out of the House in 1834, preventing his adoption for Lynn Regis.[14] In 1846, however, Bentinck was as desperate for a jockey as Disraeli was for the ride. Peel's proposal to phase out the Corn Laws over three years (introduced on 27 January) was met by blank disappointment on the Conservative benches, and the Protectionists swung into open opposition. 'Lord Henry Bentinck is going to give up hunting and give himself up to politics in order to support me!' Disraeli told Sarah.[15]

On 9 February the Protectionists moved to delay Peel's motion to go into committee on the Corn Laws. The Protectionists must 'prove to the country', wrote Disraeli, 'that they could represent their cause in debate', and Bentinck, Disraeli and a committee mobilised the country gentlemen. It was, wrote Greville, 'the dullest debate on record', but as one after another normally silent Tory member rose to declare his opposition to Repeal, dragging out the debate until 27 February, Peel acknowledged that a party split was unavoidable.[16] 'I am fighting a desperate battle here,' he wrote on 24 February to his friend Sir Henry Hardinge, Governor-General of India, then in the thick of the Sikh wars; 'shall probably drive my opponents over the Sutlej; but what is to come afterwards I know not'.[17]

The Protectionist squires made little attempt to argue their case, and Disraeli attempted to confute the Repealers in an uncharacteristically businesslike speech on 20 February. For two and a half hours he discoursed on the difficulty of fighting hostile tariffs with free imports, and argued that corn imports would lead to a deflationary drain of gold. Under Protection, Disraeli claimed, English agriculture had become the most efficient in the world, expanding its output to feed a population which had doubled in half a century; because it bore the burdens of England's territorial constitution, agriculture deserved special provision.

Disraeli's speech, wrote Greville, was poor and worthless.[18] It was not so much the weakness of his arguments – there *was* a case to be made in favour of Protection, and he raised points about retaliation and deflation under free trade which were addressed time and again during the debates of 1846. But Disraeli talking political economy did not convince. Sir George Clerk, a junior minister, showed that his figures were wrong and his facts mistaken. The most remarkable speech of the debate was Lord George Bentinck's. Rising at midnight, having eaten nothing since breakfasting on dry toast, he spoke without notes for three hours, reeling off reams of figures with the ease of a memory trained by betting. Even Greville was impressed, conceding that Bentinck's abilities might have taken him to the top in politics had he not thrown himself away on racing. To the Whig lawyer Lord Campbell, Bentinck's furious onslaught heralded the annihilation of the Conservative party; he no longer saw Peel as another Walpole, but he looked forward once more to holding office as Irish Lord Chancellor.[19]

In the division on the Corn Laws on 27 February the government won by 97 votes (337:240). A total of 231 Conservatives voted against the government, and of the 112 who voted for Repeal, about 40 were office holders. Peel owed his majority to the 227 Liberals who voted for Repeal.[20] It was an extraordinary situation, and presented dazzling opportunities for Disraeli.

'Here we are involved in a struggle of ceaseless excitement and energy,' he told a well-wisher, Sir George Sinclair. 'Deserted by our leaders, even by the subalterns of the camp, we have been obliged to organise ourselves, and choose chieftains from the rank and file.'[21]

What Disraeli was plotting in March 1846 is tantalisingly obscure. His Whig friend Lord Ponsonby, handsome, patrician, an intriguer and a womaniser, wrote that he had approached the Protectionist ex-Cabinet minister, the duke of Buccleuch about joining 'an efficient Administration'. 'I hope you will persevere,' wrote Ponsonby, 'and succeed in your endeavours to form a strong government and thereby save the country from the evils which will attend the existence of one without courage or strength: you will have a hard task, but I believe your ability is equal to anything.' A 'strong government' was Ponsonby's phrase for a Whig-Protectionist coalition, a project which originated with Ponsonby's kinsman, Lord Bessborough, with whom Disraeli was also in communication. 'You are not a bit more committed now than you were by what was said when you and Bessborough dined here,' wrote Ponsonby.[22]

The key to the 'strong government' intrigue was Palmerston. Disraeli had already perceived that Palmerston's Whig-Radical rhetoric masked High Toryism not dissimilar from his own, and saw Palmerston as potential Whig-Protectionist prime minister. Early in 1846 Palmerston was something of a loose cannon. The passing of Repeal was guaranteed so long as Peel could count on the support of Russell and the Whigs, bound by Russell's 'Edinburgh Letter' of December 1845. Palmerston, however, disliked free trade, and having been humiliated when the Whigs refused to accept him as foreign secretary in December, he was more than willing to humiliate Russell. In January Lady Palmerston and her brother, Lord Beauvale, hatched a plot for Palmerston rather than Russell to succeed Peel as prime minister: 'If the Protectionists had but common sense and would yield what ought to be yielded, I firmly believe we should beat Johnny, Peel and the League united,' wrote Beauvale.

The terms of the alliance were a moderate fixed duty on corn, and on 27 March when Palmerston made a speech praising the Protectionists and extolling a fixed duty, Disraeli dashed off a letter of support. 'I don't suppose the mighty mystery involved in it was perceptible to half a dozen individuals in the house, but it will work. The "boobies" on both sides were quite mystified. I sat among yours, and their running commentary was infinitely diverting.' Disraeli had acted as Palmerston's intermediary with Louis Philippe in December and it was partly on his advice that Palmerston made a judicious visit to Paris at Easter to patch up relations with the French court. A regular guest at Lady Palmerston's assemblies that spring, Disraeli evidently knew all about the 'mighty mystery' of a Whig-Protectionist coalition, and, prompted by Ponsonby, he agreed to abstain from criticising Palmerston in the House and to encourage the Protectionists to do the same.[23]

Palmerston's response, however, was discouragingly dampening: 'I could not refrain from affording one "pitying Tear, to grace the obsequies" of fixed Duty. Many would, I am persuaded, be glad to revive it; but to all appearances its life seems entirely extinct.'[24] Palmerston had failed to split the Whig party, which was united behind Russell in support of Repeal. The idea of a Whig-Protectionist alliance was not dead however, nor was the fixed duty. 'There is a diplomacy even in debate,' wrote Disraeli in *Lord George Bentinck*, 'Lord Palmerston threw a practised and prescient eye over the disturbed elements of the house of commons, and two months afterwards, when a protectionist ministry on moderate principles ... was not impossible, the speech of the noble lord was quoted by many as a rallying point.' For Disraeli the Corn Laws were already negotiable, whatever he might say about Protection in public, though whether the diehard Protectionists could have been persuaded is another matter. When Hobhouse expressed the fear that Peel, having broken up his own party, would break up the Whigs, Disraeli replied, 'That you may depend upon it he will, or any other party that he has anything to do with.'[25]

The Government's Irish Coercion Bill, which reached the Commons at the end of March, introduced new possibilities for political combinations. Disraeli, who was eager to seize any opportunity of defeating the government, wanted to oppose the bill, and said so at a meeting of 200 or so Protectionist members. Bentinck disagreed and persuaded the Protectionists to support Coercion in exchange for the government's agreeing to delay the Corn Bill. The Whigs maintained that Corn should receive priority over Ireland; as a result in April the government was deadlocked, unable to proceed either on Corn or Ireland.

Disraeli was ill at the end of March. 'For God's sake get quite right before you venture out,' wrote Bentinck, 'as we shall want you after Easter in earnest.' Disraeli and Mary Anne spent Easter at Bradenham, returning to a confused and uncertain political situation. The Protectionist party seemed in danger of melting away. 'The illusions of the Protectionist party that they could form a government are, I think, vanishing,' wrote Peel on 4 April. Paradoxically, they were the victim of their success; the longer they succeeded in delaying the Corn Bill, the greater its support in the country. 'I am altogether unsanguine as to our compactness,' Smith O'Brien told Disraeli, 'and believe we shall go to pieces so fast that it will soon be a question how far we shall be authorized in calling ourselves a party at all.' On

21 April, at a meeting at Bankes's house, Bentinck agreed to act as leader – a necessary sacrifice, if only to keep the party together.[26]

In the House on 24 April Disraeli accused Peel of cheering during a speech of Cobden's, when Cobden asserted that the people of England were the people living in towns, who would govern the country. Peel jumped up and denied it. 'If the Right Honourable Baronet means to say that anything I have said is false,' retorted Disraeli, 'of course I cease – I sit down.' After the rumpus had quietened, Jonathan, Peel's quick-tempered horse-racing brother, came over to Disraeli and told him that what he had said was false. Disraeli, who was astounded, said nothing but placed the affair in the hands of Bentinck; he went to bed half expecting to fight a duel in the morning. Late at night in White's Club Bentinck and Captain Rous, whom Peel had appointed as his second, agreed that Jonathan Peel should withdraw, which he duly did. No longer a matter of argument, the party split had become an affair of honour.[27]

In *Lord George Bentinck* Disraeli recalled how, late one night about this time, after the adjournment of the House, Peel remained in his seat, alone among the empty benches, plunged in thought. From behind the speaker's chair his colleagues watched as the prime minister was gently roused by the clerk who inspected the chamber before the doors were closed and the lights extinguished.[28]

The Irish Coercion Bill passed its first reading on 2 May; Bentinck and the Protectionists voted with the government and Disraeli walked out of the House. The deadlock was unblocked, enabling the government to proceed once more with the Corn Bill. Bentinck continued to obstruct, prompting Peel to deliver an impressive extempore reply (on 4 May) to the Protectionist argument that free trade in corn would destroy aristocratic influence. 'I believe it to be of the utmost importance that a territorial aristocracy should be maintained.' The only question, said Peel, was what, in a certain state of public opinion, was the most effectual way of maintaining their legitimate influence and authority. 'My firm belief is that you will more increase the just influence of the landed aristocracy by now forgoing this protection than by continuing it.' The territorial aristocracy, said Peel, had maintained its influence because 'it has always identified itself with the people; it has never pertinaciously insisted on the maintenance of a privilege when the time for forgoing that privilege had arrived'. Disraeli's response was crude and blustering, accusing Peel once again of stealing the ideas of Cobden and Bright. 'And so,' he declared, 'when the right honourable Gentleman, with a fervour of mimetic rhetoric, which has been much developed of late, turns round, and says he has not the courage, and he is surprised that we have, to oppose that which is for the benefit of ... the people; that, I say, is not the question at issue.'[29]

Disraeli himself was by no means impervious to attack. As the Radical J. A. Roebuck pointed out, he was always promising to enlighten the House with his doctrines of political economy, yet somehow he never did. Nor was he in a position to twit Peel for changing his views when he had changed from Radical to Tory, not on grounds of public good but for reasons of personal advantage. Disraeli could and did defend himself against the old charge of changing his party; far harder to rebut was the charge of the intellectual bankruptcy of the Protectionists.[30]

A week later Disraeli attempted to argue the Protectionist case. For three hours he discussed political economy, warning that Repeal would cause corn prices to fall, and pointing to the surplus of wheat in Russia, Mississippi (of all places), and Hungary; once more he tried to prove the impossibility of meeting hostile tariffs with free imports. Not until 1875, when cheap American corn flooded the British market and Europe turned to protection, were these gloomy prophecies vindicated. In 1846, in a climate of free trade economics and mechanistic, self-adjusting systems, Protection was intellectually unacceptable. What really made an impression was the last twenty minutes of Disraeli's speech when, in perhaps the greatest of his philippics, he hacked and mangled Peel, charging him with stealing the ideas of what he described (in a phrase which stuck) as the Manchester School:

> ... for between 30 and 40 years, from the days of Mr Horner to the days of the honourable Member for Stockport, the Right Honourable Gentleman has traded on the ideas and intelligence of others. His life has been one great appropriation clause. He is a burglar of others' intellect. ... I believe, therefore, that when the Right Honourable Gentleman undertook our cause on either side of the House, that he was perfectly sincere in his advocacy; but as, in the course of discussion, the conventionalisms which he received from us crumbled away in his grasp, feeling no creative power to sustain him with new arguments, ... faithful to the law of his nature, [he] imbibed the new doctrines, the more vigorous, bustling, popular and progressive doctrines, as he had imbibed the doctrines of Mr Horner – as he had imbibed the doctrines of every leading man in this country, for thirty or forty years, with the exception of the doctrine of Parliamentary reform, which the Whigs very wisely led the country upon, and did not allow to grow sufficiently mature to fall into the mouth of the Right Honourable Gentleman.[31]

Disraeli sat down to a burst of cheers such as had rarely been heard; he later claimed it was the loudest and longest cheer ever. Peel's reply was almost drowned by the hooting and screaming of the Protectionists. Turning to his left, where Disraeli sat on the benches behind and above him, he responded, 'The smallest of all the penalties which I anticipated, were the continued venomous attacks of the Member for Shrewsbury' (venomous he pronounced with a marked contemptuous emphasis). If in 1841 Disraeli held the opinion he now professed, it was a little surprising that 'he should have been ready – as I think he was – to unite his fortunes with mine in office'.[32]

Disraeli waited until the end of Peel's speech, his fifth and last great Corn Law speech, before replying. There would have been nothing dishonourable if he *had* applied for office in 1841, he declared; 'but I can assure the House nothing of the kind ever occurred. I never shall – it is totally foreign to my nature – make an application for any place.' But in 1841 when the government was formed, 'an individual, possessing, as I believe him to possess, the most intimate and complete confidence of the Right Honourable Gentleman, called on me and communicated with me'. The individual, of course, was Lyndhurst, and Disraeli concluded his uneasy statement thus: 'Whatever occurred in 1841 between the Right Honourable Gentleman and myself was entirely attributable to the intervention of another gentleman, whom I supposed to be in the confidence of the Right Honourable Baronet, and I dare say it may have arisen from a misconception.' Peel merely reiterated that it was not right that in 1841 Disraeli 'should have intimated to me that he was not unwilling to give that proof of confidence that would have been implied by the acceptance of office'.[33]

Disraeli, said Hobhouse, 'had better not have spoken'. He has often been accused of lying. Both he and Mary Anne had written to Peel in 1841. But Disraeli's letter did not actually ask for office; written in despair at his exclusion from the government, it mentioned Lyndhurst, who had led him to expect a place, and it implored Peel to save him from humiliation.[34] Disraeli seems to have kept no copy of his letter, which may partly explain why his speech was so stumbling and obscure – he could not remember exactly what it said. Peel's charge that Disraeli *wished* for office is certainly true; and if Peel carried his letter in his pocket Disraeli had good reason to fear him reading it to the House.[35]

Disraeli's denial did not lessen the effect of his attack on Peel, which intuitively expressed the feeling of the House. 'You crucified Peel,' wrote Lord Ponsonby. As lord chancellor, Lyndhurst could not decently listen to Disraeli abusing Peel, but he interrogated Campbell, who was there; and, though he thought the Corn Laws 'all a humbug', Lyndhurst could hardly conceal his satisfaction when Campbell told him how the House relished the jokes about Peel's hypocrisy, pedantry and inconsistency. 'Though I should not have spoken it myself,' wrote Lord Ashley, 'I am forced to admit the truth of it; though bitter in principle and motive, it is hardly exaggerated in imputation. This statesman's career is without precedent in the history of politicians: he has begun by opposing, and ended by carrying (not simply supporting) almost every great question of the day.'[36] At one point in Peel's reply, when he mentioned personal ambition, he was jeered for several minutes, and he broke down with tears in his eyes. 'I never saw Peel beat before,' wrote Hobhouse. It was, thought Greville, a cruel and degrading spectacle. The Protectionists hunted Peel like a fox they were eager to kill in the open.[37]

Disraeli crucified Peel; but, as Boyd Hilton has written, 'Peel was more than a little willing to shed his own mediatorial blood.'[38] Atonement was at the core of Victorian evangelicalism – that man should make retribution for worldly sins and beastliness was a welcome sign of God's grace, essential to avoid eternal damnation. Peel was a man of deep and simple evangelical faith, and in 1846 the moral authority he enjoyed with his disciples owed not a little to his mediatorial role; it was Peel who made atonement, for the worldly success of his time, for the disasters of the Irish famine.

Disraeli was too keenly attuned to the political mood not to realise the symbolic religious dimension to Peel's political death. Later in 1846, when he returned to work on *Tancred* and pondered the relations of Judaism and Christianity, he wrote that the essential object of the Christian scheme was the expiation – the idea of a sacrificial mediator, purifying the world by atoning blood. Yet the Jews, he argued, were not to blame for the crucifixion; on the contrary, they were the agents of the expiation. 'Suppose the Jews had not prevailed upon the Romans to crucify Jesus, what would have become of the Atonement?'[39] Disraeli's Judaeo-Christian interpretation of the atonement mirrored, or rather justified, his role in crucifying Peel, the mediator, redeeming the sins of politics through his crucifixion. Without the agency of Disraeli, what would have become of Peel's atonement?

The third reading of the Corn Bill passed the Commons at 4 a.m. on 16 May. Strolling back from Westminster to Grosvenor Gate late at night with Ponsonby, Disraeli discussed the House of Lords, where Bessborough, aided and abetted by Palmerston, was plotting for the Whig peers to defeat the bill. The Whig peers met at Lansdowne House on 23 May, and Disraeli was dismayed to hear the 'sinister news' that Russell had dissuaded them from opposing Repeal. He scrawled a note to Ponsonby: 'The game is over for the moment, but it is a great game, as I think that "yet a little time", and the people of England will rally round it. In the meantime, I will not execrate Peel, or his measures since they have permitted me to write you this.'[40]

For Disraeli to quote the New Testament was unusual in itself; his choice of Jesus's words, 'a little while, and ye shall not see me: and again a little while, and ye shall see me, because I go to the Father' (John 16:16) shed light on the strange elated state of his mind in the summer of 1846. Peel's disciples shall weep, but the world shall rejoice for the result of his death. The game, the great game, which Peel permitted, was a realignment of parties along new fault lines – a Whig-Protectionist coalition, or the reconstruction of the Whig party on a broad basis. As Disraeli explained in *Lord George Bentinck*: 'If indeed the whigs had been prepared to form a government on the economical principles of their own budget of 1842, the whole of the protectionist party would have arrayed itself under their banners, and the landed interest, whose honour they would have then saved, would have been theirs for ever.' Greville deplored the Protectionists' inconsistency in being 'ready to join the detested Whigs, and to concur in the whole of those Liberal measures, by a partial adoption of which Peel had already rendered himself so obnoxious to them'.[41] That Disraeli, self-appointed guardian of the Tory conscience and scourge of Peel's Whig backsliding, could contemplate a Whig coalition so eagerly suggests that his talk about the importance of party was so much claptrap.

'How was Sir Robert Peel to be turned out? Here was a question which might well occupy the musing hours of a Whitsun recess,' wrote Disraeli in *Lord George Bentinck*, and, in the first week of June, as the temperature soared into the eighties at the start of the hottest summer month in memory, Disraeli plotted Peel's destruction.[42] The Whigs were not prepared to oppose Peel until the Corn Bill passed the House of Lords later in June, and there was a real danger that once Repeal was secure, the Protectionists would melt away, allowing Peel to survive. The blow had to be struck the instant the bill passed. Irish coercion offered the best chance of gaining Whig votes, but the Protectionists' hands were tied by Bentinck's support for the first reading. Disraeli, who thought this a mistake at the time, urged him to oppose the bill, but this was resisted by the Protectionist leaders, who were embarrassed by their earlier vote. On 8 June, when the House met to debate the second reading of the Coercion Bill, nothing was decided. Bentinck left the chamber for a hurried conference with a Whip, who told him that, despite the risk of Protectionist defections, opposition to the bill was imperative: 'It may be perilous, but if we lose this chance the traitor will escape.'[43]

Bentinck responded with a violent and vindictive speech, accusing Peel of chasing and hunting his illustrious relative, Canning, to death. In 1827 Peel had refused to join Canning's government, alleging that he disagreed with Canning over Catholic Emancipation, but in 1829, according to Bentinck, Peel admitted that he had changed his mind on the Catholic issue two years before, in 1825. 'A second time has [Peel] insulted the honour of Parliament and of the country, and it is now time that *atonement* [author's italics] should be made to the betrayed constituencies.' Bentinck produced no evidence in support of his charges, which were made on the spur of the moment. Peel, who was wounded and angry, contemplated challenging Bentinck to a duel but he was dissuaded by Lord Lincoln, who remonstrated with the irate prime minister, pacing up and down Whitehall in the early morning light after the House had risen. Peel easily vindicated himself on 12 June. Meanwhile, Bentinck and Disraeli discovered that, according to reports in *The Times* and the *Mirror of Parliament*, Peel's speech of 1829 contained an admission that he told Lord Liverpool in 1825 that 'the time was come when something respecting the Catholics ought to be done'. The sentence did not appear in *Hansard*, but this report had been edited by Peel. Armed with this new ammunition, Disraeli reiterated the charge on 15 June, speaking on behalf of Bentinck, whom the rules prevented from speaking again. 'I never saw Mr Canning but once,' he told the House, remembering the visit he made with John Murray as a brash and ambitious twenty-year-old. 'I can recall the lightning flash of that eye, and the tumult of that ethereal brow; still lingers in my ear the melody of that voice.'[44]

Disraeli's speech, Greville and Hobhouse agreed, was a plausible and effective answer to Peel's defence. But it gave Peel the opportunity to vindicate himself once more, which he did triumphantly on 19 June, effectively crushing the charges against him, and demonstrating beyond all doubt that *The Times* report, which the *Mirror of Parliament* copied, was inaccurate. 'Nothing could be more miserable than the figure which the choice pair, G.B. and Disraeli, cut,' wrote Greville. At last Peel had revenged himself, exposing what he told the queen was a 'foul conspiracy' concocted by Mr Disraeli and Lord George Bentinck. The affair was of great service to Peel: 'The abortive attempt to ruin his character,' wrote Greville, 'which has so signally failed and recoiled on the heads of his accusers, has gathered round him feelings of sympathy which will find a loud and general echo in the country.'[45] The House, wrote the queen, 'ought to be ashamed of having such members as Lord George Bentinck and that detestable Mr D'Israeli. They ruin their cause – the Queen feels sure that Sir Robert will only stand higher in the country.' How right she was. 'I little thought I should ever live to praise Peel,' wrote Dickens. 'But D'Israeli and that Dunghill Lord have so disgusted me, that I feel inclined to champion him.'[46]

The Canning episode has been dismissed as a typically vicious and rancorous attack by Bentinck; Disraeli himself admitted in *Lord George Bentinck* that the charge was without foundation.[47] True, Bentinck and Disraeli failed to prove their case against Peel, but their attack on his record in 1827–9 was not as wild and misguided as might be imagined. Contemporaries saw clear parallels between Peel's duplicitous behaviour over Catholic Emancipation and his betrayal of his party over Corn Law repeal; as Ashley wrote in May, Peel agreed with Canning over the Catholic question, but acquired distinction, power and a party by leading the resistance to it.[48] Disraeli himself had successfully attacked Peel over Canning in 1845.

The wrangle over Canning was a cynical parliamentary manoeuvre; it helped to prolong the debate on Irish Coercion in the Commons, which was carefully co-ordinated to continue until the Corn Bill passed the Lords. On 25 June Peel had the satisfaction of seeing two drowsy masters in chancery mumble out at the table of the House that the Lords had passed Repeal. Two hours later, on the Second Reading of the Coercion Bill, the government was defeated by a majority of 73. Peel was defeated, as Disraeli wrote, by 'the flower of that great party which had been so proud to follow one who had been so proud to lead them'. As Peel sat on the Treasury bench, 'the Manners, the Somersets, the Bentincks, the Lowthers and the Lennoxes, passed before him'. Disraeli pictured Peel's feelings as they trooped on – 'all the men of metal and large-acred squires, whose spirit he had so often quickened ... in his fine conservative speeches at Whitehall gardens'. When the division was announced, Peel did not even turn his head. 'He looked very grave, and extended his chin as was his habit when he was annoyed and cared not to speak. He began to comprehend his position, and that the emperor was without his army.'[49]

Not all the emperor's army had deserted him. Of the 240 or so Conservatives who had voted against Repeal, nearly half voted with the government on 25 June and over fifty abstained. Only 74 Protectionists voted to destroy the government. Nor was it true, as Disraeli implied, that the Protectionists comprised the aristocracy and landed gentry of Peel's party ('Mr Bankes, with a parliamentary name of two centuries, and Mr Christopher from that broad Lincolnshire which protection had created; and the Mileses and the Henleys were there; and the Duncombes, the Liddells, and the Yorkes ...'). The proportion of squires and aristocrats in the faction supporting Repeal was roughly equal to the proportion among the Protectionists. Contrary to the rhetoric of Cobden and Bright and Disraeli, Corn Law Repeal did not divide the party along class lines. If there was a difference between the Protectionists and the Repealers, it concerned their experience of office.[50] Official men, or men who had earlier held office, supported Peel; the Protectionists, by contrast, were an army without officers. Lack of official men was at once Disraeli's liability and his opportunity, the problem that was to undermine the Protectionists' credibility as an alternative government and the reason why his leadership was unavoidable.

Peel resigned on 29 June. 'We have fallen in the face of day, and with our front to our enemies,' he told Hardinge. Disraeli wrote triumphantly to Mary Anne from the Carlton ('club crowded, confusion immense'.) 'All "Coningsby" and "Young England" the general exclamation here'.[51] But Young England was no more than a memory – as a member of the government, Smythe had voted for Repeal and so did Milnes. And the alliance between Toryism and Russell and Cobden, which had formed the hidden agenda of *Coningsby*, was now an impossibility. In his resignation speech, Peel paid an elaborate and much-criticised tribute to Cobden, and in exchange for the support which Russell had given him over the Corn Laws he undertook to support the minority government which Russell formed in July. Despite the Protectionists' role in Peel's fall, they had no place in the new government.

Disraeli was not disappointed. It is no exaggeration to say that Bentinck and Disraeli together had succeeded in smashing Peel. There was nothing inevitable about Peel's fall; as Disraeli told his friend George Mathew, had it not been for the crisis of 1846 he might 'not only have governed this country for his life, but have left its rule to his successors, and established a political dynasty as long as that of the Walpoles, Pelhams and Grenvilles'.[52] In January 1846 Peel was confident of carrying Repeal with Whig votes and remaining in office; that he failed to keep his party together was largely due to Bentinck and Disraeli. Historians have drawn attention to the organisation of the Protectionists, both inside and outside parliament, which Disraeli barely mentions in his account in *Lord George Bentinck*.[53] But, in the age of fluid parties, the parliamentary battle was critical, and this was led by Disraeli and Bentinck. 'These two men and these two alone carried on the war *usque ad internecionem*,' wrote the shrewd parliamentarian Lord Campbell. 'Their great object was (in which they fully succeeded) to make Peel personally odious to the Tory party, to provoke him to retaliate upon them, and to render a reconciliation with him utterly impossible.' The great treat, wrote Campbell, who came down from the Lords to listen to the debates, was Disraeli's invective. 'I heard them with infinite delight, perceiving that they were not only widening the breach between Peel and his party, but effectually subverting his authority both in the House and in the country. So great was the *prestige* attaching to Peel's name that he would have continued minister had his conduct not been thus assailed in a manner to make him both odious and ridiculous.'[54]

The political future was wildly uncertain. Gladstone seemed a more likely Tory leader than Disraeli. 'Some think Gladstone, fortunately for himself out of parliamt., is to be the future leader of the Tory party, & that we are all to rally under his banner, leaving Peel stranded.' The Protectionists, who still occupied their seats on the government side of the House, gave Russell's

Whig government their support. They were resolved on one thing: to retain their separate identity, not to reunite with the Peelites. 'It will require some time,' Disraeli told Mathew, 'before our party is re-organised on a comprehensive basis and before the confidence in public men is sufficiently restored to make the country in general exert itself for any leaders.'[55] Nor had Disraeli abandoned hope of a Protectionist alliance with Palmerston and the Whig right. 'Ultimately,' he told John Manners, 'there must be a fusion between the real Whigs and us', if only to govern Ireland. 'I see no other mode of establishing a strong government and arresting the vulgar middle class liberalism which pretends to be Democracy, and which is essentially hostile to the Roman Catholic population, though it may use them for its purpose.'[56]

Disraeli and Mary Anne spent the autumn of 1846 at Bradenham. Since January the parliamentary campaign had entirely absorbed his time and energies, and he succumbed at once to the languor which the change to pure air and regular habits always brought. After a fortnight, he told John Manners, it seemed impossible 'that I could ever live anywhere except among the woods and turfy wilderness of this dear county, which, though it upset Charles 1st, so exhausted its progressive spirit in 1640, that it has now neither a town, nor a railroad'.[57] He returned to the manuscript of *Tancred*, untouched since Cassel the previous winter, but as he pondered the Asian mystery and mused on the destiny of the Jews and the meaning of the atonement, his mind recurred to politics. Peel's fall, the party split and his friendship with Bentinck opened undreamed-of opportunities. What prospects for a man of imagination!

FOURTEEN

Conclusion

THIRTY-THREE years later, in December 1879, the twenty-two-year-old duke of Portland, who a fortnight before had succeeded his distant cousin, the tunnel-building 5th duke, received an invitation to Hughenden from the earl of Beaconsfield. It was a foggy winter's evening towards the end of the widower prime minister's government, and the young duke was filled with trepidation. He travelled down from Paddington with Montagu Corry, the prime minister's secretary; Beaconsfield travelled alone in a separate carriage. No guests dined with them, but Beaconsfield wore his Garter ribbon for dinner. Throughout the meal he said little. When the port arrived, he stood up. 'My lord duke,' he began, then said that he owed his success in life to two people – his wife and Lord George Bentinck. He then announced his intention of creating the duke's stepmother, Mrs Cavendish-Bentinck, a peeress – Baroness Bolsover. 'I come from a race which never forgives an injury,' he hissed, 'nor forgets a benefit.' Cutting short the duke's stammered thanks, he left the room.[1]

'What does our Ben know of dukes?' Isaac had asked in 1830, when his callow son published an extravagant novel, *The Young Duke*. Lord George Bentinck introduced Disraeli to the dazzling world of dukes. In 1846 he accompanied Bentinck on a ducal tour, staying with Portland at Welbeck and Rutland at Belvoir Castle. At Belvoir, whose doors had remained stubbornly closed to Disraeli, despite his friendship with Lord John Manners and the butter he had lavished on the Rutlands in *Coningsby*, he was received by 'two rows of servants, bowing as we passed' – a scene which reminded him of the arrival of Coningsby at the castle of his grandfather, Lord Monmouth.[2] Bentinck's friendship had magically dispelled Rutland's prejudices.

In 1848 Bentinck and his two brothers provided Disraeli with a vital loan of £25,000 which enabled him to buy Hughenden Manor, the house two miles from Bradenham which had once belonged to the Norris family.

Disraeli loved the place. Here he found peace and solace after the parliamentary session, sauntering for days through the walks Mary Anne had cut through the beech woods, or fingering the shelves in his library of theology, the classics and history. He planted trees, filling the grounds with decorative firs and cedars whose foliage grew so thick that it choked out the light. On Sundays he attended the decaying church in the park; did he reflect as he listened to the words of Cranmer's prayer book that the Englishman's day of rest was secured by the laws of Moses? 'Christianity is Judaism for the multitude, but still it is Judaism. ... Half Christendom worships a Jewess, and the other half a Jew ... Which do you think should be the superior race, the worshipped or the worshippers?'[3]

Hughenden was critically important. As the owner of an estate of 750 acres, Disraeli was a member of county society. 'I write this from my lonely Buckinghamshire chateau,' Disraeli told Prince Metternich in 1848. 'It is sylvan and feudal.' What joy to invite the once-mighty Metternich, hero of his youth, now an exile in Brighton; how delightful to confide in Lady Londonderry, mistress of Wynyard, 'I have been forced to give up every country house except my own'.[4] In anticipation of its purchase Disraeli abandoned Shrewbury at the 1847 election and stood for the county of Buckinghamshire. He was returned without contest and represented the county for the rest of his Commons career. 'This', he wrote in 1860, 'is the event in my public life which has given me the greatest satisfaction.' A county seat was the *sine qua non* for his ultimate ambition: the Tory leadership.

The leadership was the Portland family's great gift to Disraeli; their backing essential to his accession. After the fall of Peel, Disraeli talked of quitting politics, and was dissuaded by Bentinck. 'For his sake, and the inspiration of a great cause, I sacrificed, without a murmur, the domestic life to which I am attached, graceful pursuits, and perhaps an honourable fame.'[5] Lord George Bentinck tirelessly wore down the prejudice of the squires who resented Disraeli as a Jew and adventurer. 'Over and over again,' recalled Sir William Gregory, 'did Lord George ... speak with almost fury of the resistance of the squires to the prominence of the "d–d Jew" as they chose to call the man whose memory they now adore with primroses in their button-hole.' Lord George died suddenly from a heart attack in 1848, shortly after he resigned the Protectionist leadership. Disraeli was devastated. 'It is the greatest sorrow I have ever experienced.' A few weeks later he was interviewed by Lord George's brother, Lord Henry Bentinck. 'Then I went on the state of my affairs,' recorded Disraeli, 'observing that it would be no object to them and no pleasure to me, unless I played the high game in public life; and that I could not do that without being on a rock.' Lord Henry replied that Disraeli should play the great game; he would guarantee the rock – Hughenden and settlement of Disraeli's private affairs.[6]

Disraeli's relationship with the Portlands was reminiscent of the eighteenth century and the great days of aristocratic Whiggery. The Portlands had not forgotten that they were Whigs of 1688, who had only recently joined the Tories. Ironically, Disraeli, who had begun by attacking the Venetian oligarchy of 1688, was in the end promoted by it. Perhaps, as Robert Blake pondered, Disraeli remembered Monmouth's words to Coningsby:

> And it is our own fault that we have let the chief power out of the hands of our own order. It was never thought of in the time of your great-grandfather, sir. And if a commoner were for a season permitted to be the nominal Premier to do the detail, there was always a secret committee of great 1688 nobles to give him his instructions.

Consciously or not, Disraeli surely echoed Monmouth in the words he wrote to Lord Stanley in 1848. 'The office of leader of the Conservative party in the House of Commons at the present day, is to uphold the aristocratic settlement of this country. That is the only question at stake.'[7] Disraeli repaid his friend and patron by writing his political biography in 1851: 'the portraiture of an ENGLISH WORTHY,' he wrote on the last page of *Lord George Bentinck*.

Bentinck promoted him and pushed him into the Tory leadership, but Disraeli was a self-made politician; his extraordinary rise was of his own making. In 1851, when Derby made his first, unsuccessful attempt to form a Protectionist Ministry, Queen Victoria objected to Disraeli's appointment. She did not approve of his conduct to her dear Sir Robert Peel, she told Derby. 'Madam,' replied Derby, 'Mr Disraeli has had to make his position, and men who make their positions will say and do things, which are not necessary to be said or done by those for whom positions are provided.'[8]

A notorious figure from an early age, from the days of *Vivian Grey*, Disraeli lived under the hostile glare of an anti-semitic press. Changing parties was commonplace among politicians in the 1830s, but when Disraeli shifted from Radical to Tory well before he entered parliament he was compelled to justify himself to a prejudiced and unfriendly world. Not for him the easy rise of the aristocratic insider or the Oxford high flyer like Gladstone, whose career he chronicled in *Falconet*, his last, unfinished novel. As he told the House of Commons in 1846,

> I am not in a condition to have hereditary opinions carved out for me, and all my opinions, therefore, have been the result of reading and of thought. I never

was a follower of either of the two great aristocratic parties in this country. My sympathies and feelings have always been with the people, from whom I spring; and when obliged ... to join a party, I joined that party with which I believed the people sympathised. My sympathies are the same now as they were when I first addressed a public meeting long before I entered this House; and I have never given a vote in this House which has not been in sympathy with those feelings.[9]

'You go with your family, sir, like a gentleman,' Lord ·Monmouth told Coningsby, 'you are not to consider your own opinions like a philosopher or a political adventurer.'[10] Disraeli was both a philosopher and an adventurer. Radical turned Tory, democrat who became an upholder of the monarchical principle, Tory apologist of the Chartists turned High Tory Protectionist – it is hardly surprising that historians have dismissed him as an opportunist or charlatan, like Napoleon III a sphinx without a riddle. This is a superficial view.

There was always a Tory strain in Disraeli's early Radicalism. At Wycombe in 1832–3, guided by the ultra-Tory Chandos, he worked for a Tory-Radical alliance against the Whigs. He was a dandy and, in so far as it was political, dandyism embraced both the revolutionary and the reactionary: both were in revolt against sober middle-class respectability. Byron, whom the youthful Disraeli idolised, was a Whig, but the Romantic rebellion to which he belonged breathed new spirit into old Toryism. According to Disraeli, the Jews, though forced by discrimination to oppose the status quo, were by instinct conformist and Tory; his father was a Tory.

Ever since his miserable schooldays at Dr Coggan's, he had hated Unitarianism. Later, he likened it to Bentham's Utilitarianism, which he found equally repellent. 'The Utilitarians in Politics are like the Unitarians in Religion. Both omit Imagination in their systems, and Imagination governs Mankind.'[11] He remained true to his dislike of schematic systems which treated society as a self-regulating machine; he refused to believe that political institutions such as parliamentary government were panaceas which shaped man's behaviour, and he was indifferent towards the new science of political economy. His unsuccessful attempts to force his way into politics led him to formulate the anti-Whig theory of the Venetian oligarchy, which drew heavily on Isaac's work on the seventeenth century. Later, he developed a historical theory which attacked the Whig interpretation of British history as a mighty mystery; the cause of civil and religious liberty was a Whig myth, propaganda put out by the Whig oligarchy to justify their exploitation of the poor and emasculation of the monarchy. European politics he explained in terms of secret societies or the hidden influence of the Jews.

But eighteenth-century systems of management were inadequate in the age of the masses.[12] The people needed faith, and they needed leadership. As a young man he had welcomed democracy as a check on the low Whig ten-pound freeholders enfranchised in 1832, but he came to see democracy as something which must be controlled, not by spies but by imagination and by the aristocracy. The alternative was anarchy, the apocalyptic nightmare he sketched in *Sybil*.

Liberalism, in Disraeli's view, was no answer to democracy. That was the trouble with Peel's Conservatism, or Liberal Toryism: it was unable to provide the leadership needed to prevent the people seizing power. 'If Democracy be combated only by Conservatism, Democracy must triumph,' he had written in *Coningsby*. And, 'Man is made to adore and obey; but if you give him nothing to worship, he will fashion his own divinities and find a chieftain in his own passions.' Yet he recognised that Liberalism made possible his accession to the Tory leadership. 'Your being the Leader of the Tory party is the greatest triumph that Liberalism has ever achieved,' remarked Guizot.[13]

In *Tancred*, written mostly after Peel's fall, Disraeli turned from Peel's England to Europe and Asia. On the eve of the European revolutions of 1848, the book is tense with fear of the European multitudes, who are once more stirring in the throes of a new birth. The liberal prescriptions of parliamentary government, of reason, of material progress, have failed; the multitude needs faith. Tractarianism, as in Young England, was no solution; Young England taught Disraeli something of the Oxford Movement, and he quickly learned that Tractarianism was a political liability. His lack of empathy with the churchiness of Victorian Tories led him to look for other sources of faith. Aristocratic leadership and a revived monarchy, empire and the east, Judaeo-Christianity – above all, his theory of race. 'All is race; there is no other truth.' Cloudy though his ideas were, Disraeli was no charlatan. His ideas were as prophetic for the right as those of Marx for the left; both saw that the fatal weakness of liberalism was its failure to inspire the masses, and both saw their opportunity in this weakness.

It would be wrong, however, to describe Disraeli as an intellectual. For him, a life like Isaac's, spent scratching with a quill pen in the stillness of a library would have been a half-life. He neither knew nor was respected by the Victorian literary-intellectual élite, by Mill and Carlyle, by Dickens and George Eliot. He wrote nothing for periodicals like the *Quarterly* or the *Edinburgh Review*, the life-blood of the Victorian intellectual world. He craved action, light, an audience, as a small child craves attention. 'My mind is a continental mind,' he wrote in 1833. 'It is a revolutionary mind. I am only truly great in action.'[14] Again and again in his novels he fantasised about fame and power. 'I want Europe to talk of me,' says a character in *Tancred*. 'I am wearied of hearing of nothing but Ibrahim Pacha, Louis Philippe and Palmerston. I too can make combinations; and I am of a better family than all three.'[15]

He was only half in jest. The romantic aristocratic Sephardic ancestry he concocted for himself was, like many Victorian genealogies, a work of imagination, but it was crucial to his self-esteem. So was his theory of the racial superiority of the Jews, the only Caucasian race of unmixed blood, who he claimed were the secret rulers of Europe, an intellectual élite, blessed with a unique spirituality. In his twenties, his sense of alienation and worthlessness, coupled with the virulent anti-semitic abuse he encountered over *Vivian Grey*, had triggered a nervous breakdown which nearly destroyed him. Making a positive virtue of his Jewishness served a deep psychological need; it gave a rationale to the sense of worth, of his own genius, which he had imbibed from Isaac, and which his feelings of alienation as a Jew had so painfully threatened. Asserting his identity and superiority as a Jew was Disraeli's way of escaping from the despair and depression which had dogged his twenties. To feel himself men's equal, he had to lead them.

One explanation for his extraordinary rise was proposed by Walter Bagehot in 1859. He attributed Disraeli's success 'to his very unusual capacity for *applying* a literary genius, in itself limited, to the practical purposes of public life'.[16] Not only did Disraeli achieve fame, set an agenda and buy favours as the author of the political novels *Coningsby* and *Sybil*, but in parliament he applied his novelist's skill to the invention of personalities. His tirades against Peel succeeded because of his empathy with his subject; Peel was perhaps the most inspired of his literary-political creations and Disraeli studied him hour after hour in the House.[17]

As a young man, Disraeli admired the Greek orator and general Alcibiades. It was revealing choice. Alcibiades's oratory transfixed the Athenian people as Disraeli's did the Wycombe mob in 1832 or the House of Commons in 1844–6. But Alcibiades was a brilliant, amoral character who, after leading an unsuccessful expedition during the Peloponnesian War, changed sides and worked for Sparta and who, having begun as leader of the democratic party in Athens, intrigued with Persia to bring about an oligarchic revolution. True to his hero's example, Disraeli had scant respect for probity or integrity in politics – his code of behaviour was truly Machiavellian.

The wise prince, said Machiavelli, should be both lion and fox. The prince who was only the lion and never broke his word did not understand the world.[18] Disraeli could roar like a lion, and he possessed the political cunning of a fox. In 1846 he crucified Peel for betraying the Conservative party and stealing the ideas of the Whigs, while at the same time secretly intriguing with Palmerston for a Whig-Protectionist coalition. 'The strife / And struggling fell [*sic*] of party,' which he lauded in his anniversary verse to Mary Anne, 'where the prize / is power over the powerful, and to sway / The race that sways the world', was for Disraeli only partly a matter of 'the blaze of factious senates'; equally important was 'the inspiring cheer / And craft of secret councils'.[19] In *Tancred*, he created a character, Fakredeen, who is an inveterate intriguer, charming, unreliable and utterly unprincipled. 'To dissemble and to simulate; to conduct confidential negotiations with contending powers and parties at the same time; to be ready to adopt any opinion and to possess none; to fall into the public humour of the moment, and to evade the impending catastrophe; to look upon every man as a tool, and never to do anything which had not a definite though circuitous purpose; these were his political accomplishments.'[20] Writing in relaxed mood after his triumph over Peel, he created in Fakredeen a caricature of himself.

His addiction to intrigue contrasts sharply with the evangelical political morality of Liberal Tories. A Machiavellian code of behaviour was characteristic of High Tories; most Machiavellian of Victorian politicians was Palmerston, outwardly a Whig but at heart High Tory, for whom Disraeli had great respect. Disraeli's cunning was not the result of early exposure to the diplomacy of Metternich's Europe but, in part at least, of a youth spent in debt. The connexion between debt and intrigue is made clear in *Tancred*. Fakredeen, says Disraeli, was fond of his debts. 'All my knowledge of human nature is owing to them: it is in managing my affairs that I have sounded the depths of the human heart ... What expedient in negotiation is unknown to me? ... Yes, among my creditors, I have disciplined that diplomatic ability, that shall some day confound and control cabinets.'[21] Little did Benjamin Austen know, as he wearily agreed to advance Disraeli yet another loan, that he was providing a political education for the future Tory leader. In sexual intrigue, too, he learned to dissimulate and manipulate, to lie to his mistresses and cheat their husbands.

Socially, he could be affected, grand and condescending. A cruelly competitive talker, he took pleasure in exposing the stupidity of others and sulked when he was not the centre of attention. Balfour, who knew Disraeli in old age, called him a brazen mask speaking his own novels.[22] Perhaps he never felt at ease in society; perhaps, like Tancred reluctantly mounting the stairs at Deloraine House, it was only pride that prevented him from retreating. The Disraeli whom James Clay or George Smythe, Bulwer or D'Orsay knew was warm-hearted, open and generous. Nor could anyone doubt the warmth of his affection for Isaac or for Sarah.

His mother died in April 1847. A month before she died, when Disraeli made a speech on Cracow, Sarah wrote: 'Mama at last confesses that she never *before* thought Dis was equal to Mr Pitt.' It was too late. Disraeli had never forgiven his mother for not loving him best or recognising his genius, and in her old age he had become indifferent towards her. He barely grieved for her. Isaac died soon after, in January 1848. He had a heart attack while revelling in Lord Hardwicke's account of his interview with George II. ('Ministers are the Kings in this country,' said the unhappy monarch.) Isaac was buried beside Maria in the vault of Bradenham Church.[23] Isaac was eighty-one, he had been blind for seven years, and Disraeli was counting on his patrimony to help pay for Hughenden. Nonetheless, his death was a blow. 'My only consolation for the death of my father is his life,' Disraeli wrote, and in 1848 he composed his affectionate Memoir of Isaac's life. The family home at Bradenham, which Isaac had leased not owned, was broken up, and Sarah retired to a lonely spinster's life in Brighton and Hastings and later Twickenham.[24]

Sarah was his best audience; his letters to her still sparkle, but they slowed to a trickle as her place in his life was taken by Mary Anne. Their marriage had begun cynically enough: Grosvenor Gate, a respectable income, money to pay off his debts, dinner parties and a carriage; all this he had bargained for when he cold-bloodedly set out to woo a rich widow many years his senior. Her disposable wealth turned out to be far less than he expected, though her willingness to pay off his debts to the tune of around £4000 a year kept his creditors at bay. But it was Mary Anne's companionship and counsel, her warmth and mothering that he came to depend upon. No man as vain and hypochondriacal as Disraeli could resist a woman who plied him with pills and prophylactics, who cut his hair and treasured every lock, not to mention every word he wrote, who tiptoed out of bed while the genius slept late in the morning. ('All men of high imagination', he once wrote, 'are *indolent*.') Their marriage was consecrated to his political success; his books were their children. The anniversary verses he wrote her celebrate time and again the connexion between their marriage and his success.

> Beloved wife!
> Onward I feel my way; the breath of fame
> Supports my progress, and the watchful eye
> Of nations nerves my heart – and yet alone,
> Reft of thy still small voice, that gently guides
> And aids with quick perception, I should sink.

And in *Coningsby*, 'It is the Spirit of Man that says "I will be great"; but it is the Sympathy of Woman that usually makes him so.'[25]

Mean rations of sugar, a cold house and sullen servants were a small price for him to pay. He supported Mary Anne during her difficult bouts; when she became tearful, sleepless, overwrought and thin. When her runaway tongue caused raised eyebrows and smothered giggles, Dizzy was fiercely protective; her embarassing remarks were mostly about sex. She was the happiest of women, she announced at breakfast when staying with the Londonderrys, to learn that Lord Hardinge was in the next room, for she had now slept between the greatest orator and the greatest soldier. Stories multiplied about her tale of a naked Venus in a room where she was staying which she endeavoured to hide from Dizzy (why?) by staying awake half the night. Her preoccupation with sex in an age when the subject was taboo stemmed partly from the desire to shock, but it invites speculation about her relations with Dizzy; 'cold in love,' was how she described herself at the time of their marriage. Disraeli made no secret of his intense, emotional relationships with younger men like George Smythe. To avoid the jealous eye of Mary Anne he wrote secretly to Sarah; Sarah greeted him as 'My dear Dis' when she wrote to Grosvenor Gate, 'My dearest' in her secret letters to the Carlton. Disraeli was aware of the political advantages of a reputation for devoted domesticity, but after 1846 a darker side to his marriage emerges.

He tried to bury his rackety Romantic youth. Henrietta Sykes, voluptuous, feckless Henrietta, died on 15 May 1846, the day Disraeli crucified Peel in the House. Rumours about his scandalous relationship with Henrietta and Lyndhurst continued to haunt him, but he did what he could to suppress the scandal. *Vivian Grey, The Young Duke* and *Henrietta Temple* were reissued in the 1850s, carefully pruned of indiscretions and extravagances. The editing was done by Sarah; Disraeli shrank from reading his own works. 'It is worse than masturbation.'[26] In 1846 he turned over his affairs to Philip Rose, who remained his loyal and confidential man of business for life.[27]

'I get duller every day,' Disraeli would remark in his forties. No longer the vulgar dandy, he dressed soberly in a dark frock coat. In summer, a pair of stays could be seen protruding beneath the arms of his thin coat, and tell-tale grey roots occasionally gave away the black dye of his hair and pointed imperial beard.[28] 'What are forty-five or even forty-eight years,' he asks in *Tancred*, 'if a man do not get up too early or go to bed too soon, if he be dressed by the right persons, and, early accustomed to the society of women, he possesses that flexibility of manner, and that readiness of gentle repartee which a feminine apprenticeship can alone confer?'[29]

Yet Disraeli was neither so secure nor so dull as he pretended. Old debts returned to threaten him; financial crises loomed periodically, and his marriage became an unhappy prison. He took refuge in the company of young men and other women, weaving a web of deceit around his affairs.

Depression returned to dog him. After *Tancred*, which appeared in 1847, he wrote no more novels until *Lothair* in 1870. He was never able to do at one time two things which required creative power, he said, and after 1846 his creative energies were absorbed by politics.[30]

Disraeli had spent the first half of his life inventing himself, his career and his political ideas. He made his reputation by smashing Peel and splitting his party. A political adventurer, he achieved advance at the cost of Peel's destruction. After 1846, he lived with the consequences – the exclusion of his party from power for a generation: not until 1874 did the Conservatives win an election. For nearly thirty years after 1846 the imagination, the tenacity and the mental agility he had thrown into the invention of himself was dedicated to the re-invention of the Tory party. That story is the subject of another book.

APPENDIX

A Chronology of Books and Pamphlets by Benjamin Disraeli

1825 *An Inquiry into the Plans, Progress and Policy of the American Mining Companies*, [Anon] (John Murray)
Lawyers and Legislators: or, Notes on the American Mining Companies, [Anon] (John Murray)
The Present State of Mexico: as Detailed in a Report to the General Congress by the Secretary of State for the Home Department and Foreign Affairs, at the Opening of the Session in 1825, [Anon] (John Murray)

1826 *Vivian Grey*, [Anon] (2 vols, Henry Colburn)

1827 *Vivian Grey* Part II, [Anon] (3 vols, Henry Colburn)

1828 *The Voyage of Captain Popanilla*, by the author of *Vivian Grey* (Henry Colburn)

1831 *The Young Duke*, by the author of *Vivian Grey* (3 vols, Henry Colburn and Richard Bentley)

1832 *England and France: or, A Cure for the Ministerial Gallomania*, [Anon] (John Murray)
Contarini Fleming, a Psychological Auto-biography, [Anon] (4 vols, John Murray)

1833 *The Wondrous Tale of Alroy. The Rise of Iskander*, by the author of *Vivian Grey, Contarini Fleming* etc (3 vols, Saunders and Otley)
What Is He?, by the author of *Vivian Grey* (James Ridgway)
Velvet Lawn. A Sketch. Written for the Benefit of the Buckinghamshire Infirmary, by the author of *Vivian Grey* (Wycombe, E. King)

1834 *A Year at Hartlebury, or the Election*, by Cherry and Fair Star (2 vols, Saunders and Otley)
The Revolutionary Epick, the work of Disraeli the Younger, author of *The Psychological Romance* (2 vols, Edward Moxon)

1835 *Vindication of the English Constitution in a Letter to a Noble and Learned Lord*, by Disraeli the Younger (Saunders and Otley)

1836 *The Letters of Runnymede*, [Anon] (John Macrone)

1837 *Henrietta Temple, a Love Story*, by the author of *Vivian Grey* (3 vols, Henry Colburn)
Venetia, by the author of *Vivian Grey* and *Henrietta Temple* (3 vols, Henry Colburn)

1839 *The Tragedy of Count Alarcos*, by the author of *Vivian Grey* (Henry Colburn)
1844 *Coningsby; or, the New Generation*, by B. Disraeli (3 vols, Henry Colburn)
1845 *Sybil: or, the Two Nations*, by B. Disraeli (3 vols, Henry Colburn)
1847 *Tancred: or, the New Crusade*, by B. Disraeli (3 vols, Henry Colburn)
1852 *Lord George Bentinck: a Political Biography*, by B. Disraeli (Henry Colburn)
1870 *Lothair*, by B. Disraeli (3 vols, Longmans)
1880 *Endymion*, by the author of *Lothair* (3 vols, Longmans)

Notes and Sources

The standard collected edition of Disraeli's novels is still the Hughenden edition (11 vols, Longmans, 1881). For *Vivian Grey*, Lucien Wolf's scholarly edition is invaluable (2 vols, Alexander Moring, 1904). Wolf reprinted the original text of the novel, indicating the changes and cuts made in the revised edition of 1853. He also published an edition of *The Young Duke* (Alexander Moring, 1905). This is scarce.

The British Library holds the original edition of *Henrietta Temple* (Henry Colburn, 1837), which was severely pruned in later editions. The newly discovered Disraeli novel, written jointly with Sarah Disraeli and published in 1834 under the pseudonym of Cherry and Fair Star, *A Year at Hartlebury*, was published by John Murray in 1983. Disraeli's General Preface appears as the preface to *Lothair*, which is Volume I in the Longman Collected Edition of 1870–1. *Coningsby* and *Sybil* are available in Oxford World's Classics (Oxford University Press, 1982, 1981), edited by Sheila M. Smith.

Rumpal Stilts Kin, Disraeli's piece of juvenilia, was published by Michael Sadleir in a limited Roxburghe Club edition of sixty-six copies (1952). Sadleir also published an edition of *The Dunciad of Today* (Ingpen and Grant, 1928).

The Revolutionary Epick was reissued by Disraeli in a heavily revised edition (Longman, 1864). Only fifty copies of the original 1834 edition were printed. One of these is in the British Library.

W. Hutcheon (ed.), *Whigs and Whiggism* (John Murray, 1913) is a selection of Disraeli's political writings and journalism, including *What Is He?* (1833), *Vindication of the English Constitution* (1835) and *The Letters of Runnymede* (1836). The Runnymede Letters are also published in *Benjamin Disraeli: Letters* (vol II). The London Library pamphlet collection contains copies of the Mexican mining pamphlets of 1825. *Gallomania* (1832) is in the British Library. *Lord George Bentinck: a Political Biography* was reissued in a photographic reprint (Gregg International, 1969).

For Disraeli's speeches, see T. E. Kebbel, *Selected Speeches of the Late Rt. Hon. the Earl of Beaconsfield* (2 vols, Longman, 1882). *Hansard* is a basic source; speeches in *Hansard* were revised by the speaker; important speeches have therefore been checked against *The Times*.

Disraeli published no memoirs. The unpublished pieces of autobiography which he left in his papers were published by Helen M. Swartz and Marvin Swartz, *Disraeli's Reminiscences* (Hamish Hamilton, 1975). Monypenny and Buckle's *Life* is still an invaluable trove. Disraeli's Memoir of his father Isaac D'Israeli, 'On the Life and Writings of Mr Disraeli [*sic*]', is published as a preface to Isaac D'Israeli's *Curiosities of Literature* (Moxon, vol I, 1849 edn).

There is a bibliography: R.W. Stewart's *Benjamin Disraeli: A List of Writings by him, and Writings about him, with Notes* (Metuchen, N.J., Scarecrow Press (1972)).

The Disraeli Project of Queen's University at Kingston is preparing the definitive edition of his letters. J. A. W. Gunn, John Matthews, Donald M. Schurman, M.G. Wiebe (eds.), *Benjamin Disraeli: Letters*, vol I, 1815–34; vol II, 1835–37 (Toronto, University of Toronto Press, 1982). M. G. Wiebe, J. B. Conacher, John Matthews, Mary S. Millar (eds.), *Benjamin Disraeli: Letters*, vol III, 1838–41 (Toronto, 1987); vol IV, 1842–47 (Toronto, 1989); vol V, 1848–51 (Toronto, 1993).

Two collections of Disraeli's later letters are still useful: Marchioness of Londonderry (ed.), *Letters from Benjamin Disraeli to Frances Anne, Marchioness of Londonderry 1837–61* (Macmillan, 1938); and Marquis of Zetland (ed.), *The Letters of Disraeli to Lady Bradford and Lady Chesterfield* (2 vols, Ernest Benn, 1929).

Abbreviations

M & B   W. F. Monypenny and G. E. Buckle, *The Life of Benjamin Disraeli, Earl of Beaconsfield* (2 vol. edn, John Murray, 1929)

DL   Disraeli's *Letters* (followed by number of letter, unless page number is indicated)

H   Hughenden Papers

Chapter One: Isaac's Library 1804–24

1. M & B, I, 961.
2. Isaac D'Israeli, *Curiosities of Literature* (Edward Moxon, 14th edn, 1849) vol I, 5, 9.
3. Samuel Smiles, *Memoir and Correspondence of the Late John Murray* (John Murray, 1891) vol I, 43–6, 52–3; James Ogden, *Isaac D'Israeli* (Oxford, 1969), 64–5.
4. Benjamin D'Israeli, 'On the Life and Writings of Mr Disraeli', *Curiosities of Literature* (1849 edn), xlv. (Henceforth D's Memoir of Isaac).
5. Isaac D'Israeli, *The Literary Character: or the History of Men of Genius* (Colburn, 1828 edn) vol I, xxxviii; vol II, 220–1.

6. Quoted in Ogden, op. cit., 114–15.
7. ibid., 10–11. See Cecil Roth, *Benjamin Disraeli* (Philosophical Library, New York, 1952), 16.
8. D's Memoir of Isaac, xx–xxi.
9. Disraeli's ancestry was investigated by the Jewish scholar and journalist Lucien Wolf, who published his findings in *The Times* in 1904; the articles were reprinted in *Transactions of the Jewish Historical Society of England*, V (1902–5), 202–18. Wolf's account was revised by Cecil Roth in *Disraeli*, 1–10.
10. D's Memoir of Isaac, xxiii, xxv; M & B, I, 11–12.
11. D's Memoir of Isaac, xxiv; Roth, op. cit., 9.
12. D's Memoir of Isaac, xxv.
13. James Picciotto, *Sketches of Anglo-Jewish History* (Trubner & Co., 1875), 296.
14. Ogden, 194.
15. ibid., 198–9.
16. Paul Johnson, *A History of the Jews* (Weidenfeld & Nicolson, 1987), 300–9.
17. *Coningsby*, Bk IV, ch 15.
18. Picciotto, op. cit., 220–1, 275–6.
19. D's Memoir of Isaac, xxxix, xlii.
20. Ogden, 40–1. See Fiona St Aubyn (ed.) *Ackermann's Illustrated London* (Arrowhead Books, 1985).
21. Wolf, 'The Disraeli Family', *TJHSE*, V, 214–5
22. ibid., 216–7
23. M & B, I, 16; Ogden, 72–3.
24. M & B, I, 15.
25. *Vivian Grey*, Bk I, ch 1.
26. *Contarini Fleming*, Pt I, chs 2, 5.
27. DL, 675, D to Sarah Disraeli, 20 November 1837; M & B, I, 23–4; Wilfrid Meynell, *Benjamin Disraeli. An Unconventional Biography* (Hutchinson, 1903), vol I, 2–8.
28. Picciotto, 297–8. See A. L. Shane, 'Isaac D'Israeli and his Quarrel with the Synagogue – a Reassessment', *Transactions of the Jewish Historical Society of England*, XXIX (1982–6).
29. Picciotto, 299; Roth, 19.
30. John Summerson, *Georgian London* (Penguin edn, 1962), 39–40, 95–6, 313. The interior of the house was remodelled in 1911. Information supplied by Duncan Bull of the *Burlington Magazine*, which currently occupies part of the house.
31. *Vivian Grey*, Bk I, ch 2.
32. M & B, I, 28–9. Richard Jenkyns, *The Victorians and Ancient Greece* (Basil Blackwell, Oxford, 1980).

33. *Vivian Grey*, Bk I, chs 4, 13.
34. *Contarini Fleming*, Pt I, ch 7.
35. M & B, I, 32; *Vivian Grey*, Bk I, ch 6.
36. *Vivian Grey*, Bk I, ch 6; M & B, I, 30, 33.
37. Ogden, 107–8; M & B, I, 32.
38. Ogden, 117. For the Byron legend, see Rupert Christiansen, *Romantic Affinities* (Bodley Head, 1988).
39. Isaac D'Israeli, *The Literary Character*, ch 5.
40. Ogden, 77, 100; *Vivian Grey*, Bk II, ch 1.
41. Ogden, 76–7, 127; *Vivian Grey*, Bk I, ch 8.
42. M & B, I, 41–2. *Vivian Grey*, Bk IV, ch 1.
43. DL, 3, D to John Murray, n.d. [August 1820].
44. M & B, I, 36–7.
45. ibid., 37; *Vivian Grey*, Bk I, ch 7; *Contarini Fleming*, Pt 2, chs 1–2.
46. Benjamin and Sarah Disraeli, *A Year at Hartlebury* (John Murray, 1983), Appendix by John Matthews, 206–7.
47. *Rumpal Stilts Kin* was published by Michael Sadleir in a Roxburghe Club edition (1952).
48. DL, 8, D to John Murray, May 1824; 9, D to Murray, June 1824.
49. William Archer Shee, *My Contemporaries* (Hurst & Blackett, 1893), 54–5.

Chapter Two: Vivian Grey *1824–6*

1. DL, 10, D to Sarah Disraeli, 29 July 1824.
2. C. L. Cline, 'Unfinished Diary of Disraeli's Journey to Flanders and the Rhineland,' *University of Texas Studies in English (Austin)*, XXIII (1943), 105, 108. DL, 11, D to Sarah Disraeli, 2 August 1824.
3. Cline, op. cit., 100.
4. *Vivian Grey*, Bk VI, ch 1.
5. Lucien Wolf's Introduction to *Vivian Grey* (Alexander Moring, 1904), vol I, li–lii.
6. DL, 14, D to Sarah Disraeli, 19 August 1824; *Vivian Grey*, Bk V, ch 12.
7. *Vivian Grey*, Bk VI, ch 3.
8. DL, 15, D to Sarah Disraeli, 23 August 1824; *Vivian Grey*, Bk VII, ch 8.
9. DL, 16, D to Sarah Disraeli, 29 August 1824. See Isaac D'Israeli to Maria and Sarah Disraeli, 29 August 1824, quoted in Sarah Bradford, *Disraeli* (Weidenfeld & Nicolson, 1982), 12.
10. D's 'Mutilated Diary', 1 September 1833, *Letters*, vol I, p. 445.
11. *Vivian Grey*, Bk I, ch 9; Wolf's Introduction, xix.
12. *Vivian Grey*, Bk I, ch 10; M & B, I, 37. See George Steiner, *In Bluebeard's Castle* (Faber, 1971).
13. DL, 21, D to Robert Messer (draft), April 1825. Paul Johnson, *The Birth*

of the Modern (Orion, 1992), ch 11. *The Journal of Mrs Arbuthnot* (eds.) Francis Bamford and the Duke of Wellington (Macmillan, 1950) complements Disraeli's account of the boom and crash of 1825–6.

14. *Vivian Grey*, Bk III, ch 8.
15. DL, 21, D to Robert Messer (draft), April 1825.
16. *Journal of Mrs Arbuthnot*, vol I, 382 (16 March 1825).
17. DL, 20, D to John Murray, 1 April 1825.
18. DL, 21, D to Robert Messer (draft), April 1825.
19. *Journal of Mrs Arbuthnot*, vol I, 354 (11 November 1825).
20. 'Lawyers and Legislators' was published anonymously, but Disraeli could not resist the opportunity to give himself a puff. The last sentence reads: 'These sentiments come not from one who sits in Royal Councils, or mingles in the assemblies of legislative wisdom, but they come from one who has had some opportunity of investigation, some patience for inquiry, whose opinions are unbiassed by self interest, and uncontrouled [*sic*] by party influence, who, whatever may be the result, will some satisfaction, perchance some pride, that at a time when wavering and inconsistent councils were occasioning the very ruin which they affected to deprecate, when Ignorance was the ready slave of Interest, and Truth was deserted by those who should have been her stoutest champions, there was at least one attempt to support sounder principles, and inculcate a wiser policy.' (98–9).
21. DL, 21, D to Robert Messer (draft), April 1825.
22. DL, 22, D to John Murray, May 1825; 23, D to Murray, May 1825.
23. ibid., 26, 17 September 1825. Disraeli stored the Carnival of the North in his memory, describing it four years later in *The Young Duke*, which is partly set in Yorkshire.
24. ibid., 27, 18 September 1825.
25. *Vivian Grey*, Bk III, ch 1.
26. DL, 28, D to John Murray, 21 September 1825.
27. Scott's library at Abbotsford contains the following books by Isaac: *Literary and Political Character of James I* (1816); *Calamities of Authors* (1812); *Quarrels of Authors* (1814); *Literary Character* (1822 edn). (Information supplied by Fiona Campbell.) Helen M. Swartz and Marvin Swartz, *Disraeli's Reminiscences* (Hamish Hamilton, 1975), 9.
28. Smiles, op. cit., vol II, 193–5.
29. Murray's letter of recommendation is quoted in Bradford, op. cit., 14. H. J. C. Grierson (ed.), *Letters of Sir Walter Scott*, (Constable, 1935), vol IX, 245, Scott to W. Stewart Rose, 12 October 1825.
30. Andrew Lang, *Life and Letters of J. G. Lockhart* (John C. Nimmo, 1897), vol I, 368, William Wright to J. G. Lockhart, 3 October 1825. Disraeli,

continued Wright, 'has never had to struggle with a single difficulty ... At present his chief exertions as to matters of decision have been with regard to the selection of his food, his enjoyment, and his clothing, and though he is honest, and, I take it, wiser than his father, he is inexperienced and untried ...'

31. DL, 40, D to Lockhart, 23 November 1825.
32. Smiles, vol II, 198–9.
33. DL, 36, D to Lockhart, 12 November 1825.
34. *Vivian Grey*, Bk IV, ch 1.
35. Charles C. Nickerson, 'Disraeli, Lockhart and Murray: an Episode in the History of the "Quarterly Review" ', *Victorian Studies*, vol 15 (1972), 290–5. Miron Brightfield's *John Wilson Croker* (Allen and Unwin, 1940), 182–94, makes an unconvincing attempt to exonerate Croker.
36. *Disraeli's Reminiscences*, 10. Johnson, *Birth of the Modern*, 895–901.
37. DL, 37, D to Lockhart, 21 November 1825. See W. E. K. Anderson (ed.) *Journal of Sir Walter Scott* (Oxford, 1972), 15–17, 27 November 1825.
38. DL, 38, D to Lockhart, 22 November 1825.
39. ibid., 41, 24 November 1825.
40. ibid., 42, 25 November 1825.
41. Smiles, vol II, 225–6; Lockhart to Murray, 27 November 1825.
42. *Vivian Grey*, Bk V, ch 14.
43. Nickerson, op. cit., 305.
44. *Reminiscences*, 145–6. Rose Papers, I/C/3, Rose's Memorandum, 28 October 1871.
45. Murray to Sharon Turner, 16 October 1825, quoted in Robert Blake, *Disraeli* (Eyre and Spottiswoode, 1966), 47.
46. *Vivian Grey*, Bk IV, ch 4.
47. Wilfred S. Dowden ed., *Journal of Thomas Moore* (University of Delaware, 1986), vol III, 1236, 22 July 1829.
48. DL, 1802, D to Richard Wright, 18 March 1849; and note.
49. M & B, I, 83. For *Tremaine*, see Alison Adburgham, *Silver Fork Society* (Constable, 1983).
50. *Vivian Grey*, Bk II, ch 10.
51. *Contarini Fleming*, Pt II, ch 12.
52. B. R. Jerman, *The Young Disraeli* (Princeton, New Jersey, 1960), 51–2.
53. ibid., 53; Sir Henry Layard, *Autobiography and Memoirs* (John Murray, 1905), vol I, 49.
54. *Vivian Grey*, Bk I, ch 9.
55. ibid., Bk II, ch 2.
56. ibid., ch 17.

57. See Lucien Wolf's perceptive Introduction, xxxv.
58. Elie Halévy, *The Liberal Awakening* (1961 edn), 188.
59. *Vivian Grey*, Bk II, chs 1, 13, 15.
60. E. J. Stapleton, *Some Official Correspondence of George Canning* (Longmans, Green & Co., 1887), vol I, 377–8.
61. *Vivian Grey*, Bk IV, chs 1, 2.
62. ibid., Bk III, ch 5.
63. H/A/IV/A/13, Meredith to D, n.d. [1826].
64. Benjamin Disraeli, *The Dunciad of Today* (ed.) Michael Sadleir (Ingpen and Grant, 1928). Sadleir makes a convincing case for Disraeli's authorship. The manuscript of the *Star Chamber*, together with correspondence, is preserved in the Rose Papers in the Bodleian Library, (R/II/C/17 a). Why Disraeli persisted in insisting that he 'never had anything whatever to do with it' remains a mystery (see Rose's Memorandum, 28 October 1871, Rose/I/C/3). See also R. W. Stewart, *Benjamin Disraeli: A List of Writings* ... (Metuchen, N.J., Scarecrow Press, 1972), 116–20.
65. Jerman, 65; Wolf, Introduction, xliv–v.
66. DL, 48, n.4, Maria D'Israeli to John Murray, 21 May 1826.
67. M & B, I, 79.
68. R. W. Stewart, 'The Publication and Reception of Disraeli's *Vivian Grey*', *Quarterly Review*, vol 298 (1960), 414.
69. *Blackwood's Magazine*, vol xx, (July 1826), 98.
70. R. W. Steward (ed.) *Disraeli's Novels Reviewed* (Scarecrow Press, Metuchen, N.J., 1975), 115–18. In *Contarini* Disraeli claimed that he was savaged by 'the great critical journal of the north of Europe', i.e. *Blackwood's*, but the *Literary Magnet* was far more abusive.
71. *Contarini Fleming*, Pt II, ch 8.
72. The letter was deciphered by R. W. Stewart, '*Vivian Grey*', *Quarterly Review*, vol 298, 414.
73. DL, 49, D to Benjamin Austen, July 1826.
74. *Vivian Grey*, Bk III, ch 1.
75. Disraeli, *Dunciad*, 55.
76. *Endymion*, ch 2.

Chapter Three: Nervous Breakdown 1826–30

1. Wolf (ed.), *Vivian Grey*, Bk V, ch 2.
2. DL, 50, D to Isaac D'Israeli, 9 August 1826.
3. *Vivian Grey*, Bk VII, ch 7; Jerman, 75–7; Bradford, 27.
4. *Contarini Fleming*, Pt III, ch 1. See also Disraeli's 1826 travel diary, H/A/III/C.
5. DL, 51, D to Isaac D'Israeli, 21 August 1826.

6. ibid., 52, 2 September 1826.
7. ibid.
8. *Contarini Fleming*, Pt III, ch 1; DL, 52.
9. DL, 58, D to Sarah Disraeli, 15 October 1826.
10. DL, 53, D to Isaac D'Israeli, 13 September 1826.
11. ibid., 54, 26 September 1826.
12. ibid., 55, 29 September 1826.
13. ibid., 56, 29 September 1826; Roth, 29–30.
14. DL 55, D to Isaac D'Israeli, 29 September 1826.
15. ibid., 56, 29 September 1826; *Contarini Fleming*, Pt IV, ch 1.
16. DL 57, D to Isaac D'Israeli, 10 October 1826.
17. DL, 58, D to Sarah D'Israeli, 15 October 1826.
18. H/A/IV/D/21, Sara Austen to Disraeli, 1826; *Contarini Fleming*, Pt IV, ch 2.
19. D. Hudson (ed.), *Diary of Henry Crabb Robinson* (Oxford University Press, 1967), 198; M & B, I, 116; Carola Oman (ed.) *The Gascoyne Heiress* (Hodder & Stoughton, 1968), 61; *Journal of Sir Walter Scott*, 314, 11 June 1827.
20. Daniel R. Schwarz, *Disraeli's Fiction* (Macmillan, 1979), 21; *Contarini Fleming*, Pt IV, ch 2; *The Letters of Robert Browning and Elizabeth Barrett Browning* (Smith, Elder, 1899), vol I, 52.
21. *Vivian Grey*, Bk V, ch 1.
22. ibid., vol II, Bk VI, ch 4.
23. ibid., ch 6.
24. ibid., ch 7.
25. The manuscript is in the Hughenden Papers, H/E/V/A/2.
26. DL, 61, D to John Murray, 19 March 1827.
27. *Contarini Fleming*, Pt IV, ch 4.
28. DL, 63, D to Benjamin Austen, 14 July 1827.
29. DL, 64, D to Thomas Evans, 3 January 1828.
30. DL, 66, D to Sharon Turner, 10 March 1828.
31. DL, 67R, D to T. J. Pettigrew, 19 March 1828.
32. M & B, I, 120; *Popanilla*, ch 13.
33. DL, 1521, D to Philip Rose, 25 October 1846.
34. See Janet Oppenheim, '*Shattered Nerves*', (Oxford University Press, New York, 1991), 166–8; *Contarini Fleming*, Pt IV, ch 6.
35. *Vivian Grey*, Bk V, ch 7.
36. ibid., ch 15.
37. H/A/IV/D/24, Sara Austen to Disraeli, 9 April 1828; H/A/IV/D/25, Sara Austen to D, 15 April 1828; DL, 58, D to Sarah Disraeli, 15 October 1826; Stanley Weintraub, *Disraeli* (Hamish Hamilton, 1993), 76–80.
38. DL, 66, D to Sharon Turner, 10 March 1828.

39. H/A/IV/D/24, Sara Austen to D, 9 April 1828.
40. H/E/V/A/1, MSS of *Aylmer Papillon*.
41. *Popanilla*, ch 4.
42. ibid., ch 6.
43. ibid., ch 10.
44. Schwarz, op. cit., 79–80.
45. I. D'Israeli, *Commentaries on the Life and Reign of Charles I* (Colburn, 1828), vol I, xiii.
46. Stewart, op. cit., 130–1.
47. H/A/IV/D/26, Sara Austen to D, 18 August 1828; H/A/IV/A/15, William Meredith to D, 2 December 1828.
48. M & B, I, 120.
49. ibid., 124; H/A/IV/C, Note by Philip Rose, July–August 1882.
50. DL, 72, note 1; Ogden, 155–6; DL, 214, D to Samuel Carter Hall, [23 September 1832]. Today's Bradenham hams, the famous black ones, bear no relation to Isaac's. They are cured in Chippenham, Wilts, and Bradenham is the name of the firm.
51. H/A/IV/E/4, Isaac D'Israeli to D, 30 June 1830.
52. Meynell, op. cit., vol I, 24.
53. *Endymion*, ch 15.
54. H/A/IV/D/26, Sara Austen to D, 18 August 1828.
55. Ellen Moers, *The Dandy* (Secker & Warburg, 1960), 12–13, 18–19, 74–82.
56. H/B/XX/Ly/1, E. Lytton Bulwer to D, 19 February 1829. See Edward Robert Lord Lytton, *The Life, Letters and Literary Remains of Edward Bulwer, Lord Lytton By His Son* (Kegan Paul, 1883), vol II, 316.
57. DL, 75, note 3.
58. H/B/XX/Ly/2, E. Lytton Bulwer to D, 26 July 1829.
59. Moers, op. cit., 71–2; *Endymion*, ch 37; Michael Sadleir, *Bulwer: A Panorama* (Constable, 1931); C. R. Sanders, K. J. Fielding, C. D. Ryals, *The Collected Letters of Thomas and Jane Welsh Carlyle* (Duke University Press, Durham, vol 11, 1985), 49.
60. Jerman, 92–3; M & B, I, 132, n.
61. DL, 72, D to Benjamin Austen, 23 November 1829.
62. ibid., 74, 8 December 1829; and n. 3; H. J. Hanham, *The Nineteenth-Century Constitution* (Cambridge University Press, 1969), 134–5; Marquis of Zetland (ed.) *Letters of Disraeli to Lady Bradford and Lady Chesterfield* (Ernest Benn, 1929), vol I, 135. The *Letters* editors conjecture that Disraeli wished to buy an estate in Stockton in Warwickshire; Stockton, Wiltshire seems more likely in view of his later recollection about negotiations for Hindon.
63. DL, 74, D to Benjamin Austen, 8 December 1829; Weintraub, op. cit., 87.

64. DL, 75, D to Catherine Gore, 14 February 1830. In her novel *Cecil, or the Adventures of a Coxcomb* (1841), Gore quoted Disraeli's epigram in an improved form. Disraeli incorporated her version in *Coningsby*, where Sidonia says, 'Youth is a blunder; Manhood a struggle; Old Age a regret'.
65. DL, 76, D to Henry Colburn, 14 February 1830.
66. M & B, I, 127.
67. DL, 78, D to Sara Austen, 7 March 1830; Blake, 76–7.
68. M & B, I, 128–9.
69. *The Young Duke*, Bk I, ch 1.
70. ibid., ch 10.
71. H/B/XXI/C/240, James Clay to D, 21 December 1831.
72. *The Young Duke*, Bk IV, ch 8.
73. *Letters ... to Lady Bradford and Lady Chesterfield*, vol I, 113.
74. DL, 1462, D to Richard Bentley, 26 January 1846; and note.
75. See Jerman, 94–102; H/A/IV/E/19, Isaac D'Israeli to D, 4 April 1831.
76. *The Young Duke*, Bk II, ch 7.
77. ibid., Bk III, ch 18.
78. ibid., Bk IV, ch 3.
79. ibid., Bk III, ch 18.
80. ibid., Bk V, ch 6.
81. H/B/XX/Ly/4, E. Lytton Bulwer to D, 10 April 1830. See Sadleir, *Bulwer*, 188.
82. H/B/XX/Ly/5, E. Lytton Bulwer to D, 14 April 1830; DL, 81, D to Benjamin Austen, 13 April 1830.
83. DL, 86, D to Murray, 27 May 1830.
84. DL, 84, D to Evans, 9 May 1830; 87, D to Thomas Jones, 28 May 1830.

Chapter Four: The Great Asian Mystery 1830–1

1. Jerman, 108–9.
2. DL, 90 and 91, D to Isaac D'Israeli, 1 July 1830.
3. Donald Sultana, *Benjamin Disraeli in Spain, Malta and Albania* (Tamesis Books, 1976), 23; Bradford, 35.
4. H/A/IV/E/4, Isaac D'Israeli to D, 30 June 1830; Sarah Disraeli to D, 28 July 1830, quoted in Sultana, 22; DL, 92, D to Isaac D'Israeli, 14 July 1830.
5. DL, 91, D to Isaac D'Israeli, 1 July 1830; 92, D to Isaac D'Israeli, 14 July 1830; 97, D to Isaac D'Israeli, 25 August 1830.
6. Sultana, 19; DL, 92, n. 10.
7. Herbert Maxwell quoted in Viscount Chilston, *Chief Whip* (Routledge and Kegan Paul, 1961), 16.
8. DL, 93, D to Isaac D'Israeli, 26 July 1830; 95, D to Sarah Disraeli, 9

August 1830; *Contarini Fleming*, Pt V, ch 3. DL, 95, D to Sarah Disraeli, 9 August 1830.

9. DL, 97, D to Isaac D'Israeli, 25 August 1830; *Contarini Fleming*, Pt V, ch 1.
10. DL, 94, D to Maria D'Israeli, 1 August 1830.
11. Sarah Disraeli to D, 3 September 1830, quoted in Sultana, 33.
12. DL, 95, D to Sarah Disraeli, 9 August 1830; 98, D to Benjamin Austen, 14 September 1830.
13. M & B, I, 152–3; DL, 1395, D to R. S. Mackenzie, 26 February 1845.
14. H/A/IV/E/8, Sarah and Isaac D'Israeli to D, 3 September 1830.
15. DL, 97, D to Isaac D'Israeli, 25 August 1830.
16. DL, 99, D to Ralph Disraeli, 17 September 1830; Sir William Gregory, *Autobiography* (John Murray, 1894), 96; Sultana, 37.
17. H/A/IV/E/9, Sarah Disraeli to D, 2 October 1830; DL, 98, D to Benjamin Austen, 14 September 1830.
18. Robert Blake, *Disraeli's Grand Tour* (Weidenfeld & Nicolson, 1982), 19.
19. DL, 99, D to Ralph Disraeli, 17 September 1830.
20. DL, 98, D to Benjamin Austen, 14 September 1830.
21. Blake, *Disraeli's Grand Tour*, 29–33; DL, 103, D to Benjamin Austen, 18 November 1830. See Stanford J. Shaw and Ezel Kural Shaw, *History of the Ottoman Empire and Modern Turkey* (Cambridge University Press, 1977), vol 2, 29–34.
22. DL, 100, D to Isaac D'Israeli, 10 October 1830; 103, D to Benjamin Austen, 18 November 1830.
23. DL, 100, D to Isaac D'Israeli, 10 October 1830.
24. *Contarini Fleming*, Pt V, ch 10.
25. DL, 101, D to Isaac D'Israeli, 25 October 1830.
26. ibid.; *Contarini Fleming*, Pt V, ch 11.
27. DL, 101, D to Isaac D'Israeli, 25 October 1830 and n. 8; *Contarini Fleming*, Pt V, ch 12; Sultana, 57.
28. DL, 101, D to Isaac D'Israeli, 25 October 1830.
29. DL, 103, D to Benjamin Austen, 18 November 1830. There may be links between Jewishness and being pro-Turk. In 1876, when the Turks massacred the Bulgarian Christians, Disraeli as Prime Minister upheld the Turks in the face of furious public agitation. Liberal critics alleged that Disraeli was pro-Turk because he was Jewish. The Turks were the natural allies of the Jews, they alleged. The Christians of the East persecuted the Jews, but in the Turkish Empire the Jews, who were servants of the Empire, were favoured over the Christians. None of this emerges, however, from Disraeli's letters in 1830–1. See David Feldman, *Englishmen and Jews* (Yale University Press, 1994), 101–2.
30. DL, 101, D to Isaac D'Israeli, 25 October 1830.
31. H/A/IV/E/11, Sarah Disraeli to D, 4 December 1830.
32. DL, 103, D to Benjamin Austen, 18 November 1830.

33. DL, 104, D to Isaac D'Israeli, 30 November 1830.
34. DL, 103, D to Benjamin Austen, 18 November 1830; *Contarini Fleming*, Pt V, ch 19. See Richard Jenkyns, op. cit., 14–15.
35. DL, 104, D to Isaac D'Israeli, 30 November 1830.
36. Disraeli, *The Revolutionary Epick* (Longman, 1864), Preface to the original edn, 1834, viii.
37. DL, 105, D to Isaac D'Israeli, 23 December 1830.
38. HA/A/IV/E/11, Sarah Disraeli to D, 4 December 1830.
39. DL, 109, D to Isaac D'Israeli, 11 January 1831; *Contarini Fleming*, Pt V, ch 24.
40. DL, 107, D to E. Lytton Bulwer, 27 December 1830.
41. H/A/IV/E/11, Sarah Disraeli to D, 4 December 1830; Blake, *Disraeli's Grand Tour*, 62.
42. DL, 109, D to Isaac D'Israeli, 11 January 1831; H/A/IV/E/17, Sarah Disraeli to D, 25 February 1831.
43. DL, 109, D to Isaac D'Israeli, 11 January 1831; *Contarini Fleming*, Pt V, ch 25.
44. DL, 110, D to Sarah Disraeli, 20 March 1831.
45. *Contarini Fleming*, Pt VI, ch 2.
46. DL, 110, D to Sarah Disraeli, 20 March 1831; *Contarini Fleming*, Pt VI, ch 4.
47. DL, 110, D to Sarah Disraeli, 20 March 1831; *Alroy*, note 35; Blake, *Disraeli's Grand Tour*, 69.
48. Blake, *Disraeli's Grand Tour*, 71–4, 106.
49. *Tancred*, Bk IV, ch 3.
50. DL, 110, D to Sarah Disraeli, 20 March 1831.
51. ibid., 111, 28 May 1831.
52. ibid., H/A/IV/E/17, Isaac D'Israeli to D, 25 February 1831.
53. Disraeli, *Whigs and Whiggism* (John Murray, 1913), 169–72.
54. Revel Guest and Angela V. John, *Lady Charlotte* (Weidenfeld & Nicolson, 1989), 149–50.
55. DL, I, Appendix III, Mutilated Diary, 1833; *Contarini Fleming*, Pt VI, ch 7; H/A/IV/F/1, Botta to D, 3 December 1831.
56. H/A/IV/F/2, Botta to D, July 1832.
57. DL, 111, D to Sarah Disraeli, 28 May 1831; *Contarini Fleming*, Pt VI, ch 12.
58. H/A/IV/E/22, Sarah Disraeli to D, 6 June 1831.
59. H/A/IV/E/23, Sarah Disraeli to D, 1 August 1831.
60. DL, 112, D to Isaac D'Israeli, 20 July 1831; *Contarini Fleming*, Pt III, chs 19, 20.
61. The physician's report and Disraeli's notes on it are in DL, 113, n. 3.
62. DL, 114, D to Sarah Disraeli, 20 July 1831.

Chapter Five: 'I am for myself' 1831–2

1. DL, 117, D to Isaac D'Israeli, 23 October 1831.
2. DL, 119, D to Georgiana Meredith, 3 November 1831; 137, D to Georgiana Meredith, 11 February 1832.
3. *Alroy* (1845 edn), Pt I, ch 1; Pt VII, ch 11.
4. DL, 124, D to Sarah Disraeli, 12 November 1831.
5. ibid., 126, 14 November 1831; ibid., 127, 15 November 1831.
6. C. L. Cline, 'Disraeli and Peel's 1841 Cabinet', *Journal of Modern History*, XI (1939); Blake, *Disraeli*, 71–3.
7. H/B/XXI/C/240, James Clay to D, 21 December 1831.
8. *Contarini Fleming*, Pt IV, ch 2; Stewart, 136, 138; T. Pinney (ed.), *Letters of T. B. Macaulay* (Cambridge University Press, 1974), vol II, 37.
9. DL, 117, D to Isaac D'Israeli, 23 October 1831.
10. DL, 151, n. 1, H. H. Milman to John Murray, 5 March 1832.
11. *Contarini Fleming*, Pt IV, ch 5.
12. Schwarz, 31.
13. *Contarini Fleming*, Pt I, ch 21.
14. Edith J. Morley (ed.), *Henry Crabb Robinson on Books and their Writers* (J. M. Dent, 1938), vol II, 575; J. W. Warter (ed.), *Selections from the Letters of Robert Southey* (Longman, 1856), vol IV, 264.
15. *Contarini Fleming*, Pt I, ch 23.
16. ibid., Pt II, chs 9, 13.
17. ibid., Pt VII, chs 1, 2.
18. DL, 143, D to John Murray, 26 February 1832.
19. S. Smiles, vol. II, 335–8.
20. DL, 132, D to Benjamin Austen, 6 January 1832; 148, D to John Murray, 4 March 1832; 155, D to Benjamin Austen, 19 March 1832.
21. DL, 146, D to Sarah Disraeli, 1 March 1832; Jerman, 147. See Maurice Edelman, *Disraeli in Love* (Collins, 1972), ch 1. DL, 1802, note.
22. H/A/IV/E/17, Sarah Disraeli to D, 25 February 1831.
23. DL, 165, D to Sarah Disraeli, 31 March 1832; 173, D to Sarah Disraeli, 7 April 1832.
24. ibid., 126, 14 November 1831; 163, D to John Murray, 30 March 1832.
25. Miron Brightfield, op. cit., 238–9; Bradford, 46; *Crabb Robinson on Books*, II, 575; DL, 179, D to Sarah Disraeli, 14 April 1832.
26. Bradford, 48; DL, 146, D to Sarah Disraeli, 1 March 1832; 159, D to Sarah Disraeli, 26 March 1832; 165, D to Sarah Disraeli, 31 March 1832.
27. DL, 169, D to Sarah Disraeli, 2 April 1832.
28. DL, 172, D to Mary Anne Lewis, 6 April 1832.
29. Louisa Devey, *Life of Rosina, Lady Lytton* (1887), 411–12.
30. DL, 126, D to Sarah Disraeli, 14 November 1831; Paul H. Emden, *The Money Powers of Europe* (1937), 86–90.
31. DL, 140, D to Sarah Disraeli, 20 February 1832.

32. M & B, I, 210; DL, 141, D to Sarah Disraeli, 22 February 1832; 142, D to Sarah Disraeli, 24 February 1832.
33. *England and France; or a Cure for the Ministerial Gallomania* (John Murray, 1832), vii, 27. *Endymion*, ch 7.
34. *Gallomania*, 7, 34.
35. ibid., 13. J. M. Roberts, *The Mythology of the Secret Societies* (Secker & Warburg, 1972).
36. *Gallomania*, 43–6.
37. DL, 1265, D to Sarah Disraeli, 7 November 1842, n. 17.
38. DL, 163, D to John Murray, 30 March 1832; 167, D to J. W. Croker, 1 April 1832.
39. DL, 152, D to Sarah Disraeli, 9 March 1832.
40. ibid., 179, 14 April 1832.
41. General Preface (Longman, 1870), xix.
42. Stewart, 138–40; DL, D to Sarah Disraeli, 15 May 1832, n. 6.
43. C. L. Cline, 'The Failure of Disraeli's "Contarini Fleming"', *Notes and Queries*, 1 August 1942.
44. DL, 193, D to Sarah Disraeli, 26 May 1832; 194, D to Sarah Disraeli, 28 May 1832; F. L. Jones (ed.) *Letters of Mary W. Shelley* (University of Oklahoma, 1944), vol II, 62.
45. DL, 192, D to Sarah Disraeli, 24 May 1832; 193, D to Sarah Disraeli, 26 May 1832; Sir William Fraser, *Disraeli and his Day* (Kegan Paul, 1891), 187.
46. DL, 142, D to Sarah Disraeli, 24 February 1832; Bradford, 49–50.
47. DL, 195, D to Sarah Disraeli, 29 May 1832.
48. DL, 133, D to Benjamin Austen, 19 January 1832; 142, D to Sarah Disraeli, 24 February 1832; 190, D to Sarah Disraeli, 18 May 1832; Bradford, 54.
49. M & B, I, 215; Bradford, 56–7.
50. DL, 198, D to Benjamin Austen, 2 June 1832.
51. L. J. Ashford, *History of the Borough of High Wycombe* (Routledge & Kegan Paul, 1960), 247–62; W. B. Pope (ed.), *Diary of Benjamin Robert Haydon* (Harvard University Press, Cambridge, Massachusetts, vol IV, 1963), 63.
52. M & B, I, 218; Benjamin and Sarah Disraeli, *Hartlebury*, vol I, ch 20; DL, 201, D to Sara Austen, 10 June 1832.
53. C. L. Cline, 'Disraeli at High Wycombe: the Beginning of a Great Political Career', *University of Texas Studies in English*, vol XXII (1942); DL, 201, D to Sara Austen, 10 June 1832, n. 6.
54. DL, 202, n. 4, Bulwer to D, 11 June 1832.
55. DL, 169, D to Sarah Disraeli, 2 April 1832; 203, editorial comment; 219, D to *The Times*, 11 November 1832.
56. DL, 215, Address to the Electors of Wycombe, 1 October 1832.

57. DL, 216, D to Benjamin Austen, 6 October 1832.
58. Ashford, op. cit., 263–7.
59. *Hartlebury*, vol II, ch 1.
60. M & B, I, 222–3.
61. *Hartlebury*, vol II, ch 7.
62. Because Wycombe was a two-member borough, voters had the right to vote for two candidates, or 'plump' and cast only one vote. Whig voters gave one vote each to the two Whigs, Smith and Grey, who received respectively seven and one plumper. Disraeli, on the other hand, had 85 plumpers – he was the only anti-Whig candidate, and few voters chose to divide their support between Disraeli and the Whigs.
63. DL, 221, Address to Electors of County of Bucks, 12 December 1832.

Chapter Six: Henrietta 1832–4

1. DL, 224, D to J. G. Lockhart, 22 December 1832; 227, D to J. G. Lockhart, 1 January 1833; 239, D to Macvey Napier, 23 February 1833.
2. Andrew Lang, op. cit., vol II, 199–200.
3. D's Preface to 1845 edn of *Alroy*. The lengthy Notes printed at the end give references and extracts from Disraeli's reading.
4. DL, 209, D to Sarah Disraeli, 4 August 1832.
5. *Alroy*, Pt I, ch 2; DL, vol I, Mutilated Diary.
6. *Alroy*, Pt V, ch 4.
7. ibid., Pt VIII, ch 1.
8. Weintraub, 141–2; *Crabb Robinson on Books*, vol II, 421; I. Ker and T. Gornall (eds.), *Letters and Diaries of J. H. Newman* (Clarendon Press, Oxford, 1979), vol II, 110, Newman to Jemima Newman, 14 December 1828.
9. *Alroy*, Pt X, ch 22. See *Lord George Bentinck*, ch 24.
10. John Vincent, *Disraeli* (OUP, 1990), 68–70; Schwarz, 42–51.
11. Schwarz, 45; *Alroy*, Pt I, ch 1; Pt VIII, ch 4; Pt IX, ch 2.
12. DL, 228, D to Sarah Disraeli, 12 January 1833.
13. ibid., 229, 18 January 1833.
14. ibid., 230, 24 January 1833; DL, vol I, Mutilated Diary.
15. DL, 231, D to Sarah Disraeli, 29 January 1833; 233, D to Sarah Disraeli, 7 February 1833.
16. ibid., 243, 6 March 1833; 255, D to Helen Blackwood, 18 March 1833; Stewart, 17; DL, 1656, n.
17. *Letters to Lady Bradford and Lady Chesterfield*, vol II, 9; DL, 257, D to Sarah Disraeli, 26 March 1833.
18. DL, 253, n., Beckford to George Clarke, 14 March 1833; J. W. Oliver, *Life of William Beckford* (Oxford University Press, 1932), 298–9.
19. Alan Chedzoy, *A Scandalous Woman* (Allison & Busby, 1992), 54–5; DL,

234, D to Sarah Disraeli, 14 February 1833; M & B, I, 235–6.

20. DL, 235, D to Helen Blackwood, 16 February 1833; 240, D to Helen Blackwood, 23 February 1833; 244, D to Helen Blackwood, 7 March 1833.
21. ibid., 249, 10 March 1833; 255, 18 March 1833.
22. See Chedzoy, op. cit., Philip Ziegler, *Melbourne* (Collins, 1987 edn), 228.
23. M & B, I, 258–9; *Diary of B. R. Haydon*, vol IV, 50–1, 58.
24. DL, 248, D's Address to the Electors of Marylebone, 9 March 1833; 250, D's Address to the Electors of Marylebone, 12 March 1833; 255, D to Helen Blackwood, 18 March 1833.
25. DL, 251, D to Sarah Disraeli, 14 March 1833; 254, D to George Dashwood, 18 March 1833.
26. *What Is He?* is printed in Hutcheon, *Whigs and Whiggism* (John Murray, 1913), 16–22.
27. DL, 262, D to Sarah Disraeli, 8 April 1833.
28. ibid., 209, 4 August 1832; Stewart, 17–18.
29. DL, 263 n, W. J. Fox to D, 11 April 1833; 268, D to Sarah Disraeli, 25 April 1833; 269, D to Sarah Disraeli, 30 April 1833.
30. Oliver, op. cit., 301; DL, 265, n., Helen Blackwood to D, u.d.; 265, D to Helen Blackwood, 17 April 1833.
31. DL, vol I, Mutilated Diary.
32. Blake, *Disraeli*, 95–7; Reverend J. Richardson, *Recollections* (C. Mitchell, 1856), vol I, 180–5; National Trust, *Guide to Basildon Park*; DL, 267, D to Sarah Disraeli, 23 April 1833.
33. DL, 339, D to Sarah Disraeli, 16 July 1835.
34. ibid., 269, 30 April 1833; *Henrietta Temple*, Bk IV, ch 5.
35. *Lady Morgan's Memoirs* (W. H. Allen, 1862), vol II, 365.
36. DL, 270, D to Sarah Disraeli, April 1833; 282, D to Benjamin Austen, 24 June 1833.
37. *Henrietta Temple*, Bk 2, ch 4.
38. DL, 276, D to Sarah Disraeli, 5 June 1833; Bradford, 63–4.
39. DL, 273, D to Sarah Disraeli, 22 May 1833; 286, D to Sarah Disraeli, 26 July 1833. Revel Guest and Angela V. John, op. cit., 17–21.
40. DL, 275, D to Sarah Disraeli, 3 June 1833; 277, D to Sarah Disraeli, 7 June 1833. *Hartlebury*, vol I, ch 17; Weintraub, 147–8.
41. DL, 288, D to Sarah Disraeli, 10 August 1833; Blake, *Disraeli*, 99.
42. Henrietta's letters printed in Blake, *Disraeli*, 100, 103.
43. Jerman, 192, 200–1; Blake, *Disraeli*, 102–3.
44. DL, vol I, Mutilated Diary.
45. Blake, *Disraeli*, 105.
46. *Hartlebury*, vol I, ch 14.
47. ibid., vol I, ch 14; vol II, ch 1.
48. See Vincent, op. cit., 73–4.

49. *Hartlebury*, Appendix 1 (by John Matthews), 202–11.
50. DL, 304, D to Sarah Disraeli, 14 January 1834; and note.
51. DL, 296, D to Benjamin Austen, 30 November 1833; 300, D to Richard Bentley, 31 December 1833.
52. DL, 306, D to Sarah Disraeli, 29 January 1834.
53. ibid., 290, 12 November 1833; 291, 15 November 1833; Bradford, 69.
54. DL, 296, D to Benjamin Austen, 30 November 1833.
55. DL, 297, D to Sara Austen, 1 December 1833; 298, D to Benjamin Austen, 3 December 1833; 298, n., Benjamin Austen to D, 1 December 1833.
56. DL, 302, n. 1; 306, D to Sarah Disraeli, 29 January 1834.
57. DL, 307, D to Sarah Disraeli, 13 February 1834; 308, D to Sarah Disraeli, 17 February 1834.
58. *Victoria History of the Counties of England. A History of Essex* (Archibald Constable, 1907), vol II, 576.
59. DL, 290, D to Sarah Disraeli, 12 November 1833; 297, D to Sara Austen, 1 December 1833; 305, D to Sarah Disraeli, 25 January 1834.
60. DL, 297, D to Sara Austen, 1 December 1833.
61. ibid.
62. DL, 303, n., quoting Henry Layard in the *Quarterly Review*, 1889.
63. *Revolutionary Epick*, Bk I, Canto XXXII. References are taken from the original 1834 edition.
64. ibid., Canto XXXVIII.
65. ibid., Bk II, Canto XII. The last three lines are cut from the 1864 edition.
66. ibid., Bk I, Canto XLIV.

Chapter Seven: Lord Lyndhurst's Friend 1834–6

1. DL, 319, D to Benjamin Austen, 24 May 1834.
2. DL, 314, D to Sarah Disraeli, 11 March 1834; DL, vol I, Mutilated Diary.
3. *Diary of B. R. Haydon*, vol IV, 263. See Michael Sadleir, *Blessington D'Orsay* (Constable, 1933); Ernest J. Lovell, Jr., (ed.), *Lady Blessington's Conversations with Lord Byron* (Princeton University Press, 1969), 3–114; M. House and G. Storey (eds.), *Letters of Charles Dickens*, vol II (*Clarendon Press*, 1969), 58, note.
4. DL, vol I, p. 448, Mutilated Diary; Bradford, 75–6.
5. DL, 323, D to Sarah Disraeli, 2 June 1834; 324, D to Sarah Disraeli, 4 June 1834.
6. ibid.
7. ibid., 322, 28 May 1834; 338, 11 July 1834; 341, 26 July 1834.
8. ibid., 331, 19 June 1834.

9. DL, 316, n, Isaac D'Israeli to D, 14 March 1834; 331, D to Sarah Disraeli, 19 June 1834; Stewart, 148–50.
10. Sadleir, *Blessington D'Orsay*, 231.
11. 'The Infernal Marriage' is bound up with *Alroy* in the Hughenden edn. 'Infernal Marriage', Pt I, iv; Pt II, i.
12. ibid., Pt IV, iii.
13. ibid.
14. DL, 339, D to Sarah Disraeli, 7 July 1834; M & B, I, 228, 1275.
15. DL, 345, D to Lady Blessington, 5 August 1834; 346, D to Lady Blessington, 15 August 1834; 347, D to Lady Blessington, 2 September 1834; 347, n., Lady Blessington to D, 20 August 1834.
16. DL, 350, D to Lady Blessington, 17 October 1834; 351, D to Benjamin Austen, 24 October 1834. See DL, 1521, n., for the ill effects of D's smoking.
17. DL, vol I, p. 450, Mutilated Diary.
18. *Disraeli's Reminiscences*, 119–20. Lyndhurst was brilliantly but inaccurately savaged by his Whig rival Campbell in *Lives of the Lord Chancellors*, vol VIII, (1869). Sir Theodore Martin's biography of Lyndhurst (1883) adds little.
19. Jerman, 191, 230; Blake, *Disraeli*, 118.
20. Bradford, 78; *Diary of Henry Crabb Robinson*, 136.
21. DL, vol II, p. 427, Political Notebook II; DL, vol I, p. 444 Aide-Memoire, 11–15 November 1834.
22. *Coningsby*, Bk II, ch 4.
23. DL, 353, D to Lord Durham, 17 November 1834; 356, D to Lord Lyndhurst, 4 December 1834.
24. DL, vol IV, 356X, D to Lord Durham, 4 December 1834.
25. Lytton Strachey and Roger Fulford (eds.), *The Greville Memoirs* (Macmillan, 1938), vol III, 117.
26. DL, vol II, 362, D to John Matthie, 1 January 1835; DL, vol IV, 359X, D to Sarah Disraeli, 26 December 1834. *The Crisis Examined* is printed in *Whigs and Whiggism*, 23–40.
27. DL, 331, D to Sarah Disraeli, 19 June 1834; 358, D to Sarah Disraeli, 11 December 1834; 363, D to Duke of Wellington, 7 January 1835.
28. Fraser, op. cit., 72–3.
29. DL, 368, D to Benjamin Austen, 19 January 1835; 384, D to Sarah Disraeli, 21 March 1835.
30. DL, 368X, D to Lord Lyndhurst, 20 January 1835; 369, D to Sarah Disraeli, 20 January 1835; M. R. D. Foot and H. C. G. Matthew (eds.), *The Gladstone Diaries*, vol 2 (Clarendon Press, 1968), 148–9, 17 January 1835.
31. DL, 370, D to Westminster Club Secretary, 28 January 1835; 381, D to Westminister Club Secretary, 8 March 1835; 409, note 39; 384, D to

Sarah Disraeli, 21 March. DL, vol II, p. 428, Political Notebook II.
32. *Coningsby*, Bk II, ch 4.
33. DL, vol II, p. 425, Political Notebook II; 389, D to Isaac D'Israeli, 17 April 1835.
34. DL, 390, D to Isaac D'Israeli, 18 April 1835.
35. F. R. Bonham's letters recommending Disraeli to Beadon, a Taunton solicitor who acted as Disraeli's agent, and referring to £300 received from party funds, are printed in Norman Gash, *Politics in the Age of Peel* (Longmans, 1953), 462–3. The *Letters* editors make a rare error in denying that Disraeli received financial backing at Taunton (DL, 390, n. 4). See Bradford, 80.
36. DL, 392, D to Sarah Disraeli, 27 April 1835; 393, D to Sarah Disraeli, 28 April 1835. M & B, I, 285–9. Nowell C. Smith, *Letters of Sydney Smith* (Clarendon Press, 1953), vol II, 614.
37. DL, 394, D to Sarah Disraeli, 2 May 1835; and note.
38. According to the *Dorset County Chronicle*, Disraeli merely remarked that the Whigs 'could only obtain power by leaguing themselves with one whom they had denounced as a traitor' (T. E. Kebbel, *Selected Speeches* ... (Longmans, 1882) vol I, 25–31). What Disraeli really said at Taunton can never be established for certain.
39. See N. P. Willis, *Pencillings by the Way* (H. G. Bohn, 1850 edn), 365.
40. DL, 398, D to Daniel O'Connell, 5 May 1835 (*The Times*, 6 May 1835).
41. DL, 399, D to Sarah Disraeli, 6 May 1835; 400, D to Morgan O'Connell, 6 May 1835.
42. DL, 401, D to Sarah Disraeli, 9 May 1835; 402, D to Sarah Disraeli, 9 May 1835.
43. See *London Review*, vol II (January 1836), 533.
44. DL, 406, editorial comment.
45. DL, 409, D to Edwards Beadon, 2 July 1835.
46. ibid.
47. ibid., 415, 9 August 1835.
48. DL, 395, D to Sarah Disraeli, 5 May 1835; Jerman, 257.
49. DL, 408, D to Sarah Disraeli, 27 June 1835; 410, D to Sarah Disraeli, 3 July 1835.
50. Sir Philip Rose's note is printed in Jerman, 191; DL, 411, D to Sarah Disraeli, 14 July 1835.
51. Lyndhurst destroyed his papers. His biographer, Sir Theodore Martin, denies this story. But Disraeli's account, printed in DL, vol II, p. 422, Political Notebook I, is credited by G. Kitson Clark, *Peel and the Conservative Party* (Frank Cass, 1964 edn), 271–95. See also G. B. A. M. Finlayson, 'The Politics of Municipal Reform, 1835', *English Historical Review* (1966, vol. LXXXI).
52. DL, 413, D to Sarah Disraeli, 4 August 1835; 416, D to Sarah Disraeli,

11 August 1835; 419, D to Sarah Disraeli, 17 August 1835. Campbell, op. cit., vol VIII, 109.

53. DL, 416, D to Sarah Disraeli, 11 August 1835; 421, D to Sarah Disraeli, 20 August 1835.

54. *Whigs and Whiggism*, 88–9.

55. ibid., 59. In the London Library copy, which belonged to Philip Guedalla, there is a note in the margin against this passage: 'the only true thing he says'.

56. ibid., 64, 80–1, 103.

57. DL, vol II, p. 422, Political Notebook I; *Whigs and Whiggism*, 107.

58. DL, 449, D to Sarah Disraeli, 12 December 1835.

59. DL, 425, D to V. S. Reynolds, 29 August 1835; 431, D to R. Culverwell, 25 September 1835.

60. DL, 441, D to John Murray, 19 November 1835; 443, D to R. Bentley, 22 November 1835.

61. *Greville Memoirs*, III, 256.

62. The *Vindication* is printed in *Whigs and Whiggism*. Macaulay, 'Mill's Essay on Government', *Edinburgh Review*, vol. 49 (1829), 185.

63. *Whigs and Whiggism*, 123, 143, 145. DL, 472, D to Lord Eliot, 18 January 1836.

64. DL, 464, n. 2, Lord Eliot to D, 7 January 1836. *London Review*, vol II (January 1836), 537. Compare the *Vindication* with Burke, *Reflections on the Revolution in France* (Everyman, 1910), 29–31.

65. *Whigs and Whiggism*, 149, 169.

66. ibid., 162, 173. *London Review*, vol II, 543–4. Vincent, 21.

67. DL, 464, n 2, Lord Eliot to D, 7 January 1836.

68. *Whigs and Whiggism*, 198.

69. DL, 444, D to Isaac D'Israeli, 24 November 1835.

70. *Whigs and Whiggism*, 210, 212, 214–15.

71. ibid., 215, 216.

72. ibid., 219.

73. DL, 458, D to the Editor of *The Times*, 28 December 1835; 464, n. 2, Lord Eliot to D, 7 January 1836. See Richard Faber, *Beaconsfield and Bolingbroke* (Faber & Faber, 1961).

74. *Journal of Thomas Moore*, vol IV, 1737.

75. M & B, I, 322.

76. DL, vol IV, 453R, D to Sarah Disraeli, 19 December 1835. *Gladstone Diaries*, II, 221. The author of the *London Review* article (vol II, (January 1836), 533–52) is still uncertain. It is signed 'S.A.', which the *Wellesley Index to Victorian Periodicals* identifies as Mill's friend Sarah Austin (vol III, 586). Sarah Austin's biographers have disputed the identification, noting her reservations about the *London Review*, which she described as 'too Radical for my taste' (Lotte and Joseph Hamburger, *Troubled Lives:*

John and Sarah Austin (University of Toronto (1985), note 44). See however DL, 479, D to Benjamin Austen, 10 February 1836: 'Mrs Austen's copy was sent to Mrs Austin the authoress; which I greatly regret for all reasons. I have not the honour of her acquaintance, and she is a violent Whig.' This may be a veiled allusion to the *London Review* article.

77. DL, 464, D to Sarah Disraeli, 9 January 1836; 465, D to Joseph Hume, 11 January 1836; 466, D to Sarah Disraeli, 12 January 1836.
78. DL, 459, D to Isaac D'Israeli, 28 December 1835.
79. DL, 468, D to Benjamin Austen, 14 January 1836; 470, D to Richard Culverwell, 16 January 1836.
80. DL, 428, D to William Pyne, 11 September 1835.
81. DL, 479, D to Benjamin Austen, 10 February 1836, and note; 489, D to Benjamin Austen, 14 March 1836 and Austen to D, 11 March 1836; 495, D to Benjamin Austen, 4 April 1836.
82. DL, 478, D to Isaac D'Israeli, 6 February 1836. See Sir Charles Webster, *The Foreign Policy of Palmerston* (G. Bell, 1951), vol I, 422–58.
83. DL, 493, D to Sarah Disraeli, 26 March 1836.
84. DL, 475, D to Isaac D'Israeli, 29 January 1836. The Runnymede Letters are printed in DL, vol II at Appendix II: pp. 364, 368, 381, 384, 387, 393.
85. *History of The Times* (*The Times*, 1935), vol I, 438–9.
86. DL, vol II, p. 358.
87. DL, vol II, p. 416, Mutilated Diary; 484, D to Sarah Disraeli, 24 February 1836; 499, D to Sarah Disraeli, 16 April 1836.

Chapter Eight: Scrapes with Count D'Orsay 1836–7

1. DL, vol II, pp. 398, 400.
2. DL, 511, D to Sarah Disraeli, 1 July 1836; vol II, p. 342.
3. DL, vol II, p. 423, Political Notebook I; 522, D to Sarah Disraeli, 20 August 1836. See Kitson Clark, 298–319; *Greville Memoirs*, vol III, 293–305.
4. DL, 515, D to William Pyne, 21 July 1836; 516, D to Sarah Disraeli, 22 July 1836; 487, D to William Pyne, 7 March 1836. DL, vol II, p. 416, Mutilated Diary.
5. DL, 489, note; 511, D to Sarah Disraeli, 1 July 1836. M & B, I, 336, 342.
6. DL, 499, D to Sarah Disraeli, 16 April 1836; vol II, p. 416, Mutilated Diary.
7. S. M. Ellis (ed.), *Unpublished Letters of Lady Bulwer Lytton to A. E. Chalon* (Everleigh Nash, 1914), 152–3. Meynell, vol I, 11–12; *Daniel Maclise*, National Portrait Gallery (Arts Council, 1972).
8. DL, 522, D to Sarah Disraeli, 20 August 1836.

9. DL, 527, D to William Pyne, 25 September 1836.
10. ibid., 537, 27 November 1836.
11. Jerman, 282. Blake, *Disraeli*, 134; DL, 659, note 4.
12. *Henrietta Temple*, Bk II, ch 6. *National Trust Guide to Basildon Park* (1989).
13. M & B, I, 344.
14. *Henrietta Temple*, Bk III, ch 4. *Henrietta Temple* should be read in the first edition (there is a copy in the British Library) rather than the revised 1853 edition.
15. ibid., Bk III, ch 5; Bk IV, ch 1.
16. Stewart, 181.
17. *Henrietta Temple*, Bk V, ch 6; Bk VI, ch 12.
18. ibid., Bk VI, ch 10.
19. Vincent, 76.
20. *Henrietta Temple*, Bk VI, ch 11, ch 13.
21. Fraser, 176.
22. Vincent, 76; M & B, I, 348.
23. Stewart, 154–6; DL, 555, note, Lady Blessington to D, 26 December 1836; 539, D to Sarah Disraeli, 14 December 1836; 612, D to William Beckford, 17 May 1837.
24. DL, 540, D to Sarah Disraeli, 15 December 1836; 543, D to Sarah Disraeli, 19 December 1836; 570, D to Sarah Disraeli, 3 February 1837.
25. David Spring, 'Lord Chandos and the Farmers, 1818–1846', *Huntingdon Library Quarterly*, vol XXXIII, 1969–70. *Greville Memoirs*, vol III, 311.
26. DL, 532, D to the Freeholders and Farmers of Bucks, 20 October 1836.
27. DL, 536, D to Count D'Orsay, 27 November 1836; 538, D to William Pyne, 5 December 1836; 540, D to Sarah Disraeli, 15 December 1836. M & B, I, 337–9.
28. DL, vol IV, 538X, D to Sarah Disraeli, 12 December 1836.
29. ibid., 539, 14 December 1836; 540, 15 December 1836. M & B, I, 339–40.
30. DL, 544, D to E. Lytton Bulwer, 22 December 1836; Blake, *Disraeli*, 138.
31. DL, 542, D to D'Orsay, 18 December 1836.
32. DL, 544, D to E. Lytton Bulwer, 22 December 1836; 545, D to D'Orsay, 23 December 1836.
33. Blake, *Disraeli*, 138, 141; DL, 551, D to William Pyne, 8 January 1837; *Greville Memoirs*, vol III, 336–7.
34. DL, 547, D to William Pyne, 26 December 1836.
35. ibid., 551, 8 January 1837. Blake, *Disraeli*, 138–9, 140–1.
36. *Diary of B. R. Haydon*, vol IV, 285. *Diary of Crabb Robinson*, 163–4.
37. *Collected Letters of Thomas and Jane Welsh Carlyle*, vol II, 71.
38. DL, 543, D to Sarah Disraeli, 19 December 1836; 555, D to Lady

Blessington, 12 January 1837.

39. DL, 551, D to William Pyne, 8 January 1837; 552, D to William Pyne, 11 January 1837.

40. DL, 557, D to Sarah Disraeli, 17 January 1837; 558, D to Sarah Disraeli, 19 January 1837; 560, D to Sarah Disraeli, 23 January 1837.

41. ibid., 564, 27 January 1837; 568, 1 February 1837. Campbell, VIII, 117.

42. DL, 494, D to Sarah Disraeli, 4 April 1836; 559, D to Sarah Disraeli, 21 January 1837; 560, D to Sarah Disraeli, 23 January 1837.

43. ibid., 570, 3 February 1837; 573, 7 February 1837.

44. ibid., 568, 1 February 1837; 579, D to Count D'Orsay, 24 February 1837.

45. DL, 577, D to Sarah Disraeli, 15 February 1837; 578, D to William Pyne, 16 February 1837.

46. DL, 578, D to William Pyne, 16 February 1837.

47. DL, 580, D to Sarah Disraeli, 27 February 1837; 1521, note 2, Mary Anne to Disraeli, 11 June 1847.

48. DL, 593, D to John Nash, 30 March 1837.

49. DL, 587, D to William Pyne, 7 March 1837.

50. ibid., 585, 5 March 1837; 588, D to Count D'Orsay, 13 March 1837.

51. DL, 588, D to D'Orsay, 13 March 1837; 589, D to William Pyne, 18 March 1837.

52. DL, 591, D to William Pyne, 23 March 1837; 598, D to William Pyne, 5 April 1837.

53. ibid., 591, 23 March 1837; 596, 4 April 1837.

54. ibid., 596, 4 April 1837; 598, 5 April 1837; 600, 11 April 1837.

55. DL, 533, D to Benjamin Austen, 23 October 1836; 554, D to Benjamin Austen, 12 January 1837; 566, D to Benjamin Austen, 30 January 1837; 571, D to Benjamin Austen, 4 February 1837; 583, D to Benjamin Austen, 28 February 1837; 599, D to Benjamin Austen, 9 April 1837.

56. H/A/IV/C, Note by Sir P. Rose, July–August 1882.

57. J. A. Froude, *Life of the Earl of Beaconsfield* (J. M. Dent, 1914 edn), 64. DL, 600, D to William Pyne, 11 April 1837.

58. DL, 601, D to William Pyne, 16 April 1837; 602, D to William Pyne, 19 April 1837; 603, D to William Pyne, 23 April 1837.

59. DL, 604, D to Sarah Disraeli, 2 May 1837; 605, D to D'Orsay, 2 May 1837.

60. DL, 590, D to Lady Blessington, 21 March 1837.

61. 'D'Israeli's *Novels*', *Edinburgh Review*, vol 66 (1837), 68.

62. *Venetia*, Bk I, ch 12; Bk III, ch 7.

63. ibid., Bk III, ch 4; Bk IV, ch 1; Bk IV, ch 3.

64. ibid., Bk IV, ch 2.

65. *Crabb Robinson on Books*, vol II, 755. Schwarz, *Disraeli's Fiction*, 70–2.

66. *Venetia*, Bk I, ch 18.

67. Schwarz, 70–1.
68. *Venetia*, Bk VI, ch 4. See Vincent, 77–9.
69. DL, 590, D to Lady Blessington, 21 March 1837; 601, D to William Pyne, 16 April 1837.
70. *Venetia*, Bk IV, ch 18. *Letters of T. B. Macaulay*, vol V.
71. DL, 612, D to William Beckford, 17 May 1837; 613, D to Sara Austen, 23 May 1837; 622, D to Sarah Disraeli, 19 June 1837. Stewart, 163–5.
72. DL, 666, D to Sarah Disraeli, 25 October 1837; 669, D to Lady Caroline Maxse, 3 November 1837. 'D'Israeli's *Novels*', 59–60.
73. DL, 608, D to Sarah Disraeli, 5 May 1837; vol II, p. 417, Mutilated Diary. M & B, I, 373–4; *Greville Memoirs*, vol III, 363–4.
74. DL, 614, D to William Pyne, 29 May 1837; 618, D to Sarah Disraeli, 15 June 1837.
75. DL, 622, D to Sarah Disraeli, 19 June 1837; 623, D to Sarah Disraeli, 20 June 1837; 624, D to Sarah Disraeli, 21 June 1837; 638, D to Sarah Disraeli, 18 July 1837.
76. ibid., 623, 20 June 1837; 626, 26 June 1837.
77. ibid., 628, 30 June 1837.
78. *Greville Memoirs*, vol III, 132–3.
79. DL, 630, D to William Pyne, 3 July 1837; 631, D to Sarah Disraeli, 4 July 1837; 632, D's Address to Freemen & Electors of Maidstone, 8 July 1837; 633, D to Sarah Disraeli, 8 July 1837. M & B, I, 377–8.
80. DL, 640, D to Sarah Disraeli, 22 July 1837.
81. ibid., 642, 27 July 1837; 643, D to Mary Anne Lewis, 29 July 1837 and note, Mary Anne Lewis to Major Viney Evans, 29 July 1837.
82. DL, 659, D to Count D'Orsay, 31 August 1837; and note.
83. Richardson, op. cit., vol II, 180–5; *Gladstone Diaries*, vol III, 465.
84. Carola Oman, op. cit., 248.

Chapter Nine: Mary Anne 1837–9

1. DL, 646, D to Sarah Disraeli, 8 August 1837; 654, D to William Pyne, 22 August 1837.
2. DL, 646, D to Sarah Disraeli, 8 August 1837; 656, D to Mary Anne Lewis, 26 August 1837. Stanley Weintraub, *Victoria* (Unwin Hyman, 1987), 118.
3. DL, 660, D to Mary Anne Lewis, 1 September 1837; 666, D to Sarah Disraeli, 25 October 1837; 685, n., Lady Caroline Maxse to D, 17 December 1837.
4. Archer Shee, op. cit., 54–5.
5. '*Vindication of the English Constitution*. By D'Israeli the Younger', *London Review*, vol II (1836), 552. See above, ch 7, n. 76.
6. DL, 647, D to John Monckton, 10 August 1837; *Coningsby*, Bk V, ch 2.

7. DL, 672, D to Sarah Disraeli, 15 November 1837; 673, D to Sarah Disraeli, 16 November 1837.
8. ibid., 676, 21 November 1837.
9. ibid., 675, 20 November 1837; 683, 5 December 1837.
10. Weintraub, *Disraeli*, 142; DL, 450, D to Isaac D'Israeli, 15 December 1835.
11. DL, 685, D to Lady Caroline Maxse, 7 December 1837.
12. *Hansard*, Third Series, vol 39 (1837), cols 802–7; M & B, I, 406–9. Monypenny, quoting from the *Mirror of Parliament*, says 'tail', which was the word used of O'Connell and the Irish; according to the report in *Hansard*, which is probably less accurate because revised by Disraeli, Disraeli merely said, 'Why not let me enjoy that reflection'.
13. DL, 686, D to Sarah Disraeli, 8 December 1837; Wemyss Reid, *Monckton Milnes* (Cassell, 1890), vol I, 204.
14. DL, 686, D to Sarah Disraeli, 8 December 1837; Reid, op. cit., vol I, 204, 206.
15. DL, 686, n. 4, Isaac D'Israeli to D, 10 December 1837; 688, D to Sarah Disraeli, 11 December 1837; 690, D to Sarah Disraeli, 15 December 1837.
16. DL, 695, D to Mary Anne Lewis, 1 January 1838.
17. Fraser, 231.
18. Gash, *Politics in the Age of Peel*, 130–1; DL, 702, note 2.
19. DL, 700, D to William Pyne, 7 January 1838.
20. ibid., 696, D to William Pyne, 3 January 1838; 697, D to Wyndham Lewis, 4 January 1838.
21. D's Old England articles are printed in DL, vol III at Appendix II. Weintraub, *Disraeli*, 178; *Letters of Thomas and Jane Welsh Carlyle*, vol X, 6.
22. DL, 701, D to Mary Anne Lewis, 9 January 1838; 932, note 2.
23. ibid., 706, 18 January 1838; 709, D to Sarah Disraeli, 20 January 1838; 715, D to Sarah Disraeli, 24 January 1838; 716, D to Sarah Disraeli, 25 January 1838.
24. DL, 709, D to Sarah Disraeli, 20 January 1838; 730, D to Sarah Disraeli, 15 February 1838; 733, D to Sarah Disraeli, 19 February 1838.
25. ibid., 733, 19 February 1838; 738, Disraeli to Peel, 2 March 1838; 738, note 2, Peel to D, 2 March 1838; 739, D to Sarah Disraeli, 6 March 1838.
26. DL, 747, D to Sarah Disraeli, 16 March 1838; *Hansard*, Third Series, vol 41 (1838), cols 940–1.
27. DL, 747, D to Sarah Disraeli, 16 March 1838.
28. DL, 744, D to William Pyne, 14 March 1838; 745, D to Sarah Disraeli, 14 March 1838; 746, D to Sarah Disraeli, 15 March 1838.
29. See Mollie Hardwicke, *Mrs Dizzy* (Cassell, 1972).

30. ibid., 64–9; Louisa Devey, *Rosina, Lady Lytton*, 411–12.
31. Rosina took her revenge the following year, satirising Mary Anne's crocodile tears for Wyndham Lewis in her *roman à clef*, *Cheveley*. See *Unpublished Letters of Lady Bulwer Lytton*, 231–2.
32. DL, 767, D to Mary Anne Lewis, 26 April 1838; Hardwicke, 76–80.
33. Hardwicke, 69; DL, 755, 29 March 1838.
34. DL 764, D to Mary Anne Lewis, 19 April 1838; 765, D to Mary Anne Lewis, 22 April 1838.
35. Mary Anne's courtship letters are published in DL, vol III, at Appendix VI. (Henceforth cited as DL, MA Courtship). DL, MA Courtship, MA to Disraeli, 1/7 May 1838; 2/10 May 1838; 3/14 May 1838. 771, D to Mary Anne Lewis, 9 May 1838. Weintraub has suggested that this exchange refers to Lady Lyndhurst, correcting Sarah Bradford for misidentifying 'Lady L' as Lady Londonderry, but it is plain from Disraeli's reply of 9 May that Lady L *is* Lady Londonderry, and Bradford is therefore correct (*Disraeli*, 180).
36. DL, 773, D to Mary Anne Lewis, 20 May 1838.
37. ibid., 774, 31 May 1838; 776, D to the *Morning Post*, 5 June 1838.
38. DL, 777, D to Mary Anne Lewis, 6 June 1838.
39. DL, 780, note 1; 843, note 1; 844, D to Sarah Disraeli, 23 November 1838. M & B, I, 440–4; Fraser, 221–9.
40. DL, 786, D to Sarah Disraeli, 22 June 1838; 789, D to Sarah Disraeli, 25 June 1838.
41. ibid., 786, 22 June 1838; 790, 29 June 1838; 791, 2 July 1838; 793, 4 July 1838.
42. *Greville Memoirs*, IV, 72.
43. Mary Anne Account Book, 1838; DL, 796, D to Sarah Disraeli, 10 July 1838.
44. DL, 796, D to Sarah Disraeli, 10 July 1838.
45. DL, 787, D to Mary Anne Lewis, 23 June 1838; 792, D to Mary Anne Lewis, 2 July 1838; 806, D to Mary Anne Lewis, July 1838.
46. DL, 809, D to Sarah Disraeli, 10 August 1838. *Hansard*, Third Series, vol 44 (1838), cols 1121–2. Disraeli made two other speeches between Easter 1838 and the recess: on copyright (25 April 1838) and Irish Municipal Corporations (1 June 1838).
47. DL, 694, D to Lady Caroline Maxse, 31 December 1837.
48. DL, 816, D's verses to Mary Anne Lewis, September 1838.
49. DL, 815, D to William Pyne, 30 September 1838.
50. DL, 819, D to Mary Anne Lewis, 6 October 1838; 820, D to Mary Anne Lewis, 7 October 1838; 822, D to Mary Anne Lewis, 9 October 1838; 882, note 5. MA Courtship 7, MA to Disraeli, 8 October 1838.
51. DL, 827, D to Mary Anne Lewis, 18 October 1838.
52. *Count Alarcos*, Act 1, scene 2. *Count Alarcos: a Tragedy* is bound up with

The Young Duke in the Hughenden edition of D's novels.

53. ibid., Act 1, scene 4.
54. ibid., Act 3, scene 1.
55. DL, 827, D to Mary Anne Lewis, 18 October 1838.
56. DL, MA Courtship 8, MA to Disraeli, 17 October 1838; 828, D to Mary Anne Lewis, 19 October 1838.
57. DL, 831, D to Mary Anne Lewis, 25 October 1838; MA Courtship 14, MA to Disraeli, 26 October 1838.
58. DL, 832, D to Mary Anne Lewis, 28 October 1838; 843, D to Mary Anne Lewis, 23 November 1838.
59. ibid., 846, 26 November 1838; 849, D's poem to Maria D'Israeli, 1 December 1838; 850, D to Mary Anne Lewis, 2 December 1838.
60. DL, 856, n., D'Orsay to D, 25 December 1838; 857, D to Mary Anne Lewis, 23 December 1838. MA Courtship 18, MA to Disraeli, 25 November 1838; 23, MA to Disraeli, 23 December 1838.
61. DL, 859, D to Mary Anne Lewis, 29 December 1838.
62. ibid., 861, 30 December 1838.
63. DL, MA Courtship 31, MA to Disraeli, 23 January 1839.
64. DL, 868, D to Mary Anne Lewis, 22 January 1839; 869, D to Mary Anne Lewis, 23 January 1839; 871, D to Mary Anne Lewis, 25 January 1839; 875, D to Mary Anne Lewis, 30 January 1839.
65. ibid., 874, 29 January 1839.
66. DL, 876, note, D'Orsay to D, n.d.
67. DL, 880, D to Mary Anne Lewis, 7 February 1839. Mary Anne Account Book, 1839.
68. DL, 881, D to Mary Anne Lewis, 7 February 1839.
69. ibid., 882, 7 February 1839.
70. ibid., 883, 7 February 1839.
71. DL, MA Courtship 36, MA to Disraeli, 7 February 1839.
72. DL, MA Courtship 37, MA to Disraeli, 8 February 1839; 885, D to Mary Anne Lewis, 8 February 1839.
73. DL, 891, D to Sarah Disraeli, 14 February 1839; 896, D to Mary Anne Lewis, 22 February 1839.
74. DL, 905, D to Sarah Disraeli, 16 March 1839; 906X, D to Sarah Disraeli, 19 March 1839; 909, D to Sarah Disraeli, 23 March 1839.
75. ibid., 897, 25 February 1839; 908, D to David Urquhart, 23 March 1839.
76. DL, 897, D to Sarah Disraeli, 25 February 1839. *Hansard*, Third Series, vol 45 (1839), cols 1038–40.
77. DL, 904, D to Sarah Disraeli, 9 March 1839. *Hansard*, Third Series, vol 46 (1839), cols 181–2.
78. DL, 901, D to Sarah Disraeli, 4 March 1839; 910, D to Sarah Disraeli, 26 March 1839; 917, D to Sarah Disraeli, 16 April 1839; 920, D to Sarah Disraeli, 2 May 1839.

79. ibid., 899, 28 February 1839.
80. ibid., 916, 15 April 1839; 918, 19 April 1839.
81. DL, vol III, Appendix III, D's Laelius letter to *The Times*, 6 May 1839; 922, D to Sarah Disraeli, 4 May 1839.
82. DL, 921, D to Sir Robert Peel, 2 May 1839; 922, D to Sarah Disraeli, 4 May 1839; 926, D to Mary Anne Lewis, 7 May 1839.
83. DL, 929, D to Mary Anne Lewis, 10 May 1839; 930, D to Mary Anne Lewis, 11 May 1839.
84. DL, vol III, Appendix III, D's Laelius letter to *The Times*, 28 May 1839. *Sybil*, Bk IV, ch 14.
85. DL, 965, D to Sarah Disraeli, 13 July 1839. J. C. Trewin (ed.), *Journal of W. C. Macready* (Longmans, 1967), 135; Stewart, 170.
86. *Hansard*, Third Series, vol 38 (1839), cols 578–89.
87. DL, 938, D to Mary Anne Lewis, 20 June 1839; 939, D to Sarah Disraeli, 20 June 1839; 941, D to Sarah Disraeli, 24 June 1839.
88. Hardwicke, 102–3.
89. DL, 946, D to Sarah Disraeli, 28 June 1839; 947, D to Sarah Disraeli, 1 July 1839; 948, D to Sarah Disraeli, 3 July 1839.
90. ibid., 956, 8 July 1839.
91. ibid., 963, 12 July 1839; MA Courtship 50, MA to Disraeli, 11 July 1839.
92. *Hansard*, Third Series, vol 49 (1839), cols 246–52.
93. *Sybil*, Bk V, ch 1.
94. Cecil Driver, *Tory Radical. The Life of Richard Oastler* (Octagon Books, New York, 1970 edn), 407–9.
95. DL, 971, D to Sarah Disraeli, 23 July 1839.
96. *Hansard*, Third Series, vol 49 (1839), cols 731–2.
97. DL, 978, D to Sarah Disraeli, 9 August 1839; 980, D to Sarah Disraeli, 10 August 1839.
98. ibid., 982, 15 August 1839.
99. DL, 995X, D to Henry Richards, 28 August 1839; 996, D to William Pyne, 28 August 1839.
100. DL, 997, D to Maria D'Israeli, 30 August 1839.

Chapter Ten: No Office from Peel 1839–42

1. DL, 1013, D to Sarah Disraeli, 9 December 1839.
2. Blake, *Disraeli*, 159.
3. I am grateful to the Grosvenor Estate for allowing me to visit Grosvenor Gate (now 93 Park Lane). The fireplaces and plasterwork are still intact; the contents and furnishings are listed in an inventory made in 1842, printed in DL, vol IV at Appendix X. In 1848 minor alterations were made by the architect Sydney Smirke; the staircase was gilded and the hall and lobby painted green (DL, 1751 and note).

4. Fraser, 78–9.
5. DL, 1045, D to Sarah Disraeli, 12 February 1840. Weintraub, *Disraeli*, 191. Mary Anne Account Book, 1840.
6. DL, 1061, D to Sarah Disraeli, 28 May 1840; 1069, D to Sarah Disraeli, 12 June 1840; 1070, D to Lady Blessington, 12 June 1840; and note.
7. DL, 1020, D to Sarah Disraeli, 19 December 1839; Ogden, 169–85.
8. DL, 1047, D to Sarah Disraeli, 15 February 1840.
9. DL, 985, note; 1025, D to William Pyne, 1 January 1840; 1077, D to William Pyne, 13 July 1840.
10. DL, 1031, D to Sarah Disraeli, 15 January 1840.
11. M & B, I, 487. *Hansard*, Third Series, vol 51 (1840), cols 395–401.
12. DL, 1038 X, D to Sarah Disraeli, 28 January 1840; 1039, D to Sarah Disraeli, 31 January 1840.
13. *Hansard*, Third Series, vol 51 (1840), cols 725–32.
14. DL, 1043, D to Sarah Disraeli, 7 February 1840; 1044, D to Sarah Disraeli, 10 February 1840; 1049, D to Sarah Disraeli, 19 February 1840.
15. DL, 1065, D to Charles Attwood, 7 June 1846; and note, Attwood to D, 2 June 1846.
16. *Hansard*, Third Series, vol 55 (1840), cols 637–42.
17. DL, 1078, note.
18. DL, 1083, D to Sarah Disraeli, 8 August 1840. *Reminiscences*, 17–18; *Endymion*, ch 55.
19. Mary Anne Account Book, 1840. DL, 1083, D to Sarah Disraeli, 8 August 1840; 1085, D to Sarah Disraeli, 15 August 1840; 1086, D to Sarah Disraeli, 20 August 1840. See F. M. L. Thompson, 'The End of a Great Estate', *Economic History Review*, vol 8 (1955), 36–52.
20. *Carlyle Letters*, vol 12, 9–10; *Reminiscences*, 60.
21. DL, 1104, D to Sarah Disraeli, 17 October 1840; Disraeli's General Preface (1870), xii.
22. DL, 1107, D to Sarah Disraeli, 28 October 1840; 1109, D to Sarah Disraeli, 2 November 1840; 1111, D to Sarah Disraeli, 9 November 1840; 1115, D to Sarah Disraeli, 13 November 1840. Charles Whibley, *Lord John Manners and his Friends* (William Blackwood, 1925), vol I, 86–92.
23. *Endymion*, ch 22.
24. Mary Anne Account Book, 31 October and 3 December 1840.
25. DL, 1108, D to William Pyne, 1 November 1840; 1112, D's birthday verse to Mary Anne, 11 November 1840.
26. DL, 1124, D to Sarah Disraeli, 27 December 1840, and note; 1126R, D to Sarah Disraeli, 30 January 1841.
27. Whibley, op. cit., I, 66; Richard Faber, *Young England* (Faber, 1987), 24–44.
28. Whibley, I, 84–5.

29. *Hansard*, Third Series, vol 56 (1841), cols 375–82.
30. *Greville Memoirs*, IV, 369; DL, vol III, xviii.
31. DL, 1131, D to Sarah Disraeli, 26 February 1841.
32. ibid., 1041, 3 February 1840.
33. DL, vol III, Appendix IV, 11 March 1840.
34. DL, 1138, D to Sarah Disraeli, 13 March 1841; 1139, D to Sarah Disraeli, 16 March 1841; 1140, D to Sarah Disraeli, 18 March 1841; 1143, D to Sarah Disraeli, 22 March 1841; 1144, D to Sarah Disraeli, 25 March 1841.
35. DL, 1137, D to William Pyne, 11 March 1841; 1286, D to Richard Wright, 6 March 1843.
36. *Endymion*, ch 65; DL, 1151, D to Sarah Disraeli, 3 May 1841.
37. DL, 1152, D to Sarah Disraeli, 5 May 1841; 1155, D to Sarah Disraeli, 8 May 1841; 1156, D to Sarah Disraeli, 15 May 1841. *Hansard*, Third Series, vol 58 (1841), cols 454–61.
38. *Hansard*, Third Series, vol 58 (1841), col 856.
39. DL, 1158, D to Rice Wynne, 27 May 1841; 1161, D's Address to the Electors of Shrewsbury, 8 June 1841.
40. DL, 1162, D to Mary Anne Disraeli (hereafter MA), 12 June 1841.
41. DL, 1166, D to Sarah Disraeli, 21 June 1841. Fraser, 474.
42. James Sykes, *Mary Anne Disraeli* (Ernest Benn, 1928), 70.
43. DL, 1167, D to Henry Richards, 24 June 1841; 1168, D's Address to the Electors of Shrewsbury, 25 June 1841.
44. DL, 1170, D to Maria D'Israeli, 30 June 1841; 1171, D to Sarah Disraeli, 7 July 1841. Sykes, op. cit., 67.
45. The poll was: Tomline 793, Disraeli 785, Sir Love Parry 605, Christopher Temple 576.
46. *Victoria History of the Counties of England. Shropshire* (Oxford University Press, 1979), vol III, 328. DL, 1171, D to Sarah Disraeli, 7 July 1841.
47. DL, 1171, D to Sarah Disraeli, 7 July 1841; 1174, D to Sarah Disraeli, 24 July 1841; 1175, D to Sarah Disraeli, 27 July 1841.
48. DL, 1178, D to Sir Robert Peel, 17 August 1841.
49. DL, 1176, D to Sarah Disraeli, 29 July 1841.
50. ibid., 1180, 21 August 1841.
51. *Hansard*, Third Series, vol 59 (1841), cols 172–7; M & B, I, 514; DL, 1183, D to MA, 28 August 1841.
52. DL, 1185, D to MA, 2 September 1841.
53. M & B, I, 516–17. Bradford, 115–16.
54. DL, 1186, D to Sir R. Peel, 5 September 1841; 1189, D to Sir R. Peel, 8 September 1841. M & B, I, 517–18, Sir R. Peel to D, 7 September 1841.
55. M & B, I, 520; Jerman, 192.
56. Blake, *Disraeli*, 166.
57. DL, 1202, D to Sarah Disraeli, 1 February 1842.

58. ibid., 1188, 6 September 1841.
59. M & B, I, 520–1.
60. Isaiah Berlin, 'Benjamin Disraeli, Karl Marx and the Search for Identity', *Transactions of the Jewish Historical Society of England*, vol XXII (1970), 1–20.
61. DL, 1190, D to Sarah Disraeli, 14 September 1841.
62. DL, 1193, D's birthday verse to MA, 11 November 1841. MA Account Book, 1841.
63. DL, 1194, D to William Pyne, 11 November 1841.
64. DL, 1195, D to MA, 14 December 1841; 1197, D to D'Orsay, 21 December 1841.
65. DL, 1201, D to Sarah Disraeli, 29 January 1842.
66. ibid., 1203, 2 February 1842; 1204, 11 February 1842; 1211, D to MA, 21 February 1842; 1214, D to MA, 23 February 1842.
67. *Endymion*, ch 71; DL, 1233, D to MA, 15 March 1842.
68. DL, 1213, D to MA, 22 February 1842; 1214, D to MA, 23 February 1842; 1219, D to MA, 26 February 1842.
69. ibid., 1217, 25 February 1842.
70. ibid., 1221, 5 March 1842; 1222, 7 March 1842. Fraser, 52.
71. DL, 1224, D to MA, 9 March 1842.
72. *Hansard*, Third Series, vol 61 (1842), cols 220–44. See DL, 1079, D to Sarah Disraeli, 14 July 1840; Lucy Brown, *The Board of Trade and the Free-Trade Movement* (Clarendon Press, 1958).
73. This is Disraeli's version of what he said (DL, 1224, D to MA, 9 March 1842). It is broadly similar to the version in *Hansard*, Third Series, vol 61 (1842), col 280.
74. DL, 1224, D to MA, 9 March 1842.
75. ibid., 1229, 11 March 1842; 1231, 13 March 1842.
76. ibid., 1207, 17 February 1842.
77. DL, 1211, note, MA to D, 22 February 1842; 1217, D to MA, 25 February 1842.
78. DL, 1216, note 1; 1234, D to MA, 16 March 1842, and note; 1286, D to Richard Wright, 6 March 1843.
79. DL, 1240, D to Sarah Disraeli, 7 April 1842.
80. DL, 1230, D to MA, 12 March 1842. *Sybil*, Bk VI, ch 1. *Hansard*, Third Series, vol 63 (1842), cols 390–2.
81. DL, 1229, D to MA, 11 March 1842.
82. *Hansard*, Third Series, vol 62 (1842), cols 1028–31; vol 64 (1842), cols 444–60.
83. ibid., vol 65 (1842), cols 419–27.
84. *Coningsby*, Bk III, ch 1.
85. Lord John Manners's Journal, quoted in DL, 1229, note 1.
86. DL, 1231, D to MA, 13 March 1842.

87. See Faber, *Young England*, 66–73.
88. Gregory, op. cit., 93–5.
89. DL, 1257, D to Isaac D'Israeli, 13 August 1842.
90. Sykes, op. cit., 62.
91. DL, 1259, D's third wedding anniversary verses to MA, 28 August 1842.

Chapter Eleven: Sidonia and Young England 1842–4

1. DL, vol IV, Appendix V, 'Commonplace Book. 1842'. *Coningsby*, Bk IV, ch 15.
2. DL, 1264, D to Sarah Disraeli, 14 October 1842.
3. Whibley, vol I, 142–3.
4. ibid., 137, 139, 145–6, 153.
5. ibid., 143, 148–9.
6. Draft of D's Memorandum for Louis Philippe, DL, vol IV, Appendix III.
7. Faber, *Young England*, 114; DL, 1268, D to Sarah Disraeli, 21 November 1842; Whibley I, 141; *Reminiscences*, 19.
8. DL, 1269, D to Sarah Disraeli, 2 December 1842.
9. ibid., 1270, 21 December 1842; 1275, 4 February 1843.
10. DL, 1293, D to Wright, 29 March 1843; 1299, D to T. Chapman, 10 April 1843; 1309, D to Wright, 20 May 1843; 1310, D to Wright, 23 May 1843.
11. DL, 1330 and note.
12. Whibley, I, 159; Faber, *Young England*, 118–22; DL, 1281, D to Sarah Disraeli, 17 February 1843.
13. T. E. Kebbel, D's *Speeches*, (Longmans, 1882), I, 46–57; DL, 1307, D to Sarah Disraeli, 12 May 1843.
14. M & B, I, 542; DL, 1318, D to Sarah Disraeli, 27 July 1843.
15. DL, 1312, D to Sarah Disraeli, 8 June 1843; *Macaulay Letters*, IV, 133.
16. *Hansard*, Third Series, vol 71, cols 430–8; 460.
17. Gash, *Peel*, 387; *Greville Memoirs*, V, 127; *Hansard*, Third Series, vol 71, cols 833–9.
18. DL, IV, p. xix; M & B, I, 579–80; DL, 1323, D to Sarah Disraeli, 29 August 1843.
19. Lord Lamington, *In the Days of the Dandies* (William Blackwood & Sons, 1890), 124–6; DL, 1324, D to Lady Blessington, 11 September 1843.
20. Whibley, I, 185; DL, 1323, D to Sarah Disraeli, 29 August 1843.
21. DL, IV, Appendix V, IX. Disraeli later endorsed the notebook 'Mem: about 1842, I shd. think', but from internal evidence it is plain that the notes were written later. Among the entries is the King of Hanover, whom Disraeli met only in June 1843.
22. 'Policy of Ministers', *Quarterly Review*, vol LXXII (1843), 554; M & B, I, 519–20; L. J. Jennings, *The Croker Papers* (John Murray, 1885), vol

III, 7–8, 264–5, 306–7; Campbell Papers, Campbell's MSS Autobiography, vol VIII.

23. DL, 1229, D to MA, 11 March 1842.
24. M & B, I, 582; *Coningsby*, Bk IV, ch 2.
25. *Sybil*, Bk VI, ch 13; MA Account Book; DL, 1326, D to Sarah Disraeli, 28 September 1843.
26. *Coningsby*, Bk I, ch 7.
27. ibid., Bk II, chs 1, 4, 5, 6; Bk III, ch 2.
28. Whibley, I, 149.
29. Vincent, 84.
30. *Coningsby*, Bk IV, ch 4; Richard Edsall, *Cobden* (Havard University Press, 1986), 445; Vincent, 90.
31. *Coningsby*, Bk IV, chs 10, 15.
32. See Vincent, 31. Richard Davis, *The English Rothschilds* (Collins, 1983), 87.
33. *Coningsby*, Bk III, ch 1.
34. ibid., Bk IV, ch 10; Bk VI, ch 2.
35. George K. Anderson, *The Legend of the Wandering Jew* (Brown University Press, Providence US, 1965), esp. 212, 225. See P. L. Rose, *Wagner, Race and Revolution* (Faber, 1992).
36. *Coningsby*, Bk IV, chs 10, 15; DL, 1433, D to Editor of the *Morning Post*, 16 August 1845. Also, D. L. Dinkin, 'The Racial and Political Ideas of Benjamin Disraeli', MSc thesis (Bristol, 1980); Vincent, 27–37.
37. DL, 1388, D to Monckton Milnes, 29 December 1844. Norman Cohn, *Warrant for Genocide* (Eyre and Spottiswoode, 1967), 32.
38. Maurois quoted in Leon Poliakov, *The History of Anti-Semitism* (Routledge and Kegan Paul, 1975), vol III, 334.
39. *Coningsby*, Bk IV, ch 15.
40. ibid., ch 13.
41. ibid., Bk VII, ch 2.
42. Robert O'Kell, 'Disraeli's "Coningsby": Political Manifesto or Psychological Romance?', *Victorian Studies*, 23 (1979), 57–78.
43. DL, 1335, D to MA, n.d.
44. DL, 1262, D to Sarah Disraeli, 19 September 1842; 1332, D to Sir James Graham, 20 December 1843.
45. DL, 1337, D to Peel, 4 February 1844.
46. Greville Memoirs, V, 162.
47. DL, vol IV, Appendix VI.
48. DL, 1343, D to MA, 10 May 1844; M & B, I, 598, 623.
49. DL, 1345, D to John Delane, 15 May 1844.
50. Stewart, 184–6; MA Account Book; DL, 1340, D to Richard Wright, 14 March 1844.
51. Houghton Papers, Harriet Martineau to Richard Monckton Milnes, 12 June [1844]. I am indebted for this reference to Dr Valerie Sanders.

52. Stewart, 180–3.
53. James Pope-Hennessy, *Monckton Milnes. The Years of Promise*, vol I (Constable, 1949), 194; DL, 1352, D to Monckton Milnes, 2 June 1844; *Reminiscences*, 57.
54. Wemyss Reid, I, 2–8.
55. DL, 1341, D to Henry Colburn, 29 March 1844; 1364, D to Lord Lyttelton, 14 July 1844.
56. DL, 1358, D to Sarah Disraeli, 13 June 1844; 1362, D to Sarah Disraeli, 9 July 1844.
57. *Reminiscences*, 88; DL, 1403, D to Messrs Carey and Hart, 1 May 1845.
58. DL, 1356, D to Sarah Disraeli, 10 June 1844; 1358, D to Sarah Disraeli, 13 June 1844.
59. Cohen, *Lady de Rothschild and her Daughters* (John Murray, 1935), 30; DL, 1347, D to Sarah Disraeli, 16 May 1844.
60. Faber, *Young England*, 132–3; John Morley, *Life of Richard Cobden* (T. Fisher Unwin, 1906 edn), 302.
61. MA Account Book.
62. Lord Broughton, *Recollections of a Long Life* (John Murray, 1911), vol VI, 114–16.
63. Robert Stewart, 'The Ten Hours and Sugar Crises of 1844', *Historical Journal*, vol XII (1969); Broughton, op. cit., vol VI, 117–19; *Hansard*, Third Series, vol 75, col 1030; D. R. Fisher, 'Peel and the Conservative Party: the Sugar Crisis of 1844 Reconsidered', *Historical Journal*, vol XVIII (1975).
64. M & B, I, 640; *Greville Memoirs*, V, 181; *Gladstone Diary*, vol III, 383.
65. DL, 1370, D to MA, 27 August 1844; 1371, D to MA, 28 August 1844.
66. M & B, I, 631, 643–4; DL, 1372, D to T. J. Ouseley, 29 August 1844.
67. Lamington, op. cit., 92, 128–9; Gregory, 90–1.
68. *Anti-Coningsby* [by William North] (T. C. Newby, 1844).
69. F. Engels, *The Condition of the Working Class in England in 1844* (Swan Sonnenschein & Co., 1892), 293–4; Karl Marx, *The Communist Manifesto*, ed. A. J. P. Taylor (Penguin Books, 1967), 106–7.
70. Quoted in Robert M. Stewart, *Foundation of the Conservative Party* (Longman, 1976), 186.
71. Carlyle to Milnes, 17 March 1844. *Carlyle Letters*, vol 17, 311–12.
72. *Anti-Coningsby*, vol. I, 68–9.
73. Robert O'Kell, op. cit.
74. E. Strangford's Memoir in Strangford, *Angela Pisani* (Richard Bentley, 1875), vol I, xiii, xxx. DL, vol IV, xlvii; 1370, D to MA, 27 August 1844.

Chapter Twelve: 'The Great Object of my Political Life' 1844–5

1. DL, IV, xxxiv–v; 1378, n. 4; M & B, I, 644–5.
2. DL, 1379, D to Lord John Manners, 27 October 1844.
3. Wemyss Reid, I, 339; R. Shannon, *Gladstone*, vol I (Hamish Hamilton, 1982), 167.
4. James Pope-Hennessy, op. cit., 194–6; M & B, I, 646.
5. DL, 1375, n. 1, Smythe to D, 15 August 1844; *Sybil*, Bk VI, ch 13.
6. *Greville Memoirs*, vol V, 236–8; Edwin Hodder, *Life and Work of the Seventh Earl of Shaftesbury* (Cassell, 1886), vol II, 71.
7. Sheila M. Smith, *Mr Disraeli's Readers* (University of Nottingham, 1966), 21–4.
8. DL, 1379, D to Lord John Manners, 27 October 1844; 1447, n 5.
9. See Sheila Smith's Introduction to the World's Classics edition of *Sybil* (Oxford, 1981), xiv.
10. Blake, *Disraeli*, 273.
11. *Sybil*, Bk I, ch 5; Bk VI, ch 13.
12. ibid., Bk II, ch 5.
13. Vincent, 94.
14. Gladstone's Notes on *Sybil*, Gladstone Papers, Add MSS 44792, f. 49. Weintraub's tantalising references to this document (*Disraeli*, 242) sent me hastening to the British Library. I was disappointed to discover that the phrases quoted by Weintraub as Gladstone's comments on *Sybil* are in fact extracts from the novel; quotations from Disraeli rather than Gladstone. The two chapters from which Gladstone took his extracts are Bk II, chs 11, 12.
15. *Sybil*, Bk II, ch 12.
16. Robert O'Kell, 'Two Nations or One?: Disraeli's Allegorical Romance', *Victorian Studies* (1987), 220–1.
17. Martin Fido, 'From his own Observation: Sources of Working Class Passages in Disraeli's "Sybil"', *Modern Language Review*, 72 (1977).
18. Sheila M. Smith, op. cit., 22, 34, 46, 52.
19. *Sybil*, Bk V, ch 4. Sheila M. Smith, 'Willenhall and Wodgate: Disraeli's Use of Blue Book Evidence', *Review of English Studies*, vol 13 (1962).
20. See O'Kell, 'Two Nations or One?', 226–34.
21. *Letters of Macaulay*, vol IV, 202; Lord Broughton, op. cit., vol VI, 122–3.
22. *Sybil*, Bk IV, ch 15.
23. ibid., Bk V, ch 2.
24. DL, 1384, D to Lord John Manners, 29 November 1844; 1388, D to Monckton Milnes, 29 December 1844. See 1402, D to Sarah Disraeli, 1 May 1845, for D's progress on *Sybil*.

25. M & B, I, 647; DL, 1389, D to Sarah Disraeli, 20 January 1845; 1389, n. 1, MA to Sarah Disraeli, 19 January 1845; 1453 and note; *Sybil*, Bk IV, ch 6.
26. DL, 1391, D to Sarah Disraeli, 6 February 1845.
27. ibid.; Campbell Papers, MS Autobiography, 1847, vol XI, 402.
28. Gash, *Age of Peel*, 468.
29. *Hansard*, Third Series, vol 77, cols 902–10; Blake, *Disraeli*, 185.
30. DL, 1396, n. 2, Smythe to D [Feb 1845].
31. *Hansard*, Third Series, vol 78, cols 148–56.
32. DL, 1396, D to Sarah Disraeli, 3 March 1845; M & B, I, 715.
33. *Sybil*, Bk VI, ch 1; Gash, *Age of Peel*, 470–1.
34. *Hansard*, Third Series, vol 78, cols 1002–8; M & B, I, 720.
35. B. Disraeli, *Lord George Bentinck: A Political Biography* (Colburn & Co., 1852 edn), 7–8.
36. Hodder, op. cit., II, 100.
37. Wemyss Reid, I, 352.
38. DL, 1399A, n. 1, T. J. Ouseley to D, 11 April 1845.
39. Wemyss Reid, I, 356; Broughton, VI, 143.
40. Shannon, op. cit., 173–4; John Morley, *Life of W. E. Gladstone* (Macmillan, 1903) vol I, 279; DL, 1455, D to Lord John Manners, 17 December 1845.
41. *Hansard*, Third Series, vol 79, cols 55–69. *The Times* reports the laughter and cheers.
42. *The Times*, 14 April 1845. See Donald Read, *Peel and the Victorians* (Basil Blackwell, 1987), 138–46; Robert M. Stewart, *Foundation of the Conservative Party*, 190–4; Gash, *Sir Robert Peel*, 468–78; *Greville Memoirs*, vol V, 213–15.
43. DL, 1400, D to Lord Carrington, 15 April 1845.
44. DL, 1398, D to Tresham Gregg, 1 April 1845; 1478, D to Tresham Gregg, 1 April 1846; 1519, D to Lord John Manners, 19 September 1846.
45. Hodder, op. cit., I, 102–3.
46. *Croker Papers*, vol III, 31
47. DL, 1402, D to Sarah Disraeli, 1 May 1845.
48. DL, 1407, D to Lord John Manners, 12 May 1845.
49. Stewart, 204–14; *Diary of Henry Crabb Robinson*, 235.
50. DL, 1428, D to Sarah Disraeli, 19 July 1845.
51. *Sybil*, Bk IV, ch 3.
52. Sheila M. Smith, 22.
53. DL, 1424, D to Lady Londonderry, 29 June 1845.
54. DL, 1428, D to Sarah Disraeli, 19 July 1845.
55. *Lord George Bentinck*, 8.
56. DL, 1434, D to Sarah Disraeli, 23 August 1845; and n. 7.

57. Smythe's August and September 1845 letters are quoted at DL, 1434, n. 7, 1455, n. 1.
58. DL, 1427, D to James Crossley, 17 July 1845.
59. DL, 1436, D to Henry Colburn, 31 August 1845.
60. DL, 1434, D to Sarah Disraeli, 23 August 1845.
61. ibid., 1441, 6 September 1845.
62. Bradford, 164–6; Cohen, op. cit., 47–9; DL, 1434, n 2.
63. DL, 1440, D to Sarah Disraeli, 5 September 1845; 1443, D to Sarah Disraeli, 8 September 1845.
64. ibid., 1444, 17 September 1845; 1445, 5 October 1845; 1446, 26 October 1845; 1447, 10 November 1845.
65. Vincent, 97–8; Disraeli, General Preface, (1870), xiv–xv; DL, 1447, n 7.
66. *Tancred*, Bk II, ch. 8.
67. ibid., chs. 7, 8.
68. ibid., chs. 13, 14. Schwarz, 99–104.
69. *Tancred*, Bk II, ch 13.
70. ibid., ch 14.
71. ibid., ch 11.
72. Blake, *Disraeli*, 209.
73. DL, 1389, D to Sarah Disraeli, 20 January 1845; *Tancred*, Bk II, ch 9.
74. M & B, I, 620. Dinkin, op. cit., 80.
75. Cohen, 44–5.
76. DL, 1452, D to Sarah Disraeli, 5 December 1845; & n 5.
77. *Lord George Bentinck*, 7, 236–7.
78. DL, 1454, D to Palmerston, 14 December 1845.
79. Vincent, 4, 32.
80. DL, 1454, D to Sarah Disraeli, 16 December 1845.
81. DL, 1455, D to Lord John Manners, 17 December 1845.

Chapter Thirteen: The Breaking of Peel 1846

1. DL, 1460, D to Sarah Disraeli, 11 January 1846; Morley, *Gladstone*, I, 286; Smythe to Disraeli, 16 January 1846, quoted in Blake, *Disraeli*, 224; DL, 1737, D to Metternich, 30 October 1848.
2. *Hansard*, Third Series, vol 83, col 95; *Lord George Bentinck*, 55.
3. *Greville Memoirs*, V, 288.
4. *Hansard*, Third Series, vol 83, cols 111–123; *The Times*, 23 January 1846; Blake, *Disraeli*, 227.
5. Nancy Mitford, *The Ladies of Alderley* (Hamish Hamilton, 1967), 102, Lady Stanley to Mrs Stanley, 27 January 1846.
6. Betty Kemp, 'Reflections on the Repeal of the Corn Laws', *Victorian Studies*, vol 5 (1962).
7. Boyd Hilton, 'Peel: A Reappraisal', *Historical Journal*, XXII (1979), 606–8.

8. *Letters to Lady Bradford and Lady Chesterfield*, vol I, 184.
9. *Lord George Bentinck*, 38, 40, 348; M & B, I, 758.
10. *Greville Memoirs*, VI, 105–17; Gregory, 106–16; N. Gash, 'Lord George Bentinck and his Sporting World' in *Pillars of Government and Other Essays* (1986), 162–75; Angus Macintyre, 'Lord George Bentinck and the Protectionists: A Lost Cause?', *Transactions of the Royal Historical Society*, 5th series, vol 39 (1989).
11. *Croker Papers*, vol III, 146.
12. See A. A. W. Ramsay, *Sir Robert Peel* (Constable, 1928), 339, 346–7.
13. DL, 1464, D to T. J. Ouseley, 29 January 1846, and note; 1467, D to Richard Taylor et al., 3 February 1846.
14. *Letters to Lady Bradford and Lady Chesterfield*, vol I, 171.
15. DL, 1466, D to Sarah Disraeli, 29 January 1846. See Robert Stewart, *The Politics of Protection. Lord Derby and the Protectionist Party 1841–1852* (Cambridge, 1971).
16. *Lord George Bentinck*, 79; *Greville Memoirs*, V, 296–7.
17. C. S. Parker, *Sir Robert Peel* (John Murray, 1899), vol III, 301–2, 339.
18. *Hansard*, vol 83, cols 1318–46; *Greville Memoirs*, V, 302.
19. Campbell Papers, Campbell's MS Autobiography, 1847, vol XI, 407.
20. *Hansard*, Third Series, vol 84, col 354; Parker, op. cit., III, 308–10.
21. DL, 1475, D to Sir George Sinclair, 13 March 1846.
22. DL, Ponsonby to D, 17 March 1846, quoted at 1475, n. 3. See 1664, D to Ponsonby, 9 July 1848.
23. H. F. C. Bell, *Lord Palmerston* (Longmans, Green & Co., 1936), vol II, 363–9; DL, 1664, D to Ponsonby, 9 July 1848.
24. DL, 1477, D to Palmerston, 28 March 1846; and n. 3.
25. *Lord George Bentinck*, 122–3; Broughton, VI, 166–7.
26. DL, IV, xxxiv; Parker, III, 308–10; M & B, I, 771; *Greville Memoirs*, V, 308, 311; *Disraeli's Reminiscences*, 58.
27. *Hansard*, Third Series, vol 85, cols 1015–16; *Greville Memoirs*, V, 317–8; Broughton, VI, 168; M & B, I, 777.
28. *Lord George Bentinck*, 201.
29. *Hansard*, Third Series, vol 86, cols 63–4, 83.
30. ibid., cols 274–6; 279–80.
31. ibid., col 675.
32. M & B, I, 786; *Hansard*, vol 86, col 689; Gash, *Peel*, 588–9.
33. *Hansard*, Third Series, vol 86, cols 707–9.
34. Broughton, VI, 171; see above p. 254
35. Gash, *Peel*, 590; M & B, I, 789–90; Blake, *Disraeli*, 237–9; *Letters*, IV, xxxv–vi.
36. Campbell, *Lives of the Lord Chancellors*, vol VIII, 159; Hodder, vol II, 138.

37. Broughton, VI, 171; *Greville Memoirs*, V, 321; *Hansard*, Third Series, vol 86, col 692; M & B, I, 785.
38. Boyd Hilton, op. cit., 614.
39. *Tancred*, Bk III, ch 4.
40. DL, 1490, D to Lord Ponsonby, 23 May 1846; 1664, D to Lord Ponsonby, 9 July 1848.
41. *Lord George Bentinck*, 231–2; *Greville Memoirs*, V, 315.
42. *Lord George Bentinck*, 230; Alethea Hayter, *A Sultry Month* (Robin Clark, 1992 edn), 47.
43. *Lord George Bentinck*, 248.
44. *Hansard*, Third Series, vol 87, col 536; Gash, *Peel*, 595–7; *Lord George Bentinck*, 254–5.
45. *Greville Memoirs*, V, 327–9; Broughton, VI, 178; A. C. Benson and Viscount Esher (eds.), *The Letters of Queen Victoria* (John Murray, 1908), vol II, 94.
46. Read, 230; Hayter, op. cit., 106.
47. *Greville Memoirs*, VI, 120; *Lord George Bentinck*, 285–6.
48. Hodder, II, 138.
49. Sir Robert Peel, *Memoirs* (John Murray, 1858), vol II, 309–10; *Lord George Bentinck*, 299–301.
50. W. O. Aydelotte, 'The Country Gentlemen and the Repeal of the Corn Laws', *English Historical Review* LXXXII (1967).
51. Peel, op. cit., II, 309–10; DL, 1499, D to MA, 29 June 1846.
52. DL, 1514, D to George Mathew, 28 August 1846.
53. See e.g. Stewart, *Foundation of the Conservative Party*, 205–16; M. Lawson Tancred, 'The Anti-League and the Corn Law Crisis of 1846', *Historical Journal*, III (1960).
54. Campbell Papers, Campbell's MS Autobiography, 1847, vol XI, 407, 418–19.
55. DL, 1514, D to George Mathew, 28 August 1846.
56. DL, 1519, D to Lord John Manners, 19 September 1846.
57. ibid.

Chapter Fourteen: Conclusion

1. Blake, *Disraeli*, 705–6; Duke of Portland, *Men, Women and Things* (Faber, 1937), 164–5.
2. DL, 1510, D to Sarah Disraeli, 10 August 1846. See *Coningsby*, Bk IV, ch 5.
3. *Tancred*, Bk II, ch 15; Bk VI, ch 4; Bk III, ch 4.
4. DL, 1725, D to Metternich, 12 October 1848; 1874, D to Metternich, 2 September 1849; 1947, D to Lady Londonderry, 30 December 1849.
5. *Reminiscences*, 148; DL, 1733, D to Duke of Newcastle, 24 October 1848.

6. Gregory, 110–11; M & B, I, 967–8; DL, 1719, D to Sir W. Jolliffe, 25 September 1848; 1730, D to MA, 18 October 1848.
7. Quoted in Blake, *Disraeli*, 253; DL, 1755, D to Lord Stanley, 26 December 1848.
8. *Reminiscences*, 43.
9. *Hansard*, Third Series, vol 86, cols 279–80.
10. *Coningsby*, Bk VIII, ch 3.
11. Mutilated Diary, 1833, DL, vol I, Appendix III.
12. See *Tancred*, Bk IV, ch 3.
13. *Coningsby*, Bk IV, ch 13; Bk VII, ch 2; *Reminiscences*, 108.
14. Mutilated Diary, 1833, DL, vol I, Appendix III.
15. *Tancred*, Bk III, ch 5.
16. Norman St John-Stevas, *The Collected Works of Walter Bagehot* (The Economist, 1968), vol III, 488.
17. *Reminiscences*, 32–3; *Tancred*, Bk II, ch 5.
18. Niccolo Machiavelli, *The Prince* (World's Classics edn, Oxford, 1984), 59.
19. DL, 1513, D's anniversary verses to MA, 28 August 1846.
20. *Tancred*, Bk III, ch 6.
21. ibid., Bk V, ch 3.
22. Meynell, vol I, 179.
23. DL, 1541, n. 1, quoting Sarah Disraeli to D, 21 March 1847; DL, 1621, D to Lord John Manners, 29 January 1848; 1645 and note.
24. DL, 1544, D to Philip Rose, 24 March 1847; and n. M & B, I, 958–60.
25. DL, 1513, D's anniversary verses to MA, 28 August 1846; *Coningsby*, Bk IV, ch 2.
26. DL, 1722 and note; 2044, D to Lytton, 24 September 1850.
27. DL, vol IV, l–li; 1484, D to Philip Rose, 28 April 1846.
28. Meynell, vol I, 101; Fraser, 149.
29. *Tancred*, Bk I, ch 5.
30. M & B, II, 1376, 1513.

Bibliography

A Manuscript Collections

Hughenden Papers, Bodleian Library, Oxford
Rose Papers, Bodleian Library, Oxford
Hughenden Manor, Transcript of Mary Anne Disraeli's Account Books
Campbell Papers, Scraesburgh, Jedburgh

B Articles

[Austin, Sarah ?], 'Vindication of the English Constitution. By D'Israeli the Younger', *London Review*, vol II (1836)

Aydelotte, W. O., 'The Country Gentlemen and the Repeal of the Corn Laws', *English Historical Review*, vol LXXXII (1967)

Berlin, Isaiah, 'Benjamin Disraeli, Karl Marx and the Search for Identity', *Transactions of the Jewish Historical Society of England*, vol XXII (1970)

Cline, C. L., 'Disraeli and Peel's 1841 Cabinet', *Journal of Modern History*, vol XI (1939)

—— 'The Failure of Disraeli's "Contarini Fleming"', *Notes and Queries*, August 1942

—— 'Disraeli at High Wycombe: the Beginning of a Great Political Career', *University of Texas Studies in English*, vol XXII (1942)

—— 'Unfinished Diary of Disraeli's Journey to Flanders and the Rhineland', *University of Texas Studies in English*, vol XXIII (1943)

Dinkin, D. L., 'The Racial and Political Ideas of Benjamin Disraeli', (MSc Dissertation, University of Bristol, 1979–80)

Dinwiddy, J. R., 'Sir Francis Burdett and Burdettite Radicalism', *History*, vol 65 (1980)

'D'Israeli's Novels', *Edinburgh Review*, vol 66 (1837)

Eastwood, David, 'Robert Southey and the Intellectual Origins of Romantic Conservatism', *English Historical Review*, vol CIV (1989)

Fido, Martin, 'From his own Observation: Sources of Working-Class Passages in Disraeli's "Sybil"', *Modern Language Review*, vol 72 (1977)

Finlayson, G. B. A. M., 'The Politics of Municipal Reform, 1835', *English Historical Review*, vol LXXXI (1966)

Fisch, Harold, 'Disraeli's Hebraic Compulsions', in H. J. Zimmels, J. Rabbinowitz & I. Finestein (eds.), *Essays Presented to Chief Rabbi Israel Brodie* (Jews' College Publications, No. 3 (1967))

Gash, Norman, 'Lord George Bentinck and his Sporting World', in *Pillars of Government and Other Essays* (Edward Arnold, 1986)

Ghosh, Peter, 'Disraelian Conservatism: a Financial Approach', *English Historical Review*, vol XCIX (1962)

Hilton, Boyd, 'Peel: A Reappraisal', *Historical Journal*, vol XXII (1979)

Kemp, Betty, 'Reflections on the Repeal of the Corn Laws', *Victorian Studies*, vol 5 (1962)

Lawson Tancred, M., 'The Anti-League and the Corn Law Crisis of 1846', *Historical Journal*, vol III (1960)

Layard, Sir Henry, 'The Early Life of Lord Beaconsfield', *Quarterly Review*, vol 168 (1889)

Macintyre, Angus, 'Lord George Bentinck and the Protectionists: a Lost Cause?', *Transactions of the Royal Historical Society*, 5th series, vol 39 (1989)

Nickerson, Charles C., 'Disraeli, Lockhart and Murray: an Episode in the History of the "Quarterly Review"', *Victorian Studies*, vol 15 (1972)

O'Kell, Robert, 'Disraeli's "Coningsby": Political Manifesto or Psychological Romance?', *Victorian Studies*, vol 23 (1979)

—— 'Two Nations or One? Disraeli's Allegorical Romance', *Victorian Studies*, vol 30 (1987)

Shane, A. L., 'Isaac D'Israeli and his Quarrel with the Synagogue – A Reassessment', *Transactions of the Jewish Historical Society of England*, vol XXIX (1982–6)

Smith, Paul, 'Disraeli's Politics', *Transactions of the Royal Historical Society*, 5th series, vol 37 (1987)

Smith, Sheila M., 'Willenhall and Wodgate: Disraeli's Use of Blue Book Evidence', *Review of English Studies*, vol 13 (1962)

Stewart, Robert M., 'The Ten Hours and Sugar Crises of 1844', *Historical Journal*, vol XII (1969)

Stewart, R. W., 'The Publication and Reception of Disraeli's *Vivian Grey*', *Quarterly Review*, vol 298 (1960)

Thompson, F. M. L., 'The End of a Great Estate', *Economic History Review*, vol 8 (1955)

Wolf, Lucien, 'The Disraeli Family', *Transactions of the Jewish Historical Society of England*, vol V (1902–5)

C Books
London publication unless otherwise noted.

Adburghham, Alison, *Silver Fork Society* (Constable, 1983)
Anderson, George K., *The Legend of the Wandering Jew* (Providence, U.S., Brown University Press, 1965)
Anderson, W. E. K. (ed.), *Journal of Sir Walter Scott* (Oxford, 1972)
Archer Shee, William, *My Contemporaries* (Hurst & Blackett, 1893)
Ashford, L. J., *History of the Borough of High Wycombe* (Routledge & Kegan Paul, 1960)
Bamford, Francis, and Wellington, Duke of (eds.), *The Journal of Mrs Arbuthnot* (2 vols, Macmillan, 1950)
Beckett, J. C., *The Making of Modern Ireland* (Faber, 1966)
Bell, H. F. C., *Lord Palmerston* (Longmans, Green & Co., 1936)
Benson, A. C., and Esher, Viscount (eds.), *The Letters of Queen Victoria* (3 vols, John Murray, 1908)
Blake, Robert, *Disraeli* (Eyre & Spottiswoode, 1966)
—— *Disraeli's Grand Tour* (Weidenfeld & Nicolson, 1982)
Bradford, Sarah, *Disraeli* (Weidenfeld & Nicolson, 1982)
Braun, Thom, *Disraeli the Novelist* (George Allen & Unwin, 1981)
Brightfield, Miron, *John Wilson Croker* (Allen & Unwin, 1940)
Brooke, John, & Sorensen, Mary (eds.), *W. E. Gladstone, Autobiographical Memoranda 1832–1845* (Royal Commission on Historical Manuscripts. H.M.S.O., 1972)
Broughton, Lord, *Recollections of a Long Life* (6 vols, John Murray, 1909–11)
Brown, Lucy, *The Board of Trade and the Free-Trade Movement* (Oxford, Clarendon Press, 1958)
Browning, Robert, *The Letters of Robert Browning and Elizabeth Barrett Browning* (2 vols, Smith, Elder, 1899)
Burke, Edmund, *Reflections on the Revolution in France* (Everyman, 1910)
Campbell, Lord, *Lives of the Lord Chancellors* (8 vols, John Murray, 1845–69)
Chedzoy, Alan, *A Scandalous Woman* (Allison & Busby, 1992)
Christiansen, Rupert, *Romantic Affinities* (Bodley Head, 1988)
Clive, John, *Thomas Babington Macaulay* (Secker & Warburg, 1973)
—— *Not by Fact Alone* (Collins, 1989)
Cohen, Lucy, *Lady de Rothschild and her Daughters* (John Murray, 1935)
Cohn, Norman, *Warrant for Genocide* (Eyre & Spottiswoode, 1967)
Davis, R. W., *Political Change and Continuity 1760–1885: A Buckinghamshire Study* (Newton Abbot, 1972)
—— *The English Rothschilds* (Collins, 1983)
Devey, Louisa, *Life of Rosina, Lady Lytton* (Swann, Sonnenschein, Lowrey, 1887)
D'Israeli, Isaac, *Commentaries on the Life and Reign of Charles I* (5 vols, Henry Colburn, 1828–31)

—— *Curiosities of Literature* (3 vols, Edward Moxon, 1849)
—— *Curiosities of Literature* (New York, Dover, 1964)
—— *The Genius of Judaism* (Edward Moxon, 1833)
—— *The Literary Character: or the History of Men of Genius* (2 vols, Henry Colburn, 1828)
Dowden, Wilfred S. (ed.), *Journal of Thomas Moore* (6 vols, University of Delaware, 1983–91)
Drabble, Margaret (ed.), *The Oxford Companion to English Literature* (Oxford University Press, 1985)
Driver, Cecil, *Tory Radical. The Life of Richard Oastler* (New York, Octagon Books, 1970 edn)
Edelman, Maurice, *Disraeli in Love* (Collins, 1972)
Edsall, Richard, *Cobden* (Cambridge, Mass, Harvard University Press, 1986)
Ellis S. M. (ed.), *Unpublished Letters of Lady Bulwer Lytton to A. E. Chalon* (Everleigh Nash, 1914)
Engels, F., *The Condition of the Working Class in England in 1844* (Swan, Sonnenschein & Co., 1892)
Faber, Richard, *Beaconsfield and Bolingbroke* (Faber & Faber, 1961)
—— *Young England* (Faber, 1987)
Feldman, David, *Englishmen and Jews* (Yale University Press, 1994)
Fonblanque, E. B. de, *Lives of the Lords Strangford* (Cassell, Petter and Galpin, 1877)
Foot, M. R. D., and Matthew, H. C. G. (eds.), *The Gladstone Diaries* (vols 1–3, Oxford, Clarendon Press, 1968–74)
Fraser, Sir William, *Disraeli and his Day* (Kegan Paul, 1891)
Froude, J. A., *Life of the Earl of Beaconsfield* (J. M. Dent, 1914 edn)
Gash, Norman, *Politics in the Age of Peel* (Longmans, 1953)
—— *Reaction and Reconstruction in English Politics* (Oxford, Clarendon Press, 1965)
—— *Sir Robert Peel* (Longman, 1972)
Gregory, Sir William, *An Autobiography* (John Murray, 1894)
Grierson, H. J. C. (ed.), *Letters of Sir Walter Scott* (vol IX, Constable, 1935)
Guest, Revel, and John, Angela V., *Lady Charlotte* (Weidenfeld & Nicolson, 1989)
Gunn, J. A. W., Matthews, John, Schurman, Donald M., Wiebe, M. G., (eds.), *Benjamin Disraeli: Letters* (vols I and II, Toronto, University of Toronto Press, 1982)
Halévy, Elie, *The Liberal Awakening* (Ernest Benn, 1961)
Hanham, H. J., *The Nineteenth-Century Constitution* (Cambridge University Press, 1969)
Hardwicke, Mollie, *Mrs Dizzy* (Cassell, 1972)
Hayter, Alethea, *A Sultry Month* (Robin Clark, 1992)
Hilton, Boyd, *Corn, Cash, Commerce* (Oxford University Press, 1977)

——*The Age of Atonement* (Oxford, Clarendon Press, 1988)

Hodder, Edwin, *Life and Work of the Seventh Earl of Shaftesbury* (2 vols, Cassell, 1886)

House, Madeline, and Storey, Graham (eds.), *The Letters of Charles Dickens* (7 vols, Oxford, Clarendon Press, 1965–1993)

Hudson, D. (ed.), *The Diary of Henry Crabb Robinson* (Oxford University Press, 1967)

Hutcheon, W. (ed.), *Whigs and Whiggism* (John Murray, 1913)

Jenkyns, Richard, *The Victorians and Ancient Greece* (Oxford, Basil Blackwell, 1980)

Jennings, L. J., *The Croker Papers* (3 vols, John Murray, 1885)

Jerman, B. R., *The Young Disraeli* (Princeton, New Jersey, 1960)

Johnson, Paul, *A History of the Jews* (Orion, 1987)

——*The Birth of the Modern* (Weidenfeld & Nicolson, 1991)

Jones, F. L. (ed.), *Letters of Mary W. Shelley* (2 vols, University of Oklahoma, 1944)

Kebbel, T. E., *Selected Speeches of the Late Rt. Hon. the Earl of Beaconsfield* (2 vols, Longman, 1882)

Ker, I., and Gornall, T. (eds.), *Letters & Diaries of J. H. Newman* (31 vols, Oxford, Clarendon Press, 1961–1984)

Kitson Clark, G., *Peel and the Conservative Party* (Frank Cass, 1964)

Lamington, Lord, *In the Days of the Dandies* (William Blackwood, 1890)

Lang, Andrew, *Life and Letters of J. G. Lockhart* (2 vols, John C. Nimmo, 1897)

Layard, Sir Henry, *Autobiography and Memoirs* (2 vols, John Murray, 1905)

Lemprière, J., *Lemprière's Classical Dictionary* (Bracken Books, 1984 edn)

Longford, Elizabeth, *Victoria R.I.* (Weidenfeld & Nicolson, 1964)

Londonderry, Marchioness of (ed.), *Letters from Benjamin Disraeli to Frances Anne, Marchioness of Londonderry 1837–61* (Macmillan, 1938)

Lovell, Ernest J. Jr. (ed.), *Lady Blessington's Conversations with Lord Byron* (Princeton University Press, 1969)

Lytton, Earl of, *The Life, Letters and Literary Remains of Edward Bulwer, Lord Lytton By his Son* (2 vols, Kegan Paul, 1883)

Martin, Sir Theodore, *Lord Lyndhurst* (John Murray, 1883)

Meynell, Wilfrid, *Benjamin Disraeli. An Unconventional Biography* (2 vols, Hutchinson, 1903)

Mill, J.S., *The Subjection of Women* (World's Classics, Oxford University Press, 1912)

Mitford, Nancy, *The Ladies of Alderley* (Hamish Hamilton, 1967)

Moers, Ellen, *The Dandy* (Secker & Warburg, 1960)

Monypenny, W. F., and Buckle, G. E., *The Life of Benjamin Disraeli Earl of Beaconsfield* (2 vol edn, John Murray, 1929)

Morgan, Lady, *Lady Morgan's Memoirs* (2 vols, W. H. Allen, 1862)

Morley, Edith J. (ed.), *Henry Crabb Robinson on Books and Their Writers* (3 vols, J. M. Dent, 1938)

Morley, John, *Life of Richard Cobden* (2 vols, Chapman & Hall, 1881)

——*Life of W. E. Gladstone* (3 vols, Macmillan, 1903)

National Portrait Gallery, *Daniel Maclise* (Arts Council, 1972)

National Trust, *Guide to Basildon Park* (The National Trust, 1989)

——*Guide to Hughenden Manor* (The National Trust, 1988)

[North, William,] *Anti-Coningsby* (T. C. Newby, 1844)

Ogden, James, *Isaac D'Israeli* (Oxford, 1969)

Oliver, J. W., *Life of William Beckford* (Oxford University Press, 1932)

Oman, Carola (ed.), *The Gascoyne Heiress* (Hodder & Stoughton, 1968)

Oppenheim, Janet, *'Shattered Nerves'* (New York, Oxford University Press, 1991)

Parker, C. S., *Sir Robert Peel* (3 vols, John Murray, 1891–9)

Peel, Sir Robert, *Memoirs* (2 vols, John Murray, 1858)

Picciotto, James, *Sketches of Anglo-Jewish History* (Trubner & Co., 1875)

Pinney, T. (ed.), *Letters of T. B. Macaulay* (6 vols, Cambridge University Press, 1974–81)

Poliakov, Leon, *The History of Anti-Semitism* (4 vols, Routledge & Kegan Paul, 1974–85)

Pope, W. B. (ed.), *Diary of Benjamin Robert Haydon* (5 vols, Cambridge, Mass., Harvard University Press, 1960–3)

Pope-Hennessy, James, *Monckton Milnes. The Years of Promise* (Constable, 1949)

Portland, Duke of, *Men, Women & Things* (Faber, 1937)

Ramsay, A. A. W., *Sir Robert Peel* (Constable, 1928)

Read, Donald, *Peel and the Victorians* (Oxford, Basil Blackwell, 1987)

Richardson, Reverend J., *Recollections* (2 vols, C. Mitchell, 1856)

Ridley, Jasper, *Lord Palmerston* (Constable, 1970)

Roberts, J. M., *The Mythology of the Secret Societies* (Secker & Warburg, 1972)

Rose, P. L., *Wagner, Race and Revolution* (Faber, 1992)

Roth, Cecil, *Benjamin Disraeli* (New York, Philosophical Library, 1952)

Sadleir, Michael, *Bulwer: A Panorama* (Constable, 1931)

—— *Blessington D'Orsay* (Constable, 1933)

Salbstein, M. C. N., *Emancipation of the Jews in Britain: the Question of the Admission of the Jews to Parliament 1828–1860* (East Brunswick, N.J., Associated University Press, 1982)

St Aubyn, Fiona (ed.), *Ackermann's Illustrated London* (Arrowhead Books, 1985)

St John-Stevas, Norman, *The Collected Works of Walter Bagehot* (15 vols, The Economist, 1965–89)

Sanders, C. R., Fielding, K. J., Ryals, C. D. (eds.), *The Collected Letters of Thomas and Jane Welsh Carlyle* (Duke–Edinburgh Edition. 21 vols, Duke

University Press, Durham, 1970–93)

Schwarz, Daniel R., *Disraeli's Fiction* (Macmillan, 1979)

Shannon, Richard, *Gladstone* (vol I, Hamish Hamilton, 1982)

Smiles, Samuel, *Memoir and Correspondence of the Late John Murray* (2 vols, John Murray, 1891)

Smith, Nowell C., *Letters of Sydney Smith* (2 vols, Oxford, Clarendon Press, 1953)

Smith, Sheila, M., *Mr Disraeli's Readers* (University of Nottingham, 1966)

Stapleton, E. J., *Some Official Correspondence of George Canning* (2 vols, Longmans, Green & Co., 1887)

Steiner, George, *In Bluebeard's Castle* (Faber, 1971)

Stewart, Robert M., *The Politics of Protection. Lord Derby and the Protectionist Party 1841–1852* (Cambridge, 1971)

—— *The Foundation of the Conservative Party* (Longman, 1976)

Stewart, R. W., *Benjamin Disraeli: A List of Writings by him and Writings about him, with Notes* (Metuchen, N. J., Scarecrow Press, 1972)

—— *Disraeli's Novels Reviewed* (Metuchen, N. J., Scarecrow Press, 1975)

Strachey, Lytton, & Fulford, Roger (eds.), *The Greville Memoirs* (8 vols, Macmillan, 1938)

Strangford, Lord, [George Smythe], *Historic Fancies* (Henry Colburn, 1844)

—— *Angela Pisani* (Richard Bentley, 1875)

Sultana, Donald, *Benjamin Disraeli in Spain, Malta and Albania* (Tamesis Books, 1976)

Summerson, John, *Georgian London* (Penguin, 1962)

Sutherland, John, *Victorian Novelists and Publishers* (Athlone Press, 1976)

Swartz, Helen M. and Swartz, Marvin (eds.), *Disraeli's Reminiscences* (Hamish Hamilton, 1975)

Sykes, James, *Mary Anne Disraeli* (Ernest Benn, 1928)

Taylor, A. J. P. (ed.), *The Communist Manifesto* by Karl Marx (Penguin, 1967)

Times, The, *History of The Times* (vol I, The Times, 1935)

Trewin, J. C., *Journal of W. C. Macready* (Longmans, 1967)

Victoria History of the Counties of England. Shropshire (vol III, Oxford University Press, 1979)

Vincent, John, *Disraeli* (Oxford University Press, 1990)

Warter, J. W. (ed.) *Selections from the Letters of Robert Southey* (4 vols, Longman, 1856)

Webster, Sir Charles, *The Foreign Policy of Palmerston* (2 vols, G. Bell, 1951)

Weintraub, Stanley, *Victoria* (Unwin Hyman, 1987)

—— *Disraeli* (Hamish Hamilton, 1993)

Wellesley Index to Victorian Periodicals, ed. Walter E. Houghton (5 vols, University of Toronto Press, 1966–89)

Wemyss Reid, T., *Life, Letters and Friendships of Richard Monckton Milnes, First Lord Houghton* (2 vols, Cassell, 1890)

Whibley, Charles, *Lord John Manners and his Friends* (2 vols, William Blackwood, 1925)

Wiebe, M. G., Conacher, J. B., Matthews, John, Millar, Mary S. (eds.), *Benjamin Disraeli: Letters* (vols III–V, Toronto, University of Toronto Press, 1987–93)

Willis, N. P., *Pencillings by the Way* (H. G. Bohn, 1850 edn)

Wilson, Hariette, *Hariette Wilson's Memoirs* (Peter Davis, 1929)

Zetland, Marquis of, *Letters of Disraeli to Lady Bradford and Lady Chesterfield* (2 vols, Ernest Benn, 1929)

Ziegler, Philip, *Melbourne* (Collins, 1987 edn)

Index